Second Edition

International Entrepreneurship

Starting, Developing, and Managing a Global Venture

Robert D. Hisrich
Thunderbird, The Garvin School of International Management

Los Angeles | London | New Delhi
Singapore | Washington DC

Los Angeles | London | New Delhi
Singapore | Washington DC

FOR INFORMATION

SAGE Publications, Inc.
2455 Teller Road
Thousand Oaks, California 91320
E-mail: order@sagepub.com

SAGE Publications Ltd.
1 Oliver's Yard
55 City Road
London, EC1Y 1SP
United Kingdom

SAGE Publications India Pvt. Ltd.
B 1/I 1 Mohan Cooperative Industrial Area
Mathura Road, New Delhi 110 044
India

SAGE Publications Asia-Pacific Pte. Ltd.
33 Pekin Street #02–01
Far East Square
Singapore 048763

Acquisitions Editor: Lisa Cuevas Shaw
Assistant Editor: Theresa Accomazzo
Editorial Assistant: Katie Guarino
Production Editor: Astrid Virding
Copy Editor: Taryn Bigelow
Typesetter: Hurix Systems Pvt. Ltd.
Proofreader: Ellen Brink
Indexer: Kathy Paparchontis
Cover Designer: Candice Harman
Marketing Manager: Kelley McAllister
Permissions Editor: Adele Hutchinson

Printed in the United States of America

Library of Congress Cataloging-in-Publication Data

Hisrich, Robert D.
International entrepreneurship : starting, developing, and managing a global venture / Robert D. Hisrich. – 2nd ed.

p. cm.
Includes bibliographical references and index.

ISBN 978-1-4522-1739-0 (pbk. : acid-free paper)

1. Entrepreneurship. 2. International business enterprises. 3. Entrepreneurship–Case studies. 4. International business enterprises–Case studies. I. Title.

HB615.H576 2013

658'.049–dc23

2011033242

This book is printed on acid-free paper.

12 13 14 15 16 10 9 8 7 6 5 4 3 2 1

Second Edition

International Entrepreneurship

To my wife, Tina; my daughters, Kary, Katy, and Kelly;
my son-in-law, Rich; and grandchildren, Rachel, Andrew, Sarah,
as well as Kaiya. To all your global and entrepreneurial endeavors.

Contents

Preface

Starting and operating a new venture in one's own country involves considerable risk and energy to overcome all the obstacles involved. These are significantly compounded when one crosses national borders—the fate of the global entrepreneur. This book is designed to help you understand all these international obstacles and to assist you with starting and growing a successful international venture.

To provide an understanding of the person and the process of creating and growing an international venture, the second edition of the book, *International Entrepreneurship*, is divided into three parts—international entrepreneurship and entrepreneurship opportunities, entering the global market, and managing the global enterprise.

Part 1: International Entrepreneurship and Entrepreneurship Opportunities deals with the general aspects of being a global entrepreneur and identifying global opportunities. The specific issues covered include the importance of international entrepreneurship, globalization and the international environment, the impact of a culture, the global entrepreneur and his or her venture, and developing the business plan.

These chapters describing the general nature and aspects of international entrepreneurship are followed by a discussion about entering a global market in Part 2. The three chapters in Part 2 are extremely important, because without a successful global market selection and entry, obtaining sales and revenues from the global effort becomes very difficult. These three chapters address selecting a business opportunity and its global market, international legal concerns that the global entrepreneur needs to address, and alternative market entry strategies for entrance into the selected market.

The final section of the book, Part 3, deals with all aspects of managing the global enterprise. The specific areas addressed include the global monetary system, global marketing and research and development, global human resource management, and implementing a global strategy and managing the global venture.

To facilitate an understanding of the material and allow the reader to apply it in a global context, original case studies are contained in Part 4. These case studies, written by individuals from a wide range of countries, cover global entrepreneurs from these countries who are creating and growing ventures in a variety of industries. Each case study is followed by questions that will ensure the most important aspects of the case have been covered.

Acknowledgments

Many individuals—corporate executives, entrepreneurs, small business managers, professors from all over the world, and the publishing staff—have made this book possible. My special thanks goes to two individuals involved with the publishing process for their detailed comments and editorial assistance: Lisa Shaw, Senior Executive Editor, SAGE Publications; Mayan White, Editorial Assistant, SAGE Publications. Thanks go to my research assistants, Katie Nehlsen and Morgan Olson, who provided significant research and editorial assistance and to Anetta Hunek, whose website provided the Cultural Stories. And, my utmost appreciation goes to my administrative assistant, Carol Pacelli, without whom this book would have never been prepared in a timely manner.

Special thanks to the following reviewers for their help and comments and suggestions:

Charlotte Broaden, *Southern New Hampshire University*
Donald J. Kopka Jr., *Towson University*
Charles Wankel, *St. John's University New York*
Rebecca J. White, *University of Tampa*

I am deeply indebted to my wife, Tina; my daughters, Kary, Katy, and Kelly; my son-in-law, Rich; and my grandchildren, Rachel, Andrew, Sarah, as well as Kaiya for their support and understanding of my time commitment in writing this book. It is to them and their generation that this book is particularly dedicated, as the world is truly global.

Part I

International
Entrepreneurship
and
Entrepreneurship
Opportunities

Importance of International Entrepreneurship

Profile: Kandahar Treasure

Jupiterimages/Photos.com/Thinkstock

Perhaps nowhere in the world is the need for entrepreneurship as obvious as in Afghanistan post–September 11, 2001. Nearly three decades of invasion, war, and terrorist rule have left the people of Afghanistan in a wasteland of economic desperation. With few natural resources at its disposal, a fragile economy based mainly on agriculture and livestock could not support its people, with the rural areas suffering the most. War destroyed what little infrastructure there was, rendering the movement of goods and resources nearly impossible. The people learned to rely heavily on foreign aid, a temporary resource that often fails to provide relief to those who need it most.

Afghan national Rangina Hamidi saw firsthand the devastation in her home country and felt compelled to do something about it. Born in Kandahar, Afghanistan, Hamidi's family fled to Pakistan three years after the Soviet invasion. For seven years while in Pakistan, she and her sister were not allowed to go to school or receive any kind of education, as mandated by the pre-Taliban terrorists who controlled the area at the time. Fortunately, in 1988 Hamidi's family was able to immigrate to the United States, where she attended high school, and received her undergraduate degree from the University of Virginia. Understanding the power and necessity of education, Hamidi further pursued business education through a program with Thunderbird School of Global Management, created specifically to teach Afghan women how to run a proprietary business. With the mission statement, "We educate global leaders who create sustainable prosperity worldwide," Thunderbird was the ideal match for Hamidi's goal of starting a company that could improve quality of life for people in Afghanistan.

Hamidi was granted $55,000 from the nonprofit organization Afghans for Civil Society, which she used to launch her own business, Kandahar Treasure. The goal of the company is, in her own words, "a way to create an economic base for the province while supporting the advancement of women in the country." Understanding the lack of available natural resources, Hamidi identified the fine craftsmanship of the region as a source of revenue. Starting with just 20 female artisans, Hamidi bought raw materials for them to create delicately spun embroidery for decorative accessories as well as clothing. The embroidered goods were then sold in various markets around the world that would pay far more than the local market price, creating a significant profit. Being a nonprofit organization, any revenue generated was used to expand the business. Today, Kandahar Treasure employs 450 people and has considerably improved the lives of many in Afghanistan.

Hamidi, however, is not stopping there. She has plans to take the business into the for-profit sector to create a more sustainable change for her employees. The entrepreneur has seen firsthand the shortcomings of foreign aid programs, and understands that those funds may not be around forever. By allowing the company to turn a profit, the women will be better equipped to prosper independently, which is of utmost importance for survival in a male-dominated society. Hamidi sees the bigger picture, saying, "I believe in the idea that entrepreneurship can transform lives and help begin the process of rebuilding societies. . . . By focusing on private business and enhancing opportunities for ordinary Afghans to fill their days, we will not only help Afghanistan with building its economy, but also help the Afghans find jobs so they can depend on a peaceful and just way of making money for themselves and their families."

SOURCE: Adapted from Perman (2008).

Chapter Objectives

1. To understand the fundamental importance of the global venture in today's changing world
2. To introduce the concept of entrepreneurship from a global perspective, crossing national boundaries
3. To learn the key differences in operating a business in a global versus domestic environment from economic, political, cultural, and technological perspectives
4. To explain the various factors affecting the business plans of entrepreneurs entering different markets
5. To identify the major motivators for taking a business global or of conceiving a new business with a global focus
6. To become familiar with the positive and negative aspects of the decision to take one's business global

Introduction

Never before in the history of the world has there been such a variety of exciting international business opportunities. The movement of the once-controlled economies to more market-oriented ones, the advancement of the Pacific Rim and the new markets in the Middle East provide a myriad of possibilities for entrepreneurs wanting to start a new enterprise in a foreign market as well as for existing entrepreneurial firms desiring to expand their businesses globally. The world is truly global.

As more countries become market oriented and economically developed, the distinction between foreign and domestic markets is becoming less pronounced. What was once only produced domestically is now produced internationally. For example, Yamaha pianos are now manufactured in the United States, and Nestlé chocolate (started in Europe) is made all over the world. Invacare's wheelchairs, once produced only in the United States, are now made in Germany and China. This blurring of national identities will continue to accelerate as more products are introduced outside domestic boundaries earlier in the life of entrepreneurial firms.

Since the mid-1990s, organizations have been attempting to redefine themselves to be truly global. The pressure to internationalize is being felt in every type of organization: nonprofit and for-profit, public and private, large and small. This need to internationalize is accelerating because of the self-interest of these organizations as well as the effect of a variety of external events. Today, more than seven eighths of the world's economic states have some form of market economy. A few large trading blocs such as the European Union and NAFTA (the North American Free Trade Agreement between Canada, Mexico, and the United States) have emerged and are growing. Once-developing countries, like China, are economic powers.

These changes are well recognized by organizations that are investing trillions of dollars in a world economy that includes emerging markets as some of the vehicles of future growth. About 85% of the world's population lives in developing countries, most of which are in need of major investment in infrastructure development. Just ask the potato farmers in the Chuvash Republic of Russia, who saw 26% of their crop rot because of inadequate distribution and warehousing, whether there is a need for this investment in infrastructure. Or, ask the economics professor in the Czech Republic, who had to leave the university to find other employment due to the low university wages, whether massive investment in education is needed. The professor, like many human resources in these developing countries, needs training and education to provide the manpower required in the next century.

The need for physical and technological infrastructure is no more apparent than in one of the fastest-growing markets in the 2000s and early 2010s—the Pacific Rim. This area offers economically viable locations for manufacturing and trade. Over half of the world's population lives in Asia, with China containing 20% of the world's population. India alone is twice the size in population of Latin America. And then there is Japan, with its world economy, ranking high in the world in exporting and importing.

There are also new market opportunities in South America, Africa, Ukraine, Vietnam, Iraq, and other countries in transition throughout the world. These areas are becoming highly attractive to globally oriented companies that want to grow their business internationally and develop a strong market position as the economies of countries change through privatization and deregulation.

The globalization of entrepreneurship creates wealth and employment that benefit individuals and nations throughout the world. International entrepreneurship is exciting because it combines the many aspects of domestic entrepreneurship with other disciplines such as anthropology, economics, geography, history, jurisprudence, and language. In today's hypercompetitive world with rapidly changing technology, it is essential for an entrepreneur to at least consider entering the global market.

Many entrepreneurs find it difficult to manage and expand the venture they have created, especially into the global marketplace. They tend to forget a basic axiom in business: The only constant is change. Entrepreneurs who understand this axiom will effectively manage change by continually adapting their organizational culture, structure, procedures, and strategic direction, as well as their products and services in both a domestic and an international orientation. Entrepreneurs in developed countries like the United States, Japan, the United Kingdom, and Germany must sell their products in a variety of new and different market areas as early as possible to further the growth of their firms.

Global markets offer entrepreneurial companies new market opportunities. Since 1950, the growth of international trade and investment has often been larger than the growth of domestic economies, even than those of the United States and China.

A combination of domestic and international sales offers the entrepreneur an opportunity for expansion and growth that is not available solely in a domestic market.

The Nature of International Entrepreneurship

Simply stated, *international entrepreneurship* is "the process of an entrepreneur conducting business activities across national boundaries." It may consist of exporting, licensing, opening a sales office in another country, or something as simple as placing a classified advertisement in the Paris edition of the *International Herald Tribune.* The activities necessary for ascertaining and satisfying the needs and wants of target consumers often take place in more than one country. When an entrepreneur executes his or her business model in more than one country, international entrepreneurship is occurring.

The term *international entrepreneurship* was introduced around 1988 to describe the many untapped foreign markets that were open to new ventures reflecting a new technological and cultural environment (Morrow, 1988).

McDougall (1989, p. 389) defined international entrepreneurship as "the development of international new ventures or start-ups that, from their inception, engage in international business, thus viewing their operating domain as international from the initial stages of the firm's operation."

In 1997, McDougall and Oviatt introduced a broader definition of international entrepreneurship to include the study of established companies and the recognition of comparative (cross-national) analysis. They defined this field as "a combination of innovative, proactive, and risk-seeking behavior that crosses or is compared across national borders and is intended to create value in business organizations" (McDougall & Oviatt, 2000, p. 903). This definition takes into account at the organizational level the notions of innovation, risk taking, and proactive behavior. It also focuses on the entrepreneurial behavior of these firms rather than only the characteristics and intentions of the individual entrepreneurs. The key dimensions of entrepreneurship—innovativeness, proactiveness, and risk propensity—can be found and developed at the organizational level.

A good definition and understanding was presented in the introduction to an issue devoted to the topic in *Entrepreneurship Theory and Practice* (Honig-Haftel, Hisrich, McDougall, & Oviatt, 1996). The authors broadly defined international entrepreneurship as any activity of an entrepreneur that crossed a national border. This understanding was further developed in a review article (Ruzzier, Antoncic, & Hisrich, 2006). Numerous research studies and definitions have emerged focusing on a wide variety of areas, such as the international sales of new ventures (McDougall, 1989), born-global ventures (McDougall & Oviatt, 2000), role of national culture (McGrath, McMillan, & Scheinberg, 1992), and the internationalization of small and medium enterprises (Lu & Beamish, 2001). It has also been applied in many geographic contexts, such as Eastern Europe (Hisrich, 1994; Hisrich & O'Cinneide, 1991), Germany (Grichnik & Hisrich, 2004), Hungary (Hisrich & Fulop, 1993, 1995; Hisrich & Szirmai, 1993; Hisrich & Vecsenyi, 1994), Ireland (Hisrich & O'Cinneide, 1989), Israel (Lerner,

Brush, & Hisrich, 1997), Northern Ireland (Hisrich, 1988), Slovenia (Hisrich, Vahcic, Glas, & Bucar, 1998), Soviet Union (Ageev, Grachev, & Hisrich, 1995), Ukraine (Hisrich, Bowser, & Smarsh, 2006), and developing economies (Antoncic & Hisrich, 1999, 2000; Hisrich & Öztürk, 1999).

Finally, according to McDougall, Oviatt, and Shrader's definition (2003, p. 61), international entrepreneurship is "a combination of innovative, proactive, and risk-seeking behavior that crosses national borders and is intended to create value in organizations."

With a commercial history of only 300 years, the United States is a relative newcomer to the international business arena. As soon as settlements were established in the New World, American businesses began an active international trade with Europe. Foreign investors helped build much of the early industrial trade with Europe as well as much of the early industrial base of the United States. The future commercial strength of the United States, as well as the rest of the world, will depend on the ability of both entrepreneurs and established companies to be involved in markets outside their borders.

International Versus Domestic Entrepreneurship

Although both international and domestic entrepreneurs are concerned with sales, costs, and profits, what differentiates domestic from international entrepreneurship is the variation in the relative importance of the factors affecting each decision. International entrepreneurial decisions are more complex due to such uncontrollable factors as economics, politics, culture, and technology (see Table 1.1).

Economics

In a domestic business strategy, a single country at a specified level of economic development is the focus of entrepreneurial efforts. The entire country is almost always organized under a single economic system with the same currency. Creating a business strategy for a multicountry area means dealing with differences in levels of economic development; currency valuations; government regulations; and banking, venture capital, marketing, and distribution systems. These differences manifest themselves in each aspect of the entrepreneur's international business plan and methods of doing business.

❖ **Table 1.1** International Versus Domestic Business: Factors That Are Different

- Economics
- Language stage of economic development
- Type of economic system
- Political-legal environment
- Language

SOURCE: Adapted from Hisrich, R. D., Peters, M. A., & Shepherd, D. A. (2010). *Entrepreneurship* (8th ed.). Burr Ridge, IL: McGraw-Hill/Irwin, p. 134.

Stage of Economic Development

The United States is an industrially developed nation with regional variances of relative income. While needing to adjust the business plan according to regional differences, an entrepreneur doing business only in the United States does not have to worry about a significant lack of such fundamental infrastructures as roads, electricity, communication systems, banking facilities and systems, adequate educational systems, a well-developed legal system, and established business ethics and norms. These factors vary greatly in other countries and significantly affect the ability to successfully engage in international business.

Balance of Payments

With the present system of flexible exchange rates, a country's *balance of payments* (the difference between the value of a country's imports and exports over time) affects the valuation of its currency, and this valuation of one country's currency affects business transactions between countries. At one time, Italy's chronic balance of payments deficit led to a radical depreciation in the value of the lira, Italy's currency. Fiat Group Automobiles S.p.A. responded by offering significant rebates on cars sold in the United States. These rebates cost Fiat very little because fewer dollars purchased many more liras due to the decreased value of the lira. Similar exchange rate divergences have occurred for Japanese automobile manufacturers and many products made in other countries. The shrinking value of the U.S. dollar has helped U.S. firms export more due to lower prices of U.S. goods in foreign currencies.

Type of Economic System

Pepsi-Cola began considering the possibility of marketing in the former U.S.S.R. as early as 1959, following the visit of U.S. Vice President Richard Nixon. When Premier Nikita Khrushchev expressed his approval of Pepsi's taste, East–West trade really began moving, with Pepsi entering the former U.S.S.R. Instead of using its traditional type of franchise bottler in their entry strategy, Pepsi used a barter-type arrangement that satisfied both the socialized system of the former U.S.S.R. and the U.S. capitalist system. In return for receiving technology and syrup from Pepsi, the former U.S.S.R. provided the company with Soviet vodka and distribution rights in the United States. Many such *barter* or *third-party arrangements* have been used to increase the amount of business activity in countries in various stages of development and transition. Having to come up with appropriate bartering arrangements is just one of the many difficulties in doing business in developing and transition economies.

Political-Legal Environment

The multiplicity of political and legal environments in the international market creates vastly different business problems, opening some market opportunities for entrepreneurs and eliminating others. For example, U.S. environmental standards have eliminated the possibility of importing several models of European cars.

Another significant event in the political-legal environment involves price fluctuations and significant increases in the last few years in oil, other energy products, and food.

Each element of the business strategy of an international entrepreneur has the potential to be affected by the multiplicity of legal environments. Pricing decisions in a country that has a value-added tax are different from those decisions made by the same entrepreneur in a country with no value-added tax. Advertising strategy is affected by the variations in what can be said in the copy or in the support needed for advertising claims in different countries. Product decisions are affected by legal requirements with respect to labeling, ingredients, and packaging. Types of ownership and organizational forms vary widely throughout the world. The laws governing business arrangements also vary greatly with over 150 different legal systems and national laws.

❖ CULTURAL STORIES

Story 1

My wife and I were in Argentina having dinner at a fancy restaurant when it was time for dessert. The waiter asked my wife if she had decided and she said, "Could you bring me a portion of *cajeta*?" In Mexico, this is like candy-caramel made of milk. In Argentina, however, cajeta means "vagina."

I will never forget the waiter's expression.

Often, in different countries that officially speak the same language, the same word has an entirely different meaning. In this couple's case, it would have spared them embarrassment to know beforehand how the word for caramel, or "dulce de leche," differs within Spanish-speaking countries:

Argentina, Costa Rica, Spain, El Salvador, Guatemala, Paraguay, Uruguay, The Dominican Republic, and Puerto Rico: Dulce de leche

Mexico: Dulce de cajeta

Chile and Ecuador: Manjar

Venezuela and Colombia: Arequipe

Peru, Bolivia and Panamá: Manjar blanco

Cuba: Fanguito

Story 2

While studying in Shanghai in the summer of 1995, I would routinely drive around the city in a taxi to get to know the area and to chat with the taxi drivers (who were always very knowledgeable about the city).

One day, the driver asked me my English name. I told him it was "Phillip," and he looked puzzled. I asked him what "Phillip" meant to him and he replied, "good reception with many channels."

So, I have that going for me … which is nice.

SOURCE: http://www.culturalconfusions.com (Story 1 by Bernardo Alanis; Story 2 by Philip Graham).

Cultural Environment

The effect of culture on entrepreneurs and strategies is also significant. Entrepreneurs must make sure that each element in the business plan has some degree of congruence with the local culture. For example, in some countries point-of-purchase displays are not allowed in retail stores, while they are in the United States. An increasingly important aspect of the cultural environment in some countries concerns bribes and corruption. How should an entrepreneur deal with these situations? What is the best course of action to take and still maintain the needed high ethical standards? Sometimes, one of the biggest problems is finding a translator. To avoid errors, entrepreneurs should hire a translator whose native tongue is the target language.

Technological Environment

Technology, like culture, varies significantly across countries. The variations and availability of technology are often surprising, particularly to an entrepreneur from a developed country. While U.S. firms produce mostly standardized, relatively uniform products that meet industry standards, this is not the case in many countries, making it more difficult to achieve a consistent level of quality. New products in a country are created based on the conditions and infrastructure operating in that country. For example, U.S. car designers can assume wider roads and less expensive gasoline than European designers. When these designers work on transportation vehicles for other parts of the world, their assumptions need to be significantly altered.

Local Foreign Competition

When entering a foreign market, the international entrepreneur needs to be aware of the strength of local competitors who are already established in the market. These competitive companies can often be a formidable force against foreign entry, as they are known companies with known products and services. This can be particularly difficult when there is a "buy national" attitude in the country. A sustained effort stressing the unique selling propositions of the entering product or service is necessary, including a guarantee to ensure customer satisfaction, in order to compete.

Subsidies Offered by Foreign Governments

Some governments offer subsidies to attract particular types of foreign companies and investments to help further the development of the country's economy. These subsidies can take different forms, such as cash or a tax holiday for a period of time, and usually involve infrastructure development. This occurred for U.S. oil companies that built the oil fields and delivery system in the Middle East and for foreign banks that assisted in developing the banking system in China. Foreign governments can also offer subsidies to local firms to help them compete against foreign products. This is often called an *infant industry protection policy*.

Motivations to Go Global

Unless you are born global, most entrepreneurs will only pursue international activities when stimulated to do so. A variety of proactive and reactive motivations can cause an entrepreneur to become involved in international business, as is indicated in Table 1.2. Profits are, of course, one of the most significant reasons for going global. Often, the profitability expected from going global is not easily obtained. In fact, profitability can be adversely affected by the costs of getting ready to go global, underestimating the costs involved, and mistakes. The difference between the planned and actual results may be particularly large in the first attempt to go global. Anything you think won't happen, probably will, like having significant shifts in foreign exchange rates.

The allure of profits is reflected in the motive to sell to other markets. For a U.S.-based entrepreneurial firm, the 95% of the world's population living outside the United States offers a very large market opportunity. These sales can cover any significant research and development and start-up manufacturing costs that were incurred in the domestic market. Without sales to these international markets, these costs would have to be spread just over domestic sales, resulting in fewer sales and smaller profits.

Another reason for going global—the home domestic market is leveling or even declining in sales or sales potential. This is occurring in several markets in the United States with its aging demographics.

Sometimes an entrepreneur moves to international markets to avoid increased regulations or governmental or societal concerns about their products or services. Cigarette companies such as Philip Morris aggressively pursued sales outside the United States, particularly in developing economies, when confronted with increased government regulations and antismoking attitudes of consumers. Sometimes this took the form of purchasing existing cigarette companies in foreign markets, as occurred in Russia.

When the entrepreneur's technology becomes obsolete in the domestic market or the product or service is near the end of its life cycle, there may be sales opportunities in foreign markets. One entrepreneur found new sales life for the company's gas-permeable hard contact lenses and solutions when highly competitive soft lenses

❖ Table 1.2 Motivations for Going Global

- Profits
- Competitive pressures
- Unique product(s) or service(s)
- Excess production capacity
- Declining home-country sales
- Unique market opportunity
- Economies of scale
- Technological advantage
- Tax benefits

SOURCE: Adapted from Hisrich, R. D., Peters, M. A., & Shepherd, D. A. (2010). *Entrepreneurship* (8th ed.). Burr Ridge, IL: McGraw-Hill/Irwin, p. 142.

negatively affected the domestic market in the United States. Volkswagen continued to sell its original VW Beetle in Latin and South America for years after stopping its sales in the United States.

Entrepreneurs often go global to take advantage of lower costs in foreign countries for labor, manufacturing overhead, and raw materials. The "Flip Watch," made by HourPower, could not be marketed at its price point in Things Remembered and JC Penney stores without being produced in China. Waterford Crystal is manufacturing some products in Prague to help offset the higher labor costs in Ireland. This cost advantage decreases as the Czech Republic develops as a member of the European Union. There are often some cost advantages by having at least a distribution and sales office in a foreign market. Graphisoft, a Hungarian software company, found its sales significantly increased in the United States when it opened a sales office in California.

Several other motivations can motivate an entrepreneur to go global. One of the more predominant motivations is to establish and exploit a global presence. When an entrepreneur truly goes global, many company operations can be internationalized and leveraged. For example, when going global an entrepreneur will establish a global distribution system and an integrated manufacturing capability. Establishing these gives the company a competitive advantage because they not only facilitate the successful production and distribution of present products but help keep out competitive products as well. By going global, an entrepreneur can offer a variety of different products at better price points.

Traits of an International Entrepreneur

Several characteristics and traits are identifiable in international entrepreneurs regardless of the country of origin. These include ability to embrace change, desire to achieve, ability to establish a vision, high tolerance for ambiguity, high level of integrity, and knowing the importance of individuals.

Embraces Change

A global entrepreneur likes and even embraces differences in people, as well as situations. He or she constantly seeks new and exciting things and likes to "break the mold" and challenge corporate orthodoxies. Living in and learning about different cultures and ways of doing things is an exciting way to live. New ways of doing things are encouraged. Employees are taught how to manage change.

Desire to Achieve

A global entrepreneur has good business savvy and a strong desire to achieve. To succeed, an entrepreneur needs to have profit/loss experience and an ability to create value in a different culture. A possession of broad business knowledge, such as transfer pricing, foreign exchange, and international customs and laws, combined with a global mindset, provides the basis for success.

Ability to Establish a Vision

A global entrepreneur needs to establish a vision that employees and customers understand. Employees should feel that they are an important part of the global organization and essential to its success. A global entrepreneur is very optimistic, assumes that everything is possible, and establishes a limited number of short-term goals to obtain the vision. He or she focuses more on outcomes than processes, works long hours, has a high energy level, and does not fear failure.

High Tolerance for Ambiguity

The passion for learning from a variety of sources and viewing uncertainty as an opportunity instead of a threat allows a global entrepreneur to develop mental maps that will lead to achieving a vision. Incrementally moving initiatives in a variety of areas without completing one regularly is not a problem. This high tolerance for ambiguity makes utility a key virtue of any practice at the individual or company level.

High Level of Integrity

A global entrepreneur has an extremely high standard for individual and company integrity. These established standards are used inside and outside the company. The same high ethical standards are expected from all employees and activities of the venture.

Individuals are Important

A global entrepreneur focuses on the well-being of his or her employees and acts as a nurturing coach. He or she focuses on building and inspiring people and works effectively with others in teams. Spending more time listening than talking, a global entrepreneur values people—employees as well as customers—and wants to build a sustainable enterprise in a particular culture and country.

The Importance of Global Business

Global business has become increasingly important to firms of all sizes in today's hypercompetitive global economy. There can be little doubt that today's entrepreneur must be able to move in the world of international business. The successful entrepreneur will be someone who fully understands how international business differs from purely domestic business and is able to respond accordingly. An entrepreneur entering the international market should address the following questions:

1. What are the options available for engaging in international business?
2. What are the strategic issues in successfully going global?
3. How is managing international business different from managing domestic business?

Many factors affect how an entrepreneurial firm can become truly global. Since the cultural, political and legal environment, economy, and the available distribution channels vary significantly from country to country, each of these needs to be taken into account when deciding to go global as discussed in the following summary. Change and communication are important aspects of operating in a global environment, as are market selection and entry.

Summary

At no other time in human history has the potential for great wealth and prosperity been accessible to so many. This first chapter introduces the concept of international entrepreneurship, and the process that takes place when an entrepreneur conducts business activities across national boundaries. More businesses than ever before are deciding to go global early in their inception. Entrepreneurs today have numerous opportunities from which to choose. The chapter emphasizes how economics; state of economic development; balance of payments; economic system; and political-legal, cultural, and technological environments all play a large role in the establishment of an international versus domestic company. The motives for launching an international enterprise, including a large market opportunity and potential for profit, are also examined. Finally, the chapter discusses what questions an individual or company should consider before going global.

Questions for Discussion

1. What are some differences between domestic and international entrepreneurship?
2. What are the key characteristics to understand when moving a business from one country or region to another?
3. What potential problems might an entrepreneur encounter when entering a new country?
4. What does an entrepreneur need to be aware of before entering a foreign market?

Chapter Exercises

1. Define international entrepreneurship and describe an example of an international entrepreneur and his or her business.
2. Explain the differences between domestic and international entrepreneurship and how these affect a global venture?
3. What are the motivations for taking a business global? What factors influence this decision?

Note

Portions of this chapter are adapted from Chapter 5 of Hisrich, R. D., Peters, M. A., & Shepherd, D. A. (2010). *Entrepreneurship* (8th ed.). Burr Ridge, IL: McGraw-Hill/Irwin.

References

Ageev, A. I., Grachev, M. V., & Hisrich, R. D. (1995). Entrepreneurship in the Soviet Union and post-socialist Russia. *Small Business Economics, 7,* 1–121.

Antoncic, B., & Hisrich, R. D. (1999, May). The role of entrepreneurship in transition economies: Insights from a comparative study. *Proceedings of the 1999 Conference on Entrepreneurship,* 214–215.

Antoncic, B., & Hisrich, R. D. (2000, April). Intrapreneurship model in transition economies: A comparison of Slovenia and the United States. *Journal of Developmental Entrepreneurship, 5*(1), 21–40.

Grichnik, D., & Hisrich, R. D. (2004). Entrepreneurship education needs arising from entrepreneurial profiles in a unified Germany: An international comparison. In A. Miettinen, L. Landoli, & M. Raffa (Eds.), *Internationalizing Entrepreneurship Education and Training Conference Proceedings* (pp. 157–160). Napoli: Edizione Scientifiche Italiane.

Hisrich, R. D. (1988, July). The entrepreneur in Northern Ireland: Characteristics, problems, and recommendations for the future. *Journal of Small Business Management, 26*(5) 32–39.

Hisrich, R. D. (1994). Developing technology joint ventures in Central and Eastern Europe. In L. Dana (Ed.), *Advances in Global High-Technology Management: International Management of High Technology* (pp. 111–130). Greenwich, CT: JAI.

Hisrich, R. D., Bowser, K., & Smarsh, L. S. (2006). Women entrepreneurs in the Ukraine. *International Journal of Entrepreneurship and Small Business, 3*(2), 207–221.

Hisrich, R. D., & Fulop, G. (1993, March). Women entrepreneurs in controlled economies: A Hungarian perspective. *Proceedings of the 1993 Conference on Entrepreneurship,* 590–592.

Hisrich, R. D., & Fulop, G. (1995, July). Hungarian entrepreneurs and their enterprises. *Journal of Small Business Management, 33*(3), 88–94.

Hisrich, R. D., & Grachev, M. V. (1993, November). The Russian entrepreneur. *Journal of Business Venturing, 8,* 487–497.

Hisrich, R. D., & Grachev, M. V. (1995). The Russian entrepreneur: Characteristics and prescriptions for success. *Journal of Managerial Psychology, 10*(2), 3–9.

Hisrich, R. D., & O'Cinneide, B. (1989, April). The entrepreneur and the angel: An exploratory cross-cultural study. *Proceedings of the 1989 Conference on Entrepreneurship,* 530–531.

Hisrich, R. D., & O'Cinneide, B. (1991, May). Analysis of emergent entrepreneurship trends in Eastern Europe: A public policy perspective. *Proceedings of the 1991 Conference on Entrepreneurship,* 594–596.

Hisrich, R. D., & Öztürk, S. A. (1999, Fall). Women entrepreneurs in a developing economy. *Journal of Management Development, 18*(2), 114–124.

Hisrich, R. D., Peters, M. A., & Shepherd, D. A. (2010). *Entrepreneurship* (8th ed.). Burr Ridge, IL: McGraw-Hill/Irwin.

Hisrich, R. D., & Szirmai, P. (1993). Developing a market oriented economy: A Hungarian perspective. *Entrepreneurship and Regional Development, 5*(1), 61–71.

Hisrich, R. D., Vahcic, A., Glas, M., & Bucar, B. (1998, May). Why Slovene public policy should focus on high growth SME's. *Proceedings of the 1998 Conference on Entrepreneurship,* 487–489.

Hisrich, R. D., & Vecsenyi, J. (1994). Graphisoft: The entry of a Hungarian software venture into the U.S. market. In R. D. Hisrich, P. P. McDougall, & B. M. Oviatt (Eds.), *Cases in international entrepreneurship* (pp. 80–96). Homewood, IL: Irwin.

Honig-Haftel, S., Hisrich, R. D., McDougall, P. P., & Oviatt, B. M. (1996, Summer). International entrepreneurship: Past, present, and future. *Entrepreneurship Theory and Practice, 20*(4), 5–7.

Lerner, M., Brush, C., & Hisrich, R. D. (1997, July). Israeli women entrepreneurs: An examination of factors affecting performance. *Journal of Business Venturing, 12*(4), 315–339.

Lu, J. W., & Beamish, P. W. (2001). The internationalization and performance of SMEs. *Strategic Management Journal, 22,* 565–586.

McDougall, P. P. (1989). International versus domestic entrepreneurship: New venture strategic behavior and industry structure. *Journal of Business Venturing, 4,* 387–399.

McDougall, P. P., & Oviatt, B. M. (1997). International entrepreneurship literature in the 1990s and directions for future research. In D. L. Sexton & R. W. Smilor (Eds.), *Entrepreneurship 2000,* (pp. 291–320). Chicago: Upstart.

McDougall, P. P., & Oviatt, B. M. (2000). International entrepreneurship: The intersection of two research paths. *Academy of Management Journal, 43*, 902–908.

McDougall, P. P., Oviatt, B. M., & Shrader, R. C. (2003). A comparison of international and domestic new ventures. *Journal of International Entrepreneurship, 1*, 59–82.

McGrath, R. G., MacMillan, I. C., & Scheinberg, S. (1992). Elitists, risk-takers, and rugged individuals? An exploratory analysis of cultural differences between entrepreneurs and non-entrepreneurs. *Journal of Business Venturing, 7*(2), 115–135.

Morrow, J. F. (1988). International entrepreneurship: A new growth opportunity. *New Management, 5*(3), 59–60.

Perman, S. (2008). Doing business in Afghanistan. *Bloomberg Businessweek: Entrepreneur's Journal.* Retrieved from http://www.businessweek.com/smallbiz/content/aug2008/sb20080822_264781.htm

Ruzzier, M., Antoncic, B., & Hisrich, R. D. (2006). SME internationalization research: Past, present, and future. *Journal of Small Business and Enterprise Development, 13*(4), 476–497.

Suggested Readings

Articles/Books

Javidan, M., Steers, R., & Hitt, M. (Eds.). (2007). *The global mindset: Advances in international management.* Greenwich, CT: JAI.

Having a global mindset is fundamental to influencing people from a wide variety of cultures and heritages. Today's managers need to cultivate a global mindset to remain competitive themselves and make their businesses more competitive in an international context. The book's contributors show managers how to develop a global mindset. Being able to shape the thinking and actions of employees is a fundamental skill that any global manager needs to make the global company more integrated and responsive to different customer needs.

Prashantham, S. (2008). *The internationalization of small firms: A strategic entrepreneurship perspective.* New York: Routledge.

The author provides an in-depth look at how small firms are currently growing internationally through a case study of the software industry in India. Contrary to contemporary opinion, Prashantham explains how "going global" is no longer reserved for medium- to large-sized corporations.

Samli, A. C. (2009). *International entrepreneurship: Innovative solutions for a fragile planet.* New York: Springer.

The author of this book makes the case that entrepreneurship may be the only hope for developing economies to break out of the cycle of poverty and reliance on foreign aid. Samli discusses the measures developing governments and societies must take to encourage and support entrepreneurial efforts, in hopes of creating sustainable economic development.

Strong, M. (2009). *Be the solution: How entrepreneurs and conscious capitalists can solve all the world's problems.* Hoboken, NJ: John Wiley.

Strong's manifesto gives an insightful look into the good that can come from conscious capitalism in the form of social entrepreneurism. He discusses how capitalism can create global prosperity regardless of position, industry, or field of work. He gives practical examples of how social entrepreneurship can create wealth and well-being for people all over the globe.

Zucchella, A., & Scabini, P. (2008). *International entrepreneurship: Theoretical foundations and practices*. New York: Palgrave Macmillan.

Zucchella lays a foundational framework for the relatively new field of international entrepreneurship. Although there has been some recent research done on the topic, this book attempts to create an academic structure for the field of study.

2

Globalization and the International Environment

Profile: Wing Zone

Stockbyte/Stockbyte/ThinkStockPhotos

With the United States being the largest economy in the world, many U.S.-based firms fail to look beyond domestic borders for expansion opportunities. However, with the recent economic recession stymying growth potential, some savvy companies have thought to do just that. Wing Zone, a restaurant based out of Atlanta, Georgia, is one such example. With fewer than 200 units, international expansion seemed ridiculous a few years ago, but upon a closer look, CEO and cofounder Matt Friedman saw a unique opportunity for his small business.

Looking at the financial statements from the fast food giants of the world, such as McDonalds, Kentucky Fried Chicken (KFC), Taco Bell, and Pizza Hut, more than 60% of revenue is generated outside of the United States. Of course, it will take a few years for any small company to see a profit from newly established international operations, but the lack of capital investment for franchising expansion in the United States in the past decade makes international expansion a plausible venture for small and medium-sized enterprises (SMEs) such as Wing Zone.

To Friedman's delight, Wing Zone's restaurant concept makes sense outside of the United States as well. Chicken is one of the most widely eaten foods in the world, accepted in almost all, if not all, omnivorous cultures. Beyond that, spicy foods are a staple in many diets, including those in Latin America, India, and Southeast Asia. Thus, Wing Zone's main attraction, buffalo-style spicy chicken wings, makes sense to introduce to the global market.

Despite the financial risk, Friedman is excited about the opportunity to expand into other countries. He realizes, however, that to be successful, a great deal of time must be devoted to researching different markets to identify fit as well as *how* to best enter that new market. After months of research, Friedman chose Panama City, Panama, as the test market due to eating habits, the presence of a middle class, and an established understanding of food delivery, which is a core element of Wing Zone's business model. By allowing plenty of time for tweaks, especially with supply chain issues, Friedman successfully launched the first of many international Wing Zone franchise restaurants. This success has led to talks with franchisees all over the world, including others in Latin America, Europe, the Middle East, and even Japan.

In an overdeveloped market like the United States, competition is fierce and the little guys often are eaten alive by corporate giants. For Wing Zone, international expansion was a genius way to bypass the competition by entering new markets where its product was the first of its kind. The blue ocean will not last for long, but if a small company can establish its name and brand identity early on, it will have an advantage over competitors who subsequently enter the market. Innovation and creative thinking led Matt Friedman to success as an international entrepreneur.

SOURCE: Adapted from Daley (2011).

Chapter Objectives

1. To understand the implications of taking a business or venture global
2. To define the critical questions that each entrepreneur must answer before taking a company global

3. To describe various organizations' aims at enhancing global ventures
4. To identify and define strategic issues faced by entrepreneurs
5. To determine methods for analyzing the environment in which a venture is operating
6. To analyze the key components of planning and taking a venture global

Introduction

To be a global entrepreneur, one needs to establish an international vision. The level of international skills and knowledge of the company, industry, and market will help determine the international strategy. If you have not had any international experience, you may want to avoid a plan that needs significant overseas market involvement at the outset, such as a foreign sales office or an R&D alliance. Your success in global business will ultimately reflect how well you identify and leverage your core competencies and that of your venture.

Strategic Effects of Going Global

While going global presents a variety of new environments and new ways of doing business, it is also accompanied by a new array of problems. The mechanisms of carrying out business internationally involve a variety of new documents, such as commercial invoices, bills of lading, inspection certificates, and shipper's export declarations as well as compliance with domestic and international regulations.

The proximity to customers and ports is an issue. Physical and psychological closeness to the international market significantly affects some global entrepreneurs. Geographic closeness to the foreign market may not necessarily provide a perceived closeness to the foreign customer. Sometimes cultural variables, language, and legal factors make a foreign market that is geographically closer seem psychologically distant. For example, some U.S. entrepreneurs perceive Canada, Ireland, and the United Kingdom to be much closer psychologically due to similarities in culture and language.

Three issues are involved in this psychological distance. First, the distance envisioned by the entrepreneur may be based more on perception than reality. Some Canadian and even Australian entrepreneurs focus too much on the similarities with the United States market, losing sight of the vast differences. Such differences are in every international market to some extent and need to be taken into account to avoid costly mistakes. Second, closer psychological proximity does make it easier for an entrepreneurial firm to enter a market. It may be advantageous for the entrepreneur to go global by first selecting a market that is closer psychologically to gain some experience before entering markets that are perceived as more distant. Finally, the entrepreneur should also keep in mind that there are more similarities than differences between individual entrepreneurs regardless of the country. Each has gone through the entrepreneurial process, taken on the risks, passionately loved the business idea, and struggled for success.

Additionally, choosing operations in countries that not only have a physical and psychological advantage but also advantages such as trade agreements and current operations of other companies from the entrepreneur's home country, often makes entering and succeeding in a country more manageable. Today, close to 300 regional trade agreements (RTAs) exist, while an additional 100 are proposed or under negotiation. Of these, 90% are free trade agreements making trade across these borders much easier. Some of the most popular include the European Union (EU), the European Free Trade Association (EFTA), the North American Free Trade Agreement (NAFTA), the Southern Common Market (Mercosur), the Association of Southeast Asian Nations (ASEAN), Free Trade Area (AFTA), and the Common Market of Eastern and Southern Africa (COMESA). These RTAs do not include additional agreements made bilaterally between nations, which will be discussed later in the chapter.

With outsourcing becoming a reality for many entrepreneurs, it is important for them to understand that free trade agreements—with their possible reductions in costs and duties on goods being imported—can create further opportunities. Some disputes affecting certain industries and regional trade blocs perhaps prevent, more than aid, the trade process.

Strategic Issues

Four strategic issues are important to an entrepreneur going global: (1) the allocation of responsibility between the United States and foreign operations; (2) the nature of the planning, reporting, and control systems to be used throughout the international operations; (3) the appropriate organizational structure for conducting international operations; and (4) the potential degree of standardization. Each of these issues affects a firm's organizational structure through three primary stages.

- *Stage 1.* When making the first movements into international business, an entrepreneur typically follows a highly centralized decision-making process. Since the entrepreneur generally has access to a limited number of individuals with global experience, a centralized decision-making network is usually used.
- *Stage 2.* When the business is successful, it is no longer possible to use a completely centralized decision-making process. The multiplicity of environments becomes far too complex to handle from a central headquarters. In response, an entrepreneur often decentralizes the entire international operation.
- *Stage 3.* The process of decentralization carried out in Stage 2 becomes more difficult once further success is attained. Business operations in the different countries end up in conflict with one another. The U.S. headquarters is often the last to receive information about problems. When this occurs, some authority and responsibility are pulled back to the home country base of operations. A balance is usually achieved with the home country headquarters having reasonably tight control over major strategic marketing decisions and the in-country operating unit having the responsibility for the tactical implementation of corporate strategy. Planning, reporting, and control systems are important for international success at this stage.

Opportunities and Barriers to International Trade

Beginning around 1947 with the development of trade agreements and the reduction of tariffs and other trade barriers, there has been an overall positive atmosphere concerning trade between countries. Regardless of this positive atmosphere, the global entrepreneur needs to be aware of risks and barriers that exist. Understanding each market and its specific culture and environment will assist in achieving success within those markets.

World Trade Organization

The leading international organization on trade, and one of the longest-lasting agreements, is the World Trade Organization (WTO). Begun in 1947 under U.S. leadership as the General Agreement on Tariffs and Trade (GATT), the WTO was officially established in January 1995, under the Uruguay Round (1986–1994), as a multilateral agreement among nations with the objective of liberalizing trade by eliminating or reducing tariffs, subsidies, and import quotas. WTO membership includes more than 150 nations that create policies in rounds. The WTO has had numerous rounds of tariff reductions. Mutual tariff reductions are typically negotiated between member nations.

Monitored by the Dispute Settlement Board (DSB) of the WTO, which was established in 1995 along with the WTO, member countries are able to bring disputes to this mechanism if they feel that a violation has occurred. Often these cases are brought against more than one nation by more than one country, forming something similar to a bloc. If the investigation uncovers a violation, violating countries are asked to change their policy and conform to the agreed-upon tariffs and agreements, or barriers in other sectors can be levied by prosecuting countries to compensate for lost revenues. With over 400 cases already brought before the WTO DSB with successful trials, decisions, and according actions, trade has been protected among developed and developing nations.

A case brought against the United States and its steel industry exemplifies the WTO DSB's role and its unilateral actions against dumping. The U.S. Congress used an antidumping fine to aid U.S. steel companies under the name of the Byrd Amendment. Creating an environment solely beneficial to the U.S. steel companies, the U.S. Congress had allowed this "fine" to be directed solely into the coffers of U.S. companies affected as a result of dumping. With a myriad of countries claiming unfair trade practices, Japan, the European Union, Mexico, South Korea, and a variety of others took the case to the DSB, and after appeal, the United States lost and the other countries were allowed to levy taxes against similar industries (World Trade Organization, 2003). Under the ruling, these nations could levy up to 72% of the money raised and distributed during the life of this amendment affecting other industries such as U.S. paper, farm goods, textiles, and machinery ("WTO Rules in Favor of EU," 2004).

Important from an entrepreneurial aspect, these types of cases can affect industries and sectors in which the entrepreneur's new venture is operating. Understanding the implications for each business venture helps determine the direction and strategy for each undertaking.

Increasing Protectionist Attitudes

Although the support for the WTO varies and was relatively low in the 1970s, it increased in the 1980s due to the rise in protectionist pressures in many industrialized countries. The renewed support reflected three events. First, the world trading system was strained by the persistent trade deficit of the United States, the world's largest economy, a situation that caused adjustments in such industries as automobiles, semiconductors, steel, and textiles. Second, the economic success of a country perceived as not playing by the rules (e.g., Japan and then China) has also strained the world's trading system. Japan and China's successes as the world's largest traders and the perception that their internal markets are, in effect, closed to imports and foreign investment have caused problems. Finally, in response to these pressures, many countries have established bilateral voluntary export restraints to circumvent the WTO. China did this during the economic prosperity of the 1990s due to the pressures from the world, particularly the United States.

Trade Blocs and Free Trade Areas

Around the world, nations are banding together to increase trade and investment between nations in the group. One agreement between the United States and Israel, signed in 1985, establishes a free trade agreement (FTA) between the two nations. All

❖ CULTURAL STORY

For the Chinese New Year in 2000, my company—a pan-Asian systems integrator—wished to give each employee a *hong bao* (a traditional red packet usually containing a gift of money for a special occasion) with approximately two or three U.S. dollars. The employees would have normally considered this a very thoughtful gift, but something went terribly wrong.

The conversion came to four Singapore dollars. What the headquarters failed to realize was that four is a very unlucky number in Chinese culture. This is because the word for four and the word for death are identical except for the tone that is used.

Morale and productivity plummeted as staff felt Western management somehow wished them ill will. After learning eight is a lucky number in Chinese and knowing that four plus four equals eight, management attempted to resolve the situation by sending a second packet of four Singapore dollars.

The local Singaporean staff did not see it that way. They thought the management now wished them double the bad luck and to "die twice."

At this point, I am managing 15 people across seven countries, with most of them thinking that management wants them to suffer in some way. Not fun.

SOURCE: http://www.culturalconfusions.com (Story by Philip Graham).

tariffs and quotas, except those on certain agricultural products, were phased out over a 10-year period. In 1989, an FTA went into effect between Canada and the United States that phased out tariffs and quotas between the two countries, which are each other's largest trading partners.

Many trading alliances have evolved in the Americas. In 1991, the United States signed a framework trade agreement with Argentina, Brazil, Paraguay, and Uruguay to support the development of more liberal trade relations. The United States has also signed bilateral trade agreements with Bolivia, Chile, Colombia, Costa Rica, Ecuador, El Salvador, Honduras, Peru, and Venezuela. The North American Free Trade Agreement (NAFTA) among the United States, Canada, and Mexico is an agreement to reduce trade barriers and quotas and encourage investment among the three countries. Similarly, the United States, Argentina, Brazil, Paraguay, and Uruguay operate under the Treaty of Asunci6n, which created the Mercosur trade zone, a free trade zone among the countries.

Another important trading bloc is the European Union (EU). Unlike NAFTA and other agreements like it, the EU is founded on the principle of supranationality; member nations are not able to enter into trade agreements on their own that are inconsistent with EU regulations. As nations are added, the EU trading bloc becomes an increasingly important factor for entrepreneurs doing international business.

Entrepreneur's Strategy and Trade Barriers

Clearly, trade barriers pose problems for the entrepreneur who wants to become involved in international business. First, trade barriers increase an entrepreneur's costs of exporting products or semi-finished products to a country. If the increased cost puts the entrepreneur at a competitive disadvantage with respect to indigenous competitive products, it may be more economical to establish production facilities in the country. Second, voluntary export restraints may limit an entrepreneur's ability to sell products in a country from production facilities outside the country, which may also warrant establishing production facilities in the country to compete. Finally, an entrepreneur may have to locate assembly or production facilities in a country to conform to the local product content regulations of the country.

Important Considerations

In addition to these outside considerations, the entrepreneur also needs to be aware of the internal features of a country that affect a business. Examining these political, economic, social, technological, and environmental factors is known as a PESTE analysis. Such in-depth consideration can protect the entrepreneur from future concerns or difficulties. When Intel Corporation wanted to expand, it was not sure where to take its operations. Negotiating with Costa Rica, Brazil, Mexico, and Chile in Latin America, the company finally decided to open operations in Costa Rica based on its political stability during government transitions, the quality of the workforce and its labor unions, and government incentives that would not handcuff the company. In making its decision, Intel dealt with all facets of the PESTE.

No matter the size of the company, this analysis takes careful planning and evaluation. As witnessed when Microsoft took Windows into China in 1993, a lack of careful planning and analysis can produce bad results. Not only did Microsoft have minimal sales of Windows to Chinese consumers, but in early 1994 the company was blacklisted by the Chinese government. Microsoft founder Bill Gates went to China to make a personal appeal to Chinese President Jiang Zemin. He argued that China should join much of the rest of the world in adopting Windows as its standard operating system. Gates was ignored. Instead, he was told that if he was going to sell to the Chinese customer, he needed to better understand their culture.

Microsoft also faced piracy concerns, problems created by software that did not have full capabilities. Additionally, understanding that the majority of its business fell in the hands of the government required an economic and social concern that was not fully understood by the company before entry. It took a decade, but in 2006 Gates and Microsoft finally found a solution to the opposition of the Chinese government and gained inclusion in one of the biggest markets in the world (Khanna, 2008).

To understand what is required for effective planning, reporting, and control in international operations, the entrepreneur should consider situational analysis, strategic planning, organizational structure, operational planning, and controlling the program (see Table 2.1).

Situational Analysis

Once an entrepreneur completes the situational analysis outlined in Table 2.1, several other questions should be asked: What are the unique characteristics of each national market? What characteristics does each market have in common with other national markets? As with many regional markets, deciding between one market and another can make the difference between building and growing the business and/or facing extensive competition from similar companies. When the computer company Dell entered Latin America, the company was able to successfully leverage its knowledge of the national market in Brazil by addressing these questions. In Brazil, states are able to negotiate their own tax incentive packages to entice companies to invest. Realizing this, Dell asked each state to create the best package for the company before deciding where to locate. This understanding of the market was critical in Dell's entry and success in this market.

By beginning to cluster the markets, the entrepreneur increases his or her ability to understand how to operate within these environments. Can any national markets be clustered together for operating and/or planning purposes? What dimensions of markets should be used to cluster markets? These, too, are questions that should be answered as the market is chosen—the answers could help ensure the future success of the company.

Strategic Planning

After deciding on the market, the entrepreneur needs to strategically plan and carefully implement. Who should be involved in marketing decisions? What are the major assumptions about target markets? Are these valid?

Defining the target market is critical to strategic planning for marketing, bringing the product to market, and pricing. A company must define and clearly delineate

❖ Table 2.1 Requirements for Effective Planning, Reporting, and Control in International Operations

Situational Analysis

1. What are the unique characteristics of each national market? What characteristics does each market have in common with other national markets?
2. Can any national markets be clustered together for operating and/or planning purposes? What dimensions of markets should be used to cluster markets?

Strategic Planning

3. Who should be involved in marketing decisions?
4. What are the major assumptions about target markets? Are these valid?
5. What needs are satisfied by the company's products in the target markets?
6. What customer benefits are provided by the product in the target markets?
7. What are the conditions under which the products are used in the target markets?
8. How great is the ability to buy our products in the target markets?
9. What are the company's major strengths and weaknesses relative to existing and potential competition in the target markets?
10. Should the company extend, adapt, or invent products, prices, advertising, and promotion programs for target markets?
11. What are the balance-of-payments and currency situations in the target markets? Will the company be able to remit earnings? Is the political climate acceptable?
12. What are the company's objectives, given the alternatives available and the assessment of opportunity, risk, and company capability?

Structure

13. How should the organization be structured to optimally achieve the established objectives, given the company's skills and resources? What is the responsibility of each organizational level?
14. Given the objectives, structure, and assessment of the market environment, how can an effective operational marketing plan be implemented? What products should be marketed, at what prices, through what channels, with what communications, and to which target markets?

Controlling the Program

15. How does the company measure and monitor the plan's performance? What steps should be taken to ensure that marketing objectives are met?

SOURCE: Adapted from Hisrich, Peters, & Shepherd (2007), pp. 526–527.

what the target market wants from the product. What needs are satisfied by the company's products in the target markets? What customer benefits does the product in the target markets provide? What are the conditions under which the products are used? How easy is it to purchase the product?

Analyzing the strengths and weaknesses of the company in this way makes it easier to evaluate where the company stands in comparison to its competitors, and how to better extend, adapt, or invent new products, prices, advertising, and promotion programs to meet these needs.

Structure

After understanding the environment in which the entrepreneur is entering and strategically assessing how to take advantage of this, the next step is to determine the structure of the company. How should the organization be structured to achieve the established objectives, given the company's skills and resources? What is the responsibility of each organizational level? These questions will assist in the company entering and growing in the global market.

Operational Planning

Just as important as the structure is the operational planning. Even with a strong organizational structure, operations need to be outlined to give the company the best chance to satisfy the target market. Given the objectives, structure, and assessment of the market environment, how can an effective operational marketing plan be implemented? What products should be marketed, at what prices, through what channels, with what communications, and to which target markets?

Controlling the Program

How does the company measure and monitor the plan's performance? What steps should be taken to ensure that marketing objectives are met? One key to successful strategic planning is an understanding of the market. While environmental analysis focuses on this dimension of the planning process, the first step in identifying markets and clustering countries is to analyze data on each country in the following six areas. First, are the market characteristics: the size of market, rate of growth, stage of development, stage of product life cycle and saturation level, buyer behavior characteristics, social and cultural factors, and physical environment. The second area is the marketing institutions such as the distribution systems, communication media, and marketing services to reach the customer whether it's in advertising or research. The third is the industry conditions, focusing on competitive size and practices and technical development of the product. This can help the entrepreneur to adapt, extend, or invent new products or services. The legal environment is the fourth area, which will be covered in a later chapter. Critical resources make up the fifth area. This includes available personnel who have the skills and potential required. The sixth consideration is the political environment. An understanding of the present and future outlook of the government, especially in emerging economies, is most important before market entry.

Summary

Chapter 2 presents the fundamental strategic questions that every entrepreneur needs to ask as he or she prepares to enter the global market. When considering international expansion, an entrepreneur needs to be able to handle the many problems that arise when dealing with multiple countries that have their own regulations, culture, and economy. Also, the entrepreneur needs to consider the effect that the physical or psychological closeness to a foreign market has on the company's decision to enter that market. This psychological closeness is based on individual perception, which may be different from reality. This chapter describes strategic issues that the global entrepreneur faces, including allocation of responsibility; nature of planning, reporting, and control systems; appropriate organizational structure; and potential degree of standardization. The evolution of the organization as it becomes international starts with highly centralized decision making; it evolves into a decentralized structure; and finally, it reorganizes into a decentralized structure in which major decision making and controls can come directly from headquarters.

Questions for Discussion

1. What are the most critical strategic factors to consider before entering a foreign market?
2. How does the control of foreign operations change as the enterprise grows?

Chapter Exercises

1. Describe each of the major issues and considerations an entrepreneur must address when launching his or her product or company in a new country.
2. Choose a country besides your home country and create a comparative table that describes the key environmental factors (economic, political, etc.) in that country versus your home country. What major differences exist? What is one major attribute that you must consider when doing business in the foreign country?
3. Suppose you are the CEO of a small firm that is taking its business into a new country. You are fortunate to have two gifted managers who have volunteered to handle the operational issues for this project, but you must choose just one to send to the new country. One of the managers has extensive work experience in all the operational aspects of running a business, and the other manager is from the new country and previously ran a business there. Which manager will you send and why?

Note

Portions of this chapter are adapted from Chapter 5 of Hisrich, R. D., Peters, M. A., & Shepherd, D. A. (2010). *Entrepreneurship* (8th ed.). Burr Ridge, IL: McGraw-Hill/Irwin.

References

Daley, J. (2011, May). No boundaries. *Entrepreneur,* 98–103.

Hisrich, R. D., Peters, M. A., & Shepherd, D. A. (2007). *Entrepreneurship* (7th ed.). Burr Ridge, IL: McGraw-Hill/Irwin.

Khanna, Tarun. (2008, March 28). Microsoft's China foibles. *Forbes.* Retrieved from http://www.forbes.com/books/2008/03/28/entrepreneurs-microsoft-china-oped-books-cx_tk_0328khanna.html

World Trade Organization. (2003, December 10). *United States—Definitive safeguard measures on imports of certain steel products* (WTO Dispute Settlement DS252). Retrieved from http://www.wto.org/english/tratop_e/dispu_e/cases_e/ds252_e.htm

WTO Rules in Favor of EU in US Trade Row. (2004, August 31). *BBC News* [online]. Retrieved from http://news.bbc.co.uk/1/hi/business/3615030.stm

Suggested Readings

Dittmer, L., & Yu, G. T. (2010). ***China, the developing world, and the new global dynamic.*** **Boulder, CO: Lynne Reinner.**

This book delves into the complexity of the Chinese market, noting changes in the trading, political, and social environment since the end of the Cold War. Multiple academics discuss China's current identity in a global context with an emphasis on China's closer relationship to emerging markets than the developed superpowers. The book also touches on the importance of China in today's global economy, as well as its relationships with other countries in Southeast Asia, Africa, the Middle East, and Latin America.

Eichengreen, B., Landesmann, M., & Stiefel, D. (2008). ***The European economy in an American mirror.*** **London: Routledge.**

Based on the studies of numerous scholars, this compilation of papers collectively provides an analysis comparing current economic trends in the United States and the European Union. Topics such as business competitiveness, employment, and fiscal policy round out an intelligent and somewhat objective discussion of economic and social issues currently affecting both sides of the Atlantic. Though academic in nature, the papers are easy to digest.

Kuivalainen, O., Sundqvist, S., & Servais, P. (2007). Firms' degree of born-globalness, international entrepreneurial orientation and export performance. ***Journal of World Business, 42,*** **253–267.**

Despite the recent increase in "born-global" studies, there has been little research on how the scale and scope of being a born-global firm affects performance: Most of the earlier research takes no account of either the number of or the distances between the countries on firm or export performance. This article begins with a review of the existing literature on born-globals, and subsequently explores the relationship between entrepreneurial orientation (EO) and two different born-global strategies, namely true born-global and apparently born-global (born-international), and the effectiveness of these two born-global pathways. The results of an empirical study on 185 Finnish exporting firms show that those that qualified as true born-globals had better export performance. Furthermore, depending on the degree of born-globalness, different dimensions of EO are of importance.

Lerner, J., & Schoar, A. (2010). ***International differences in entrepreneurship.*** **Chicago: University of Chicago Press.**

With the importance of entrepreneurship to a country's overall economic condition in mind, the authors of this book present a study of how social, political, and environmental factors affect entrepreneurship across various countries. In a truly global look at the world's differences, the authors present empirical data using real, current case studies from various countries to support their arguments. From regulatory constraints to cultural differences to credit policies, this book provides an excellent summary of what countries are doing right and wrong to support or reduce entrepreneurial ventures.

Vashistha, A. (2009). *Globalization wisdom: The 7 secrets of great globalizers.* Singapore: Global Business Press.

In his book, Vashistha attempts to reveal the seven "secrets" every CEO needs to know to take his or her company global, regardless of the size of the firm. Through his own experience with over 200 large corporations, Vashistha has summarized the best practices of the most successful global firms for others to mimic. Citing highly regarded firms such as Lenovo, Cisco, and Virgin, this book offers practical advice for any executive looking toward globalization.

Zucchella, A., Palamara, G., & Denicolai, S. (2007). The drivers of the early internationalization of the firm. *Journal of World Business, 42,* 268–280.

Building on a literature review, a theoretical framework on going international is proposed and tested through an analysis of a sample of 144 small and medium-sized enterprises. The positive association between precocity and niche positioning of the business enforces the relevance of entrepreneurship because focalization is a reflection of entrepreneurial orientation and strategic decisions.

3

Cultures and International Entrepreneurship

Profile: Jack Ma

Photodisc/Photodisc/ThinkStockPhotos

Alibaba

Ten thousand businesspeople and hobby traders got together in Hangzhou, China, a city near Shanghai, to talk about e-commerce. The group gathered to discuss things with other online traders and listen to 42-year-old boyish Jack Ma, founder of Alibaba, an e-commerce company. Jack Ma is thought of as the founder and guru of the Internet in China. This popularity of a businessperson in China is very unique, as many are viewed suspiciously. This recognition reflects the impact Jack Ma has had enabling the Chinese to become entrepreneurs, making money by creating and starting a business in a controlled economy.

Jack Ma's company, Alibaba, is the largest online business-to-business (B2B) company in the world, a result of acquiring Yahoo! China. Alibaba is the most popular online auction site in Asia. The company's popularity ranks with the giants in the online space, such as Amazon, eBay, Google, and Yahoo!.

He is also at the forefront of the online community and social networking. Jack Ma opened Taobao in 2003 for instant messaging and added this feature to Alibaba's websites as well. Buyers and sellers can get to know each other through instant messaging and voice mail and putting up personal information and even photographs. In terms of China, this has helped build trust in the community of friends throughout the country. Taobao quickly attracted over 20 million users, mostly from the under-30 Chinese web users, in part by offering an informal blog-like format.

Alibaba, reflecting the founder's vision, is unique by having two B2B websites—one in English (www.alibaba.com) and one in Chinese (www.china.alibaba.com). The English website is a platform for firms around the world and the Chinese website a platform for domestic Chinese transactions. These websites allow China's small and medium-sized enterprises (SMEs) to build markets in part by providing the opportunity to trade with each other and build global supply chains. In fact, some people buy goods on Alibaba and resell them on eBay.

Since most Chinese do not have credit cards, they are serviced by AliPay, an online payment system of Alibaba that keeps cash in escrow until the goods arrive. AliPay is actually an online bank with thousands of credit histories and is under watch by the Chinese banking regulations committee. This has allowed Alibaba to significantly increase its market share, mostly by taking market share from eBay.

In addition, Alibaba's purchase of Yahoo! China has allowed the company to be at the cutting edge of the intersection of paid searches and e-commerce. With online advertising growing significantly and small firms being the biggest users of paid searches, Alibaba is in a strong competitive position against Baidu, the main search engine in China.

Even though his success is in the technology area, Jack Ma is far from a geek; in fact, he is not even a technologist. He insists on simplicity and rejects any feature that he cannot easily understand. Jack Ma actually relates the success of Alibaba to simplicity, uncomplicated technology, no business plan, and scarce resources such as money. The company, however, has not faced the lack of money due in part to his friendship with Jerry Yang of Yahoo!, the early backing of Goldman Sachs and Softbank, and the

$1 billion paid by Yahoo! for a 40% stake in Alibaba when it was taken over. Jack Ma is not only well financed but has access to significant capital whenever needed.

SOURCES: "China's Pied Piper" (2006); http://www.alibaba.com.

Chapter Objectives

1. To introduce the importance of culture in the feasibility and success of taking a company global
2. To describe how language, verbal or nonverbal, can influence the marketing of a product or service and how clients and consumers interpret those messages
3. To delineate how societal structure and religion affect decisions made by consumers, and how to best understand these influential sociocultural forces
4. To discuss how economic and political philosophy sway the decisions of a culture and therefore the global entrepreneur
5. To emphasize the importance of learning about the manners and customs of different cultures to successfully launch ventures
6. To provide an understanding of the meaning of culture within contexts
7. To show how to analyze cultures when preparing to enter new markets

Introduction

The ever-increasing amount of international business, the opening of new markets, and hypercompetition have provided the opportunity for entrepreneurs to start or expand globally. To be successful in their global efforts, entrepreneurs must understand and consider the culture of each country. Strategic plans must tailor products and services to different attitudes, behaviors, and values. Clothing, for example, is a cultural product. Suits that sell well in Italy may have little success in Japan. Styling and colors vary by culture. What sells well in the United States may have a limited market elsewhere. Additionally, for continued success, the global entrepreneur needs to meet and understand the cultural needs of suppliers and the potential workforce to maintain and/or expand the business.

Nature of Culture

Probably the single most important aspect that must be considered in global entrepreneurship is crossing cultures. The word "culture" comes from the Latin word *cultura*, which means "cult or worship." Although culture has been variously defined, the term generally refers to common ways of thinking and behaving that are passed by the family unit or transmitted by social organizations, and are then developed and reinforced through social pressure. Culture is learned behavior and the identity of an individual and society. Most would agree that culture is adaptive (humans have the capacity to change or adapt), learned (acquired by learning and experience, not inherited), shared (individuals as members of a group share their culture), structured (culture is integrated into a structure), symbolic (culture has symbols with meaning), and transgenerational (it is passed on from generation to generation).

Culture encompasses a multitude of elements including language, social structure, religion, political philosophy, economic philosophy, education, and manners and customs (see Figure 3.1). Each of these affects the cultural norms and values of a country and groups within the country.

Values are basic beliefs individuals have regarding good/evil, important/unimportant, and right/wrong. These are shared beliefs that are internalized by each individual in the group. The more entrenched the values and norms are in a group, the less the tendency for change. In some countries, there is a generally positive attitude toward change. Any change is viewed negatively in other countries, particularly when it is introduced by a foreign entity. For example, although change is fairly well

❖ Figure 3.1 Cultural determinants.

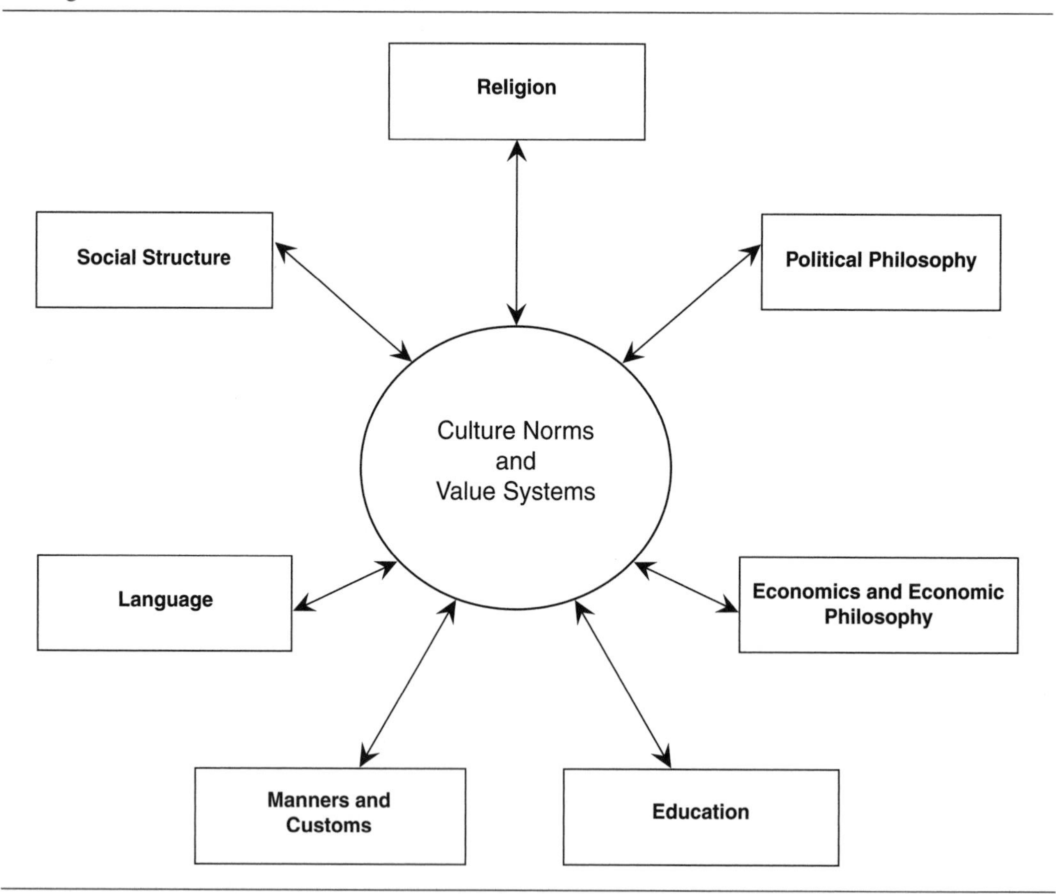

SOURCE: Hisrich, R. D., Peters, M. A., & Shepherd, D. A. (2010). *Entrepreneurship* (8th ed.). Burr Ridge, IL: McGraw-Hill/Irwin, p. 140.

accepted in some sectors in the United States, this is not the case in Japan, where there is stronger resistance to change.

At the same time, similarities in values exist between cultures. Research has shown that managers from four different countries (Australia, India, Japan, and the United States) have similar personal values that relate to success (England & Lee, 1974). Not only was there a reasonably strong relationship between values and success across the four countries, but the value patterns could be used in selection and placement decisions.

While values and culture are relatively stable and do not change rapidly, change does occur over time. This can be seen in the values of Japanese managers both inside and outside of the country. One study found that Japanese managers felt that traditional attitudes and organizational values such as lifetime employment, formal authority, group orientation, paternalism, and seniority were less important than they had been in the past (Reichel & Flynn, 1984). Similarly, there is evidence that individualism is gaining traction in Japan. Instead of denouncing individualism as a threat to society, many Japanese are starting to view individualism as a necessity for the country's economic well-being, which has contributed to the start of an awakened entrepreneurial attitude and spirit in the country.

Additionally, global entrepreneurs need to be aware of other cultural dimensions that will play significant roles in negotiations and the ability to succeed with local suppliers and customers. Recent studies have analyzed the five cultural dimensions of power—distance, individualism, masculinity, uncertainty avoidance, and long-term orientation. These dimensions give insight into the way the seven cultural determinants discussed next play a further role in how an entrepreneur approaches a new market (Hofstede, 2001). Additional studies have taken the five cultural dimensions one step further, focusing on the leadership of individuals within these cultural norms (Javidan, Dorman, de Luque, & House, 2005).

Seven Cultural Determinants

Language

Language—sometimes thought of as the mirror of culture—is composed of verbal and nonverbal components. Messages and ideas are transmitted by the spoken words used, the voice tone, and the nonverbal actions such as body position, eye contact, or gestures. Entrepreneurs and their teams must have command of the language of the country in which business is being done. It is important for information gathering and evaluation, for communication with all involved, and eventually in advertising campaigns. Even though English has generally become the accepted language of business, dealing with language almost always requires local assistance whether it is a local translation, a local market research firm, or a local advertising agency.

One U.S. entrepreneur was having a difficult time negotiating an agreement on importing a new high-tech microscope from a small entrepreneurial firm in St. Petersburg, Russia. The problems were resolved when the entrepreneur realized that translations were not being done correctly and hired a new translator that reported to him. Examples of some very problematic translation errors by some U.S. companies are shown in Table 3.1.

❖ Table 3.1 Potential Translation Problems

Lost in Translation		
Even the best-laid business plans can be botched by a careless translator. Here is how some of America's biggest companies have managed to mess things up.		
Kentucky Fried Chicken	English: "Finger lickin' good."	Chinese: "Eat your fingers off."
Adolph Coors Co.	English: "Turn it loose."	Spanish: "Drink Coors and get diarrhea."
Otis Engineering Corp.	English: "Complete equipment."	Russian: "Equipment for orgasms."
Parker Pen Co.	English: "Avoid embarrassment."	Spanish: "Avoid pregnancy."
Perdue Farms Inc.	English: "It takes a tough man to make a tender chicken."	Spanish: "It takes a sexually excited man to make a chick affectionate."

SOURCE: Adapted from Piech (2003).

Equally important to verbal language is the nonverbal or hidden language of the culture. This can be thought of in terms of several components—directness, expressiveness, context, and formality. From a nonverbal standpoint, the directness and contextual uses of language can play a very large role in understanding a culture. Very low-context cultures use words and language to express themselves, and very high-context cultures use body language, facial expressions, and movements to convey their meaning. Consider four countries from different parts of the world. Argentina and China tend to be very high-context cultures, requiring an entrepreneur to understand that not everything is going to be expressed with words, but potentially more with actions. Doors closed to offices, copying individuals on e-mails, preferring telephone use to talking face-to-face are examples of high-context clues that bring insight into certain cultures; in each case, subtle actions show the intentions or desires of the individuals. Germany and Denmark, on the other hand, are very low context, managing and negotiating very forthrightly. From a directness perspective, these cultures often explicitly express their wishes or desires when doing business, while others view this type of forwardness to be rude. Almost all Asian and Latin cultures tend to carry a more indirect approach to communication, preferring not to tackle issues in a confrontational manner (Training Management Corporation, 2008).

The expansion of Canada's Bank of Nova Scotia into the Mexican market through obtaining an increased stake in the Mexican bank, Grupo Financiero Inverlat, offers insight into what can happen when people from cultures with opposite communication orientations interact. With meetings being conducted in English, Canadian managers, being more direct and low context, found their manner of communication, paramount to making decisions, not being understood and many of the Mexicans felt the same way. Instead of letting the Mexican managers discuss and carry on side conversations in meetings as was necessary for a very indirect and high-context culture, the more rigid style of the Canadians led to discontent among each party involved (Campbell, 1997).

Both verbal and nonverbal language affect business relationships, and for entrepreneurs, the types of communication styles in different cultures need to be considered and understood. In many countries, for example, it is necessary to know a potential business partner on a personal level before any transactions occur or business is even discussed. One global entrepreneur in Australia met the president, the management team, and their families, each on a different social occasion, before any business between the two companies was discussed.

Social Structure

Social structure and institutions also affect the culture facing the global entrepreneur. While the family unit in the United States usually consists of parent(s) and children, in many cultures it extends to grandparents and other relatives. This, of course, radically affects lifestyles, living standards, and consumption patterns.

Social stratification can be very strong in some cultures, significantly affecting the way people in one social stratum behave and purchase. India, for example, is known for a relatively rigid, hierarchical social class system, which can offset the acceptance of new products/services.

Reference groups in any culture provide values and attitudes that influence behavior. Besides providing overall socialization, reference groups develop a person's concept of self and provide a baseline for compliance with group norms. As such, they significantly affect an individual's behavior and buying habits.

The global entrepreneur also needs to recognize that the social structure and institutions of a culture will affect the relationships of managers and subordinates. In some cultures, cooperation between managers and subordinates is elicited through equality, while in others the two groups are separated explicitly and implicitly.

❖ CULTURAL STORY

I was building a market in Mexico in the late 1980s for a privately held one-man-founded U.S. manufacturing firm. In my presentation in Spanish, I kept referring to the founder as *"El Señor."* I noticed smiles everywhere every time I said it.

I finally asked my agent what I was saying that prompted responses like that. He explained that, within the context of the presentation, "the" not only had made the founder appear like a God based on his accomplishment of founding the company, but was actually calling him "God"—the article *"El"* before *"Señor,"* implied God.

Luckily, the audiences were well educated enough and experienced enough in dealing with gringos to be understanding.

SOURCE: http://www.culturalconfusions.com.

Religion

Religion in a culture defines certain ideas that are reflected in the values and attitudes of individuals and the overall society. The effect of religion on entrepreneurship, consumption, and business in general will vary depending on the strength of the dominant religious tenets and the level of these tenets' influence on values and attitudes of the culture. Religion also provides the basis for some degree of transcultural similarity as shared beliefs and attitudes can be seen in some of the dominant religions of the world—Christianity, Islam, Hinduism, Buddhism, and Judaism. Nonreligious or secularist societies are also powerful forces affecting behavior.

Political Philosophy

The political philosophy of an area also affects culture. Because this topic will be treated separately later in this chapter, suffice it to say here that the rules and regulations of the country significantly affect the global entrepreneur and the way he or she conducts business. For example, embargoes or trade sanctions, export controls, and other business regulations may preclude a global entrepreneur from doing business in a particular culture or at the very least will affect the attitudes and behaviors of people in that culture when business is done.

Economics and Economic Philosophy

Economics and the economic philosophy affect the culture of a country and the global entrepreneur. The country's overall view of trade or trade restrictions, attitudes toward balance of payments and balance of trade, convertible or nonconvertible currency, and overall trading policy affect not only whether it is advantageous to do business in a certain market, but the types and efficiency of any transactions that occur. Some countries use import duties, tariffs, subsidization of exports, and restrictions on the importation of certain products to protect the country's own industry—often called infant industry protection—and maximize the gain of more exports than imports. Think how difficult it would be to do business in a country that restricts the exportation of the profits of an international company. Or how difficult it is to do business in a culture that is anti-materialism and more equalitarian.

Education

Both formal and informal education affects the culture and the way the culture is passed on. A global entrepreneur not only needs to be aware of the education level as indicated by the literacy rate of a culture, but also the degree of emphasis on particular skills or career paths. China, Japan, and India, for example, emphasize the sciences and engineering more than many Western cultures do. Slovenia has a very high literacy rate.

The technology level of a company's products may be too sophisticated depending on the educational level of the culture. This also influences whether customers are able to use the product or service properly and understand the firm's advertising or other promotional messages.

Manners and Customs

Manners and customs, the final aspect of culture, need to be carefully dealt with and monitored. Understanding names and customs is particularly important for the global entrepreneur when negotiating and giving gifts. In negotiations, unless care is taken, the global entrepreneur can come to an incorrect conclusion because the interpretations are based on his or her frame of reference instead of the frame of reference of the culture. The silence of the Chinese and Japanese has been used effectively in negotiating with American entrepreneurs when American entrepreneurs interpret this incorrectly as a negative sign. Agreements in these countries, as well as other countries in Asia and the Middle East, may take much longer because there is a desire to talk about unrelated issues. Aggressively demanding last-minute changes is a tactic used by Russian negotiators.

Probably the area that requires the most sensitivity is gift giving. Gifts can be an important part of developing relationships in a culture, but one must take great care to determine whether it is appropriate to give a gift, the type of gift, how the gift is wrapped, and the manner in which the gift is given. For example, in China a gift is given with two hands and is usually not opened at that time but rather in privacy by the recipient.

Cultural Dimensions and Leadership

Hofstede's Five Cultural Dimensions

Having looked at the seven cultural determinants that can be the basis for understanding any culture, understanding the five cultural dimensions described by Hofstede (2001)—power distance, individualism, masculinity, uncertainty avoidance, and long-term orientation—gives the entrepreneur further insight into how these determinants often play out in a business setting. Power distance, or the hierarchical gap between the least powerful (lowest-level employee, lowest-regarded individual in society) and the most powerful, and the acceptance of this position demonstrates to the entrepreneur the level of power and inequality that a society possesses. If an entrepreneur wanted to do business in South Korea, for example, it would be important for decisions to be made and discussed with only the top-level individuals. Power distance is high in this culture, and these managers would be the only individuals capable of rendering and carrying out decisions in general. Without this knowledge, the entrepreneur could be stuck negotiating for months with people of little to no importance, not furthering the enterprise in the least.

The second dimension, individualism, reflects how decisions are made, taking into account societies that include either a strong, integrated group mentality with typically unyielding loyalty and unquestioning authority, or a very individualistic mentality with the priority being the individual and the importance of regarding solely oneself and immediate family. In collectivistic societies, such as those in Latin America and Asia, decision making is often based on what is best for the society, group, or company as a whole.

The third dimension, masculinity, is an aspect of social structure because society determines the importance and role of gender. In many Latin American countries, women have often been viewed as important figureheads in the household, but their role in business was limited. These roles, however, are constantly changing as evidenced in Latin America by the election of two women presidents, Michelle Bachelet in Chile and Cristina Fernandez de Kirchner of Argentina in 2006 and 2007, respectively, both residing in societies regarded as being on the masculine side of the spectrum (Reel, 2007).

The fourth dimension is uncertainty avoidance. This measures the tolerance a society has for ambiguity and whether the members of society feel comfortable in situations that are not typical or structured in a manner in which the members are not accustomed. In uncertainty avoidance cultures, the people follow strict laws, rules, and security measures, and they do not openly accept opinions separate from their own. In cultures on the opposite side of the spectrum, the rules are few and far between and people often have difficulty expressing their emotions. In a country with a low uncertainty avoidance index, bribes are often considered not only acceptable but necessary for transacting business. This is something entrepreneurs need to be aware of.

Finally, the long-term orientation of a culture is based on the values of that specific society. In a culture with a long-term orientation, thrift and perseverance are the two values that are most important, whereas a short-term-oriented individual has a respect for tradition, social obligations, and the appearance of "face." In Japan, for instance, the name of the company for which one works is the basis for respect and gives "face" to the individual who works there, especially if he or she is someone of seniority. Table 3.2 indicates the positioning of many countries on each of these dimensions.

❖ Table 3.2 Geert Hofstede's Five Cultural Dimensions by Country

Country	Power Distance Index (PDI)	Individualist (IDV)	Masculinity (MAS)	Uncertainty Avoidance Index (UAI)	Long-Term Orientation (LTO)
Argentina	49	46	56	86	
Australia	36	90	61	51	31
Austria	11	55	79	70	
Bangladesh[a]	80	20	55	60	40
Belgium	65	75	54	94	
Brazil	69	38	49	76	65
Bulgaria[a]	70	30	40	85	
Canada	39	80	52	48	23
Chile	63	23	28	86	
China[a]	80	20	66	30	118

(continued)

❖ Table 3.2 (continued)

Country	Power Distance Index (PDI)	Individualist (IDV)	Masculinity (MAS)	Uncertainty Avoidance Index (UAI)	Long-Term Orientation (LTO)
Czech Republic[a]	57	58	57	74	13
Denmark	18	74	16	23	
El Salvador	66	19	40	94	
Estonia[a]	40	60	30	60	
Finland	33	63	26	59	
France	68	71	43	86	
Germany	35	67	66	65	31
Greece	60	35	57	112	
Hong Kong	68	25	57	29	96
Hungary[a]	46	80	88	82	50
India	77	48	56	40	61
Indonesia	78	14	46	48	
Iran	58	41	43	59	
Ireland	28	70	68	35	
Israel	13	54	47	81	
Italy	50	76	70	75	
Japan	54	46	95	92	80
Malaysia	104	26	50	36	
Malta[a]	56	59	47	96	
Mexico	81	30	69	82	
Morocco[a]	70	46	53	68	
Netherlands	38	80	14	53	44
New Zealand	22	79	58	49	30
Norway	31	69	8	50	20
Peru	64	16	42	87	
Philippines	94	32	64	44	19
Poland[a]	68	60	64	93	32
Portugal	63	27	31	104	
Romania[a]	90	30	42	90	

(continued)

❖ Table 3.2 (Continued)

Country	Power Distance Index (PDI)	Individualist (IDV)	Masculinity (MAS)	Uncertainty Avoidance Index (UAI)	Long-Term Orientation (LTO)
Russia[a]	93	39	36	95	
Singapore	74	20	48	8	48
South Africa	49	65	63	49	
South Korea	60	18	39	85	75
Spain	57	51	42	86	
Sweden	31	71	5	29	33
Switzerland	34	68	70	58	
Taiwan	58	17	45	69	87
Turkey	66	37	45	85	
United Kingdom	35	89	66	35	25
United States	40	91	62	46	29
Uruguay	61	36	38	100	
Venezuela	81	12	73	76	
Vietnam[a]	70	20	40	30	80

SOURCE: Used by permission from Geert Hofstede.
[a]Estimated values.

GLOBE and Leadership

Building on Hofstede's five determinants, the GLOBE (Global Leadership and Organizational Behavior Effectiveness) project focuses on how better understanding cultural dimensions can improve the leadership of the entrepreneur, creating success from the top down. This research program also includes gender egalitarianism, power distance, and uncertainty avoidance, and a future orientation (similar to Hofstede's long-term orientation), but adds assertiveness and performance, and human orientation as well. Building on the idea of the determinant individualism or collectivism, the authors focus on institutional and in-group collectivism, separating to what degree individuals of society are rewarded for collective actions and to what degree individuals express pride in their organizations.

Assertive cultures are those that enjoy competition in business, such as the United States and Austria, whereas less assertive ones, such as Sweden and New Zealand, prefer harmony in relationships and emphasize loyalty and solidarity. Understanding this environment can help the entrepreneur from a marketing and competitive intelligence point of view, while giving additional techniques for better managing local suppliers, customers, and the workforce.

Performance orientation and human orientation give rise to how an enterprise operates based on the rewards offered to the individuals for excellence and additionally how the collective encourages and rewards their individuals for being fair, caring, and generous. From a performance perspective, Singapore and many Western nations score very high where training and development are emphasized; Russia and Greece are good examples of cultures where family and background are more important. As for human orientation, Egypt and Malaysia emphasize the collectivistic nature and reward individuals, whereas Germany and France are not so disposed in this way.

Global entrepreneurs can better understand how to take advantage of a market if they understand the culture. By having a better understanding, entrepreneurs can enter a market with less risk and a better guarantee of success knowing they can reach the target consumers, suppliers, workforce, and know how to manage them according to their dispositions.

This area is further elaborated upon in Chapter 10.

Summary

A full understanding of the culture of the new market that a company plans to enter is vital to the venture's success. Chapter 3 outlines the important cultural considerations that each global entrepreneur must take into account as he or she decides to enter a new market or partner with individuals or companies from a different country. Culture generally refers to common ways of thinking and behaving that are passed on from parents to their children or transmitted by social organizations, developed, and then reinforced through social pressure. Every entrepreneur must keep in mind that by nature culture is adaptive, learned, shared, structured, symbolic, and transgenerational. This chapter also describes how social structure, language, religion/belief system, political philosophy, economic philosophy/system, customs, and manners can affect a country's culture. A few examples show how an entrepreneur needs to be aware of and adapt to cultural differences. An entrepreneur's understanding of a different culture can make or break a new venture.

Questions for Discussion

1. Why does an entrepreneur need to be aware of the culture of the country that he or she is entering?
2. How should an entrepreneur act in a country with high power distance?
3. Why do you need to be culturally aware when you receive gifts in different countries?

Chapter Exercises

1. With a partner, discuss an instance of cultural misunderstanding that has personally happened to you. Could this misunderstanding have been avoided? If so, how?
2. Choose one of the cultural scenarios in the chapter. How would you have avoided the same cultural problems that the company faced?

3. Pick a foreign country where you would like to do business. Write a brief report explaining the cultural differences between your country and that country, and describe how you would handle them.

4. Find an article about a company that attributes its failure in a foreign country to misunderstanding the local culture. What could the company have done to prevent this failure?

Note

Portions of this chapter are adapted from Chapter 5 of Hisrich, R. D., Peters, M. A., & Shepherd, D. A. (2010). *Entrepreneurship* (8th ed.). Burr Ridge, IL: McGraw-Hill/Irwin.

References

Campbell, D. D. (1997, February 15). *Grupo Financiero Inverlat* (Version: [A], 9497L00). Ontario, Canada: Ivey Management Services.

China's Pied Piper. (2006, September 21). *The Economist.* Retrieved from http://www.economist.com/node/7942225

England, G. W., & Lee, R. (1974, August). The relationship between managerial values and managerial success in the United States, Japan, India, and Australia. *Journal of Applied Psychology, 59*(4), 411–419.

Hofstede, G. (2001). *Culture's consequences: Comparing values, behaviors, institutions, and organizations across nations.* Thousand Oaks, CA: Sage.

Itim International. (n.d.). *Geert Hofstede cultural dimensions.* Retrieved from http://www.geert-hofstede.com/hofstede_dimensions.php

Javidan, M., Dorman, P. W., de Luque, M. S., & House, R. J. (2005). In the eye of the beholder: Cross cultural lessons in leadership from project GLOBE. *Academy of Management Executive, 20*(1), 67–90.

Piech, A. (2003, June) Speaking in tongues. *Inc., 25*(6), 50.

Reel, M. (2007, October 31). South America ushers in the era of the presidenta. *The Washington Post,* A12.

Reichel, A., & Flynn, D. M. (1984). Values in transition: An empirical study of Japanese managers in the U.S. *Management International Review, 23*(4), 69–79.

Training Management Corporation. (2008). *The cultural navigator—Cultural orientation inventory.* Retrieved from www.culturalnavigator.com

Suggested Readings

Dana, L. P. (2007). *Asian models of entrepreneurship: From the Indian Union and the Kingdom of Nepal to the Japanese archipelago: Context, policy, and practice.* Hackensack, NJ: World Scientific.

While entrepreneurship is a global phenomenon, its nature is affected by the unique characteristics of the different countries and regions in the world. This book provides vivid examples of the differences in entrepreneurship and entrepreneurial activity among and within countries in Asia, in particular Japan, China, Singapore, and South Korea.

Katsioloudes, M., & Hadjidakis, S. (2007). *International business: A global perspective.* Oxford, UK: Butterworth-Heinemann.

Using a purely multinational perspective instead of the traditional U.S. perspective, this text examines international business. Most important, it includes interviews with politicians and business executives from numerous countries, including the United States, Canada, Mexico,

Brazil, Colombia, Argentina, India, Hong Kong, Taiwan, China, Japan, South Korea, Germany, Italy, and Russia, to give a better understanding of international business from not only the U.S. perspective but the "reverse" perspective as well.

Sebenius, J. K. (2002, March). The hidden challenge of cross-border negotiations. *Harvard Business Review, 80*(3), 76–85.

Cross-border negotiations are highly affected by cultural differences that go far deeper than surface behaviors and cultural characteristics. The author examines how the processes involved in negotiations and the ways people from different cultures reach agreements affect cross-border negotiations.

Zhou, L. (2007). The effects of entrepreneurial proclivity and foreign market knowledge on early internationalization. *Journal of World Business, 42,* 281–293.

Foreign market knowledge can come either from the pursuit of entrepreneurial activities across national borders or the slower building of experience in foreign markets. The author examines the role of foreign market knowledge in early internationalization. This study furthers the theoretical development of international entrepreneurship.

4

Developing the Global Business Plan

Profile: TOMS Shoes

Digital Vision/Digital Vision/Thinkstockphotos

Entrepreneurial inspiration can occur anywhere, as happened to Blake Mycoskie, founder of TOMS, a very successful shoe company with an extraordinary business model. For him, inspiration struck while on vacation in Argentina as he witnessed extreme poverty in many parts of the country. Many of the people in the smaller villages, including most of the children, did not own shoes, a condition that can cause numerous health problems as well as general discomfort. He wanted to take action to help the problem, but rather than a one-time charitable contribution, he envisioned a sustainable solution that could provide ongoing help to the people who had so lovingly invited him into their lives.

On the same trip, Mycoskie noticed the *alpargatas,* a simply made, inexpensive shoe that sold for less than $2, worn by the majority of Argentinians. He decided that he could use the simple design of the shoes, and reinvent them using high-quality materials and production methods to create a product that could be sold in the United States and other developed markets. With knowledge from previous entrepreneurial ventures, Mycoskie decided to start his own company producing *alpargata*-inspired shoes manufactured in Argentina. For every pair of shoes sold, he would donate the same pair to a child in need. His "one-for-one" concept was simple enough, but many thought that such an altruistic business model could never succeed. With a fixed cost of around $9 per pair selling at about $40 retail, in conjunction with the cost of the extra pair given to charity, the margin seemed slim for a consumer product. However, in pursuit of sustainability rather than profitability, Mycoskie snubbed the naysayers and proceeded with his plan, commissioning 250 pairs of shoes from an Argentinian manufacturer and transporting them back to his apartment in the United States.

With the problem of distribution looming, Mycoskie began cold-calling vendors in the Los Angeles area, trying to find an outlet that would sell his shoes. One upscale boutique heard his story and believed the product would appeal to its customer base. With an order of 150 pairs, TOMS was in business. With the help of this boutique owner, word spread quickly about TOMS "one-for-one" mission, and attracted media attention. After an article about the brand was published in the *Los Angeles Times*, Mycoskie received orders for 2,200 pairs in one day. With less than 100 pairs left in his apartment headquarters, the young entrepreneur was not ready to meet such high demand. "As any good entrepreneur would do," he said, he immediately ran an ad to hire interns, three of whom he hired just a few days later. Handing over the keys to his apartment as well as the customer list and instructions to call every one and let them know that their shoes would be shipped in "more like three months than three days," Mycoskie jumped on the first airplane to Argentina to find a solution to his supply dilemma.

Once he found enough manufacturers to handle the supply demand, TOMS had nowhere to go but up. Within the first year of business, the company sold 10,000 pairs of shoes, which he matched and gave to those in need to make good on his promise. Mycoskie created what he called a "shoe drop" in which he and many colleagues, friends, and like-minded supporters flew to Argentina and hand delivered 10,000 pairs of shoes to barefooted children. They filmed the experience and turned it into a documentary revealing the difference that TOMS could make. Word spread like wildfire.

In an instant, TOMS had an abundance of media buzz, celebrity endorsers, and word-of-mouth advertising, with zero cost to the company.

Whether meticulously calculated or wholly accidental, TOMS's business model was successful and business is booming. NGOs, charities, and nonprofits around the globe want to partner with TOMS. Mycoskie, who refers to himself as "Chief Shoe Giver" rather than CEO, encourages the business with a strong online presence through Twitter, a corporate blog, and multiple documentaries of "shoe-drops" posted on YouTube for all curious viewers to see. Celebrities such as Liv Tyler, Keira Knightly, Kirsten Dunst, and the Hanson brothers have endorsed the shoes on their own account, having no official affiliation with the brand. Mycoskie is quick to commend this free word-of-mouth advertising for TOMS's success. Citing other major shoe brands, such as Nike, that must spend a good percentage of their revenue on marketing to stay competitive, TOMS has enjoyed free marketing, allowing the "one-for-one" business model to work. The company has expanded throughout the world, selling shoes in most major markets as well as online. Since its beginning in 2006, TOMS has given away more than a million pairs of shoes to children in need in more than 20 different countries.

SOURCES: Adapted from CNBC (2009) and TOMS (2011).

Chapter Objectives

1. To know the internal and external purposes of a global business plan
2. To be able to identify all the parts of the business plan and their purposes for each department or organizational function of the company
3. To understand how each audience of stakeholders will use the plan and which section will be each stakeholder's key focus
4. To be able to draft a global business plan from the outline and sample provided
5. To be able to monitor and improve the business plan

Introduction

In today's highly competitive business environment, there is perhaps nothing more important than planning and, specifically, developing a business plan. In any organization, there are many different types of plans—financial, human resource, marketing, production, sales, and so on. These plans may be short term or long term, strategic or operational, and may vary greatly in scope. In spite of the differences in scope and coverage, each plan has a common purpose: to provide guidance and structure on a continuing basis for managing the organization in a rapidly changing hypercompetitive environment. This chapter will first look at an opportunity analysis plan. Then the purpose and aspects of a global business plan are discussed. The chapter concludes with a discussion of the do's and don'ts of a plan.

Opportunity Analysis Plan

Every innovative idea and opportunity needs to be carefully assessed by the global entrepreneur. A good way to do this is to develop an opportunity analysis plan. An opportunity analysis plan is *not* a business plan, as it focuses on the idea and the market (the opportunity) for the idea—not on the venture. It also is shorter than a business plan and does not contain any formal financial statement of the business venture. The opportunity analysis plan is developed to serve as the basis for the decision to either act on the opportunity or wait until another (and one hopes better) opportunity comes along. A typical opportunity analysis plan has four sections: (1) a description of the idea and its competition, (2) an assessment of the domestic and international market for the idea, (3) an assessment of the entrepreneur and the team, and (4) a determination of the steps needed to make the idea the basis for a viable business venture.

The Idea and Its Competition

This section focuses on one of the major areas of the opportunity analysis plan: the idea itself and the competition. The product or service needs to be described in as much detail as possible. A prototype or schematic of the product is often helpful in fully understanding all its aspects and features. All competitive products and competitive companies in the product (service) market space need to be identified and listed. The new product/service idea should be compared with at least three competitive products/services that are most similar in filling the same identified market need. This analysis will result in a description of how the product/service is different and unique and will indicate its unique selling propositions. If the idea does not have at least three to five unique selling propositions versus competitive products/services on the market, the global entrepreneur will need to more carefully examine whether the idea is really unique enough to compete and be successful in the market.

The Market and the Opportunity

The second section of the opportunity analysis plan addresses the size and the characteristics of the market. Market data should be collected for at least 3 years, so that a trend is apparent for the overall industry, the overall market, the market segment, and the target market. This can be done through gathering as much secondary (published) data as possible. For example, if you had an idea for a motorized wheelchair for small children that was shaped like a car, you would get market statistics on the health care industry (overall industry), wheelchairs (overall market), motorized wheelchairs (market segment), and children needing wheelchairs (target market). This funnel approach indicates the overall industry market size as well as the size of the specific target market.

Not only should the size of these markets be determined but also their characteristics. Is the market made up of a few large companies or many small ones? Does the market respond quickly or slowly to new entrants? How many (if any) new products are introduced each year in the market? How geographically dispersed is the market? What market need is being filled? What social conditions underlie this market? What other products might the company also introduce into this market? Based on this section of the opportunity analysis plan, the entrepreneur should be able to determine both the size and the characteristics of the market, and whether it is large enough and suitable enough to warrant the time and effort required to proceed and perhaps actually enter the market.

Entrepreneur and Team Assessment

Next, both the entrepreneur and the entrepreneurial team need to be assessed. At least one person on the team needs to have experience in the industry area of the new idea. This is one characteristic that correlates to the probability of success of the venture. Several questions need to be answered, such as why does this idea and opportunity excite you? Will this idea and opportunity sustain you once the initial excitement has worn off? How does the idea and opportunity fit your personal background and experience? How does it fit your entrepreneurial team? This section of the opportunity analysis plan is usually shorter than the previous two sections and allows the entrepreneur to determine if indeed he or she is really suited to successfully move the idea into the market.

The Next Steps

This final section of the opportunity analysis plan delineates the critical steps that need to be taken to make the idea a reality in the marketplace. The steps need to be identified and put in sequential order, and the time and the money needed for each step needs to be determined. If the idea cannot be self-financed, then sources of capital need to be identified. The entrepreneur should always keep in mind that most entrepreneurs tend to underestimate both the costs and the time it will take by about 30%.

Some questions to answer when developing an opportunity analysis plan are listed in Table 4.1.

Purpose of a Global Business Plan

Given the hypercompetitive environment and the difficulties of doing business outside your home country, a global business plan is an integral part of strategically managing an organization. A global business plan is a written document prepared by the entrepreneur and the team that describes all the relevant external and internal elements in going global. By describing all the relevant external and internal elements involved in starting and managing a global organization, the business plan integrates the functional plans such as finance, marketing, and organizational plans, thereby providing a road map for the future of the organization.

Often a global business plan is read by a variety of stakeholders and can have several different purposes. It needs to be comprehensive enough to address the issues and concerns of advisers, bankers, consultants, customers, employees, investors, and venture capitalists. It can also have such purposes as to obtain financial resources,

❖ **Table 4.1** Questions for the Development of an Opportunity Analysis Plan

Description of the Product or Service Idea and Competition

1. What is the market need for the product or service?
2. What are the specific aspects of the product or service (include any copyright, patent, or trademark information)?
3. What competitive products are already available and filling this need?
4. What are the competitive companies in this product market space? Describe their competitive behavior.
5. What are the strengths and weaknesses of each of your competitors?
6. What are the NAIC and SIC codes for this product or service?
7. What are the unique selling propositions of this product or service?
8. What development work has been completed to date on the idea?
9. What patents might be available to fulfill this need?
10. What are total industry sales over the past 5 years?
11. What is anticipated growth in this industry?
12. How many new firms have entered this industry in the past 3 years?
13. What new products have been recently introduced in this industry?

An Assessment of the Market

1. What market need does the product/service fill?
2. What are the size and past trends over the last 3 years of this market?
3. What are the future growth prospects and characteristics of this market?
4. What social conditions underlie this market need?
5. What market research data can be marshaled to describe this market need?
6. What does the international market look like?
7. What does the international competition look like?
8. What is the profile of your customers?

Entrepreneurial Self-Assessment and the Entrepreneurial Team

1. Why does this opportunity excite you?
2. What are your reasons for going into business?
3. Why will this opportunity sustain you once the initial excitement subsides?
4. How does this opportunity fit into your background and experience?
5. What experience will you need to successfully implement the business plan?
6. Who are the other members of your team?
7. What are their skills and experience?

Next Steps for Translating This Opportunity Into a Viable Venture

1. Examine each critical step.
2. Think about the sequence of activity and put these critical steps into some expected sequential order.
3. Determine the amount of time and the amount of money each step will require. If you cannot self-finance (provide this money), where would you get the needed capital?

obtain other resources, develop strategic alliances, or provide direction and guidance for the organization. Although a global business plan can serve these various purposes, its most frequent use is to obtain financial resources. Bankers, investors, and venture capitalists will not take an investment possibility seriously without a comprehensive global business plan. Some will not even meet with a global entrepreneur without first reviewing the business plan. A well-developed global business plan is important because it (1) provides guidance to the entrepreneur and managers in decision making and organizing the international direction of the company, (2) indicates the viability of an organization in the designated global market(s), and (3) serves as the vehicle for obtaining financing.

Aspects of a Global Business Plan

Given the importance and purpose of a global business plan, it is important that it be comprehensive and covers all aspects of the organization. The plan will be read by a variety of individuals, each of whom is looking for a certain level of detail (Taylor, 2006). As is indicated in Table 4.2, the global business plan can be divided into several areas, each of which has several sections.

❖ Table 4.2 Outline of an International Business Plan

I. **Title Page, Table of Contents, and Executive Summary**

Three-page description of the project.

II. **Introduction**

The type of business proposed and an in-depth description of the major product/service involved. A description of the country proposed for market entry, the rationale for selecting the country, identification of existing trade barriers, and identification of sources of information.

III. **Analysis of the International Business Opportunity**

A. Economic, Political, and Legal Analysis of the Trading Country

1. The trading country's economic system; economic information important to the proposed product/service; and the level of foreign investment in that country.
2. The trading country's governmental structure and stability, and how the government regulates trade and private business.
3. Laws and/or governmental agencies that affect the product/service such as labor laws and trade laws.

B. Trade Area and Cultural Analysis

1. Geographic and demographic information; important customs and traditions; other pertinent cultural information; and competitive advantages and disadvantages of the proposed business opportunity.

(continued)

❖ Table 4.2 (Continued)

IV. Operation of the Proposed Business

A. Organization
   Type of ownership and rationale; start-up steps to form the business; personnel (or functional) needs; proposed staffing to handle managerial, financial, marketing, legal, production functions; proposed organizational chart; and brief job descriptions.

B. Product/Service
   1. Product/service details include potential suppliers, manufacturing plans, and inventory policies.
   2. Transportation information: costs, benefits, risks of the transportation method, documents needed to transport the product.

C. Market Entry Strategy

D. Marketing Strategy Plan
   1. Pricing policies: what currency will be used, costs, markups, markdowns, relation to competition, factors that could affect the price of the product such as competition, political conditions, taxes, tariffs, and transportation costs.
   2. Promotional program: promotional activities, media availability, costs, and 1-year promotional plan outline.

V. Financials

A. Projected Income and Expenses
   1. Pro forma income statements for first 3 years operation.
   2. Pro forma cash flow statements for first 3 years of operation.
   3. Pro forma balance sheet for the end of the first year.
   4. A brief narrative description of the planned growth of the business, including financial resources, needs, and a 3-year pro forma income statement.

B. Sources and Uses of Funds Statement
   1. Country statistics
   2. Partner information
   3. Relevant laws

VI. Appendix (Exhibits)

Executive Summary

The first area, although the shortest, is perhaps the most significant, particularly when the purpose is to secure financing. This area consists of the title page, table of contents, and executive summary. The title page should contain the following information: (1) the name, address, telephone and fax numbers, and e-mail address of the organization; (2) the name and position of the principal individuals in the organization; (3) three to four sentences briefly describing the nature of the organization and the purpose of the business plan; and (4) a statement of confidentiality, such as "This is confidential business plan number 3, which cannot be reproduced without permission." This statement is important, as each numbered business plan needs to be accounted for by recording the person and organization of the individual receiving it and the date of receipt. When trying to obtain financing, this is particularly essential as follow-up can be scheduled at the appropriate time, which is about 30 days from the receipt date and then regular 30-day intervals. As one venture capitalist commented, "One way I get a feel for the hunger and drive of the entrepreneur is by waiting to see if he or she initiates follow-up at the appropriate time."

The table of contents is perhaps the easiest part of the business plan to develop. It should follow the standard format with major sections and appendixes (exhibits) indicated along with the appropriate page numbers.

The final part of the first primary area of the global business plan—the *executive summary*—is the most important, particularly when the purpose of the plan is to secure financing or other resources. The executive summary should be no more than three pages. It is frequently used by upper-level managers, investors, venture capitalists, and bankers to determine if the entire business plan is worth reading and analyzing. The executive summary becomes the screen or hurdle that determines if more detailed attention will be given to the plan. Imagine a typical venture capitalist, who receives more than a hundred 150-page business plans per month. He or she needs to employ some mechanism for screening this large number down to perhaps 10 to 15 for more focused initial attention.

Given its importance, the executive summary should be written last and be written and rewritten until it highlights the organization in a concise and convincing manner, covering the key points in the business plan. The executive summary should emphasize the three most critical areas for the success of the organization. In order of importance, these are the characteristics, capabilities, and experiences of the entrepreneur and management team; the nature and degree of innovativeness of the product or service and its market size and characteristics; and the expected results in terms of sales and profits over the next 3 years.

Introduction

The second section of the global business plan is the *introduction*, where the focus is on the new global initiative, the product/service to be offered, and the country to be entered. A detailed description of the global initiative provides important information on the size and scope of the opportunity. Besides delineating the mission and purpose of the initiative, an in-depth discussion of the product/service to be offered should be provided. The questions in Table 4.3 will help the global entrepreneur prepare this section.

The introduction also needs to discuss the proposed country, the selection process, existing trade barriers, and sources of information (see Table 4.2). Even though these terms are further developed in later sections of the global business plan, they should be summarized in this introductory section. Some key questions that should be considered by the global entrepreneur concerning the needed environmental and industry analysis in developing this section are provided in Table 4.4.

Economic, Political, and Legal Aspects of the International Business Opportunity

The third section of the global business plan addresses the *international business opportunity*. Since this important area has been addressed in Chapter 3 (Cultures and International Entrepreneurship) and will be covered in Chapter 7 (Alternative Entry

❖ Table 4.3 Describing the Venture

1. What is the mission of the new venture?
2. What are your reasons for going into business?
3. Why will you be successful in this venture?
4. What development work has been completed to date?
5. What is your product(s) and/or service(s)?
6. Describe the product(s) and/or service(s), including patent, copyright, or trademark status.
7. Where will the business be located?
8. Is the building leased or owned? (State the terms.)
9. What office equipment will be needed?
10. Will this equipment be purchased or leased?

SOURCE: Adapted from Hisrich, R. D., Peters, M. A., & Shepherd, D. A. (2010). *Entrepreneurship* (8th ed.). Burr Ridge, IL: McGraw-Hill/Irwin, p. 206.

❖ Table 4.4 Issues in Environmental and Industry Analysis

1. What are the major economic, technological, legal, and political trends on a national and an international level?
2. What are total industry sales over the past 3 years?
3. What is anticipated growth in this industry?
4. How many new firms have entered this industry in the past 3 years?
5. What new products have been recently introduced in this industry in the last 3 years?
6. Who are the competitive companies?
7. What are the competitive products or services?
8. Are the sales of each of your major competitors growing, declining, or steady?
9. What are the strengths and weaknesses of each of your competitors?
10. What trends are occurring in your specific market area?
11. What is the profile of your customers?
12. How does your customer profile differ from that of your competition?

SOURCE: Adapted from Hisrich, R. D., Peters, M. A., & Shepherd, D. A. (2010). *Entrepreneurship* (8th ed.). Burr Ridge, IL: McGraw-Hill/Irwin, p. 205.

Strategies), only an overview will be presented here. Two focus areas should be addressed in this section—the target country's culture and the overall economic, political, and legal environment of the country. It is important to understand the economic system operating in the country, including the various financial institutions and particularly the banking system. Frequently, especially in developing countries, it can be difficult to get funds transferred in and out of a country. In one country where one of the author's companies was doing business, currency needed to be hand carried into the country with transactions taking place in cash because the banking system operated very slowly at a very high cost per transaction; funds were not available in a timely manner.

The government structure and its stability as well as the various laws affecting trade and businesses need to be examined. This is particularly important in deciding the best organizational structure, which is discussed in section four of the global business plan

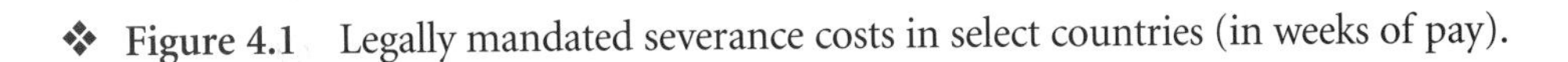

❖ **Figure 4.1** Legally mandated severance costs in select countries (in weeks of pay).

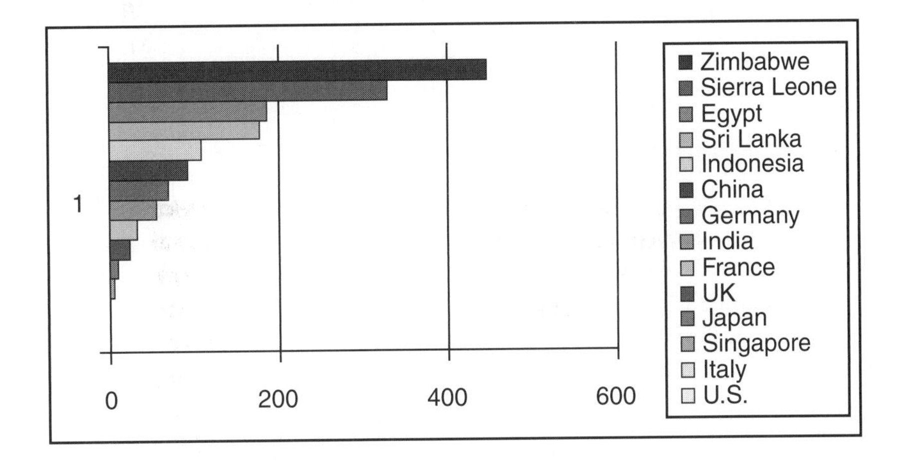

U.S.	0	Germany	69.3
Italy	1.7	China	91.0
Singapore	4.0	Indonesia	108.3
Japan	8.6	Sri Lanka	177.7
UK	22.1	Egypt	186.3
France	31.8	Sierra Leone	328.7
India	55.9	Zimbabwe	446.3

(see Table 4.2). Also, trade and labor laws often affect a country entrance decision as well as the effect of doing business there. McDonald's, when entering Hungary in 1988, needed to get special dispensation from labor law from the Hungarian government (then under control of the Soviet Union) to be able to fire workers who were not performing to its standards. Some countries have very high legally mandated severance costs, making it less desirable to do business there. As is indicated in Figure 4.1, while there are 0 weeks in pay in severance costs legally mandated in the United States, it is 8.6 weeks in Japan, 55.9 weeks in India, 91.0 weeks in China, 186.3 weeks in Egypt, and 446.3 weeks in Zimbabwe. Even though Indonesia should be well positioned to attract manufacturing because of the country's low wages and high productivity, its labor law requiring 108.3 weeks of pay in severance costs is a major deterrent to companies investing in manufacturing facilities there. One factory producing Lee Cooper brand jeans facing a cash-flow problem found it more economical to declare bankruptcy with all its workers losing their jobs rather than downsizing and laying off enough of the 1,500 employees to keep the business going at a lower level of output.

The second part of this section—cultural analysis—is equally important. The customs and traditions of the country need to be analyzed as well as any competitive products or services available. This will lead the global entrepreneur to identify the competitive advantages and disadvantages of the particular business opportunity.

The fourth section of the global business plan—the operation of the proposed business—is a most significant one. The organization, product/service, market entry strategy, and overall marketing strategy all need to be delineated.

Organizational Plan

The *organizational plan* is the part of the business plan that describes the venture's form of ownership—such as, proprietorship, partnership, or corporation in the United States. If the venture is a partnership, the terms of the partnership should be included. It is also important to provide an organizational chart indicating the line of authority and the responsibilities of the members of the organization. Some of the key questions the entrepreneur needs to answer in preparing this section of the business plan are

- What is the form of ownership of the organization?
- If a partnership, who are the partners and what are the terms of agreement?
- If incorporated, who are the principal shareholders and how much stock do they own?
- How many shares of voting or nonvoting stock have been issued and what type?
- Who are the members of the board of directors? (Give names, addresses, and resumes.)
- Who has check-signing authority or control?
- Who are the members of the management team and what are their backgrounds?
- What are the roles and responsibilities of each member of the management team?
- What are the salaries, bonuses, or other forms of payment for each member of the management team?

This information provides a clear understanding of who controls the organization and how other members will interact when performing their management functions.

Product/Service

The *product/service* to be produced and/or offered needs to be succinctly described. For technology-based products, this section should provide information on the nature of the technology, the unique differential advantage the technology has over rivals, and the degree that the technology is protectable by patents, copyrights, or trade secrets.

Market Entry Strategy

This section of the global business plan describes the *market entry strategy*, the focus of Chapter 7. Suffice it to say here that the various alternative entry strategies need to be carefully considered by the global entrepreneur and the one most appropriate for the country/product/market situation selected. The entry strategy needs to take into account potential suppliers, manufacturing plans, inventory policies, and an operations plan.

❖ CULTURAL STORIES

Story 1

Two colleagues and I were invited to speak at a conference in Amman. At the conclusion of the program, the host invited us to dinner at a beautiful Lebanese restaurant. An extensive English-language menu was brought out from which we were to make our food selections. As I thumbed through the pages, I noticed that the desserts preceded the entrees in the menu, and being naturally curious about the culture, I asked if eating dessert before the main meal was traditional practice in Lebanon.

Everyone laughed, naturally, since it is well known that Arabic is read in the opposite direction than English. The host kindly jumped in and selected a wonderful variety of dishes for us, and we ended up having a delightful evening.

Story 2

Twenty-five years ago when my family first moved to the United States from Poland, my mom heard it was popular for kids to celebrate their birthdays at McDonalds, and decided that's where she would have my third birthday party.

She picked up the phone book, looked up "McDonald," selected a location that was closest to our house, and called the number. When a woman answered the phone, my mom informed her, "I would like to have my daughter's birthday party at your place." The woman finally understood what was going on and responded, "I would love to host a birthday party here, but my house is just too small."

It turns out that my mom, not realizing the difference between the white pages and the yellow pages, had attempted to schedule a party at someone's house with the last name of McDonald rather than the fast-food chain!

SOURCE: http://www.culturalconfusions.com (Story 1 by Gina Frazier; Story 2 by Anetta Hunek).

Operations Plan

The *operations plan* goes beyond the manufacturing process (when the new venture involves manufacturing) and describes the flow of goods and services from production to the customer. It might include inventory or storage of manufactured products, shipping, inventory control procedures, and customer support services. A nonmanufacturer such as a retailer or service provider would also need this section in the business plan to explain the chronological steps in completing a business transaction. For example, an Internet retail sports clothing operation would need to describe how and where the products offered would be purchased, how they would be stored, how the inventory would be managed, how products would be shipped, and how a customer would log on and complete a transaction. In addition, this would be a convenient place for the entrepreneur to discuss the role of technology in the business transaction process. For any Internet retail operation, some explanation of the technology requirements needed to efficiently and profitably complete a successful business transaction should be included in this section.

It is important to note here that the major distinction between services and manufactured goods is that services involve intangible performances. This implies that they cannot be touched, seen, tasted, heard, or felt in the same manner as manufactured products. Airlines, hotels, car rental agencies, theaters, and hospitals, to name a few, rely on business delivery or quality of service. For these firms, performance often depends on location, facility layout, and personnel, which can in turn affect service quality (including such factors as reliability, responsiveness, and assurance). The process of delivering this quality of service is what distinguishes one new service venture from another and thus needs to be the focus of its operations plan. Some key questions or issues for both the manufacturing and nonmanufacturing new venture include

- Will you be responsible for all or part of the manufacturing operation?
- If some manufacturing is subcontracted, who will be the subcontractors? (Give names and addresses.)
- Why were these subcontractors selected?
- What are the costs of the subcontracted manufacturing? (Include copies of any written contracts.)
- What will be the layout of the production process? (Illustrate steps if possible.)
- What equipment will be needed immediately for manufacturing?
- What raw materials will be needed for manufacturing?
- Who are the suppliers of new materials and what are the appropriate costs?
- What are the costs of manufacturing the product?
- What are the future capital equipment needs of the venture?

Marketing Plan

The *marketing plan* is an important part of the business plan because it describes how the product(s) or service(s) will be distributed, priced, and promoted. Marketing research evidence to support any of the critical marketing decision strategies, as well as for forecasting sales, should be described in this section. Specific forecasts for product(s) or service(s) are indicated to project the profitability of the venture. Budget and appropriate controls needed for marketing strategy decisions are also needed. Potential investors regard the marketing plan as critical to the success of the new venture. The global entrepreneur should make every effort to prepare as comprehensive and detailed a plan as possible so that investors can be clear as to what the goals of the venture are and what strategies are to be implemented to effectively achieve these goals. Marketing planning will be an annual requirement (with careful monitoring and changes made on a weekly or monthly basis) for the entrepreneur and should be regarded as the road map for short-term decision making.

Financials

The final area of the global business plan covers the financials. Like the other aspects, the *financials* are an important part of the plan. They determine the potential investment commitment needed for the new venture and indicate whether the business plan is economically feasible.

Generally, three financial areas are discussed in this section of the business plan. First, the global entrepreneur should summarize the forecasted sales and the appropriate expenses for at least the first 3 years, with the first year's projections provided monthly. It includes the forecasted sales, cost of goods sold, and the general and administrative expenses. Net profit after taxes can then be projected by estimating income taxes.

The second major area of financial information needed is cash flow figures for 3 years, with the first year's projections provided monthly. Since bills have to be paid at different times of the year, it is important to determine the demands on cash on a monthly basis, especially in the first year. Remember that sales may be irregular and receipts from customers also may be spread out, thus necessitating the borrowing of short-term capital to meet fixed expenses, such as salaries and utilities.

The last financial item needed in this section of the business plan is the projected balance sheet. This shows the financial condition of the business at a specific time. It summarizes the assets of a business, its liabilities (what is owed), the investment of the entrepreneur and any partners, and retained earnings (or cumulative losses). Any assumptions considered for the balance sheet or any other item in the financial plan should be listed for the benefit of the potential investor.

Appendix (Exhibits)

The *appendix* of the business plan generally contains any backup material that is not necessary in the text of the document. Reference to any of the documents in the appendix should be made in the plan itself. Letters from customers, distributors, or subcontractors are examples of information that should be included in the appendix. Any documentation of information—that is, secondary data or primary research data used to support plan decisions—should also be included. Leases, contracts, or any other types of agreements that have been initiated also may be included in the appendix. Finally, price lists from suppliers and competitors may be added.

Do's and Don'ts of the Global Business Plan

The global business plan needs to carefully articulate all aspects of the global venture. Some of the do's and don'ts of preparing this important document are listed in Table 4.5. Two do's focus on the all-important executive summary—write it last and make sure it is a powerful statement focused on the recipient and objectives of the global business plan. The market entry strategy, marketing plan, and obtaining market research data are also important.

❖ **Table 4.5** Do's and Don'ts of a Global Business Plan

Do:	Don't:
• Write the executive summary last and revise it until it is a succinct and powerful statement of you, your company, and its goals. • Tailor the executive summary to each recipient of the business plan. • Include a dated and numbered statement of confidentiality to create a proper follow-up schedule. • Include information about the potential economic, legal, and political hurdles your company may face in a foreign market. • Clearly delineate the ownership of the company and its organizational structure. • Present multiple market entry strategies and assess each proposed strategy. • Describe in full the operations plan, including costs, from manufacturing or acquiring inventory to sales and shipment. • Strengthen your marketing plan by referring to in-depth market research. • Provide detailed sales and expense forecasts as well as projected cash flows and a balance sheet.	• Write the executive summary first and make minimal revisions. • Treat the business plan as a one-time report instead of a living document that should be constantly reviewed and updated. • Skip any of the sections of the business plan. • Use outdated data and figures when creating the operations plan and the financial projections. • Ignore market research when defining your market plan. • Limit your company to only one form of market entry strategy. • Hastily prepare the sales and expense forecasts, and other financial data. • Be the only editor of the business plan.

Sample Global Business Plan

A sample global business plan created by a student, Joseph Naaman, for his company, Maktabi, can be found starting on page 373.

Summary

This chapter takes an entrepreneur through the important process of creating a business plan, which is integral in strategically managing an organization. Business plans are used by global entrepreneurs to examine the internal and external factors that affect a company's decision to go global. A well-developed global business plan provides guidance in decision making and organizing the international direction of the company; indicates the viability of an organization in the designated global market(s); and serves as the vehicle for obtaining financing. Each section of the business plan is described, including each section's necessary content. The primary sections of the business plan are the executive summary; introduction; political, legal, and economic aspects of the new opportunity; organizational plan; product/service; market entry strategy; operations plan; marketing plan; financials; and appendix.

Questions for Discussion

1. What role does a business plan play for a global entrepreneur?
2. What are the key sections of the plan?
3. What additional information is needed for a global plan that would not be needed for a strictly domestic business?

Chapter Exercises

1. Create a table containing each section of the business plan, its primary audience, and its primary function and importance.
2. Explain the role of the financial section of the business plan, including where the information comes from, who the primary audience is, and what internal planning function this section serves.
3. Suppose you are an American donut company that has decided to launch a donut bakery and cafe in Shanghai, China. The company grosses US$25 million per year from donut and café sales, US$5 million of which is attributed to its bakery-cafés in Australia and New Zealand. Create an executive summary to convince a Chinese venture capitalist to invest in this project.
4. Consider your own business or business idea and outline a business plan for it. Identify which areas of the business plan will need more research, brainstorming, and calculations and what steps are needed to address these areas.

References

CNBC (Producer). (2009). *The entrepreneurs: TOMS shoes* [Television program]. New York: Author.

Hisrich, R. D., Peters, M. A., & Shepherd, D. A. (2008). *Entrepreneurship* (8th ed.). Burr Ridge, IL: McGraw-Hill/Irwin.

Taylor, M. (2006, May 27). Healthy living to be made out of wellness: Investors will only be interested if you have a business plan with significant room for growth. *South China Morning Post*, p. 8.

TOMS. (2011, June 8). *TOMS company overview.* Retrieved from http://www.toms.com/corporate-info/

Suggested Readings

Fried, J., & Hansson, D. H. (2010). *Rework*. New York: Crown Business.

Told from the perspective of successful entrepreneurs Jason Fried and David Heinemeier Hansson, this book delves into the world of entrepreneurship from a nontraditional yet successful point of view. Based on their own experience launching and managing a software company that specializes in web-based productivity software, the authors describe their own unique methods of running a business while maintaining work–life balance and staying true to themselves. In a manifesto-like style, the authors give simple tips and suggestions on how to survive in the competitive environment of the 21st century with innovative but provocative ideas.

Gruber, M. (2007, November). Uncovering the value of planning in new venture creation: A process and contingency perspective. *Journal of Business Venturing, 22(6), 782.*

This article describes how the different founding environments affect the planning process, regimes and new ventures. Select planning activities and swift planning are recommended for entrepreneurs in highly dynamic environments, while a broader approach to planning is better in slower environments. The author's findings overall suggest entrepreneurs should use a flexible, tool kit approach to venture planning.

Jordan, R. (2010). *How they did it: Billion dollar insights from the heart of America.* Northbrook, IL: RedFlash Press.

This book is a compilation of 45 stories told by some of the most successful entrepreneurs in the United States. These real-life stories not only inspire entrepreneurial spirit but also give great tips and ideas about how to grow a one-person operation into a multimillion-dollar for-profit company. In a kind of history lesson of contemporary entrepreneurship, author Robert Jordan allows readers to learn from the mistakes and achievements of those who have made it, and to share their secrets with budding entrepreneurs.

Part 2

Entering the Global Market

5

Selecting International Business Opportunities

Profile: Frontera Foods

Jupiterimages/Brand X Pictures/ThinkStockPhotos

Most businesses create a product, and then hire a celebrity to endorse it. Frontera Foods broke the mold by creating its own celebrity rather than outsourcing the job. As a young chef, Rick Bayless wanted nothing more than to bring the authentic flavors of Mexico to the United States. Having spent 6 years discovering, cooking, and savoring the local cuisines in different parts of Mexico, Bayless had a passion for the food. Growing up in a family of restaurateurs, Bayless fulfilled his destiny in 1987 with the opening of his own Mexican-style restaurant, the Frontera Grill in Chicago, Illinois. Touted by locals for its exquisite cuisine, Frontera was especially known for the fresh homemade salsa served with every meal. One of his biggest fans was marketing executive Manuel Valdes, who frequented the restaurant. Every visit he would inevitably say, "Someone should bottle this stuff," in reference to the delicious salsa he so enjoyed. Bayless agreed and the partnership was born.

The first major hurdle in selling Bayless's salsa in retail stores was the manufacturing process. Bayless refused to accept the premade or processed ingredients that manufacturers currently used. Luckily, he finally found a small manufacturing plant that was already used to mass-producing foods using fresh ingredients and traditional Mexican cooking techniques, as Bayless wanted. With the chef overseeing the process, they began to produce and jar salsas. The company obtained distribution, but as a specialty product rather than a staple. Using only fresh, high-quality ingredients was expensive; the salsa had to be priced accordingly. At about $4 per jar, Frontera salsa was about twice as expensive as competitive products. In addition, the company was using truly Mexican flavors that American consumers were not familiar with such as *chipotle* and *habanero*. The entrepreneurs realized that they would have to educate the American public about these flavors if they wanted Frontera salsa to gain momentum in the market.

Concurrently, the Food Television Network and celebrity chefs such as Bobby Flay and Emeril Lagasse were gaining popularity and recognition. Taking advantage of the trend, a decision was made to make Bayless a TV star. Rather than vying for a spot on the Food Network, they chose to produce a show themselves and distribute it on public television. *Mexico: One Plate at a Time* starring Rick Bayless appeared on PBS, fulfilling the need to educate American consumers about the Spanish names of Mexican foods and flavors, as well as Bayless's personal mission to bring true Mexican cuisine to the United States. The show was a success and both Bayless and Frontera gained name and brand recognition. Today, Americans use terms like *chipotle* (pronounced correctly) as frequently as the words *salsa* or *jalapeno*.

The TV show propelled Frontera from specialty shops to being a staple at Whole Foods market. Subsequently, the firm has enjoyed double-digit sales growth year after year, and expanded its line to more than 100 different products. Most recently, Frontera Foods partnered with Macy's to create Frontera Fresco, a quick-service restaurant featuring food inspired by Mexican street fare. Ever in pursuit of innovation and the "next big thing," 3.5% of profits go to new product development in hopes of keeping the company at the forefront of the Hispanic food market.

SOURCE: Adapted from CNBC (2009) and Bayless (2011).

Chapter Objectives

1. To develop an understanding of how to best select the most appropriate foreign market for each venture
2. To determine the best indicators for entry into a foreign country or market
3. To identify primary and secondary sources of information on specific foreign market industries or sectors
4. To recognize how to collect country market data
5. To demonstrate the importance of positioning the venture correctly and how to pursue competitive intelligence to enhance this strategy
6. To learn how to assess competitive strengths and weaknesses in foreign markets and determine a strategy to combat them

Introduction

With so many potential markets and prospective countries available, critical issues for the global entrepreneur are foreign market selection (the focus of this chapter) and entry strategy (the focus of Chapter 7). Should the global entrepreneur enter the top prospective country or should he or she employ a part of a country or multi-country approach? Should he or she choose the largest market possible or one that is easier to understand and navigate? Is a more-developed foreign market preferable to one that is developing?

These are just some of the questions confronting the global entrepreneur when deciding which market to enter. The market selection decision should be based on past sales and competitive positioning, as well as assessment of each foreign market alternative. Data need to be systematically collected on both a regional and a country basis. A region can be a collection of countries, such as the European Union, or an area within a country, such as the southeastern part of China.

A systematic process is needed to select the best market in terms of market potential, ease of entry and ease of doing business. This helps the entrepreneur to avoid relying on assumptions and gut feelings. Any statistical data should be collected for at least a three year period so any trends are evident. This collected data will also be used to develop the marketing plan and appropriate entry strategy.

Foreign Market Selection Model

Although there are several market selection models available, a good method employs a five-step approach: (1) develop appropriate indicators, (2) collect data and convert into comparable indicators, (3) establish an appropriate weight for each indicator, (4) analyze the data, and (5) select the appropriate market from the market rankings.

In Step 1, appropriate indicators are developed based on past sales, competitive research, experience, and discussions with other global entrepreneurs. Specific indicators for the new company are needed in three general areas: overall market indicators, market growth indicators, and product indicators. Market size indicators generally center on population, per capita income, market for the specific product for consumer products and sales, and profits of particular companies for industrial products. In terms of market growth, the overall country growth should be determined as well as the growth rate for the particular market of the venture. Finally, appropriate product indicators, such as existing exports of the specific product category to the market and the number of sales leads and interest, should be established.

In Step 2, data for each of the indicators are collected and converted to facilitate comparison. Both primary data (original information collected for the particular requirement) and secondary data (published data already existing) need to be collected. Typically, secondary data are gathered first to establish what information needs to be collected through primary research. When collecting international secondary data, there are several problems that vary to some extent based on the stage of economic development of the country. These problems include (a) comparability (the data can be grouped differently in each country); (b) availability (some countries have much more country data than others, usually reflecting the stage of economic development); (c) accuracy (sometimes the data have not been collected using rigorous standards or are biased due to the interests of the government of the country; the latter is particularly a problem in nonmarket-oriented economies); and (d) cost of the data. The United States has the Freedom of Information Act, which makes all government-collected data that does not pertain to security or defense available to all. This is not the case in all countries. For example, one global entrepreneur was interested in opening the first Western health club in Moscow. He was going to charge two rates: a higher hard currency rate to foreigners and a lower ruble rate to Russians and other citizens of countries in the former Soviet Union. In determining the best location, he was interested in finding areas of the city where most foreigners lived. After significant searching to no avail and a high degree of frustration, he finally was able to buy the data needed from the former KGB (Soviet Union security branch).

When researching foreign markets, you will usually want economic and demographic data such as population, GDP (gross domestic product), per capita income, inflation rate, literacy rate, unemployment rate, and education levels. There are many sources for this and other foreign information at government agencies, websites, and embassies. One important source of data is STAT-country name, such as STAT-Austria. The STAT-USA database has good information, including a large number of international reports—Country Reports, Country Analysis Briefs (CABS), Country Commercial Guides (CCGs), Food Market Reports, International Reports and Reviews, Department of State Background Notes, and Import/Export Reports. Other good sources of data are trade associations and embassies.

The data for each selected indicator are then converted to point scores so each indicator from each country can be numerically ranked against the others. Various methods can be used to assign these values, each of which involves some judgment by the global entrepreneur. Another method is to compare country data for each indicator against global standards.

Step 3 establishes appropriate weights for the indicators that reflect the importance of each in predicting foreign market potential. For one company manufacturing hospital beds, the number and types of hospitals, the age of the hospitals and their beds, and the government expenditure on health care were the best country indicators in selecting a foreign market. This procedure results in each indicator receiving a weight that reflects its relative importance. The assignment of points and weights, as well as the selection of indicators, vary greatly from one global entrepreneur to another and indeed are somewhat arbitrary. Regardless, this requires intensive thinking and internal discussion, which results in better market selection decisions.

Step 4 involves analyzing the results. When looking at the data, the global entrepreneur needs to evaluate them carefully. A "what if" analysis can be conducted by changing some of the weights and seeing how the results vary.

Step 5 is the selection of a market to enter and follow-up markets so that an appropriate entry strategy can be determined and a market plan developed. China, India, Ireland, and Germany are countries ICU Global, a videoconferencing provider, is targeting, according to founder and chief executive Stephen McKenzie. McKenzie feels it is easy to expand into other countries even when you are a small business as long as you can provide "the same quality assurance to end users." He adds, "Technology allows you to provide full-support, virtual operations in other countries." The countries in question have been selected because they offer the greatest opportunities for ICU Global. "It's good to have a base in Germany because you can easily access the rest of Europe," McKenzie says. "Meanwhile, Ireland has a large number of companies from continental Europe and the United States investing in it, so there is good opportunity in the context of new technology. Then, there's a thriving technology center in India" (Woods, 2008).

Developing Foreign Market Indicators

While some global entrepreneurs, especially those who have had success in their domestic markets, have an idea of the best foreign markets to enter based on sales or past experience, most do not. Thus, for those in this latter group, it is important to identify some indicators for potential success in foreign markets to assist in the selection process.

Internal Company Indicators

Several internal company indicators can be used to develop foreign market indicators, including competitive information, information from fellow global entrepreneurs, previous leads and sales, and trade show information. Foreign markets with good potential are ones that a company's competitors are entering.

Another good internal way to establish foreign market indicators is to discuss the various markets with noncompeting global entrepreneurs. These individuals can provide significant information based on their experience in specific foreign markets and advice on the potential of your company's product success in those markets. Sometimes you can even establish a mentoring relationship with a more experienced global entrepreneur.

A third source for developing marketing indicators is your company's past sales and leads. Leads and actual sales, while doing business domestically, from out-of-country markets are by far the best indicators of foreign market potential. Care needs to be taken to ensure that potential leads really are meaningful and not just distributors trying to establish product lines for their country. A sale in a foreign country signifies that at least for one customer your product can compete.

The final sources for developing foreign market indicators are leads from domestic and foreign trade shows. These gather firms and buyers in a particular product area and provide a great opportunity to gather market information to determine market potential in various countries. They also provide an opportunity to gather competitive information on both domestic and foreign products.

Primary Versus Secondary Foreign Market Data

One of the most important aspects of any market selection decision is market and demographic information on the foreign country. This can be secondary data (data that are already published) or primary data (original data gathered specifically for the particular decision). Although primary data are generally more accurate, it is also more costly and time-consuming to collect versus data that already exist and have been collected by third parties. It is usually best for the global entrepreneur to start the data-gathering process by first identifying the secondary data available about the foreign country.

Secondary Data

The first step in obtaining secondary data is to identify the classification codes associated with the company's product/service. These include the Standard Industrial Classification (SIC), the North American Industry Classification System (NAICS), the Standard International Trade Classification (SITC), and the International Harmonized Commodity Description and Coding System (Harmonized System), each of which will be discussed in turn.

The SIC code is appropriate for an initial appraisal of the extent and nature of the need in a foreign market, particularly for industrial products. Standard industrial classifications—the means by which the U.S. government classifies manufacturing industries—are based on the product produced or operation performed. Each industry is assigned a 2-, 3-, or, where needed for further breakdown, 4-digit code.

To determine the primary market demand using the SIC method, first determine all potential customers that have a need for the product or service being considered. Once the groups have been selected, the appropriate basis for demand determination is established and the published material on the industry groups obtained from the *Census of Manufacturers*. Then, the primary demand can be determined based on the size of the group and the expenditure in the product area. The website for using the SIC code is www .osha.gov/oshstats/sicser.html.

The North American Industry Classification System (NAICS) is a newer system replacing the SIC system. This newer system is based on a 6-digit code versus the 4-digit code of the SIC system and has new industries, particularly in the service and technology sectors, that were not included in the SIC system. The NAICS system is used in the United States, Canada, and Mexico, allowing for greater country comparisons than previously available. The website for the NAICS system is www.census.gov/epcd/www/naics.html.

Once the global entrepreneur has obtained the codes for his or her product/service, these can be converted to the code system used in the European Union. Each NAICS Rev. 1.1 code is shown with its corresponding *International Standard Industrial Classification* (ISIC) Rev. 3.1 code on an easily accessible website (http://unstats .un.org/unsd/cr/registry/regso.asp?Ci=26&Lg=1).

The final two coding systems are more useful for international data. The Standard International Trade Classification (SITC), developed by the United Nations in 1950, is used to report international trade statistics. It classifies products and services based on a 5-digit code, but frequently data are available at only the 2- or 3-digit code level. Each year, approximately 140 countries report their import and export trade statistics to the United Nations. The data are compiled and printed in the United Nations' *International Trade Statistics Yearbook*. The data are also available at http://unstats .un.org/unsd.

The final and perhaps best system for obtaining international data is the Harmonized Commodity Description and Coding System, better known as the International Harmonized Commodity Codes. Each product or service is identified by a 10-digit number that is broken down by chapter (first 2 digits), heading (first 4 digits), subheading (first 6 digits), and the commodity code (all 10 digits). Here are some sample codes:

Name	*International Harmonized Commodity Code*
Peanut butter	2008.11.1000
Grand pianos	9201.20.0000
Farmed Atlantic salmon	0302.12.0003

Care must be taken when using the International Harmonized Commodity codes because there may be differences between countries, as well as variance within a country depending on whether the codes are used for exporting or importing products. In the United States, for example, the purpose of the commodity codes is different for importing and exporting. For importing, the code is used to determine the import duty (if any); for exporting, the primary use of the code is for statistical reporting. This results in two sets of commodity codes in the United States: one set for importing and one set for exporting. The exporting system of classification is labeled Schedule B, and the importing system of classification is called the Harmonized Tariff Schedule, maintained by the Office of Tariff Affairs and Trade Agreements.

Problems in Collecting Secondary Data

There are several problems in collecting international secondary data. The first, and perhaps the most troublesome one is *accuracy*. Often, countries are not particularly rigorous in their data collection, resulting in data not reflective of the true situation in a country. Sometimes, particularly in more controlled countries, the data are collected to satisfy a political agenda, rather than statistical reliability.

The second problem is *comparability*—the data available in one country may not be comparable to the data collected in another country. This may be due to the different methodologies used, errors in the data collection, or differences in applying the commodity coding system.

Lack of current data in a country is a third problem. In many countries, the frequency of data collection is much more sporadic than in more developed countries. In dynamically changing economies, 4- to 5-year-old data are obsolete and not very valuable in decision making.

The final problem in secondary data is the *cost*. In many countries, the data may only be available at a fairly high price.

Sources of Country Market Data

Finding useful, accurate data for your country selection decision can sometimes be challenging. Even for the global entrepreneur who has had experience collecting data in the United States, the process of collecting data in other countries is much more difficult and usually more expensive. There are several sources for both country market and industry data discussed in the following sections.

Country Industry Market Data

Economic and country data on such things as age, population, gross domestic product, inflation, literacy, and per capita income is often available from a variety of sources depending on the country. The CIA's *World Factbook* provides data on various aspects of a country, such as demographics of population, economic indicators, geography, military, politics, and resources available. The Country Commercial Guides (CCG) are produced for most countries on a yearly basis. Each guide contains the following information on a country: executive summary, economic trends and outlook, political environment, marketing U.S. products and services, leading sectors for U.S. exports and investments, trade regulations and standards, investment climate, trade and project financing, and business travel. It also has numerous appendices in such areas as country data, domestic economy, trade, investment statistics, U.S. and country contacts, market research, and trade event schedules. These are invaluable to the global entrepreneur in understanding the numbers and trade possibilities in a country. Even though this data is mainly U.S. focused, the reports contain valuable information for global entrepreneurs regardless of country. The National Trade Data Bank (NTDB), maintained by the U.S. Department of Commerce, is also an important database available to the global entrepreneur at virtually no cost. The NTDB database comprises international reports, trade statistics, research, and leads on trading opportunities.

Another source of country market data is STAT-USA. This international data source, managed by an agency of the U.S. Department of Commerce, is enormous and includes the just-discussed NTDB, GLOBUS (Global Business Opportunities) database, and the State of the Nation database. Contributed to by many governmental agencies, the STAT-USA website has a multitude of international and national reports available, including

- African Development Bank Business Opportunities
- Asia Commerce Overview
- Bureau of Export Administration (BXA) Annual Report
- Computer Markets
- Country Analysis Briefs (CABS)
- Directory of Feasibility Studies and Projects
- Fish and Fishery Product Imports and Exports
- Food Market Reports
- Foreign Labor Trends
- International Automotive Industry
- Latin American/Caribbean Business Bulletin
- Minerals Yearbook
- Steel Monitoring Report
- Telecommunications Information and Reports
- Trade Associations and Publications
- U.S. Foreign Trade Reports
- U.S. International Trade in Goods and Services
- World Agricultural Production Reports
- World Bank International Business Opportunities

Because this is just a small sampling of the reports and data available, it is important that every global entrepreneur look into STAT-USA when collecting the needed international data. Each country also has data on its STAT-(country name), such as STAT-Brazil.

One of the best sources of information is the World Bank, which uses various criteria to rank every country on the ease of doing business there. The index ranks countries (economies) from 1 to 178 and is calculated by averaging the percentile rankings on each of the 10 topics covered in *Doing Business: Economy Rankings* (2008). The criteria being ranked include ease of doing business, ease of starting a business, dealing with licenses, registering property, getting credit, protecting investors, paying taxes, trading across borders, enforcing contracts, and closing a business. The rankings for selected countries are shown in Table 5.1. Singapore, New Zealand, and the United States were ranked 1, 2, and 3, respectively, on the ease of doing business. Australia, Canada, and New Zealand were ranked 1, 2, and 3, respectively, on the ease of starting a business.

❖ Table 5.1 Rankings of Countries on Various Business Criteria

Economy	Ease of Doing Business Rank	Starting a Business	Dealing With Construction Permits	Registering Property	Getting Credit	Protecting Investors	Paying Taxes	Trading Across Borders	Enforcing Contracts	Closing a Business
Singapore	1	4	2	15	6	2	4	1	13	2
Hong Kong SAR, China	2	6	1	56	2	3	3	2	2	15
New Zealand	3	1	5	3	2	1	26	28	9	16
United Kingdom	4	17	16	22	2	10	16	15	23	7
United States	5	9	27	12	6	5	62	20	8	14
Denmark	6	27	10	30	15	28	13	5	30	5
Canada	7	3	29	37	32	5	10	41	58	3
Norway	8	33	65	8	46	20	18	9	4	4
Ireland	9	11	38	78	15	5	7	23	37	9
Australia	10	2	63	35	6	59	48	29	16	12
Saudi Arabia	11	13	14	1	46	16	6	18	140	65
Georgia	12	8	7	2	15	20	61	35	41	105
Finland	13	32	55	26	32	59	65	6	11	6
Sweden	14	39	20	15	72	28	39	7	52	18
Iceland	15	29	31	11	32	74	35	79	3	17
Korea, Rep.	16	60	22	74	15	74	49	8	5	13
Japan	18	98	44	59	15	16	112	24	19	1
Thailand	19	95	12	19	72	12	91	12	25	46
Germany	22	88	18	67	15	93	88	14	6	35
Belgium	25	31	41	177	46	16	70	44	21	8
France	26	21	19	142	46	74	55	26	7	44

Switzerland	27	80	37	14	15	167	16	43	28	41
Israel	29	36	121	147	6	5	82	10	96	40
Netherlands	30	71	105	46	46	109	27	13	29	11
Portugal	31	59	111	31	89	44	73	27	24	21
Austria	32	125	57	33	15	132	104	25	9	20
Taiwan, China	33	24	95	32	72	74	87	17	90	10
South Africa	34	75	52	91	2	10	24	149	85	74
Mexico	35	67	22	105	46	44	107	58	81	23
UAE	40	46	26	4	72	120	5	3	134	143
Slovenia	42	28	63	97	116	20	80	56	60	38
Chile	43	62	68	45	72	28	46	68	68	91
Spain	49	147	49	54	46	93	71	54	52	19
Romania	56	44	84	92	15	44	151	47	54	102
Poland	70	113	164	86	15	44	121	49	77	81
Vietnam	78	100	62	43	15	173	124	63	31	124
China	79	151	181	38	65	93	114	50	15	68
Italy	80	68	92	95	89	59	128	59	157	30
Jamaica	81	18	47	106	89	74	174	104	128	24
Pakistan	83	85	98	126	65	28	145	81	155	67
Egypt, Arab Rep.	94	18	154	93	72	74	136	21	143	131
Greece	109	149	51	153	89	154	74	84	88	49
Morocco	114	82	98	124	89	154	124	80	106	59
Argentina	115	142	168	118	65	109	143	115	45	77
Russia	123	108	182	51	89	93	105	162	18	103

(continued)

❖ Table 5.1 (Continued)

Economy	Ease of Doing Business Rank	Starting a Business	Dealing With Construction Permits	Registering Property	Getting Credit	Protecting Investors	Paying Taxes	Trading Across Borders	Enforcing Contracts	Closing a Business
Uruguay	124	139	141	159	46	93	155	132	102	57
Costa Rica	125	116	131	52	65	167	155	69	130	114
Mozambique	126	65	155	144	128	44	101	133	132	129
Brazil	127	128	112	122	89	74	152	114	98	132
Tanzania	128	122	179	151	89	93	120	109	32	113
Iran	129	42	143	156	89	167	115	131	49	111
Bolivia	149	166	98	139	116	132	177	125	136	58
Sudan	154	121	139	40	138	154	94	143	146	183
Iraq	166	174	102	96	168	120	54	179	141	183
Afghanistan	167	25	149	170	128	183	53	183	162	183
Congo, Rep.	177	176	83	133	138	154	180	180	158	128
Central African Republic	182	161	148	141	138	132	182	182	173	183
Chad	183	182	101	137	152	154	179	171	164	183

SOURCE: The World Bank: Economic Rankings, "Doing Business" (2008).

Trade Associations

Trade associations in the United States and throughout the world are also a good source for industry data about a particular country. Some trade associations do market surveys of their members' international activities and are strategically involved in international standards issues for their particular industry.

Trade Publications and Periodicals

There are numerous domestic and international publications specific to particular industries that are also good sources of information. The editorial content of these journals can provide interesting information and insights on trends, companies, and trade shows by giving a more local perspective on the particular market and market conditions. Sometimes trade journals are the best, and often the only source of information on competition and growth rates in a particular country.

Competitive Positioning

One aspect of success in both international and domestic markets is competitive positioning—knowing the competition very well and being able to position your company and product in that product/market space. In positioning your company internationally, it is even more important to identify the strategy of each competitive company. The strategy will significantly affect the manner and commitment of a company in an international market, which in turn affects the nature and degree of its competitive behavior in that market. A competitive company's international strategy may not be the same as yours. If the global entrepreneur emphasizes the competitive analysis too much without taking into account the competitive company's strategy, then he or she can create a reactive strategy that can be totally ineffective and inappropriate. This is particularly important in developing economies where some companies use a "hit or miss" strategy, realizing that many of the markets will lose money and will not be viable over a long period of time.

The global entrepreneur should begin competitive positioning by first documenting the current strategy of each primary competitor. This can be organized by using the form method indicated in Table 5.2. Information on competitors can be gathered initially by using as much public information as possible and then complementing this with a marketing research project. Newspaper articles, websites, catalogs, promotions, interviews with distributors and customers, and any other marketing or company information available should be reviewed. Articles that have been written on competitors can be found by using a computer search in any university or local library. These articles should be analyzed for information on competitor strategies and should identify the names of individuals who were interviewed, referenced, or even mentioned in the articles. Any of these individuals, as well as the author of the article, can then be contacted to obtain further information. All the information can then be summarized in the form in Table 5.2. Once the competitors' strategies have been summarized, the global entrepreneur should begin to identify the strengths and weaknesses of each competitor, as shown in the table.

❖ Table 5.2 An Assessment of Competitor Market Strategies and Strengths and Weaknesses

	Competitor A	Competitor B	Competitor C
Product or service strategies			
Pricing strategies			
Distribution strategies			
Promotion strategies			
Strengths and weaknesses			

SOURCE: Hisrich, R. D., Peters, M. P., & Shepherd, D. A. (2010). *Entrepreneurship: Starting, Developing, and Managing a New Enterprise* (8th ed.). New York: McGraw-Hill, page 226.

The information in Table 5.2 can then be used to formulate the market positioning strategy of the new venture. Will the new venture imitate a particular competitor or will it try to satisfy needs in the market that are not being filled by any other company? This analysis will enlighten the global entrepreneur and provide a solid basis for developing the market entry plan for the international market.

One method for analyzing a market opportunity and determining your competitive position is indicated in Table 5.3. Using this evaluation process, various elements of the opportunity are evaluated, such as (1) the creation and length of the opportunity, (2) its real and perceived value(s), (3) its risks and returns, (4) its competitive environment, (5) its industry, and (6) its fit with the personal skills and goals of the entrepreneur.

It is important that the global entrepreneur understand the nature and root cause of the opportunity. Is it technological change, market shift, government regulation, or competition? These factors and the resulting opportunity result in a different market size and time dimension. The market size and the length of the window of international opportunity form the primary basis for determining the risks and rewards involved. The amount of capital needed determines the returns and rewards.

In this evaluation, the competition is carefully analyzed. Features and potential price for the product/service need to be evaluated against those of competitive products presently in the product/market space in the country. If any major problems and competitive disadvantages are identified, modifications can be made or a new market investigated.

The relative advantages of the product/service versus competitive products can be determined through use of the following questions: How does the new idea compare with competitive products in terms of quality and reliability? Is the idea superior or deficient compared with products currently available in the market? Is this a good market opportunity? These questions and others can be used in a conversational interview. Here, selected individuals are asked to compare the idea against products presently filling that need. By comparing the characteristics and attributes of the new idea, some uniqueness of the idea can be determined.

❖ Table 5.3 Determining the Company's Competitive Position

Factor	Aspects	Competitive Capabilities	Company's Idea/ Capability	Differential Advantage	Unique Selling Proposition
Type of Need Continuing need Declining need Emerging need Future need					
Timing of Need Duration of need Frequency of need Demand cycle Position in life cycle					
Competing Ways to Satisfy Need Doing without Using present way Modifying present way					
Perceived Benefits/Risks Utility to customer Appealing characteristics Customer tastes and preferences Buying motives Consumption habits					
Price Versus Performance Features Price-quantity relationship Demand elasticity Stability of price Stability of market					
Market Size Potential Market growth Market trends Market development requirements Threats to market					
Availability to Customer Funds General economic conditions Economic trends Customer income Financing opportunities					

SOURCE: Hisrich, Robert, *Marketing Decisions for New and Mature Products,* 2ND, ©1991. Printed and electronically reproduced by permission of Pearson Education, Inc., Upper Saddle River, New Jersey.

To accurately evaluate the idea, it is helpful to define the potential needs of the market in terms of timing, satisfaction, alternatives, benefits and risks, future expectations, price-versus-product performance features, market structure and size, and economic conditions (see Table 5.3). These factors need to be evaluated in terms of the idea's competitive strength relative to each factor. This comparison with competitive products will indicate the strengths and weaknesses of the idea.

Once the idea has been evaluated in terms of the need and the market, an initial value determination should be done. In determining the value of the product/service in the international market, financial scheduling—such as cash outflow, cash inflow, contribution to profit, and return on investment—needs to be evaluated in terms of other ideas. Using the form in Table 5.4, the dollar amount of each of the aspects can be determined as accurately as possible so that a quantitative evaluation can be performed. These figures will be revised later as better information becomes available.

Finally, the product/service/international market must fit the personal skills and goals of the global entrepreneur. It is particularly important that the entrepreneur be able to put forth the necessary time and effort required to make the venture succeed. Although many global entrepreneurs feel that the desire can be developed along with the venture, typically this does not materialize and therefore causes problems in the venture's success. A global entrepreneur must believe in the idea so much that he or she will make the necessary sacrifices to develop the idea into a sound business model that will be the basis for a successful new venture in the international market.

International Competitive Information

There are many good international sources for competitive information. These include company information, databases, journals, newspapers, trade associations, and personal interviews.

Company Information

Particularly with publicly traded companies, the company itself provides a significant amount of data useful to the global entrepreneur. This is often the best and

❖ CULTURAL STORY

I was living in Colombia and one of the vice presidents from the Argentina headquarters had just arrived. It was just 10:00 a.m. and an assistant offered him a *tinto.*

In Spanish, *vino tinto* means "red wine." The VP was confused and could not understand how Colombians could start drinking so early, not to mention at work!

He later discovered that *tinto* is the slang for "coffee"—at least in the city of Medellin.

SOURCE: http://www.culturalconfusions.com (Story by Bernardo Alanis).

easiest source of competitive information and is usually very accurate, particularly for companies in developed economies. All company literature and information regarding their international activities should be collected. Sometimes this is very

❖ Table 5.4 Determining the Value of the Product/Service in the International Market

Value Consideration	Cost (in $)
Cash Outflow R&D costs Marketing costs Capital equipment costs Other costs	
Cash Inflow Sales of new product Effect on additional sales Salvageable value	
Net Cash Flow Maximum exposure Time to maximum exposure Duration of exposure Total investment Maximum net cash in a single year	
Profit Profit from new product Profit affecting additional sales of existing products Fraction of total company profit	
Relative Return Return on shareholders' equity (ROE) Return on investment (ROI) Cost of capital Present value (PV) Discounted cash flow (DCF) Return on assets employed (ROA) Return on sales	
Comparisons Compared to other investments Compared to other product opportunities Compared to other investment opportunities	

SOURCE: Hisrich, Robert, *Marketing Decisions for New and Mature Products,* 2ND, ©1991. Printed and electronically reproduced by permission of Pearson Education, Inc., Upper Saddle River, New Jersey.

easily obtained at international trade shows, where more detailed information is available from the individuals staffing the company's booth. Of course, the website of the company should be thoroughly explored, as well as the websites of overseas customers and distributors. Companies continually put more and more important information on their websites.

The international advertising of each competitive company should also be examined. This will help develop the market entry strategy and marketing campaign. This is also particularly helpful in providing much-needed pricing information. Whenever possible, be sure to determine if the advertisement was placed by the company or the distributor in the international market. If the advertisement mentions only one distributor as the contact and provides no details on how to reach the company, or if there are products featured from more than one manufacturer, the advertisement was probably placed by the distributor. This is important because the manufacturer's direct involvement in the placement of the advertisement suggests that this particular market is a priority. Direct placement of advertisements in a market indicates a higher level of commitment and involvement in the particular market. The advertisements also provide insight into how the competitive company is competing in the particular market; a company's competitive strategies may vary from one international market to the next.

International Databases

Four primary databases provide good sources of international competitive information. These are the Directory of United States Exporters, Port Import Export Report Service (PIERS), United Nations' *International Trade Statistics Yearbook*, and United States Exports by Commodity. Each will be discussed in turn.

The Directory of United States Exporters, published each year by the *Journal of Commerce*, is a combination of some information from PIERS and company responses to a questionnaire. The data for each company includes

- Address
- Telephone and fax numbers
- Number of employees
- Year established
- Bank SIC code
- Modes of transportation used
- Contact names and titles
- Commodity code and description of products exported
- Destination countries
- Annual 20-foot equivalent units of containers (TEUs)
- Annual number of shipments
- Company PIERS identification numbers

Sometimes one of the most important pieces of information—destination country—is not reported directly but simply indicates worldwide. The Directory of United States Exporters is available in both print and CD-ROM versions directly from the *Journal of Commerce* and can often be used at the state trade assistance center.

The second useful database is the Port Import Export Report Service (PIERS). The information in this database comes from the manifests of vessels loading international cargo outbound from the United States, as well as the manifests of all inbound shipments (imports). Although not every item is available in every situation, the information in the PIERS database includes

- Product description
- PIERS product code
- Harmonized tariff code and description
- U.S. and overseas port name
- Container size, quantity, TEU count, and cubic feet
- Steamship line and vessel name
- Manifest number
- Cargo quantity and unit of measure
- Cargo weight
- Voyage number
- Estimated cargo value
- Payment type
- Bank name
- Shipment direction
- U.S. and overseas origins and destinations
- Marks and numbers
- Name and address of U.S. importer (imports only)
- Bill of lading number
- Name and address of U.S. exporter
- Container number
- Name and address of foreign shipper (imports only)
- Customs clearing district (imports only)
- Name and address of notify party
- Arrival and departure dates in U.S. ports

The PIERS database has been expanded to include the shipping activities of most ports of Latin American countries and Mexico.

Journals, Newspapers, and Trade Associations

Journals, newspapers, and trade associations provide another very valuable source of information on competition. Most trade journals are very industry specific and often focus on international activities in that industry. There are also industry trade journals in foreign markets. From these, competitive product and other competitive information, distribution lists, advertisements, and other industry data can be easily obtained at little or no cost through the various search and retrieval options available. Many are available on the Internet.

While not usually as valuable, newspapers can also provide competitive information, particularly the local newspaper in the city where the competitive company is headquartered. The local newspaper often provides information not found anywhere else in its coverage of the company and interviews with company managers.

Finally, trade associations in the industry often have summary data on sales and pricing in the industry. Most trade associations track international trends and data. Even just a list of association members provides information about the companies interested in a particular industry.

Personal Interviews

Probably the best and most comprehensive source of competitive information comes from personal interviews with individuals who really know the competitor company and international market. By interviewing staff writers of journals and newspapers, the global entrepreneur can obtain up-to-date information and speculation. Even though they are not company specific, government contacts in a particular country can provide information about competitive trends and challenges. Industry experts can provide detailed information on the industry and usually on companies in that industry. And, best of all, foreign customers and distributors can provide detailed information about the local market and the activities of competitors.

While you need to analyze foreign markets and the competition, and adapt your product or service to meet local market needs to expand internationally, you will also need a person to run the operation. No one knows this better than Bruce McGaw, president of Bruce McGaw Graphics, a West Nyack, New York, fine-arts poster publisher. "As smart as I am about the American market, my knowledge doesn't necessarily apply abroad," admits McGaw. Rather than sending one of his U.S. employees to establish a London distributorship, he decided to search for a local manager to run his United Kingdom operation. Because he did not want to "run over there every other week," he began searching for "someone talented, who would take the ball and run with it." The individual needed the following:

- Significant industry experience and real marketplace intelligence
- An understanding that customer service was central to the company's success
- The ability to take charge and run the business as if it were "his own little business"

McGaw found the right individual—a customer whose business was struggling. McGaw Graphics bought the company and the individual became the UK manager. Five years later, European sales accounted for $3.5 million of the company's total $15 million in revenue; the UK operation was considered a market leader. McGaw used a similar strategy in France when he acquired a business run by an American. "Where you set up your business is not as important as finding the right person to run it," says McGaw. Although his strategic plan includes expansion into Germany, Italy, and Spain, McGaw will not move until he finds the right managers (Fenn, 1995).

Summary

This chapter deals with how global entrepreneurs should research and select the best foreign market(s) to launch their company or their business. Finding the best market is only possible with thorough research using multiple resources. The chapter describes an effective five-step foreign market selection process that a global entrepreneur should use: (1) develop appropriate indicators, (2) collect data and convert into comparable indicators, (3) establish an appropriate weight for each indicator, (4) analyze the data, and (5) select the appropriate market from the market rankings. A global entrepreneur must determine the best indicators for whether or not the company will do well in the foreign market and then collect information based on those indicators from federal and international commerce and trade institutions, as well as from competitors and other global entrepreneurs that are working in the same market. At least 3 years of detailed information needs to be collected and analyzed to develop a trend. The information will be either from primary sources, which is a more costly and time-consuming process, or secondary sources, which is normally much easier to access but not as specific. The main problems that a global entrepreneur will find with secondary data are its lack of accuracy, comparability between countries/regions, lack of current data, and potentially high costs. Analyzing the strengths and weaknesses of competitors' strategies can provide guidelines for developing the best strategy and determining the most appropriate market.

Questions for Discussion

1. What types of information should entrepreneurs seek out before deciding which foreign market to enter?
2. What are the different types and sources of information that are available?
3. What are some potential problems with data collected in another country?
4. Jean-Marie is considering expanding her bakery business from France into Croatia. What information would help her determine a good location to start her business there?

Chapter Exercises

1. Pick a business and create the key indicators that you will use to analyze the new market.
2. Using the same business you chose for Exercise 1, outline the information that you will need to collect about the new market.
3. Finally, create a list of competitors in the new market and identify primary sources to interview about these competitors.

References

Bayless, R. (2011). *About Frontera Foods.* Retrieved from http://www.rickbayless.com/

CNBC (Producer). (2009). *The Entrepreneurs: Frontera Foods* [Television program].

Doing Business. (2008). *Economy rankings.* Retrieved from http://www.doingbusiness.org/rankings

Fenn, D. (1995, June). Opening up an overseas operation. *Inc., 17*(8), 89.

Hisrich, R. D. (2004). *How to fix and prevent the 13 biggest problems that derail business.* New York: McGraw-Hill.

Hisrich, R. D., Peters, M. P., & Shepherd, D. A. (2010). *Entrepreneurship* (8th ed.). New York: McGraw-Hill.

Woods, C. (2008, April 8). ICU Global grabs international opportunities. *Real Business.* Retrieved from http://realbusiness.co.uk/news/icu_global_grabs_international_opportunities

Suggested Readings

Harvard Business Review. (2011). *Thriving in emerging markets.* Boston: Harvard Business Press.

This collection of articles from the *Harvard Business Review* highlights the difficulties and best practices of doing business in emerging markets. The articles cover many topics relevant to any company considering expansion in emerging markets including talent acquisition, bottom of the pyramid profitability, risk management, and business model adaptation.

Keichel, W. (2010). *The lords of strategy: The secret intellectual history of the new corporate world.* Boston: Harvard Business Press.

Author Walter Keichel explains how four men changed history by creating what is known today as corporate strategy. He argues that 50 years ago, businesses went about their daily routines without a vision or goal for the future of the company, comparing it to engineers who work on a project without a clear understanding of physics. Written like a novel, Keichel describes the lives and works of Bruce Henderson (founder of Boston Consulting Group), Bill Bain (creator of Bain & Company), Fred Gluck (managing director of McKinsey & Company), and Michael Porter (Harvard Business School professor and esteemed academic).

Ramamurti, R., & Singh, J. V. (2010). *Emerging multinationals in emerging markets.* Cambridge, UK: Cambridge University Press.

The work of many respected international business specialists, this book is a compilation of research done on multinationals in emerging markets, specifically the BRIC (Brazil, Russia, India, and China) countries as well as Mexico, Israel, Thailand, and South Africa. Their findings show that, like multinationals in developed markets, those in emerging markets have more differences than similarities, but all have unique competitive advantages as well as aggressive globalization strategies. Thanks to a thorough discussion of *how* these companies are winning business, the authors answer many questions useful to any company considering going global.

Sun, T. (2010). *Inside the Chinese business mind: A tactical guide for managers.* Santa Barbara, CA: Praeger.

It has been proven time and again that cultural barriers between the East and West can spell disaster for U.S. companies trying to enter the immense Chinese market. In his book, Ted Sun explains the differences between American and Chinese managers and why the gap between them can be so devastating for business. Through a survey of over 200 U.S. and Chinese business leaders, he shows some basic principles he developed via survey results as well as his own experiences as a Chinese national working in the Western world.

World Bank. (2010). *World development indicators.* Herndon, VA: Author.

World Development Indicators (WDI) is an annual publication of data about development from the World Bank. Over 900 indicators in more than 80 tables are included in the 2007 WDI, covering worldview, people, environment, economy, states and markets, and global links.

International Legal Concerns

Profile: Brooklyn Industries

Felipe Dupouy/Lifesize/ThinkStockPhotos

As young starving artists trying to survive in New York City, Lexy Funk and Vahap Avsar were trying to establish a production company to produce documentaries and TV commercials. Having little money but being very resourceful, Avsar needed a particular bag to carry his things around the city. He found a vinyl ad poster in a dumpster, and decided the material was strong enough to make into a messenger bag. Being handy with a sewing machine, he soon turned his vision into a hip and decorative homemade bag.

Rather than continuing their struggle in the production industry, they decided to take Avsar's idea and run with it. Starting out with one sewing machine and two pairs of hands, demand for their products quickly outgrew their current living situation. They decided to rent an old building in Brooklyn where they could start a proper bag-making factory. The entrepreneurs named their brand "Brooklyn Industries" to reflect their patronage to the city.

Shortly after establishing the factory, the company began experiencing many problems, especially with their human resources. It was difficult to find people who were competent sewers willing to work for nominal pay and were legal to work in the United States. Many applicants would have fake green cards or no identification whatsoever. The legal workers they could find were from many different countries including Turkey, Colombia, Tibet, and Ecuador. Since each country has a distinct working culture, the output from the workers fluctuated. There was little consistency, especially in the quality of the goods. Beyond that, not knowing if the workers were truly legal was a constant concern. With police raiding factories all over the city, exposing illegal migrant workers and fining their employers, the focus of the two owners faltered. They were so busy worrying about their workers and the quality of their products that the remainder of the business suffered.

Luckily, Funk and Avsar had befriended a man with a factory close to theirs in Brooklyn, who had since closed his factory and outsourced the work to China. Funk was skeptical at first, having heard such negative criticism in the press about Chinese companies running factories like sweatshops, disregarding workers' rights, and overall corruption in the system. Because their situation looked dire, however, Avsar took a trip to China to form his own opinion. His impression was predominantly positive, especially knowing firsthand the hardships that go into running a factory. He noted the cleanliness and good conditions in which the employees worked, as well as the efficiency of a well-run factory. Brooklyn Industries' factory never reached a point of enjoying economies of scale or production. Although outsourcing the work to China proved more expensive than expected, the entrepreneurial duo decided to take advantage of the opportunity to focus on what they did best—retail.

Through the mentorship of their manufacturing friend, Funk and Avsar were able to grow their small company to $13 million in revenue in 2009. Above all, they learned that communication and common goals help to build intercultural relationships more than anything else. Over time, their Chinese counterparts became more like partners to grow and learn from, rather than people to be concerned about. They always make sure to ask about the conditions in the factory, as well as workers' compensation and benefits. If they are unhappy with a policy or situation, they voice those complaints to their Chinese partners. Over time, the relationship has grown, along with the trust and respect between the two parties. Without the opportunity to outsource, Brooklyn Industries may not be the prosperous company it is today.

SOURCE: Adapted from "Why Brooklyn Industries Manufactures in China" (2009).

Chapter Objectives

1. To determine the best method for operating in countries based on the legal and political concerns faced
2. To understand the impact of morality and ethics in global business
3. To illustrate the various types of legal and regulatory systems faced by an entrepreneur in a global venture and how to navigate these arenas
4. To assess the level of corruption and bribery in a foreign country and how it affects the business environment in that country
5. To learn the elements of political risk and what factors to consider when entering a new market
6. To know the different legal traditions and how they affect property rights, contract law, product safety, and product liability

Introduction

The legal and political systems confronting the global entrepreneur vary significantly around the world. Generally, the political system needs to be analyzed according to its degree of collectivism versus individualism and the degree of democracy versus totalitarianism. Although related, there is a gray area as some countries have a mixture of collectivism and individualism.

In collectivism, a system stressing the primacy of communal goals, the needs of a society as a whole are more important than individual freedom. Therefore, an individual may not have the right to do something if it is counter to the good of society. Socialism and Marxism are two examples of collectivism. Individualism, the opposite of collectivism, is a system where the individual has the freedom to pursue his or her own economic and political activities. In this case, the interests of the individual usually take precedence over the interests of society. Similarly, democracy and totalitarianism are opposites on the political spectrum. While democracy is a political system in which government is by the people, exercised either directly or through elected representatives, totalitarianism is a system of government where one person or political party exercises absolute control over everything and no opposing political parties are allowed.

Although most global entrepreneurs prefer to do business in stable and freely governed countries, good business opportunities often exist in different conditions. It is important to assess each country's policies as well as its stability. This assessment is referred to as *political risk analysis.* There is some political risk in every country, but the degree of risk from country to country varies significantly; and even in a country with a history of stability and consistency, these conditions could change. There are three major types of political risk that might be present: operating risk (risk of interference with the operations of the venture), transfer risk (risk in attempting to shift assets or other funds out of the country), and the biggest risk of all—ownership risk (risk where the country takes over the property and employees). Of course, conflicts and changes in the solvency of the country are major risks to a global entrepreneur in particular countries. This can take such forms as guerilla warfare, civil disturbances, and even terrorism, where the global entrepreneur's company and employees are the target. Just look at the protests in various countries in the Middle East. As evidenced by the 9/11 attacks on the World Trade Center and Pentagon, international terrorists can target U.S. interests both in and out of the country.

The legal system of a country also affects the global entrepreneur. The legal system comprises the rules and laws that regulate behavior as well as the processes by which the laws are enforced. A country's laws regulate the business practices in a country, the manner in which business transactions are executed, and the rights and obligations of the parties involved in any business transaction.

Political Activity

There are two primary areas of political activity that can affect the global entrepreneur: trade sanctions and export controls, and regulations of global business behavior.

Trade Sanctions and Export Controls

The term *trade sanction* refers to a government action against the free flow of goods and services, or even ideas, for political purposes. Sanctions can be used to influence the type and amount of trade in a particular category and can be extended to prohibit all trade in that category—a *trade embargo.* The United States, for example, has a trade embargo on Cuba prohibiting most trade except humanitarian aid.

Trade sanctions and embargoes have been used by countries as a foreign policy tool for centuries. The purposes of such actions have ranged from upholding human rights to stopping nuclear proliferation and terrorism to forcing countries to open their home markets.

Export controls are used to restrict the flow of specified goods and services to a country. The United States and other industrialized nations have established strong export controls to deny or at least limit the acquisition of strategically important goods. In the United States, these controls are based on the Export Administration Act and the Munitions Control Act. A list of commodities needing approval in the form of an export license has been established by the Department of Commerce working with such government agencies as the Defense, Energy, and State departments.

Given the increase in availability of products of all types, the rapid dissemination of information and innovation on a global basis, and the speed of change and new technology advancement, the denial of any product has become much more difficult to enforce. Export controls based on capacity criteria, which once occurred in computer technology, are mostly irrelevant because the technology changes so quickly, obsolescing previous capacity constraints. For example, about 75% of sales in the data processing industry each year are from new products and services introduced in the previous 2 years. Given the rapidly changing technology and worldwide information dissemination via the web, export controls are becoming less and less enforceable.

Political Risk

Given these conflicts and differences in the political environments in countries, the global entrepreneur must manage the *political risks* involved. Generally, political risk tends to be lower in countries that have a history of stability and consistency. Political risk has three major components: ownership risk, operating risk, and transfer risk.

Ownership risk is the possibility of loss of property and life. International terrorists frequently target business facilities, operations, and personnel.

Operating risk refers to interference in ongoing operations in a foreign country. Countries can impose new controls in prices and production or restrict access to resources or labor markets. These can disrupt or even close down the foreign operations of the global entrepreneur.

The final aspect of political risk—*transfer risk*—affects the movement of funds within a country or between countries. Transfer risk can result in currency and remittance restrictions that can be problematic to the foreign entrepreneurial venture (this is elaborated on in Chapter 8).

The global entrepreneur must manage these risks. One way to reduce the risk of government intervention is to demonstrate a concern for the society of the host country and to be a good global citizen. This attitude is reflected in such actions as pay, good working conditions, good hiring and training practices, contributing to the economic development of the region, and having a joint venture with local national partners who will share in the sales and profits of the venture. The global entrepreneur needs to monitor political developments so appropriate action can be taken.

Finally, the global entrepreneur should consider purchasing insurance that covers at least some possible losses. In the United States, the Overseas Private Investment Corporation (OPIC) provides three types of risk insurance for currency inconvertibility, expropriation of resources, and political violence at a cost that is not particularly prohibitive. Of course, the best risk management is good country selection as discussed in Chapter 5.

Legal Considerations and Regulations

Among the main difficulties in being a successful global entrepreneur are the challenges resulting from the many different legal and regulatory environments. Even though there are a variety of legal and regulatory systems apparent, each is based on one of four foundations: common law, civil law, Islamic law, and socialist law.

The common law system, stemming from English law, is the foundation of the legal system in such countries as Australia, Canada, the United Kingdom, and the

United States. The civil law system, stemming from Roman law, is the basis of law in such countries as France and some countries in Latin America. Derived from the Qur'an and the teachings of the Prophet Mohammed, Islamic law prevails in most Islamic countries. Finally, socialist law is derived from the Marxist socialist system and influences, to some degree, the law and regulations in China, Cuba, North Korea, and Russia.

These foundations result in a variety of dissimilar laws and regulations of business, which are modified by the treaties and conventions in each country. To handle this facet of going international, the global entrepreneur needs to have an overall sense of the legal system of a country. When needing legal counsel, ideally the legal firm hired would have its headquarters in the United States with an office in the host country. Several key legal areas important to every global entrepreneur are property rights, contract law, product safety, and product liability.

Countries vary in the degree to which their legal systems protect the property rights of individuals and businesses. The property rights of a business are the resources owned, the use of those resources, and the income earned from their use. Besides buildings, equipment, and land, the protection of intellectual property is also a concern. Intellectual property, such as a book, computer software code, a music score, a video, a formula for a new chemical or drug, or another unique idea, needs to be protected when going outside the United States. The three major ways of protecting intellectual property in the United States are patents, copyrights, and trademarks. Few countries have strong enforceable laws protecting intellectual property. For example, videos can be purchased in China at 10% of the cost in the United States, sometimes even before being officially released. Even the *Entrepreneurship* book, which the author coauthored, has legal editions in several languages including Arabic, Chinese, Hungarian, Indonesian, Portuguese, Russian, Serbian, Slovenian, and Spanish, and has an illegal edition in the Iranian language because Iran does not recognize world corporate copyright laws. Before entering a country, the global entrepreneur needs to assess the country's protection of the intellectual property involved and the costs if copied illegally.

Another area of concern is the contract law of the country *and* how it is enforced. A contract specifies the conditions for an exchange and the rights and duties of the parties involved in this exchange. Contract law varies significantly from country to country, in part reflecting two types of legal tradition—common law and civil law—previously discussed. Common law tends to be relatively nonspecific, so contracts under this law are longer and more detailed with all the contingencies spelled out. Because civil law is much more detailed, contracts under it are much shorter.

In addition to the law itself, the global entrepreneur needs to understand how contract law might be enforced and the judicial system securing this enforcement. If the legal system of the country does not have a good track record of enforcement, the contract can contain an agreement that any contract disputes will be heard in the courts of another country. Because each entrepreneur might have some advantage in his or her home country, a third country is usually selected. This aspect is very important for global entrepreneurs operating in developing economies with little or even a bad history of enforcement and other anti-business countries. One company exporting Hungarian wine into Russia made sure any disputes in all its Russian contracts were heard in the Finnish court system instead of the Russian one.

The final overall area of concern is the law of the country regarding product safety and liability. Again, the laws have significant variances between countries from very high liability and damage awards in the United States to very low levels in Russia. When doing business in a country where the liability and product safety laws are not as stringent as in one's home country, should you follow the more relaxed local standards or adhere to the stricter standards of your home country at the risk of not being competitive and losing the business?

Intellectual Property and Organizational Form

Intellectual property, which includes patents, trademarks, copyrights, and trade secrets, represents important assets to the global entrepreneur. Often global entrepreneurs, because of their lack of understanding of intellectual property, ignore the steps needed to try to protect these assets.

Because all business is regulated by the laws of the country a global business locates in, the global entrepreneur needs to be aware of any regulations that may affect the venture. At different stages of the start-up, the entrepreneur will need legal advice, which will vary based on such factors as whether the new venture is a franchise, an independent start-up, or a buyout; whether it produces a consumer versus an industrial product; whether it is nonprofit or for-profit; and whether it involves exporting or importing.

The effect on the global entrepreneur and the venture, particularly in the case of intellectual property, reflects the disparity in laws of various countries, particularly emerging ones. For example, China, since entering the World Trade Organization (WTO) in 2001, has strengthened the rights of the owners of intellectual property and is continuing to do so. Even though China's intellectual property laws and the laws of other industrialized nations are not fully harmonized, a global entrepreneur can usually receive and enforce intellectual property rights in China, depending to some extent on the region of China.

The form of company as well as the type of franchise agreement offers many options to consider. The global entrepreneur should understand the advantages and disadvantages of each type of organization as it relates to such issues as liability, taxes, continuity, transferability of interest, costs of setting up, and attractiveness for raising capital in the country of interest.

Patents

A *patent* is a contract between the government of a country and the global entrepreneur. In exchange for disclosure of the invention, the government grants the inventor exclusivity regarding the invention in the country for a specified amount of time. At the end of this time, the invention becomes part of the public domain.

The patent gives the global entrepreneur a negative right because it prevents anyone else from making, using, or selling the defined invention. Even if the global entrepreneur has been granted a patent, he or she may find during the process of producing or marketing the invention that it infringes on the patent rights of others. There are usually several types of patents:

- *Utility patents.* A utility patent grants the global entrepreneur protection from anyone else making, using, and/or selling the identified invention; it usually protects new, useful, and unobvious processes such as film developing; machines such as photocopiers; compositions of matter such as chemical compounds or mixtures of ingredients; and articles of manufacture such as the toothpaste pump. A utility patent in the United States has a term of 20 years, beginning on the date of filing with the Patent and Trademark Office (PTO). The time period and filing process varies by country.
- *Design patents.* These patents cover new, original, ornamental, and unobvious designs for articles of manufacture. A design patent reflects the appearance of an object and is granted for a 14-year term in the United States. Again, this time period varies by country. Like the utility patent, the design patent provides the global entrepreneur with a negative right, excluding others from making, using, or selling an article having the ornamental appearance given in the drawings included in the patent. Companies such as Reebok and Nike are very interested in obtaining design patents as a means of protecting their original designs. These types of patents are valuable for global ventures that need to protect molded plastic parts, extrusions, and product and container configurations.
- *Plant (factory) patents.* These are issued under the same provisions as utility patents and are for new varieties of plants. Few of these types of patents are issued in the United States.

Patents in the United States are issued by the PTO. In addition to patents, this office administers other programs such as the Disclosure Document Program, whereby the inventor files disclosure of the invention, gaining recognition that he or she was the first to develop or invent the idea. In most cases, the inventor will eventually patent the idea. A second program is the Defensive Publication Program. This gives the inventor the opportunity to protect an idea for which he or she does not wish to obtain a patent. It prevents anyone else from patenting this idea but gives the public access to the invention.

With international trade increasing each year, the need was recognized for an international patent law to protect firms from imitations by providing some protection in global markets. In response, the Patent Cooperation Treaty (PCT) was established in June 1970 to facilitate patent filings in multiple countries in one office rather than filing in each separate country. Administered by the World Intellectual Property Organization (WIPO) in Geneva, Switzerland, it provides a preliminary search that assesses whether the filing firm will face any possible infringements in any country. The company can then decide whether to proceed with the required filing of the patent in each country. There is a 20-month time frame to file for these in-country patents. There are some significant differences in patent laws in each country. For example, patent laws in the United States allow computer software to receive both patent and copyright protection. In the European Union, patent protection is not extended to software (Pike, 2005).

In China, patent applications are filed with the State Intellectual Property Office (SIPO) in Beijing. The enforcement varies throughout the country because the local SIPO offices are responsible. Since China is a signatory of the Patent Cooperation Treaty, the country can be designated when a patent is filed in the United States or any time within 12 months after this filing. Unlike the United States and the European Union, where each patent application is examined based on its merits, Chinese patent applications are examined only if the applicant makes a request for examination. Otherwise, if no request is made, the application will be abandoned.

The use of business method patents has emerged with the growth of Internet use and software development. Amazon.com owns a business method patent for the single clicking feature used by a buyer on its website to order products. Priceline.com claims a patent regarding its service whereby a buyer can submit a price bid for a particular service. Expedia was forced to pay royalties to Priceline.com after being sued for patent infringement. Many firms that hold these types of patents have used them to competitively position themselves as well as provide a steady stream of income from royalties or licensing fees. Whether these types of patents will hold up over a long period of time is still not clear (Scheinfield & Sullivan, 2002).

❖ CULTURAL STORY

At a division of General Motors in Dayton, Ohio, Kathleen was responsible for a specific product line and I was the business development person for the division.

Prior to our arrival, the division had entered into a joint venture in Japan. We had just hired a marketing person in Japan named "Hirofumi," to watch out for our interests there. Everyone just called him Hiro.

One day, the Japanese joint venture partners came to the U.S. for a meeting. Kathleen's boss, Bob, was at the head of the table with Kathleen on his left. The Japanese were on his right facing Kathleen. I was against the wall behind the Japanese.

Bob started to explain that we had hired "Hiroshima" to help us out in Japan. Kathleen's eyes got as wide as saucers while I was unabashedly aghast at the faux pas but had no need to hide my reaction as I was behind the Japanese. After our initial eye contact, Kathleen refused to look at me as I was laughing, albeit silently. Then the boss called him "Hiroshima" a second time! We were totally incredulous and embarrassed. The picture of Kathleen trying to hold it together in front of the Japanese is a priceless memory.

Needless to say, the joint venture failed.

SOURCE: http://www.culturalconfusions.com (Story by Jonathan Katz).

Trademarks

A *trademark* is a word, symbol, design, slogan, or even a particular sound that identifies the source or sponsorship of certain goods or services. Unlike a patent, a trademark can last indefinitely, as long as the mark continues to be used in its indicated function. For all registrations in the United States, the trademark is given an initial 10-year registration with 10-year renewable terms. In the 5th year, the global entrepreneur needs to file an affidavit with the PTO indicating that the mark is currently in commercial use. If no affidavit is filed, the registration is canceled. Between the 9th and 10th years after registration, and every 10 years thereafter, the global entrepreneur must file an application for renewal of the trademark. If this does not occur, the registration is canceled. Trademark law in the United States allows the filing of a trademark solely on the intent to use the trademark in interstate or foreign commerce. The filing date often becomes the first date of use but this varies by country.

Generally, throughout the world, there are four categories of trademarks: (1) coined marks denote no relationship between the mark and the goods or services (e.g., Mercedes, Kodak) and offer the possibility of expansion to a wide range of products; (2) an arbitrary mark is one that has another meaning in the language of the United States (e.g., Apple) and is applied to a product or service; (3) a suggestive mark is used to suggest certain features, qualities, ingredients, or characteristics of a product or service (e.g., Halo shampoo) and suggests some describable attribute of the product or service; and (4) a descriptive mark must have become distinctive over a significant period of time and gained consumer recognition before it can be registered. Registering a trademark can offer significant advantages or benefits to the global entrepreneur in each country.

In China, trademark applications are filed with the China Trademark Office. Registered trademarks have more protection in China than unregistered ones in a situation similar to the United States. Unlike the United States, however, China has a "first to file" trademark system that does not require evidence of prior use or ownership of the trademark. Early filing and a good Chinese translation of the trademark are essential based on input from a native Chinese speaker familiar with the goods or services. Without this accurate translation, often-unintelligible trademarks result in the Chinese language.

Copyright

A *copyright* protects original works of authorship. The protection in a copyright does not protect the idea itself, and thus it allows someone else to use the idea or concept in a different manner. Copyright law has become especially relevant because of the tremendous growth in the use of the Internet, especially in downloading music, literary work, pictures, videos, and software.

Copyrights in the United States are registered with the Library of Congress and usually do not require an attorney. To register a work, the global entrepreneur sends a completed application (available online at www.copyright.gov), two copies of the work, and the required filing fees (the initial filing fee). The term of the copyright is the life of the global entrepreneur plus 70 years in the United States. This time period also varies by country.

Besides computer software, copyrights are desirable for books, scripts, articles, poems, songs, sculptures, models, maps, blueprints, printed material on board games, data, and music. In some instances, several forms of protection may be available.

Chinese copyrights are registered at the National Copyright Administration (NCA) in Beijing. Even though China recognizes protection for original works of authorship from countries belonging to the international copyright conventions without the works being specifically registered in China, to adequately enforce the copyright, the global entrepreneur should register the copyright with the NCA. Two of the author's books in the Chinese language are registered with the NCA, protecting these well-selling Chinese editions.

Trade Secrets

The global entrepreneur may prefer to maintain an idea or process as confidential and to keep it as a *trade secret.* The trade secret will have a life as long as the idea or process remains a secret.

A trade secret is not covered by any laws, but is recognized under a governing body of common laws in some countries. Employees involved in working with an idea or process may be asked to first sign a confidential information agreement that will protect the global entrepreneur against the employee giving out the trade secret either while an employee or after leaving the global venture. A simple example of a trade secret nondisclosure agreement is illustrated in Figure 6.1.

The amount of information to give employees is a difficult decision and is often determined by the global entrepreneur's judgment. Usually global entrepreneurs tend to protect sensitive or confidential company information from anyone else by simply not making the information available.

Most global entrepreneurs who have limited resources can choose not to protect their ideas, products, or services. This can become a serious problem because obtaining competitive information legally is easy to accomplish unless the global entrepreneur takes the proper precautions. It is usually easy to learn competitive information through such means as trade shows, transient employees, media interviews or announcements, and even websites.

Under China's Unfair Competition Law (UCL), protection is available for trade secrets as well as unregistered trademarks and packaging. The Fair Trade Bureau of the State Administration for Industry and Commerce (SAIC) in Beijing enforces the law. The enforcement of this law by the Chinese courts and administrative agencies, however, varies greatly from province to province.

Licensing

Licensing is an arrangement between two parties, where one party has proprietary rights over some information, process, or technology protected by a patent, trademark, or copyright. This arrangement, specified in a contract (discussed later in this chapter),

❖ Figure 6.1 A simple nondisclosure agreement.

WHEREAS, New Venture Corporation (NVC), Anywhere Street, Anyplace, U.S.A., is the Owner of information relating to; and

WHEREAS, NVC is desirous of disclosing said information to the undersigned (hereinafter referred to as "Recipient") for the purposes of using, evaluating, or entering into further agreements using such trade secrets as an employee, consultant, or agent of NVC; and

WHEREAS, NVC wishes to maintain in confidence said information as trade secrets; and

WHEREAS, the undersigned Recipient recognizes the necessity of maintaining the strictest confidence with respect to any trade secrets of NVC,

Recipient hereby agrees as follows:

1. Recipient shall observe the strictest secrecy with respect to all information presented by NVC and Recipient's evaluation thereof and shall disclose such information only to persons authorized to receive same by NVC. Recipient shall be responsible for any damage resulting from any breach of this Agreement by Recipient.
2. Recipient shall neither make use of nor disclose to any third party during the period of this Agreement and thereafter any such trade secrets or evaluation thereof unless prior consent in writing is given by NVC.
3. Restriction on disclosure does not apply to information previously known to Recipient or otherwise in the public domain. Any prior knowledge of trade secrets by the Recipient shall be disclosed in writing within (30) days.
4. At the completion of the services performed by the Recipient, Recipient shall, within (30) days, return all original materials provided by NVC and any copies, notes, or other documents that are in the Recipient's possession pertaining thereto.
5. Any trade secrets made public through publication or product announcements are excluded from this Agreement.
6. This Agreement is executed and delivered with the State of ______ and it shall be construed, interpreted, and applied in accordance with the laws of that State.
7. This Agreement, including the provision hereof, shall not be modified or changed in any manner except only in writing signed by all parties hereto.

SOURCE: Adapted from Hisrich, R. D., Peters, M. P., & Shepherd, D. A (2010). *Entrepreneurship* (8th ed.). Homewood, IL: McGraw-Hill/Irwin, page 172.

requires the licensee to pay a royalty or some other specified sum to the holder of the proprietary rights (licensor) in return for permission to copy the patent, trademark, or copyright. Licensing has significant value as a marketing strategy to holders of patents, trademarks, or copyrights to grow their businesses in new markets when resources or experience in those markets is lacking. It is also an important marketing strategy for global entrepreneurs who want to start a new venture but need permission to incorporate the patent, trademark, or copyright with their ideas.

Although licensing opportunities are often plentiful, they must be carefully considered as part of the global entrepreneur's business model. Licensing is an excellent option for the entrepreneur to increase revenue in a global market without the risk and costly start-up investment. To be able to license requires the global entrepreneur to have something to license, which is why it is so important to seek protection for any new product, information, or name with a patent, trademark, or copyright.

Contracts

When starting a new venture, the global entrepreneur will be involved in a number of negotiations and *contracts* with vendors, property owners, and clients. A contract is a legally enforceable agreement between two or more parties as long as certain conditions are met. It is very important for the global entrepreneur to understand the fundamental issues regarding contracts.

Often business deals are concluded with a handshake. Ordering supplies, lining up financing, or reaching an agreement with a partner are common situations in which a handshake consummates the deal. When things are operating smoothly, this procedure is sufficient; if disagreements occur, the global entrepreneur may find that because there is no written contract he or she is liable for something never intended. The global entrepreneur should never rely on a handshake if the deal cannot be completed within 1 year.

Nearly 5 years after bringing its popular ice cream to Russia, Ben & Jerry's Homemade Inc. has pulled out. Legal, tax, and management problems, which plague many Western investors in Russia, forced the South Burlington, Vermont, ice cream maker to rethink a production and sales joint venture that started in 1992 in the spirit of a "social mission" with the northern province of Karelia, said Bram Kleppner, Ben & Jerry's manager of Russian operations.

Kleppner said the company's financial loss on Russian operations had been minimal, under $500,000, but the real drain had been executive time spent trying to resolve, among other problems, a court case with one of its partners. Operations were also partly financed through an $850,000 grant from the U.S. Agency for International Development. "We simply don't have the people and resources to run a business in Russia," Kleppner said by telephone from Vermont. "We're a small company. You tie up two or three senior managers and you end up having a measurable effect on the company's performance" (McKay, 1997).

Ben & Jerry's started the joint venture, Iceverk, mainly as a goodwill gesture, to prove that high-quality ice cream could be made by Russian employees using mostly local ingredients. The ice cream, including the company's signature flavors like Chunky Monkey and Cherry Garcia, quickly became a local hit. Three "scoop shops" in the Karelia region, next to Finland, were among the busiest in Ben & Jerry's entire chain. Employing 100 local employees, the joint venture also distributed ice cream to Moscow and St. Petersburg, had five franchisees, and posted sales of $1 million a year.

But the venture never turned a profit, according to Kleppner. Expansion led to quality control problems, with shipments of ice cream often arriving melted and refrozen. An unexpected change in the tax status for joint ventures sent tax liabilities soaring, with the venture unable to meet the increased tax burden. And, like scores of other joint ventures in Russia, this one went bad when a local financial institution, PetroBank, successfully sued Ben & Jerry's for the return of a 20% stake the U.S. partner insisted it had legally bought back.

Ben & Jerry's turned over its 70% equity stake in the venture to a third partner, Karelia's capital city of Petrozavodsk. The company also donated installed equipment and did not collect the debts of about $150,000 owed to the joint venture. The venture now makes and sells ice cream under a new trademark, said Alexander Mukhin, head of the Petrozavodsk municipal-property committee (McKay, 1997).

Business Ethics in a Global Setting

A global entrepreneur must consider how to conduct business in an ethical manner throughout all parts of his or her firm's operations. By operating ethically, a global venture will be better able to secure repeat business and make a profit, while also adding value to the consumer. Consumers want to have a clear conscience about the type of company that their purchases support, and knowing that a company has high ethical standards guarantees this peace of mind.

Ethics are the principles that guide an entrepreneur's decision making and should be based on three basic values: integrity, transparency, and accountability. Integrity requires the entrepreneur to conduct all operations and transactions with honesty and respect for the law, including refraining from bribery and other forms of corruption. Transparency demands that the entrepreneur undertakes internal and external functions in an open manner and does not try to hide or disguise the firm's actions. Finally, accountability requires the firm to accurately record all transactions and take responsibility for its decisions and actions. Conducting business in foreign markets should not change or alter the ethical principles that the entrepreneur follows. In short, while the entrepreneur must continue to grow the firm's bottom line, he or she must also make sure that these decisions are made with integrity, transparency, and accountability.

Countries often establish laws and regulations to ensure that the business activities of foreign firms are within moral and ethical boundaries that are considered appropriate. Of course, what is considered morally and ethically appropriate ranges considerably from one country to the next, resulting in a wide range of laws and regulations as well as enforcement activities. A global entrepreneur must consider a country's laws and regulations while conducting business activities in an ethical manner. Sometimes this causes the global entrepreneur to choose between paying substantial fines or losing business.

One particular regulatory activity that affects global entrepreneurship is antitrust law. These laws empower government agencies to closely oversee and regulate joint ventures with a foreign firm, acquisition of a domestic firm by a foreign entity, or any other foreign business activity that can restrain competition or negatively affect domestic companies and their business activities. Some countries use these laws to protect their "infant industries" as they attempt to establish themselves and grow.

Global entrepreneurs are also strongly affected by laws against bribery and corruption. In many countries, payments or favors are expected in return for doing business or gaining a contract. To establish a foreign operation, obtain a license, or even access electricity and water, global entrepreneurs are often asked to pay bribes to government officials at all levels. Due to the increased incidence of this, the United States passed the Foreign Corrupt Practices Act in 1977, making it a crime for U.S. executives of publicly traded companies to bribe a foreign official to obtain business. Although this act has been very controversial and its enforcement varies, the global entrepreneur must carefully distinguish between a reasonable way of doing business in a particular country and illegal bribery and corruption. The work of the nonprofit Transparency International provides a good resource for judging the level of corruption, real and perceived, in a foreign country. Table 6.1 provides the rankings for the level of perceived public sector corruption for a selection of countries based on Transparency International's annual survey. While New Zealand, Denmark, and Singapore are ranked 1 (not corrupt), Egypt is ranked 98, Argentina 105, and Iraq 175. While the United States is ranked 22, Mexico is ranked 98.

Finally, the global entrepreneur is confronted with the general standards of behavior and ethics. Is it all right to cut down the rain forest and employ people at above national wages? Can you manufacture a product under different working conditions than those that occur in the United States yet pay wage levels far higher than average in the country? Can you fire employees in a country? Some countries severely restrict this even though the individual has not been working hard or, even worse, stealing from the company. These are just some of the issues confronting the global entrepreneur as he or she does business in certain foreign countries. One can only hope that global entrepreneurs will assert leadership in establishing standards that help promote a quality of life throughout the world.

Ethics and expectations of ethics do vary by country, depending in part on whether the country is based on the philosophies of Aristotle and Plato or Confucius, for example. In developing countries without a codified system of business laws that have been in place and enforced for a period of time, there is a great temptation to use bribes (facilitation payments) to expedite the business deal. Warner Osborne, chairman and CEO of Seastone LC, in working with thousands of companies during his 20-plus years' experience in China and other countries, advises, "We make sure all partners we work with know we won't tolerate that [facilitation payments—bribes]." He says when dealing with foreign firms, "We begin by establishing the ground rules—including the ethical rules that are critical to us—one-on-one verbally." (Dutton, 2008) These rules, of course, need to be fully understood by each employee.

Summary

A thorough understanding of a country's political and legal system is vital to the success of a new venture in a foreign country. This chapter provides an overview of the major political and legal considerations that a global entrepreneur needs to

❖ Table 6.1 Public Sector Corruption Perceptions Index (2010)

Economy/Country	Ranking	Score
New Zealand	1	9.3
Denmark	1	9.3
Singapore	1	9.3
Finland	4	9.2
Sweden	4	9.2
Canada	6	8.9
Netherlands	7	8.8
Australia	8	8.7
Switzerland	8	8.7
Norway	10	8.6
Iceland	11	8.5
Hong Kong, China	13	8.4
Ireland	14	8
Germany	15	7.9
Japan	17	7.8
United Kingdom	20	7.6
United States	22	7.1
France	25	6.8
Estonia	26	6.5
United Arab Emirates	28	6.3
South Africa	54	4.5
Turkey	56	4.4
Mexico	98	3.1
Egypt	98	3.1
Argentina	105	2.9
Bolivia	110	2.8
Vietnam	116	2.7
Nigeria	134	2.4
Iraq	175	1.5
Somalia	178	1.1

SOURCE: Transparency International.

NOTE: The rankings come from the 2010 *Transparency International Corruption Perceptions Index*. This index measures the perceived levels of public sector corruption in a given country from the opinions of both businesspeople from that country as well as country analysts from various international and local institutions. The scores fall on a scale of zero to 10 for each country, with 10 implying a highly clean public sector and zero implying a highly corrupt public sector. This data is useful for global entrepreneurs as they choose new markets to enter and assess the costs, risks, and ethical issues that they might face in doing business in a foreign market. Transparency International produces this index annually and publishes the results on its website at www.transparency.org.

understand before entering a new market. A political system, which governs a country, needs to be analyzed according to its degree of collectivism versus individualism and the degree of democracy versus totalitarianism. A country will use certain political tools, such as trade sanctions and export controls and regulations to impact the business in that country. Also, different political systems allow (and expect) different levels of corruption and bribery. Conducting political risk analysis assesses threats to the ownership, operation, and finances of an entrepreneur's organization from a country's political system and stability. A country's legal system and, in particular, its protection of both intangible and tangible property rights must also be understood by the global entrepreneur. Four different traditions of law influence the legal systems around the world: common law, civic law, Islamic law, and socialist law. Legal counsel can be particularly useful to the global entrepreneur in interpreting and enforcing contracts, property rights, liability, and product safety.

Questions for Discussion

1. How can an entrepreneur mitigate potential political and legal risks prior to them happening?
2. What are the four different types of legal systems, and which countries follow each of these systems?
3. How should a contract be structured differently in a country with common law compared to one with civil law?

Chapter Exercises

1. Pick one of the BRIC countries (Brazil, Russia, India, China) and analyze its political structure (collective vs. individual and democratic vs. totalitarian) compared with your home country. What is the greatest difference that exists? What is your assessment of the political risk to a business entering that country?
2. Research and explain the difference between outright bribery and corruption versus a "facilitation payment."
3. Find an article describing a legal dispute that a multinational corporation has had outside its home country. What is the legal tradition of the foreign company? What is the major legal issue of the dispute and is there a different understanding of that issue in the home country versus the foreign country?

References

Dutton, G. (2008, May). Do the right thing. *Entrepreneur, 36*(5), 92.

Hisrich, R. D., Peters, M. A., & Shepherd, D. A. (2010). *Entrepreneurship* (8th ed.). Burr Ridge, IL: McGraw-Hill/Irwin.

McKay, B. (1997, February 7). Ben & Jerry's post-cold war venture ends in Russia with ice cream melting. *Wall Street Journal* (Eastern ed.), p. A14.

Pike, G. H. (2005, May). Global technology and local patents. *Information Today, 22*(5), 41–46.

Scheinfield, R. C., & Sullivan, J. D. (2002, December 10). Lawyers and technology Internet-related patents: Are they paying off? *New York Law Journal*, p. 5.

Why Brooklyn Industries manufactures in China. (2009, November 20). *Bloomberg Businessweek: Entrepreneur's Journal*. Retrieved from http://www.businessweek.com/smallbiz/content/nov2009/sb20091119_311230.htm

Suggested Readings

Articles/Books

American Bar Association. (2010). *The American Bar Association legal guide for small business*. Chicago, IL: Author.

The American Bar Association provides this guide as a reference for all legal issues regarding starting, operating, and ending a business. For U.S.-owned and -operated businesses, it is a practical guide for entrepreneurs in any stage of business who require legal guidance.

Blaas, W., & Becker, J. (2007). *Strategic arena switching in international trade negotiations*. Hampshire, UK: Ashgate.

This book analyzes rule making in international trade across multilevel and multiarena perspectives to explain the arena preferences of both state and nonstate actors. It also shows how the rules of different arenas relate to one another and why certain institutional designs can serve one group better than another.

Eicher, S. (2009). *Corruption in international business: The challenge of cultural and legal diversity*. Burlington, UK: Gower.

Many entrepreneurs enter foreign markets completely unaware of the extent of corruption in that country's system. This book intends to shed some light on corruption practices by exposing students to some common methods of corruption and how to identify and combat them. Understanding why and how corruption exists can greatly increase chances of success for those faced with such ethical quandaries.

Jolly, A. (2011). *The handbook of European intellectual property management* (3rd ed.). London: Kogan Page.

True to its title, this book is written as a practical guide for intellectual property management in the European Union. By first spelling out the difficulty of politically managing intellectual property (IP) laws and regulations in a region where each country has its own set of rules, the authors are then able to explain the best ways for businesses to protect IP, and therefore their competitive advantage within the EU.

World Trade Organization, Legal Affairs Division. (2007). *WTO analytical index: Guide to WTO law and practice* (2nd ed., Vols. 1–2). Cambridge, UK: Cambridge University Press.

This book assists in the identification of existing jurisprudence and relevant decisions in any WTO agreement. As such, the book can assist anyone working in countries abiding by WTO law, serving as a guide to legal interpretations of WTO-based agreements.

Website

The website www.stopfakes.gov/smallbusiness was created by the U.S. Patent and Trademark Office (USPTO) to help small businesses consider the benefits of strong intellectual property (IP) protection, both in the United States and overseas. Although every IP-based business is vulnerable to piracy and counterfeiting, small businesses can be at a particular disadvantage because they lack the resources and expertise available to larger corporations. Small businesses may also lack familiarity with the process of protecting intellectual property: Research conducted in the spring of 2005 by the USPTO indicates that only 15% of small businesses that do business overseas know a U.S. patent or trademark provides protection only in the United States.

7

Alternative Entry Strategies

Profile: Blank Label

Kraig Scarbinsky/Lifesize/ThinkStockPhotos

Through a mixture of good timing, ingenuity, and a smart partnership, two university students created a global company with just the click of a button. Blank Label is an online retail store that sells made-to-order dress shirts for men. At age 23, Fan Bi from Sydney, Australia, came up with the business concept while on vacation in Shanghai. At a local market, Bi was shopping for a dress shirt he could buy off the rack, as he was accustomed, but what he found changed not only his perspective on clothes shopping, but his life as well. Rather than ready-made garments with sizes attached, customers sorted through fabric, which was then stitched to their exact size specifications. These custom-made shirts not only fit better but also were less expensive than those of similar quality at off-the-rack stores. Bi dreamt of bringing personalized shirts to the global community, especially to college students who often need professional clothing but have little money to purchase nice pieces.

Lacking experience in online retailing, Bi found a business partner in Danny Wong, a 19-year-old student at Babson College, where Bi was studying abroad. Wong had the e-commerce and online marketing knowledge that Bi needed to get his company off the ground. As a team, they launched a website in 2009 on which consumers could not only buy a custom-fit dress shirt but could also help to design the shirt to appeal to their personal style. They adopted the term "co-created" to describe the consumer experience of first choosing a fabric, customizing it by size and design, and then adding monogramming or even their own label before clicking "Add to Cart." With a focus on the *experience* of creating one's own shirt, Bi and Wong hope to revolutionize the way people shop for clothes. They sum up their convictions on their website: "Too long [have] the 'appointed' designers branded their fans like they were advertisements of their own egos. . . . Then in came a platform where you could design your own dress shirt, a bridge to quality tailoring, and ready and excited customer service to help you through this. Enter YOU as the designer, the co-creator. Enter the revolution."

Reaching a global market and working together from halfway around the world, the young entrepreneurs are truly a product of their generation. For them, globalization is not a threat or challenge, but rather an opportunity to reach the most customers possible. As of April 2011, Blank Label has generated over $350,000 in revenue with more than 7,000 customers worldwide. The web-based company has potential for enormous growth. As Fan Bi stated, "Thanks to the Internet, you can work with the best people in the world, not just the best people in your neighborhood." Perhaps the same is true for their customer-base as well.

SOURCE: Adapted from Holland (2011); *Our Story* (2011).

Chapter Objectives

1. To determine the best overall strategy for bringing a venture to market through relevant factors.
2. To understand how each different market entry strategy works and which one applies best to your business.

3. To explain the various market entry methods and their advantages and disadvantages.
4. To determine the most appropriate type of entry mode and the best way to engage this market.
5. To understand the benefits of entrepreneurial partnering with home-country entrepreneurs and how to select a partner in a foreign market.

Introduction

Once the business and market opportunity has been selected, it is important that the global entrepreneur develop a strategy to go international. This global strategy outlines the actions the company will take to obtain the international goals established and successfully enter the international market(s) selected. To be profitable (making sure that total revenues are greater than total costs), the global entrepreneur must be competitive and offer something that has value to customers at a price that they are willing to pay. This requires that the global entrepreneur be very attentive to the value of what is being offered for sale, as well as reducing the costs of the offering.

Formulating the Global Strategy

To develop a sound global strategy, a global entrepreneur frequently undertakes the following steps: (1) scan the external environment, (2) determine the strengths and weaknesses of the entrepreneur and the company, and (3) develop the goals and strategy. Each of these will be discussed in turn.

Scan the External Environment

Environmental scanning is a way to provide a good sense of the geographic area being considered for global business. Two main features of this were the focus of Chapters 5 and 6: selecting the international business opportunity and understanding international legal concerns. Other areas of interest where forecasts are also done include competition, consumer data, the overall economy, and political stability. A typical environmental scanning will evaluate and forecast the following:

- Markets for the products/services
- Per capita income of the population
- Labor and raw material availability
- Exchange rates, exchange controls, and tariffs
- Inflation rate
- Competitive products/services available
- Positioning
- Political risk

The resulting forecasts and assessments provide the global entrepreneur with a risk profile and the profit potential of several geographic areas. This will serve as the basis for an accurate decision to be made about which global market(s) to enter.

Determine the Strengths and Weaknesses of the Company

Along with environmental scanning, it is important for the global entrepreneur to assess the strengths and weaknesses of the company. This assessment provides an understanding of the venture's financial, managerial, marketing, and technical capabilities, as well as the critical factors for success that could affect how well the venture will perform. The goal of this analysis is for the global entrepreneur to match as closely as possible the external opportunities identified through the scanning of the environment with the internal strengths of the entrepreneur and the venture. When the people and resources are present to develop and maintain the critical factors for success, the correct market entry strategy can be successfully implemented.

Develop the Goals and Strategy

Although a global entrepreneur already has some general goals that initiated the environmental scanning, more specific goals obtained from both the external and internal analysis need to be established. Goals are usually established in the areas of finance, human resources, marketing, and profitability.

Profitability is key in going global; in general, a venture should achieve higher profitability from its international business than its domestic activities to compensate for the additional effort, management costs, and risk. For those ventures having significant success in their domestic markets, achieving additional market share at home is often very costly and difficult. Global markets offer an ideal alternative for increasing growth and profitability. Based on the established strategic goals, the global entrepreneur will need to develop specific operational goals and controls, which will ensure that the overseas group operates in a way that supports the strategic goals in the plan.

Timing of Market Entry

Once the market(s) has been selected and the global strategy formulated, it is important to determine the best timing of the market entry. One consideration is whether to enter a market before other foreign firms—first mover advantage—or after other foreign businesses have been established in the market—second mover advantage. First mover advantages associated with early market entry include (1) preempting competitive firms and capturing sales by establishing a strong brand name, (2) creating switching costs tying customers to your company's products or services, and (3) building sales volume that provides an experience curve and cost advantages over later market entrants.

The global entrepreneur also has some disadvantages, often referred to as pioneering costs, in being the first entrant into a foreign market. Pioneering costs can often be avoided or minimized by late entrants into the foreign market. Because these costs can be particularly problematic and high when the business system in the foreign market is very different from the firm's home market, considerable effort, expense, and time are needed to learn the new market situation. The highest cost is business failure due to a lack of understanding of doing business in the foreign market. Other pioneering costs include the cost of educating the foreign market customer about the product through promotion and advertising. In developing economies where the rules and regulations governing businesses are still evolving, the first mover may have extra costs of reformulating the company's strategy to take into account any changes that occur. Sometimes the entire business model used in market entrance is invalidated.

The second mover has the advantage of observing and learning from the entrance and mistakes made by early entrants. The later entrant can use a business model that takes these mistakes into account, as well as any changes in the business laws and regulations of the foreign market. The reduction in liability and costs and the increase in learning raise the probability of success for global entrepreneurs entering a foreign market after several other foreign firms have already entered.

Scale of Entry

A final issue that a global entrepreneur needs to address before selecting an entry mode into a foreign market is the scale of entry. Entering a market on a large scale involves a significant amount of time and resources and significantly increases risk. This requires a strategic commitment to the market that has long-term effects on the global entrepreneur and is a decision that is very difficult to reverse.

It also signals to the competition the firm's commitment and can influence the nature and reaction of incumbent firms. This strategic commitment to a foreign market will make it easier to attract customers and establish a base of sales, and may also make other companies deciding to enter the market at least reconsider because they will have to compete with the first firm in the market in addition to national companies. On the negative side, a full-scale commitment will alert incumbent firms and could elicit a vigorous competitive response.

The strategic commitment to enter a foreign market on a large scale decreases the flexibility of the global entrepreneur. Committing heavily to one market leaves fewer resources available to support entrance and expansion in other markets. Few firms have the resources needed to have many large-scale market entries.

Although large-scale market entries are neither always good nor always bad, it is important for the global entrepreneur to think through carefully the implications of such a decision because it will definitely change the competitive landscape. It is important to identify the nature of the competitive reactions, realizing that large-scale entry will increase sales substantially and provide economies of scale of production and distribution while providing some barriers to entry due to the company's presence and/or switching costs.

A small-scale market entry allows the global entrepreneur to learn more about a foreign market with limited exposure. Information can be obtained about the foreign market before significant resources are committed. This increases the venture's flexibility and reduces the risk. The potential long-term rewards are likely to be lower, however, because it will be more difficult and time-consuming to build market share and capture all the first mover advantages.

Foreign Market Entry Modes

There are various ways a global entrepreneur can market products internationally. The method of entry into a market and the mode of operating overseas are dependent on the goals of the entrepreneur and the company's strengths and weaknesses. The modes of entering or engaging in international business can be divided into three categories: exporting, nonequity arrangements, and direct foreign investment (see Table 7.1).

Exporting

Usually an entrepreneur starts doing international business through exporting. *Exporting* normally involves the sale and shipment of products manufactured in one

❖ Table 7.1 Various Entry Modes

Entry Mode	Advantage	Disadvantage
Exporting	Ability to realize location and experience curve economies	High transport costs Trade barriers Problems with local marketing agents
Turnkey contracts	Ability to earn returns from process technology skills in countries where FDI is restricted	Creating efficient competitors Lack of long-term market presence
Licensing	Low development costs and risks	Lack of control over technology Inability to realize location and experience curve economies Inability to engage in global strategic coordination
Franchising	Low development costs and risks	Lack of control over quality Inability to engage in global strategic coordination
Joint ventures	Access to local partner's knowledge Sharing development costs and risks Politically acceptable	Lack of control over technology Inability to engage in global strategic coordination Inability to realize location and experience economies
Wholly owned subsidiaries	Protection of technology Ability to engage in global strategic coordination Ability to realize location and experience economies	High costs and risks

SOURCE: Hisrich, R. D., Peters, M. P., & Shepherd, D. A (2010). *Entrepreneurship* (8th ed.). Homewood, IL: McGraw-Hill/ Irwin, page 147.

country to a customer located in another country. There are two general classifications of exporting: direct and indirect.

Indirect Exporting

Indirect exporting involves having a foreign purchaser in the local market or using an export management firm. For certain commodities and manufactured goods, foreign buyers actively seek out sources of supply and have purchasing offices in markets throughout the world. An entrepreneur wanting to sell into one of these overseas markets can deal with one of these buyers. When this occurs, the entire transaction is handled as though it were a domestic transaction with the goods being shipped out of the country by the foreign buyer. This method of exporting involves the least amount of knowledge and risk for the entrepreneur.

Export management firms, another avenue of indirect exporting, are located in most commercial centers. These firms provide representation in foreign markets for a fee. Typically, they represent a group of noncompeting manufacturers from the same country with no interest in becoming directly involved in exporting. The export management firm handles all the selling, marketing, and delivery of the entrepreneur's products, in addition to any technical problems, in the export process to the foreign country.

One method for indirect exporting is using the Internet. This is exemplified in Green & Black's decision to open an online shop to expand its operations internationally. The organic chocolatier's retail site went live on November 15, 2006, enabling both United States and United Kingdom consumers to buy its products online for the first time. Products include gift items ranging from dinner party to birthday selections, as well as Green & Black's flagship bar products. Customers tailor their gift by picking their own assortment of bars, which is presented in a ribbon-wrapped gift box. The products are also tailored for occasions such as Christmas and Mother's Day.

Green & Black's senior brand manager, Katie Selman, indicated that the launch of the online shop was the first time the company had offered a gifting service to customers. "The online shop allows customers to create tailor-made gifts, which shows they put that little bit more thought into them." The brand is entering a competitive arena. Hotel Chocolat, which launched more than 10 years ago, originally as a catalogue retailer, has been selling products online for the last 5 years (Charles, 2006).

Another form of indirect exports for the global entrepreneur, particularly in the United States, is through home shopping networks. TV shopping on networks such as QVC and Home Shopping Network (HSN) has resulted in products getting instant brand recognition as well as selling thousands of units. QVC and HSN reach nearly 200 million homes in the United States with the following viewer demographics: 75% women between the ages of 25 and 54 with an average household income of $60,000. These home shopping networks conveniently provide quality at an affordable price and sometimes even feature celebrities.

Home shopping networks are particularly open to global entrepreneurs with innovative new products and a background and story that are interesting to their viewers. Both QVC and HSN attend relevant trade shows to find new product opportunities;

they both also accept online submissions at www.qvcproductsearch.com and www.hsn.com/corp/vendor. Both networks look for unique products that are usually recognizable and have broad appeal. One entrepreneur who invented a cleaning compound for outdoor furniture was amazed when 100,000 18-oz. bottles of his cleaning compound sold in one session on QVC. Laurie Feltheimer, founder of Hot in Hollywood, in California, a company specializing in trendy clothes and accessories modeled on Hollywood fashions, recently called HSN's CEO. She soon had a personal meeting to present her concept to the network. Now supplying HSN alone is a multimillion-dollar business. According to Feltheimer, who appears on HSN six to eight times each year, "At this point, I am really happy with my business at HSN. It is growing, it's keeping me busy and interested, and I don't see any reason to complicate my life any further" (Wilson, 2008).

Direct Exporting

If the entrepreneur wants more involvement without any financial commitment, *direct exporting* through independent distributors or the company's own overseas sales office is a way to get involved in international business. Independent foreign distributors usually handle products for firms seeking relatively rapid entry into a large number of foreign markets. This independent distributor directly contacts potential foreign customers, and takes care of all the technicalities of arranging for export documentation, financing, and delivery for an established rate of commission.

Entrepreneurs can also open their own overseas sales offices and hire their own salespeople to provide market representation. When starting out, the entrepreneur may send a domestic salesperson to be a representative in the foreign market. As more business is done in the overseas sales office, warehouses are usually opened, followed by a local assembly process when sales reach a level high enough to warrant the investment. The assembly operation can eventually evolve into the establishment of manufacturing operations in the foreign market. Entrepreneurs can then export the output from these manufacturing operations to other international markets.

Dieter Kondek, a German-born entrepreneur, was talking with friends at a dinner party, expressing his distaste for the lighting designs of the hotel and resort developments opening around his home in Cape Coral, Florida. At that point a friend mentioned a German company, Moonlight, that manufactures glowing orbs that can light a room, illuminate a path, or float in a pool.

"They create light like the moon," says Kondek. "This is what was fascinating to us." He researched the company and found that the polyethylene globes can withstand temperatures from minus 40° to 170° Fahrenheit, range in size from 13 to 30 inches in diameter, and are powered with rechargeable batteries or hardwired into an outlet. Kondek also found out that Moonlight's products were decorating wealthy homes in Europe, Asia, and the Middle East, but were not in the United States. So, after 30 years in the high-tech field, Kondek, along with his wife and two friends, launched Moonlight U.S.A. and became the exclusive U.S. distributor. Worldwide, Moonlight has sold more than 10,000 balls, which cost from $325 to $1,000, and Kondek believes that the United States can eventually make up half the company's sales (Centers, 2008).

Nonequity Arrangements

When market and financial conditions warrant the change, a global entrepreneur can enter into international business by one of three types of *nonequity arrangements:* licensing, turnkey projects, and management contracts. Each of these arrangements allows the global entrepreneur to enter a market and obtain sales and profits without direct equity investment in the foreign market.

Licensing

Licensing involves a global entrepreneur who is a manufacturer (licensor) giving a foreign manufacturer (licensee) the right to use a patent, trademark, technology, production process, or product in return for the payment of a royalty. The licensing arrangement is most appropriate when the entrepreneur has no intention of entering a particular market through exporting or direct investment. Since the process is low risk, yet provides a way to generate incremental income, a licensing agreement can be a good method for the global entrepreneur to engage in international business. Unfortunately, some entrepreneurs have entered into these arrangements without careful analysis and later found that they have licensed their largest competitor into business or that they are investing large sums of time and money to help the licensee adopt the technology or knowledge being licensed.

Wolverine World Wide, Inc., opened a Hush Puppies store in Sofia, Bulgaria, through a licensing agreement with Pikin, a local country combine. Similar arrangements were made a year later in the former USSR with Kirov, a shoe combine. Stores in both countries are doing well.

Turnkey Projects

Another method by which the global entrepreneur can do international business without much risk is through *turnkey projects.* The underdeveloped or lesser-developed countries of the world have recognized their need for manufacturing technology and infrastructure and yet do not want to turn over substantial portions of their economy to foreign ownership. One solution to this dilemma has been to have a foreign entrepreneur build a factory or other facility, train the workers, train the management, and then turn it over to local owners once the business is operational, hence the name turnkey operation.

Entrepreneurs have found turnkey projects an attractive alternative. Initial profits can be made from this method, and follow-up export sales can result. Financing is provided by the local company or the local government, paying the entrepreneur for work completed over the life of the project.

Management Contracts

The final nonequity method the global entrepreneur can use in international business is the *management contract.* Several entrepreneurs have successfully entered international business by contracting their management techniques and skills. The management contract allows the purchasing country to gain foreign expertise without giving ownership of its resources to a foreigner. For the global entrepreneur, the management contract is a way of entering a foreign market without a large equity investment.

Direct Foreign Investment

The wholly owned foreign subsidiary has been a preferred mode of ownership for global entrepreneurs using *direct foreign investment* for doing business in international markets. Joint ventures and minority and majority equity positions are also methods for making direct foreign investments. The percentage of ownership obtained in the foreign venture by the global entrepreneur is related to the amount of money invested, the nature of the industry, and the rules of the host government.

Minority Interests

Japanese companies have been frequent users of the minority equity position in direct foreign investment. A *minority interest* can provide a firm with a source of raw materials or a relatively captive market for its products. Global entrepreneurs have used minority positions to gain a foothold or acquire experience in a market before making a major commitment. When the minority shareholder has something of strong value, the ability to influence the decision-making process is often far in excess of the amount of ownership.

Joint Ventures

Another direct foreign investment method used by global entrepreneurs to enter foreign markets is the *joint venture.* Although a joint venture can take many forms, in its most traditional form two firms (for example, one U.S. firm and one German firm) get together and form a third company in which they share the equity.

Joint ventures have been used by global entrepreneurs most often in two situations: (1) when the global entrepreneur wants to purchase local knowledge as well as an already-established marketing or manufacturing facility, and (2) when rapid entry into a market is needed. Sometimes joint ventures are dissolved and the entrepreneur takes 100% ownership.

Even though using a joint venture to enter a foreign market is a key strategic decision, the keys to its success have not been well understood. The reasons for forming a joint venture today are also different from those of the past. Previously, joint ventures were viewed as partnerships and often involved firms whose stock was owned by several other firms. Joint ventures in the United States were first used by mining concerns and railroads as early as 1850. The use of joint ventures, mostly vertical joint ventures, started increasing significantly during the 1950s. Through the vertical joint venture, two firms could absorb the large volume of output when neither could afford the diseconomies associated with a smaller plant.

What has caused this increase in the use of joint ventures, particularly when many have not worked? The studies of success and failure of joint ventures have found many different reasons for their formation. One of the most frequent reasons an entrepreneur forms a joint venture is to share the costs and risks of a project. Projects where costly technology is involved frequently require resource sharing. This can be particularly important when an entrepreneur does not have the financial resources necessary to engage in capital-intensive activities. Another reason for forming a joint venture is to obtain a competitive advantage. A joint venture can preempt competitors, allowing an entrepreneur to access new customers and expand the market base. Joint ventures are frequently used by global entrepreneurs to enter markets and economies that pose entrance difficulties or to compensate for a company's lack of foreign experience. This has been the case for the transition economies of Eastern and Central Europe and the former USSR.

Majority Interests

Another equity method for the global entrepreneur to enter international markets is to purchase a majority interest in a foreign business. In a technical sense, anything over 50% of the equity in a firm is *majority interest.* The majority interest allows the entrepreneur to obtain managerial control while maintaining the acquired firm's local identity. When entering a volatile international market, some entrepreneurs take a smaller position, which they increase up to 100% as sales and profits increase.

Mergers

A global entrepreneur can obtain 100% ownership to ensure complete control. Many U.S. entrepreneurs desire complete ownership and control in cases of foreign investments. If the global entrepreneur has the capital, technology, and marketing skills required for successful entry into a market, there may be no reason to share ownership.

Mergers and acquisitions have been used significantly to engage in international business, as well as domestically within the United States. During periods of intense merger activity, global entrepreneurs may spend significant time searching for a firm to acquire and then finalizing the transaction. Any merger should reflect basic principles of any capital investment decision and make a net contribution to shareholders' wealth, but the merits of a particular merger are often difficult to assess. Not only do the benefits and cost of a merger need to be determined, but special accounting, legal, and tax issues must also be addressed. The global entrepreneur needs a general understanding of the benefits and problems of mergers as a strategic option, as well as an understanding of the complexity of integrating an entire company into present operations.

There are five basic types of mergers: horizontal, vertical, product extension, market extension, and diversified activity. A *horizontal merger* is the combination of two firms that produce one or more of the same or closely related products in the same geographic area. They are motivated by economies of scale in marketing, production, or sales. An example is the acquisition of convenience food store chain Southland Stores by 7-Eleven Convenience Stores.

A *vertical merger* is the combination of two or more firms in successive stages of production that often involve a buyer-seller relationship. This form of merger stabilizes supply and production and offers more control of these critical areas. Examples are McDonald's acquiring its store franchises and Phillips Petroleum acquiring its gas station franchises. In each case, these outlets become company-owned stores.

A *product extension merger* occurs when acquiring and acquired companies have related production and/or distribution activities but do not have products that compete directly with each other. Examples are the acquisitions of Miller Brewing (beer) by Philip Morris (cigarettes), and Western Publishing (children's books) by Mattel (toys).

A *market extension merger* is a combination of two firms producing the same products but selling them in different geographic markets. The motivation is that the acquiring firm can economically combine its management skills, production, and marketing with that of the acquired firm. An example of this type of merger is the acquisition of Diamond Chain (a West Coast retailer) by Dayton Hudson (a Minneapolis retailer).

The final type of merger is a *diversified activity merger.* This is a conglomerate merger involving the consolidation of two essentially unrelated firms. Usually, the acquiring firm is not interested in either using its cash resources to expand shareholder wealth or actively running and managing the acquired company. An example of a diversified activity merger is Hillenbrand Industries (a caskets and hospital furniture manufacturer) acquiring American Tourister (a luggage manufacturer).

Mergers are a sound strategic option for a global entrepreneur when synergy is present. Synergy is the qualitative effect on the acquiring firm brought about by complementary factors inherent in the firm being acquired. Synergy in the form of people, customers, inventory, plant, or equipment provides leverage for the joint venture. The degree of the synergy determines how beneficial the joint venture will be for the companies involved. Several factors cause synergy to occur and make two firms worth more together than apart.

The first factor, economies of scale, is probably the most prevalent reason for mergers. Economies of scale can occur in production, coordination, and administration; sharing central services such as office management and accounting; financial control; and upper-level management. Economies of scale increase operating, financial, and management efficiency, thereby resulting in lower costs, fewer employees, and better earnings.

The second factor is taxation or, more specifically, unused tax credits. Sometimes a firm has had a loss in previous years but not enough profits to take tax advantage of the loss. Corporate income tax regulations allow the net operating losses of one company to reduce the taxable income of another when they are combined. By combining a firm with a loss with a firm with a profit, the tax-loss carryover can be used.

The final important factor for mergers is the benefits received in combining complementary resources. Many entrepreneurs will merge with other firms to ensure a source of supply for key ingredients, to obtain a new technology, or to keep the other firm's product from being a competitive threat. It is often quicker and easier for a firm to merge with another that already has a new technology developed—combining the technological innovation with the acquiring firm's engineering and sales talent—than to develop the technology from scratch.

CULTURAL STORIES

Story 1

A friend of mine from Poland bought an expensive watch in a big, respected department store. Sometime later, the watch stopped ticking. He immediately took it back to the store and explained that the watch does not function properly.

An elegant sales person, after examining the watch, stated with an expert's confidence while nodding her head, "second hand."

My friend, infuriated, raised his voice and stated, "No, I bought it here!"

Story 2

My friend was traveling around small towns across Russia, developing contracts and purchasing textiles from local factories.

Together with several Russians, we were discussing (in Russian) his job at a Canada Dry party in Moscow, and he mentioned that he frequently had to attend banquets with local mayors and other dignitaries. Somebody asked him what he discussed with these dignitaries, to which he replied, "Politiki, Sport, Ekonomiki, Pollutsya."

There was a stunned silence at the table, and it fell to me to enlighten him on the finer points of Russian (his was quite good, but not quite good enough).

"Pollutsya" in Russian, does not mean pollution, but to put it delicately, the resulting mess from a wet dream. He had been using this conversational gambit for quite a while, including with several female mayors!

SOURCE: http://www.culturalconfusions.com (Story 1 by Bozena Hunek; Story 2 by Brian Rovetta).

Entrepreneurial Partnering

One of the best methods for a global entrepreneur to enter an international market is to partner with an entrepreneur in that country. These foreign (in-country) entrepreneurs know the country and culture and therefore can facilitate business transactions while keeping the global entrepreneur current on business, economic, and political conditions.

There are several characteristics of a good partner. A good partner helps the global entrepreneur achieve his or her goals, such as market access, cost sharing, or core competency obtainment. A good partner also shares the global entrepreneur's vision and is unlikely to try to opportunistically exploit the partnership for his or her own benefit.

How do you select a good partner? First, you need to collect as much information as possible on the industry and potential partners in the country. This information needs to be collected from embassy officials, members of the country's chamber of commerce, firms doing business in that country, and customers of the potential partner. The global entrepreneur will need to attend any appropriate trade shows. References for each potential partner should be checked and each reference asked for other references. Finally, it is most important that the global entrepreneur meet several times with a potential partner to get to know the individual and the company as well as possible before any commitment is made.

Summary

This chapter discusses developing a market entry strategy, choosing the right time for market entry, defining the scale of entry, and finally establishing the best mode of entry. To develop a sound entry strategy, a global entrepreneur must (1) scan the external environment, (2) determine the strengths and weaknesses of the entrepreneur and the company, and (3) develop the goals and strategy. The global entrepreneur must always keep in mind that the international business should be more profitable than the domestic business to compensate for the higher risk involved. The timing for market entry centers on whether the global entrepreneur is the first to enter the foreign market or enters after other competitors have already established their businesses. The primary advantages for "first movers" are preempting competitors and gaining market share; creating switching costs that tie the customer to the entrepreneur's product/services; and building sales volume to maintain profitability after competitors enter the market. A later entry into a foreign market allows a global entrepreneur to learn from the mistakes of the first entrant while also reducing some of the pioneering costs. The global entrepreneur must then weigh the advantages and disadvantages of entering a market on a large scale to command the market, or on a small scale to make sure the foreign market is right for the product or service. Finally, the best mode for entering the market must be defined. Market entry falls into three categories: exporting (indirect or direct), nonequity arrangements (licensing, turnkey projects, and management contracts), and direct foreign investment (wholly owned foreign subsidiaries, joint ventures, majority and minority equity positions, and mergers). The chapter concludes by discussing one more option for entry into a foreign market—partnering with an entrepreneur from that country.

Questions for Discussion

1. What are the different ways to enter a foreign market? What are the advantages and disadvantages of each?
2. What factors should a global entrepreneur consider when deciding on an entry strategy?
3. Anastasia is considering introducing her new line of high-end food products into Mexico. She has heard through a friend that one of her competitors is planning to do the same. Give the arguments as to why it can be better to be the first mover into the market and why it might be better to be the second.

Chapter Exercises

1. Using your own company or business idea, choose a new market for your product or service. Define the external environment, your own and your company's strengths and weaknesses, and a basic strategy to enter that market.

2. What are the advantages of a first mover strategy? What are the best market conditions in which to use this strategy?
3. Imagine that you are the inventor of unique, robotic dolls that have been very successful and popular in your home country. You see a great opportunity in bringing this product to Germany. Conduct a basic analysis of the German market and suggest the best entry mode (exporting, nonequity, or direct foreign investment) for your product.

Note

Portions of this chapter are adapted from Chapter 5 of Hisrich, R. D., Peters, M. A., & Shepherd, D. A. (2010). Entrepreneurship (8th ed.). Burr Ridge, IL: McGraw-Hill/Irwin.

References

Centers, J. (2008, April 1). Great balls of light. *Fortune Small Business, 18*(3), 25.

Charles, G. (2006, October 18). Green & Black's in web shop. *Marketing,* p. 12. Retrieved from http://www.marketingmagazine.co.uk/news/rss/599139/Green---Blacks-web-shop/

Hisrich, R. D., Peters, M. P., & Shepherd, D. A. (2008). *Entrepreneurship* (8th ed.). Homewood, IL: McGraw-Hill/Irwin.

Holland, J. (April 2011). Two college entrepreneurs dress for success. *Entrepreneur, 84.* Retrieved from http://www.entrepreneur.com/article/219343

Our story. (2011). Retrieved from BlankLabel.com: http://www.blanklabel.com/story.aspx

Wilson, S. (2008, May). Big break. *Entrepreneur, 36*(5), 102–108. Retrieved from http://www.entrepreneur.com/article/192754

Suggested Readings

Articles/Books

Clydesdale, G. (2010). *Entrepreneurial opportunity: The right place at the right time.* New York: Routledge.

As a scholar of entrepreneurship, Greg Clydesdale presents the case that the market environment is not given enough weight when analyzing the success or failure of a new venture. Through an analysis of public policy and real-life case studies, he offers strategies for how new businesses can add value, reduce costs and broaden market spectrum to increase their chances for success in the given market environment.

Draper, W. H., III. (2011). *The startup game: Iniside the partnership between venture capitalists and entrepreneurs.* New York: Palgrave Macmillan.

The author of this book offers a compelling argument that the relationship between entrepreneurs and venture capitalists is critical for the success of any economy. Having worked for a venture capital firm for many years himself, Bill Draper gives an insider's view into the world of venture capitalists and their relationship with the people and/or companies in which they invest. He argues that the need for capital can be an impetus for innovation, citing many of the world's most innovative companies to support his argument.

Ellis, P. D. (2007). Paths to foreign markets: Does distance to market affect firm internationalization? *International Business Review, 16*, 573–593.

This paper examines whether distance to a market affects firm internationalization, especially when viewed as geographic, cultural, or psychic distance. Using the location of markets, the sequence of market entry, the rate of international expansion, and the relationship between sequentially linked markets, this paper gives a comprehensive assessment of whether distance does impact internationalization.

Fernandez, J. A., & Underwood, L. (2009). *China entrepreneur: Voices of experience from 40 international business pioneers.* Hoboken, NJ: John Wiley.

This book gives inexperienced entrepreneurs who would like to start a venture in China what the authors have termed a "second-mover advantage," in that they share all of the secrets to success and failure that they have learned through their own journeys as well as the journeys of others. With extensive experience in the Chinese business world, the authors offer street-tested insights to every aspect of starting a business including talent acquisition, finding the right business partners, licensing and other legal issues, customer acquisition, and more.

Jayachandran, C., Thorpe, M., Subramanian, R., & Nagadevara, V. (2011). *Business clusters: Partnering for strategic advantage.* New Delhi, India: Routledge.

A compilation of academic papers on business clusters, this book was developed from a research symposium in Dubai in January 2009. It discusses clustering as a corporate strategy and a source of competitive advantage, as well as the associated difficulties such as performance measurement and management. Assertions are backed by practical evidence from case studies from numerous countries around the world.

Part 3

Managing the Global Entrepreneurial Enterprise

8

The Global Monetary System

Profile: Tiffany & Co.

Ryan McVay/Digital Vision/ThinkStockPhotos

Tiffany & Co. launched in Asia in the plush business area of Ginza, Tokyo, in May 1972. This move replaced its previous Japanese retail operations in the upscale department store chain—Mitsukoshi Ltd.—where Tiffany had 29 boutiques. Even though sales in the Mitsukoshi boutiques were exceptional, even when the Japanese economy slowed, the company was not happy giving away the great retail margins. When Mitsukoshi did not have the capability to invest in expansion, Tiffany paid $115 million for the Japanese operations and inventory. This was one of the reasons for the $10 million loss for the company in 1993.

Tiffany rapidly expanded its presence in Japan by opening a lot of upscale new shops on its own as well as boutiques in Mitsukoshi and Daimaru Inc., a rival department store chain. The terms of the leases in the two chains are much more favorable—paying an operating fee based on sales, not on the margins. Since 1993, Tiffany has experienced strong growth and returns in the Japanese market. In 1993, the company earned 19% of the entire company's revenues from Japan, which increased to 28% in 1994. Even during recessionary times, Tiffany has done well in Japan. A significant part of the sales, around 35%, are from wedding-related items, where Japanese couples are not price sensitive.

This success in Japan has provided the opportunity for Tiffany to expand throughout Asia. It has opened stores in such places as Singapore, Hong Kong, and Korea.

SOURCE: http://www.tiffany.com.

Chapter Objectives

1. To analyze various types of financial management tools in managing exchange rate variations for global businesses
2. To understand the financial implications of doing business globally
3. To understand foreign exchange and the foreign exchange market
4. To understand the global capital market
5. To explain balance of payment concerns and the role of international organizations
6. To learn about protecting a business from the financial exposure in international financial transactions

Introduction

Probably the most difficult aspect of doing international business for most global entrepreneurs involves understanding the global monetary system, foreign exchange, and foreign exchange rates. The purpose of this chapter is to explain the nature of foreign exchange, foreign exchange transactions, and the manner in which foreign exchange rates are established and fluctuate. Following the discussion of the international monetary system and international capital markets, the chapter concludes by discussing the role of the International Monetary Fund (IMF) and the World Bank.

Foreign Exchange

Foreign exchange, an important aspect of doing international business, can be viewed as the system of converting a national currency into another currency and transferring currency from one country to another. It includes deposits, credits, and foreign currency as well as bills of exchange, drafts, letters of credit, and travelers checks.

Aspects of the Foreign Exchange Market

The foreign exchange market provides the platform for foreign exchange transactions where national currencies are bought and sold against one another. It serves three important functions. First, the foreign exchange market transfers purchasing power from one country to another and from one currency to another. By so doing, it facilitates international commerce and trade and capital movement. Second, the foreign exchange market provides credit. This credit function plays an important role in increasing international trade. Finally, the foreign exchange market provides hedging facilities by covering export risk. This hedging facilitation provides a mechanism for exporters and importers to protect themselves against losses from any fluctuations in the exchange rate occurring during the time of the transaction.

There are two primary types of exchange in the foreign exchange market: spot exchange and forward exchange. The spot exchange is a type of foreign exchange transaction that requires the immediate delivery or exchange of currencies. Usually, even though the terms of the transaction are established, the actual settlement takes place in two days. The rate of exchange effective for this type of transaction is the spot rate and its market is called the spot market. The forward exchange involves a transaction between two parties where the delivery is made on a future date by one of the parties for payment in domestic currency by the other party using the price agreed upon in a contract. The rate of exchange in a forward exchange transaction is called the forward exchange rate and the market is known as the foreign market. By having a forward exchange contract, the exporters and importers are protected against any exchange rate fluctuations that may occur during the time of the contract.

The foreign exchange market plays an important role in making global transactions possible. Because a global network of banks, brokers, and foreign exchange dealers connect electronically, the market provides easy access to a company in any country, usually through a bank in the local economy. Even though it is a worldwide network, there are three primary trading centers: London, New York, and Tokyo. There are also several major secondary centers: Frankfurt, Hong Kong, Paris, San Francisco, Singapore, and Sydney. Of these, due to historical and geographic reasons, London is the most important trading center.

There are several interesting features of the market that are important to the global entrepreneur. First, the U.S. dollar plays a very important role because most transactions involve dollars. A manufacturer with Japanese yen wanting to buy Swiss francs will often purchase U.S. dollars to buy the needed Swiss francs. Dollars are easy to use in any transaction. Besides the U.S. dollar, other important currencies are the European euro, the Japanese yen, and the British pound.

Second, the foreign exchange market is always open. Even during the few hours that all three primary trading centers (London, New York, and Tokyo) are closed, trading continues in secondary markets, particularly San Francisco and Sydney.

Finally, all the markets, and particularly the primary and secondary trading centers, are so closely integrated and connected electronically that the foreign exchange market acts as a single market. This means there are no significant differences in exchange rates quoted in any trading center, even those outside the primary and secondary ones. Since there are so many companies involved, any exchange rate discrepancies are small and corrected immediately as dealers attempt to make a profit through arbitrage, or buying a currency low and selling it at a higher price.

Nature of the Foreign Exchange Market

What are the foreign exchange market and its accompanying rates? The foreign exchange market is the open market for converting the currency of one country to the currency of another country at the rate of convertibility determined by the market at the time of the transaction (the foreign exchange rate). The main function of the foreign exchange market is to convert the prices of the goods and services in one country's currency into the currency of another. Each country (or group of countries) has its own currency: Australia (Australian dollars); Canada (Canadian dollars); China (renminbi); France (euro); Germany (euro); Japan (yen); United Kingdom (British pound); and the United States (U.S. dollars). Each currency is converted into another at the exchange rate operating on the date that the exchange occurs. Some hypothetical exchange rates are presented in Table 8.1 (see page 134).

Such exchange rates operate for foreign tourists exchanging currency in a country and are used in the currency transactions in international trade. A company converts the money it receives from sales of its exports, income from licensing agreements, and income from its foreign investments into home country currency or the currency of another country where payments need to be made. Companies also convert home country currency into that of a country where they are interested in investing or buying goods and services. Some companies purchase foreign currencies (hedging) in case there are any significant changes in the exchange rates.

Foreign Exchange Rate Fluctuations

The foreign exchange market can be used to provide some protection for the global entrepreneur against wide fluctuations in exchange rates. This is accomplished through three basic mechanisms: currency swaps, forward exchange rates, and spot exchange rates.

Currency swaps are used to protect against fluctuations and foreign exchange risk when there is a need to move in and out of a currency for a limited period of time. For example, many companies do business in Europe, buying and selling from member countries. Let us say, for example, Alcoa buys and sells finished goods and parts with its wholly owned plant in Hungary and wants to ensure that the US$1 million that it will need to pay some bills in Hungary at EUR .76/US$1 is available at a known exchange rate. It also will collect EUR 20 million in 75 days when some accounts are due. If today's spot exchange rate is US$1 = EUR .76 and the forward foreign exchange is US$1 = EUR .90, Alcoa can enter into a 75-day forward exchange currency swap for converting EUR 20 million into U.S. dollars (US$). Since the euro is at a premium on the 75-day market, the company will receive US$22.2 million (EUR 20 million /.90 = US$22.2 million). Of course, this could be reversed if the euro was trading at less than EUR .76/US$1 in 75 days.

When the global entrepreneur and another company agree to execute a transaction and exchange currency immediately, the transaction is called a spot exchange. In this type of transaction, the spot exchange rate is the rate that the currency of one country is converted into the currency of another country on a particular day. This rate also applies when someone is traveling to London and wants to convert euros into British pounds at a London bank. The spot exchange rate may not be the most favorable exchange rate because the value of the currency is determined by the interaction of demand and supply of each country's currency with respect to the currency of other countries on that particular day.

A final form of protection for the global entrepreneur against widely fluctuating currencies is the forward exchange rate. Forward exchange can be used by two parties to exchange currency and execute a deal at some specific date in the future. The exchange rate used in this type of transaction is called the forward exchange rate and is usually quoted 30, 90, or 180 days into the future. Let us assume a U.S. company and a Swiss company are doing a US$5 million transaction in 90 days, where the Swiss company is purchasing US$5 million of computer software and equipment. Both companies want to enter into a 90-day forward exchange contract. Today the Swiss franc is trading at SF.806/US$1. Since the two companies feel that in 30 days forward it will be SF.808/US$1, 90 days forward it will be SF.812/US$1, and 180 days forward it will be SF.818 /US$1, they enter into a 90-day forward contract guaranteeing that the Swiss company would not pay more than US$6.16 million (US$6.16 million = US$5 million ÷ SF.812/US$1) for the software and equipment. The higher foreign exchange rate in 90 days reflects the expectation that the U.S. dollar would appreciate against the Swiss franc over the next 90 days.

For most global entrepreneurs, foreign exchange should not be a profit driver for their venture. Companies that spend too much time trying to predict or speculate on changes in foreign exchange rates usually end up losing focus on their core product or service and will then lose out in the marketplace. By using the tools previously discussed, global entrepreneurs can improve the predictability of their business and reduce one of the potential risks inherent in international business.

The Global Capital Market

A global capital market benefits both borrowers and investors because it brings together those from around the world who want to invest money and those who want to borrow money better than any single domestic market. For the borrowers, the global capital market increases the funds available for borrowing and lowers the cost of capital. In a domestic market, the pool of investors is limited to those who live in the

❖ Table 8.1 Examples of Foreign Exchange Rates

Country	Currency	Dollar	Euro	Pound	Country	Currency	Dollar	Euro	Pound
Argentina	Peso	3.1063	4.0181	6.0819	New Zealand	NZ$	1.4350	1.8563	2.8097
Australia	A$	1.2954	1.6757	2.5364	Nigeria	Naira	128.075	165.671	250.765
Bahrain	Dinar	0.3771	0.4878	0.7383	Norway	NOKrone	6.3105	8.1629	12.3556
Bolivia	Boliviano	7.9950	10.3420	15.6538	Pakistan	Rupee	60.7300	78.5573	118.906
Brazil	Real	2.1374	2.7649	4.1850	Peru	New Sol	3.1980	4.1368	6.2616
Canada	C$	1.1828	1.5300	2.3159	Philippines	Peso	49.1350	63.5586	96.2039
Chile	Peso	544.650	704.532	1066.40	Poland	Zloty	3.0440	3.9375	5.9599
China	Yuan	7.7745	10.0567	15.2221	Romania	New Leu	2.6343	3.4075	5.1577
Colombia	Peso	2262.20	2926.27	4429.27	Russia	Ruble	26.5591	34.3555	52.0014
Costa Rica	Colon	518.375	670.544	1014.95	Saudi Arabia	Saudi Riyal	3.7508	4.8518	7.3438
Czech Republic	Koruna	21.8198	28.2250	42.7221	Singapore	S$	1.5398	1.9918	3.0148
Denmark	DKr	5.7627	7.4544	11.2831	Slovakia	Koruna	27.2506	35,2500	53.3553
Egypt	Egyptian £	5.7063	7.3814	11.1726	South Africa	Rand	7.3163	9.4640	14.3249
Estonia	Kroon	12.0958	15.6465	23.6830	South Korea	Won	940.450	1216.52	1841.35
European Union (0.7730)	EUR	1.2936	—	1.5137	Sweden	Krona	7.0070	9.0639	13.7194
Hong Kong	HK$	7.8112	10.1041	15.2939	Switzerland	Swiss Franc	1.2546	1.6229	2.4564

Hungary	Forint	198.724	257.060	389.093	Taiwan	T$	32.9720	42.6509	64.5576
India	Rupee	44.2050	57.1814	86.5512	Thailand	Baht	34.2750	44.3365	67.1088
Indonesia	Rupiah	9122.50	11800.40	1786.40	Tunisia	Dinar	1.3156	1.7018	2.5759
Iran	Rial	9231.00	11940.80	18073. 80	Turkey	Lira	1.4275	1.8465	2.7950
Israel	Shekel	4.2540	5.5028	8.3292	United Arab Emirates	Dirham	3.6729	4.7511	7.1913
Japan	Yen	121.905	157.690	238.684	United Kingdom	English £	1.9580	0.6607	—
Kenya	Shilling	70.5000	91.1953	138.036	United States	US$	—	1.2936	1.9580
Kuwait	Dinar	0.2893	0.3742	0.5664	Uruguay	Peso	24.2750	31.4010	47.5293
Malaysia	M$	3.5025	4.5307	6.8577	Venezuela	Bolivar	4389.25	5677.72	8593.93
Mexico	New peso	11.0824	14.3357	21.6988	Vietnam	Dong	16050.00	20761.50	31425.10

particular country, so there is an upper limit on the supply of funds available. A global capital market increases the number of investors and supply of funds available from the larger pool.

Also, the broader pool obtained in a global market eliminates the limited liquidity found in a domestic capital market, and this also lowers the cost of capital. This means that the dividend yield and expected capital gains on equity investments, as well as the interest rate on loans (debt), are lower. This lower price of obtaining capital is very important to companies all over the world. This is particularly beneficial in less-developed countries, where the pool of investors tends to be smaller than in more developed economies.

From the investor's perspective, the global capital market provides a wider range of investment opportunities than is available in any domestic market. This allows investors to reduce their risk by diversifying their portfolios over a wide range of industries geographically dispersed. As the number of investments increases in an investor's portfolio, generally the risk in the portfolio declines until it approaches the systematic risk of the market. Systematic risk is the risk associated with the value in a portfolio attributable to macroeconomic forces affecting all firms in an economy and not a specific individual firm. Because the movement of stock and interest rates are country specific and are not perfectly correlated across countries, the investor's risk is reduced by investing in various countries. By doing this, the losses incurred when an investment(s) in one country goes down are offset by gains in investment(s) in another country. This low correlation of value and interest rates among countries reflects the different macroeconomic policies and different economic conditions on a country-by-country basis. It also reflects the capital controls in place in some countries that restrict cross-border capital flows.

Balance of Payments

A key concern today is disparity in the balance of payments between countries. The balance of payments measures all the international economic transactions between two countries. There are hundreds of thousands of international transactions, such as imports, exports, repatriation of profits, grants, and investments that occur each year, all of which are recorded and classified.

By definition, the balance of payments must balance or there is an error in counting. While there can be an imbalance in currency or trade between two countries, the entire balance of payment of every country is always balanced. In recording all international transactions over a period of time, the balance of payments is tracking the flow of purchases and payments between every country. Two types of business transactions dominate the balance of payments: real assets (the exchange of goods and services for other goods and services, through either barter or, more commonly, money) and financial assets (the exchange of financial claims such as stocks, bonds, loans, purchases, or sales for other financial claims or money). The balance of payments consists of two primary subaccounts—the current account and the capital and financial account—and two minor subaccounts—the official reserve account and the net errors and omissions account. Each of these will be briefly discussed in turn.

The current account includes all international economic transactions with income or payment within the year. It includes goods trade, services trade, income, and current transfers. Goods trade consists of the export and import of goods, the oldest form of international economic activity. Many countries attempt to keep a balance or, even better, a surplus of exports over imports. Services trade deals with the export and import of services. Significant activity in services trade involves construction services, financial services provided by banks, and travel services of airlines. Income is mostly current income from investments made in previous periods. Any wages or salaries paid to nonresident workers of subsidiaries of out-of-country companies are also considered income. Finally, current transfers are composed of any financial settlements in change of ownership of real assets or financial items as well as a one-way transfer, gift, or grant from one country to another.

While every country has some trade, most of the trade involves merchandise (goods trade). The balance of trade, which is widely discussed in the business press, refers to the balance of imports and exports of goods trade only. This, for large industrialized countries like Japan, the United States, and the United Kingdom, is misleading because it does not include the other three areas of the current account, particularly services trade, which can also be very large and significant.

The capital and financial account of the balance of payments measures all international transactions of financial assets and has two major subaccounts—the capital account and the financial account. The capital account is composed of all the transfers of financial assets and the acquisition of nonproduced and nonfinancial assets. This is a very small part of the total combined account. The financial account is by far the largest component of this dual account and consists of three parts: direct investment, portfolios investment, and other long-term and short-term capital transfers. Each of the financial assets is classified by the degree of control over the particular asset the claim represents. In a portfolio investment, the investor has no control, but in a direct investment, the investor exerts some degree of control over the asset.

One minor subaccount of the balance of payments—the official reserve account—is composed of the total currency and metallic reserves held by the official monetary authority of the government of each country. Most of these revenues are in the major currencies of the world used in international trade and financial transactions. Another minor subaccount of the balance of payments is the net errors and omissions account. This very small account, as the name implies, makes sure that the balance of payments is always in balance.

Role of the International Monetary Fund and World Bank

In addition to the balance of payments, another area important for the global entrepreneur to understand is the role of the International Monetary Fund (IMF) and the World Bank. Both the IMF and the World Bank were established in 1944 when representatives from 44 countries met at Bretton Woods, New Hampshire (USA), to design a new international monetary system. The overall goal of the meeting was to design an economic order that would endure and facilitate the economic growth of the world following the end of World War II. While the IMF was established to maintain order in the international monetary system, the World Bank was established to promote general economic development. Each will be discussed in turn in terms of its importance for the global entrepreneur.

International Monetary Fund (IMF)

Due to the worldwide financial collapse after World War II, competitive currency devaluations, high unemployment, and hyperinflation occurring particularly in Germany in 1944, the IMF was established to avoid a repetition of these events. The discipline part of the equation was achieved through the establishment of a fixed exchange rate, thereby helping to control inflation and improving economic discipline in countries. This fixed exchange rate lasted until 1976 when a floating exchange rate was formalized and established.

Some flexibility was built into the system in the form of the IMF lending facilities and adjustable parities. Most members of the IMF make available gold and currencies to the IMF to lend to member countries to cover short-term periods of balance-of-payment deficits to avoid domestic unemployment in that country due to a tightening monetary or fiscal policy. The IMF funds are lent to countries to bring down inflation rates and reduce the country's balance-of-payment deficits. Because a persistent balance-of-payment deficit would deplete a country's reserves of foreign currency, a loan to reduce this deficit helps a country avoid devaluing its currency. When extensive loans from the IMF fund are given to a country, that country must submit to increasingly stringent supervision by the IMF of its macroeconomic policies.

The system of adjustable parities established by the IMF allows for the devaluation of a country's currency by more than 10% if the IMF feels that this will help achieve a balance-of-payment equilibrium in the country. The IMF felt that in these circumstances, without devaluation the member country would experience high unemployment and a persistent trade deficit.

The World Bank

The World Bank, officially named the International Bank for Reconstruction and Development (IBRD), was established initially to help finance the rebuilding of Europe following World War II. Because the U.S. Marshall Plan accomplished this, the World Bank focused instead on such areas as lending money to third world countries. The focus was on power stations and transportation as well as agriculture, education, population control, and economic development.

The World Bank makes loans for projects in developing economies through two schemes. The first one, the IBRD scheme, raises money for the project through the sale of bonds in the international capital market. The second scheme involves International Development Association (IDA) loans from money supplied by wealthier member nations. A global entrepreneur may have the opportunity to be involved in one of these funded projects.

❖ CULTURAL STORIES

Story 1

When we lived in Mexico, several engineering students asked us to review resumes they had written in English. Our students had excellent English skills and wanted their resumes to be perfect.

One student was concerned about reusing verbs and had used a thesaurus to help create more variety. He did well until the bullet point about "practicing intercourse" with clients. We tried to explain that "conversing" might be better, and he insisted that the thesaurus told him his choice was perfect—until we had him look it up in the dictionary.

The word was finally understood and the story spread—everyone was asking if they could get a job with him.

Story 2

I was working at a local newspaper in San Diego and one of my responsibilities was the Latino community. One year at Christmastime, I sent an e-mail to more than 50 Latino leaders in San Diego and Tijuana wishing them a Happy New Year. What I said was Feliz Ano, forgetting to include the ~ over the n.

Instead of wishing them Happy New Year, I wished them a "Happy Anus." Boy, was I embarrassed.

SOURCE: http://www.culturalconfusions.com (Story 1 by Jamie Mattson; Story 2 by Jeri Denniston).

Trade Financing

One of the keys to successful global expansion is having funds available. One alternative to acquiring these funds, and often the only option available to the global entrepreneur, is *bootstrap financing*. This approach is particularly important at start-up and in the early years of the venture when capital from debt financing (i.e., in terms of higher interest rates) or from equity financing (i.e., in terms of loss of ownership) is very expensive.

In addition to the monetary costs, outside capital has other costs as well. First, it usually takes about 6 months to raise outside equity capital or to find out that there is no outside capital available. During this time of raising equity capital, the global entrepreneur may not focus enough on the important areas of marketing, sales, product development, and operating costs. A business usually needs capital when it can least afford the time to raise it. One company's CEO spent so much time raising capital for global expansion that sales and marketing were neglected to such an extent that the forecasted sales and profit figures on the pro forma income statements were not met for the first 3 years after the capital infusion. This led to investor concern that, in turn, required more of the CEO's time.

Second, the availability of capital increases the global entrepreneur's impulse to spend. It can cause a company to hire more staff before they are needed and to move into more costly facilities. A company can easily forget the basic axiom of venture creation: staying lean and mean.

Third, outside capital can decrease the company's flexibility. This can hamper the direction, drive, and creativity of the global entrepreneur. Unsophisticated investors are particularly a problem because they often object to a company's moving away from the focus and direction outlined in the business plan that attracted their investment; this often occurs in taking the venture into international markets. This attitude can encumber a company to such an extent that the needed change cannot be implemented or implemented only very slowly after a great deal of time and effort has been spent in consensus building. This can substantially demoralize the global entrepreneur who likes the freedom of not working for someone else.

Finally, outside capital may cause disruption and problems in the venture. Capital is not provided without the expectation of a return. Sometimes equity investors pressure the entrepreneur to continuously grow the company so that an exit (payback) can occur as soon as possible or at least within a 5- to 7-year period. This emphasis on short-term performance can be at the expense of the long-term success of the company.

In spite of these potential problems, a global entrepreneur at times needs some capital to finance international growth; without outside capital, this growth can be slow or nonexistent if internal sources of funds are used. Outside capital should be sought only after all possible internal sources of funds have been explored. And, when outside funds are needed, the global entrepreneur should not forget to stay focused on the basics of the business. Two good sources of external funds for expanding the business are from family and friends, and commercial banks.

Family and Friends

Family and friends are a common source of capital to go international, particularly if their origins are from the country to be entered. These individuals are most likely to invest due to their past knowledge and relationship with the entrepreneur as well as knowledge of the country. Family and friends usually provide a small amount of equity funding for the global venture. Although it is often easier to obtain money from family and friends, like all sources of capital, there are positive and negative consequences. Although the amount of money provided may be small, if it is in the form of equity financing, upon funding, the family members or friends have an ownership position in the venture and may feel they have the right to direct input into the operations of the venture. This may have a negative effect on employees and facilities and distract from focus on sales and profits. On the other hand, family and friends are usually more patient in desiring a return on their investment.

To avoid problems in the future, the global entrepreneur should present the possible positive and negative consequences and the nature of the risks of the investment opportunity in the international market. The business arrangements should be strictly business. Any loans or investments from family or friends should be treated in the same businesslike manner as if the financing were from an impersonal investor. Any loan should specify the rate of interest and a proposed repayment schedule of interest and principal. If the family or friend is treated the same as an investor, future conflicts can be avoided. Everything should be in writing as it is amazing how short memories become when money is involved.

The global entrepreneur should carefully consider the effect of the investment on the family member or friend before accepting. Particular concern should be paid to any hardships that might result should the international market not be successful. Each family member or friend should invest because they feel it's a good international opportunity, not because they feel obligated.

Commercial Banks

Commercial banks can be a good source of funds for global expansion when collateral is available. The funds are in the form of debt financing and, as such, require some tangible guaranty or collateral—some asset with value. This collateral can be in the form of business assets (land, equipment, or the building of the venture), personal assets (the entrepreneur's house, car, land, stocks, or bonds), the assets of the cosigner of the note, or the assets of doing business (accounts receivable, inventory). There are several types of bank loans available to the global entrepreneur. To ensure repayment, these loans are based on the assets and/or the cash flow of the venture, such as accounts receivable, inventory, or equipment.

Accounts receivable provide a good basis for a loan to do international business, particularly if the customer base is well known and creditworthy. For creditworthy customers, a bank may finance up to 80% of the value of their accounts receivable. When the customer is a foreign government, a global entrepreneur can develop a factoring arrangement whereby the factor (the bank) actually "buys" the accounts receivable at a value below the face value of the sale and collects the money directly from the foreign purchaser. In this case, if any of the receivables is not collectible, the factor (the bank) sustains the loss, not the global entrepreneur. The cost of factoring the accounts receivable is of course higher than the cost of securing a loan against the accounts receivable, because the bank has more risk when factoring. The costs of factoring involve the interest charge on the amount of money advanced until the time the accounts receivable are collected, the commission covering the actual collection, and protection against any possible uncollectible amount.

Inventory is another of a firm's assets that is often a basis for an international loan, particularly when the inventory is more liquid and can be easily sold. Usually, the finished goods inventory can be financed for up to 50% of its value.

Equipment can be used to secure long-term financing, usually on a 3- to 10-year basis. Equipment financing can fall into any of several categories: financing the purchase of new equipment, financing used equipment already owned by the company, sale-leaseback financing, or lease financing. When new equipment is being purchased or presently owned equipment is used as collateral, usually 50% to 80% of the value of the equipment can be financed depending on its salability. Given an entrepreneur's tendency to rent rather than own, sale-leaseback or lease financing of equipment is widely used. In the sale-leaseback arrangement, the global entrepreneur "sells" the equipment to a lender and then leases it back for the life of the equipment to ensure its continued use.

The other type of debt financing frequently provided by commercial banks and other financial institutions is cash flow financing. These conventional bank loans include lines of credit, installment loans, straight commercial loans, long-term loans, and character loans. Lines of credit financing is perhaps the form of cash flow financing most frequently used by global entrepreneurs. In arranging for a line of credit to be used as needed, the company pays a commitment fee to ensure that the commercial bank will make the loan when requested and then pays interest on any outstanding funds borrowed from the bank. Frequently, the loan must be repaid or reduced to a certain agreed-upon level on a periodic basis.

One problem for the global entrepreneur is determining how to successfully secure an international loan from a bank. Banks are generally cautious in lending money, particularly to new ventures and ventures doing business in global markets. Regardless of geographic location, commercial loan decisions are made only after the loan officer and a loan committee carefully review the borrower and the financial track record of the business.

These decisions are based on both quantifiable information and subjective judgments. The bank's lending decisions are made according to the five Cs of lending: character, capacity, capital, collateral, and conditions. Past financial statements (balance sheets and income statements) are reviewed for key profitability and credit ratios, inventory turnover, aging of accounts receivable, the entrepreneur's capital invested, and commitment to the business. Future projections on the international market size, sales, and profitability are also evaluated to determine the ability to repay the loan. Several questions are usually raised regarding this ability: Does the entrepreneur expect to have the loan for an extended period of time? If problems occur, is the entrepreneur committed enough to spend the effort necessary to make the business a success? Does the business have a unique differential advantage in a growth market? What are the downside risks? Is there protection (such as life insurance on key personnel and insurance on the plant and equipment) against disasters? The intuitive factors, particularly the first two Cs, character and capacity, are also taken into account. This part of the loan decision—the gut feeling—is the most difficult part to assess. The global entrepreneur must present his or her capabilities and the prospects for the company in a way that elicits a positive response from the lender. This intuitive part of the loan decision becomes even more important when there is little or no track record, limited experience in financial management, a nonproprietary product or service (one not protected by a patent or license), or few assets available.

Some of the concerns of the loan officer and the loan committee can be reduced by providing a good loan application and global business plan. Although the specific loan application format of each bank differs to some extent, generally the application format is a mini business plan that consists of an executive summary, business description, owner/manager profiles, international business projections, financial statements, amount and use of the loan, and repayment schedule. This information provides the loan officer and loan committee with insight into the creditworthiness of the individual and the venture, as well as the ability of the venture to make enough sales and profit to repay the loan and the interest.

The global entrepreneur should evaluate several banks, select the one that has had positive loan experiences in the particular business area, make an appointment, and then carefully present the case for the loan to the loan officer. Presenting a positive business image and following the established protocol are necessary to obtain a loan from a commercial bank. The global entrepreneur needs to establish a good relationship with a globally oriented bank.

Letters of Credit

The use of letters of credit in international trade has significantly increased in the past years, particularly in the United States. A letter of credit is simply a letter from one bank to another bank requesting that the second bank do something (usually pay money to someone) once certain conditions are fulfilled, such as the receiving or shipping of merchandise. Banks issue letters of credit for a fee, and some banks take the money from the customer's account or freeze that money in the account until needing to release the money to another bank when the terms and conditions are met, which can be 3 to 4 months later.

Suppose a German manufacturer wants to buy some component parts from a supplier in China. How could the transaction take place? The German company could send a check along with the order or wire transfer the money to the bank of the Chinese company. In this transaction, the German manufacturer could not be guaranteed that the component parts will be received. Instead, the Chinese company could ship the component parts to the German manufacturer along with an invoice for the amount due. When doing this, the Chinese company could not be assured that payment will be received. This is where a letter of credit plays an important role. The two companies need to reach an agreement on when the seller (the Chinese company in this case) gets paid and provide that information to the bank of each company.

This is very important when the bank issuing the letter of credit (the bank of the German company) does not take control of the amount of money of the letter of credit when it is issued. In this case, the buying company (the German company) may have 60 to 90 days before the actual money is withdrawn. If the payment is specified at a certain time and condition, the selling company (the Chinese company) can usually get most of the amount of the letter of credit by drawing a draft for this amount at its receiving bank. The receiving bank will discount the draft at the prevailing discount rate. If the discount rate is 8% and the payment period is 90 days, then the discount will be 2% (90/360 on a quarter of 8%). This can be a very inexpensive way of getting money now instead of later. Some banks, often in the United States, take the money from the issuer's account (the German company) once the letter of credit is issued.

Banks vary on their application form for obtaining a letter of credit. All forms contain such information as the demographic information on the buying and selling company, the exact items being purchased, and the specific requirements of the transaction including how payment is to be made. The agreement between the buyer and seller may specify that payment is to be made after the items have been inspected or upon shipment or the presentation of the appropriate documents. Also included may be the latest shipping date acceptable to the buyer and who is responsible for freight.

The exact cost of a letter of credit varies greatly by bank and by country. There is always a bank charge for writing the letter of credit, and it can vary from $200 to $500. There is also a percentage charge for the amount of money involved. This ranges from .5% to 2.5%. Even at the highest fee and percentage, letters of credit enable the global entrepreneur to more easily buy and sell internationally.

Summary

The creation, use, and effects of the global monetary system are discussed in this chapter. Since there are numerous currencies being used all over the world, a global entrepreneur must understand foreign exchange rates and how the foreign exchange market works. When a product or service is sold in a foreign country, this market converts the prices of goods and services in one country into the currency of another. The global entrepreneur will use the foreign exchange market whenever making a global sale, receiving income from foreign agreements and investments, receiving payments from foreign countries, investing in a foreign country, purchasing goods or services from a foreign country, or taking part in currency speculation. Exchange rate fluctuations can affect the costs and profits of a global enterprise. There are three mechanisms to reduce the risk of currency fluctuations: currency swaps, forward exchange rates, and spot exchange rates. The U.S. dollar is the primary currency used in international transactions along with the European euro, the Japanese yen, and the British pound. The chapter concludes with an overview of two major international financial institutions, the International Monetary Fund (IMF) and the World Bank, both of which could be important to a global entrepreneur.

There are many sources of capital for a small company. Banks can provide letters of credit that prove the creditworthiness of a company to its potential customers in foreign markets. Letters of credit shift the credit responsibility from the individual or company to an established bank. This can prove necessary when both buying and selling in the international market where there is often limited knowledge.

Questions for Discussion

1. What are the potential effects of a change in the ∈/NZ$ exchange rate for an Italian entrepreneur who frequently does business in New Zealand?
2. How would a weak Swiss franc benefit a Swiss entrepreneur who exports much of his product?
3. Explain the different roles of the International Monetary Fund and the World Bank.
4. Mike just signed a US$1-million contract to sell small engines to a Slovenian manufacturer. Delivery will take place in 1 month, but he does not expect to receive his payment in euros for 3 months. What are the potential risks? What are some of the ways to mitigate these risks?

Chapter Exercises

1. Choose a foreign currency and visit the website www.Xe.com to familiarize yourself with how the exchange rate between your home currency and that foreign currency functions.
2. Pick a country that has recently dealt with severe currency devaluation and research how that devaluation has affected foreign investment and holdings in that country.
3. Select a country besides your own and see how the balance of payments works between your country and that foreign country.
4. Go to the International Monetary Fund and World Bank websites (www.imf.org and www.worldbank.org) to familiarize yourself with their roles in the global economic system. How do these roles differ?

Suggested Readings

Books

Brown, G. (2010). *Beyond the crash: Overcoming the first crisis of globalization.* Glencoe, IL: Free Press.

Former British Prime Minister and Chancellor of the Exchequer Gordon Brown gives a compelling argument for why the global financial crisis occurred, and what can be done to avoid such disasters in the future. As a person with a great deal of access and high regard in the public sector, Brown offers a unique perspective of the global meltdown from the inside, as well as an intelligent analysis of the crisis in a historical context.

International Monetary Fund. (2010). *Balance of payments statistics yearbook.* Washington, DC: Author.

The ***Balance of Payments Statistics*** **Yearbook**, usually published in December, contains balance of payments statistics for most of the world, compiled in accordance with the International Monetary Fund's **Balance of Payments Manual**.

Motianey, A. (2010). *Supercycles: The new economic force transforming global markets and investment strategy.* New York: McGraw-Hill.

International economist and strategist Arun Motianey explains the global economy in detail, drawing from historical events as well as current policy and trends. Through his analysis, he offers a plan for how to predict market fluctuations and invest accordingly. He intelligently discusses the 21st-century economic crisis from a broad and global perspective.

Plunkett, J. (2010). *The next boom: What you absolutely, positively have to know about the world between now and 2025.* Houston, TX: BixExces Press.

In this book, Jack Plunkett predicts an economic boom in the near future, defined as the years 2013 to 2025. In an optimistic, but not idealistic tone, Plunkett describes the political, social, economic, and environmental factors that he believes will lead the world into an era of global prosperity.

Rogers, S. (2009). ***Entrepreneurial finance: Finance and business strategies for the serious entrepreneur.*** **New York: McGraw-Hill.**

This book guides the reader through the financial aspect of the entrepreneurial process from start to finish, including capital procurement, operational management, and either buy-out or dissolution of the firm. The author provides both an academic and practical overview of finance management for entrepreneurs.

Websites

www.imf.org
The IMF is an international organization of 185 member countries that promotes international monetary cooperation, exchange stability, and orderly exchange arrangements; fosters economic growth and high levels of employment; and provides temporary financial assistance to countries to help ease balance of payments adjustment.

www.worldbank.org
The World Bank is a good source of technical and financial assistance for developing countries. It is a group of entities headquartered in Washington, D.C.

www.xe.com
This is a currency site that provides up-to-date information on currencies as well as trading, currency education, data, and tools.

Global Marketing and R&D

Profile: Spanx

Polka Dot RF/Polka Dot/ThinkStockPhotos

Sara Blakely, founder of Spanx, is the face behind a successful brand of body shaping underwear. In a small one-bedroom apartment, while selling fax machines daily, Blakely spent her nights concocting a solution to every woman's battle of the bulge. A pair of white pants inspired her to cut the feet off of a pair of control-top pantyhose in order to appear slimmer in the not-so-flattering white garment. Her idea worked well, giving her backside the shape she desired, but the legs of the pantyhose kept rolling up. A little help from some elastic at the bottom would fix the problem right up, and Blakely knew she had a winning product—a modern approach to the traditional girdle.

She immediately set out to get her "shapewear" manufactured, pitching her idea to every hosiery manufacturer she could find. Nearly 2 years of total rejection in the male-dominated industry had Blakely discouraged but not defeated. Finally, she received a call from a man who agreed to make her product. When she asked him what had changed his mind, he simply said that he had two daughters and they seemed to understand her vision. The entrepreneur quickly began producing prototypes to show to department stores. In order to gain distribution, Blakely literally had to demonstrate to one buyer how Spanx works by asking her to follow her into the ladies room. Wearing the infamous white pants, Blakely simply put the shapewear on in a stall and showed the buyer the "before and after" difference. The department store chain put Spanx in seven stores that week.

A new twist on an old idea, Spanx skyrocketed almost overnight. Celebrities in image-obsessed Hollywood began endorsing the product, even showing their undergarments to the press. Actress Gwyneth Paltrow was quoted as saying that everyone in Hollywood wears Spanx. Once Oprah touted Spanx as one of her "favorite things," and the company sold 50,000 items due to that media exposure alone. Spanx enjoys an extraordinary demographic reach, appealing to women of all ages from the 17-year-old wanting to look perfect in her prom dress to the 65-year-old who wants to maintain her appearance. Spanx retail sales in 2007 reached $250 million, as it created more than 100 new products in the 8 years since its inception. Every product has the same sales pitch: it works, and it is comfortable.

The genius behind Spanx's success is Sara Blakely and the inspiration she brings to the marketing campaign. As the face of the brand, the target audience relates to her, heightening the brand's credibility. Her name as well as her cartoon figure appears on the packaging giving consumers a sense of intimacy, as with a close friend. The brightly colored packaging is fun and attractive with amusing product names such as "Slim Cognito" and "Undie-tectable." Even the website maintains this sense of entertaining banter by advertising, "Free shipping: No butts about it!" The company has made every effort to brand the product to be hip and uninhibited, just like the unrestrained characters featured in the TV show and movie, *Sex and the City.* The trend for women to be open, honest, and free to discuss topics thought to be taboo in the past was at full force in the early 2000s and Spanx jumped directly on board. For a company that knows its customers intimately, appealing to their modern desires was a sure way to success.

Blakely attributes much of her success to her customers. The innovation behind new Spanx products has come directly from the women who use and love the product. As Blakely and her team have come to realize, if one woman complains about a problem she has with her body or clothing, chances are that thousands of other women have the same complaint. Simply listening to customers' needs has accelerated Spanx into the highly lucrative, but nearly impossible to attain position of the brand name being synonymous with the product. As Kleenex is to tissues, so now is Spanx to body shaping underwear. Having expanded tremendously in just a decade, Spanx now ships to 60 different countries and has extended its lines to include swimwear, apparel, and even men's undergarments. With quite literally a world full of customers, Sara Blakely is reshaping the undergarment industry one derrière at a time.

SOURCE: Adapted from CNBC (2009) and Spanx Inc. (2011).

Chapter Objectives

1. To understand how telecommunications technology will affect the global entrepreneur through marketing products and services
2. To understand the role of innovation for a global entrepreneur
3. To describe innovation and how often this determines the future of organizations and ventures
4. To learn how to adapt a product to the market it is entering
5. To determine how to best introduce products to the market while maintaining top quality
6. To define the product life cycle and how to plan and develop this process
7. To show how to evaluate new products for suitability to enter a market
8. To understand the global marketing mix and its key components

Introduction

The four major problems in the areas of marketing and research and development facing the global entrepreneur when entering or expanding in an international market(s) are (1) the technological environment, (2) product policy and the total quality issue, (3) adopting the best research and development strategy, and (4) developing and implementing the best marketing strategy. Each of these problems has accelerated due to rapidly changing technologies, shorter and shorter product life cycles, changing consumer tastes, and changing economies, particularly in emerging markets. Depending on the nature of the global market, there can be significant problems in each of the four areas, particularly in the short run. When General Electric (GE) purchased a controlling interest in Tungstrum, the Hungarian light bulb manufacturing company, it expected to turn the company around, solve the total quality issue, and sell light bulbs to the countries in the European Union in a much shorter period of time than actually occurred. The GE manager in charge of the Tungstrum operation was continually heard saying, "In 6 months we will have light bulbs for Europe." Six months turned into 3 years before the product was sufficient to sell in Europe. Yet, in 2005–2006, GE moved much of its research and development in light bulbs to Tungstrum in Hungary.

Technological Environment

The technological environment varies greatly from country to country and changes at lightning speed. There are several ways in which technology will affect the global entrepreneur in the next decade. First, and perhaps foremost, is the use of social media. The Internet allows individuals from around the world to obtain information from millions of sources. Second, automatic translation in various media is available, allowing people to communicate in their own language with individuals all over the world. Third, satellites play an increasing role in communication and learning, enabling people in even very remote areas to receive voice messages and data through handheld telephones. Fourth, there is the increasing use of nanotechnology to create products on a micro level. Fifth, advances in biotechnology will transform agriculture and medicine. And, sixth, more and more people have purchasing power as countries move into more market economics. The resulting issues in telecommunication and e-business are discussed in more detail in the following sections.

Telecommunications

Previously, one of the biggest obstacles in global business, particularly in less-developed and emerging markets, was telecommunications; this is rapidly changing. Since it is no longer necessary to hardwire, economies are leapfrogging from phones being unavailable to cellular phones being available everywhere, even in the remotest parts of China and Africa. Because of the quick and relatively inexpensive installation of this new infrastructure and the merging technology of the computer and telephone, a growing number of people, even in rural areas of Asia, are accessing the web through cell phones, allowing business transactions to take place in the remotest of areas. During the next decade, the further merger of wireless technology and the Internet will radically change the way people communicate and will open even more markets in less-developed countries and rural areas. Cellular phones are also making an impact in developed countries like Finland, Norway, and Sweden, where more than 75% of each country's population are cellular subscribers.

With telecommunication services providing an efficient communication system, many governments believe this is the key to their economic development and the attraction of foreign direct investment. Some telecommunication operations are state run, such as many in the Asia-Pacific region, but an increasing number are private-sector companies. Some former state-owned companies that have been privatized, often with the help of foreign companies, include Korea Telecom, Philippines Global Telecom, and Thailand's Telecom Asia. Most of the investment needed to privatize and expand the telecommunication systems in developed and developing countries will come from outside those countries.

E-Business

As the number of individuals and companies having access to the Internet continues to expand, the role of e-business in international commerce will similarly have an increasing effect on the global entrepreneur. This includes both the business-to-business and the business-to-consumer markets. Two areas of e-business will have a significant effect on global consumers: retailing and financial services. Eventually, there will be a convergence of business transactions, money, and personal computers making electronic cash available. The forerunner of this is in existence already: prepaid smart cards. Twenty-four-hour buying and selling throughout global worldwide markets is now a regular event and will continue to grow.

This worldwide e-commerce system (both business-to-business and business-to-consumer) has significantly affected the role of financial institutions. Companies do not have to wait as long for their money after a sales transaction occurs, substantially reducing the days in accounts receivable and the funding required for these.

This speed in cash obtainment in turn affects the foreign currency markets. Today, if a company in China buys goods in the United States and wants to pay in Chinese renminbi (RMB), a system is needed for converting RMBs to U.S. dollars. This is now handled by regulated foreign exchange markets as discussed in Chapter 8. The system's move to a single common exchange market using the prevailing exchange rates makes the transaction seamless and, most of all, faster.

Product Policy and Total Quality

Goods or services are the core of a global entrepreneur's international operations; success depends a lot on how well the goods or services offered satisfy the wants and needs of the market, and how they are different (their unique selling proposition) from competitive products and services available. This important issue will be discussed in terms of product adaptation and total quality.

Product Adaptation

There are two major factors that affect the degree to which a domestic product needs to be changed for a global market: the domestic product itself and characteristics of the international market on both a country and local basis. The needed changes can range from minor ones, such as translating the label, to major ones, such as physical product changes. Changes needed generally include such things as brand names, instructions-on-use labels, logos, measurement units, packaging, and product features and design.

Aspects of the Domestic Product

The type and characteristics of the domestic product significantly affect the degree (if any) of modifications needed for an international market. A global entrepreneur needs to ensure that the product does not contain ingredients that violate the legal requirements or religious or social customs of a country. For example, in Islamic countries vegetable shortening needs to be used rather than animal fats. In Japan, it is illegal to have any formaldehyde in hair and skin products. In India, mutton needs to be used instead of beef. In many countries, the product may not be operable in the global market due to the major differences in electric power systems.

A major difficulty confronting the global entrepreneur is having the required parts, repairs, or servicing for a product. If the product breaks down and repairs and service are not up to standard, the product and company image suffer and future sales become difficult. Sometimes a product designed for use in one way in the domestic market will be used for entirely different purposes in the global market. It is important that the global entrepreneur provide good training for the individuals providing the repairs and service. This is usually most easily accomplished through outsourcing to a local firm under a contract.

Brand names and aesthetics provide another challenge. Since the brand name conveys the image of the product or service, it is important to standardize it as much as possible across global markets. Standardizing the name is particularly difficult due to translation problems, especially when a variety of products are going to many different countries. Sometimes, the global entrepreneur must standardize other elements such as colors, packaging, and symbols while maintaining the brand name.

Packaging is an area where the global entrepreneur generally makes some modifications to enter the global market. This in part reflects the longer time that the product remains in the distribution system and the differences in the channel members of the distribution itself. Usually, the international package uses more expensive materials, such as the air-tight, reclosable containers used in the global distribution of food products.

The labeling of the packaging usually needs modification. Sometimes this means conforming to the legal requirement that everything is bilingual, such as French and English in Canada, and Finnish and Swedish in Finland. Global government regulations often require more informative labeling about the content and percentage of ingredients on food products, for example. This provides for better consumer education and protection. Not conforming to the content, language, or description laws of the country will often cause a product to be held up in customs, such as when the author was importing wine from Hungary that did not have the alcohol content of the wine correctly provided on the label.

Characteristics of the Global Market

Typically, the characteristics of the global market(s) mandate many product modifications. These often result from government regulations, some of which may be protecting domestic industry or responding to political controversies among nations. Not only must the global entrepreneur be aware of the present regulations but also exceptions and possible future changes. Products entering some global markets, such as the European Union, must comply with the product standards established by the European Union as well as adopt the overall system approved by the International Standards Organization.

Tariff and nontariff barriers also affect product adaptations. If tariffs are so high that the domestic product is not price competitive, then a less costly version may have to be developed. Nontariff barriers, such as bureaucratic red tape, product standards, required testing or approval procedures, or domestic product subsidies, can also affect product adaptation. Because some nontariff barriers may be intended to protect domestic products and industries, they may be the most difficult to overcome.

Competitive products and features often affect product adaptation. Already established in their domestic market, these competitive products must be carefully analyzed to determine any product changes needed for competitive positioning. Ideally, the changes made will not only establish a strong competitive market position but will be hard to duplicate by domestic product manufacturers.

The stage of economic development of the foreign market and the economic status of potential users can also affect the product. As the economy of a country becomes stronger, buyers are usually better able to afford and demand better product alternatives. Sometimes the economic stage of a country requires that the product be significantly simplified or downgraded due to the lack of purchasing power or usage conditions.

Purchase decisions are also affected by the attitudes, behavior, beliefs, and traditions of the purchaser in the global market. The global entrepreneur must be very aware of which of these cultural aspects affect the changes needed in the product to gain customer approval and result in sales. Such cultural aspects particularly affect the product's positioning in the market—the perception of the consumers of the global product with respect to competitive products. For instance, Coke entered the Japanese and European Union markets using the name Coke Light instead of Diet Coke so as not to confront consumers with the idea of weight loss. The promotional theme behind Coke Light was not weight loss but rather figure maintenance.

Training the Global Managers

Training global managers for overseas assignments is very important. Proper training can help global managers understand the culture, customers, and work habits of the specific market situation. The most common topics covered in this cultural training include business etiquette, customs, economics, history, politics, and social etiquette of the country.

The type of training also reflects the global entrepreneur's overall philosophy of international management. Some global entrepreneurs prefer to send their own people to fill an overseas position, but others prefer to use host-country locals. The management philosophy of global entrepreneurs tends to be one of the following three: (1) ethnocentric philosophy (putting home-country people in key international positions); (2) geocentric philosophy (integrating diverse regions of the world through a global approach to decision making); or (3) polycentric philosophy (using local host-country nationals in key international positions). The venture with the ethnocentric philosophy usually does the training at the headquarters in the home country while the polycentric philosophy has the local key managers do the training in the host country.

Leadership in an International Context

The leadership style of a global entrepreneur tends to fall in one of three categories: (1) authoritarian (focuses on work-centered behavior to ensure task accomplishment); (2) paternalistic (uses work-centered behavior along with a protective employee-centered concern); or (3) participative (uses both a work-centered and a people-centered approach). Different approaches to each of these occur in various parts of the world.

Of course, an outstanding global entrepreneurial leader is a transformational one—a visionary leader with a sense of mission who is able to motivate employees to embrace the vision, new goals, and new ways of doing things. These global leaders have several things in common regardless of the culture of operation. First, the transformational global leader is charismatic and has the admiration of employees. He or she increases confidence, loyalty, and pride at all levels of the organization. Second, a global transformational leader gets employees to question old paradigms and accept new ways of doing things, effectively articulating the vision and mission. Finally, a transformational global leader determines the needs of employees and further develops these individuals so they are more effective and efficient.

The leadership in a particular country needs to reflect the culture of the country. This has been studied in the GLOBE project, which evaluated the cultural dimensions of performance orientation, assertiveness, future orientation, humane orientation, institutional collectivism, in-group collectivism, gender egalitarianism, power distance, and uncertainty avoidance across many countries. As shown in Table 9.1, countries vary on each of these dimensions. While the United States and Russia (individualistic countries) scored high on performance improvement, Singapore and Sweden (collectivistic countries) scored high on institutional collectivism. In terms of power distance (the degree to which members of an organization should expect power to be distributed equally), entrepreneurial companies in high power-distance countries such as Brazil, France, and Thailand tend to have more hierarchical decision-making processes with limited participation and communication. A good global entrepreneurial leader takes into account the country dimensions in the leadership style employed in the particular country.

Total Quality Issues

One major issue for the global entrepreneur is total quality; international customers want their expectations met or exceeded regardless of the provider. This is true even in developing economies where some products and services provided in the past have not been of high quality. To accomplish this, the global entrepreneur needs to focus on quality, cost, and innovation.

China, India, Ireland, and Germany are all countries ICU Global, a video conferencing provider, is targeting, according to founder and chief executive Stephen McKenzie. Currently, the company has six people in the United Kingdom with an anticipated turnover of £3 million. McKenzie feels it is easier for a small business to expand into other countries as you can provide "the same quality assurance to end users." He adds, "Technology allows you to provide full-support, virtual operations in other countries" (Woods, 2008).

The countries that offer the greatest opportunities are selected for expansion. "It's good to have a base in Germany because you can easily access the rest of Europe," McKenzie relates. "Then, there's a thriving technology center in India." McKenzie also has taken advantage of being born in Germany and the possibilities in India due to a former employee returned home to the subcontinent. "Therefore, there was an opportunity to move into the main cities in India," he says.

ICU Global started in China by doing research and development with a Chinese company. McKenzie notes, "It's a situation that will only grow" (Woods, 2008).

Some global entrepreneurs falsely believe that by increasing the quality of their product or service to a very high level, costs would also increase, resulting in a need to raise the price too high. Companies measuring quality in terms of defective parts per million have found that as the error rate (expressed in terms of sigma) fell (the level of sigma increased) so did the cost of producing the product. In other words, quality and cost are inversely related. A global entrepreneur can produce quality at a lower cost per unit when producing with low error rates than when producing with higher error rates.

❖ **Table 9.1** Cultural Clusters Classified on Societal Culture Practices

Cultural Dimension	High-Score Clusters	Mid-Score Clusters	Low-Score Clusters
Performance Orientation	Confucian Asia Germanic Europe Anglo	Southern Asia Sub-Saharan Africa Latin Europe Nordic Europe Middle East	Latin America Eastern Europe
Assertiveness	Germanic Europe Eastern Europe	Sub-Saharan Africa Latin America Anglo Middle East Confucian Asia Latin Europe Southern Asia	
Future Orientation	Germanic Europe Nordic Europe	Confucian Asia Anglo Southern Asia Sub-Saharan Africa Latin Europe	Middle East Latin America Eastern Europe
Humane Orientation	Southern Asia Sub-Saharan Africa	Middle East Anglo Nordic Europe Latin America Confucian Asia Eastern Europe	Latin Europe Germanic Europe
Institutional Collectivism	Nordic Europe Confucian Asia	Anglo Southern Asia Sub-Saharan Africa Middle East Eastern Europe	Latin Europe Latin America
In-Group Collectivism	Southern Asia Middle East Eastern Europe Latin America Confucian Asia	Sub-Saharan Africa Latin Europe	Anglo Germanic Europe Nordic Europe
Gender Egalitarianism	Eastern Europe Nordic Europe	Latin America Anglo Latin Europe Sub-Saharan Africa Southern Asia Confucian Asia Germanic Europe	Middle East

(Continued)

❖ Table 9.1 (Continued)

Cultural Dimension	High-Score Clusters	Mid-Score Clusters	Low-Score Clusters
Power Distance		Southern Asia Latin America Eastern Europe Sub-Saharan Africa Middle East Latin Europe Confucian Asia Anglo Germanic Europe	Nordic Europe
Uncertainty Avoidance	Nordic Europe Germanic Europe	Confucian Asia Anglo Sub-Saharan Africa Latin Europe Southern Asia	Middle East Latin America Eastern Europe

SOURCE: Javidan, Dorfman, de Luque, & House (2006).

A similar false belief surrounds high technology. Many global entrepreneurs falsely think that the best way to exploit any new technology is to get to an international market first and charge premium prices. Now they realize that often the best way to exploit the advantage of a new high technology is to lower the price in an international market. This allows the company to grow its market share as quickly as possible, driving less efficient competition from the market while increasing overall revenues and profits. Paradoxically, some high-tech global entrepreneurs can thrive at the same time their prices are falling the fastest. Because this can result in significantly reduced margins and lower return on investment (ROI), these global entrepreneurs are compensating by generating more revenues through increased uses.

All this requires global entrepreneurs to outsource more and more of their manufacturing and focus on developing new technologies. They also need to continually add features that increase the value to keep their product from becoming generic or sold almost strictly on price. This requires the effective use of benchmarking—identifying what leading-edge competitors are doing and using this to produce improved products or services. Whenever possible, a global entrepreneur should employ mass customizations—tailor-making mass production products to meet the expectations of the customer. Indeed, offering quality goods and services always pays off.

International Research and Development

Developing a good international research and development process requires focus on three areas: (1) defining what innovation is to the company, (2) performing opportunity analysis, and (3) understanding the product life cycle.

❖ CULTURAL STORY

Story 1

My husband and I met a guy named Nacho in a sports bar in Argentina. We got to talking about Nacho's cousin who was in "jail." We told him we were sorry to hear that. Nacho looked at us with a confused face and said, "but it's a good school." That's when we realized he meant "Yale."

Story 2

When my Chinese was pretty elementary I told my girlfriend's father that I used to deliver furniture in high school. I did not know the word for deliver, so looked up "send" and used the word "tou" (ÿ)—but instead I had informed him that, in high school, I was a furniture thief.

SOURCE: http://www.culturalconfusions.com (Story 1 by Jessica Reser; Story 2 by Stuart Schulte).

Innovation

Innovation is the key to the future of any company. As technologies change, old products decrease in sales and old industries decrease and sometimes die. Inventions and innovations are the building blocks of the future of any international organization. As Thomas Edison reportedly said, "Innovative genius is 1% inspiration and 99% perspiration."

There are a variety of views regarding what constitutes innovation. To some, it is a new technological breakthrough. For others, it is a new invention or way of doing things. Still for others, innovation is a new design or new business model. For some, it is managing chaos or turbulence. The only commonality among these many views is "new." Indeed, while innovation requires something new and involves creativity and invention, true innovation requires one more thing—delivering customer value. Until the innovation is on the market delivering some new value to customers, it is not really innovation. In the marketplace, innovation can take a variety of forms, such as a new design, a new delivery system, a new package, a new production process, a new invention, or a radical new technological breakthrough.

Types of Innovation

There are various levels of innovation based on the uniqueness of the idea. Figure 9.1 presents three major types of innovation, in decreasing order of uniqueness: breakthrough innovation, technological innovation, and ordinary innovation. As you would expect, the rarest innovations are of the breakthrough type. These extremely unique innovations often establish the platform on which future innovations in an area are developed. Given that they are often the basis for further innovation in an area, these innovations should be protected as much as possible by strong patents, trade secrets, or copyrights. Breakthrough innovations include such ideas as penicillin, the steam engine, the computer, the airplane, the automobile, the Internet, and nanotechnology.

❖ Figure 9.1 Types of innovation and their frequency.

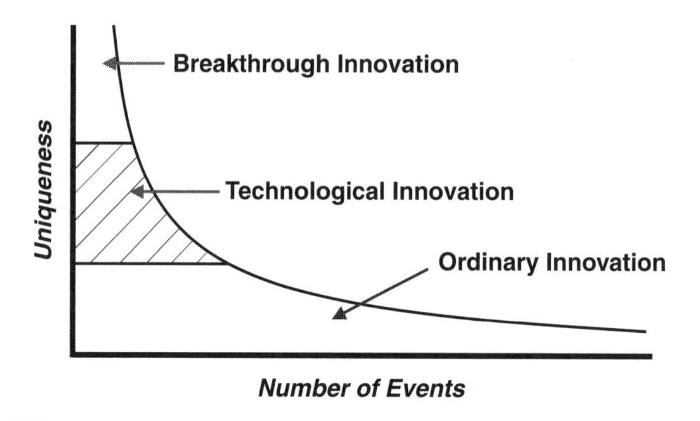

SOURCE: Hisrich, R. D., Peters, M. P., Shepherd, D. A. (2010). *Entrepreneurship* (8th ed.). Chicago: McGraw-Hill/Irwin, p 107.

The next type of innovation—technological innovation—occurs more frequently than breakthrough innovation and in general is not at the same level of scientific discovery and advancement. Nonetheless, these are very meaningful innovations, because they do offer advancements in the product/market arena. As such, they usually need to be protected. Such innovations as the personal computer; the flip watch for containing pictures, and voice and text messaging; and the jet airplane are examples of technological innovations.

The final type of innovation—ordinary innovation—is the one that occurs most frequently. These more numerous innovations usually extend a technological innovation into a better product or service or one that has a different—usually better—market appeal. These innovations often come from market analysis and market pull, not technology push. The market has a stronger effect on the innovation (market pull) than the technology (technology push). One ordinary innovation was developed by Sara Blakely, who wanted to get rid of unsightly panty lines while also being able to wear open-toed shoes and sandals. To do this, she cut off the feet of her control-top pantyhose to produce footless pantyhose. Investing her total money available (US$5,000), Sara Blakely started Spanx, an Atlanta-based company, which in 5 years had annual earnings of US$20 million.

Defining a New Innovation (Product or Service)

One of the dilemmas faced by global entrepreneurs is defining a "new" product or identifying what is actually new or unique in an idea. Fashion jeans became very popular even though the concept of blue jeans was not new. What was new was the use of names such as Sassoon, Vanderbilt, and Chic on the jeans. Sony made the Walkman one of the most popular new products of the 1980s, although the concept of cassette players had been in existence for many years.

In these examples, the newness was in the consumer concept. Other types of products, not necessarily new in concept, have also been defined as new. When coffee companies introduced naturally decaffeinated coffee, which was the only change in the product, the initial promotional campaigns made definite use of the word *new* in the copy.

Other old products have simply been marketed in new packages or containers but have been identified as new products by the manufacturer. When soft drink manufacturers introduced the can, some consumers viewed the product as new, even though the only difference from past products was the container. The invention of the aerosol can is another example of a change in the package or container that added an element of newness to old, established products, such as whipped cream, deodorant, and hair spray. Flip-top cans, plastic bottles, aseptic packaging, and the pump have also contributed to a perceived image of newness in old products. Some firms, such as detergent manufacturers, have merely changed the colors of their packages and then added the word *new* to the package and their promotional copy. Pantyhose are another product that has undergone significant marketing strategy changes. L'eggs (a division of Hanes Corporation) was the first to take advantage of merchandising in supermarkets using special packaging, lower prices, and a new display.

In the industrial market, firms may call their products "new" when only slight changes or modifications have been made in the appearance of the product. For example, improvements in metallurgical techniques have modified the precision and strength of many raw materials that are used in industrial products, such as machinery. These improved characteristics have led firms to market products containing the improved metals as "new."

In the process of expanding their sales volume, many companies add products to their product line that are already marketed by other companies. For example, when a drug company added a cold tablet to its product line and a longtime manufacturer of soap pads entered the dishwasher detergent market, both advertised their products as new. In both cases, the product was new to the manufacturer but not new to the consumer. With the increased emphasis on diversification in the world economy, this type of situation is quite common today. Firms are constantly looking for new markets to exploit in order to increase profits and make more effective use of their resources. Other firms are simply changing one or more of the marketing mix elements to give old products a new image.

Classification of New Products

New products may be classified from the viewpoint of either the consumer or the firm. Both points of view should be analyzed by the global entrepreneur, because both the ability to establish and attain product objectives and consumer perception of these objectives can determine the success or failure of any new product.

From a Consumer's Viewpoint

There is a broad interpretation of what may be labeled a new product from the consumer's viewpoint. One attempt to identify new products classifies the degree of newness according to how much behavioral change or new learning is required by the consumer to use the product. This technique looks at newness in terms of its effect on the consumer rather than whether the product is new to a company, is packaged differently, has changed physical form, or is an improved version of an old or existing product.

The continuum proposed by Thomas Robertson (shown in Figure 9.2) contains three categories based on the disrupting influence that product innovation has on

❖ Figure 9.2 Continuum for classifying new products.

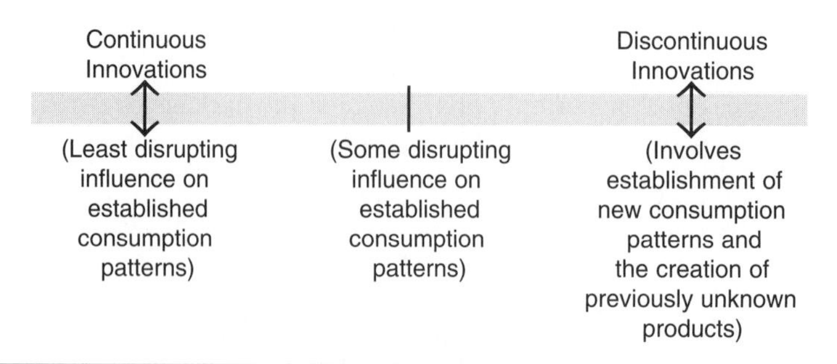

SOURCE: Adapted from Robertson (1967).

established consumption patterns. Most new products tend to fall at the continuous innovations end of the continuum. Examples are annual automobile style changes, fashion style changes, package changes, or product size or color changes. Products such as compact discs, Sony Walkmans, and the iPod tend to be in the middle of the continuum. Truly new products, called discontinuous innovations, are rare and require a great deal of new learning by the consumer because these products perform either a previously unfulfilled function or an existing function in a new way. The Internet is one example of a discontinuous innovation that has radically altered our society's lifestyle. The basis for identifying new products according to their effect on consumer consumption patterns is consistent with the marketing philosophy that satisfaction of consumer needs is fundamental to a venture's existence.

From a Firm's Viewpoint

The innovative global entrepreneurial firm may find it necessary to classify its new products. One way to classify the objectives of new products is shown in Figure 9.3. In this figure, an important distinction is made between new products and new markets (i.e., market development). New products are defined in terms of the amount of improved technology, whereas market development is based on the degree of new segmentation.

The situation in which there is new technology *and* a new market is the most complicated and difficult—and it has the highest degree of risk. Since the new product involves new technology and customers who are not currently being served, the firm will need a new and carefully planned marketing strategy. Replacements, extensions, product improvements, reformulations, and remerchandising involve product and market development strategies that range in difficulty depending on whether the firm has had prior experience with a similar product or with the same target market.

Opportunity Recognition

Some entrepreneurs have the ability to recognize a business opportunity—a skill that is fundamental to the entrepreneurial process as well as growing a business.

❖ Figure 9.3 New product classification system.

Technology Newness →

Market Newness ↓

Product Objectives	No Technological Change	Improved Technology	New Technology
No market change		Reformation Change in formula or physical product to optimize costs and quality	Replacement Replace existing product with new one based on improved technology
Strengthened market	Remerchandising Increase sales to existing customers	Improved product Improve product's utility to customers	Product life extension Add new similar products to line; serve more customers based on new technology
New market	New use Add new segments that can use present products	Market extension Add new segments modifying present products	Diversification Add new markets with new products developed from new technology

SOURCE: Hisrich, R. D., Peters, M. P., Shepherd, D. A. (2010). *Entrepreneurship* (8th ed.). Chicago: McGraw-Hill/Irwin, page 110.

A business opportunity represents a possibility for the entrepreneur to successfully fill a large enough unsatisfied need that sufficient sales and profits result. Significant research has yielded several models of the opportunity recognition process.

Recognizing an opportunity often results from the knowledge and experience of the individual entrepreneur and, when appropriate, the entrepreneurial business. This prior knowledge results from a combination of education and experience; the relevant experience could be work-related or could result from a variety of personal experiences or events. The other important factors in this process are entrepreneurial alertness and entrepreneurial networks. The interaction between entrepreneurial alertness and the entrepreneur's prior knowledge of markets and customer problems has a tremendous effect on success. Those entrepreneurs who have the ability to recognize meaningful business opportunities are in a strategic position to successfully complete the product planning and development process and launch new ventures.

Opportunity Analysis Plan

The global entrepreneur should carefully assess every innovative idea and opportunity. One good way to do this is to develop an opportunity analysis plan, as discussed in Chapter 4. An opportunity analysis plan is *not* the business plan; it focuses on the idea and the market (the opportunity) for the idea—not on the venture. It also is shorter than a business plan and does not contain any formal financial statements of the business venture. The opportunity analysis plan is developed to serve as the basis for the decision to either act on the opportunity or wait until another (and one hopes better) opportunity comes along. A typical opportunity analysis plan has four sections: (1) a description of the idea and its competition; (2) an assessment of the domestic and international market for the idea; (3) an assessment of the entrepreneur and the team; and (4) a discussion of the steps needed to make the idea the basis for a viable business venture (see Chapter 4).

Product Planning and Development Process

Once ideas emerge from idea sources or creative problem solving, they need further development and refinement. This refining process—the product planning and development process—is divided into five major stages: idea stage, concept stage, product development stage, test marketing stage, and commercialization. It results in the start of the product life cycle (see Figure 9.4).

Establishing Evaluation Criteria

At each stage of the product planning and development process, criteria for evaluation need to be established. These criteria should be all-inclusive and quantitative enough to screen the product carefully in the particular stage of development. Criteria should be established to evaluate the new idea in terms of market opportunity, competition, the marketing system, financial factors, and production factors.

A market opportunity in the form of a new or current need for the product idea must exist. The determination of market demand is by far the most important criterion of a proposed new product idea. Assessment of the market opportunity and size needs to consider the characteristics and attitudes of consumers or industries that may buy the product, the size of this potential market in dollars and units, the nature of the market with respect to its stage in the life cycle (growing or declining), and the share of the market the product could reasonably capture.

Current competing producers, prices, and marketing efforts should also be evaluated, particularly in terms of their effect on the market share of the proposed idea. The new idea should be able to compete successfully with products and services already on the market by having features that will meet or overcome current and anticipated competition. The new idea should have some unique differential advantage based on an evaluation of all competitive products and services filling the same consumer needs.

The new idea should have synergy with existing management capabilities and marketing strategies. The firm should be able to use its marketing experience and other expertise in this new product effort. For example, General Electric would have a far less difficult time adding a new lighting device to its line than Procter & Gamble. Several factors should be considered in evaluating the degree of fit: the degree to which the ability and time of the present sales force can be transferred to the new product; the ability to sell the new product through the company's established channels of distribution; and the ability to piggyback the advertising and promotion required to introduce the new product.

The proposed product or service should be supported by and contribute to the company's financial well-being. The manufacturing cost per unit, the marketing

❖ **Figure 9.4** The product planning and development process.

Idea Stage		**Concept Stage**		**Product Development Stage**		**Test Marketing Stage**		**Commercialization Stage Product Life Cycle**			
Idea	Evaluate	Laboratory development	Evaluate	Pilot production run	Evaluate	Semi-commercial plant trials	Evaluate	Introduction	Growth	Maturity	Decline

SOURCE: Hisrich, Robert, *Marketing Decisions for New and Mature Products,* 2ND, ©1991. Printed and electronically reproduced by permission of Pearson Education, Inc., Upper Saddle River, New Jersey.

expense, and the amount of capital need to be determined along with the break-even point and the long-term profit outlook for the product.

The compatibility of the new product's production requirements with existing plant, machinery, and personnel should also be evaluated. If the new product idea cannot be integrated into existing manufacturing processes, additional plant and equipment costs will need to be taken into account. All required materials for production need to be available and accessible in sufficient quantity.

Global entrepreneurs need to formally evaluate an idea throughout its evolution. They must be sure that the product can be the basis for a new venture. This can be done through careful evaluation that results in a go or no-go decision at each of the stages of the product planning and development process: the idea stage, the concept stage, the product development stage, and the test marketing stage.

Idea Stage

Promising new product and service ideas should be identified and impractical ones eliminated at the *idea stage*, allowing maximum use of the company's resources. One evaluation method successfully used at this stage is the systematic market evaluation checklist, where each new idea is expressed in terms of its primary values, merits, and benefits. Consumers are presented with clusters of new product or service values to determine which, if any, new product or service alternatives should be pursued and which should be discarded. A company can test many new alternatives with this evaluation method; promising ideas can be further developed and resources will not be wasted on ideas that are incompatible with the market's values.

It is important to determine both the need for the new idea as well as its value to the company. If there is no need for the suggested product, its development should not be continued. Similarly, the new product or service idea should not be developed if it does not have any benefit or value to the firm. To accurately determine the need for a new idea, it is helpful to define the potential needs of the market in terms of timing, satisfaction, alternatives, benefits and risks, future expectations, price-versus-product performance features, market structure and size, and economic conditions. A form for helping in this need determination process is shown in Table 9.2. The factors in this table should be evaluated not only in terms of the characteristics of the potential new product/service but also in terms of the new product/service's competitive strength relative to each factor. This comparison with competitive products/services will indicate the proposed idea's strengths and weaknesses and, more important, its unique selling propositions.

The need determination should focus on the type of need, its timing, the users involved with trying the product/service, the importance of controllable marketing variables, the overall market structure, and the characteristics of the market. Each of these factors should be evaluated in terms of the characteristics of the new idea being considered and the aspects and capabilities of present methods for satisfying the particular need. This analysis will indicate the extent of the opportunity available.

In determination of the value of the new product/service to the firm, financial scheduling—such as cash outflow, cash inflow, contribution to profit, and return on

❖ Table 9.2 Determining the Need for a New Product or Service Idea

Factor	Aspects	Competitive Capabilities	New Product Idea Capability
Type of Need Continuing need Declining need Emerging need Future need			
Timing of Need Duration of need Frequency of need Demand cycle Position in life cycle			
Competing Ways to Satisfy Need Doing without Using present way Modifying present way			
Perceived Benefits/Risks Utility to customer Appeal characteristics Customer tastes and preferences Buying motives Consumption habits			
Price Versus Performance Features Price–quantity relationship Demand elasticity Stability of price Stability of market			
Market Size and Potential Market growth Market trends Market development requirements Threats to market			
Availability of Customer Funds General economic conditions Economic trends Customer income Financing opportunities			

SOURCE: Hisrich, Robert, *Marketing Decisions for New and Mature Products*, 2ND, ©1991. Printed and electronically reproduced by permission of Pearson Education, Inc., Upper Saddle River, New Jersey.

❖ Table 9.3 Determining the Value for a New Product or Service Idea

Factor	Cost (in $)
Cash Outflow R&D costs Marketing costs Capital equipment costs Other costs	
Cash Inflow Sales of new product Effect on additional sales of existing products Salvageable value	
Net Cash Flow Maximum exposure Time to maximum exposure Duration of exposure Total investment Maximum net cash in a single year	
Profit Profit from new product Profit affecting additional sales of existing products Fraction of total company profit	
Relative Return Return on shareholders' equity (ROE)	
Return on Investment (ROI) Cost of capital Present value (PV) Discounted cash flow (DCF) Return on assets employed (ROA) Return on sales	
Compared to Other Investments Compared to other product opportunities Compared to other investment opportunities	

SOURCE: Hisrich, Robert, *Marketing Decisions for New and Mature Products*, 2ND, ©1991. Printed and electronically reproduced by permission of Pearson Education, Inc., Upper Saddle River, New Jersey.

investment—needs to be evaluated in terms of other product/service ideas as well as investment alternatives. With the use of the form shown in Table 9.3, the dollar amount of each of the considerations important to the new idea needs to be determined as accurately as possible so that a quantitative evaluation can be made. These figures can then be revised as better information becomes available and the product/service continues to be developed.

Concept Stage

After a new product or service idea has passed evaluation at the idea stage, it is further developed and refined through interaction with customers. In the *concept stage*, the refined idea is tested to determine consumer acceptance. Initial reactions to the concept are obtained from potential customers or members of the distribution channel when appropriate. One method of measuring consumer acceptance is the conversational interview in which selected respondents are exposed to statements that reflect the physical characteristics and attributes of the product or service. Where competing products (or services) exist, these statements can also compare their primary features. Both favorable and unfavorable product features can be discovered by analyzing consumers' responses. Favorable features can then be incorporated into the new product or service.

Features, price, and promotion need to be evaluated for both the concept being studied and any major competing products by asking the following questions:

- How does the new concept compare with competitive products or services in terms of quality and reliability?
- Is the concept superior or deficient compared with products and services currently available on the market?
- Is this a good market opportunity for the firm?

Similar evaluations should be done for all aspects of the marketing strategy.

Product Development Stage

In the *product development stage*, consumer reaction to the physical product or service is determined. One tool frequently used at this stage is the consumer panel, in which a group of potential consumers is given product samples. Participants keep a record of their use of the product and comment on its virtues and deficiencies. This technique is more applicable for product ideas and works for only some service ideas.

The panel of potential customers might also be given a sample of the product and one or more competitive products simultaneously. Then one of several methods—such as multiple brand comparisons, risk analysis, level of repeat purchases, or intensity of preference analysis—can be used to determine consumer preference.

Test Marketing Stage

Although the results of the product development stage provide the basis of the final marketing plan, a market test can increase the certainty of successful commercialization. This last step in the evaluation process, the *test marketing stage*, provides actual sales results, which indicate the acceptance level of consumers. Positive test results indicate the degree of probability of a successful product launch and company formation. This is not frequently done by a global entrepreneur due to time and cost constraints.

Developing the Global Marketing Mix

Once an international market is selected, the global entrepreneur needs to develop the appropriate marketing mix—product, price, distribution, and promotion. A first step is to determine the extent to which these elements can be standardized.

Standardization

This critical decision on the degree of standardization will affect the global entrepreneur when entering international markets. Should a cross-national strategy rather than a fully localized strategy be adopted? Some factors that favor standardization include a shrinking world marketplace; the increasing use of English as the language of business; economies of scale in production; and economies in research, development, and marketing. Other factors favor a more localized (market-specific) strategy, such as different buyer behavior patterns, different uses, government regulations, and severe local market differences and distinctiveness. Generally, the global entrepreneur needs to use a flexible marketing strategy that thinks globally but acts locally. This approach incorporates differences into the global marketing strategy that can be implemented locally.

Pricing Decisions

Pricing decisions are much more complicated in international versus domestic markets due in part to currency and cost differences and government regulations and policies. Two critical issues involved in pricing decisions are foreign market pricing and transfer (intracompany) pricing.

Foreign Market Pricing

The factors affecting the price in a particular market (costs, competitive prices, customer price sensitivity and behavior, market structure and conditions, and objectives of the company) vary from market to market, requiring pricing decisions to vary as well. The global entrepreneur should avoid the ease of having a uniform pricing policy and use price as a competitive factor in the marketing program in each country. Although individual prices should reflect the specific conditions of a market, prices should also be coordinated on a worldwide basis, particularly when economic integration is occurring across markets. One way to do this is to set maximum and minimum prices within which the local countries' price can be established. This approach allows flexibility in pricing to reflect local market conditions, but does not allow so much price deviation that a price–quality relationship can be established and cross-border shopping can be discouraged.

Almost every global entrepreneur needs to confront the issue of export pricing. Export pricing generally uses a standard worldwide price, different prices for domestic and export products, or market-differentiated pricing. When the global entrepreneur uses standard worldwide pricing, domestic and export products are priced the same based on average unit costs of fixed, variable, and export cost. When using dual pricing that differentiates between domestic and export prices, the global entrepreneur can use either cost plus pricing or marginal cost pricing. Cost plus pricing means that a margin is put on top of the full allocation of domestic and foreign costs. While this ensures that a margin or return occurs, the result can be a price too high for the market. The marginal cost method for pricing exports uses the direct costs for producing and selling for export as the floor of the pricing decision. Any research and development costs, and domestic production and marketing costs are not used. A margin is then added to this floor cost.

The aforementioned export pricing methods focus on costs, not demand. One demand-oriented pricing method—market-differentiated pricing—focuses on competitive prices in a market to establish an export price. Unique export costs, such as any cost for modifying the product, costs of the export operation, and any costs for entering the foreign market, are taken into consideration.

Transfer Pricing

Transfer pricing is pricing items for sale to other members of the company. It is often referred to as intracompany pricing. The pricing of intracorporate sales can have a significant effect on the price of the product in the international market and therefore on global sales and profits. Various factors affect both the method and the level of transfer pricing, such as import duties, taxes, tariffs, government regulations, and rules concerning repatriation of profits. A low transfer price on goods shipped to a subsidiary and a high transfer price on goods imported from it results in a maximum tax liability for the subsidiary, which is beneficial if the tax in the subsidiary country is substantially lower than the tax in the home country of the company.

Generally, a global entrepreneur will use one of four methods for transfer pricing: (1) transfer at the price that unrelated parties would have reached on the transaction, or arm's length pricing; (2) transfer at the price of direct cost; (3) transfer at the price of direct cost plus any additional expenses; or (4) transfer at a price derived from the end-market price. Often, a company can have its price challenged by either the home country tax authority, who thinks that the price is too low, or the tax authority in the foreign country, who thinks the price is too high. Companies win these challenges only 50% of the time. Given this incident rate, it is far safer for the global entrepreneur to use the arm's length pricing method when establishing the company's transfer price. This also helps establish the company's image as a good global citizen.

Distribution Decisions

One of the most difficult aspects of international business is understanding and using the channel of distribution in the international market, because each country varies significantly in this aspect. Distribution decisions can be the hardest to change, and may require the global entrepreneur to give up some degree of control over the product being sold.

Establishing the Channel

The selection of the best channel members is very important to being successful in international business. This process is called determining the channel design—the length and width of the channel. The best channel design is influenced by a number of factors, the most important ones being the culture of the market, the type of product, the competition, and the customer.

The global entrepreneur needs to carefully examine the overall culture of the market and the culture of the existing distribution system. Of all of the marketing activities, the distribution systems have the most variance from one culture to another. Part of this is due to the country's legislation, which directly affects the distributors and agents operating there. In some countries, only a few selected distributors are permitted to distribute for foreign companies. In other countries, only distributors 100% locally owned can do this distribution. In others, no dealers are allowed.

The type of product or service to be distributed and its price point is the second factor affecting channel design. A short channel is usually best for bulky, expensive, perishable, or specialized products, those that require after-sale service, as well as the services themselves. Staple items can have a longer channel. The positioning and price point also affect channel choice, because the channel itself helps create an image for the product or service being offered. The channel member also absorbs some of the risk for the customer who is dealing with a known home-court entity, not a foreign company.

Of course, competition affects the channel design decision. The global entrepreneur needs to carefully evaluate the channels used by competitors. These channels may be the best or even the only ones accepted by both the trade and customers alike. When this occurs, these same channels should be used, but more effectively and efficiently. Whenever possible, a totally unique distribution approach is better because it will become a unique selling proposition of the company that is difficult to replicate.

The final and most important factor in the channel design is the customer. The demographic composition of the target market should be the basis for the channel design because it is the essential link between the foreign company and the customers in the target market. The buying process of the customer and the many aspects of the buying decision affect how the product or service should be made available for purchase. Sometimes two or more different channels of distribution are needed to effectively reach customers with different characteristics.

Selecting and Managing the Channel

Once the channel design has been determined, it is important for the global entrepreneur to carefully select the channel members that will represent the company. This selection process is as important as hiring and recruiting within the company. An ineffective or bad distribution decision can set the company back for years, or even permanently, in a foreign market. Trade directories such as Dun & Bradstreet, telephone directories, and the U.S. Department of Commerce can be used to identify possible company representatives that might be suitable.

Each identified prospect should be carefully screened on both performance and professional criteria; as much information as possible should be collected on each prospect. Once the channel members are in place and the channel is operating, it needs to be carefully managed. A good cooperative channel relationship will establish the best possible link between the foreign company and the local customer.

Promotion Decisions

The final decision the global entrepreneur needs to make in conjunction with pricing and distribution decisions is the promotion mix decision—selecting and implementing the right combination of advertising, publicity, personal selling, and sales promotion that will expedite sales in the selected target market.

Started in 1994, Blue Tomato is a snowboard company based in Austria founded by a former champion in the sport. From the beginning, the company used its roots in the sport to keep close to its customers and followed its young customer profile onto the Internet in 1999. Success followed rapidly and within 7 years Internet sales accounted for 90% of total revenues.

The adoption of an online sales presence immediately provided the company with almost every international market. One barrier to this can be language. Since Blue Tomato's biggest market was Germany, the company's first website presence was correctly done in the firm's native German. The Internet also led to certain other developments for Blue Tomato that affected its international growth. It enabled the company to increase the sales mix by keeping more products available and reducing its dependence on seasonal markets. The Internet also enabled the company to vary and refine its service offerings through different languages and pricing strategies.

Blue Tomato again used many available options in the networked world to access international markets with an effective multichannel strategy:

- a snowboard catalog distributed to customers and stockists in two languages, in addition to a regular newsletter;
- direct contact with customers by e-mail and telephone, with customer service lines staffed by experienced snowboarders;
- promotions at various snowboarding events;
- partnerships with other related websites;
- sponsorship of top snowboarding professionals; and
- sponsorship of snowboarding facilities.

Internally, communications and structure seem to work well. The company makes the most of the casual snowboarding lifestyle and work ethic, while it splits the operations of the retail and training centers. Although many sports companies that are created by people intimately involved in the sport have done well initially, many fail as the initial surge of interest in product offerings wanes. Blue Tomato is still achieving 100% growth with 80% of sales in international markets (Foscht, Swoboda, & Morschett, 2006).

Advertising

The important issues in establishing a good advertising campaign for the foreign market are the advertising budget, the media strategy, and the message. The global entrepreneur needs to first establish an overall promotion budget for all areas of the promotion mix (advertising, publicity, personal selling, sales promotion, and social media) and then determine the amount that should be allocated to advertising. This budgeted amount for advertising should be enough to accomplish the sales objectives of the firm. Often a percentage of the sales objective (somewhere around 3% to 7%, depending on the industry) is used to establish the first year's advertising budget.

The type of media to use is very dependent on the market being entered. For example, if entering Peru or Mexico, a higher percentage of the advertising budget will be allocated to television as 84% of the media spending in Peru and 73% of the media spending in Mexico is spent on television advertising. If entering Bolivia, outdoor advertising would be used often, as 48% of the media budget there is spent in this area. If entering Kuwait or Norway, concentration would be in print media, with 91% and 77% of media spending in print advertising for each country, respectively.

Probably the most errors come in the third sphere of planning a good advertising campaign—the message, particularly by U.S. global entrepreneurs. Careful consideration needs to be given to culture, language, economic development, and lifestyles when creating the best message for a specific global market. Although it is nice if a single world brand can be established throughout the foreign markets of the venture, many global entrepreneurs abandon identical campaigns for more localized ones, making sure that the advertising message is customized to the particular local global market.

Publicity

Strong publicity can be helpful in entering a foreign market by portraying the foreign company as a good global citizen interested in the well-being of a particular culture or country. The global entrepreneur should consider partnering with a non-governmental organization (NGO) in the country to work on issues in the country such as diversity, energy, or health care. Any way that a solid company image can be established greatly benefits sales in a foreign market.

Personal Selling

In the early stages of market entry, most global entrepreneurs rely heavily on personal contacts. Personal selling is particularly important in high-priced industrial goods. Usually a local country salesperson, when properly trained, can be more effective than someone from outside the country, especially in those countries with high levels of nationalism.

Sales promotion activities such as trade shows, coupons, samples, premiums, point-of-purchase materials, and give-aways can be especially effective when tailored to the specific product or service being offered and to the culture of the company. To be effective, the sales promotion campaign must be accepted and used by the channel members. When carefully crafted and implemented, a well-designed sales promotion effort can be very cost effective when entering and developing a foreign market.

Summary

This chapter discusses how effective international research and development and marketing can help the global entrepreneur handle the challenges of rapidly changing technology, shorter product life cycles, changing consumer tastes, and changing economies. Advances in telecommunications, such as cellular technology, the Internet, social media, and e-business, are allowing greater connectivity between producers and consumers. To satisfy consumer needs and wants and to be unique, products need to be adaptable to changing consumer tastes and preferences. Products also must be customized to the local culture to be successful. The global entrepreneur needs to use a good international research and development process, including defining what innovation is to the company, performing opportunity analysis, and understanding the product life cycle. When entering a new market or launching a new product, each global entrepreneur must deal with (1) the technological environment, (2) product policy and the total quality issue, (3) adopting the best research and development strategy, and (4) developing and implementing the best marketing strategy. The product planning and development process (idea stage, concept stage, product development stage, test-marketing stage) results in commercialization and the start of the product life cycle. To successfully commercialize in a global market, the global entrepreneur needs to establish the best marketing mix (pricing, distribution, and promotion). Identifying the best distribution channel, as well as selecting the best in-country representatives in the foreign market, are important decisions for the global entrepreneur. Finally, the promotion of the product consists of identifying the right mix of advertising, publicity, personal selling, sales promotion, and social media within a predetermined budget. The global entrepreneur must also identify the best types of media to use in the foreign market and carefully craft an advertising message that resonates with the local culture.

Questions for Discussion

1. What are the three types of innovation? Give an example of each.
2. What is the purpose of creating an opportunity analysis plan? How does it differ from a business plan?
3. What factors should be considered when an entrepreneur sets a price for a product or service in a foreign market?

Chapter Exercises

1. Pick a foreign market and a product. Research the alterations that are necessary for the product to be allowed in that market (e.g., package design, labeling).
2. Using that same product, find research that indicates the product will be successful in the country that you are choosing to enter.
3. Take one of your product ideas and outline how that product will be carried through from the idea stage to commercialization.
4. You are a paper clip holder manufacturer launching your product in a new market. Identify how you will have to alter your product, pricing, distribution, and communication. What is the best distribution channel for this product? How will you develop the channel distribution?

Note

Portions of this chapter are from Hisrich, Robert, *Marketing Decisions for New and Mature Products,* 2ND, ©1991. Printed and electronically reproduced by permission of Pearson Education, Inc., Upper Saddle River, New Jersey.

References

CNBC (Producer). (2009). *The Entrepreneurs: Spanx* [Television broadcast]. Englewood Cliffs, NJ: Author.

Foscht, T., Swoboda, B., & Morschett, D. (2006). Electronic commerce-based internationalization of small, niche-oriented retailing companies: The case of Blue Tomato and the snowboard industry. *International Journal of Retail & Distribution Management, 34*(7), 556–572.

Hisrich, R. D., & Peters, M. P. (1991). *Marketing decisions for new and mature products* (2nd ed.). Upper Saddle River, NJ: Pearson Education.

Hisrich, R. D., Peters, M. P., & Shepherd, D. A. (2007). *Entrepreneurship* (7th ed.). Chicago: McGraw-Hill/Irwin.

Javidan, M., Dorfman, P., de Luque, M. S., & House, R. J. (2006, February). In the eye of the beholder: Cross cultural lessons in leadership from project GLOBE. *Academy of Management Executive, 20*(1), 67.

Robertson, T. (1967, January). The process of innovation and the diffusion of innovation. *The Journal of Marketing, 31*(1) 14–19.

Spanx Inc. (2011). Retrieved from http://www.Spanx.com

Woods, C. (2008, April 18). *ICU Global grabs international opportunities.* Retrieved from http://realbusiness.co.uk/news/icu_global_grabs_international_opportunities

Suggested Readings

Articles/Books

Bell, S. (2010). ***International brand management of Chinese companies.*** **Heidelberg, Germany: Physica-Verlag.**

This dissertation provides a glimpse into the marketing strategies of Chinese corporations, providing insight on doing business in China as well as how Chinese businesses are adapting their models to be successful abroad. Using the models and marketing efforts of successful Japanese and Korean companies, Chinese companies are mimicking and expanding on these models to appeal to Western consumers. The author discusses the strengths and weaknesses of the Chinese branded companies, and how branding affects competition.

Fitzgerald, E., & Wankerl, A. (2010). ***Inside real innovation: How the right approach can move ideas from R&D to market—and get the economy moving.*** **Hackensack, NJ: World Scientific Publishing Co.**

Through their own real-world experiences, the authors explain innovation from the ground up, providing a genuine sense of how innovation occurs in the context of business. They prove that, contrary to popular belief, innovation is not a linear procedure that starts with research and ends with a product or service at market but instead is an iterative process that systemically repeats until the pieces come together perfectly. The book argues that innovation is not what it once was in the United States and then indicates how businesses can build a better process for survival in the future.

Nwankwo, S., & Gbadamosi, T. (2011). *Entrepreneurship marketing: Principles and practice of SME marketing.* New York: Routledge.

This book offers a real-world look at how marketing efforts, or lack thereof, can make or break SMEs (small and medium-sized enterprises), especially in the global market. With an entrepreneurial focus, the authors provide readers with simple but crucial guidelines to successfully marketing a small business in a global context.

Wang J. (2011, March 22). Upcycling becomes a treasure trove for green business ideas. *Entrepreneur.* Retrieved from http://www.entrepreneur.com/article/219310

An interesting insider at several startups, the author presents good examples of how even the smallest companies can change consumer attitudes. The "green" trend in the United States has led to the invention of "upcycling": taking used materials and transforming them into something greater in value. This article describes the struggles and successes of companies that are championing the movement.

Young, R. B., & Javalgi, R. G. (2007). International marketing research: A global project management perspective. *Business Horizons, 50,* 113–122.

This article provides internal client-side marketing research managers with a proper framework for conducting international market research projects. The article also addresses the factors and challenges that conducting research across national borders present, including constructing questionnaires and the finer points of primary data collection.

Global Human Resource Management

Profile: Bonobos

Thinkstock Images/Comstock/ThinkStockPhotos

Andy Dunn set out to do the impossible with his partner, Brian Spaly, and started a company that sold their own line of clothes exclusively on the Internet. Experts on both e-commerce as well as the fashion industry warned them that to do both simultaneously would be incredibly difficult since clothes never sell online without brand recognition, and website retail never succeeds without traffic from existing customers. Nevertheless, the two entrepreneurs proceeded with their clothing line for men sold exclusively on their website.

The company, Bonobos, did well in its first year. During the second year, however, sales nearly tripled, which was more demand than the company of eight employees could handle. Dunn's inexperience left him clueless as to how to scale the company in order to grow it lucratively. Profitability dwindled despite an increase in revenue and the young CEO knew he had to make some changes.

Dunn's first order of business was to determine what was going wrong, and why the financials were diminishing. After taking a good, hard look at himself, he realized that as CEO, he was not the best at every function the company needed to survive. He was trying to wear too many hats, and therefore not wearing any of them well. In short, he needed help to run the company, but more specifically, he needed functional and industry *expertise.*

At its inception, Dunn and Spaly had stated that one of the goals of Bonobos was to have extraordinary customer service. Dunn noticed that as orders flooded in, they were unable to keep up the level of customer service they once had. He immediately opened a position for head of customer service and filled it quickly with someone who had managed the principal Apple store in New York City. The additional expertise paid off and performance metrics increased significantly. Noting the transformative power of industry talent, Dunn hired engineers from Zappos, buyers from Old Navy, and designers from Banana Republic, Club Monaco, and others.

Dunn's acknowledgement of his as well as the company's weaknesses allowed him to see the gaps in performance and fill them appropriately. Dunn stated, "My job as CEO, I now realize, is easy. All I have to do is recruit superstars." Of course, the CEO must make the company an attractive place to work to attract those superstar employees. Dunn offers the advice of being humble enough to know your own weaknesses and limitations, and then earnestly ask for others' help. People who are truly good at their jobs simply want to have enough autonomy to carry out their tasks independently, without micromanagement or bureaucratic restriction. Giving that kind of autonomy willingly has put Bonobos at an advantage with an all-star lineup of employees. In his experience, Dunn believes the path to success lies first and foremost in understanding your own flaws.

SOURCE: Adapted from "To Recruit the Best, Admit Weaknesses" (2009).

Chapter Objectives

1. To determine the importance of motivating employees and various methods to accomplish this across cultures
2. To illustrate the importance of hiring global-minded employees for the success of a venture and training these employees to succeed

3. To demonstrate the leadership necessary to inspire and recruit personnel
4. To understand the critical role of proper human resource management in a successful global enterprise
5. To identify the major sources of people and how to access them
6. To show ways of training for a global business

Introduction

The importance of having good global managers and a quality international workforce cannot be overemphasized. Although the focus of the venture does change, this importance and need does not.

In the early stages of going global, the focus is on understanding cultural differences, the political risks, and the best way to enter the international market. Typically, this first stage can involve the marketing or sales manager or the global entrepreneur being responsible for selecting a market and beginning some export activities. Usually, next an export manager and small staff with international experience are hired externally. This staff handles the paperwork and facilitates the international transaction and documentation. As the level of global business progresses, the global human resource activity involves assessing existing personnel and their abilities to handle the needed global markets and functions. Plans are then developed and implemented for the recruitment, selection, and training of employees for the needed positions.

The global entrepreneur needs to make sure that clear career paths for managers assigned overseas are established and a clear system of human resource management is operant. This provides promotion criteria and eliminates many of the perceived problems in motivating managers to want foreign assignments. The global venture can also more easily determine which individuals in the company are able and willing to accept overseas assignments. This important area can be addressed by looking at motivation across cultures, sources and types of human capital, selection criteria and procedures, the global mindset, compensation policies, and the hiring process.

Motivation Across Cultures

Motivation is a psychological process by which unsatisfied needs lead to drives that seek to achieve goals or incentives that at least partially satisfy these needs. As such, the process has three elements: needs, drives, and goal attainment. Although the process is universal in nature, the specific content needs and goals that are pursued are significantly influenced by the local culture. For example, in the United States, personal achievement is an important need and individual success through promotion and money is an important goal. In China, on the other hand, group affiliation is an important need and harmony a desired goal. While a key incentive for individuals in the United States is money, it is respect and power for individuals in Japan, and respect, family considerations, and a good personal life in Latin America.

The effect of culture on motivations changes over time, particularly with any significant changes in the economic or political environment of the country. As more countries move toward market economies, the ways in which individuals in these countries are motivated continually changes as well.

Culture also significantly affects the view of quality of life in a country, which directly affects the view of work and the type of work. In Sweden, there is a fairly high degree of individualism, which is reflected in the emphasis on individual decision making on the job. Conversely, in Japan there is a high degree of uncertainty avoidance, which is reflected in the structured tasks of most jobs in which individuals can have security and know what is to be done and how it is to be done.

The importance of work in an individual's life (work centrality) also varies by culture. Japan has the highest level of work centrality, followed by Israel with a moderately high level. There are average levels of work centrality in Belgium and the United States and moderately low levels in Germany and the Netherlands. This means, depending on the country, other areas of interest such as church, family, or leisure are more important to differing extents.

Sources and Types of Human Capital

The location and nationality of the candidates for a particular job are significant issues in global human resources. This usually changes as the global venture moves through the stages of internationalization. In the start-up stage, outside expertise is usually hired; as the venture expands and gains more foreign operations, it starts to develop more of its own personnel for international operations. As this staff continues to expand and grow, the venture will rely less on home-country personnel and have more host-country nationals in management positions.

There are four basic sources of personnel for global ventures: home-country nationals (expatriates), host-country nationals, third-country nationals, and inpatriates.

Home-Country Nationals (Expatriates)

Home-country nationals, often called expatriates or expats, are citizens of the country where the venture of the global entrepreneur is headquartered. These individuals are willing to work for the global venture in a foreign country for a period of time. The major advantages of using expats in a foreign country are that they know the culture of the venture; relate easily and efficiently to corporate headquarters; have the particular technical or business skills needed; put the venture ahead of the country and will therefore promote the interests of the venture; and are less likely to take the venture's knowledge and set up a competing business.

There are many disadvantages to using expats. Firms often have reintegration and retention problems because a high percentage of expats leave the venture after an overseas experience. The costs of relocation, housing, education, and overseas living allowance are usually high. Some expats return early before completion of the assignment. Finally, there are longer start up and wind down times and a shortsighted focus.

Host-Country Nationals

Host-country nationals, or local managers hired by the global entrepreneur, are a particularly good source of middle- and lower-level managers. Some foreign governments, and even customers, expect and can even stipulate that a firm hire host-country nationals to further the country's employment and training. Most global ventures use home-country managers to start the operation in a country and turn this position over to a host-country manager as soon as he or she is trained and ready to assume the position. The decision to use host-country nationals depends on such factors as the nature of the industry, the complexity and life cycle of the product, the functional areas that need staffing, and the availability of a country's resources. The service sector typically uses the largest number of host-country nationals.

Third-Country Nationals

A third source of managers is third-country nationals. These managers are citizens of a country that is neither the home country of the venture nor the host country of operation. These managers are typically used in the later stages of the internationalization process of the venture or when there are no host-country nationals with the needed expertise. Often third-country managers have technical expertise or are from cultures quite similar to the culture of the host country.

Third-country managers tend to build a career with the company in the host country and are often lured away by competitive companies needing management talent in that particular market. These third-country national managers, particularly if they have been with the venture in a different country, are often able to achieve corporate objectives more quickly and more effectively than either expats or host-country nationals. They also bring a broader perspective to the management position.

❖ CULTURAL STORY

I arrived in the U.S. in the early 80s and was still a freshman in college, studying English. I went to the library on campus one morning and asked for the person who had been helping me the previous night.

The librarian looked at me and said "So-and-so is in the John."

I looked at her very puzzled and wondered if she had meant to say, "in a meeting with John," so I asked, "Do you know how long he's going to be in a meeting?"

She said "no he's not in a meeting he's in the John".

I asked, "Where is John?"

Then she said, "Oh, the women's restroom is on the left." And that's when I guessed that "The John" is probably another word for the restroom. Still to this day I wonder why the women's restroom is not "The Mary" or "The Margaret."

SOURCE: http://www.culturalconfusions.com (Story by Shaden Shawky).

Inpatriates

In recent years, a new type of manager has emerged—an inpatriate. This is an individual from the host country or a third-country national who works in the home country. These managers are a new breed, who can truly manage across borders and are thus truly global managers. They are very good at developing the global core competency of the venture.

Selection Criteria

Making an effective selection decision for an overseas assignment can be a major problem for the global entrepreneur. Traits that are used in this process range from the ideal to the real. Over time, a venture establishes more defined, accurate international selection criteria based on experience. Normally, the selection criteria include technical knowledge; experience; knowledge of the area and language; interest in and appreciation of overseas work and the specific culture; adaptability of the family; and demographics, such as age, education, sex, and health.

Technical competence in the functional area needs to be at a high level, because an overseas manager usually has far more responsibility and less support than a domestic manager. The individual selected needs to be self-sufficient in making decisions and running the business. This technical competence is usually reflected in outstanding past performance and solid, diverse experience in the company and industry. Experienced corporate managers going overseas also ensure the continuation of the company culture in the overseas location.

Although knowledge of the area, culture, and language are important, the level of importance varies. The ability to speak and understand the language of the host country is by far the most important. A manager who does not know the language of the country may get by with the help of associates and translators, but still will never fully understand or be a part of the situation. This is still the case even though knowledge of English is widespread and, in most cases, the language of international businesses regardless of country.

Another factor in the selection is the manager's interest in an international assignment and appreciation of the culture of the specific country. This desire, knowledge, and adaptability to change are important for success in the overseas assignment. Some managers go through an "exhilaration curve"—they are very excited at the beginning of the overseas assignment, but after a time frustration and confusion with the new environment set in like a delayed culture shock. An appreciation and knowledge of the particular culture allows the overseas manager to more easily become a part of the new culture and operation. This allows for total integration and a much more successful experience in the new position.

This ability to integrate into the culture also depends on the manager's family situation, because living overseas usually puts more strain on other family members than on the manager. If the family is not happy, the manager often performs poorly and is frequently terminated or leaves the company. The characteristics of the family as a whole are important. Is the marriage stable? Does the family work together? Are there any behavioral problems with the children? Most firms today are interviewing both the spouse and the manager before deciding on an overseas assignment. A family that has successfully lived abroad previously is usually a less risky choice.

Finally, demographic characteristics are important selection criteria in an overseas assignment. Reflecting a minimum age and experience requirement, many overseas assignments are filled by managers in their mid-30s or older. Although the number of women in overseas assignments is increasing, it is significantly lower than the number of men. To a certain extent, this reflects the view of women in some cultures. Any overseas manager must also be in good physical and emotional health. Many host countries have radically different environmental conditions than the home country that could aggravate existing health problems or cause new ones to occur. An overseas manager needs to be dependent and self-reliant. He or she must be able to make decisions and work at various levels in the organization without the support staff usually available in the home country.

The Global Mindset

The globalization of the business world has brought individuals and organizations from many different parts of the world together as customers, suppliers, partners, or creditors. The success of global corporations is increasingly dependent on their ability to bridge cultural gaps and to work effectively in environments different from their home country.

To succeed in their roles, global entrepreneurs need to influence individuals and groups inside and outside their organization from different parts of the world to help achieve organizational goals. Global mindset is a set of individual attributes that facilitate the influence process. Global entrepreneurs who have a global mindset are better able to influence individuals, organizations, and systems that are different from their own. They are better able to understand and interpret global issues and more effectively understand the viewpoints of people from other parts of the world.

What are the components of global mindset? Global mindset consists of three major groups of individual attributes: intellectual capital, psychological capital, and social capital. Intellectual capital consists of

- Knowledge of the global business and industry
- Knowledge of the global political and economic systems
- Ability to build and manage global value networks
- Ability to build and manage global teams
- Ability to understand and manage the tension between corporate requirements and local needs and challenges
- Understanding of other cultures and histories
- Understanding cultural similarities and differences
- Knowledge of other languages
- Ability to adapt, learn, and cope with complex cross-cultural and global issues

Psychological capital consists of the following attributes:

- Self-confidence and self-efficacy

- Resiliency
- Curiosity
- Fearlessness and risk-taking propensities
- Quest for adventure
- Desire and passion for learning about and being in other cultures
- Openness and ability to suspend judgment
- Passion for cultural diversity
- Adaptability
- Ability to connect with people from other parts of the world
- Collaborativeness
- Ability to generate positive energy in people from other parts of the world and to excite them

Social capital is the ability to work with people from other parts of the world, the ability to generate positive energy in people from other parts of the world, and, most important, the ability to build trusting relationships with people from other cultural backgrounds. Trust is the most critical factor in building long-term relationships with others, whether they are employees, colleagues, supervisors, customers, or partners. Building trust in a cross-cultural setting is more complex because even the definition of trust is culture specific. The outcome of trust is universal.

The combination of intellectual, psychological, and social capital composes the global mindset, which enables global entrepreneurs to be successful. It helps them develop behavioral tools to influence those from different sociocultural systems to contribute to the achievement of organizational goals. A measuring instrument has been developed that allows an organization to determine the extent of the global mindset of any of its employees (www.thunderbird.edu/globalmindset).

Selection Procedures

In addition to establishing the appropriate selection criteria, the global entrepreneur also needs to establish the best selection procedure. The selection procedure can employ interviewing, testing procedures, or both.

Most global firms use interviews to screen and select managers for overseas assignments. Usually, both the manager and the spouse are interviewed. Often the interview is conducted by several people in the venture to ensure that the responses are heard correctly and all the needed information is obtained. Developing and using standard interview questions and a format assists in the process.

There are many different tests available. One test determines the nature and extent of the global mindset. Just a few of the over 2,000 employment tests are listed in Table 10.1. These tests are either cognitive tests or personality tests generally used by many global companies. Care must be taken to use the right test, because using the wrong test can result in the selection of the wrong person or can even dismiss some very qualified individuals. The results of the test used and the performance of the individual should be recorded and compared so that a good testing instrument is developed.

❖ Table 10.1 Testing Procedures for International Managers

Global Personality Inventory

This 300-question test is used to test executives, mid- to senior-level managers, and senior salespeople. The cost is around US$40 to $50 per individual tested.

Hogan Personality Inventory

This test, using true or false responses to attitude and biographical questions, measures individuals on personality areas such as ambition and prudence, and occupational scales such as clerical potential or service orientation. The cost per individual tested is US$25 to $175, depending on the amount of detail in the report.

Multidimensional Aptitude Battery II

This 303-question test measures the ability to reason, plan, and solve problems of technical, managerial, and professional individuals. The cost is US$190 for a 25-test kit.

Occupational Personality Questionnaire

This test asks candidates to choose the statement that is most and least like them from a set of 104. The test can measure general profile or specific leadership or sales potential traits. The cost is US$30 and higher depending on the measurement desired.

NEO Personality Inventory

This test measures executives or managers on five scales: agreeableness, conscientiousness, extroversion, neuroticism, and openness to experiences. The test costs US$245 for a 25-test kit.

Personality Research Form

This 352-question test is appropriate for any level of employee. It measures 22 job-relevant personality traits. The cost is US$80 for a 5-test kit.

Watson-Glaser Critical Thinking Appraisal

This test of 40 rather difficult questions appraises such things as creativity and problem-solving skills of all levels of executives and managers. The test costs between US$10 and $20 per individual.

Wesmann Personnel Classification

This test uses a combination of verbal and numerical questions to predict on-the-job performance and the ability to learn of managers at all levels. The cost is US$7 to $15 per individual tested.

16PF

This test of 185 questions measures 16 personality factors of managers in leadership positions. The cost is US$8 to $20 per individual tested.

Compensation Policies

The global venture's compensation program needs to provide an incentive to leave the home country and take the foreign assignment, maintain an established standard of living in that country including family needs, and facilitate return to the home country. Salaries and costs of global managers can be three to five times higher than their home-country counterparts. While the overall compensation package will vary from country to country as well as from company to company, the compensation of most managers overseas includes base salary, salary-related allowances, nonsalary-related allowances, and taxes.

The base salary of the manager, of course, is dependent on the responsibilities and duties of the position. The foreign position salary should have equity and comparability with the domestic position, reflecting the normal salary received in the home country. For example, a manager in a German venture would receive a base salary for working in Spain that reflects the salary structure of the venture in Germany.

In addition to the base salary, there is usually a foreign service premium, valued at 10% to 25% of the base salary. Sometimes the percentage decreases each year the manager is abroad, such as 20% for the first year and 15% for the second. Sometimes the percentage slides in salary increments such as 25% of the first US$50,000 base salary; 20% for the second US$50,000; and 10% for any base salary over US$100,000. Sometimes a ceiling is set for the total amount of foreign service premium received.

There are several nonsalary allowances paid such as benefits, cost-of-living allowances, housing allowances, and hardship allowances. The benefit packages are usually 25%–30% of the base salary for health care and insurance and need to be carefully evaluated in the international setting. The cost-of-living allowance makes sure that the global manager can maintain as closely as possible the same standard of living as he or she would have in the home country. This is usually calculated by selecting a percentage of base salary that would be spent at the foreign location. Almost all firms provide a housing allowance that is commensurate with the global manager's salary level and position. Because this is usually the largest cost, most firms establish a range within which the global manager must find housing. Most ventures pay for utilities in the housing unit outright. Finally, in some instances, there are hardship allowances to account for working and living in a very difficult environment; the percentage paid varies by the degree of difficulty.

Nonsalary-related allowances typically include (1) allowances related to housing, such as a home sale, rental protection, shipment and storage of household goods, or household furnishings in the host-country location; (2) automobile coverage, including selling a car in the home country and purchasing a car in the host country; (3) travel expenses to host country and one or two trips each year for the manager and his family to return to the home country, called home leave; (4) temporary living expenses; and (5) a relocation allowance to pay for any additional expenses of the move.

The final aspect of the compensation package is taxes. A global manager may have two tax bills—one for the host country and one from the home country. It is usually good to have in place a tax-equalization plan in which the global venture pays the difference if the tax rate in the host country is higher than what would be paid in the home country or keeps the difference if the tax rate is lower. The plan would take into account differences (higher or lower) if taxes are paid in both the home and host country.

Basic economic and noneconomic compensation options are indicated in Figures 10.1 and 10.2.

The Hiring Process

The global entrepreneur needs to establish a standardized hiring process that can be used throughout the global operation of the venture. This includes having an established system for selecting and hiring that can be used repeatedly. Some entrepreneurs do not feel hiring can be reduced to a series of processes, and instead rely more on feeling and judgment. In hiring for global positions, a more established systematic approach will provide a fuller, more balanced view of the candidates and the opportunity to hire the best individual.

The systematic approach includes developing a standardized interview format and testing procedures. Because a traditional interview results in a subjective, narrow view of a candidate in which most interviewers prefer candidates similar to themselves, a more structured behavioral interview should be established. A behavioral interview involves several interviewers defining qualities needed, asking the same questions to

❖ **Figure 10.1** Compensation options: Employee economic reward package.

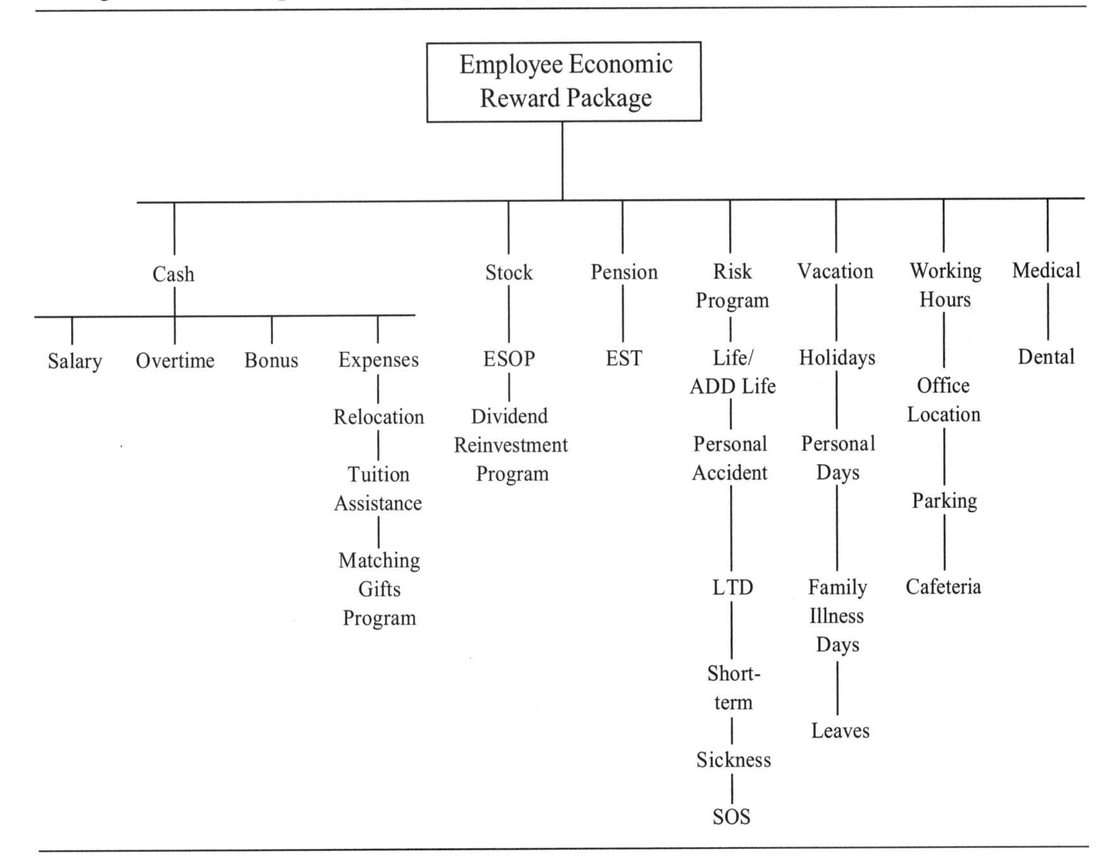

SOURCE: Hisrich (2004).

❖ Figure 10.2 Compensation options: Employee noneconomic reward package.

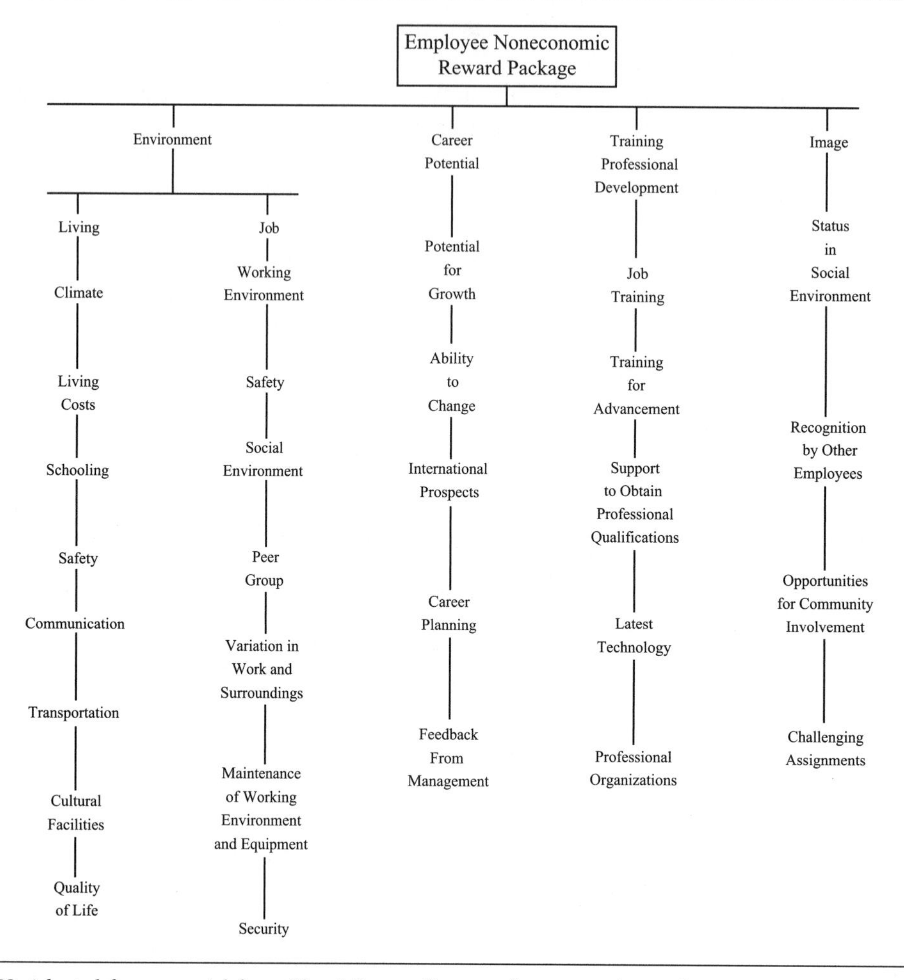

SOURCES: Adapted from material from Girard Torma, director of compensation and international human resources, Nordson Corporation; Hisrich (2004).

each candidate to give past examples of how they demonstrated those qualities, and taking copious notes. How the candidate has responded on a past job is indicative of how he or she will respond in a future job—a principle of historicity. Eventually, a standard template for what is needed for a global manager is established that can be modified for various managerial levels.

These behavioral interviews need to be combined with some tests, which can often be administered online. It is usually better to use both a cognitive test measuring cognitive abilities and a personality test that measures personality traits. Table 10.1 contains examples of each type of test. Cognitive tests generally have a slightly closer correlation with job success than personality tests.

Summary

This chapter focuses on how to identify and recruit the right people for the global venture. In selecting the right people, the global entrepreneur needs to understand the implications of cultures on motivation. What motivates individuals in one country, whether wealth, status, or group membership, varies greatly from other countries. The global entrepreneur could decide to staff the overseas venture with individuals from the home country (expatriates), individuals from the host country (local or host-country managers), individuals from neither the host or home countries (third-party nationals), or individuals from host or third-party countries in the home country (inpatriates). The choice of manager or employee is based on what the firm believes is needed to be successful—for example, a deep understanding of the firm's culture and vision (expatriate) or the ability to motivate individuals from different cultures (third-party nationals) or thorough knowledge of the local country and culture (home-country nationals).

For the sake of consistency and easing the hiring process, a global entrepreneur needs to establish specific hiring criteria and processes, which should involve a mixture of interviews and tests to understand better both the cognitive abilities and personality of prospective managers. The principle of historicity states that how a candidate has responded on a past job is indicative of how he or she will respond in a future job. The manager in the overseas venture must also be able to handle varying amounts of support staff, compared to his or her home-country counterparts. In addition, because the overseas ventures normally contain a mix of expatriate and third-party national managers, a global entrepreneur must keep in mind the need to interview spouses when determining if the overseas position fits with the candidate. As the global entrepreneur builds the overseas workforce, particular attention needs to be paid to compensation of the international manager, including maintaining the same base pay between the home-country managers and host-country managers while also covering relocation costs and perhaps offering a foreign service premium. Once the best managers have been selected by the global entrepreneur, providing the proper training is fundamental to the manager's success in the overseas venture. Finally, the global entrepreneur needs to provide the visionary leadership to inspire, teach, and guide the managers to make the global venture a success.

Questions for Discussion

1. Why would an expatriate manager be better in one situation but a host-country manager better in another?
2. What traits in a manager make him or her a good candidate for a foreign assignment?
3. What components, besides salary, are important parts of a compensation package for an expatriate assignment?
4. How can you train and prepare a manager for a role in a different country?

Chapter Exercises

1. Imagine that you are leading a small company and need to find someone to handle your operations in the new market that you are entering. What characteristics are the most desirable for this employee to have? Why?
2. What are the advantages and disadvantages of relying on an expatriate, a third-country national, an inpatriate, or a home-country national to oversee your operations in a new market?
3. Choose one of the management styles and analyze how that style works well for a multicountry operation.

References

Hisrich, R. D. (2004). *Small business solutions: How to prevent and fix the 13 biggest problems that derail business.* New York: McGraw-Hill.

To recruit the best, admit weaknesses. (2009, December 29). *Businessweek.* Retrieved from http://www.businessweek.com/smallbiz/content/dec2009/sb20091224_646669.htm

Suggested Readings

Articles/Books

Barrett, R., & Mayson, S. (2010). *International handbook of entrepreneurship and HRM.* Northampton, MA: Edward Elgar.

This book describes the need for and the processes to properly control human resource management to obtain sustainable entrepreneurship. Specifically dealing with small companies, the author offers insight on the intersection of human resources management and entrepreneurship, and why it is so important to the success of new ventures. Through theoretical as well as practical advice, the authors explain how human resources can help small business owners build an organization and adapt to a changing landscape.

Engardio, P. (2007, August 20). A guide for multinationals: One of the great challenges for a multinational is learning how to build a productive global team. *Businessweek.* Retrieved from http://www.businessweek.com/magazine/content/07_34/b4047405.htm

This article discusses the need for multinational corporations to provide better coordination and collaboration across their globally dispersed workforces. With the ultimate goal of creating superfast, efficient organizations, multinationals must essentially undergo a management revolution that recognizes the move away from hierarchical, single outfits to fluid organizations with shifting networks of suppliers and workers.

Morgan, G. (2011, May). The business of better benefits. *Entrepreneur,* 81–82.

This article discusses the importance of offering employee benefits, especially for small companies. The author points out that offering fair (or the best the company can financially provide) benefits packages can exponentially promote human resource recruitment, retention, and overall contentedness. He also briefly explains different options and how they can profit both the employee as well as the employer.

Punnett, B. J. (2009). *International perspectives on organizational behavior and human resource management.* Armonk, NY: M. E. Sharpe.

Focusing on multiple variables in a country's environment, this book discusses the impact of cross-national issues beyond just cultural differences on organizational behavior and management. Arguing that politics, social issues, and governmental regulations have just as much impact on the business environment as culture, the author discusses how these other factors affect human resources.

Rickard, C., Baker, J., & Crew, Y. (2009). *Going global: Managing the HR function across countries and cultures.* Farnham, UK: Gower.

Based on the results of a consulting firm that has transformed the HR departments of numerous Fortune 500 companies such as Pepsi Americas, Accenture, and BP, this book describes why the HR function is so desperately needed in the current competitive environment, and how to transform it into a strategic component of the company. Challenging the role and purpose of an HR department as implemented in the traditional way, the authors explain how many of those traditional responsibilities should be passed down to managers so that the HR department can focus on building human resources strategically as part of the overall corporate strategy.

Website

Society for Human Resource Management (http://www.shrm.org)
The Society for Human Resource Management (SHRM) consists of over 205,000 individual members with 550 affiliated chapters in more than 100 countries. Founded in 1948, the association provides comprehensive resources to HR professionals and advances the human resource profession and its vital role in creating and implementing organizational strategy.

11

Implementing and Managing a Global Entrepreneurial Strategy

Profile: Red Bull

Jupiter Images/Comstock/ThinkStockPhotos

Born in a small town in Austria, Dietrich Mateschitz had big dreams of an extraordinary life, exactly the life he is living today. At 38, he was not happy working as the international marketing director of Blendax, a German consumer goods company. The monotony of everyday life was getting to him as he was seeking something bigger; but he just did not know what. On a trip to Thailand in 1982, Mateschitz found what he was looking for. The Thai people liked to drink an unappetizing beverage called Krating Daeng. Curious, he tried it one day. He immediately noticed the positive effects as his jet lag subsided. Instantly, he knew he wanted to sell this type of beverage in the West, and went about making plans to arrange it. He quickly found a business partner in Chaleo Yoovidhya, who was from Thailand and already had experience selling the tonic in Southeast Asia. The duo headed west to pursue their endeavor.

Being a savvy businessman, Mateschitz knew the most crucial component to selling the new beverage would be marketing. He spent over a year and a half consulting with an ad agency in Frankfurt, Germany, to create the product's design and slogan until it was perfect. Another critical piece, they decided was to add carbonation to the drink to better appeal to the target audience. Once the product was ready for distribution, Mateschitz revealed one last stroke of genius that truly solidified Red Bull as a success: the pricing. He priced one can of the beverage at $2, which at the time was significantly higher than any other canned soft drink on the shelf. He explained the method to his madness, "If we'd only had a 15% price premium, we'd merely be a premium brand among soft drinks and not a different category altogether." Mateschitz accomplished the nearly impossible feat that independent entrepreneurs and corporate conglomerates dream of: He created a brand new category called "energy drinks."

Red Bull would not enjoy its blue ocean for long. Imitators stepped up to the plate almost immediately, followed by the large beverage companies creating new lines of energy drinks to add to their portfolios. For a while, the company reveled in being the first mover, but how would Red Bull, a foul-tasting sugary caffeine rush, maintain its celebrity status as the number one preferred energy drink? Mateschitz answered that question while also showing his true intentions for Red Bull. He never wanted to produce a consumer product to compete with all the other consumer products in the world; he wanted to create a *brand.* Touting the "performance enhancing" effects of the caffeine-laden drink, the company sponsored extreme sports athletes all over the world, from Formula 1 racers to BASE jumpers. Anything that could be considered extreme and exciting, Red Bull had its name on it. Rather than sticking to the traditional routes of marketing and advertising, the company began to not only sponsor events but to produce them. It built stadiums for extreme sports, bought airplanes and race cars, and created sports teams (Mateschitz personally owns four soccer teams). Now Mateschitz and Red Bull have entered into the media arena with the subsidiary Red Bull Media House, as well as a partnership with Bunim/Murray Productions (creator of the *Real World* reality TV series) to create a reality show featuring Red Bull athletes. Beyond that, Red Bull has produced magazines, websites, virtual videos, and TV shows and films. The firm's first full-length documentary entitled *The Art of Flight* was released in theaters in the United States in fall 2011.

In short, Mateschitz created an empire. Although it seems foolish for a soft drink guru to wander into the world of media (much larger, more successful corporations have failed doing the same), it all seems to be part of a master plan, a plan that generated $5.175 billion revenue in 2010. To round it out, Mateschitz has created a mystique by keeping to himself, rarely giving interviews, and displaying an almost Howard Hughes-like eccentricity. At 70 years old, he relishes riding horses, flying planes, and racing motorcycles. To his delight, thanks to his mystique in conjunction with the rest of his efficient formula, Red Bull is growing faster than ever.

SOURCE: Adapted from McDonald (2011).

Chapter Objectives

1. To analyze the various organizational structures that best meet the needs of the enterprise
2. To understand the need for performance evaluation and benchmarking as relevant techniques for controlling a venture
3. To understand global organizational structures and the benefits and drawbacks of each
4. To learn how to control the global venture and the use of needed measurements and evaluations

Introduction

The recent changes in the world marketplace have been rapid and significant. More and more countries are moving toward market-oriented economies. Competition is at a very high level with companies needing to remain competitive by matching or preempting competitive moves. There is a growing scale and mobility in the world's capital markets. Given these opportunities and challenges in the global marketplace, it is imperative that the global entrepreneur establishes a strategic planning process to match the products of the venture with markets and maximize the employment of company resources to strengthen the long-term competitive advantage of the venture.

Global Strategic Planning

The global strategic planning process has the following three stages: (1) developing the core global strategy, (2) developing the global program, and (3) implementing and controlling the global effort.

Developing the Core Global Strategy

The global strategic plan starts with a clear definition of the business model and the core strategy of the venture. An assessment of the realities of the global market and its economics usually modifies both. To establish a global strategy on a country-by-country basis, the global entrepreneur needs to start by identifying the underlying forces that impact whether or not the business will be successful in the global marketplace. Planning across a broad range of markets balances the risks and resource requirements and develops a long-term position for profitability. To develop this type of plan, one must understand the common features of consumer needs and benefits desired and buying processes as well as competition.

The resources of the venture need to be taken into account to determine the capacity for creating and sustaining a competitive position in the global marketplace. Although deep pockets are not a necessity, a realistic view of the costs and a long-term time frame of at least 5 years are important.

Key decisions need to be made about the nature of the competitive strategy for market entrance and which market(s) to enter. These basic strategies are available: cost leadership, differentiation, and a hybrid approach. When employing a cost leadership strategy, global entrepreneurs should plan to offer a very similar product or service at a lower cost than their competitors. This strategy does not imply that the product is a commodity, but rather that the venture has some efficiencies that allow the product to be offered at a lower price. A differentiation strategy focuses on some unique aspect of the product or service (its unique selling proposition) that clearly separates it from competitive products presently on the market. One hybrid strategy for global market entrance and expansion is to combine a strong differentiation strategy with cost containment. This can be accomplished through economies of scale of both production and marketing activities.

The first country chosen (previously discussed in Chapter 5) is particularly important because it serves as a vehicle for market entrance and expansion. This decision takes into account internal strengths of the venture as measured by resources available, market share, product fit, contribution margin, and country attractiveness as measured by market size and growth rate, degree of competition, and the economic and political environment of the country. Combining the original country market choice and the internal strengths of the company along with synergies for expansion and future market entries provides a solid strategy for the global venture. Care must be taken to ensure that there are sufficient company resources for the expansion, which was not the case for GU Sports, even though GU developed another strategy to get around this apparent weakness.

GU Sports (Sports Street Marketing) was founded in Berkeley, California, in the early 1990s by Dr. William Vaughan. The mission from day one was to provide athletes the best exercise-specific nutrition products available. After formulating the world's first energy bar, Vaughan was disappointed that the bar, due to its high level of fat, fiber, and protein, did not work for athletes while they were training and racing. "How can we call it an energy bar for athletes when all it does is shut down the system for 45 minutes or so while the body digests all those useless-to-athletes ingredients?" asked a frustrated Vaughan (Malik, 2006/n.d.). So, in the late 1980s, he began experimenting with carbohydrates in gel form. Because gels did not require any ingredients for solidity (fat, fiber, and protein), they could transport energy to working muscles within minutes without any stomach distress. The perfect food for athletes during workouts, training, and racing was invented. After extensive testing and trial use by all types of athletes, in 1991 GU Energy Gel was perfected (https://guenergy.com/gu-story). The 1- or 1½-ounce foil packets of gel offered carbohydrates combined with electrolytes, sodium, and/or amino acids that quickly dissolve into the bloodstream (Malik, 2006/n.d.).

Sold primarily through specialty shops or online to top high-endurance competitors, GU needed to enter the mainstream consumer market to reach other athletes preparing for triathlons, marathons, and other adventure sports. Malik (2006/n.d.) reports that in the increasingly competitive landscape of energy-gel sales, GU Sports found itself having an unusual entrepreneurial problem. How could it grow the market size while still keeping its dominant market share? One way was to encourage sports-nutrition rival companies to emerge.

When US$15 million in U.S. gel sales would be achieved, GU would have a strong market position with a 50% share, PowerBar (acquired by food giant Nestlé SA in 2000) would have a 35% market share, and Clif Bar Inc., would have a 15% market share, according to Matt Powell, analyst at industry data source Sports-OneSource.

Nestlé increased distribution and marketing campaigns for Power-Bar Gels, which GU's Will Garratt, Jr., the vice president of marketing for GU, felt would "definitely create a better awareness" to the general public (Malik, 2006/n.d.). This type of market expansion had both potential and risks for a small company such as GU.

GU took many steps to remain competitive with the larger companies, such as developing new products with different tastes. With 25 employees, it manufactured its own product in a 6-hour process that produced 18,000 units selling for US$1.25 each. Approximately 90% of its sales were in the United States, but other countries where the product was gaining market shares included South America, South Africa, Australia, and New Zealand. According to Garratt, the company's gel sales increased "about 20% in each of the past 5 years along with the gel market," but with increased competition, it "had to fight a lot more for the same growth by increasing spending on grass-roots advertising and sponsorships" (Malik, 2006/n.d.).

Developing the Global Program

Once the core global strategy is established, the overall global program needs to be developed and implemented. Actually, this process occurs in concert with the strategy formulation. Although the core product or technology used to produce the product may be standardized, the product or service itself needs to reflect local market conditions to the extent possible. Localization is particularly needed in the marketing program. The overall marketing plan and position needs to be global, but the tactical elements of the plan should be market specific—very localized. Production, customer service activities, and warehousing need to be concentrated as much as possible to obtain any cost savings rather than being present in each country. Frequently, resources in one global market are used to fight competitive advances in other global markets to maintain the venture's competitive advantage.

Implementing and Controlling the Global Effort

Successful global entrepreneurs understand the need to balance local and global concerns. Local differences need to be taken into account when standardizing programs and policies by the headquarters, and as much autonomy as possible needs to go to the local country organization. Over-standardization and inflexibility in planning and implementation are probably the two biggest problems in executing the global program. Good local market research helps ensure that the product launch in a specific country reflects the characteristics of the market conditions in that country. Without this, the launch could fail. On the other hand, too much local customization can cause the venture to lose its overall global position. A successful global entrepreneur carefully balances local needs and overall global strategy. This means that neither headquarters nor local country managers are entirely in charge. Without the local managers and their commitment, however, no global program can be successful.

This success in part depends on the free flow of information between each country and headquarters as well as among country organizations themselves. In this way, ideas are exchanged and the overall venture and its values strengthened. This can also be accomplished through periodic meetings of the global managers or worldwide conferences.

Any personnel interchange facilitates this. The more experience each manager has in working with others from different nationalities, the better the integration and working relationships become. Managers become familiar with different markets and people. This is particularly important for managers at headquarters, who will then become more sensitive in developing and implementing global policies. Once a global strategy or program has been developed, it is usually better to permit local managers to develop and implement their own specific local programs within specified parameters and subject to approval. This develops a spirit of cooperation and trust that does not occur when local managers are forced to strictly adhere to the global strategy.

This also prevents the not-invented-here syndrome from occurring that can accompany local resistance and imitation. The global entrepreneur can take some proactive actions as well to help minimize the occurrence of this syndrome. One way is to make sure that local managers participate in the development of the venture's global strategies and programs. Another way is to give local managers a discretionary budget that they can use to respond to local competition and customer needs. A final way is to encourage local managers to submit ideas for consideration at the corporate level. Establishing this balance between headquarters and local country managers along with the right organizational structure, the topic of the next section, allows the global entrepreneur to establish a truly global culture that favors no specific country and has managers with a global mindset.

Sustainability

One key issue that needs to be addressed in the global venture is sustainability. Al Gore's book and movie, *An Inconvenient Truth*, stimulated consumer interest in the sustainability movement, making it a significant global concern for organizations all over the world that are attempting to integrate it into their strategic visions.

The level of concern about sustainability and the greening of the environment vary by country. In countries like Germany, where the population density is much higher than in the United States, consumers have become concerned about environmental concepts much faster than in the United States in part because of government mandates. Even though there are degrees of concern, the number of concerned people is getting larger in every country in the world.

Endorsing green movements as well as the issues of sustainability makes a global venture more profitable, often even in the short run. Sustainability can involve making money. Dial Corporation is producing concentrated detergents to reduce packaging wastes. Intel Corporation is developing microchips that cut the amount of energy wasted in home electronics. Arizona Public Service encourages employees to shut down energy-wasting computer monitors when they are not in use. Wal-Mart is examining hybrid-diesel trucks for its massive fleet.

Global Organizational Structure

As a venture moves from a totally domestic orientation to a global one, its organizational structure must change to reflect the new orientation. The organizational structure will vary depending on the stage of internationalization of the venture. The type of organization that is appropriate is one that facilitates the development of worldwide strategies while maintaining flexibility in implementing at the local market level. This concept is captured in the phrase "organize to think and plan globally but act locally."

Overall Organizational Structure

Important factors in choosing and implementing a specific organizational structure include the focus of decision making (where decision-making authority within the organization will reside), the roles of the different entities in the organization, the needed coordination and communication, and the needed controls. These factors are the basis for the global entrepreneur's decision to use one of the following three organizational approaches: (1) little emphasis on the international activities of the venture, (2) recognizing the ever-growing importance of the international activities occurring, and (3) being a truly global organization with no domestic/international split.

In the early stage of international development, the company's international activities are usually coordinated by the domestic operation. Because these early activities tend to be of such a small size, they really have no effect on the organizational structure of the venture. Often the transactions are actually facilitated using entities outside the organization, such as an export management company or freight forwarder, as discussed in Chapter 7. As international sales increase and become more important to the venture, export operations are often separated from domestic operations in a separate entity in the overall organizational structure, such as an export department. This is the first step toward internationalizing the venture. At this stage, any international licensing activity takes place in the research and development and legal areas. The faster the growth in international sales, the more quickly the export department becomes obsolete. The amount of coordination and control needed at a certain point requires a more formal international organizational structure, which often results in the establishment of an international division.

The international division centralizes all the non–home-country activities of the venture to better serve the global customers. While this division oversees and has responsibility for the sales, information about the market, and other market opportunities, manufacturing and other functional activities remain in the domestic division. To avoid conflict, coordination between the divisions is necessary. This coordination is often achieved through a joint staff that interacts regularly to discuss problems and develop the strategic plans for the venture.

As the international sales grow in size, diversity, and complexity, the international division also tends to become obsolete, requiring a new organizational structure to be implemented. There are several structural formats available, as discussed in the following section.

Types of Organizational Structures

There are several types of global organizational structures available for implementation by the global entrepreneur. These include area structure, customer structure, product structure, mixed structure, or the matrix structure. The *global area structure* is a widely used approach that uses geographical areas as its basis. For example, a U.S. entrepreneurial company could organize its activities into four areas: Asia-Pacific, Europe, North America, and South America. The areas can be designated based on cultural similarity, such as Asia, or historical connections between the countries, such as the Balkans. No preference in funding is given to the headquarters in the United States, as personnel for each of the areas support and monitor the activities and develop the companywide global strategy. The increased use of the global area structure reflects such regionalization activities as NAFTA (the North American Free Trade Agreement) and the European Union. The area approach aligns itself well with having one marketing concept because each geographic area defined has similar characteristics and can be given similar marketing attention. It works particularly well for those entrepreneurial ventures that have narrow product lines with similar end users and uses, since they are so closely related. When there are many diverse product lines or diverse end users and uses, the global area approach may not be the best one to employ.

The *global customer structure* is used when the customer groups served are dramatically different. This is often called "verticals." Customer groups include consumer, governmental, and industrial. Another group could be along the lines of industry, such as the automobile industry, the printing industry, or the mining industry. Even though the products for each customer group may be similar or even identical, the buying process is so different that a specific marketing and service approach is needed. Some groups may require industry specialists.

The *global product structure* is the organizational form most often used by global entrepreneurs. This approach places the responsibility for global activities in each product area. This approach allows improved cost efficiency through the centralization of manufacturing. It is frequently used by consumer-product firms, where the world market share of a product helps determine its competitive position. The global product structure balances functional input to the product with the ability to quickly respond to any specific product problems. This allows each product to be adapted to the extent needed for each foreign market. Coordination between the product groups in each market is essential as well as having managers who have adequate country market experience. Problems, however, can occur, particularly when a customer buys multiple products from the venture.

The *mixed global structure*, as the name implies, uses two or more of the possible global structures, providing significant attention to the area, customer, and/or product. It is often used in a transition period following a merger or acquisition or before implementing the final global organizational structure—the global matrix structure.

The *global matrix structure* is a complex structure adopted mainly by large entrepreneurial corporations for planning and controlling many independent businesses, resources, and geographic areas. The matrices developed vary in the number of dimensions and allow for better cooperation between business managers, product managers, and area managers, as each person must work with the others to obtain the company's objectives. Problems and conflicts can occur because most managers report to at least two people. Often even minor problems have to be solved through committee discussion, which seriously reduces the reaction time of a venture. This is particularly a problem in today's hypercompetitive environment, which requires a quick response time. Some companies using a matrix organization have changed to one of the other four global organizational structures: area, customer, product, or mixed in order to avoid conflicting reporting systems.

❖ CULTURAL STORIES

Story 1

On a bus with my friend in Japan, we saw an old woman board. The bus was crowded and my friend decided to offer her his seat. He stood up and said, in his newly learned Japanese, *"Sawatte kudasai."* The lady looked puzzled.

He should have said *suwatte kudasa*—"please sit." Instead, he had asked her to "touch it." She finally understood, laughed, and sat down.

Story 2

The first time I lived in Mexico City, after several weeks of tacos, I treated myself to a good 'ol American hamburger and chocolate malt at Sanborn's. Upon finishing, the waitress asked me if I wanted anything more, *"Quiere algo mas?"* I replied, in a loud and confident tone, *"No, yo estoy lleno"*—"No, I'm full.

She started laughing and told the other waitresses what I had said, and they also began to laugh and point at me. After inquiring, I learned that I had announced to them that I was pregnant.

(I am a man, by the way.)

SOURCE: http://www.culturalconfusions.com (Story 1 by David Johnson; Story 2 by Mark Wilson).

Authority and Global Decisions

Although the organizational structure is important, it does not necessarily indicate where the authority for decision making and control resides. This is a critical decision for the global entrepreneur and can be referred to as the degree of centralization of the venture. Many global entrepreneurs prefer a high degree of centralization in which all the strategic decisions are made at headquarters (often by them) and the controls are tight. Sometimes this high degree of centralization occurs in some functions, such as finance, human resources, and research and development, while in other functions, such as marketing, it does not. The more autonomy each global structural unit is given and the lighter the controls, the more decentralized the venture becomes. Since each unit is its own profit center, most of the information flow between the structural units is financial.

The more a venture is decentralized, the better able its global units are to market effectively and react quickly at the local level. This encourages a high level of participation at the local level and usually results in much higher corporate morale.

Because a high degree of decentralization seriously modifies the control aspect of headquarters, some companies are now using coordinated decentralization. In this hybrid model, the overall company strategy is developed at headquarters and each global structural unit is allowed to adjust and implement this strategy within agreed upon parameters.

Controlling the Global Venture

In today's hypercompetitive environment, it is imperative that the global venture establish a system for evaluating performance and controlling the venture. Part of this system would be internal and external benchmarking. External benchmarking, when the data are available, allows the global entrepreneur to evaluate his or her performance against competitors of similar size in the same industry. The problem is that frequently the data are not available to do this.

Every venture, however, can regularly do internal benchmarking. This provides needed information for control purposes and for sharing best practices throughout the company. This knowledge transfer is most important for growing a truly global organization.

The control of both the outputs of the international activities (sales, production, profits, growth) and behavior (culture, employee behavior, management capabilities) can be accomplished either through bureaucratic, formalized control or through cultural control.

Formalized Versus Cultural Control

While formalized control relies on rules and regulations that indicate the needed level of output, cultural controls rely on shared beliefs and expectations of personnel in the venture. A formalized control system relies on a standardized budget, reporting system, and policy manuals. The budget and reporting system is the major control mechanism for a local country operation and establishes the nature of the relationship between these local entities and headquarters. As much uniformity as possible should occur without sacrificing the ability of local country units to grow and respond in a timely manner. Establishing the appropriate manuals for each major function facilitates uniformity and reduces report preparation time.

When emphasizing the values and culture of the venture, or cultural control, evaluations are based on the extent to which there is a fit between the individual or entity and the norms. This requires extensive informal personal interaction and training on the corporate culture and the way things are done. Sound cultural control requires that good selection and training programs are established in the venture. Regardless of the positioning on the formalized, cultural continuum, it is important for the global entrepreneur to understand and use some control techniques as discussed in the next section.

Measurement and Control Techniques

There are several useful performance measures: financial performance, personnel performance, and quality performance. Financial performance of a local country operation is based on sales, profit, and return on investment (ROI). Profit is affected by management capabilities as well as external, uncontrollable factors, such as currency value and exchange rates. If a local country's currency value decreases (devaluation), sales will increase because the price of the products will be lower for foreign buyers. The opposite occurs when the value of the local currency increases.

Control using personnel performance as a measure needs to be done periodically. This appraisal of each manager's output and behavior is done differently in different cultural settings. Turnover among global managers should be minimized, but no turnover may indicate that evaluations are too infrequent or standards and expectations are too low. The last control technique, based on quality performance, makes sure the goods and services and the operation of the local country unit and headquarters are at the highest possible level of quality. This can occur by using total quality management techniques, quality circles, and employee reward and recognition systems. A well-run global venture will employ performance measures in each of these three areas to ensure that a proper control system is operational.

Managing Chaos

Chaos and change are two dimensions of every global entrepreneurial venture. Change is an opportunity as well as a challenge for global entrepreneurs who can live with chaos. The scale and complexity of change and chaos are even greater for global entrepreneurs than their domestic counterparts, particularly in today's hypercompetitive business environment. To understand change and be better able to manage chaos, it is important for the global entrepreneur to understand the dynamics that occur according to Prigogine's concept of far-from-equilibrium dynamics, Heisenberg's Uncertainty Principle, and Zadeh's fuzzy logic.

Ilya Prigogine's concept of far-from-equilibrium dynamics reflects his comprehensive and judicious understanding of the history of science (Prigogine & Stengers, 1984). He felt that the paradigm of Newton, particularly its treatment of change and chaos, does not apply to many important phenomena. According to Prigogine, while the state of a system stabilizes around its equilibrium, fluctuations disturb this equilibrium, making its behavior unpredictable before the system returns to equilibrium and becomes predictable again. While this is true for some systems, many common and important systems are so far-from-equilibrium that they can be destructive. Still some order forms at the edge of chaos. In those conditions, the process of self-organization can form and proliferate, not by imposing order into the chaos, but by negotiating it and creating a new complex form of order.

Heisenberg's Uncertainty Principle (1950) proposes that it is not possible to measure with equal precision the position and the momentum of a quantum element (Heisenberg, 1950). Although mainly applicable to the quantum world, it also applies to the macroworld of organizations when the position and movement are interdependent and change rapidly and unpredictably, sometimes resulting in things becoming the opposite when at the extreme. The new resulting position and momentum cannot be predicted from the previous states of each, making uncertainty more the norm in most systems.

Zadeh views this dynamic through fuzzy logic in which categories are opposites and multivalent (Zadeh & Yager, 1987). Both Z and not Z can coexist to some degree according to Zadeh, particularly as the complexity of the system increases. In these cases, managers do not have the ability to make precise and relevant statements and predictions until a threshold is reached. "It is then that fuzzy statements are the only bearers of meaning and relevance" (Zadeh & Yager, 1987). Fuzzy logic provides an understanding of change for managers when they do not attempt to achieve absolute precision.

These three principles, as well as the art of managing chaos, are illustrated particularly well in the cases of Google and Enron. Larry Page and Sergey Brin, Google's founders, introduced the concept on Stanford University's internal website in 1996, and Google was a commercial enterprise by 1998. With the majority of the world's Internet users using Google as their search engine, no wonder the company has increased in sales, profits, and value, and handles more transactions every day than the combination of the New York, London, Frankfurt, and Paris stock exchanges. Google embraces chaos, and profits from it with a work environment employees call the "Google way of working," where mistakes are viewed as tools for learning and employees are encouraged to come up with outrageous ideas. The informal environment—there is no dress code or rules for behavior—recognizes that the most valuable resource of the company is the mind and thought processes of its employees. Google indeed thrives by managing this chaos.

Enron provides another classic example, in another perspective, of managing chaos (McLean & Elkind, 2003). At Enron, change was continuous, sometimes going as intended but more often than not producing paradoxical outcomes. The company was a constantly changing entity on an exponential growth curve that was accelerating over time. The change blurred boundaries, with the potential for great success and catastrophic losses coexisting for many years. Enron can be viewed from each one of the theoretical perspectives of managing chaos. It became a company driven by steeper and steeper growth curves and expectations, and having to hit quarterly targets expected by Wall Street despite having a far-from-equilibrium world of distortions. This unmanaged chaos eventually led to illegal accounting practices and the company's bankruptcy.

Summary

This chapter focuses on the need for a global entrepreneur to define and execute a strategic plan, establish the best organizational structure, and use proper benchmarking and control techniques to realize the full potential of his or her company. The strategic plan is rarely established before the business is launched and is often a continuous work in progress in which the global entrepreneur uses numerous indicators to adjust and refine the strategy. The basis for the strategic plan lies in defining the core strategy of the venture through the careful examination of the underlying forces that affect the business's success in the global marketplace and the business's resources. Two basic strategies that can be employed are differentiation and cost leadership. Once the strategy has been chosen, the global entrepreneur institutes a global program in which he or she takes the standardized product and adapts it to the local market(s), taking into consideration the culture and mores of the particular locality. As the global venture grows, the global entrepreneur normally needs to reorganize and adapt the organization to handle the greater demands of more markets or products. First, the global entrepreneur must address (1) how much to emphasize the international activities of the venture, (2) how much recognition the ever-growing importance of the international activities demand, and (3) what being a truly global organization with no domestic/international split entails. The answers to these questions will help the global entrepreneur decide which type of organizational structures to use, such as global area structure, global customer structure, global product structure, global mixed structure, and global matrix structure. Finally, the global entrepreneur needs to establish whether a centralized or decentralized decision-making and control structure is best for the firm. The global entrepreneur must also evaluate financial performance, personnel performance, and quality performance to create benchmarks to measure the success of the firm.

Questions for Discussion

1. To what situations is a cost leadership strategy better suited? When might a differentiation strategy be better?
2. Describe the different organizational structures and at what stage in the venture they might be best for an entrepreneurial enterprise.
3. How does organizational control change as a venture achieves more success in a foreign market?

Chapter Exercises

1. Find articles about a company that attributes its success to meeting the goals set forth in its strategic plan. What is the company's core strategy? Identify its indicators of success beyond profitability.
2. Suppose you are the owner of a successful electric-powered, environment-friendly scooter company and plan to launch your product in India. Pick either the cost leadership or differentiation strategy and explain how you bring the scooter to India. Will you have to alter the design at all? What difficulties could the Indian market pose, and how will your strategic plan deal with them?
3. Create a table listing the common organizational structures for a global firm and find examples of multinational companies that use each type of structure.
4. Discuss with a partner the best way to lead a global firm. Which method is better—formalized or cultural leadership? Why?

References

Heisenberg, W. (1950). *The physical principles of the quantum theory.* New York: Dover.

Malik, N. S. (n.d.). Risky business: GU Sports could benefit from Nestle energy gels, but competition stiffens. Retrieved from http://wsjclassroomedition.com/monday/mx_06nov13.pdf (Reprinted from *The Wall Street Journal: Monday Extra,* November 13, 2006).

McDonald, D. (2011). Red Bull's billionaire maniac. *Bloomberg Businessweek.* Retrieved from http://www.businessweek.com/magazine/content/11_22/b4230064852768.htm

McLean, B., & Elkind, P. (2003). *The smartest guys in the room: The amazing rise and scandalous fall of Enron.* New York: Portfolio.

Prigogine, I., & Stengers, I. (1984). *Order out of chaos: Man's new dialogue with nature.* New York: Bantam.

Zadeh, L. A., & Yager, R. R. (1987). *Fuzzy sets and applications: Selected papers.* New York: Wiley.

Suggested Readings

Articles/Books

Businessweek. (2008). ***Global business power plays: How the masters of international enterprise reach the top of their game.*** **Washington DC: Brookings Institution Press.**

This book provides insights on how to grow a business into a global corporation by sharing the stories of some of the most successful companies in the world. Through these real-world cases, the author extricates powerful strategies and best practices that an entrepreneur can replicate in his or her own business. From Howard Schultz with Starbucks to Xu Danhua with Huawei, the book offers lessons in leadership and business strategy from the best of the best.

Hempel, J. (2011, May). Trouble@Twitter. ***Fortune Magazine, 2,*** **66–76.**

This article outlines the ups and downs that the highly successful social media website Twitter has experienced since its inception, and the potential that it has not yet realized. Highlighting problems in top management and the board of directors, it is a lesson in leadership and the importance of good management in establishing a company's direction, especially in start-ups.

Hitt, M. A., Ireland, R. D., & Hoskisson, R. E. (2011). ***Strategic management concepts and cases: Competitiveness and globalization*** **(9th ed.). Mason, OH: South-Western.**

This book reveals the problems and provides answers on how to effectively build a management strategy that creates competitive advantage. Building from older theories, the authors discuss contemporary strategic management and how it can be used to create sustainable competitiveness for companies wanting to compete globally. With examples from over 600 companies, this book offers a wealth of knowledge regarding how to best use strategic management to increase chances of success.

Katz, J. S. (2010). ***Competing for global dominance: Survival in a changing world.*** **Silicon Valley, CA: Super Star Press.**

Citing Silicon Valley as the gold standard for how to effectively market and grow a company in the 21st century, this book discusses how different the market is since the rise of globalization, which created a marketplace unconstrained by time or distance. The author discusses issues that entrepreneurs will face and how small businesses can be positioned to survive in such an environment.

Porter, M. E. (2006, November/December). What is strategy? ***Harvard Business Review, 74*****(6), 61–78.**

This article explains the differences between enhanced operational effectiveness and a viable, adaptable strategy, which is the true basis of sustained profitability and competitive advantage. Operational effectiveness is a company's ability to perform a particular, single activity better than its rivals. Strategic positioning and strategy, on the other hand, focus on how to perform activities that are different from your rivals or how to carry out the same activities in a different way. The author emphasizes how operational improvements through total quality management, benchmarking, partnering, and so forth will not necessarily create sustainable profitability, unless superior leadership is guiding the process.

Part 4

Cases

- Beijing Sammies
- Federal Express
- Fitz-Ritter Wine Estate
- Intelligent Leisure Solutions
- Logisys
- Mayu LLC
- Motrada Ltd.
- Parsek LLC
- Sedo.com
- Trimo
- UniMed and EduMed

Case I

Beijing Sammies

Christopher Ferrarone

When Sam Goodman opened a new Sammies cafe in Beijing's Motorola Building, he cut prices by 50% for the first three months to attract customers. The initial period was very successful but when he returned prices to normal, sales dropped dramatically and fell short of targets. The local store manager, when presenting the figures, suggested that Goodman simply lower the sales targets. Goodman was frustrated; the manager had failed to address any of the issues that were keeping customers from returning. There were countless orders that went out with missing utensils, in the wrong bag, or [with items] simply left out. Delivery orders were being sent hours late or to the wrong location. This typified Goodman's early experience. The market was showing interest in Beijing Sammies' products, but he knew that without exceptional service, good food would not be enough. Goodman questioned whether he could find employees who were thinkers and problem solvers and he wondered how to improve upon the business to turn Beijing Sammies into a sustainable and profitable enterprise.

According to Goodman, face and money were the two most important subjects. With experience as a student and businessman in China, he knew one must observe the cultural beliefs:

> Face is a huge issue here, and as the economy develops, so is money. If one is not relevant, the other is. Once you recognize this is crucial, it was not hard to learn. The difficult part is incorporating it into the business. We need to offer a superior experience in order for customers to justify paying more. This means providing a quality product with excellent service. It sounds easy, but in China the concept of service is not the same as in the West. I just can't seem to get my employees to understand that there is a way to serve the customer while also keeping the company's interest at heart. It is an "all for us" or "all for them" mentality here.

Author's Note: This case was prepared under the supervision of Boston College Professor Gregory L. Stoller as the basis for class discussion rather than to illustrate either effective or ineffective handling of an administrative situation.

Throughout the company's initial years, Goodman sought to teach a service-oriented approach to his employees. In doing so, he ironically learned that face was as much of an important issue for Beijing Sammies' customers as it was for its employees.

Beijing Sammies' Origins

Canadian native Sam Goodman started Beijing Sammies in 1997. Aside from producing food for the everyday, walk-in customer, Sammies provided fare for company meetings, presentations, picnics, and gifts. Sammies was open for breakfast, lunch, and dinner and delivered all products to its customers. The menu included a selection of sandwiches, salads, bagels, brownies, cookies, coffee, soda, and tea (see Figure 1).

Goodman started the company with personal savings and money borrowed from family. He opened his first cafe at the Beijing Language and Culture University with the goal of providing people with a place to "hang out" and enjoy homemade Western food.

By 2003, Beijing Sammies had five outlets—four "deli-style" cafes and one kiosk. The stores were traditional in terms of layout and size for fast food restaurants. Two Sammies cafes were 1,200 square feet and the other two were roughly 800 square feet

❖ Figure 1 A menu from Beijing Sammies.

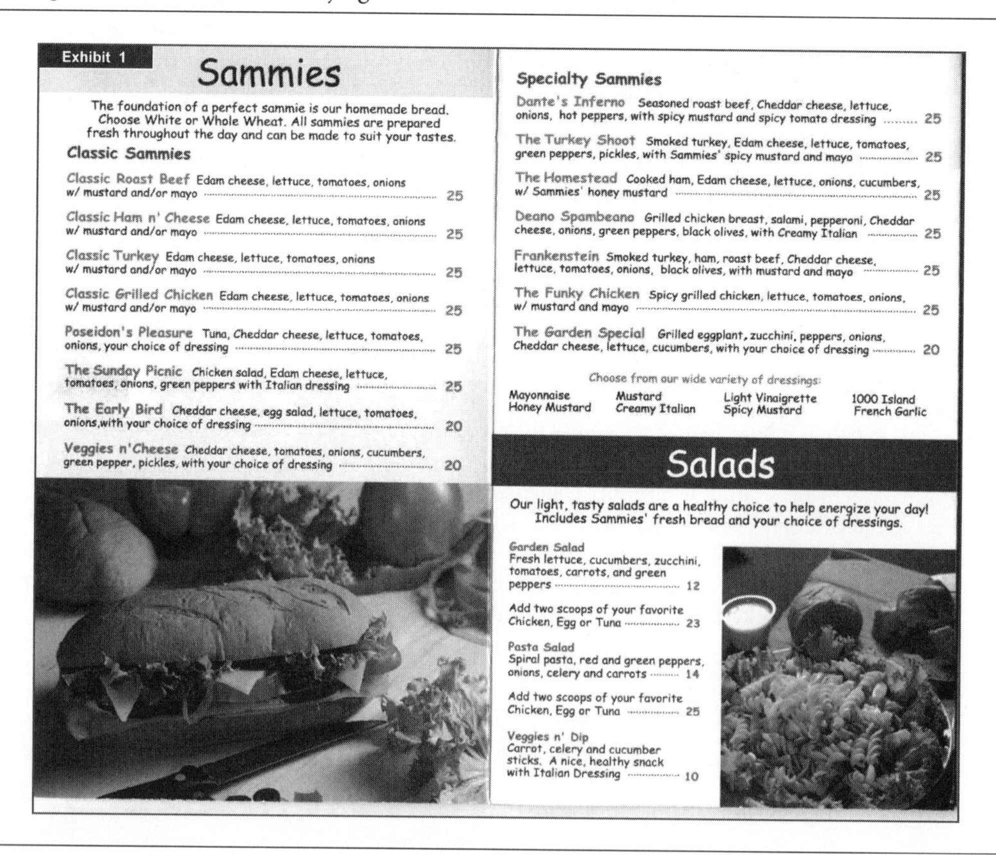

Exhibit 1

Sammies

The foundation of a perfect sammie is our homemade bread. Choose White or Whole Wheat. All sammies are prepared fresh throughout the day and can be made to suit your tastes.

Classic Sammies

Classic Roast Beef Edam cheese, lettuce, tomatoes, onions w/ mustard and/or mayo 25

Classic Ham n' Cheese Edam cheese, lettuce, tomatoes, onions w/ mustard and/or mayo 25

Classic Turkey Edam cheese, lettuce, tomatoes, onions w/ mustard and/or mayo 25

Classic Grilled Chicken Edam cheese, lettuce, tomatoes, onions w/ mustard and/or mayo 25

Poseidon's Pleasure Tuna, Cheddar cheese, lettuce, tomatoes, onions, your choice of dressing 25

The Sunday Picnic Chicken salad, Edam cheese, lettuce, tomatoes, onions, green peppers with Italian dressing 25

The Early Bird Cheddar cheese, egg salad, lettuce, tomatoes, onions,with your choice of dressing 20

Veggies n'Cheese Cheddar cheese, tomatoes, onions, cucumbers, green pepper, pickles, with your choice of dressing 20

Specialty Sammies

Dante's Inferno Seasoned roast beef, Cheddar cheese, lettuce, onions, hot peppers, with spicy mustard and spicy tomato dressing 25

The Turkey Shoot Smoked turkey, Edam cheese, lettuce, tomatoes, green peppers, pickles, with Sammies' spicy mustard and mayo 25

The Homestead Cooked ham, Edam cheese, lettuce, onions, cucumbers, w/ Sammies' honey mustard 25

Deano Spambeano Grilled chicken breast, salami, pepperoni, Cheddar cheese, onions, green peppers, black olives, with Creamy Italian 25

Frankenstein Smoked turkey, ham, roast beef, Cheddar cheese, lettuce, tomatoes, onions, black olives, with mustard and mayo 25

The Funky Chicken Spicy grilled chicken, lettuce, tomatoes, onions, w/ mustard and mayo 25

The Garden Special Grilled eggplant, zucchini, peppers, onions, Cheddar cheese, lettuce, cucumbers, with your choice of dressing 20

Choose from our wide variety of dressings:

Mayonnaise, Honey Mustard, Mustard, Creamy Italian, Light Vinaigrette, Spicy Mustard, 1000 Island, French Garlic

Salads

Our light, tasty salads are a healthy choice to help energize your day! Includes Sammies' fresh bread and your choice of dressings.

Garden Salad
Fresh lettuce, cucumbers, zucchini, tomatoes, carrots, and green peppers 12

Add two scoops of your favorite Chicken, Egg or Tuna 23

Pasta Salad
Spiral pasta, red and green peppers, onions, celery and carrots 14

Add two scoops of your favorite Chicken, Egg or Tuna 25

Veggies n' Dip
Carrot, celery and cucumber sticks. A nice, healthy snack with Italian Dressing 10

each, while the kiosk was a stand-alone structure with open seating inside the lobby of a corporate building. All of the cafe locations had enclosed seating that was maximized, as there was no need for self-contained kitchens.

The Central Kitchen

Goodman found that revenues of the first cafe were driven as much by corporate delivery orders as they were by the local walk-in customers. This motivated Goodman to open more cafes and a centralized kitchen in 1998. Located in Beijing's Chao Yang District, the kitchen ran from 10 p.m. to 5:30 a.m. each day making the sandwiches and baked goods for all of Sammies' locations. Between 5:30 and 6 a.m., trucks delivered the goods from the kitchen to each Sammies outlet. No cooking was done at any of the Sammies locations. Every sandwich, cookie, and muffin was prepared, baked, and packaged centrally. Only coffee and smoothies were prepared onsite at individual retail cafes.

While the central kitchen created a number of efficiencies for Beijing Sammies, what Goodman liked even more was the quality control that it provided:

> It is much easier for me to teach the kitchen staff how to make the food correctly than it is to teach all of the employees at each location. At the kitchen I can make sure that the product going out to all of the stores is consistent. In the end that's what I am striving for, to offer a consistently great product with superior service. Only having one kitchen to manage makes this task much easier.

The central kitchen not only provided Beijing Sammies with efficiencies with ingredients, machines, and manpower, but also allowed for larger customer capacity at each cafe location and enabled the employees to uniquely focus on customer service.

The Sammie

The idea behind Beijing Sammies originated from Goodman. Moving to Hong Kong after college and subsequently moving to Beijing to attend Beijing Language and Culture University, Goodman yearned for a place to hang out and eat a traditional sandwich or "sammie" that reminded him of home. Three years later Beijing Sammies was named Beijing's #1 Western food delivery service by City Weekend magazine.

Modeled after Goodman's version of a New York deli, Beijing Sammies' staple is the "sammie." Each sammie started with homemade bread made every night at Sammies' kitchen. Customers could order from a menu of standard sammies or could create their own. Goodman found the pre-set menu best for the local customers while many foreigners frequently customized their sandwiches:

> Having a menu of pre-crafted sandwiches is a necessity. Many of the Chinese customers simply do not know how to order. They do not understand the notion of selecting different types of deli meats and condiments for a sandwich. I didn't even think about this at first. Personally, I know exactly what goes with roast beef and what goes with turkey.

> When we opened our first location many people came in and left without ordering. They didn't know how, and did not want to look foolish ordering something inappropriate. Many times, and this still happens, people come in and just order whatever the person in front of them ordered. Putting complete sandwiches together allows the inexperienced customer to come in and feel more comfortable about ordering.

Creating premade selections of sandwiches worked so well for Sammies that Goodman put together an "Ordering Tips" section on the menu. The section not only suggested what types of products to order for breakfast and what products to buy for lunch, but also provided a guide for corporate clients to ensure correct portions and variety for meetings. In addition, Sammies trained sales clerks to act as customer service representatives who could assist both the walk-in client and growing base of corporate delivery clients with their orders.

Corporate Clients and Sammies Rewards

As Beijing Sammies realized a growing corporate delivery base, Goodman adapted the model to provide the business client with as much flexibility and customization as possible. Sammies set up corporate accounts, online ordering, flexible payment options, and a rewards program (see Figure 2).

Corporate customers who registered with Beijing Sammies could choose weekly or monthly payment terms whereby Beijing Sammies would send out itemized statements and invoices. Clients could choose to set up a debit account as well. Under the debit account, clients prepaid a certain amount (usually a minimum of rmb1000[1]) that was credited to an account and deducted each time an order was placed.

Along with the flexible payment options, corporate customers could become enrolled in the Bonus Points program, which offered credits based on the frequency and size of orders (see Figure 3). Customers who spent between rmb500 and 750 receive an rmb50 credit, orders between rmb750 and 1000 an rmb75 credit, and orders over rmb1000 are given an rmb100 credit. Furthermore, each time a client cumulatively spent over rmb5000 they were rewarded with an rmb500 credit. All of this could be done over the Beijing Sammies website, www.beijingsammies.com, where customers could log in and manage their account.

The Bonus Points program was offered to the walk-in customer as well. Customers who registered with Beijing Sammies online could become enrolled in the program. Every registered customer received a point for each rmb they spent. Every 10 points could be redeemed for 1 rmb off the next order. Extra points could be received for filling out surveys, referring new customers, or attending selected special events. The point system was well received by Beijing Sammies' customers and contributed to a solid base of returning foreign clients.

Charity Sponsorship

Beijing Sammies served large numbers of foreigners and consequently, Goodman felt a strong responsibility to sponsor charity, youth, and community events focused around the expat community in Beijing:

❖ Figure 2 Beijing Sammies' introductory e-mail.

OUR NEW SILK ALLEY SAMMIES CAFE IS ALSO OPEN!

Drop on by to enjoy some of your Sammies favorites . . . and more!

- Enjoy our wider breakfast selection
- Choose from café beverages and goodies
- Select from smoothies, espresso, cappuccinos, and our selection of baked goods
- Warm, inviting café atmosphere—whether you're networking, on a date, getting a meal-to-go or getting social, Sammies Xiu Shui Jie café is the place to be!

Located at the Silk Alley/Xiu Shui Jie south entrance on Chang An Jie, in the Chaoyang District; open every day from 07:30 to 24:00.

WHERE EAST EATS WEST

*THANKS FOR REGISTERING! NOW YOU CAN ORDER ALL YOUR SAMMIES FAVORITES THROUGH THE WEB!

Browse online and order our delicious Sammies sandwiches, salads, baked goods including muffins, cookies, brownies, biscotti, and bagels. Great for business meetings, social events, breakfast, lunch, or dinner! Registration allows you to enjoy the following:

SAVE TIME

One-time registration of delivery information—no need to re-explain your contact info at every order. Just log in, order, and then submit for successful delivery every time you come to the Web site.

SAVE MONEY

Bonus points for future discounts—sign up and receive bonus points based on every RMB you order, which you can redeem for future discounts and Sammies products.

IMPROVED EFFICIENCY

Online ordering and delivery—order directly from our Web site menu and we'll deliver to you!

CUSTOM-MADE ORDERS

Customize your Sammies, and track your orders with our new menu and online ordering interface.

RE-ORDER YOUR FAVORITES

Quick ordering of your favorite Sammies items—registered users can re-order from a recorded list of past favorite orders.

ORDER 24 HOURS A DAY

Order hours or days in advance.

Questions? Please e-mail our helpful customer service staff at beijingsammies @yahoo.com. Tell a friend to visit us at www.beijingsammies.com.

The Canadian community in Beijing and around China in general is pretty strong. As a foreign student here, I really appreciated the sense of kinship that I felt even though I was far away from home. In addition, the foreign businesses and tourists have been very supportive of Beijing Sammies so I really enjoy and feel compelled to participate in the community's events.

Along with providing snacks and food, Beijing Sammies helped certain organizations by allowing promotional and ticket sale efforts to be staged from Sammies' locations. Sammies' sponsorship events included

- Special Olympics
- Canadian Day and U.S. Independence Day
- Sporting and school events held by the Western Academy of Beijing and the International School of Beijing
- Annual Terry Fox Run for Cancer
- ACBC Baseball Events

❖ Figure 3 Beijing Sammies' corporate clients.

- Nokia China Investment
- U.S.A. Embassy
- Canada Embassy
- Intel PRC, Corp.
- Boeing
- AEA SOS
- American Chamber of Commerce
- Agilent
- Andersen Consulting
- Australia Embassy
- APCO Associates Inc.
- Benz
- Ford Foundation
- Henkel
- Hewlett-Packard
- IBM China Ltd.
- Motorola China Electronics, Ltd.
- Western Academy of Beijing
- Reuters

Sammies' Evolution

Starting out with $25,000 borrowed from friends and family back in Canada, Goodman opened Beijing's first sandwich shop. To help get past the bureaucracy involved with opening the cafe, Goodman located a Chinese partner. After an initial four months of business, Beijing Sammies was a hit. The store was so successful that the new partner attempted to strong-arm Goodman out of the company by locking him out. In response, Goodman rallied some friends and broke into the shop one night and removed the appliances and supplies. The partner agreed to be bought out.

Soon after Goodman regained control, his landlord disappeared. The government demanded the tenants cover his back taxes. When they could not, it demolished the whole row and left the tenants with the bricks. Goodman was able to sell them for $25.

Goodman responded by opening a cafe at the Beijing Language and Culture University. Again, Sammies opened to a steady stream of customers, particularly from foreign students and local corporations.

In 1998, after realizing success with the first cafe in its newfound location, Goodman found another business partner. Together they planned to invest $350,000 more into Beijing Sammies. The next step was to build a centralized kitchen and add more cafe locations. Soon after construction started, however, the funds supposedly coming from the newfound business partner dried up and Goodman was left financing the new kitchen on his own.

At the end of 1998, Sammies had a central kitchen with great capacity but no new store locations to deliver to. Goodman was able to generate yet another round of financing. With some Western investment and all of the profits from his previous two years in business, Goodman was able to put $150,000 together and open three new cafes.

In addition to the first cafe located at Beijing Language and Culture University, Sammies cafes were opened between 1998 and 2001 at the Silk Alley Market, 1/F Exchange Beijing, and the Motorola Building. A Sammies kiosk was also opened at the China Resource Building (see Figure 4). The expansion allowed Goodman to more adequately serve the Beijing area while also firmly establishing Beijing Sammies in an increasingly competitive environment:

> Overall, I see the expansion into multiple cafes as a success. Two of the cafes are doing well while the two others have not met sales targets yet. The kiosk, because of less rent, is doing moderately well but is still not as busy as I'd like it to be. 2002 looks to be our best year to

❖ Figure 4 Beijing Sammies' locations.

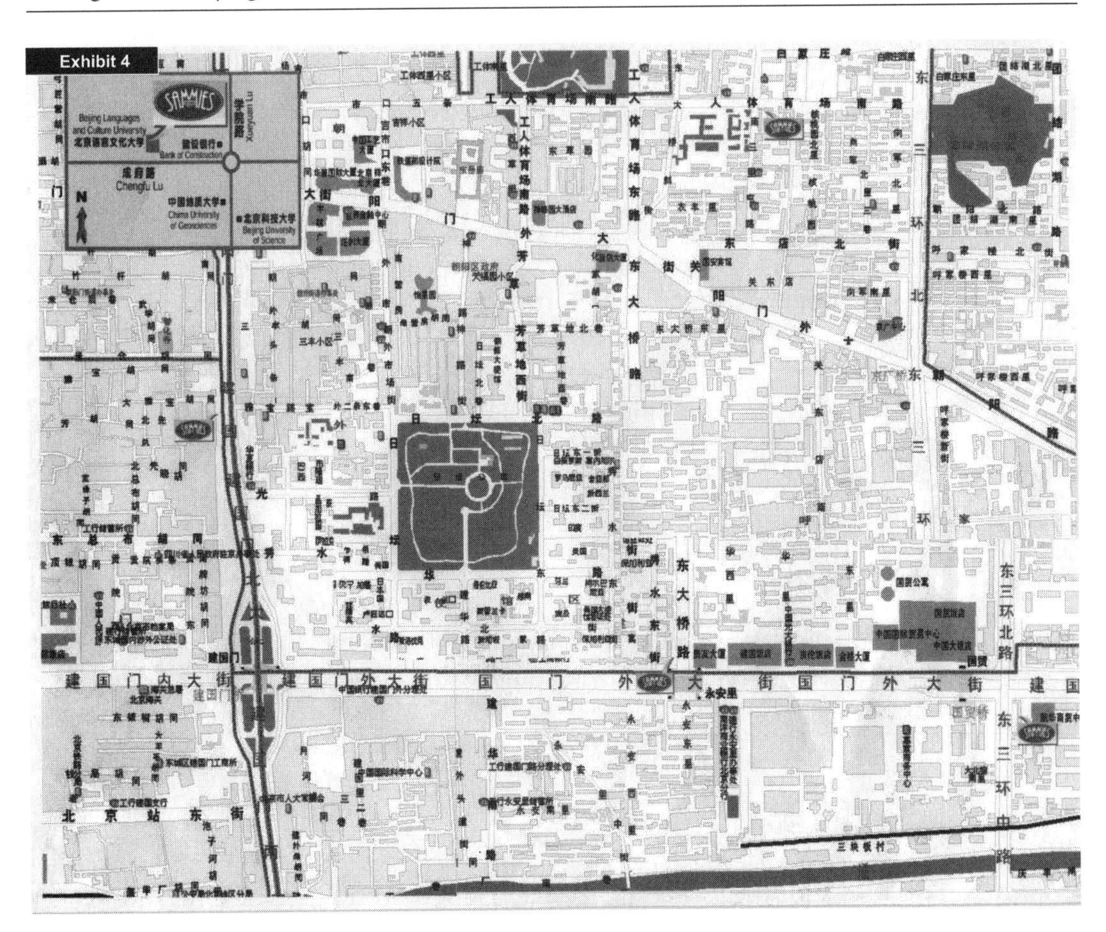

date with a revenue increase of 54%, and an operating profit of $20,000. However, due to the fact that the central kitchen is its own cost center, we will record a $24,000 loss (including depreciation). 2003 should show our first profits.

By the end of 2001, Beijing Sammies was recording monthly revenues over rmb500,000 and by 2003, the company had recorded positive net income in certain months (see Tables 1 and 2, and Figure 5).

Competition

The economic expansion of the late 1990s dramatically changed dining in Beijing. Private establishments that catered to China's emerging middle class replaced old state-run restaurants. Most traditional meals were under $5 per person. Peking duck and other local specialties were the most popular, but new restaurants opened that offered regional tastes from all around Asia. Additionally, the number of Western-style restaurants targeting tourists, expatriates, and younger, trendy Chinese customers increased.

Sam Goodman viewed all restaurants physically close to Sammies as competitors:

> As far as I'm concerned, everyone in Beijing who orders lunch is a potential customer and every restaurant serving it is a competitor. There are those who stick to the traditional Chinese meal, but who is to say that they will never try Sammies?
>
> I do not want to restrict Sammies to serving just Western businesses or students. We are delivering not only to Western businesses but to traditional Chinese companies as well. While we rely on Western students for our walk-in business, we do have Chinese customers who come to Sammies every day. There are others who only come once in a while. These people go to the Chinese restaurants when they don't come here. So I must think broadly in terms of who my customers are and who my competition is. Of course the Western restaurants like McDonald's, Subway, Schlotzskys, and Starbucks are the most obvious competitors. Competition in this business is day-to-day as people rarely eat lunch at the same location each afternoon.

Like most major cities, Beijing had an array of restaurant choices ranging from traditional Chinese to Mexican, German, Scandinavian, Italian, Swiss, and English Continental.

The Great Wall of China

As Beijing Sammies adapted to the competitive environment, Goodman increasingly turned to the delivery business for revenue. But the model did not work as planned, due to the lack of experience Goodman had in delivery logistics. Corporate clients were more demanding and lunch delivery complicated. Goodman states,

> We started out delivering from a central source. At first, things did not go as planned. Quite frankly, I was an inexperienced manager and made quite a few mistakes. The delivery model here in China is very different from the West. Clients have no understanding of what

goes on behind the scenes, and they do not understand that it is nearly impossible for us to take a large delivery order for a corporate luncheon and bring it to them ten minutes later. I didn't plan for all of the possible problems that a different culture would bring. I should have put more effort and time into educating the customer about the product. This definitely had a negative impact on the business at first.

In addition to overcoming the existing perceptions and expectations of the customer, Goodman learned about the prevailing attitude of the employees. One of his biggest challenges was not securing the hard-to-come-by ingredients, dealing with the local government, or raising capital, but rather teaching his employees the concept of service. For many of Beijing Sammies' employees, service was little more than opening the store in the morning and closing it at night. To Goodman, service was much more. It was what he believed would differentiate Beijing Sammies from the other Western food establishments, and what would cause the traditional Chinese consumer to pay more money for lunch. Service was not only delivering the product on time, with the correct number of forks and knives, but was also helping the customer to understand the product.

According to Goodman,

> For most of my employees it doesn't matter "how" you get things done—it just matters that you get the end result. The concept of face for them manifests itself with the feeling that appearance is much more important than the service or quality of the product. While for the customer, the service provided by us is part of the final product.

Just as the client base did not understand the wait for a delivery, the employees did not understand the product that Beijing Sammies was trying to sell:

> The staff does not understand the urgency needed in running a service-oriented business. The whole concept of service is new in China. The business traditions are very strong here. I don't know if it's because of the issue of face and pride, the political history, or something else, but our employees have a very difficult time understanding how we need to deliver service as much as we need to deliver a sandwich.

For Sam Goodman, the initial years of operations proved that Beijing Sammies could hold a niche. While he was pleased to see Beijing Sammies growing toward profitability, he was concerned about whether it could ever become cash-flow positive, and if so, whether he could sustain it. In addition, Goodman was no closer to finding the type of employee who would adopt his concept of service than he was when he started, and he wondered if the answer lay in increased automation, training, or somewhere else.

Note

1. Conversion rate was rmb8.3 = $1.

❖ Table 1 Beijing Sammies' Income Statement for 2002 (in Chinese renminbi)

Beijing Sammies	Kitchen Office	Kitchen Production	Kitchen Delivery	Kitchen Café	By Café	SA Café	CR Café	EB Café	2002YTD RMB	2002YTD USD
										0.120479942 Conversion factor
Revenue			2,007,921.19		1,562,707.90	2,413,590.26	253,667.83	308.161.39	6,546,048.56	788,667.55
Cost of Goods Sold	17,886.73		641,106.51		458,643.00	660,387.10	85,284.58	116,182.07	1,979,489.98	238,488.84
Gross Profit	−17,886.73		1,366,814.68		1,104,064.90	1,753,203.15	168,383.25	191,979.32	4,566,558.58	550,178.71
Gross Margin			68.07%		70.65%	72.64%	66.38%	62.30%	69.76%	69.76%
Taxes	8,983.00		99,884.24		26,129.18	126,258.34	8,716.06	15,408.20	285,379.02	34,382.45
Salary	583,260.12	308,911.56	267,225.53		295,125.60	280,945.80	43,670.25	90,302.94	1,869,441.80	225,230.24
Insurance	57,067.01	24,131.97			12,160.29	6,641.12	2,151.96	0.00	102,152.34	12,307.31
Rent Related	185,246.10	102,917.10	82,331.60	41,165.80	104,000.00	585,000.00	28,199.80	85,322.84	1,214,183.23	146,284.73
Utilities	38,075.39	41,237.04	22,891.23	2,531.10	45,492.79	7,103.90	7,587.91	6,598.31	171,517.66	20,664.44
Office Expenses	131,989.31	445.38	5,750.55		4,298.84	14,296.32	3,451.76	17,737.90	177,970.07	21,441.82
Marketing/Advertising	29,687.74		25,129.00		18,306.60	41,151.07	17,203.88	43,155.50	174,633.78	21,039.87
Transportation	37,798.57	256.75	20,545.85		4,286.23	743.60	0.00	237.90	63,868.90	7,694.92
Maintenance	68,965.65	6,357.00	1,560.00		12,139.01	21,128.90	1,843.40	1,625.00	113,618.96	13,688.81
Entertainment	16,660.54	1,033.50	2,388.10		6,477.25	1,123.20	0.00	789.10	28,471.69	3,430.27
Law & Other Expenses	47,623.29					0.00	0.00	0.00	47,623.29	5,737.65
Bank Charges	−91.60					−103.48	7.15	39.00	−148.93	−17.94
Others	1,238.08	5,987.22	10,414.69		6,236.88	4,112.19	250.76	43.63	28,283.44	3,407.59
HR	8,580.00						0.00	0.00	8,580.00	1,033.72
Legal/Gov't Charge	33,566.00					533.00	0.00	0.00	34,099.00	4,108.25
Low Cost and Short-Lived Articles	14,581.58	21,594.56	4,869.28		5,411.90	2,859.58	0.00	13,277.94	62,594.84	7,541.42
CK Service Fee	−327,302.43		100,396.06		78,135.40	120,679.51	12,683.40	15,408.07		
Total Expenses	935,928.34	512,872.07	643,386,13	43,696.90	618,199.96	1,212,473.04	125,766.30	289,946.32	4,382,269.07	527,975.52
Gross Income	−953,815.07	−512,872.07	723,428.55	−43,696.90	485,864.94	540,730.11	42,616.95	97,967.00	184,289.51	22.203.19
Amortization Pre-Operating Costs	154,683.52							15.468.34	154,683.36	18,636.24
Amortization Renovations	71,500.00							16,300.87	92,852.02	11,186.81
Depreciation Expense	49,392.72	144,283.10	2,296.71		16,088.84	10,502.70	11,881.35	24,125.41	241,254.13	29,066.28
Total	275,576.24	144,283.10	2,296.71	0.00	16,088.84	10,502.70	11,881.35	55,89462	488,789.51	58,889.33
Net Income	-1,229,391.31	-657,155.17	721,131.84	−43,696.90	459,776.10	530,227.41	30,735,60	−153,861.62	−304,500.00	−36,686.14

Beijing Sammies	Jan 02	Feb 02	Mar 02	Apr 02	May 02	Jun 02	Jul 02	Aug 02	Sep 02	Oct 02	2002YTD	
											RMB	US$
												0.120479942 Conversion factor
Revenues	474,490.19	340,345.07	633,584.38	636,305.41	714,801.13	768,954.55	819,787.15	743,912.26	659,126.31	754,742.12	6,546,048.56	788,667.55
Cost of goods sold	116,310.43	112,891.03	209,662.56	221,218.57	185,420.17	221,374.62	271,224.40	216,298.58	210,682.54	214,407.10	1,979,489.98	238,488.84
Gross profit	358,179.76	227,454.05	423,921.82	415,086.84	529,380.96	547,579.93	548,562.76	527,613.68	448,443.78	540,335.02	4,566,558.58	550,178.71
Gross margin	75.49%	66.83%	66.91%	65.23%	74.06%	71.21%	66.92%	70.92%	68.04%	71.59%	69.76%	69.76%
Taxes	21,449.26	15,003.20	21,514.52	21,744.06	31,754.91	24,373.65	42,118.17	32,275.32	25,169.18	49,976.76	285,379.02	34,382.45
Salary	195,127.49	200,044.95	179,709.69	197,527.25	172,055.86	208,886.93	151,037.11	172,597.30	181,573.80	210,881.44	1,869,441.80	225,230.24
Insurance	9,027.64	8,697.01	10,910.74	10,991.92	7,642.39	10,484.72	12,577.94	10,606.44	10,606.44	10,607.09	102,152.34	12,307.31
Rent related	118,045.59	118,045.53	118,045.66	118,045.92	118,046.11	112,665.80	99,665.80	124,581.20	142,870.82	144,170.82	1,214,183.23	146,284.73
Utilities	14,993.68	20,974.36	13,872.64	13,989.55	14,436.11	18,413.58	16,504.80	14,210.99	19,398.47	24,723.49	171,517.66	20,664.44
Office expenses	7,002.19	9,775.81	10,184.63	15,715.78	23,112.66	15,346.73	21,650.58	29,671.43	33,736.55	11,773.71	177,970.07	21,441.82
Marketing/advertising	2,080.00	8,476.00	5,473.00	7,670.00	17,500.60	24,986.00	23,403.09	33,382.75	24,166.45	27,495.88	174,633.78	21,039.87
Transportation	3,458.00	1,738.10	4,951.70	3,695.64	4,497.74	11,303.50	5,270.98	18,112.15	5,557.37	5,283.72	63,868.90	7,694.92
Maintenance	7,800.00	5,281.25	309.40	4,564.30	6,630.00	38,958.40	26,887.90	9,034.61	7,272.20	6,880.90	113,618.96	13,688.81
Entertainment	3,216.20	6,073.60	3,313.70	2,471.30	852.80	4,378.14	546.00	461.50	4,406.35	2,752.10	28,471.69	3,430.27
Law and other expenses	1,798.33	1,798.33	6,998.33	1,798.33	14,798.33	1,798.33	8,038.33	6,998.33	1,798.33	1,798.33	47,623.29	5,737.65
Bank charges	104.00	78.00	−379.54	−13.17	163.15	−425.63	176.80	117.00	9.36	21.10	−148.93	−17.94
Other	845.00	234.00	7,179.64	4,312.10	3,208.14	3,867.12	3,867.12	3,606.10	1,757.47	3,273.87	28,283.44	3,407.59
Hr	650.00	975.00	4,615.00	975.00	1,365.00	8,580.00	0.00	0.00	0.00	1,365.00	8,580.00	1,033.72
Legal/gov't charge	1,950.00	1,950.00	16,016.00	1,950.00	1,950.00	2,483.00	1,950.00	1,950.00	1,950.00	1,950.00	34,099.00	4,108.25
Low cost and short-lived articles	2,171.00	1,295.84	3,055.00	10,031.27	10,522.07	5,995.31	3,622.32	20,954.62	3,919.89	1,027.00	62,594.32	7,541.36
Total expenses	389,718.38	400,440.96	405,770.11	414,494.24	424,937.72	482,856.60	417,316.94	478,559.73	464,192.68	503,981.21	4,382,268.55	527,975.46
Gross income	−31,538.62	−172,986.92	18,151.72	592.60	104,443.24	64,723.33	131,245.82	49,053.95	−15,748.90	36,353.81	184,290.03	22,203.25
Amortization preoperating costs	15,468.34	15,468.34	15,468.34	15,468.34	15,468.34	15,468.34	15,468.34	15,468.34	15,468.34	15,468.34	154,683.36	18,636.24
Amortization renovations	7,150.00	7,150.00	7,150.00	7,150.00	7,150.00	7,150.00	7,150.00	16,300.87	13,250.58	13,250.58	92,852.02	11,186.81
Depreciation expense	24,125.41	24,125.41	24,125.41	24,125.41	24,125.41	24,125.41	24,125.41	24,125.41	24,125.41	24,125.41	241,254.13	29,066.28
Total	46,743.75	46,743.75	46,743.75	46,743.75	46,743.75	46,743.75	46,743.75	55,894.62	52,844.32	52,844.32	488,789.51	58,889.33
Net income	−78,282.37	−219,730.67	−28,592.03	−46,151.14	57,699.49	17,979.58	84,502.07	−6,840.67	−68,593.23	−16,490.51	−304,499.48	−36,686.08
Cumulative net income	−78,282.37	−298,013.04	−326,605.07	−372,756.22	−315,056.73	−297,077.14	−212,575.08	−219,415.74	−288,008.97	−304,499.48		

❖ Table 2 Beijing Sammies' Income Compared for 2001 and 2002 (in Chinese renminbi)

	Jan	Feb	Mar	Apr	May	Jun	Jul	Aug	Sep	Oct	Nov	Dec	Total	Average	%	Total USD	Average USD
																0.12048 conversion factor	
Revenues-Total																	
2002	474,490	340,345	633,584	636,305	714,801	768,955	819,787	743,912	659,126	754,742	0	0	6,546,049	654,605	32.94%	788,668	78,867
2001	195,360	221,729	273,194	322,826	360,585	487,627	485,567	479,232	495,706	501,579	565,923	534,743	4,924,071	410,339		593,252	49,438
Revenues-CD																	
2002	125,663	101,290	209,557	173,213	226,170	269,890	360,783	338,797	92,303	110,257	0	0	2,007,923	200,792	12.52%	241,914	24,191
2001	118,331	167,267	157,382	190,320	164,654	161,971	153,994	142,709	138,926	111,007	146,241	131,628	1,784,429	148,702		214,988	17,916
Revenues-BY																	
2002	150,800	55,375	173,870	202,190	213,181	245,040	86,393	20,944	191,542	223,374	0	0	1,562,708	156,271	1.18%	188,275	18,827
2001	77,029	54,462	115,812	132,506	122,457	161,166	130,244	112,095	136,210	155,964	173,991	172,487	1,544,423	128,702		186,072	15,506
Revenues-SA																	
2002	171,306	166,733	221,391	231,774	255,840	229,739	286,696	260,326	273,640	316,147	0	0	2,413,592	241,359	66.65%	290,789	29,079
2001	0	0	0	0	73,473	164,492	172,101	197,597	197,532	216,702	221,035	205,347	1,448,279	193,104		174,489	23,265
Revenues-CR																	
2002	26,722	16,949	28,768	29,128	19,612	24,287	28,860	26,354	27,414	25,579	0	0	253,672	25,367	72.63%	30,562	3,056
2001	0	0	0	0	0	0	29,229	26,832	23,036	17,908	24,656	25,284	146,944	24,491		17,704	2,951
Gross Profit																	
2002	358,180	227,454	423,922	415,087	529,381	547,580	548,563	527,614	448,444	540,335	0	0	4,566,559	456,656	33.45%	550,179	55,018
2001	136,161	155,046	181,279	216,507	243,420	334,135	340,288	353,393	340,074	360,762	406,459	354,387	3,421,909	285,159		412,271	34,356
Total Expenses																	
2002	389,718	400,442	405,770	414,495	424,938	482,856	415,874	478,560	439,563	503,981	0	0	4,356,196	435,620	25.44%	524,834	52,483
2001	199,170	212,702	203,262	204,741	292,468	293,136	271,625	318,711	367,199	358,769	367,961	383,097	3,472,840	289,403		418,408	34,867
Salary																	
2002	195,127	200,045	179,710	197,527	172,056	208,887	151,037	172,597	181,574	210,881	0	0	1,869,442	186,944	5.67%	225,230	22,523
2001	130,803	135,100	123,547	123,572	136,526	141,993	143,111	165,208	161,795	163,081	169,485	174,984	1,769,204	147,434		213,154	17,763

	Jan	Feb	Mar	Apr	May	Jun	Jul	Aug	Sep	Oct	Nov	Dec	Total	Average	%	Total USD	Average USD
																0.12048 conversion factor	
Rent Related																	
2002	118,046	118,046	118,046	118,046	118,046	112,666	99,666	124,581	142,871	144,171	0	0	1,214,183	121,418	28.69%	146,285	14,628
2001	36,833	36,833	36,833	36,833	93,180	93,180	71,500	71,500	112,666	118,045	118,048	118,047	943,497	78,625		113,672	9,473
Insurance																	
2002	9,028	8,697	10,911	10,992	7,642	10,485	12,578	10,606	10,606	10,507	0	0	102,152	10,215	174.55%	12,307	1,231
2001	0	0	0	260	0	3,894	5,203	6,003	4,694	6,516	5,049	5,589	37,207	3,101		4,483	374
Utilities																	
2002	14,994	20,974	13,873	13,990	14,436	18,414	16,505	14,211	19,398	24,723	0	0	171,518	17,152	−0.10%	20,664	2,066
2001	11,239	13,459	7,232	8,932	11,063	11,041	13,607	16,717	24,505	18,764	17,195	17,936	171,690	14,307		20,685	1,724
Office Expenses																	
2002	7,002	9,776	10,185	15,716	23,113	15,347	21,651	29,671	33,737	11,774	0	0	177,970	17,797	63.35%	21,442	2,144
2001	5,437	4,486	5,652	7,899	9,877	9,994	8,281	12,463	9,611	10,245	10,773	14,229	108,948	9,079		13,126	1,094
Marketing/Advertising																	
2002	2,080	8,476	5,473	7,670	17,501	24,986	23,403	33,383	24,166	27,496	0	0	174,634	17,463	42.87%	21,040	2,104
2001	1,950	7,150	2,842	3,900	19,682	17,508	6,838	14,598	9,460	9,494	17,076	11,736	122,234	10,186		14,727	1,227
Transportation																	
2002	3,458	1,738	4,952	3,696	4,498	11,304	5,271	18,112	5,557	5,284	0	0	63,869	6,387	149.15%	7,695	769
2001	1,158	1,131	2,298	2,662	2,989	1,219	2,428	2,522	2,510	2,626	1,651	2,439	25,635	2,136		3,088	257
Maintenance																	
2002	7,800	5,281	309	4,564	6,630	38,958	26,888	9,035	7,272	6,881	0	0	113,619	11,362	588.67%	13,689	1,369
2001	735	371	3,785	1,707	98	1,110	1,365	1,754	1,252	1,273	681	2,366	16,498	1,375		1,988	166
Entertainment																	
2002	3,216	6,074	3,314	2,471	853	4,378	546	462	4,406	2,752	0	0	28,472	2,847	−13.33%	3,430	343
2001	0	520	4,976	5,881	2,896	0	1,123	255	12,332	372	759	3,738	32,852	2,738		3,958	330
Law & Other Expenses																	
2002	3,748	3,748	23,014	3,748	16,748	4,281	9,988	8,948	3,748	3,748	0	0	81,718	8,172	123.09%	9,845	985
2001	3,613	6,500	6,500	2,665	3,848	0	867	4,767	6,136	867	867	0	36,630	3,053		4,413	368
Taxes																	
2002	21,384	15,003	21,515	21,744	31,755	24,374	42,119	32,275	25,169	49,977	0	0	285,315	28,531	83.43%	34,375	3,437
2001	6,871	5,950	8,639	8,813	6,360	6,163	13,657	15,219	16,592	25,346	16,892	25,046	155,546	12,962		18,740	1,562

❖ Figure 5 Beijing Sammies' income chart for 2001 and 2002 (in Chinese renminbi).

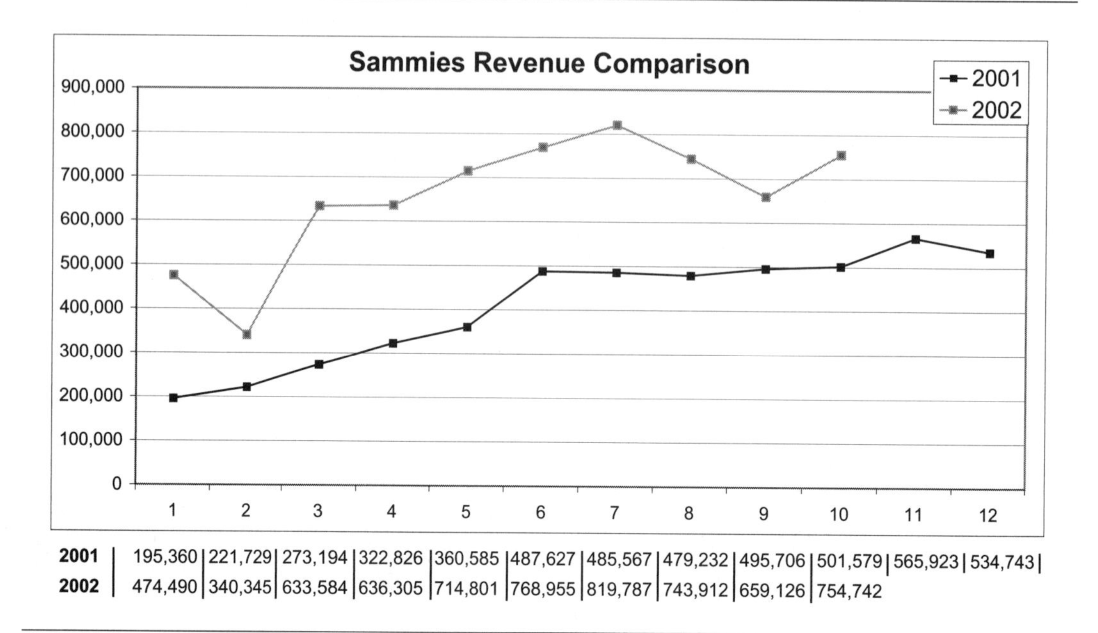

Case Questions

1. Describe the nature of the industry in terms of size and characteristics.
2. What are the critical factors for success in this industry?
3. To date, how is Beijing Sammies doing?
4. Discuss the skills and attributes of Sam Goodman. Discuss the skills that he needs. Why do you think he is having a difficult time hiring employees that can perform up to his expectations?
5. Discuss the aspects of doing business in China that may be different from doing business in the European Union or the United States.
6. Discuss the value propositions of Beijing Sammies. What are the company's unique selling propositions?
7. Analyze the financial performance and results of all aspects of the company. Where can significant improvements be made?
8. If being sold, determine the value of the company today.
9. What are Sam Goodman's next steps in terms of building and funding his business?

Case 2

Federal Express

Leo Dana

Federal Express, or FedEx, came to China in 1984, and since then China has become a major hub in the company's growing international operations. The FedEx strategy in China is simple—have a vibrant business in Asia's largest economy. The company's first direct flight from Southern China to North America with next-day service launched in 2003, and in 2005 it launched flights to Europe from China. FedEx now serves more than 200 Chinese cities, with plans to add 100 additional cities over the next few years. Today, China is growing exponentially and one of FedEx's greatest challenges will be to maintain the capacity to keep up with this growth.

Industry Background[1]

Before the U.S. airfreight industry developed, all that existed was the U.S. airmail system. All air transport of packages occurred by means of the U.S. Postal Service. Time-sensitive shipments were not possible because airfreight was not transported on its own planes; rather, package delivery and transport depended on the scheduled service of passenger airlines.

In 1977, the U.S. government deregulated the airfreight industry and the industry changed dramatically. Airfreight companies were able to acquire their own aircraft to create a privatized industry for the express air delivery service. Large-scale overnight deliveries soon became the heart of the airfreight industry. This system, commonly called the hub-and-spoke system, is characterized by all packages being shipped to a central distribution center then resorted and distributed to their destinations across the country. This system was started by FedEx and is still the method used by most airfreight firms today.

Many overnight airfreight companies joined the industry in the 1980s. But by 1999, only five companies dominated the industry: the U.S. Postal Service, Federal Express, United Parcel Service (UPS), DHL Worldwide Express, and Airborne Express.

Source: Used by permission from Leo Dana.

Express deliveries accounted for most of the growth in the airfreight industry. Air express deliveries made up 60% of air shipments in 1998, with overnight letters and envelopes claiming 27% of both shipments and revenues for the industry.

As the airfreight industry matured, companies integrated their services and refined their offerings. They guaranteed morning and afternoon deliveries, set higher weight limits, and expanded tracking and automated billing services. According to the Colography Group, an Atlanta-based research firm specializing in the airfreight and air express industries, there were 2.8 billion domestic air shipments made in 1998. The U.S. Postal Service (USPS) moved 1.3 billion express and priority mail parcels and represented 45% of the domestic market. In late 1999, the USPS announced an affiliation with DHL Worldwide for expedited global service to 65 countries.

The Growth of an Entrepreneur

Frederick W. Smith, a Memphis native whose father made his fortune by founding a bus company, conceived the idea to begin an air cargo company while studying at Yale University during the 1960s. He authored a paper describing the concept of a freight-only airline that would fly all packages to one central point, where they would then be distributed and flown out again to their respective destinations. His proposed operations would occur overnight when airports were less crowded, and with the proper logistics, the packages would reach their destination by the next day. Whether it was the novelty of his idea, that his professor was a staunch supporter of the current system of airfreight, or that it was written in one night and turned in late, the first presentation of Smith's grand idea earned him a solid C.

Smith's idea was about more than a creative term paper, however. He had seen how the technological base of the country was changing. More companies were becoming involved in the production of mass-produced technology, such as computers, and Smith was convinced that his air cargo plan would help control their inventory costs. Overnight delivery from a single distribution center to anywhere in the United States could satisfy customers' needs without a company needing to duplicate investment in inventory to be stored in regional warehouses. Smith even considered the Federal Reserve Banks a potential customer, with the vast quantities of checks that had to be shipped to all parts of the country every day.

The key to Fred Smith's company would be its ability to service a large segment of the business community from the very beginning, and the key to launching such a service was cash. Smith went to Chicago and New York, confident that he would return with the funds necessary to start his venture. Progress turned out to be slower than he anticipated, but he was relentless and through his technical knowledge of the airfreight industry he was finally able to find an enthusiastic backer in New Court Securities. This Manhattan-based, Rothschild-backed venture-capital investment bank contributed around US$5 million in capital to his start-up. New Court's support encouraged others to jump on Fred Smith's bandwagon. Five other institutions, including General Dynamics and Citicorp Venture Capital, Ltd., decided to commit funds. Smith eventually returned to Memphis with US$72 million. This was the largest venture-capital start-up deal in American business history.

FedEx's Capabilities

FedEx began its operations in April 1973, at which time it introduced a fully integrated door-to-door overnight delivery, small-package express service. The firm introduced the hub-and-spoke system of route structures, which was later adopted by passenger airlines. Federal Express carried computer components and later documents and packages. Until 1977, Federal Express used a fleet of Falcon 20 twinjets. Then, the Cargo Reform Act allowed the firm to purchase larger jets.

During the 1980s, Smith decided to take his company global and Federal Express expanded to Europe. In 1988, financier Saul Steinberg (who owned 16.5% of Tiger International) approached Federal Express and offered to sell Tiger International's Flying Tigers cargo airlines. At the time, Federal Express served only five airports outside the United States: Brussels, London, Montreal, Tokyo, and Toronto.

In 1989, Smith's Federal Express paid US$895 million for Tiger International. The acquisition of Flying Tigers led to increased advertising by Federal Express. The acquisition was trumpeted as a purchase of both capital and international knowledge and global experience:

> By joining forces with Flying Tigers, we not only acquired 40 years' worth of international shipping experience, we also created the world's largest full-service cargo airline, Federal Express—The Best Way to Ship It Over There. (Federal Express advertisement, 1990)

The Federal Express corporation subsequently acquired other firms in Australia, Canada, France, and Mexico. Smith defined the business as time-definite transportation and distribution throughout the world.

In 1992, Federal Express received publicity when Cessna ran an ad about Federal Express's use of a big, tough, and reliable aircraft—the Cessna Grand Caravan. This type of airplane can haul 340 cubic feet of cargo up to 1,000 nautical miles at speeds of up to 180 knots. With an optional cargo pool, the Caravan's capacity is increased to 451 cubic feet (Cessna Aircraft Company, n.d.). Federal Express reportedly had over 200 Cessna Grand Caravans. Yet that same year, Federal Express reported its first loss of US$147 million. Experts suggested that this was a result of growing too fast. Nevertheless, by 1993 Federal Express had expanded operations to 180 countries, up from 127 in 1992. A new corporate image was established in 1994 with an abbreviated company name—FedEx. The carrier continued to grow as an industry leader, but international competition was significant and included the following:

- *DHL Worldwide Express:* Unlike other U.S.-based express firms, DHL started with a very international outlook, working with maritime shippers along the Pacific Rim. DHL expanded by chartering flights and subcontracting to other firms. In addition, it developed its own route network with a hub in Cincinnati.
- *Emery Worldwide:* In contrast to other firms that focused on documents or the small-package market, Emery's primary target market was identified as the business-to-business commercial shipper. In 1989, Emery Worldwide was acquired by Consolidated Freightways (CF), and its operations merged with those of CF AirFreight. In 1991,

Emery President W. Roger Curry oversaw a major restructuring. The firm opted to move away from envelope services, and this enabled it to downsize its personnel by 2,000 employees and to reduce its ground fleet by 1,800 vehicles.

- *TNT Express Worldwide:* The Australian firm TNT is a provider of worldwide door-to-door express service, with world headquarters in Amsterdam. TNT also has a U.S. head office, led by David Siegfried in Miami Lakes, Florida. TNT operates direct all-cargo flights between Europe and the United States as well as between the United States and the Pacific Rim, including Australia and Southeast Asia. The firm specializes in same-day service. Its fleet includes Boeing 727 trijets and four-engine BAe 146 jets.
- *United Parcel Service of America, Inc. (UPS):* Based in Louisville, Kentucky, UPS owns and operates the world's largest privately owned package distribution and courier system. The firm launched its air service in 1953. Yet for its first couple of decades, it owned no aircraft. Instead, it leased space in commercial aircraft. In 1981, it bought its first airplanes, a fleet of seven Boeing 727s, operated by a contractor. In 1990, UPS revenues reached US$13.6 billion. This was more than the entire express industry earned in 1987. By 1992, UPS had ordered 162 aircraft. In addition, it used 259 more on a charter basis. Today, more than 335,000 employees operate 2,400 UPS facilities, more than 132,000 vehicles, and more than 500 dedicated aircraft. The firm's 1,500 daily flights serve over 600 airports in about 200 countries. UPS has an US$800-million aircraft hub and package sorting facility at Louisville International Airport. It is designed to service 100 airplanes and sort 300,000 packages per hour. UPS created the following worldwide services: (1) UPS SonicAir, a fast service available 24 hours daily; (2) UPS Worldwide Expedited, a low-cost, door-to-door service taking up to 5 days, and (3) UPS Worldwide Express, guaranteed rush service for urgent deliveries, often overnight. Yet modest quarterly earnings were offset by the growth of international business operations. With a regional office in Singapore, UPS has Asian gateway operations at several airports, including Hong Kong, Taipei, Tokyo, Singapore, and Seoul. UPS provides a daily average of 50 regional flights, serving all the major countries in Asia.

Federal Express obtained permission to launch its freight operations in China in 1995 through an acquisition from Evergreen International Airlines. Under this authority, Federal Express is the sole U.S.-based, all-cargo carrier with aviation rights to the world's most heavily populated nation. Today, FedEx has the world's largest airfreight fleet, including McDonnell-Douglass MD-11s, and Airbus A-300s and A-310s. The planes have a total daily lift capacity of more than 26.5 million pounds. In a 24-hour period, the fleet travels nearly 500,000 miles while its couriers log 2.5 million miles a day—the equivalent of 100 trips around the earth. Today, FedEx delivers to more than 210 countries ("FedEx History," n.d.).

China Market Information

In 2004, the European Union (EU) became China's top trading partner. China's exports during this same year to the EU grew at a faster rate than China's overall export growth. China's trade with the United States continues to be strong, and the United States is the number one single-nation trading partner with Asia's largest economy. In 2006, China traded US$262.7 billion with the United States, up 24.2% from 2005. China's trade with its other top-10 trading partners also increased significantly during those years. Japan–China trade increased 12.5%, Hong Kong–greater China trade increased 21.6%, and South Korea–China trade grew 20%. In Europe, Germany's trade with China grew by 23.6%, putting it in the fifth position of China's top trade partners for 2006.

Federal Express continues its growth and high performance today with a 13% increase in revenues to $39 billion in 2011, a 22% increase in earnings per share, and a 23% increase in net earnings year over year. The company remains the industry leader providing delivery service to more than 220 countries and territories. FedEx continues to achieve significant growth in Brazil, China, and India,

Toward the Future

FedEx China's headquarters are in Shanghai, and from here the company serves more than 220 countries and territories. Within China, FedEx delivers to more than 200 cities and employs more than 6,000 people. The company has hubs in three airports: Capital Airport in Beijing, Pudong Airport in Shanghai, and Bao'an Airport in Shenzhen. MD-11 and A-310 aircraft make 26 flights a week to and from Beijing, Shanghai, and Shenzhen. Despite covering more than 200 cities within China, FedEx had only 100 drop-off locations domestically as of 2008.

FedEx has built its business on the basis of moving fast with new technology and providing impeccable service. In March 2007, it completed a US$400-million acquisition of its Chinese partner firm and now has full authority over the brand's actions in the country ("FedEx Takes Full Control," 2007). As FedEx continues to extend its corporate strategy to include the relatively new focal point, China, how can it expand its operations? How should it monitor and plan its growth in China, a country with a centrally controlled economy? Can FedEx maintain the capacity to keep up with China's growth?

Note

1. Information for this section was compiled from Allbusiness.com (www.allbusiness.com/transportation-by-air/air-transportation-scheduled/3779842-3.html).

Case Questions

1. In April 2008, Delta Airlines announced its intention to merge with and absorb Northwest Airlines, formerly known as Northwest Orient. Delta Airlines had already grown through the acquisition of Northeast in 1972 and Western Airlines in 1986. Northwest was also a large airline, having absorbed Republic Airlines, itself a merger of North Central Airlines, Southern, and later Hughes Airwest. Republic had an important hub in Memphis, as did Federal Express. The result would be a global airline with hubs in Asia and Europe as well as across the United States. Will an enlarged Delta Airlines be a threat for FedEx?
2. How can FedEx maintain the capacity to keep up with China's growth?
3. What risk does FedEx encounter when subcontracting?

4. In 2008, crude oil cost more than US$100 per barrel and this was reflected in the price of jet fuel at the pump. Why might this be of concern to FedEx?

5. How might a devalued American dollar hurt FedEx?

References

FedEx advertisement. (1990, May). *Air Cargo World, 5,* 14–15.

FedEx history. (n.d.). Retrieved from http://fedex.com/us/about/today/history/

FedEx takes full control in fast-growing China. (2007, March 2). *Commercial Appeal.* Retrieved from http://m.commercialappeal.com/news/2007/mar/02/

Case 3

Fitz-Ritter Wine Estate

225 Years of Tradition and Entrepreneurship

Lambert T. Koch, Marco Biele, and Sean Patrick Sassmannshausen[1]

The Fitz-Ritter Wine Estate was founded in 1785. In 1837, the estate broadened to include champagne production facilities. Today the young owner, Johann Fitz, is the managing director of both companies, the ninth generation of his family to lead the business.

German wine producers have been facing global challenges for several years. This case shows how an entrepreneurial spirit through generations of leadership has contributed to the survival of a vineyard. It also shows how a medium-sized business can cope with global challenges if it commits itself to take advantage of international opportunities. In this complex environment, Johann Fitz has to make decisions concerning strategic positioning, customer relations, distribution channels, new business segments, investments, and how to manage the international business.

Introduction

Johann Fitz opens the door to his office on a Monday morning, holding the first bottle of a brand new product in his hands. The combination of premium sparkling wine and passion fruit will be the new FitzSecco passion fruit, a variant for the younger generation of wine drinkers. Johann is excited and rushes to the phone to call Alice, his mother, who has been responsible for the estate's marketing and exports for the last two decades. Impatiently,

SOURCE: Used by permission from Lambert Koch, Marco Biele, and Sean Patrick Sassmannshausen.

he dials her number. While he is waiting, he looks at his watch. He wonders why his mother does not answer the phone; it is only her voice mail. Johann opens his e-mail, searching for correspondence from his mother: "August 25—New York wine exhibition; August 27—Chicago; August 29—Detroit." New York City is 7 hours behind; no wonder she is not answering the phone. He peruses the attached spreadsheet with the latest figures of Fitz-Ritter's exports. Johann is calculating some key figures, unsure how to continue with the export business. Should he, as the new head of the company, expand foreign businesses or should he concentrate on domestic projects? Things are changing more rapidly on the domestic market, while the export market requires great attention and expenses, but achieves relatively smaller sales volumes. The doorbell rings. Johann switches off his laptop. With a number of construction plans stacked under his arm, he prepares to meet two men from the local monument protection office, guiding them into the historical cross-vault cow barn. "I will call her later," he is thinking, "now it is time for my next project."

Johann Fitz is part of the ninth generation of his family at Fitz-Ritter Wine Estate, succeeding his father Konrad Fitz, who ran the family business for 37 years. The young vintner inherited his passion for wine from his parents. At first, this passion remained unknown to him; his interests lay in other areas. Only weeks ago, however, he took over the lead of the Fitz-Ritter Wine Estate, right after completion of his studies in economics at the University of California, Berkeley. The wine estate, founded in 1785, is located on the fringes of Bad Dürkheim, a wine-growing spa town at the edge of the Rhine Plain in southwestern Germany (see Figure 1). Famous for its high-quality white wine, it is one of the largest wine estates in the area. Its 22 hectares (approximately 52 acres) are situated in the largest German wine-growing region, the "Pfalz" (Palatinate).

Johann is a new type of vintner, combining respect for the traditional family business with an entrepreneurial spirit. In the last 20 years, the German wine market has changed immensely. Globalization had a tremendous effect on the European wine industry. Conservative strategies and antiquated structures prevented German wine estates from achieving global competitive positions. A few years ago, however, a young generation of vintners entered leading positions at an increasing number of wine estates, determined not to be smothered with so-called "protective state intervention," but to face competition and react successfully to market forces. "Being a young German vintner is not just an occupation, it is a movement. These days, it is not just about age, it needs a certain entrepreneurial mind-set to be a young German vintner," claims Johann Fitz.

In the summer of 2006, Johann inherited a renowned family business, well-known for producing more than just quality wine. Growing the first Chardonnay ever in Germany and launching a small museum and boutique wine store, Alice and Konrad Fitz were always ahead of their local competitors in terms of innovative thinking and entrepreneurial spirit. "The production of premium wine and champagne needs passion," says Konrad Fitz. "Unfortunately, some German vintners lost track some decades ago, trying to compete with New World wine estates in mass production. Thereby, the decreasing quality of some German wines, combined with high production costs, almost ruined the international standing of German wine and many wine estates."

❖ Figure 1 Antique engraving of the estate's building and grounds.

SOURCE: Johann Fitz.

The Fitz-Ritter Wine Estate: A Family Business Since 1785

Johann Fitz, a merchant who decided to make a change and start something new, founded the Fitz-Ritter Wine Estate in 1785. The vineyard is located at the famous *Deutsche Weinstraße* (German Wine Street), which crosses an area known for its warm, sunny climate and ideal grape-growing conditions. The origins of the Champagne Factory, the family's sparkling wine production facility, in some ways reflect the entrepreneurial spirit that would continue to spur the family and its winery. In 1832, Johann Fitz (the "Red Fitz") spearheaded the German vintners' protestations for the elimination of customs duties on wine exports (see Figure 2). Because of this, and his involvement at the Hambacher Fest (a peaceful demonstration calling for more liberty), he was persecuted by the police of the Bavarian king. The Red Fitz took refuge in France, hiding in the Champagne region where he studied the production of champagne. Later he returned home, accompanied by a cellar master, and together with some members of his family, cofounded one of the first German champagne

❖ Figure 2 The "Red Fitz" cofounded Fitz-Ritter's sparkling wine operation.

SOURCE: Johann Fitz.

producers, the Dürkheim Champagne Factory. It is now the oldest sparkling wine producer in the area and the third oldest in Germany.

In 1842, even though the Red Fitz was still wanted by the political police, the Dürkheim Champagne Factory became the supplier to the royal Bavarian court. As time and tastes changed, it became clear that the king would rather maintain his supply of champagne than imprison a political antagonist, a sign that the Red Fitz was making some quality wines. Thus, traditional wine and champagne production can be traced back more than 225 years. Now, Johann Fitz, several generations removed from the Red Fitz, has taken over from his father Konrad Fitz, and is attempting to lead the company into a new and different age.

The family's entrepreneurial spirit is shown today in its vision and willingness to explore new opportunities to expand its business. On the ground floor of the Fitz-Ritter estate, the family business operates the Bacchus Boutique, a gift shop founded by Alice Fitz, who has been responsible for marketing and export for many years. After Alice married Konrad Fitz, she became familiar with the wine business (see Figure 3). "First I fell in love with Konrad, but soon, I fell in love with the wine business too,"

❖ Figure 3 The Fitz family: Alice, Konrad, and Johann.

SOURCE: Johann Fitz.

she said. Her attempts at contributing something to the business were supported by her earlier studies in business and economics. One of the first actions she took was to launch the Bacchus Boutique, which at the time was a new idea among traditional wine makers and disregarded as foolish by many of them. But later, when it proved to be a success, it was imitated by almost all of them. In line with the boutique gift shop, Alice organizes charity events and classical concerts on the estate site. The company also sponsors art galleries and wine festivals. Alice recalls,

> Even Johann cannot imagine the shape this estate was in when we took it over. In 1970 no one here had ever heard the word marketing. To German vintners, it was absolutely unknown to build a brand by cultural or social endorsement and event marketing. Now, this concept is broadly accepted, but most wine estates are too small to follow our strategy. Nevertheless, most of the bigger estates and cooperatives have created their own brand strategy nowadays, but we still have some first mover advantages because our events had been well established at the time competitors entered.

Along with the boutique and the Fitz-Ritter branding, international expansion was an area in which the winery was leading its German counterparts. Alice began the effort with a focus on the U.S. market because she was American and more familiar with it. According to VDP (*Verband Deutscher Prädikat s-und Qualitaetsweingueter*, the Association of German Prädikat Wine Estates), today's export average is about 20% of the total wine production, with a trend toward increasing growth (VDP, n.d.).

Fitz-Ritter started the export business in the late 1970s. It all happened more or less coincidentally. While Alice's American mother was on vacation in Germany, they began thinking about how to deliver wine into the United States, not for business, but for their own needs. Soon came the idea of expanding, and the export business into the United States was born. A few years later, when Konrad and Alice went to wine exhibitions, importers from Japan, Great Britain, and the Netherlands became interested in Fitz-Ritter wines and started to order. "But everything started more or less with the export into the United States," Alice emphasizes.

The wine is shipped to the United States and unloaded and cleared by an importer, who needs an alcohol license. Moreover, the importer is also responsible for the distribution of the wine. Although Alice travels across the United States to promote the wine at trade fairs, often meeting directly with consumers, she is not allowed to sell directly to them, but rather sells to distributors through the importer due to restrictive import laws in the United States. This system poses great challenges to smaller establishments such as Fitz-Ritter that are trying to enter the market.

The importers and distributors intermediary positions are very important for the export business as a whole. "You rely on the effort and contacts of your importer and your distributors," Konrad Fitz says. Alice adds,

> It has a lot to do with trust, and loyalty is hard to find. It took us years to identify trustworthy importers and distributors in the United States and other markets. It is a time- and money-consuming trial-and-error process. Trust is an emotion in the beginning, and proof only occurs when time passes by. Even if you have found a trustworthy, talented, and ambitious distributor, you still need to do a lot of sales promotion all by yourself. And if you are not present to offer the new vintage, the importer and distributors will forget you very soon. While Fitz-Ritter was obliged to give exclusive rights to one importer, this importer has many German wines in his portfolio. Exclusiveness is part of an adhesion contract: None of the licensed importers will negotiate exclusive contracts, so a family business like Fitz-Ritter only makes up a small portion of the importer's portfolio and thus, only relatively small efforts will be spent on sales promotion. Moreover, in a family business selling products made by good craftsmanship, customers want to know the entrepreneurial family behind the product, so they can judge the product and the reliability of delivery by the people representing the company. Furthermore, the financial stability of the importer you choose is, of course, vital. In the United Kingdom, we trusted one import agent and were absolutely gutted. For this reason, we are not present in the UK market anymore, and we are still looking for a trustworthy importer to take on this market.

Alice has traveled all across the United States to promote her German wines, speaking with distributors and presenting at national and international exhibitions. The Fitz-Ritter Gewurztraminer was especially embraced by Americans because of its semiarid or smooth taste, and the fact that it is full of herbs and flavor with a low amount of alcohol. "While most German exporters focused on the Riesling, soon the Gewurztraminer became our hot seller within the United States, where we positioned ourselves within a niche market," explains Alice. "But our Riesling is demanded, too," Konrad adds. Business in the United States today, however, is getting more challenging because of factors such as the strengthening of the euro as compared to the U.S. dollar, the presence of more competitive wineries on the export scene, and difficult relationships with intermediaries who want their share of the profits, making it hard to sell premium wine. Fitz-Ritter is present in many states, though sales are concentrated in some New

England states, New York City, Michigan, and California. Massachusetts has proven to be one of the toughest U.S. markets to enter. It is costly to penetrate all states with personal sales promotion; one promotional tour costs an average of EUR5,000, and up to five tours are necessary each year. Thus, Alice tries to build personal relationships and loyalty with distributors, who consequently can focus more on increasing volume.

"The business has changed a lot," says Konrad Fitz. Today, the winery has to sell its wine at exhibitions and through more innovative distribution channels. Several decades ago, the winery sold exclusively to commission agents without any direct sales. Commission agents actually traveled from door to door, offering their product portfolio. To their potential customers, usually stay-at-home mothers and wives, they offered the opportunity to taste the wine and learn more about each product before buying any bottles. Thus, the wine distribution business was slow, but it was reliable, and good traders knew their business very well, knowing the high-purchasing customers in their area and their customers' tastes and price ranges, resulting in reasonable sales levels.

Now the door-to-door business model is antiquated. As the population became more urban and mobile, and high crime rates introduced hesitation to opening doors to strangers, door-to-door salesmen were increasingly treated with mistrust and uncertainty. A new distribution model was needed, and Johann Fitz saw this early on: "When I entered the business, I instinctively knew we desperately needed new distribution channels. This is why I started an online shop. There was the risk that retailers would ban us because we decided to introduce direct customer services via the Internet, but thus far all is fine. We notice that online trade is an additional business with a certain set of customers and thus does not harm other distribution channels." (The online shop can be accessed at www.shop.fitz-ritter.de.)

The choice of grape varietals is also something that Johann must seriously focus on (see Figure 4). It requires long-term planning and a willingness to accept a level of risk. As Johann describes it, "If we decided to produce different types of grapes on

❖ **Figure 4** Wine acreage in Bad Dürkheim.

SOURCE: Johann Fitz.

some acres, this would mean that on these acres over a period of at least 3 years, no grapes will be harvested at all. Planting vines is a long-range strategic decision; change needs 3 years at least and bears some risks, and the amortization of the plants takes many years. If your decision is led by trend and fashion, you better make sure that the kind of grape won't be out of fashion again soon."

Vines have a productive life of 60 to 70 years; it takes 3 to 4 years after planting for them to produce their first harvest, 5 to 7 years to achieve full productive capacity, and up to 35 years to produce the best-quality grapes needed for wine. There is a correlation between age of vines and quality. In addition, the vintner can take many actions to increase quality. Most activities are labor intensive and therefore costly. For Fitz-Ritter premium wines, for instance, workers cut off 50% of each bunch of grapes in spring, causing the energy and sugar of the vine to concentrate in the remaining grapes, resulting in much more intense flavor.

Two thirds of Fitz-Ritter's acreage is planted with Riesling grapes. The best spots are the rolling hillsides named Herrenberg, Spielberg, Abtsfronhof, and Michelsberg. Due to their geographic situation and special soil, these hills offer the foundation for premium wine, especially the number one premium class, Grosse Gewaechse (Great Growth), the label for the highest premium wines of the Association of German Prädikat Wine Estates (VDP). Each vine is officially documented by the VDP with the aim to guarantee the highest quality. Quantities are limited and growing and harvesting of grapes, as well as wine production, has to be carried out traditionally by hand, combined with the most modern innovations in sustainable enology for the gentle treatment of grapes and wine during the process. Thus, production remains a craft, not an industrial process, and as a result is more expensive. A wine with its own personal character representing richness and complexity in taste is the reward for vintners, cellar masters, and consumers. Table 1 shows an excerpt of the comprehensive product portfolio of wines that the Fitz-Ritter Wine Estate produces today.

The German Wine Industry and the Global Wine Market

"The Riesling Renaissance" (Lynam, 2001) and "Following hard times, German Rieslings rise again" (Wolkoff, 2006) are news headlines German winemakers are pleased to read. Such headlines restore their pride. After years of difficulty, the German wine industry is hoping that its fortunes are in fact changing, though it must continue to adapt to a shifting competitive environment. Domestic competition is getting tougher, the economic strength of the German people has increased, and foreign wines are now well-known entities with a good cost-to-quality ratio. These factors combine to keep Germany as the number one importer of wine in the world. And though this growing demand should bode well for domestic producers, many things have occurred that make it less than certain that they will be able to capitalize on the opportunity.

German wines, Riesling for example, have a reputation of excellence, but the last 50 years put a "variety of demons" on them (Wolkoff, 2006). In the first two decades after World War II, Germans were drinking German wines, except for a small market segment at the higher end of the price scale, which was occupied by famous French

❖ Table 1 Fitz-Ritter Wine Estate Products and Prices (in Euros)

No.	Wine	Price B2B[a]	Price E to C[b]	No.	Wine	Price B2B[a]	Price E to C[b]
619	2005 Dürkheimer Rittergarten Riesling	2.80	5.60	613	2006 Dürkheimer Blanc de Noir	3.95	7.10
621	2006 Dürkheimer Abtsfronhof Riesling	3.20	6.40	616	2006 Dürkheimer Spielberg Chardonnay	5.15	9.30
624	2006 Riesling Classic	3.20	6.40	425	2004 Dürkheimer Abtsfronhof Gewurztraminer	6.20	10.90
335	2003 Ungsteiner Herrenberg Riesling	7.70	13.50	627	2006 Dürkheimer Abtsfronhof Gewurztraminer	4.60	8.40
536	2005 Michelsberg Dürkheimer Riesling GG[c]	11.45	19.00	339	2003 Dürkheimer Hochbenn Riesling "Ice Wine"	62.00	93.00
533	2005 Kanzel Ungstein Riesling GG[c]	12.05	20.00	938	1999 Dürkheimer Abtsfronhof Riesling Selection	46.00	70.00
511	2005 Dürkheimer Dornfelder red wine	3.30	6.60	645	2006 Cuvée "Red Fitz"	4.10	7.40
612	2006 Pinot Noir	4.30	7.90	415	2004 Cuvée "Revoluzzer"	8.10	14.20
218	2004 Dürkheimer Cabernet Dorsa	9.00	14.90	314	2003 Dürkheimer Pinot Noir	9.90	16.50
416	2004 Dürkheimer Spielberg Chardonnay	9.95	16.50	001	Rittergold "dry" (0.75 liters) sparkling wine	2.85	5.70
A	FitzSecco Blanc	2.60	5.20	003	Riesling "dry" (0.2 liters) sparkling wine	0.90	1.85
B	FitzSecco Rosé	2.60	5.20	003	Riesling Extra Brut (0.75 liters) sparkling wine	4.50	8.10
C	FitzSecco Passion Fruit (0.75 liters)	2.85	5.70	E4	2006 Fitz-Ritter Riesling (1 liter)	2.45	4.90
D	FitzSecco Passion Fruit (0.2 liters)	0.90	1.80	F3	2006 Fitz-Ritter (1 liter) red wine	1.85	4.70

SOURCE: Fitz-Ritter price list (modified).
[a]Business-to-business prices (B2B) modified for classroom calculations only.
[b]E to C: Prices for direct sale from the estate to private customer.
[c]GG = *Gross Gewaechse*, or "Great Growth."

red wines. The giant overseas wine estates were not yet founded or at least not yet recognized. Transportation costs were high, creating a natural barrier to market entry, at least for non-European producers. But over the years, the situation changed. Wine consumption increased, and foreign wine became more and more fashionable; at first Italian wines, then wines from Spain and other European origins. During this time, the so-called New World wine producers (Australia, Chile, New Zealand, South Africa, and the United States) began to learn the skills and grow the grapes necessary to compete in the global market. Decreasing transportation and production costs, combined with an increase in quality, made it possible for them to enter and aggressively compete in the European market. The market entry coincided with fierce price competition among German discounters and supermarket chains, such as ALDI, LIDL, Metro Group, and Tengelmann Group.

To succeed, discounters search for a cheap supply of a good and stable-quality wine. Therefore, the ideal wine for these retailers is a generic, medium-quality one that can be produced in quantities great enough to satisfy growing demand. New World wine producers have been able to match these criteria. Moreover, they are able to differentiate themselves by marketing the exotic origins of their wines, places like South Australia, Napa Valley, Chile, New Zealand, and South Africa—regions that have become as fashionable as Italy, France, or Spain.

For a long time, the European producers, particularly the French, Spanish, and German vintners, held to their traditions and downplayed the overseas producers and their products. Consequently, the Old World winemakers were shocked when they finally realized the increasing demand for as well as the increasing quality of their competitors' products. This realization came as they saw the rising market share of the New World producers (for more detail, see Bartlett, 2003). New methods of wine growing, new production systems, and technical innovations resulted in competitive advantages for the New World vintners. They were able to produce comparable wine with lower costs and flood Europe with it. The response of European vintners was to call for state intervention and protection to keep these wines out. Soon, numerous regulations were issued in relation to grape varieties, controlled cultivated land, and sugar content. Price guarantees were given by the European Union (EU) and national agricultural subsidies in France and Spain that were meant to support vintners by converting the overproduction of low-quality wines into cash. Prices were stabilized by state intervention; wine that could not be sold on the market was simply purchased by the EU or national state authorities.

Attempts to respond to the entrance of the New World wine producers were a disaster for German winemakers. The Germans tried to copy the successful strategy from overseas producers by mass producing white wine. The production was increased at the expense of quality. One major obstacle was the New World producers' ability to increase cultivable land by buying additional unimproved land very cheaply, whereas in Europe that strategy was impossible. The German wine producers faced geographical and regulatory limits that prevented them from increasing their cultivable land because all viticulture areas were already allocated (see Table 2). Therefore, increasing the production meant increasing the output of a given vineyard by trying to get

❖ Table 2 Viticulture Companies in Germany[a]

Company Size From ... to ... EGE[b]	Number of Companies		
	1999	2003	+/−
< 8	12,233	10,688	12.6
8 − < 16	4,123	3,696	−10.4
16 − < 40	4,716	4,210	−10.7
40 − < 100	3,656	3,561	−2.6
100 − < 250	648	1,193	84.1
> 250	55	97	76.4
	25,431	**23,445**	**−7.8**

SOURCE: Adapted from Bundesministerium für Ernährung, Landwirtschaft und Verbraucherschutz [Federal Ministry of Food, Agriculture and Consumer Protection], 2009, Ubersicht 66: Spezialisierte weinbaubetrieb [Figure 66: Specialized wineries], p. 119.

[a]Includes only companies with a contribution margin above 75% from wine production.

[b]EGE is a European unit; 1 EGE = 1,200 contribution margin.

more wine out of each grape. This in turn lowered the quality significantly. Decreasing quality resulted in decreasing reputation. In addition, productivity increased slowly in comparison with overseas wine industries because the landscape of many German vineyards does not allow the use of heavy machinery and robots. Vineyards are typically located on very steep hillsides alongside river valleys such as the Rhine, Moselle, and Main. Another setback for German vintners was suffered from changes in international consumer demand in the 1990s, when there was a dramatic shift in consumption from light white wines toward red wines. The conclusion after one generation of investment in mass production was that because of the small size of many estates, and limited acreage and steep hillsides of many vineyards, domestic production could not ever be expected to cover domestic demand. For importers, this gap made it much easier to enter the German market.

Germany is the largest importer of wine in the world, with demand continuing to grow. Unfortunately for German producers, this increasing demand is mostly being satisfied by imports from outside the country. There are a variety of reasons for this development. Wine drinking habits have changed in the last few decades; in many parts of society, drinking wine is subject to changes in fashion and lifestyle. This is not only true for the upper classes, but also for students, skilled labor, middle classes, and pensioners. These changing habits in the consumption and perception of wine were first surveyed in the world's largest nonproducing wine market, England. The marketing departments for New World producers identified Great Britain as an ideal target market because its growing demand offered opportunities for new entrants, allowing them to win the so-called "Battle of Britain" (Bartlett, 2003, p. 8) in the wine industry. Success

❖ Figure 5 German exports into the United States from 1996 to 2006.

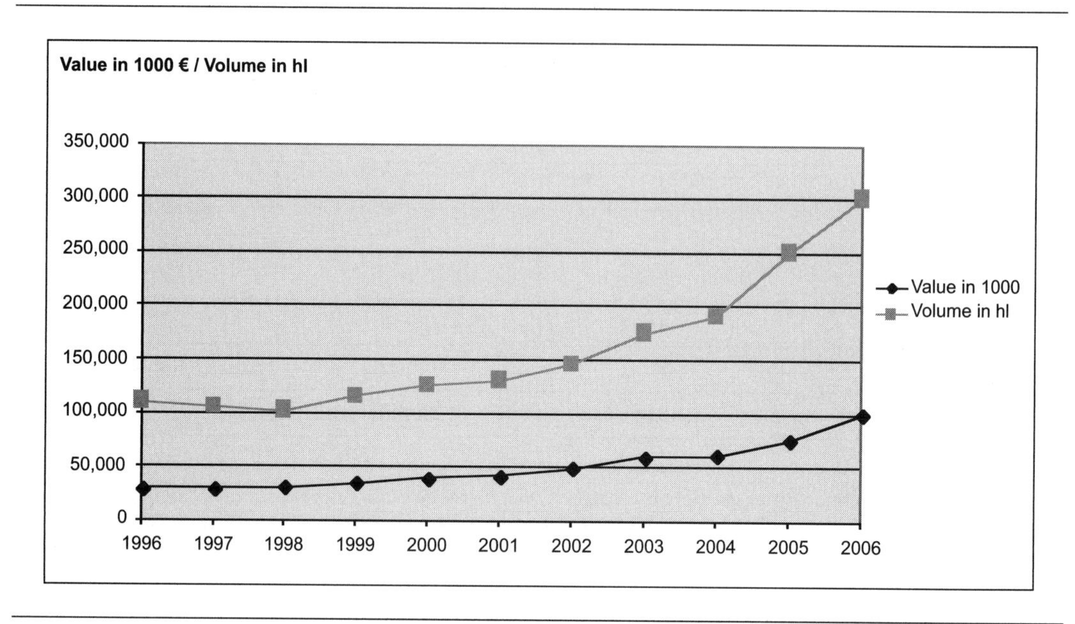

SOURCE: Verband Deutscher Weinexporteure e.V. (VDW, n.d.).

on the English market is regarded as an indicator for international competitiveness: "If you make it there, you'll make it everywhere," as wine marketing managers say.

Since advertising presents drinking wine as the common upper-class lifestyle, copying this style makes members of the middle classes feel part of the upper class. This opens new and growing market segments around the world. The largest market for German wine is the United States. Figure 5 shows German wine exports to the United States increasing. The growth coincided with the first of the new generation of young German vintners who successfully started discovering their abilities to produce first-class white wines, especially Riesling. German exports of wine are also increasing outside the European market (see Table 3).

The most important export markets for German wine, especially white wine, are the United States, Japan, Canada, and Russia; whereas in Europe the largest markets for German wines are Great Britain, the Netherlands, Sweden, Norway, France, and Belgium. Table 3 underlines the changing export trend among German wine estates, which seem to have withdrawn from highly competitive markets like Great Britain and France. They are focusing more on growing markets like the United States, the Scandinavian countries, and especially Russia. There are also opportunities in Asia (e.g., India and China) that have yet to be sought.

The 2006 trade agreement between the European Union and the United States marked a turning point in the liberalization of the global wine market. The ultimate achievement of this treaty is the mutual acceptance of wine-growing methods and the protection of semi-generic names, for example Burgundy, Port, or Champagne. The

❖ Table 3 The Global Wine Market in 2006

		2006			Annual Percentage Change (05/05)		Percentage Share 2006	
		Value	Volume					
Rank	Countries	1.000 EUR	hl	EUR/hl	Value	Volume	Value	Volume
1	EEC 25	354,661	2,185,513	162	9.7	2.5	63.2	75.2
2	Others	206,573	720,822	287	36.6	40.6	36.8	24.8
3	Great Britain	128,342	825,122	156	1.2	-8.1	22.9	28.4
4	USA	100,350	301,649	333	29	21.2	17.9	10.4
5	Netherlands	69,104	476,526	145	17.7	17	12.3	16.4
6	Norway	25,602	85,529	299	53.1	17.2	4.6	2.9
7	Sweden	23,687	176,100	135	5.8	-2.1	4.2	6.1
8	Russia	22,765	169,132	135	113.9	172.6	4.1	5.8
9	Japan	22,759	62,394	365	1.6	0.9	4.1	2.1
10	France	18,542	104,334	178	-3.9	-4.4	3.3	3.6
11	Canada	15,308	57,211	268	49.4	40.7	2.7	2.0
12	Switzerland	13,804	24,569	640	68,6	22.9	2.5	0.7
13	SUMMARY	561,234	2,906,335	193	18.2	9.9	100.0	100.0

SOURCE: VDW (n.d.).

agreement's goal to open the market contrasts to previous attempts by Old World producers to shield themselves from the pressure of the New World winemakers (see Table 4). However, globalization, lower transportation costs, and a growing desire for overseas products resulted in increasing pressures to liberalize the world market for wine.

But the market is far from being truly open. The EU is still paying huge amounts in state subsidies to wine producers to support the domestic wine industry. Old-fashioned thinking relies on the faith that state subsidies and import quotas can manage increasing demand for foreign wine, a notion that is proving to be far from accurate. In the face of these market pressures, wine producers have to rely on innovation to retain their market position, something Johann Fitz recognized early on.

Johann Fitz and the New Entrepreneurial Spirit in the German Wine Industry

Johann Fitz is one of the young German vintners who realized he had to change his business model to compete. In addition to the online shop and the new product,

❖ **Table 4** Development of the Institutional Setting in the Global and Domestic Wine Markets

Past	Present
Germany	**Germany**
German Wine Law 1971; WeinG 1994 Strict regulations of viticulture methods; rejection of non-European viticulture methods; strict rules for labeling; classification into four categories (quality wine with "prädikat," quality wine of certain regions, land wine, table wine)	German Wine Law 1971; WeinG 1994; modification of wine law planned Criticism of top wine producers (e.g., VDP); additional classification without legal protection. Goal: better differentiation of quality vineyards, common international labeling standards
EEC	**EEC**
Each country has its own wine law; strong regulations; rejection of non-European viticulture methods	Treaty between EEC and United States (2006); mutual acceptance of viticulture method
United States	**United States**
Bureau of Alcohol, Tobacco, and Firearms (ATF) Approved Viticulture Areas (AVA); percentage of grapes used from AVA area is important for classification	Treaty between EEC and United States guarantees protection of semi-generic names
World	**World**
Conglomerate of bilateral treaties; Old World vs. New World, state protection; protectionism against new viticulture methods especially in EEC	Conglomerate of bilateral treaties; tendency toward more liberalization; downsizing protectionism

FitzSecco passion fruit, one of his first projects as successor to Konrad Fitz was the refurbishment of the historical cross-vault cow barn (see Figure 6). It was converted into a ball and dining room with a winter garden, where dignified events can take place. Johann's idea of a modern wine estate is as simple as his mission statement: Deliver high-quality wine in combination with features to retain customers. For example, he hosts weddings in the room and uses various techniques to build brand awareness: "If you celebrate your wedding here, you will receive a lifetime discount and a tailored label for your special day. This is the perfect way to win over customers for our vineyard." The difficulty for vintners in such a highly competitive market is customer retention; Johann believes this is a way to achieve that.

To Johann, the transformation of the historical cross-vault cow barn into a ballroom is a symbol of the new spirit he brought into the company. Even though he was unsure about taking over the family business, he now is searching for opportunities and change. "It required a little convincing, but soon I knew that I wanted to run the company and implement new ideas," Johann recalled.

> My parents were leading the vineyard with an entrepreneurial mindset, and I want to continue this track. And continuation means change. Like many human beings, my

attention and power is limited. I need to concentrate on just a few projects at a time. Consequently, I have to develop the estate step by step. I need a priority list, showing which projects or opportunities are crucial for success and then concentrate investments on first things first.

This is why he is still unsure about building the export business with its inherent risks. "Export is an affair of my mother's heart," Johann explains. "She put so much effort in it, but the weak dollar is wearing the profits down." A small company like Fitz-Ritter has to pass through 100% of all currency changes.

> Our INCO [international commercial] terms usually refer to CIF [cost, insurance, and freight, which applies especially when carried on ships] and CIP [carriage and insurance paid, which applies in the case of airfreight]. In the international wine business, it is commercial custom for prices to be negotiated in foreign currencies on the day of order. Payment is due after delivery. Hence, we carry the risk of exchange rates, and I can tell you, we have not been lucky with the euro to U.S. dollar ratios during the past few years. Just to increase the price in U.S. dollars is not the answer, because we soon would bust market prices and our wine would become unsellable.

But Johann is optimistic: "I will find a solution and make a decision, one way or the other." He is someone who likes to tackle a problem. "I am a person who likes to put my hand on it," he adds. Recounting a story from his years of study at the University

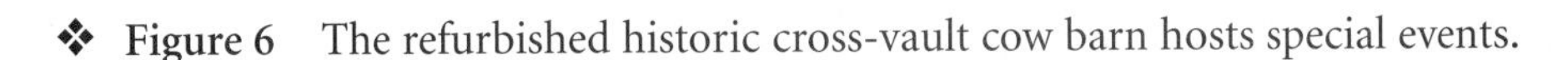

❖ **Figure 6** The refurbished historic cross-vault cow barn hosts special events.

SOURCE: Johann Fitz.

of California, Berkeley, he says, "During the summer I took part in a management program and there was a competition where students had to run a very small company. I was the manager of a painting company. It was exciting. I did all the planning and administrative processes myself, but I employed a few people for operational work. I did very well and finally won the competition. It was a great experience. But then after winning, I was supposed to explain and teach my strategies and ideas to other students, but there I failed badly," he says with a smile on his face. "I am a person who just does things, but I am not one to talk about it. I am not a coach or a teacher."

Although Johann's ideas proved a promising opportunity to build a connection between customers and the brand, he had to be careful not to stray too far from the core business.

> We have returns on investment from wine production, but the surplus reserve cannot cover the entire project. It can only contribute a little equity to the amount of cash needed. So I faced the task of financing the project. First, I limited the need for capital by having a clear focus on our core competence. The project is intended to foster our sales of wine, during the event and for future delivery. It is not designed to run a restaurant. This would mean the need to employ a chef, cooks, waiters, and so on. Therefore I decided to outsource the catering. Guests are free to choose any caterer they like, and thus all the diverse demands for cuisine that may occur can be easily fulfilled. The only product I put restrictions on is wine and champagne. It has to be purchased from the Fitz-Ritter Wine Estate or the Sektkellerei Fitz KG (the official name of the sparkling wine business). Aside from that, the outsourcing of catering is to our advantage because the expense is detached from our variable costs. Consequently, the need for capital is equated with the costs of transforming the site. The break-even point will be reached almost with the first bottle sold after the interests on the invested capital are paid.

Table 5 shows the investment costs and the sources of funds.[2]

In the financial plan, KfW-Mittelstandsbank plays a decisive role. This public financial institution was created to help Germany recover from World War II and to distribute aid from George C. Marshall's European Recovery Program (ERP). Most European countries used the money from the program for immediate development, but the German government chose a different model: They founded the KfW Bank as a fund holder. The KfW did not spend the money on subventions, but invested it by offering loans to innovative small and medium-sized enterprises (SMEs). Hence, the aid, once given by the United States, still accumulates interest and remains available to the German economy. The market for informal equity is not well developed. For this reason, the KfW-Mittelstandsbank offers not only investment loans but also mezzanine capital. On condition that the entrepreneur will get involved with 15% equity, up to an additional 25% of total investment can be financed by the mezzanine capital program. The remaining 60% of investment can be covered by an investment loan.

The new project looks promising. Although it has only just been started, 15 couples have already booked the room and the garden for their wedding parties at a rate of EUR2,100 per day. In addition to the rent, Johann plans to sell around 100 bottles per

❖ Table 5 Entrepreneurial Finance for an SME in Germany—An Example.

Total Investment	**500,000€**					
Sources of Capital						
Equity from surplus reserve	75,000€					
Mezzanine capital from KfW-Mittelstandsbank (Capital for Entrepreneurship Program)	125,000€					
Investment loan from KfW-Mittelstandsbank (Entrepreneurship Loan)	300,000€					
Interest Rates and Amortizations (Year 1 starts on January 1, 2008)						
Mezzanine Capital						
Year	1	2	3	4	Years 5–6	Years 7–15
Interest (%)[a]	0.0	3.0	4.0	5.0	6.50	6.50
Amortization[b]	0.0	0.0	0.0	0.0	0.0	13.888.89€ p.a.
Investment Loan						
Year	1	2	3	Years 3–20		
Interest (%)[a]	Max. 4.45–7.30 (depending on rating), Fitz-Ritter is rated A (4.45)					
Amortization[b]	0.0	0.0	0.0	17,674.06€ p.a.		

[a]Interest rates are subject to change (for actual rates, see www.kfw-mittelstandsbank.de).
[b]If required by the entrepreneurial enterprise, amortization can be expedited.

event at retail prices (see Table 1). At least 40 to 45 events per year could be scheduled throughout the season. “Aside from the cash that we put into the project, we used our estate’s garden and the cross-vault next to it, both representing assets that have been idle for many years but soon will contribute to our business.” Market analysts state that the average German couple spends EUR14,000 on their wedding. In addition, many companies, clubs, associations, and private persons are looking for unique locations to make their function a special event. Thanks to word of mouth, Internet advertisements, and a “Google strategy,”[3] the business plan expects the number of events to increase to 60 or even 70 per year in the fourth year. Operation of the facility began in May 2008.

Confident in his future plans, Johann is taking the necessary steps to achieve his strategy to become the best wine company in the region. “We work very hard on increasing the quality of our wines,” he emphasizes. From the first seeding to the harvest, the vintner’s family and its employees are controlling most aspects of the business—even filling the wine bottles, labeling, marketing, and selling will be done by the small group of people at the Fitz-Ritter winery.

"Today, this is special," says Konrad Fitz, "We do everything on our own. It is demanding but we believe that you can taste it. High-quality wine is our passion, and we control the total process" (see Figure 7).

Johann's next plan is to increase the quality of wine by investing in human resources and industry know-how. "You can always increase the quality of wine. We have achieved a lot but still have some space left to climb up the ladder to the top German vineyards," says Johann. The shift in methods of to achieving quality has been drastic during the last 15 years, along with the way that that quality is measured and communicated. The Internet and other types of easily accessible mass media create more transparency; consumers and reviewers can quickly share their wine experiences with others. Recommendations and ratings are popular. Some of the so-called experts have a lot of power; they influence consumer behavior and thus give incentives for higher quality. Today, markets reward quality much more than they did years or decades ago.

One struggle for Johann is finding a good supply of grapes to meet growing demand. Increasing acreage is not an option because of the high cost of land in Germany. "Purchasing good wine from another vintner is another possibility, especially in the cuvée and sparkling wine production," the young vintner adds. This strategy is feasible and can help to bypass bottlenecks in delivery, especially with his latest innovation, FitzSecco passion fruit. As Johann explains,

❖ **Figure 7** The Fitz-Ritter wine cellar.

SOURCE: Johann Fitz.

> It is a product for young people who like to enjoy good quality wine with the flavor of passion fruit. It is a stylish product, which is brand new and already the "in" drink here in our region. Demand is higher than we thought, so for production, quality wine has to be bought in addition to our own volume. With this new flavored sparkling wine, Fitz-Ritter is targeting young people, especially young women. It has a great potential to become the next hot seller for our vineyard.

In addition, FitzSecco passion fruit will soon be available in smaller piccolo bottles (0.2 liters), with the latest trend in bottling, the "twist and plop" cap. Due to its low alcohol content and fruity, refreshing taste, it is a good alternative to the alco-pops sold at pubs and clubs. "Changing our product portfolio, I can imagine dedicating our entire acreage to the production of premium wines of the highest quality and rounding out the portfolio with quality wine bought from other vintners," Johann adds. "The additional wine would be placed in the medium price range and in the production of cuvées for Champagnes, sparkling wines, and FitzSecco" (Figure 8).

Perspectives and Discussions

The Fitz-Ritter company is facing a crucial period in its history where several decisions will have to be made that depend massively on the strategy Johann wishes to pursue. The wine industry has changed and continues to evolve. In Germany and elsewhere

❖ **Figure 8** Wine testing.

SOURCE: Johann Fitz.

in Europe, smaller wine estates already had to react to the challenges of a global wine industry. In Germany, the consolidation process has started but has yet to reach its inflection point. Rumors persist that some of the largest German vineyards have received takeover offers from overseas.

The passage of leadership from Konrad to Johann is just beginning, and the company must react to this change. Steps have been taken by Fitz-Ritter to make this transition as smooth as possible; Johann received an education in enology, economics, and entrepreneurship. Konrad Fitz has retired, but is still on the estate to help with his rich experience. Alice is willing to promote exports for several more years. The company is 100% family owned. Nevertheless, future plans have to be made—it is just not enough to rest on what has been achieved so far.

The new projects Johann Fitz has executed thus far are all in line with the overall strategy of the company: the development of a premium wine estate that combines tradition and innovation. Projects have included:

- The introduction of new products such as the FitzSecco passion fruit sparkling wine
- A reorganization of product portfolio, stressing those products with the highest quality and prices
- The reorganization of distribution channels in the domestic market, including the establishment of an Internet shop
- The historical cross-vault cow barn project to increase direct sales onsite, which also has the potential to increase customer loyalty
- New labels and elegant designs for bottles containing the most expensive wines (see Figure 9)
- Investments in human resources; for example, hiring of a famous first-class enologist and employing a cellar master of excellent craftsmanship

Yet still more decisions lie ahead for Johann. Because every project mentioned above bears the risk of failure, it is necessary to have alternative plans. At this point, many questions remain and many options are available.

❖ **Figure 9** New products and new designs for bottles and labels.

Why not concentrate on the domestic market and leave the cost-intensive and difficult job of export to the competition? Even though she has decades of experience, Alice admits, "Export business is a perplexing and troublesome job, with markets not easy to understand." Domestic demand is sufficient, especially if the historical cross-vault cow barn project turns out fine. So why should Johann Fitz continue with the export business? Should the 25% of given production capacity that is used for international business be dedicated to the domestic market in the near future?

What about distribution and product portfolio? Do changes in climate offer any new opportunities for differentiation of the product portfolio? Are there any growth strategies Fitz-Ritter should take advantage of? In which areas of the Fitz-Ritter business can one recognize such opportunities for growth? Are exhibitions and Internet appearance enough to survive? How can the company use its latest innovation, the FitzSecco passion fruit? What could the marketing plan for FitzSecco passion fruit look like? How can Johann gain and retain more young customers?

These difficult questions are on Johann's mind when he returns from the cow barn refurbishment site. The monument protection officials felt comfortable with how the ancient renaissance character of the building has been preserved. After taking leave from the officials, Johann enters his office. The phone is ringing. It is Alice calling, with excitement in her voice: "Johann, our premium wine is positively reviewed by today's New York Times and to boot, the Wine Spectator ranked the Michelsberg and the Kanzel Ungestein Riesling above 90 points. So to speak, we have just entered the international champions' league at a top rank."

"What news, and the day has just started," Johann says. "Our strategy seems to be turning out fine, and tonight we shall definitively open one of the best bottles of champagne from our cellar." But before this, Johann makes good use of the day, considering the rewards of the challenging export business from a new perspective, rethinking his opportunities, and reweighing his options.

Appendix

❖ Table A1 Fitz-Ritter Wine Estate Growing Areas and Yield

Growing Area	Acreage	% of acreage[a]	Wine	Use in Production	Potential Quality[a]
Dürkheim Abtsfronhof	3.2 ha (7.9 acres)	35	Riesling	A++, A+++, and A+S	C–A+++ and A+S
		30	Gewurztraminer	A++, A+++	C–A+++ and A+S
		20	Chardonnay	SWP[b]	C–A+++
		15	Sauvignon Blanc	SWP	C–A+++
Dürkheim Fronhof	0.8 ha (1.98 acres)	100	Riesling	B, A, SWP	C–A++

(continued)

Table A1 (Continued)

Growing Area	Acreage	% of acreage[a]	Wine	Use in Production	Potential Quality[a]
Dürkheim Fuchsmantel	0.56 ha (1.38 acres)	100	Riesling	B, A, SWP	C–A++
Ungsteiner Herrenberg/ Kanzel	1.44 ha (3.46 acres)	100	Riesling	A+++	C–A+++ and A+S
Dürkheim Hochbenn	4 ha (9.88 acres)	100	Riesling	B, A, SWP, A+S	C–A+++ and A+S
Wachenheimer Mandelgarten	2 ha (4.94 acres)	50	Pinot Gris	B, A, SWP	C–A+
		50	Pinot Blanc	B, A, SWP	C–A+
Michelsberg	0.7 ha (1.73 acres)	100	Riesling	A+++	C–A+++ and A+S
Rittengarten	1.86 ha (4.6 acres)	40	Riesling	A	C–A+++
		25	Dornfelder	A, A+, A++	C–A+++
		20	Cabernet Sauvignon	A++, A+++	C–A+++
		15	Cabernet Dorsa	A++	C–A+++
Durkheimer Spielberg	0.7 ha (1.73 acres)	100	Chardonnay	A++	C–A+++
Others	5.74 ha (14.1 acres)	100	Diverse	A+, A++, A+++	C–A+++

[a]Figures adapted and modified by the authors for classroom use only.
[b]SWP = usage for sparkling wine production.

❖ Table A2 Purchasing Prices for Wine (Cuvée Production)[a]

Wine	C	A	B	A+–A+++ and A+S
Average White	0.75	0.8	0.90	No Purchasing Possible
Average Red	0.80	0.85	0.95	No Purchasing Possible
	In percentage of wholesale price			

[a]Figures for classroom calculations only.

❖ Table A3 Wine Segments Based on Quality Assessment[a]

Per Bottle	Table Wine	Average	Quality	Premium	Top	Top Special	Specialty
Price range wholesale	< 1.25	1.00–2.00	2.50–3.50	3.50–5.50	6.00–10.00	10.00–18.00	> 20.00
Average margins for retailers	100%	> 100%	100%	> 80%	> 75%	> 66%	> 50%
Price range estate to consumer	< 2.50	2.50–4.99	5.00–7.00	7.01–9.99	10.00–14.99	15.00–30.00	> 30.00
Average profit in wholesale (in euros)	0.05	0.10	0.20	0.30	0.50	1.00	2.00
Code[b]	C	B	A	A+	A++	A+++	A+S
Average liters per hectare	140,000	100,000	65,000	50,000	30,0000	20,000	5,000

[a]Figures adapted and modified by the authors for classroom calculations only.
[b]VDP wines are classified "A" at least.

❖ Table A4 Development of Exchange Rates

Currency	10-19-2007	12-29-2006	12-30-2005	12-21-2004	12-31-2003	12-31-2002	12-28-2001
Euro/U.S. Dollar	1.425 USD	1.317 USD	1.180 USD	1.362 USD	1.263 USD	1.049 USD	0.881 USD
Euro/British Pound	0.698 GBP	0.672 GBP	0.685 GBP	0.705 GBP	0.705 GBP	0.651 GBP	0.609 GBP
Euro/Yen	165.51 JPY	156.93 JPY	138.90 JPY	139.65 JPY	135.05 JPY	124.39 JPY	115.33 JPY

SOURCE: Raw data from www.bankenverband.de.

Notes

1. Institute for Entrepreneurship and Innovation Research, University of Wuppertal, Germany.
2. To protect the company's interests, all financial data and sources of funds have been subject to modification. Nevertheless, the data given are realistic and the source of financing is the most important for entrepreneurial start-ups and business successes in Germany. It was chosen to give the case a universal validity for entrepreneurial finance in Germany.
3. Searching for a wedding reception location within 100 miles of Bad Dürkheim at www.google.de, one would find the "historical cross-vault cow barn" among the first hits. The city of Frankfurt, financial capital of German economy, is located within this area.

Case Questions

1. Do you agree with the owner that there is a fit regarding the company's strategy and resources?
2. What is Fitz-Ritter's competitive advantage? How did the company manage to survive in a highly competitive wine business?
3. Regarding the company's strategy, what do you think is the most important thing the new owner has to do? And why?
4. Concerning Fitz-Ritter's export business, how should the owner reorganize the export business? Does he need a new strategy for it? If he does, what would be your suggestion to the owner? Why would you continue with the export business? And why not?
5. Why is the Association of German Prädikat Wine Estates so important for the company? How do you think Fitz-Ritter could improve its network? If you do not think it is important, why not? Where do you see arguments for and against the partnership?
6. Johann Fitz wants to strengthen the firm's position in the market and he is thinking about how to grow—do you see any potential areas for growth? How could he use the new FitzSecco?
7. Fitz-Ritter's product portfolio embraces about 40 different products. Where are the strengths and weaknesses in its product portfolio?
8. Imagine you are the new owner. What are the next steps and why? Where do you see areas to improve?

References

Bartlett, C. A. (2003). *Global wine wars: New World challenges Old.* Boston: Harvard Business School Publishing.

Bundesministerium für Ernährung, Landwirtschaft und Verbraucherschutz [Federal Ministry of Food, Agriculture and Consumer Protection]. (2009). *Ertragslage garten-und weinbau 2009: Daten-analyse* [Earnings from horticulture and viticulture 2009: Data analysis]. Retrieved from http://www.bmelv-statisik.de

Lynam, R. (2001, March). The Riesling Renaissance. *Hong Kong Business, 18*(225), 98.

Verband Deutscher Prädikat s-und Qualitaetsweingueter (VDP). (n.d.). [Website]. Retrieved from www.vdp.de/verband/daten-zahlen-fakten/

Verband Deutscher Weinexporteure e.V. [Association of German Wine Exporters]. (n.d.). Retrieved from www.vdw-weinexport.de

Wolkoff, I. (2006, June 2). Following hard times, German Rieslings rise again. *Medical Post, 42*(20), 39. Prädikat

Case 4

Intelligent Leisure Solutions

Robert Hisrich and Cristina Ricaurte

Introduction

Intelligent Leisure Solutions (ILS) is a group of five companies based in Brazil working to create, implement, and manage intelligent solutions. As a completely technology-based solutions company, ILS is unique in its approach to travel, real estate, technology, and sustainable tourism. With high growth in the tourism industry, Intelligent Leisure Solutions' founding entrepreneur, Robert Phillips, is working to find the most appropriate, innovative growth strategy for expansion and sustainability of the business.

Geographic Background

Brazil is located on the eastern Atlantic Coast of South America with a slightly smaller geographic area than the United States (see Figure 1). With the fifth largest country population in the world, it is home to more than 200 million people. Brazil's economy is larger than that of all other South American countries, characterized by developed mining, manufacturing, agricultural and service sectors, and is increasing its presence in world markets. After the global recession in 2008, Brazil was one of the first emerging markets to begin recovering with about a 5% growth in 2010 (Central Intelligence Agency [CIA], 2010).

Brazil's economy is now the eighth largest in the world. It has recently acquired a temporary seat on the United Nations Security Council until the end of 2011 and is seeking a growing international role and geopolitical influence (Economist Intelligence Unit, 2010a). Brazil's government, led by Dilma Rousseff of the Worker's Party, welcomes private sector concessions, although bureaucracy still impairs efficiency.

Source: Used by permission from Robert Hisrich and Cristina Ricaurte.

❖ Figure 1 Map of Brazil.

SOURCE: CIA (2010).

Foreign direct investment is welcomed, although domestic investors receive priority in certain areas, especially in the oil and energy sectors. Development of the export industry continues to be a priority and trade barriers are expected to be lowered. Brazil's tax system is poorly structured and tax evasion is widespread while the tax breaks applied to lessen the burden of the financial crisis of 2008 are scheduled to be lifted; yet, the overall tax burden will continue to be high. Both foreign and national companies spend considerable resources toward managing their tax issues. Compliance with environmental law is a new crucial aspect of doing business in Brazil, and intellectual property rights must be respected (Economist Intelligence

Unit, 2010b). The looming 2014 World Cup and 2016 Olympics are expected to bring an increase in public–private partnerships (Economist Intelligence Unit, 2010a).

Brazil's middle class is expanding due to the prosperity brought about by sound macroeconomic policies since 2000 (Euromonitor International, 2010). For the first time in Brazil's history, 50% of its citizens, more than 94 million people, belong to the middle class. Many low-income Brazilians have benefitted from new opportunities for stable jobs in the past decade. Because more people are being hired in the formal economy, access to working benefits such as health care, transportation, and food has increased. The real average monthly income grew 2.3% between 2008 and 2009 (Euromonitor International, 2010); this new middle class has access to certain products and services for the first time in their lives and are demanding more products and higher quality of service.

Lower fertility rates are also contributing to higher disposable incomes. Brazil's fertility rate of 1.9 children per woman in 2009 has allowed parents to spend more on consumer goods and services (Euromonitor International, 2010). This has also resulted in a rise in demand for travel services, as families are increasingly able to afford vacations.

Brazil has a very young population, with 33.2% of its population in its twenties and thirties (see Table 1). This segment of the population is technology savvy with financial independence and the means to travel (Euromonitor International, 2010). They tend to travel to different regions of Brazil and to other countries over

❖ Table 1 Brazil's Consumer Segmentation, 2010–2020 (in thousands)

	2010	2015	2020	Growth (%)
Babies/Infants (0–2 years)	9,084	8,070	7,656	−15.7
Kids (3–8 years)	20,236	17,859	16,005	−20.9
Tweenagers (9–12 years)	13,928	13,490	11,865	−14.8
Teens (13–19 years)	23,347	24,104	23,627	1.2
People in their twenties	35,258	33,749	33,335	−5.5
People in their thirties	29,875	33,207	34,611	15.9
Middle-aged adults (40–64 years)	50,359	56,508	62,662	24.4
Older population (65+ years)	13,335	15,877	19,290	44.6

SOURCE: Euromonitor International (2010).

the holidays, and are looking for comfort and efficiency in their services. The annual disposable income will increase by 2020 (see Table 2). The number of families in the US$75,000 income bracket will more than double from 1.7 million households in 2010 to 3.6 million in 2020 (Euromonitor International, 2010).

The tourism industry in Brazil grew 22% from 2003 to 2007, almost 3% more than the overall Brazilian economy during that time (Euromonitor International, 2010). Leisure and recreation spending is expected to grow by 65% by 2020 (see Table 3) with more Brazilians traveling during Carnival, Christmas, and other vacation times. Many Brazilians are starting to buy vacation packages through travel agencies and airlines that can be paid for in installments; the amount spent in this area grew 27.5% from 2005 to $5 billion Brazilian reals in 2009 (see Table 4) (Euromonitor International, 2010). People in the upper and upper-middle classes are the primary customers for these packages.

History of the Entrepreneur and Company

Robert Phillips, founder and CEO of Intelligent Leisure Solutions, has a BS in electrical engineering and an MS in space power. He worked in space power and in oil exploration in the United States and received an MBA from Thunderbird School of Global Management in 1994. He is a U.S. citizen who spent most of his childhood living in South America, specifically in Brazil, Bolivia, and Colombia (Guthry, 2010).

Phillips began Intelligent Leisure Solutions in 1998 while working at Odebrecht, the largest engineering, construction, chemical, and petrochemical company in Latin America. As an internal consultant for tourism, tourism development, and real estate projects in Brazil, Phillips acted as a liaison between McKinsey and Ernst & Young, two large consulting firms in the United States, who were hired to evaluate tourism industry possibilities for Odebrecht. When Odebrecht decided not to invest in the tourism

❖ Table 2 Annual Disposable Income Per Household, 2010–2020

	2010	2015	2020	Growth (%)
Above US$500	55,224	60,306	65,374	18.4
Above US$1,000	54,662	59,873	65,026	19.0
Above US$5,000	45,673	52,420	58,709	28.5
Above US$10,000	32,705	40,290	47,466	45.1
Above US$25,000	11,969	16,801	22,052	84.3
Above US$45,000	4,535	6,696	9,238	103.7
Above US$75,000	1,790	2,654	3,697	106.6
Above US$150,000	569	798	1,069	87.9

SOURCE: Euromonitor International (2010).

NOTE: Constant value at 2009 prices.

❖ Table 3 Consumer Expenditure by Broad Category (in billions of reals), 2010–2020

Product	2010	2015	2020	Growth (%)	CAGR[a] (%)
Food and nonalcoholic beverages	527	678	839	59.3	4.8
Alcoholic beverages and tobacco	40	50	61	51.2	4.2
Clothing and footwear	68	80	90	31.5	2.8
Housing	313	397	492	57.4	4.6
Household goods and services	107	135	163	52.8	4.3
Health goods and medical services	95	126	160	68.9	5.4
Transport	281	372	469	67.1	5.3
Communications	118	160	209	77.8	5.9
Leisure and recreation	72	95	119	65.1	5.1
Education	153	204	259	69.6	5.4
Hotels and catering	56	68	79	40.5	3.5
Miscellaneous goods and services	296	390	487	64.6	5.1
TOTAL	**2,126**	**2,755**	**3,427**	**61.3**	**4.9**

SOURCE: Euromonitor International (2010).
NOTE: Constant value at 2009 prices.
[a]CAGR = compound annual growth rate.

❖ Table 4 Consumer Expenditure on Package Holidays (in millions of reals), 2005–2009

Product	2005	2006	2007	2008	2009	Growth (%)
Package holidays	3,976	4,301	4,635	4,941	5,071	27.5

SOURCE: Euromonitor International (2010).
NOTE: Constant value at 2009 prices.

❖ Table 5 Awards and Honors Won by Intelligent Leisure Solutions Companies

- Winner – 2008 UN World Tourism Org Ulysses Award for Innovation in Tourism Enterprises
- Nominee – 2009 and 2010 World Travel Award as World's Leading Travel Agency
- Nominee – 2010 World Travel Award as World's Leading Travel Management Company
- Winner – 2009 and 2010 World Travel Award as S. America's Leading Travel Agency
- Winner – 2008, 2009, and 2010 World Travel Award as S. America's Leading Travel Management Company
- Winner – 2008 and 2010 World Travel Award as Central America's Leading Travel Agency
- Robert Phillips, managing partner, elected President of American Society of Travel Agents (ASTA), Brazil Chapter
- Selected as an Affiliate Member of the UN World Tourism Organization by Brazilian Ministry of Tourism

sector, Phillips saw a market opportunity and developed a Web-based travel company to sell Brazil to the world. Focused completely on Internet marketing, the company was unique among travel companies in Brazil in its innovative marketing strategy. In 2003, Phillips left Odebrecht to start DiscoverBrazil.com, a self-funded, Web-based travel company (now Intelligent Travel Solutions, or ITS), with the help of two partners, both colleagues from Odebrecht.

DiscoverBrazil.com began selling travel from Phillips' home office, and expanded to offer Central and South American luxury vacation packages, growing to 11 travel consultants, four websites, and monthly sales of US$300,000. The team acquired expert knowledge in Internet marketing and technology through their application of solely Internet marketing during their first few years of operations, allowing them to attain first-place results in Google's and Yahoo's search engine results pages (SERPs) for their business keywords.

Phillips and the team began setting up websites for Brazilian companies using the Internet marketing techniques they had developed for the Discover Brazil sites. Within weeks, these sites attained first placements in SERPs, something that usually took at least 3 to 6 months to achieve in the travel sector in English. In 2007, Intelligent Web Solutions (IWS) was created out of these results, and soon after, Intelligent Content Solutions (ICS) was created when Phillips partnered with another entrepreneur with translation experience. The result was an award-winning, integrated service that included Web marketing, Web business services, Web content creation, and translation service (see Table 5).

Organizational Structure

Intelligent Leisure Solutions Consulting (ILSC) is an efficient outsourcing service, with a broad network of specialized partners for each outsourced service. Demand is identified, and innovative, intelligent solutions are created, turning this demand into business opportunities. ILSC started with two employees. In 2007, the company had 26 employees. The company was restructured because of the financial crisis of 2008 and foreign exchange debt to 12 employees, which then grew again to 16 employees in 2009 (Guthry, 2010).

Throughout the creation of IWS, ICS, ITS, and IRES (Intelligent Real Estate Solutions), Phillips continued his work with ILSC, which helped fund new projects. In 2009, Phillips brought three new partners into ILSC who helped Discover Brazil evolve into a group of five companies. Due to tax structure requirements in Brazil, companies need to be kept separate to qualify for certain tax incentives.

The group has incorporated Internet technology into the horizontally integrated leisure chain. The companies in the group offer a range of services from leisure development to the marketing and distribution of products. It is able to use shared knowledge between the five companies resulting in a strategic advantage. The group considers itself unique in that it has its own business laboratory (ITS) where it is able to test and develop its integrated services and Web techniques.

Intelligent Leisure Solutions is made up of five companies, each focusing on its own market niche:

Intelligent Leisure Solutions Consulting (ILSC) is a leisure, real estate, travel, tourism, and entertainment development consulting company with customers ranging from independent project owners, banks, investment funds, universities, and municipal, state, and federal governments. The company has a strong international and multicultural team located within Brazil. Its strategic advantage is its knowledge of the entire travel real estate market and its all-in-one solutions for tourism consulting, Web marketing, real estate brokerage, and travel consulting. With rapidly growing tourism and real estate industries in Brazil, ILSC hopes to capitalize on increased foreign investors in the next decade. Sample clients include the Ministry of Tourism of Brazil, the Secretariat of Tourism of Bahia, the World Bank, the Inter-American Development Bank, the CERT Foundation, Sapiens Park, and Zank Boutique Hotel. ILSC is also the exclusive representative for Odebrecht and Gehry Technology in Brazil and has recently won the bid to provide services for the Panama Metro and the Olympics and World Cup arenas in Brazil.

Intelligent Real Estate Solutions (IRES) offers complete real estate brokerage solutions in Brazil with clients such as international investors, banks, and funds investing in real estate and real estate projects in Brazil. This member company also has a cross-cultural and multilingual team that is able to provide foreign investors with services in their own languages. Because most ILSC clients need real estate consulting and brokerage services, IRES is able to offer these additional services as part of an integrated solution.

Intelligent Web Solutions (IWS) offers Internet marketing and business plan consulting and development, specializing in both search engine optimization and search engine marketing. Customers of IWS want a presence online and include small, medium, and large companies, artists, banks, universities and governments. Since few companies in the tourism sector offer content creation solutions, IWS offers this combined with project management and global services knowledge.

IWS believes it will be able to grow efficiently because of the lower costs of Internet marketing compared to traditional marketing, offering cost savings up to 90%. Internet marketing can reach anyone around the world with access to the Internet.

Since any company interested in using Internet marketing is a potential IWS client, the firm capitalized on this by holding its second Internet Marketing Road Show in 2010. Through this, Intelligent Leisure Solutions entered the European market in 2009 with two new large clients.

Sample clients include in Spain—Universitat Oberta de Catalunya (www.uoc.edu) and Costa Brava of Girona (www.costabrava.org); in Argentina—Festival de Verão and Pepsi (www.sociallize.com.br), and Finca don Otaviano (www.FincadonOtaviano.com.ar); in Brazil—Carlinhos Brown (www.CarlinhosBrown.com.br), Physio Pilates (www.PhysioPilates.com), and Odebrecht Real Estate and Tourism projects, including Reserva do Paiva (www.reservadopaiva.com), Hangar Business Park (www.hangarsalvador.com.br), Boulevard Side (www.boulevardside.com.br), Quintas Private (www.quintasprivate.com.br), Mitchell (www.mitchell.com.br), and The Planet Fashion Wear (www.theplanet.com.br).

Intelligent Content Solutions (ICS) provides full-service Web content creation and translation to both individuals and companies needing translations and Web copywriting services. The company offers Web site translation into any language through its international team working within Brazil and its consultants located around the world. Only techniques that have been tested in the business laboratory (ITS) are offered to clients. Since companies increasingly want to sell their products globally, ICS has many opportunities for growth.

Intelligent Travel Solutions (ITS) offers personalized luxury travel solutions in Central and South America to individual travelers, travel agencies, tour operators, schools, universities, churches, other institutions, companies from diverse sectors, and countries offering incentive trips. All ITS's employees are multicultural and multilingual consultants, not travel agents, who apply in-house Web marketing techniques to establish the image of Central and South America as luxury travel destinations.

ITS is the first Web-based tour operator in Brazil and it promotes local development of sustainable tourist activity through excellence in its services. Opportunities for growth can be seen in applying this low-cost model to smaller regional and specialty travel websites.

Obstacles Faced

- **2008 Economic Crisis**—This represented a significant challenge to Intelligent Leisure Solutions as the decrease in demand led to a loss in revenue for the business. This was addressed by restructuring the business to travel consultants working from home instead of from corporate office space. This allowed the company to cut costs and implement a differentiated commission structure (Guthry, 2010).
- **Human Resources**—In Phillips' words, "What I have found to be one of the primary obstacles is human resources and human resource selection. If I were hiring a lawyer or a finance guy, that's all pretty standard. But when you go to set up an Internet-based travel company, who do you use as your foundation?" Phillips identified capable staff and implemented quality training, procedures, and a business culture appropriate for each company.

❖ Table 6 Intelligent Leisure Solutions' Estimated Net Operational Profit, 2005–2009 (in U.S. dollars)

	2005	2006	2007	2008	2009
Estimated Operational Profit (net)	$120,000	$360,000	$480,000	$390,000	$640,000

SOURCE: Guthry (2010).

- **Lack of Understanding of the Need for the Products**—Since IWS offers an integrated travel solution, something not currently seen on the market, many prospective clients need to be educated about the company's products. The sales strategy for Intelligent Leisure Solutions was designed to first educate consumers about the product, overcome skepticism of the Web-based approach, and effectively present the quality of its products. A network of past clients was then built to demonstrate credibility and generate new clients.
- **Project Management Standards**—These standards, not yet developed in the industry, were developed by the group through trial and error.

Financial Information

Intelligent Leisure Solutions was initially self-funded by Phillips until 2005, when it received investments from two individuals. It has been funded periodically by investments throughout the life of the business. The business is currently being funded by the group's operations (see Table 6).

Industry Overviews

Marketing Consulting Industry Overview

The management and marketing consultancy market in the United States had a value of $106.9 billion in 2009 (Table 7; Figure 2), with a compound annual growth rate (CAGR) of 4.4% between 2005 and 2009 (Datamonitor, 2010d). This market has experienced steady growth and is forecasted to reach $161.2 billion in 2014, an increase of 50.7% since 2009, representing a CAGR of 8.6% between 2009 and 2014 (Figure 3). The largest segment of the management and marketing consultancy market in the United States is corporate strategy with 27.8% of the total market, while the operations management segment accounts for 26.5% (Table 8). The United States represents 39.3% of the global market value (Datamonitor, 2010d).

The size of this market is the total revenues received from corporate strategy services, operations management services, information technology solutions, human resource management services, and outsourcing services. Since management and marketing consultancies provide objective external advice to improve business performance, this service involves specific professional knowledge, which can be costly.

❖ Table 7 U.S. Management and Marketing Consultancy Market Value, 2005–2009

Year	Dollars (in billions)	Euros (in billions)	Growth (%)
2005	90.0	64.7	—
2006	99.7	71.7	10.8
2007	108.4	78.0	8.8
2008	113.6	81.7	4.8
2009	106.9	76.9	5.9
CAGR 2005–2009			**4.4**

SOURCE: Datamonitor (2010d).

❖ Figure 2 U.S. management and marketing consultancy market value, 2005–2009.

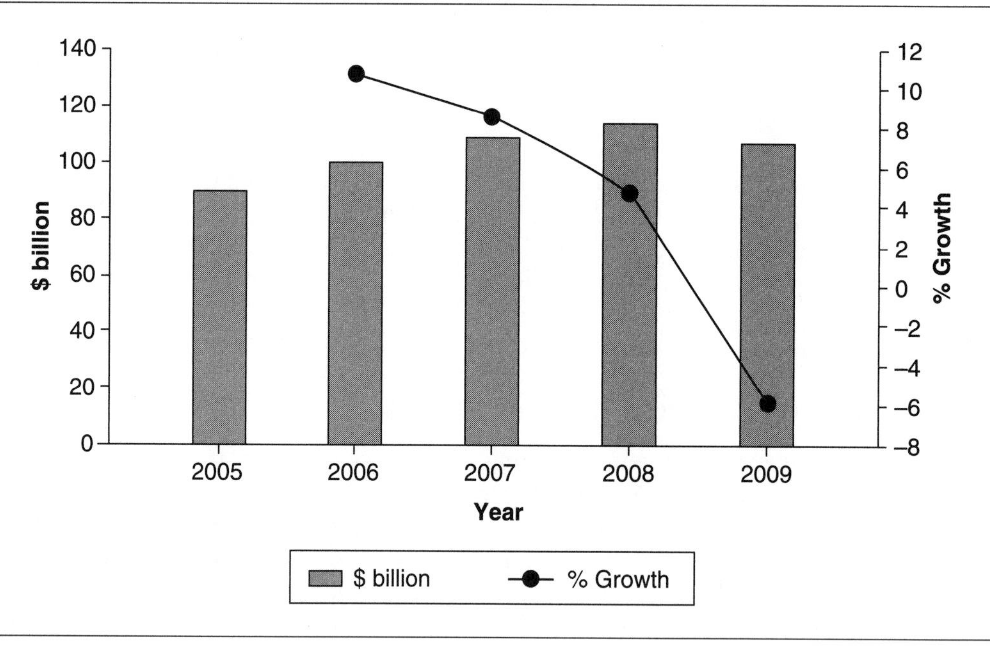

SOURCE: Datamonitor (2010d).

Strong brand reputations are important in this industry, as evidenced by the success of large global organizations such as PriceWaterhouseCoopers and Deloitte. The time and experience required to build this reputation presents a strong barrier to entry in this industry. Also, many large organizations employ in-house analysts and marketing teams as a substitute for consultancy services.

❖ Figure 3 U.S. management and marketing consultancy market value forecast, 2009–2014.

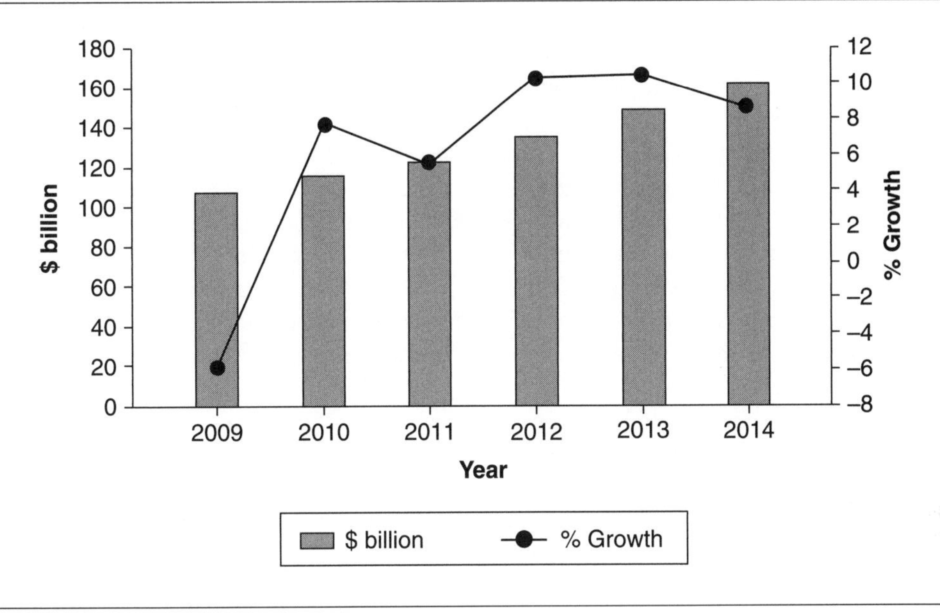

SOURCE: Datamonitor (2010d).

❖ Table 8 U.S. Management and Marketing Consultancy Market Segmentation

Category	Share (%)
Corporate Strategy	27.8
Operations Management	26.5
Human Resources Management	10.6
Information Technology	8.8
Other	26.3
Total	**100**

SOURCE: Datamonitor (2010d).

The leading management and marketing consulting firms employ economies of scale and are multinational and multidisciplinary. Reputation for cost-effectiveness and an excellent track record are keys to success in this market. There is significant fragmentation within the market with smaller companies focusing on specific markets and industries and servicing particular buyers that they are more suited for (Datamonitor, 2010d).

Internet Marketing Industry Overview

The Internet marketing industry consists of the search engine marketing industry and the social media industry. The search engine marketing industry is segmented into money spent on paid search marketing and search engine optimization (SEO), as well as spending on search engine marketing technology (Econsultancy, 2010). The North American search engine marketing industry grew from $13.5 billion in 2008 to $14.6 billion in 2009. Due to the recession, market conditions were difficult and 2009 was a relatively slow year for the industry (Figure 4) (Econsultancy, 2010).

Of the four media forms—Internet/social media, newspaper, magazine, and TV—only the percentage of time spent using Internet/media is on the rise, while the percentage of time spent using the other forms is decreasing. This has led to an increase in companies shifting spending into search engine marketing from other marketing and IT activity (Figure 5) (Econsultancy, 2010). In 2009, there were 1.8 billion global Internet users, a 13% increase from 2008, with just under half (46%) from five countries: Brazil, China, India, Russia, and the United States. In the United States alone, there were 240 million users, a 4% increase from 2008, indicating a 76% penetration rate per 100 inhabitants. In Brazil, there were 76 million users, up 17% from 2008, indicating a 39% penetration rate (Meeker, Devitt, & Wu, 2010).

According to a survey done by Econsultancy of 1,500 client-side advertisers and agency respondents, the number of companies using SEO has remained at 90% since 2007, while paid search marketing has increased from 78% in 2009 to 81% in 2010 (Figure 6). More than half of companies surveyed expected to spend more on paid search and SEO in 2010 than they did in 2009, anticipating an average increase in spending of 37% and 43%, respectively (Econsultancy, 2010).

❖ Figure 4 Value of North American search engine marketing industry, 2004–2010.

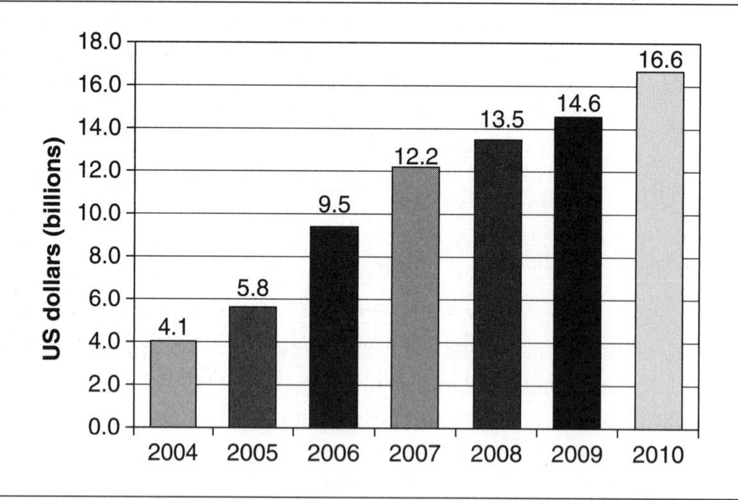

SOURCE: Econsultancy (2010).

❖ Figure 5 Funds for search marketing programs being shifted from which marketing/ IT programs?

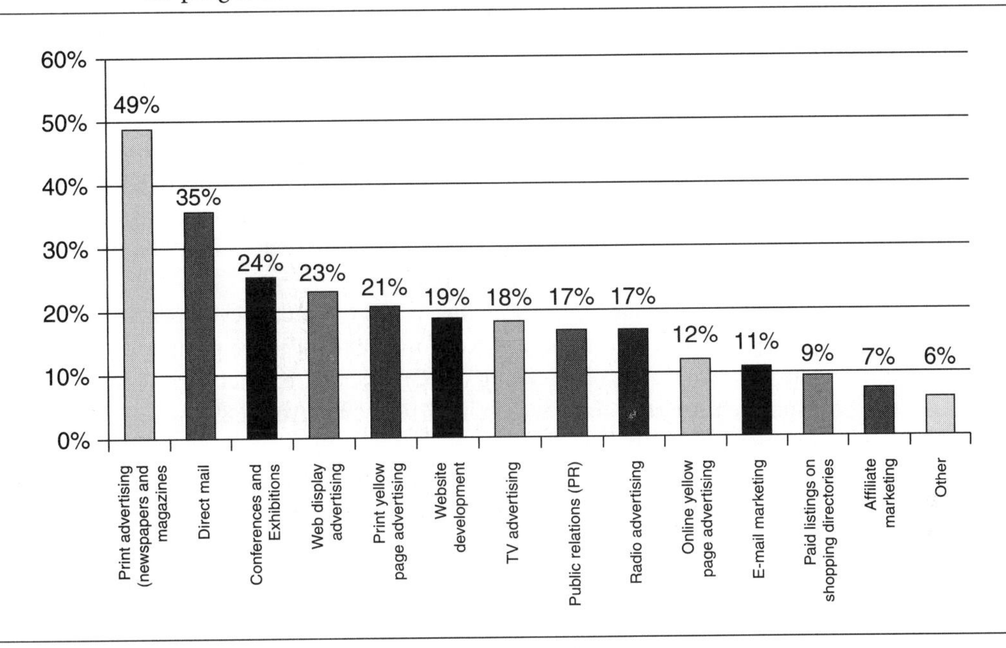

SOURCE: Econsultancy (2010).

❖ Figure 6 Type of organizational Internet marketing activity.

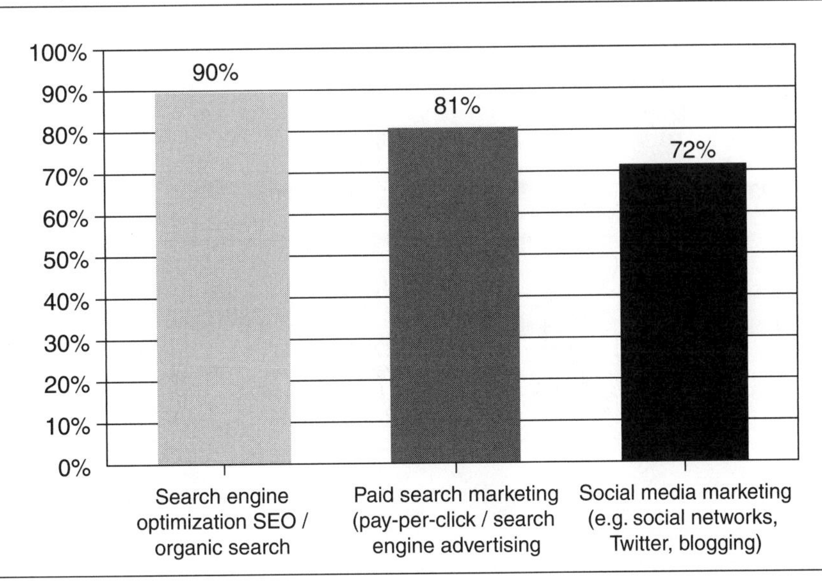

SOURCE: Econsultancy, "State of Search Engine Marketing Report 2010," in association with SEMPRO (2010).

One fifth of companies surveyed spent over $1 million on paid search in 2009, compared to a modest budget of less than $25,000 for social media marketing for 73% of companies (Figure 7). This includes 23% of companies reporting a budget of zero for social media marketing (Econsultancy, 2010). Yet the use of social marketing is on the rise. Fifty-nine percent of companies say their budgets for social media marketing will increase in 2010 (Econsultancy, 2010).

With 1.5 billion visits to social networks every day (Parker & Thomas, 2010), 74% and 73% of companies report using Facebook and Twitter, respectively, to promote their brand (Figure 8) (Econsultancy, 2010). Facebook is the largest social network in English-speaking countries with 620 million global visitors in 2009, while Twitter boasts 102 million users (Meeker et al., 2010).

Google's dominance as a search engine is clear. Ninety-seven percent of companies are paying to advertise on Google AdWords, and 71% are paying to advertise on Google search network, with 56% using the Google content network (Figure 9). Only 50% of respondents used Yahoo! Search in 2010, a drop from 68% in 2009 and 86% in 2008 (Econsultancy, 2010).

For many marketers, the measurement of return on investment (ROI) for paid search, social media marketing and SEO is a particular challenge. Forty-three percent of respondents report ROI measurement for paid search as one of their top three challenges, while 42% say the same for both social media marketing and SEO (Econsultancy, 2010).

❖ Figure 7 Company social media marketing budgets, 2009.

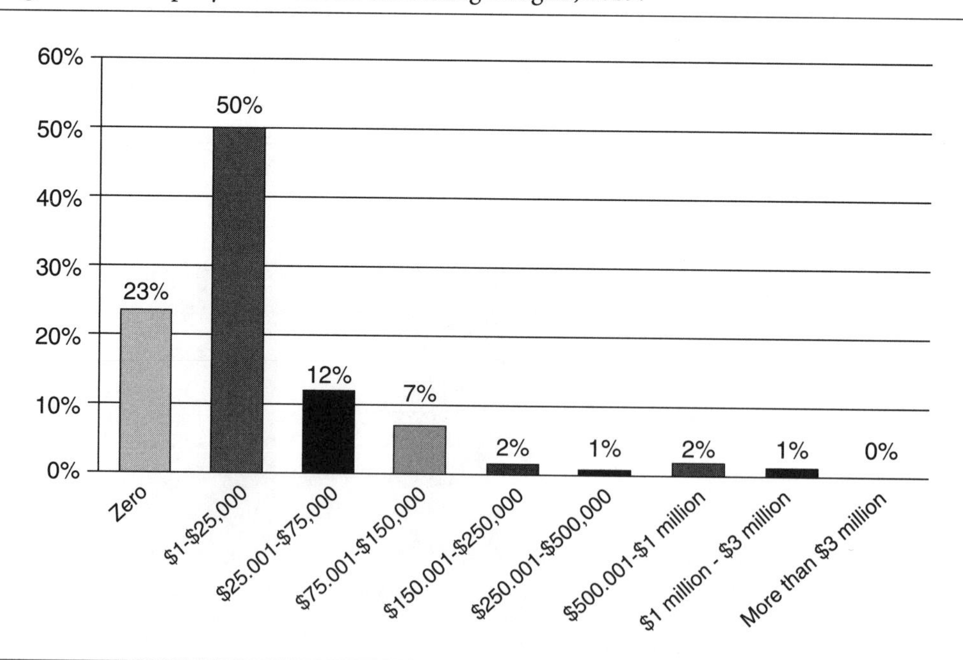

SOURCE: Econsultancy (2010).

❖ Figure 8 Social media sites used to promote brand/company by company usage rate, 2010.

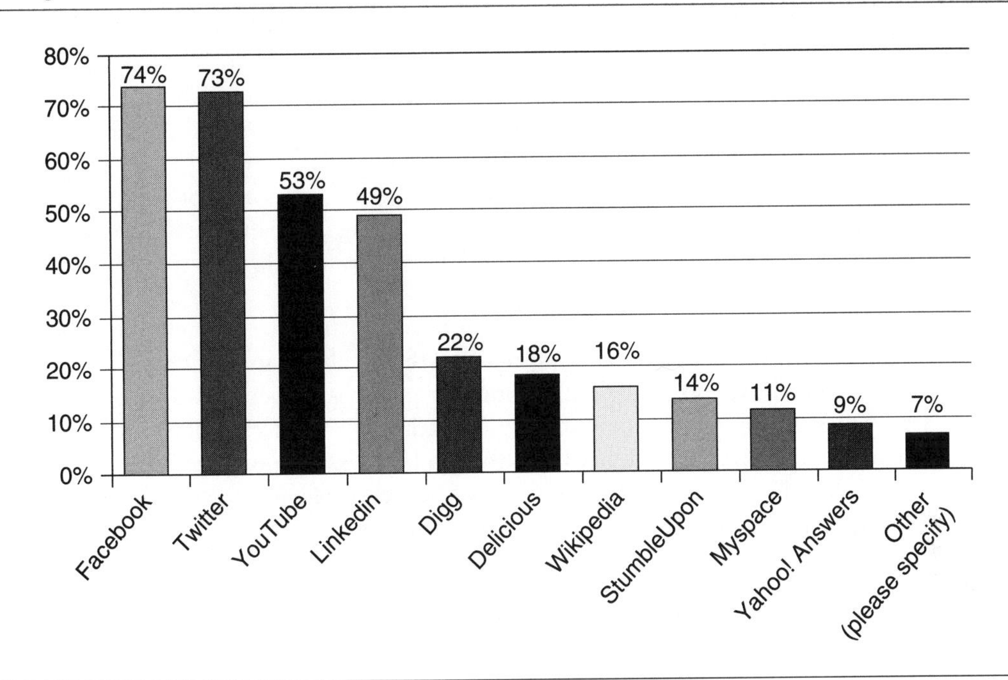

SOURCE: Econsultancy (2010).

❖ Figure 9 Percentage of companies paying to advertise on each search engine.

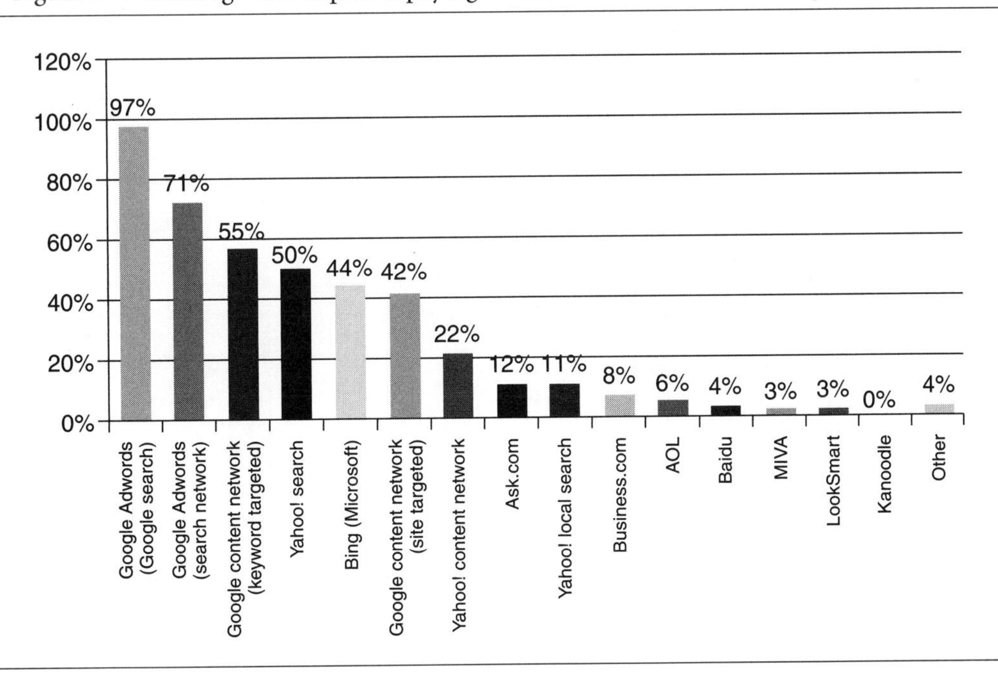

SOURCE: Econsultancy (2010).

Global Real Estate Management and Development Industry Overview

The size of the global real estate management and development industry is $461 billion, a decrease of 8% since 2009. It had a compound rate of change of –0.3% since 2005. No growth was expected in 2010, but steady growth was expected in 2011 and was forecasted to increase to $511 billion by 2014, with an expected CAGR of 2.1% for the period 2009–2014 (Figure 10) (Datamonitor, 2010c).

The residential segment of the industry accounts for 56.7% of the industry with the nonresidential segment being 43.3%. The leading companies in the industry are in Europe and the United States, accounting for 36.3% and 33.7%, respectively (Table 9) (Datamonitor, 2010c).

Buyers within the industry range in size and financial strength so large buyer power is mitigated by strong financial strength and ability to negotiate with key players, keeping buyer power moderate. Supplier power is moderate, with a large number of construction contractors offering essential key services. Substantial capital is required for entry into the market, although business or mortgage loans can provide access to this capital, and the likelihood of new entrants into the market is moderate. Competition is significant in the industry, reflecting the uncertain business environment and an unstable financial situation.

Players in the market try to differentiate themselves by the types of property or services, such as brokerage, offered. The global real estate management and development industry is highly fragmented, and name recognition is important. The top four companies in the industry account for only 3.9% of the industry's size. Of these top four companies, one is headquartered in the United States and the remaining three in Japan (Datamonitor, 2010c).

❖ **Figure 10** Global real estate management and development industry value forecast, 2009–2014.

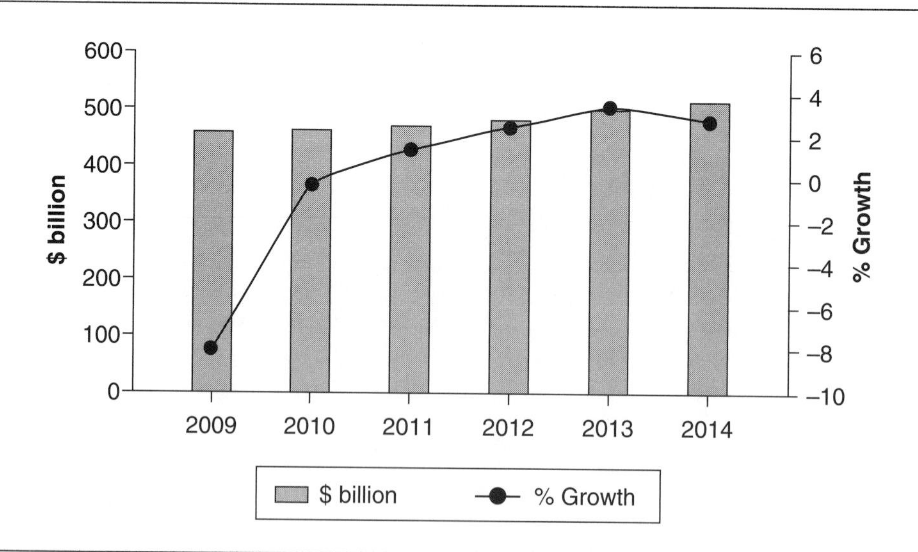

SOURCE: Datamonitor (2010c).

❖ Table 9 Global Real Estate Management and Development Industry Segmentation, 2009

Region	Share (%)
Europe	36.3
United States	33.7
Asia-Pacific	20.9
Rest of the world	9.1
Total	**100**

SOURCE: Datamonitor (2010c).

Global IT Consulting Industry Overview

In 2009, the size of the global information technology (IT) consulting and other services market was $498.2 billion, with a CAGR of 5.1% from 2005 to 2009. The market declined by 0.6% in 2009, but is expected to increase in the years ahead. The industry is forecasted to grow to $561.5 billion by 2014 (Figure 11) (Datamonitor, 2010b).

The sales of integration and development services was the most significant segment of the industry, with revenues of $246.7 billion, a total of 49.5% of the market's value. The top markets were the Americas (51.9%) and Europe (27.8%).

The industry is highly fragmented, with large, multinational players operating with numerous small firms. Key customers are businesses and government agencies, which range in size and financial strength. Brand recognition is crucial to the industry because quality IT service is a key factor in the success of the customer's businesses. Suppliers have highly skilled employees and provide both hardware and software. Because customers are dependent on being provided dependable service from their suppliers and switching costs are high, supplier power is strong overall. While small companies can differentiate themselves by specializing in certain industries such as health care or financial services, the overall likelihood of new entrants is moderate.

The top four companies in the industry account for 13.8% of industry sales (Datamonitor, 2010b). Competition is intense as the key companies continue to grow and have focused on diversification to lessen the degree of competition.

Global Internet Software and Services Industry Overview

This industry is composed of companies developing and marketing Internet software and/or providing Internet services, including online databases and interactive services, Web address registration services, database construction, and Internet design services (Datamonitor, 2010a). The size of this industry is $893.7 billion (Figure 12), an increase of 9.1% in 2009, representing a CAGR of 14.7% (Datamonitor, 2010a). It is forecast to increase 75.4% to $1,567.7 billion by 2014 (Figure 13).

❖ Figure 11 Global IT consulting and other services market value forecast, 2009–2014.

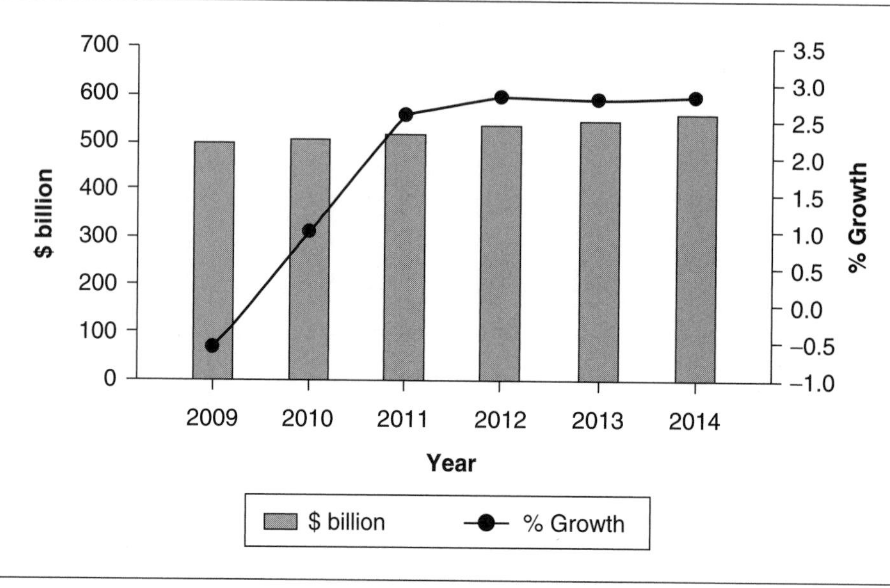

SOURCE: Datamonitor (2010b).

❖ Figure 12 Global Internet software and services industry value, 2005–2009.

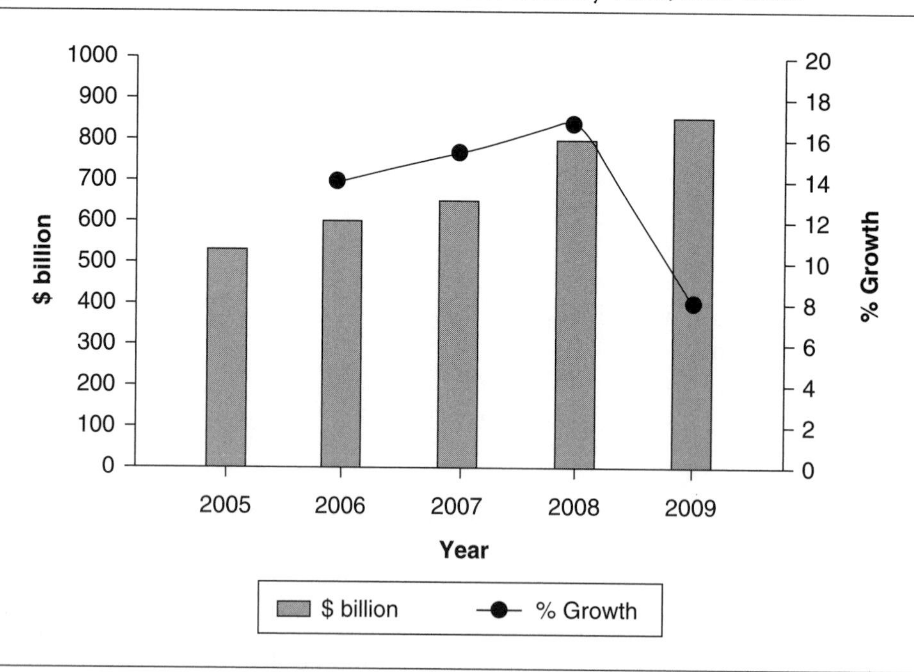

SOURCE: Datamonitor (2010a).

❖ Figure 13 Global Internet software and services industry forecast, 2009–2014.

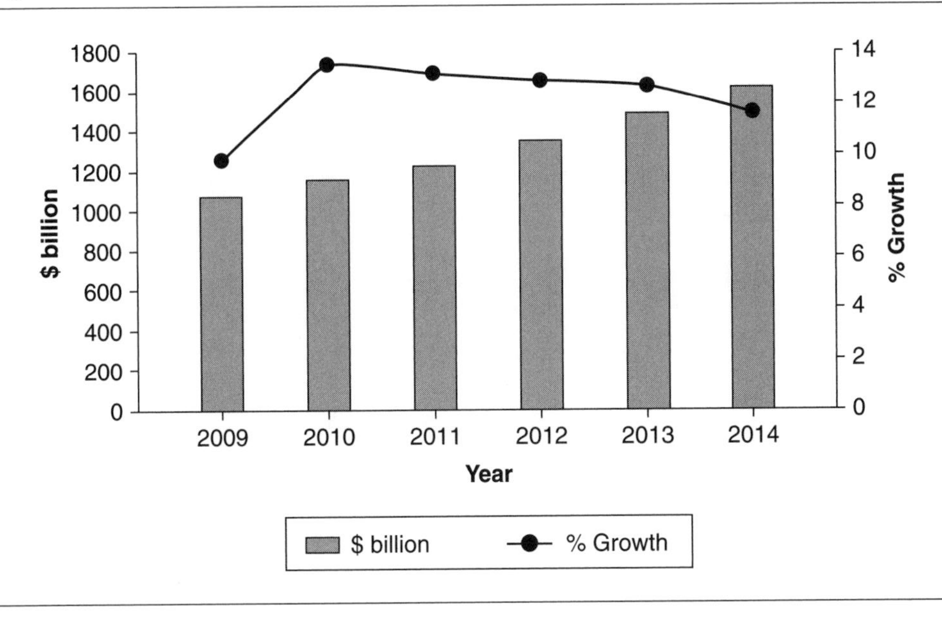

SOURCE: Datamonitor (2010a).

❖ Table 10 Global Internet Software and Services Industry Forecast, 2009–2014

Year	Subscribers (billions)	Growth (%)
2009	1.3	11.6
2010	1.4	11.0
2011	1.6	9.7
2012	1.7	9.1
2013	1.9	8.5
2014	2.0	7.9
CAGR: 2009–2014		**9.2**

SOURCE: Datamonitor (2010a).

The industry is split into two segments—the broadband segment, by far the largest (74.4% of the industry's overall size), and the narrowband segment (25.6%). Asia-Pacific is the largest regional segment of the global Internet software and services industry, accounting for 41.2% of the market's volume, followed by the Americas region with 33.2% of the global industry. The industry is forecasted to increase its subscribers up to 2 billion by 2014, a 55% increase since 2009 (Table 10) (Datamonitor, 2010a).

The industry is highly fragmented with large multinational companies accounting for only 8% of the global market. Because brand recognition is so important in the industry, companies such as Google and Yahoo! have global recognition and buyers such as individual consumers tend to frequent the brand. Commercial buyers do not consider brand recognition a significant factor in purchasing. Buyer power is moderated by the large pool of potential customers.

Supplier power is high, as many companies tend to rely on sole suppliers with strong negotiating skills. Entry in the industry is dependent upon high levels of technical expertise and R&D investments. While a strong growth trend has attracted new entrants, intellectual property is a strong barrier, as are the costs to comply with regulations such as the Digital Millennium Copyright Act (Datamonitor, 2010a).

Solutions

Robert Phillips feels that the company can grow through increased operations, new projects, new investors, and increased consulting. To do this, Phillips proposes the following for each of the group's companies (Guthry, 2010).

- **ILSC**—To capitalize on opportunities provided by the 2014 Brazil World Cup and the 2016 Summer Olympics, Phillips proposes solidifying the relationships the company has with other international companies, such as Advanced Leisure Services of Spain, Target Euro of Italy, and Gehry Technology of the United States. Additionally, a new website should be created for ILSC using the company's innovative Web marketing techniques.
- **IRES**—In this group, a leader needs to be identified to step in and grow the business, finish the IRES website, and begin offering high-end Brazilian properties online.
- **IWS**—In this group, a portfolio of success stories needs to be created and a strategy implemented to achieve international recognition and awards, update the website and translate this website into multiple languages to reach new clients, and partner with value-added providers. Additionally, IWS will work to strengthen the Internet Marketing Roadshow, which was put together by IWS to help companies understand what ILS does and why it is needed.
- **ITS**—In this group, a complete revision of ITS's existing websites must be done, as well as the creation of a new website structure applying new technologies and trends that have developed since the site was launched and allowing for rapid expansion into new destination areas and markets by replication. Also, opportunities in the Brazilian tourism industry offered by the 2014 Brazil World Cup and the 2016 Summer Olympics must be capitalized on.
- **ICS**—In this group, film, documentary, and training video dubbing and subtitling needs to be developed and offered as part of its service portfolio.
- **Overall**—Phillips proposes to continue to maintain the spillover effect between the companies to capitalize on shared knowledge, be up-to-date on trends and developments in tourism and Internet technology through continuous research, maintain the group's financial sustainability, and replicate the group's success stories by applying its successful website business model and operational system to new websites. Also, many of the companies' websites, some more than 8 years old, have not been redone since their initial creation and will be updated shortly.

Case Questions

1. How should Phillips go about solidifying the relationships Intelligent Leisure Solutions has with other international companies? How can these relationships benefit ILS?
2. How should Phillips identify a leader to grow the real estate solutions business? Because finding qualified employees for such a niche business was one of Phillips' biggest obstacles when starting the business, what are the pros and cons of hiring from within? From outside?
3. Is documentary and film dubbing too far outside Intelligent Leisure Solutions' core line of products? How could this affect the group's focus?
4. Does Intelligent Leisure Solutions need to develop a presence offline? Will its online presence be enough to capitalize on the 2014 World Cup and 2016 Summer Olympics?
5. Does Phillips demonstrate a clear vision for Intelligent Leisure Solutions? How does this impact the group's ability to grow sustainably?
6. Which of the following traits of a fast-growing firm (clear vision, retention of small company traits, market-driven behaviors, belief in customer service, shared focus, and increasing flexibility) does Intelligent Leisure Solutions exhibit that may lead it to quick growth?
7. Phillips seems to be focusing on all four growth strategies: penetration strategies (existing market, existing product), product development strategies (existing market, new product), market development strategies (new market, existing product), and diversification strategies (new market, new product). Is there one that he should focus on first?

References

Central Intelligence Agency. (2010). *The world factbook.* Retrieved from https://www.cia.gov/library/publications/the-world-factbook/index.html

Datamonitor. (2010a). *Global Internet software & services: Industry profile.* Retrieved from http://www.marketresearch.com/Datamonitor-v72/Global-Internet-Software-Services-6445589/

Datamonitor. (2010b). *Global IT consulting & other services.* Retrieved from http://www.datamonitor.com/store/Product/global_it_consulting_other_services?productid=D3F44101-8292-4FBE-9614-1C6ED508C2CA

Datamonitor. (2010c). *Global real estate management & development.* Retrieved from http://www.companiesandmarkets.com/Market-Report/global-real-estate-management-development-market-report-624768.asp

Datamonitor. (2010d). *Management & marketing consultancy in the United States: Industry profile.* Retrieved from http://www.amazon.com/Management-Marketing-Consultancy-United-States/dp/B004FFWN4W

Economist Intelligence Unit. (2010a). *Country forecast Brazil.* Retrieved from http://www.eiu.com/index.asp?layout=displayIssue&publication_id=490003649

Economist Intelligence Unit. (2010b). *Country report Brazil.* Retrieved from http://www.eiu.com/index.asp?layout=displayIssue&publication_id=1720000972

Econsultancy. (2010). *State of search engine marketing report 2010.* Retrieved from http://econsultancy.com/us/reports/sempo-state-of-search-2010

Euromonitor International. (2010). *Consumer lifestyles in Brazil.* Retrieved from http://www.euromonitor.com/consumer-lifestyles-in-brazil/report

Guthry, D. (2010). *Thunderbird 2010 Alumni Entrepreneur of the Year nomination: Robert Phillips.* Glendale, AZ: Walker Center for Global Entrepreneurship.

Meeker, M., Devitt, S., & Wu, L. (2010, November 16). *Ten questions Internet execs should ask & answer.* San Francisco: Morgan Stanley. Retrieved from http://www.morganstanley.com/institutional/techresearch/pdfs/tenquestions_web2.pdf

Parker, G., & Thomas, L. (2010). *The socialisation of brands: Wave 5.* New York: Universal McCann. Retrieved from http://www.umww.com/global/knowledge/download?id=1791&hash=F1C9F17E9E5CB4A2681D744A9AD018B3413C00BFad20708460e44685b4e8a7cb5612c496&fileName=Wave%205%20-%20The%20Socialisation%20Of%20Brands.pdf

Case 5

Logisys

A Small Company With International Potential

Problem to Analyze: Managing Company Development

***Dominika Salwa*[1]**

Introduction

Logisys is a small company established by young engineers from Krakow, Poland. Due to the qualifications and abilities of the founding partners, the company is thriving and making a mark in its industry. After receiving the prestigious European Auto-ID Award and the gold medal at the International Fair in Poznan, Poland, within its first year and a half of existence, the future of Logisys seems very bright. But one question remains: As the company enters the international scene, will it use its carefully gained competitive advantages to help unlock the potential that still lies within?

First, we will take a look at how the idea for the product was born, and then we will see how a plan of action was slowly, but successfully carried out.

Before the Beginning: An Idea Is Born

The Logisys founders met while working at another company, Incam. During the year and a half that they were there, the company went through a period of growth that

Author's Note: The author would like to thank the entrepreneurs from Logisys, Bartosz Jacyna, and Lukasz Musialski, for their help in developing this case.
Source: Used by permission from Dominika Salwa.

impressed both its workers and potential customers. This initial success, however, was shadowed by internal issues, including a stormy relationship between Incam's founders that generated a multitude of problems and lowered the morale of the employees. These problems spurred some employees and shareholders to discuss purchasing Incam and creating a new company. These employees were Martin Rosiek, a shareholder who was also responsible for Incam's finances and proprietary matters; Bart Jacyna, a hired manager who helped develop and restructure Incam; and Luke Musialski, an engineer and project manager.

Jacyna, a graduate of the Academy of Economics in Krakow, suddenly left Incam to pursue a career opportunity in Germany that did not materialize. Unemployed, but reluctant to go back to Incam, Jacyna stayed in contact with his former colleagues while he searched for a career or company that he could be passionate about. Jacyna had excelled as manager at Incam, where he created a flatter organizational structure with better management and administrative practices. He had also served as a mediator for Incam's quarrelsome founders. His sudden departure made the atmosphere even more unpleasant, since there was no one else to fulfill the main managerial functions.

The idea of purchasing Incam was raised again as Jacyna and his former coworkers pondered their options during casual conversations at social gatherings. This idea was rejected, since the likelihood of all of the shareholders selling out was not guaranteed. An alternative option was needed.

One day, Musialski announced, "I've got an idea for a product." After a promising preliminary test, Jacyna, Rosiek, and Musialski began the process of establishing a new company built around the new product. The creation of Logisys gave the trio confidence that their personal dreams (ambitions) would be protected and realized. Also, they were able to attract three crucial engineers and IT (information technology) specialists from Incam to their new venture, which augured a bright future for Logisys. Rosiek began to sever his ties with Incam by selling off his shares. With the new company established and staffed, Jacyna and Musialski turned to working on product concepts and strategy.

Difficult Beginnings: New Place, New Company, New Challenges

> Gentlemen, we are people who actually don't know anything about business. We know something about technology. We know already something about carrying out an information technology project. But, we know nothing about sales, zero about the market, and just a bit about running our own company. The main condition for our success is not what we know already, but how fast we learn what we don't.

This was Jacyna describing, in a circle of his new partners, the situation they were in when they established Logisys in May 2005. His sincerity and straightforwardness came from the strong relationships the partners had formed while working at Incam, as well as their knowledge of the basic business and strategic challenges that the new company faced.

The founding of Logisys provided Jacyna with the chance to find a career that he could be passionate about. Musialski, the creator of Logisys's hallmark product, had more reservations since he had not planned on leaving Incam so soon. However, he was drawn to the idea of a new company built around his product idea and with the right people leading it. Rosiek saw Logisys as a place where as a co-owner he could work at a decisive level with people he could trust. The three computer specialists hired from Incam saw their move to Logisys as a stepping-stone in the development of their careers in Poland. The market for computer specialists was flourishing, offering opportunities for high earnings and attractive work environments. Jacyna, Musialski, and Rosiek could not guarantee that the engineers would stay at Logisys for long. What Logisys could offer them, however, was creative freedom, full independence, and the necessity of using their intellects.

The company's first headquarters was a couch in Musialski's house, which was moved after a few weeks to a small flat. At first, Jacyna primarily took care of the basic administrative, legal, infrastructure, and strategic planning tasks related to establishing Logisys. He registered the company in a court and handled other regulatory issues, created the first financial plans, and hired an accounting firm. He also purchased basic office equipment (desks, phones, computers, stamps, etc.), worked on the website concept, looked for the best name for the new product, and handled design of the logo and other visual identifications for Logisys. Musialski and the rest of the team focused on the concept for the new product, which was a huge innovation in logistical processes operations. Rosiek was still working on leaving Incam.

The Conception of a New Product: Thoughts on Agilero

One of the major projects at Incam was the integration of automatic identification devices. Musialski's new product idea focused on the same area.

His solution that became pivotal to Logisys was connectivity software, or middleware, that provided a linking component for the integration of automatic identification devices. Why? Quite simply, a tool was needed to bridge the gap between the "eyes and ears" of sophisticated systems—auto-ID equipment or industry automation (automatics)—and the devices and technology that already existed in highly sophisticated systems. Automatic identification technologies (which are mainly represented by radio terminals, bar code scanners, RFID [radio frequency identification] printers and readers, automatic scales, and measurement systems) complicate the integration of projects. Not all companies are ready for this. Also, systems providers often get lost in this jumble of new devices and their applications. A market existed for a tool that could integrate all of the devices and applications with the main system in a cohesive, fluid manner. This was exactly the gap that Logisys filled, thanks to its new integration platform, Agilero (see Figure 1). The system had a different approach to solving the linkage problem than any other on the market.

From defining the idea to the actual implementation of the product took a long time. Agilero's architecture had to be thoroughly thought out to meet both present and future market requirements. In order to accurately assess the market requirements, the

❖ **Figure 1** Schema of logistic processes operation before and after applying Agilero.

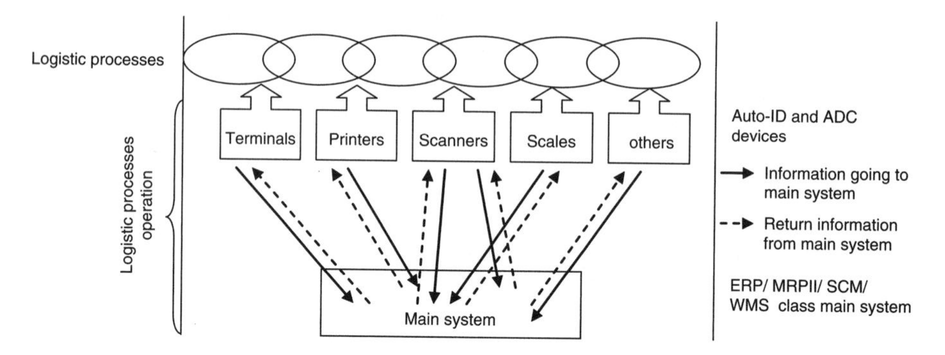

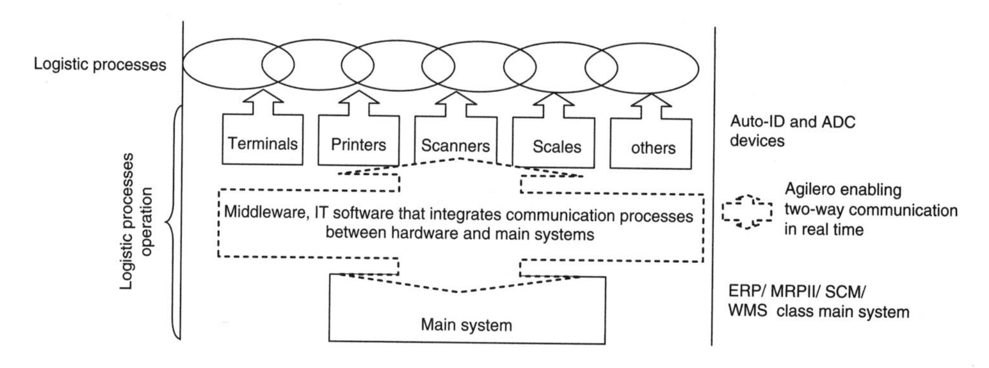

SOURCES: Dominika Salwa, Bartosz Jacyna.

creators analyzed approximately 160 implementation requirements and then defined functional features of the integration platform:

Reliability—guaranteed minimal risk of system going down. The system works online, offline, or in batch mode. The batch system allows for the possibility of data transmission after putting it into the communication dock.

Integration ability—certainty that the new solution is easy to match to existing and future systems, regardless of the type or brand of the device, the medium of transmission, and the standard of communication with the main system.

Flexibility—guarantee that the system will be able to develop with increasing and changing user needs.

Efficiency—certainty that system will be a strong link in the enterprise development chain.

Security—guarantee that system and data are always in trustworthy hands. Only designated individuals can access them.

The close focus on the conception of the product was a good investment, since it allowed for the prediction of potential problems and reduced the number of corrections needed at the beginning of implementation. Agilero is an integration platform based on SOA (service-oriented architecture). It is the only all-in-one integration platform in Poland (maybe even in Europe), without any competitors using the same approach.

"We're Still Novices, But We're Heading in the Right Direction"

At the end of June, Rosiek, exhausted from the final formalities of divesting himself of his partnership at Incam, finally officially joined the Logisys team. The Logisys founder had given up trying to purchase Incam, since the co-owners had demanded double or triple its estimated worth. Rosiek had to take a deep breath. As Incam's founder, he was emotionally attached to the company. Shortly after joining Logisys, he went on a previously reserved 3-week holiday.

Meanwhile, the premise of the product needed verification. During the summer holiday period, the Logisys entrepreneurs spent the time arranging their first business meetings with potential partners and essentially visiting half of Poland, including Warsaw, Poznan, and Gorny Slask. On their first "tour list" were 12 companies, where they presented the Agilero product idea, collected opinions, made potential contacts, and first and foremost, learned. Each meeting was thoroughly discussed and analyzed according to Musialski's thesis that "unaware knowledge is useless." July and August proved to be a good time for these meetings, since most companies had free schedules and agreed to see them without the typical long wait for a meeting. In spite of having taken first steps into the market, the results were rather poor. At that time, however, the germs of a future partnership started coming together.

At the end of 2005, Logisys signed a partnership agreement with Softex Data, a company with RFID device competence, where different RFID applications have been tested since 2004. Softex treated RFID as its future market, as its current markets were already mature and stagnant.

Logisys made preliminary contacts with several companies, including Anixandra (the largest distributor of LXE brand handheld computers in Poland) as well as Unitech, and the Cisco net Koncept-L (supplier of Symbol, PSC, Unitech, and Psion brand devices); and Talex (integrator, SAP, and Axapty main systems, logistics, transport, and telecommunications solutions supplier). Future plans centered around dealing with companies specializing in: the implementation of ERP/MRP II class main systems, logistic consultancy, supplying IT solutions to the logistic processes operation, and suppliers of auto-ID and ADC (automatic data capture) devices.

The Market: "We Create It"

To understand the criterion for choosing potential business partners, one should pay attention to the specificity of the Logisys product's location in the market of products and services connected to the management systems of logistic processes (see Figure 2). An important market discovery was the identification of who most often decides to

❖ **Figure 2** The place of Logisys products and services in logistic processes.

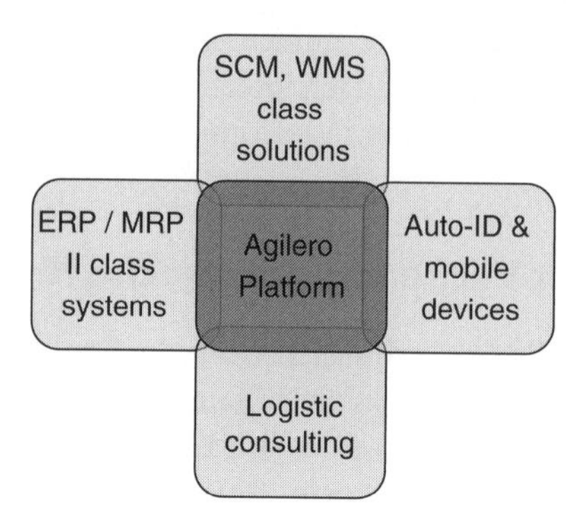

SOURCE: Logisys.

implement middleware or to use another platform of terminal management. Typically customers—final users—follow the suggestions of the system integrators and device suppliers, since the customers often do not know how necessary or useful the middleware class software application is.

The lack of customer knowledge of the role of the Agilero platform influenced the way Logisys perceived the market and took action. As Jacyna said, "We do something that the average customer doesn't understand at all. He doesn't know that what we do is very useful. We built awareness of the market, thereby creating it." Musialski added,

> This "component" [middleware] is often skipped. Everybody thinks around this "component" that somehow it'll go in, someone will cover it. . . . With the passing of time it turns out that no one covers it and no one even feels like doing it, because there's a cost. . . . And precisely in the middle there is a gap, exactly in that juncture.

Although the missing component in the integration between devices and systems—middleware—is logical, Musialski noted, "Logic isn't an argument good enough to make a thing exist [in the awareness of the customer—the final user]."

Potential Logisys partners (that means companies whose decisions make the shape and architecture of solutions for logistic processes management) are aware of the necessity of middleware, but usually in Poland they use makeshift and single solutions. These solutions enable integration, but are potentially costly in the long term.

Musialski concludes the market analysis by noting,

> We do realize that the market we act in is uneducated. To survive we have to educate it! Our great mission is to teach the market what it should look like in normal life. Maybe we differ from other companies which might or might not intentionally practice the "red ocean strategy" in the Polish market. We claim that enlarging the cake (blue ocean strategy) is worth more. Customers should be convinced that they may make a profit by using such solution.

Teaching customers this way foretells Logisys's chances for the future. Companies with an awareness of the significance of quality systems and devices in the functioning of their own logistic processes will appreciate the middleware Agilero.

Outside—Making a Move, Inside—Solving Problems

In January, 2006, Logisys's product was almost ready to introduce into the market. The first order came from Rosiek in mobile technologies; it was the first sale. The Wincor Nixdorf company needed an updated version of a solution that Rosiek had previously developed. Logisys took on the task of making new versions of his previous solution. As the first order and the first sale, it was a coincidental rather than intentional move by Logisys. They were trying to obtain their first customers.

Meanwhile, attention to the company's internal matters was needed. Jacyna was responsible for management and administration. He continued to work on the website and first marketing materials. Musialski remained the product manager of Agilero, controlling the design and preparation of the first prototype by the former Incam engineers. Musialski was responsible for all the decisions connected with technology.

Despite everyone's commitment, something was wrong. Each partner felt work discomfort and growing tension. Rosiek felt left out; Jacyna and Musialski thought he had only himself to blame. Since the situation involved friendship, it was particularly delicate. The problem primarily arose from differences in the role that Logisys played in the lives of the shareholders involved in building the company.

Further complicating the situation, the partners were providing the funding to run the company in its start-up phase and these funds were running out. At the beginning of January 2006, Musialski, Jacyna, and Doris, Jacyna's wife, made a most difficult and emotional business decision: They would part with Rosiek and buy out his share of the company.

Musialski bought the full 5% of Rosiek's shares. Soon after, Jacyna decided to sell 3% of his shares to Musialski. He thought that this would better reflect Musialski's noncapital contribution when creating the company. So, at that point, Musialski owned one third of the company's shares and Jacyna and Doris owned the rest.

Rosiek's leaving was a turning point for the company. Musialski and Jacyna now fully realized their huge responsibility, but that only amplified their determination to accomplish the aims and tasks of the company.

Becoming conscious of their weakness was also landmark. As Jacyna recollected,

> We thought we were wonderful, that we had a technology, but no one wanted to listen to us. It doesn't matter how it works, but what it gives. We could talk for hours how it works, but when we needed to tell what advantage it provided, we faltered.

The company also needed funds. To address that problem, Logisys signed an investment contract with Doris without changing the structure of company's ownership. Doris raised capital from her parents to provide development with funds from an outside source for 1 year.

From a Name to a Marketing Strategy

Jacyna began to consider company and product names, considering both Mobisys and Logisys. As combinations of prefixes of the words *mobile* or *logistics* and *systems*, they both addressed directly the company's need to explain its function. Logisys was chosen as the company name. Yet, opinion was divided when it came to Agilero—the name of the product. This name comes from the word *agile*, which describes largely the benefits of the product. The ending—*ro*—was to signal the harmonious spirit of the southern European countries. In the name selection for Agilero, Logisys worked with the company Media United and directly with a patent office. There were a few guidelines for the name: unregistered, explicitly readable in a few main languages, and with a free Internet domain.

Musialski did not initially like the Agilero name much, but the time pressure and Jacyna's imploring requests to trust him took precedence. After a few months, Musialski admitted that the name was good: "It's not globally optimal, but at least local." In spite of the irritating confusion between the product name and the singer Christina Aguilera, the memorable name became a definite plus.

Jacyna and Musialski also arranged the company's brand. Media United came up with the gray and orange Logisys logo. Quite by accident, the Agilero logo emerged from the Logisys logo. While working on the Logisys logo, a Media United employee cropped it down to the *og* part of the name. The effect was sensational. The fragment was immediately adopted as Agilero's logo (see Figure 3). "We were at once united in that issue," recollected one outside partner.

During the development stage, the partners had decided that the Agilero platform should not be dependent on Logisys to exist. Therefore, uniting the company and product by the logos and not the names was an intentional move. They wanted to keep the company and product brands separate.

The founders also decided not to use traditional titles for the various positions in the company. Using manager or president of the board seemed very exaggerated and a bit pompous considering the company's size and the age of those involved. Instead, the

❖ Figure 3 The logos of Logisys and Agilero.

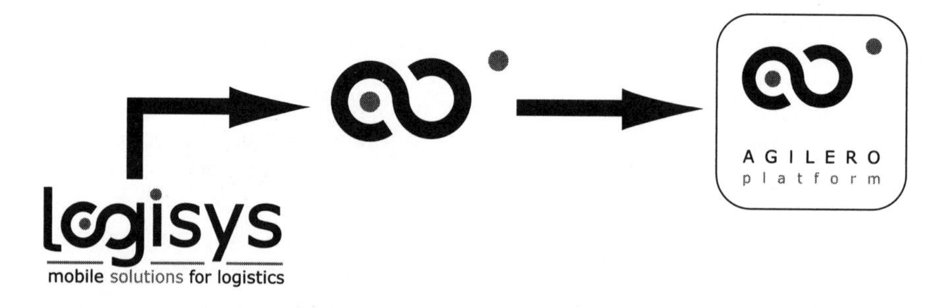

SOURCE: Logisys.

founders decided to use the name "partner" for the various employees. As a marketing strategy, this title implies that the "partner" has the ability to make decisions and has greater management and knowledge of the supplied services. Jacyna led the process of naming the positions by copying consulting companies.

The company finally decided to hire LAP Development, a consulting company, to design the marketing strategy. This inspired Logisys's employees, as the company evolved from an unfocused and unimaginative position to having well-organized, self-contained information making Logisys more understandable to potential partners and customers. New, good-looking promotional brochures that illustrated Logisys's work were developed in Polish, English, and German.

In late 2005, almost a year after Logisys began to cooperate with LAP Development, another critical problem came to light. The company's tagline, "Mobile solutions for demanding people," was wrong. Many potential customers were misinterpreting its meaning. This misunderstanding should have been resolved much earlier, when LAP Development first suggested that the motto be changed from "Mobile solutions for demanding people" to "Mobile solutions for logistics."

Developing the Company's Operational Capacity

A thorough marketing strategy required both discipline and time. New development opportunities began to appear on the market in 2006, and Jacyna needed to give some tasks away to focus on business development. Therefore, Logisys decided to add an office manager who would manage the office, its administration, and the company.

The company used Searchlight, a personnel consultancy company, to recruit its employees. Jacyna approached the employee selection process very carefully, because each new employee became a crucial company asset. Jacyna also thought that as the firm developed, each employee should specialize in some particular company function.

Searchlight offered five candidates. From the interviews, Jacyna narrowed the choice to two people. At first, Agnes seemed to be a good choice, but Jacyna believed her specific style of work organization would not be accepted at Logisys. Despite the stress of competition, the other candidate, Dominic, remained calm and reasonable, which influenced Logisys's decision to hire her.

At about the same time, Logisys landed a new business partner for the venture. The Hogart Company, noticing customer interest in the Agilero platform, decided to sign a partnership contract with Logisys. Hogart valued the concept of Agilero: "On the one hand it corresponds best to logistic processes requirements. On the other hand it has open architecture that increases the field of application and integration," commented one Hogart manager. Hogart is a leader in the implementation of Oracle systems in Poland and a recognized IT consultant in the implementation of management operating systems and the service of integration applications. In 2006, Hogart was named best provider of ERP (enterprise resource planning) systems for industry.

Another opportunity appeared on the horizon—participation in the Euro-ID Messe, or fair, in Köln, Germany. Logisys decided to take part in the messe.

A Prize Brings New Opportunities

Surfing the Internet, Jacyna happened on the Euro-ID Messe, organized in Germany, and he sent in an application. He purchased a special software kit called Demopoint, which was tailored to small, start-up companies, so that the team could prepare a demo of the Agilero platform. In addition, Jacyna applied for the prize awarded at the fair.

Jacyna's effort was rewarded with a great surprise. Musialski and Jacyna received a message that they had won the Euro-ID Award 2006, in the bar code category (it was emphasized that the Agilero solution also integrates devices based on RFID technology). What a joy, what a success, what a chance for the only Polish company attending the fair! This award provided the way for Logisys to become known abroad.

One of the first results of the new recognition was a partnership offer from the RFID Konsortium. The RFID Konsortium consisted of about 10 small German companies that came together to provide a joint solution for the implementation of RFID tagging in supply chains of German retail giants, METRO and REWE. The companies modernized the tagging of goods by changing the bar code to a radio tag, which became the new standard. Until then, tagging was mainly on a level of palettes. RFID implementation enables tracking at the level of the carton on the palette. The change to RFID tagging transfers the responsibility of logistic processes to the supplier. This new situation means that suppliers track batches of their goods and care for the stock of customers. RFID tagging enables carrying out this strategy.

The creator of RFID Konsortium had started out providing consulting services for fresh food producers (fruits, vegetables, meat, salads, flowers, and so on). He noticed that these mainly small and medium-sized companies were not ready for such new tracking technology. About 3,000 out of 10,000 of METRO's and REWE's suppliers are fresh food suppliers (so-called *Frischbereich*) and only 300 of them are big companies that understand RFID tagging and can afford to implement the required changes.

RFID Konsortium was created as a way for these small and medium-sized enterprises to be able to use the RFID technology. It gathers companies (see Table 1) that each have a certain slice of knowledge of the market in IT and RFID. Thus, the Konsortium provides very comprehensive service for companies that deal with the *Frischbereich* business.

Offering the middleware Agilero, Logisys holds an important position in the consortium. First, as the producer of Agilero, it influences the entirety of the offered product. It lets consortium members omit license granting by a third party. Second, Agilero integrates devices independently of the type, brand, or role in the whole process. When it comes to *Frischbereich* suppliers' diverse logistic processes, it does not increase costs.

Together member companies of the RFID Konsortium can serve a large number of customers. Separately, each company could only serve just a small portion of the market.

Important Staff Rotations

Despite the success at Euro-ID Messe fair, two crucial engineering employees gave notice. The job market in Poland in the IT trade had become an employee's market

❖ **Table 1** Companies Belonging to RFID Konsortium and Their Fields of Specialization

Company	Description
Schmitt	EDI solutions based on EDI EUREXc products
BWT	Weigh systems
Sato	Printers, bar code labels, and RFID producer
Michael Letterer	Consultancy in the area of technical processes, map project management
DeMann	Logistic automatics, RFID device assembly
PS4B	Programming company
Sys-Pro	ERP supplier for food trade
UBCS	Consultancy in processes, changes management, and business cooperation
VDEB	Small and average-sized consultancy and IT companies' union in Germany
Logisys	Middleware to the integration between devices and superior systems

SOURCE: RFID Konsortium (www.rfid-konsortium.de).

with numerous opportunities for finding interesting, well-paying jobs. Logisys was still in the initial development stage and could not afford those financial demands.

After a short period of crisis, the partners reached the conclusion that the situation was not as bad as they had supposed. One of the former Incam engineers stayed with the company and Agilero was by and large ready. This engineer, named Tom, was aware of the opportunities that Logisys held for him and the job suited him very well. In spite of his young age, he was a mature worker. Tom also got a raise—more than he had expected. In return, he signed a contract for a 6-month period, which protected the interests of the company. Tom took over responsibility for research and development, especially for Agilero.

Meanwhile, more potential partners and customers started to implement Logisys's solutions. Wix Filtron company, a customer of Hogart, decided to implement Agilero, which was very important and time-consuming.

The next customer was Merlin.pl, the biggest online bookstore in Poland. With Logisys's service, the company became twice as efficient in packing and sending its products without increasing costs. This was a huge success and another good reference for Logisys.

A can-packaging company (a leading producer of aluminum drink containers in Central Europe) and Dako (a wrapping-paper print house) were next to use Logisys's product to increase the efficiency of their processes. The Agilero platform was also implemented in a laboratory of the High School of Logistics at the Logistics and Storing Institute (the largest institution of logistic education in Poland).

At this point, the company needed to turn its attention to the organization of many areas of management and structuring information in- and outflow.

Introducing a New Organizational Order

The organizational structure of all small enterprises develops very dynamically. One person handles many different tasks and positions. Then as the company continues to develop and grow, it must sort out and name these different positions and the duties connected with them.

In the case of Logisys, there were three partners, but only two of them functioned as managers, determining what was going on in the company. They shared tasks according to their abilities and competencies. Since Musialski was the designer of Agilero and developed the product concept with the former Incam engineers, he naturally became the project manager, consultant, and seller.

Initially, Jacyna took care of office administration and business development and added marketing a year later. Hiring Dominic to take over the time-consuming business support functions and general office administration freed Jacyna to focus on project development.

With the departure of the two computer specialists Logisys had to find new employees. Luckily, two more former Incam workers, Peter and Luke, joined the team. Additionally, two more trainees, Jack and William, were employed to handle extra work. The whole IT team focused on improving Agilero and completing other projects ordered by customers.

During the second half of 2006, the rest of the positions at Logisys crystallized. Tom, who had been part of Agilero's design team from the beginning, became a project manager and Agilero's product manager. Peter was placed in customer service and support. Luke and Tom in cooperation with Peter ran the entire research and development department.

By the end of 2006, Logisys urgently needed to complete numerous marketing tasks. So, the company hired Ann, a student, for a marketing internship, during which she slowly took on many of Jacyna's marketing tasks.

A breakdown of employee roles in each department is presented in Table 2. Arranging the organizational structure required the placement of each person within the correct section and with the proper tasks. Moreover, an internal document, "My Logisys," was created for each worker. This document served as an operations manual for each employee, explaining the company's identity, vision and mission, goals, strategies, and what values it represents. The document also brought the structure of the organization and career development paths closer. The final section, "Help," contains everything from a dictionary of useful Logisys terms, and advice for getting along with irritating coworkers, to answers to simple but vital questions like "Who will clean up my desk?" and "Where is the coffee?"

❖ Table 2 Departments, Their Functions, and Individual Positions in Logisys

Department	Function	Personnel Positions
Research and Development	• Agilero's development • Device testing • Device certification	manager, analyst, designer, device tester, developer, documenter, instructor, application tester, servicer
Service and Support	• Coordination of contact (applications) with the customer in service and diagnostic issues • Commission and collection of service activities realization • The completion of service proceedings according to service contracts	manager, diagnostic tester, supporter, customer service, coordinator
Development	• Technical support of Agilero's implementation • The completion of service repairs	manager, system analyst, designer, tester, developer, documenter, instructor, implementer, servicer
Consulting	• Developing substantive competencies of Logisys • Sales/providing customers with knowledge and analytics • Generating advisory IT projects through sales support	manager, consultant, analyst, sales support, knowledge manager
Marketing	• Developing and making the knowledge about the market available • Managing partner relationships • Coordinating the production of advertising tools and coordinating promotional activities	manager, marketing analyst (information manager, researcher), PR specialist and manager, event-, creative-, site-manager and specialist, graphic designer, copywriter
Sales	• Coordinating sales and trade activities (especially during the early contact stage with a customer) • Global management of relations with customer • Sales plans accomplishment	manager, sales specialist, partner relations specialist
Project Management	• Range, time allocation, risk and project budget management • Project realization management and coordination • Generating additional orders and projects for current customers	manager, sales support, project preparation, project accomplishment, customer service (at designing and after implementation)

(continued)

❖ Table 2 (Continued)

Department	Function	Personnel Positions
Administration (Business Support)	• Providing Logisys employees with a good work environment • Managing the company's legal and financial safety • Providing reserves and competence of the company	marketing manager, business developer, finance manager, area manager

SOURCE: Logisys.

The Identity of Logisys and Crucial Issues

After discussing it with their lawyer, the Logisys partners chose to become a limited liability company, which is typical for small enterprises. This type of legal incorporation status gave the company more flexibility to revise its status and organization in the future.

Specific traits of the founders were directly translated into Logisys's identity, culture, and style of task completion. Jacyna —determined, with great business sense, unassuming, attentive observer—is up-to-date on matters that concern him. As he admits, he likes attaining the few visions that he has on his scorecard. He judges his own abilities as low, however, seeing a serious gap between what he knows and what he thinks he should know. While a lack of knowledge sometimes translates into avoiding tasks, Jacyna instead is adept at involving and encouraging other people to find the right person to take on those tasks. He knows how important knowledge is for organizing and he works to acquire it at the right time. He values coworkers. He says when something appeals to him, but he can also bluntly say when something is wrong. He treats many things seriously. He keeps a short distance between himself and business matters.

Musialski, always smiling, has a more distant relationship with business matters. As a great theorist, he can win over the person he is talking to, even if he does not have it right. He has a typical scientific mind, demanding that everything be presented to him "in black and white," including the justification. Otherwise, he will not believe. For example, with the name Agilero, Musialski did not want to believe the mind-boggling marketing truths that Jacyna explained to him. Although he usually gets to the bottom of the matter, he became resigned to the name and let it go through without fully believing. Now he appreciates this part of marketing, saying, "Most people take decisions, let's say, irrationally. They don't have any objective reasons that would let them take this one, not the other decision. All these reasons are subjective." He calls marketing building these subjective reasons. Musialski can accumulate and process information in amazing ways. He sees details that Jacyna arranges generally, fulfilling his role as a partner.

Together, the two managing partners seem to have achieved a synergy that neither of them could on their own. They both like doing things properly, which is reflected in the company. This probably explains why Logisys won not only the European Auto-ID

Award 2006, but also the gold medal at the International Fair in Poland in August 2006. These awards and a growing reputation for quality, helped to create and sustain perceptions of Logisys as a solid partner in the market.

Once again, it is the managing partners' features that underlie the value of the company. Logisys is characterized by professionalism, quality, knowledge, communication, continuous improvement, independence, responsibility, focus on outcomes, and care for the good name of the company. The partners aspire to having the company be recognized as a substantive leader. They do not consider reducing price at the cost of quality at all. In the long-term perspective, they can achieve satisfying success only by maintaining high product quality and service at an appropriate price. "Logisys competes through quality and range," repeat the partners.

The partners began to create Logisys's image through substantive, informative articles in the trade press. This marketing effort made them recognizable as specialists in their field.

In spite of the high quality of management for such a small enterprise, the company still contends with problems characteristic of small enterprises at this developmental stage. The market is not precisely described, well identified, or characterized. The company's reserves "are developing," but they are not ready for many large implementation projects. Since the company lacks trade experience, it needs a good sales specialist who could develop contacts. Everything is a process. Nothing can be fulfilled immediately and that is why proper planning and care of the company's development are so important.

Finances

Logisys is a typical "start-up" company, established with a plan to specialize in one area: advisory IT services. As with every small company, it had to invest money first, and only after a time expect a return on the invested capital.

Money to run the business came from three sources: the contribution of the co-owners, extra money from shareholders, and the investment contract signed with Doris. The company's first revenues from sales in 2005 and 2006 did not cover the operational costs (see Table 3). The company planned to reach a cost-revenue balance by the first half of 2007.

Plans for the Future

Logisys developed in a way characteristic of small enterprises. Based on intellectual capital, without a clearly defined market, people wanted to make the idea a reality. Logisys has a chance to join the circle of typical pioneering enterprises that make it. These successful enterprises stand out from others because their founders clearly described a vision of the company's development. Logisys seems to prove this general rule.

Further company development will depend on the ability to learn quickly, as Jacyna often emphasizes, as well as on the ability to predict and acquire needed human, financial, and material resources. Human resources seem to be especially crucial for well-balanced company development in the long run. The managing partners often emphasize human resources, because each worker that comes to the company has a chance to be promoted. Promotion stages include the following levels: junior, specialist,

❖ Table 3 Logisys's Balance Sheet in 2005

ASSETS							
+/-	Pos.			Position name	Year's beginning 2005-01-01	Year's ending 2005-12-31/ Year's beginning 2006-01-01	Year's ending 2006-12-31
-	A			Fixed assets	0,00	5,419,68	17,855,74
	-	I		Intangible assets	0,00	0,00	0,00
			1	Costs of finished development works	0,00	0,00	0,00
			2	Comapany's value	0,00	0,00	0,00
			3	Other intangible assets	0,00	0,00	0,00
	-	II		Tangible fixed assets	0,00	3,319,68	15,755,74
		-	1	Property, plant and equipment	0,00	3,319,68	15,755,74
			2	Engaged fixed assets	0,00	0,00	0,00
			3	Down payments for fixed assets	0,00	0,00	0,00
	-	III		Long-term debtors	0,00	0,00	0,00
			1	From subsidiary and associated companies	0,00	0,00	0,00
			2	From other companies	0,00	0,00	0,00
	-	IV		Long-term investments	0,00	2,100,00	2,100,00
			1	Properties	0,00	0,00	0,00
			2	Intangible assets	0,00	2,100,00	2,100,00
		-	3	Long-term financial assets	0,00	0,00	0,00
			4	Other long-term investments	0,00	0,00	0,00
	-	V		Long-term deferred expenses	0,00	0,00	0,00
			1	Deferred income tax	0,00	0,00	0,00
			2	Other deferred expenses	0,00	0,00	0,00
-	B			Current assets	50,000,00	53,632,77	164,664,57
	-	I		Stocks	0,00	0,00	0,00
			1	Materials	0,00	0,00	0,00
			2	Half-finished and under way products	0,00	0,00	0,00

❖ Table 3

+/-	Pos.	Position name			Year's beginning 2005-01-01	Year's ending 2005-12-31/ Year's beginning 2006-01-01	Year's ending 2006-12-31
			3	Ready products	0,00	0,00	0,00
			4	Goods	0,00	0,00	0,00
			5	Advance payment for supply	0,00	0,00	0,00
	-	II	Current receivables		0,00	12,515,20	151,162,15
		-	1	From subsidiary and associated companies	0,00	0,00	0,00
		-	2	From other companies	0,00	12,515,20	151,162,15
	-	III	Short-term investments		50,000,00	40,699,08	12,270,29
		-	1	Short-term financial assets	50,000,00	40,699,08	12,270,29
			2	Other short-term investments	0,00	0,00	0,00
		IV	Short-term deferred expenses		0,00	418,49	1,232,13
	TOTAL ASSETS				50,000,00	59,052,45	182,520,31

LIABILITIES

+/-	Pos.	Position name		Year's beginning 2005-01-01	Year's ending 2005-12-31/ Year's beginning 2006-01-01	Year's ending 2006-12-31
-	A	Shareholders' equity		50 000,00	50,295,10	–249,037,59
		I	Share capital	0,00	50,000,00	50,000,00
		II	Due payments on share capital (negative quantity)	0,00	0,00	0,00
		III	Own shares (negative quantity)	0,00	0,00	0,00
		IV	Reserve capital	0,00	150,000,00	150,000,00
		V	Revaluation capital	0,00	0,00	0,00
		VI	Other reserve capitals	0,00	0,00	0,00
		VII	Prior years' profit (loss)	0,00	0,00	–149,704,90

(continued)

❖ Table 3 (Continued)

+/-	Pos.	Position name				Year's beginning 2005-01-01	Year's ending 2005-12-31/ Year's beginning 2006-01-01	Year's ending 2006-12-31
		VIII	Net profit (loss)			0,00	−149,704,90	−299,332,69
		IX	The deduction from net profit in working year (negative quantity)			0,00	0,00	0,00
-	B	Liabilities and reserves for liabilities				0,00	8,757,35	431,557,90
	-	I	Reserves for liabilities			0,00	0,00	0,00
			1	Reserve for deferred income tax		0,00	0,00	0,00
			2	Provisions for pension and similar benefits		0,00	0,00	0,00
			3	Other provisions		0,00	0,00	0,00
	-	II	Long-term liabilities			0,00	0,00	384,546,40
		-	1	To subsidiary and associated companies		0,00	0,00	384,546,40
		-	2	To other companies		0,00	0,00	0,00
	-	III	Current liabilities			0,00	8,757,35	47,011,50
		-	1	To subsidiary and associated companies		0,00	0,00	0,00
		-	2	To other companies		0,00	8,757,35	47,011,50
			3	Special funds		0,00	0,00	0,00
	-	IV	Accrued expenses and deferred income			0,00	0,00	0,00
			1	Negative company's value		0,00	0,00	0,00
		-	2	Other accrued expenses and deferred income		0,00	0,00	0,00
	TOTAL SHAREHOLDERS' EQUITY AND LIABILITIES					50,000,00	59,052,45	182,520,31

SOURCE: Logisys.

self-reliant, operational-tactical management, and strategic management. Not every employee, however, goes through every stage. The company might employ an experienced specialist in a specific field. Then, he or she may move from the specialist level to project manager. Such plans might apply, for instance, to workers sought after to develop the sales department. Plans for human resources include employing an intern in the development department, a person to coordinate the RFID Konsortium project in Berlin, and a production manager.

Logisys has a clearly charted strategy for activities and strategic plans for the next few years. The company is going to implement standards for the completion of projects and design documents and evaluations of projects and production range. Contracts will be implemented on the projects to allow the company to reach income-costs balance.

Activities connected to marketing will include achieving the status of an expert in integration of mobile devices and auto-ID in Poland. Publications in the press and marketing through partners and equipment suppliers will be useful to achieve this aim. Pricing policies will be revised.

In the finance field, priority will be given to the full balance of current income and costs.

Organizational change is needed in the structure of the company to improve employees' efficiency. The ultimate effect will be increased salaries for the employees.

Logisys has a chance for international sales, especially through the Agilero platform

Participation in the RFID Konsortium is the mainspring of Logisys's international development, allowing for quicker entry into the German market. Austria should easily be the next market, since it has a similar mentality and organizational style as Germany. The first prize at the Euro-ID Messe 2006 and the gold medal at the International Fair in Poland are confirmation of Logisys's and the Agilero platform's quality. The company left the Polish market's borders and is recognized by other nations. Information of Swedes' interest in suggested solutions have come to the company. The British market also shows potential opportunities. There may be many digressions in the development of potential foreign markets, since 2007 was concentrated on Poland and the RFID Konsortium.

If growth and development of the company maintain their current rate as planned, 2008 may be a landmark year in terms of achievement, company size, supplied markets, partnerships, and so on. The year 2008 could also see a change in the company's business model. Assuming that Agilero evolves into a separate, easy-to-sell product, the company will face the decision concerning implementation of two business models—Agilero (a product) and Logisys (a consultancy)—as separate entities.

Glossary of Terms

ADC (automatic data capture) is a key to success in a range of enterprises' information strategies. Accurate, reliable data download allows the optimization of company processes. The growing importance of ADC is visible in every trade, especially in logistics and transport.

Automatic identification is a technology that identifies the units of a logistic process. Bar code and radio tag technology are most often used in automatic identification. Image recognition technology also exists, but is less popular and used in very specific conditions. Auto-ID devices identify logistic units, such as bar code readers (also called scanners), mobile terminals, and bar code printers.

EDI (electronic data interchange) is a set of standards for streamlining electronic information interchange outside and inside the enterprise.

Main systems of enterprises are IT systems used to streamline enterprise management. These systems enable optimization of resources. These include:

- **ERP** (enterprise resource planning)
- **MRP II** (manufacturing resource planning)
- **SCM** (supply chain management)

Among types of main systems found are SAP, Axapta, JDEdwards, Navision, and others.

RFID (radio frequency identification) is identification technology that uses properly modulated radio waves to carry the data. RFID tagging technology introduces a new quality of optimization of logistic processes. An RFID tagging label contains a chip with an antenna that enables data gathering and transmission by radio. Appropriate logistic information is not placed on documents (it is natural that they are unreliable) but on logical units themselves, thanks to RFID labels.

Note

1. Dominika Salwa is an assistant professor in the Department of International Management at Krakow University of Economics, Krakow, Poland.

Case Questions

1. Try to identify Logisys's development stage. Justify your opinion in detail. Compare your answer with company development stages according to L. Greiner. What are the similarities and differences?

2. Create the vision and strategic goals for Logisys.

3. Present an analysis of strong and weak features of Logisys and chances and threats that the environment makes.

4. Plan the recruitment process for a position of office manager in Logisys. Consider three stages of recruitment procedure.

5. What activities are hidden in the role of 'project preparation' for a project manager?

6. Show changes in the organizational chart considering the number of workers and their positions. Try to create an organizational chart of Logisys considering co-owners' plans that concern the company's development in the first half of 2007.

7. Perform elements of implementation of the marketing function and its importance for Logisys.
8. Where might have the personal problems between three partners originated?
9. What was the key to the selection of business partners? Why did the Hogart Company decide on a partnership contract with Logisys?
10. Assess the financial standing of Logisys in 2006.
11. Try to draw on a graph how the financial situation of the company would look in a relation to its development phase (use the schema of the phases of life cycle).
12. Concept questions: Try to perform further development of Logisys and Agilero, taking into account opportunities and threats that national and international markets pose.

Case 6

Mayu LLC

Kate Robertson

Introduction

After graduating from college with a BS in business administration, Kate Robertson was not seeking a traditional office job. Instead, she was looking for an adventure, one that would fulfill her never-ending wanderlust and allow her to unleash her entrepreneurial spirit. She joined the Peace Corps as a Small Business Development Volunteer and was sent to a rural community high in the Andes Mountains of Peru. During the 2 1/2 years that Kate lived in Peru, she became enamored with the country. After months of teary-eyed goodbyes, she returned to Chicago in early 2010 with an idea. Kate would create Mayu LLC, a company that would sell hand-knit fashion accessories made with pure Peruvian Alpaca fiber by the artisans with whom Kate worked in the Peace Corps. Kate believed that by establishing this small social enterprise, she could remain connected to her Peace Corps community. The company would not only provide additional income to Peruvian women, but also fulfill a market need for knitwear that was both one-of-a-kind and stylish.

To test the waters, Kate returned from the Peace Corps with two giant rice sacks full of alpaca shawls, scarves, and blankets. Seeing the positive reactions of friends and family, Kate decided that starting Mayu was indeed an excellent idea. As the demand was there and the weather was cold, she dove in head first without creating a formal business plan. One year later, as Mayu was growing, Kate was faced with a number of challenges and realized she had better answer a couple of questions before moving ahead.

1. Assuming demand continued to grow, how would she scale operations in Peru? She had already accepted a full-time job in Chicago and would be working on Mayu on a part-time basis.

2. How would she take Mayu from an in-person, event-based company to a successful online store if people could not see and feel the Alpaca fiber? She needed an online marketing strategy.

Source: Used by permission from Kate Robertson.

3. Admitting that finance was not her strong suit, Kate worried that the pro forma financial data she had calculated were missing something. She was looking for feedback on what she had done.
4. What fraction of equity would need to be given up assuming outside capital would be sought for expansion?
5. Should she partner with several individuals who had asked her to help them also import knitwear from Peru? She wanted to protect her "trade secret"—the artisans who she had worked hard to train.

Company and Product

Mayu, which means river in Quechua, the native language of Mayu's Peruvian artisans, imports and sells alpaca accessories including hand-knit scarves, hats, shawls, wraps, gloves, and blankets. Mayu's pro bono attorney incorporated the company as an LLC and Mayu is now a registered trademark. Kate developed the following mission for the company:

> Mayu strives to be the industry leader in the sale of high-quality, one-of-a-kind, ultra-classic alpaca accessories. Mayu offers social value by increasing the livelihood and contributing to the personal and professional development of their female producers in Peru. At the same time, Mayu transparently and honestly educates American consumers about the origins of Mayu's ethical fashion accessories. Superb customer service, mutual-respect, and triple bottom line initiatives (people, planet, profit) are the elements guiding Mayu's business activities.

After many shopping excursions in Lima's markets and Internet research on alpaca accessories currently offered in the market, Kate defined the unique selling propositions of Mayu's products. The exclusive, stylish designs were handmade with eco-friendly Alpaca fiber, were fairly traded (Mayu is a member of the Fair Trade Federation), and were of the highest quality, lasting a lifetime. This product offering was different from the mass-produced, machine made accessories found in brick-and-mortar and Internet-based shops in Peru and the United States. Kate also noticed that most of these products were not actually knit with pure alpaca yarn. Instead, they were typically a combination of alpaca and other wools of lesser quality. Another uniqueness was that Mayu's products used purely Peruvian materials and labor and had an interesting story behind them. The story reflected Kate's Peace Corps experience and direct relationship with the artisans.

Industry and Current Trends

Clothing and Accessories

Kate's research indicated that the demand for clothing and accessories was driven by personal income and fashion trends and that women purchased approximately 64 items of clothing per year. According to 2010 IBISWorld Clothing & Accessories stores industry forecasts, the industry was valued at $7.0 billion with profits of $772.8 million and of all the accessory products sold, 18% involved neckwear, scarves, and hats. The accessories market had seen annual growth of 5.1% over the previous

5 years and was expected to reach 7% annual growth from 2010 to 2015. The market size of the women's outerwear and clothing industry had consistent growth between 2003 and 2008. Although the recent economic downturn had impacted the accessories market as the consumer sentiments index fell by 4.1% during the preceding years, the index was expected to rise by 13.6% in 2010. Per capita disposable income in the U.S. was also on the rise from its lowest values in 2008. As a result, Kate thought that her target market would not be severely impacted. Studies showed that even in times of economic downturn, consumers shifted buying behavior to more classic, forever pieces, which is precisely what Mayu offered.

E-Commerce

The e-commerce industry was growing steadily, having annual growth of 6.6% from 2005 to 2010 and annual revenues over $93.8 billion. Fortunately, online sales were expected to continue growing at an even faster rate of 10.5% from 2010 to 2015. Looking at these statistics, it was clear that online retailing was a growing medium for the purchase of specialty items such as those knit by Mayu's artisans in Peru. Of all online businesses in 2010, 15% were clothing and accessories retailers. Due to increased connectivity, positive perceptions of online security, and ease of conducting transactions, online companies such as Mayu could be expected to benefit from this growth.

Trends

Kate knew that growing awareness of fair trade and ethical fashion and the recent signs of a "green revolution" would be beneficial to Mayu. There was no doubt that consumers were becoming more responsible shoppers, and Mayu offered a solution to the market's increasing demand for products that offered social value. With that, the consumer market was developing a need for transparency and traceability throughout supply chains, especially for products from the developing world. The implementation of corporate social responsibility programs and establishment of not-for-profit advocacy organizations was proof that the 21st-century business environment was changing, and companies would be unable to survive without considering the consequences of their behaviors. The Mayu website contained information about the Mayu product life cycle, and Kate intended to further expand the site to allow for even greater transparency.

According to surveys administered by the Fair Trade Federation, the trend toward fair trade shopping in the United Sates was growing quickly. By 2010, 71.4% of American consumers knew about fair trade and 88% considered themselves conscious consumers. In 2009, fair trade organizations averaged annual sales of $517,384, compared to $499,892 in 2006, and 72.4% of these organizations were for-profit entities, showing that social, mission-driven businesses were valid substitutes for the traditional "charity-based" not-for-profits. Established fair trade companies were growing with increasing numbers of employees and volunteers and increasing impact in the countries where the production of their goods took place.

As for consumer trends, A.T. Kearney indicated that in 2009, the market for sustainable products was estimated at $118 billion, while, according to the Boston Consulting Group, firms with a "true commitment to sustainability" outperformed industry peers, especially in the retail sector. These trends reiterate American society's desire to create positive change through purchasing habits.

The concept of ethical fashion was also gaining momentum, which would also benefit Mayu's eco-friendly products. The 2009 Cone Consumer Environmental Survey, which was conducted by Opinion Research Corporation, indicated that 34% of American consumers were likely to buy environmentally responsible products and 25% more Americans had greater interest in the environment today than they did one year ago. As a result, there was an increased expectation for companies to produce and sell environmentally conscious products. Seventy percent of Americans indicated that they were paying attention to what companies were doing with regard to the environment. This interest indicates that the "green revolution" is more than just a passing trend.

A 2008 study by Conscious Innovation claimed that products and services that help customers live a sustainable life and fulfill their "help me to be a conscious consumer" desire would also thrive. Consumer behaviors for purchasing clothing and gifts have changed from previous years and are expected to continue being influenced by conscious choices.

Competition

A broad range of competition existed in the industry including both online and brick-and-mortar shops selling accessories, and while some items were handmade, most were machine made. All were available in a variety of raw materials, including alpaca, cashmere, wool, and cotton.

Kate defined direct competition as online retail stores selling alpaca accessories and clothing. There were a number of e-commerce sites selling alpaca accessories but none of them sold products as unique as Mayu's. The following websites were good examples of the competition:

- Peruvian Connection—www.peruvianconnection.com
- Alpaca Direct—www.alpacadirect.com
- Purely Alpaca—www.purelyalpaca.com
- Alpaca Boutique—www.alpacaboutique.com

Mayu differentiated itself from this primary competition because of the quality and uniqueness of its products. Kate thought that the Mayu website was a higher caliber and appealed to a more fashion-forward and conscious clientele. Once customers landed on the Mayu site, they were attracted to the stylishness, sleekness, and simplicity. The site was professional, personalized, aesthetically pleasing, and most important, up-to-date with current social media and "green" shopping trends. While Mayu's prices were comparable to the competition, customers received greater value when purchasing from Mayu. Mayu provided excellent and timely customer service and a personalized touch to potential and past customers. Ease of communication with Mayu created a positive shopping experience, despite the online nature of the business.

Kate defined secondary competition as online and brick-and-mortar retail stores selling knitwear made from raw materials such as cotton, cashmere, silk, or wool. Most of these companies have an advantage over Mayu in that they are more established and therefore, had greater brand awareness and Internet presence. These larger companies have excess capital and budgets to spend on marketing and other business development activities. Mayu differentiated itself through its personal story and social mission. Kate wanted Mayu to appeal to shoppers interested in supporting independent and local companies as opposed to those who purchased from "big-box" retailers who often lacked transparency, originality, personality and ethical behavior. The following companies are among those considered secondary competition:

- Anthroplogie—www.anthropologie.com
- Nordstrom—www.nordstrom.com
- Neiman Marcus—www.neimanmarcus.com

Marketing

Target Market

Based on her research, Kate planned to target educated women between the ages of 32 and 62, who make up 67% of the accessories market. This range allowed Mayu to target a majority of women aged 15 to 65, who represent 90% of total consumer spending. Kate expected that this market would be more socially aware and understanding of global issues and would be consumers that were more responsible. It was shown that luxury shoppers, defined as consumers who earn over $100,000 per year, are more educated and demanding so workmanship, longevity, and artistry play a large role in their purchasing behaviors.

Because Mayu is striving to become an Internet business, it has access to the entire world. In order to narrow its online marketing, Kate thought she should focus on three Standard Metropolitan Statistical Areas (SMSAs)—Chicago, New York City, and San Francisco. The reasons for choosing these particular cities are that they have appropriate weather and large populations of educated and affluent female consumers. Chicago was a natural starting point, as it is Mayu's home base with existing relationships. San Francisco has a high concentration of socially conscious female consumers and New York City's inhabitants are fashion forward and the country's trendsetters.

Price

Mayu's pricing structure is cost-based pricing. Kate used the traditional industry markup of between 200% and 250% to calculate both wholesale and retail prices. The base price that Mayu pays its artisans in Peru covers labor, raw materials, and transportation in Peru. Once the products arrive in the United States, Kate added on international shipping from Peru and customs duties to generate the total cost of each item (cost of goods sold). In some instances, however, Mayu receives slightly lower or slightly higher margins than the industry standard, depending on the product and what she thought the market could pay for each item.

Distribution

Distribution will be discussed in terms of in-personal events, online, and wholesale.

In-Person Events

Until now, Mayu's greatest source of revenue had been from high-end, in-person weekend holiday events. Mayu had been invited to at least 10 such events and sales ranged from $0 to $2,500 per event. Participation fees were usually 10% of revenues. Because Kate worked full time, one of her family members or her future part-time employee would staff weekday events in the fall and spring. Mayu would make itself available for private "shopping parties" throughout the Chicago area. During a party like this, the host would invite friends over for an evening of Mayu shopping. To entice hosts to have a party, items would be offered at a 10% discount from online prices and hosts would be compensated with a generous Mayu gift card.

Online

Although the majority of Mayu's sales took place during holiday shopping events, Kate's goal was to increase online sales and decrease her reliance on labor intensive and sometimes "hit-or-miss" events. She knew it would be a challenge to sell high-end products through a website, especially without a well-established brand. The beauty of the alpaca was most apparent when customers could touch the materials and try on the products. She did offer swatches of the alpaca to interested consumers but overall, the biggest problem was driving customers to her website with a limited marketing budget and convincing them that the higher-priced items were worth the investment.

Kate purchased a social media platform at $1,000 per year. Through the platform, Mayu could efficiently target numerous social media websites with the click of a button. This was an excellent strategy to build links and increase an online presence. Kate also managed a blog, which was part of the Mayu website. There, she blogged about topics related to Peru, alpaca, fair trade and the Mayu story; photos, videos, articles, and other prose made up the content. In addition, Kate knew that Google AdWords would provide direction in terms of online marketing. She paid $250 per month on a seasonal basis to a group of professionals who would create an AdWords account and she would have to start with a $500 monthly budget for the actual pay-per-click ads.

Kate planned to buy certain advertising banners on websites during the winter months and especially before the holidays. The cost of such ads would be about $100 per month; this was for second-tier publications that had some type of an eco-fashionista following. She budgeted $500 per month for the ads.

Kate already had a functioning website created at a very reasonable price of $1,000, including six months of site adjustments and modifications. Website logistics such as domain names, security encryption, payment services, and other related costs were low and thus, led to very low start-up costs. These monthly costs totaled about $50.

Wholesale

Kate received inquiries from retailers who were interested in stocking Mayu products, but during the first year, the orders were small and margins were even smaller. The minimum order was $500 and lead time was typically no more than 6 weeks, depending on the time of year. By slightly changing her prices, Kate believed she could increase wholesale orders and therefore benefit from sales volume. The question remained though whether the artisans would be able to keep up with the increased demand. The chance of decreasing the price she paid the knitters in Peru was slim so costs savings had to be found elsewhere on the value chain.

To increase wholesale accounts, Mayu planned to hire three sales representatives, one to cover the West Coast, another for the East Coast, and one for the Midwest. Research indicated that the sales representatives would be compensated at least 10% of total sales. She had heard nightmarish stories from her friends about their experiences with sales representatives, so it was important to find the perfect ones who would best represent the Mayu line. An additional middleman would decrease Mayu's profits further, but to gain brand recognition, get the products distributed, and start striving for volume, the investment in a team of sales reps was necessary, especially because Kate could not "pound the pavement" on her own.

Mayu would also continue to open drop-ship arrangements (affiliate marketing) with online boutiques that posted Mayu's products on their sites. When a product is sold, Mayu ships the item from the Chicago warehouse and is compensated a defined price, generally 55% to 60% of the retail sales price. These drop-ship relationships are convenient, risk free, and without cost to Mayu.

Eventually, Kate planned to participate in trade shows such as Chicago's StyleMax to place Mayu's alpaca accessories in front of thousands of retailers. These events cost at least $5,000 for 4 days and profitability is not guaranteed. Kate decided to wait on these events for the first couple of years unless she could partner with a similar small business to share a booth and costs.

Promotion

During its short life, Mayu had received free publicity, which directly boosted sales. The company was mentioned on reputable blogs and in print publications, and was covered in local magazines. Publicists seemed to enjoy the Mayu story and readers were intrigued by what Kate had accomplished in the Peace Corps. The publicity did lead to additional sales but on a small scale. Kate considered hiring her friend, a PR specialist. The rate for the season would be $3,000 with the objective to get Mayu featured in fashion publications' holiday gift guides. There was, of course, no guarantee that editors would choose to feature the Mayu brand.

Mayu implemented a referral program to help spread needed word-of-mouth sales. Past Mayu customers were given a $25 Mayu gift card each time they referred someone who purchased something from Mayu.

Operations

Peru

Kate knew that it would be difficult to manage Mayu from her home base in Chicago without frequent visits to Peru. Fortunately, she was able to communicate with the producers via telephone and occasionally by e-mail. The fact that the artisans were not computer literate and did not have consistent access to cellular phones (not to mention the frequent power outages) made communication a challenge. By living in Peru, Kate had learned to be both flexible and adaptable to the Peruvian operating environment. She placed orders and dealt with logistical issues with the designated group leader, Maria Rosemberg de Huerta. Another obstacle Kate faced was ensuring that the products had a certain level of quality and consistency. The Peruvians were less demanding and had different ideas of what constituted high quality. In addition, the artisans were frequently dishonest, claiming certain products would arrive on a certain date, when in reality, they had not even been knit yet.

The nearest regional city is 3 hours by bus and Lima, the capital of Peru, is an 8-hour trip from the village where the knitters reside. This means that Mayu's artisans have to travel long hours to access their bank accounts and to send shipments to Kate from the Federal Express office. They are always faced with the risk that large quantities of cash or finished products could be stolen during the journey. Similarly, raw materials have to be ordered via the Internet and delivered to the community by overnight bus from Lima. The cost of the raw material ranges from US$27 to $30 per kilogram for pure alpaca wool and is paid for by the artisan group. The price variation depends on whether the fiber is dyed or natural and prices are slightly susceptible to general economic conditions in Peru. Kate and the artisans jointly decide the pricing structure of the products and Kate compensates the artisans per unit produced. This price includes labor and material costs. Kate pays the artisans via wire transfer at a rate of US$11 to $85 per item knit. Typically, Kate would pay for the products up front so the artisans would be able to purchase the raw materials.

When it became necessary to scale, Kate knew that quality control, logistics, and creating a solid organizational structure would be the biggest challenges. She thought she could hire a part-time employee who would work 5 months out of the year and be compensated $1,750 for the duration of the position.

United States

Kate was responsible for operations in the United States and overseeing production in Peru. From her home, she managed the website, online content, social media, marketing, and customer service aspects of Mayu and also attended sales events. She created an internship program and began employing students on an unpaid, 10 to 15 hour per week basis. Although it was time consuming, Kate felt that the use of interns could be a mutually beneficial experience and that "two heads were better than one." Once products arrived from Peru, Kate's mother was responsible for counting, ironing, and tagging inventory and outbound logistics such as shipping and handling. Kate knew that her mother would continue doing this forever so she planned to hire seasonal help for three months (November through January). The part-time help would be paid about $1,200 per month.

Team

Although Kate was receiving advice from a number of individuals, she did not have a formal advisory board. Her father provided her with legal advice, her uncle was a CPA, and her web designer guided her on all aspects of managing a website. Kate wanted to widen her support network and started thinking about contracting a product designer who excelled in knitwear, a professional photographer, and a clothing model as well as a team that could optimize her website. She knew that it was not in her budget to hire anyone on a full-time basis so she decided she could hire the necessary help on a per-project basis. Kate is a good networker and excels in finding high-quality help at minimum prices.

Mayu's Short Term Plan

To take Mayu to the next level, Kate plans to hire a fashion designer and is already in contact with a woman who specializes in knitwear. The design fees per collection will be about $5,000 and include arrangements with a professional photographer, model, and hair and makeup team. The designer will take care of the creative vision behind Mayu. Kate will travel to Peru periodically to work with the artisans to create new collections. Each trip to Peru will cost about US$700 to $1,000.

Financials

The financial statements for the company include a 3-year pro forma income statement (Table 1); the first-year pro forma income statement by month (Table 2); and a 3-year pro forma cash flow statement (Table 3).

❖ Table 1 Mayu's Projected 3-Year Income Statement (in Dollars)

	Year 1	Year 2	Year 3
Net Sales	32,000	44,800	58,240
Cost of Goods Sold	6,400	8,960	11,648
Gross Income	**25,600**	**35,840**	**46,592**
Operating Expenses			
Advertising (*5mo.)	2,500	2,500	2,500
Marketing & Promotion (AdWords *5 mo. & PR)	6,750	6,750	6,750
Social Media Platform	1,000	1,000	1,000
Dues & Subscription (FTF etc)	300	300	300
Payroll Expenses			
Part-Time Employee Peru	1,750	1,750	1,750
Part-Time Employee USA	3,600	3,600	3,600
Product Design Fees	5,000	5,000	5,000
Administrative Expenses			
Website Logistics & Design	600	700	800
Travel to Peru	1,000	1,000	1,000
Office Expenses	500	700	900
Total Operating Expenses	**23,000**	**23,300**	**23,600**
Operating Income	**2,600**	**12,540**	**22,992**
Income Before Taxes	2,600	12,540	22,992
Net Income	**2,600**	**12,540**	**22,992**

❖ Table 2 Mayu's Projected First-Year Income Statement by Month (in Dollars)

	Q1			Q2			Q3			Q4			
	January	February	March	April	May	June	July	August	September	October	November	December	Year 1
Net Sales	3,500	3,000	2,000	500	500	0	0	500	1,000	3,000	10.000	8,000	32,000
Cost of Goods Sold	700	600	400	100	100	0	0	101	200	600	2,000	1,600	6,400
Gross Income	**2,800**	**2,400**	**1,600**	**400**	**400**	**0**	**0**	**400**	**800**	**2,400**	**8,000**	**6,400**	**25,600**
Operating Expenses													
Advertising (*5mo.)	500	500	0	0	0	0	0	0	0	500	500	500	2,500
Marketing & Promotion													
(AdWords *5 mo. & PR)	1,350	1,350	0	0	0	0	0	0	0	1,350	1,350	1,350	6,750
Social Media Platform	1,000	0	0	0	0	0	0	0	0	0	0	0	1,000
Dues & Subscription (FTF etc)	300	0	0	0	0	0	0	0	0	0	0	0	300
Payroll Expenses													
Part-Time Employee Peru	583	0	0	0	0	0	0	0	0	0	583	583	1,750
Part-Time Employee USA	1,200	0	0	0	0	0	0	0	0	0	1,200	1,200	3,600
Product Design Fees	0	0	0	0	0	0	2,500	2,500	0	0	0	0	5,000
Administrative Expenses													
Website Logistics & Design	600	0	0	0	0	0	0	0	0	0	0	0	600
Travel to Peru	0	0	0	0	0	0	1,000	0	0	0	0		1,000
Office Expenses	500	0	0	0	0	0	0	0	0	0	0	0	500
Total Operating Expenses	**6,033**	**1,850**	**0**	**0**	**0**	**0**	**3,500**	**2,500**	**0**	**1,350**	**3,133**	**3,133**	**23,000**
Operating Income	**(3,233)**	**550**	**1,600**	**400**	**400**	**0**	**(3,500)**	**(2,100)**	**800**	**1,050**	**4,867**	**3,267**	**2,600**
Income Before Taxes	(3.233)	550	1,600	400	400	0	(3,500)	(2,100)	800	1,050	4,867	3,267	2,600
Net Income	**(3,233)**	**550**	**1,600**	**400**	**400**	**0**	**(3,500)**	**(2,100)**	**800**	**1,050**	**4,867**	**3,267**	**2,600**

❖ Table 3 Mayu's Projected 3-Year Cash Flows (in Dollars)

	Year 1	Year 2	Year 3
Cash In			
Cash Sales	32,000	44,800	58,240
Total Cash In	32,000	44,800	58,240
Total Cash Available	32,000	44,800	58,240
Cash Out			
Inventory	6,400	8,960	11,648
Operating Expenses			
Advertising (*5mo.)	2,500	2,500	2,500
Marketing & Promotion (AdWords *5 mo. & PR)	6,750	6,750	6,750
Social Media Platform	1,000	1,000	1,000
Dues & Subscription (FTF etc)	300	300	300
Payroll Expenses			
Part-Time Employee Peru	1,750	1,750	1,750
Part-Time Employee USA	3,600	3,600	3,600
Product Design Fees	5,000	5,000	5,000
Administrative Expenses			
Website Logistics	600	700	800
Travel to Peru	1,000	1,000	1,000
Office Expenses (tag etc)	500	700	900
Estimated Income Tax Payment	0	0	0
Total Cash Out	29,400	32,260	35,248
Beginning Cash Balance	500	3,100	15,640
Ending Cash Balance	3,100	15,640	38,632

Case Questions

1. Assuming demand continued to grow, how would Kate scale operations in Peru? She had already accepted a full-time job in Chicago and would be working on Mayu on a part-time basis.
2. How would Kate take Mayu from an in-person, event-based company to a successful online store if people could not see and feel the Alpaca fiber? She needed an online marketing strategy.
3. Admitting that finance was not her strong suit, Kate worried that the pro forma financial data she had calculated were missing something. She was looking for feedback on what she had done.

4. What fraction of equity would Kate give up assuming she would soon be seeking capital to expand operations?

5. How would Kate be able to partner with the many Americans who had asked her to help them also import knitwear from Peru? She did not want to give away her "trade secret" of the artisans whom she had worked hard to train.

Case 7

Motrada Ltd.

Paul M. Frentz, Guillaume Hébrard, and
Kathrin Macdonald

Introduction

Motrada Handels GmbH is a software/Internet services company that develops, sells, and provides a business-to-business (B2B) remarketing service with an online Internet application. This application is specifically designed for the easy sale of used products. The application is able to generate a new platform, based on customer needs, in approximately five hours. The number of platforms that can be built upon the generic core application is unlimited. Currently, Motrada is concentrating on platforms for the used car market in Europe. In the future, the company's focus will expand to additional products and to global markets.

The Beginning

Guillaume Hébrard spent most of his professional career in car sales and knew the industry in Austria and its customers inside and out. For example, he knew that an elderly couple choosing between red and blue upholstery would be back in four days ordering green. When students began their search by looking for the least expensive version of the smallest car, Guillaume knew they would end up buying the car with the cool fender design (despite its cost). He would then throw in detailing extras, converting the student into a faithful customer. Guillaume was very successful at retaining his customers, selling multiple cars to the same clients over long periods of time.

One day in early 2005, Guillaume leaned back in his leather chair, and folded his hands behind his neck. His eyes scanned the large showroom, and he attempted to guess how much rent his boss paid for this place. No doubt, it was expensive but there was still not enough room for all the cars the customers were interested in. All too often, he had to show his customers details in brochures or ask them for patience until a particular car was delivered to his location.

Source: Used by permission from Kathrin Macdonald.

Guillaume was well versed in technology and very confident on the Internet. In fact, he was so confident on the Internet that he did most of his shopping online. This made him wonder, with such an adept resource at their fingertips, why did people still buy cars in showrooms? Internet technology was fast with the advent of broadband, many households and businesses had access, and eBay was just starting to be the next big thing. Suddenly it came to him—Guillaume decided to take car buying online.

Personal Background

Guillaume was born and raised in Southern France and moved to Vienna, Austria, in 1996 when he was 24. He moved to Austria as part of a program run by the French government. This program sent young men abroad to work for French companies in place of military service. He did not speak much German, except for the remnants of an ERASMUS (foreign exchange) semester in Innsbruck, Austria, and aside from a few friends from his school days, he had no network in the country. He went to Vienna without any expectations of either enjoying or prolonging his stay. He had no idea that he would base a significant portion of his professional career there.

Guillaume specialized in accounting at his business school in Rouen, France, which led to an initial appointment with Citroen in Austria. He spent his time at Citroen building a strong network of friends based on common interests (i.e., skiing and climbing) and fully immersing himself in learning the skills necessary to perform successfully in his industry. Rewarding his hard work, Citroen offered him a full-time position with the company and asked him to support their sales team in a financial and controlling position. They also gave him the responsibility of consulting for licensed Citroen dealers in Austria. After success in this position, Citroen promoted him to business and sales director of a subsidiary in Vienna. In this position, he was responsible for the branch's new and used car sales, garage services, and spare parts sales. It was during this time that Guillaume became aware of the problems and inefficiencies within the used car market.

The B2B Used Car Market

In Austria, as in most of Europe, it is normal for major car companies and dealers to accept a used vehicle in exchange for part of the sale price of a new one. Fifty percent of these used vehicles are sold directly to private buyers. The other 50% are sold to dealers. The business-to-business portion of the used car market caught Guillaume's attention primarily because the vehicles being sold in this market are usually damaged, sold before repair, and without warranty. Selling these cars presents many challenges. If a seller wants to get a used vehicle off his or her hands quickly, the chances of getting a good price for the vehicle are low for the following reasons:

- There is little time or desire to invest in an expert estimate of the vehicle's value.
- One cannot expect a good price for a vehicle that is no longer under warranty.
- The purchasing dealer is averse to paying a high price for a vehicle that will be difficult to sell quickly or for a significant profit. The purchasing dealers are going to push the price down because they are aware that they have the stronger position.

- The purchasing dealers only purchase from companies they trust, which forces used car sellers to build a good reputation. Dealers generally purchase from networks of 10 to 15 trusted dealers.

A black market is thriving because of the inability to establish a market price for used cars in the B2B marketplace. Salespersons sell a vehicle at a low price and charge the purchasing dealer an unofficial fee. Accordingly, the purchasing company maintains low expectations for the vehicles' quality. The purchasing dealer usually enters into the deal with an end buyer in mind for the used car. Any money paid in the form of a "fee" to the salesperson is lost to the legitimate car-sales or car-leasing company since it represents how much the dealer would really be prepared to pay for the vehicle if going through official channels. Since there are no reliable data on these fees, it is impossible to size the actual demand of the B2B used car market.

A New Business Concept

Now in a leadership position, Guillaume was responsible for a sales team and had to choose between accepting the black market tendencies and maintaining his integrity. Maintaining his integrity would force him to attempt to change the way the market conducted its business. If he were successful in this transformation, he would be able to channel significant profits back into the company. Guillaume interviewed colleagues and peers in other companies and countries to gain their insight. He realized that the challenges he faced were the same all over the world and, in general, they were being ignored. This was unacceptable to Guillaume. He knew that transparency in the market was necessary to increase the selling price of the used cars to their real market value, and in turn, increase firm profits.

For Guillaume, the solution to this problem was to auction the cars, creating a competitive situation where the sale would be awarded to the highest bidder. Guillaume was not the first to think of this model—for example, British Car Auctions (BCA) holds physical car auctions exclusively for registered car dealers. Auctions tend to widen the market, to push prices up, and to improve the security of deals. The drawbacks of auctions are that they require a lot of space, they cannot be held until there are enough cars to make it worthwhile, and the dealers have to go to the place of the auction and decide on the spot which vehicles interest them and which do not. Also, auctions would not inherently increase trust in the industry and did not account for the necessity of "awarding" sales for strategic reasons.

In an effort to mitigate these challenges, Guillaume decided to build an Internet auction platform. An Internet solution could widen the market to include more buyers and create better market dynamics. At the same time, it could allow for restriction possibilities, such as allowing the seller to offer cars to a smaller circle of buyers. The platform could have standardized descriptions to alleviate trust issues. The platform would regulate descriptions to assure honesty from the seller and minimize the risk of nonpayment on the part of the buyer. As the Austrian market was limited in both geography and inventory, Guillaume knew from the start that the platform would have to be international.

Market Data

Based on current trends, the European used car market will continue to play a role in the overall car market. This forecast is based on the following observations:

- Worldwide overproduction of cars
- Product innovation—new cars turn into used cars faster and faster
- Better quality—cars are driven longer and can be traded more often
- The Internet is making globalization and targeting foreign markets easier
- E-trading is currently growing faster than any other distribution channel
- All players in the market are looking for more efficient distribution channels for used cars.

Based on this information, Guillaume decided to launch his online B2B sales platform with the used car market as his launch market. He chose this market for two reasons: first, because of its size and value, and second, because of its current lack of profitability and its inefficient organization.

The European Automotive Industry and Market Segment Growth

The car industry can be divided into two main segments: the new car business and the used car business. Vehicles registered for the first time are classified as new; all others are used. These two segments are closely related because new cars are quickly converted to used cars. According to the European Automobile Manufacturers' Association (ACEA), the 2006 European market consisted of approximately 32 million used cars (see Table 1).

Approximately 45% of the 32 million cars being traded are in the business-to-consumer (B2C) sector (14.4 million). Based on a statistical survey by Citroen Europe, 35% of the 14.4 million used cars were traded on a B2B level before they were sold to the end customer, moving from one car dealer to another. As a result, in 2006 the target market consisted of approximately 5.09 million vehicles.

In the B2B sector, the Internet is currently used for exchanging information but not as a sales channel. Only about 1% of all cars sold are sold via the Internet, which amounts to about 50,000 vehicles. The use of the Internet in daily business and e-business is becoming more common. The Internet will continue to gather momentum as a distribution channel and outgrow its role solely as an information provider. Forecasts for the development of this market segment are quite promising (see Figure 1 and Table 2).

❖ Table 1 Used/New Car Sales (in thousands of euros)

	New Cars Total			Used Cars Total		
Market	2006	2003	2006/2003	2006	2003	2006/2003
EU 25	14,995	14,713	+1.9%	31,926	31,305	+ 2.0%
EU 5[a]	9,596	9,175	+4.6%	19,345	18,527	+ 4.4%

SOURCE: ACEA (www.acea.be).

[a]The EU 5 = Austria, France, Germany, Italy, and Spain.

The Leasing Market Segment

In the European car market, there are approximately 890 leasing companies. In 2006, the number of cars financed by leasing contracts was about 4.09 million (see Table 3).

❖ Figure 1 Used car market trades.

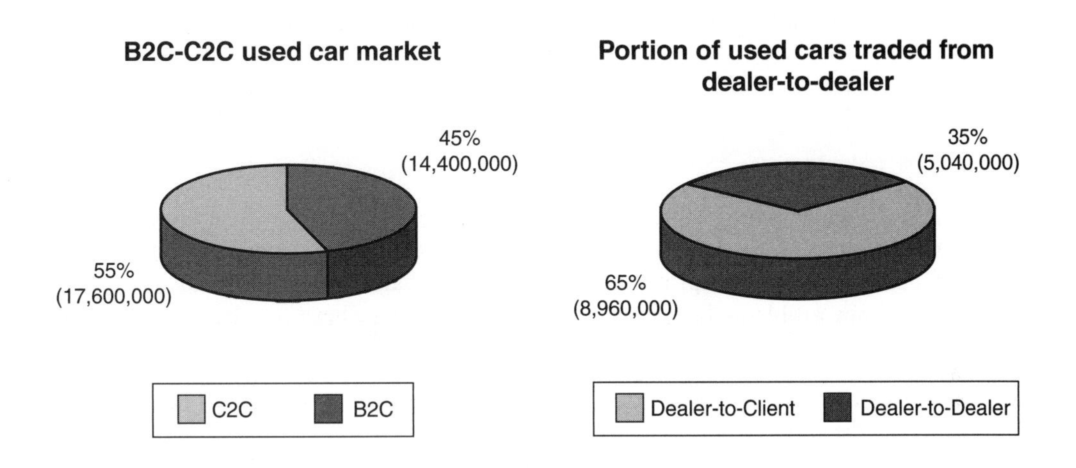

SOURCE: ACEA (www.acea.be).

❖ Table 2 Business-to-Business Market (in thousands)

Market	2006		2007		2008		2009	
	Volume	Market	Volume	Market	Volume	Market	Volume	Market
B2B market[a]	5,090		5,141		5,193		5,245	
B2B e-market[b]	76	1.5%	154	3%	260	5%	420	8%
Used car market share[c]	0.15	0.2%	3	2%	6.5	2.5%	12.5	3%

SOURCE: ACEA (www.acea.be).
[a]Projection: Annual growth of 1%.
[b]Projection: We are at the beginning of the development of the e-market.
[c](with reference to the B2B and e-market).

❖ Table 3 Car Leasing Market

Markets 2006	Number of Leased Cars	Leasing Returns (per annum)
EU 25	4,090	1,227
EU 5	2,175	733

SOURCE: Leaseurope, European Federation of Leasing Company Associations, Belgium, Germany, Austria, France, Italy, Spain, according to industry expectations, about 30% of the vehicles become leasing returns (www.leaseurope.org).

The number of cars financed via leasing rose from 1999 to 2006 with remarkable speed. According to national leasing associations, this development will continue. Table 4 shows an estimate for the number of potential clients.

Leasing companies are looking for efficient remarketing tools:

- Annually, more than 1 million vehicles need to be remarketed by leasing companies.
- Importers are using demonstration vehicles and short registrations to raise their market shares artificially. These vehicles also need professional remarketing.
- Wholesalers are looking for an option for car sales without guarantee requirements (as opposed to B2C, warranties for used cars can be limited or excluded in the B2B market).

Founding Motrada

It was a while before Guillaume took his own idea seriously and he spoke to very few people about it. He did not spend much time drawing up a financial plan, and instead focused on getting his project off the ground so that he could eventually leave Citroen. The main problems he confronted in the planning phase for the Motrada start-up regarded

- The concept: Is it feasible? Is it good? Where should he begin? Will the market accept the idea?

❖ Table 4 Potential Market for Leased Cars

Market 2006	Car Leasing Companies	Car Importers	Licensed Car Dealers	Licensed Car Dealers (more than 1,000 vehicles sold yearly)[a]
EU 25	887	585	118,000	5,900
EU 5	402	303	50,000	2,500

SOURCES: Leaseurope (www.leaseurope.org); CECRA, the European Council for Motor Trades and Repairs (www.cecra.org).
[a]Assumes that 5% of all car dealers are relevant customers.

❖ Table 5 Market Share Statistics

	2007		2008		2009	
Shares of the EU 5 Market	%	No.	%	No.	%	No.
Leasing companies	3.7	15	10.0	40	14.9	60
Importers	1.7	5	6.6	20	10.0	30
Wholesale dealers	1.2	30	4.0	100	8.0	200

SOURCE: ACEA (www.acea.be).

- The technical issues: Setting up an Internet platform is a big deal. The requirements and specifications would be enormous and need to be very specific. Where will he find the right business partners?
- The people: Who? He realized quickly that it would be impossible to go it alone.
- The money: How was he going to manage financially? How long could he last without making a profit?

Guillaume knew that if he started worrying about money, he would not even take the first step. Therefore, he rounded up about EUR70,000 from his "family, friends, and fools" and began his business.

Phase 1: First Start

The team he pulled together consisted of two consultants and him. The consultants were responsible for writing the business plan, finances, business structure, and programming. Guillaume stuck with his specialty—sales.

This first attempt failed for several reasons. All three members of the team had full-time jobs, and were unable to commit the necessary time to the venture. The team also did not have a good working relationship. Despite all this, Guillaume was committed to the success of his idea. He knew there was a market out there for his product.

Phase 2: Better Team and Second Start

Guillaume built a friendship with Martin Putschek who ran a mini-incubator. Martin, who worked with a financial partner and a private investor, focused on seed companies. He took an active part in Motrada's second launch attempt in early 2004, as he had the necessary contact network to find two professional programmers willing to take on the workload at an affordable price.

Once Martin started working with Guillaume, things started to move more quickly. The team recruited Ceus Media—the new programmers—in March 2004, before the specifications had been written. They wrote the specifications in two months and, unfortunately, the first version of the program, released in August, was far from Guillaume's original vision. It was a terrible disappointment.

Later, Guillaume described this disappointment: "It is always a problem writing specifications that are precise enough. If you want everything to be exactly like the image you are seeing in your mind's eye you have to be extremely precise and that can take years: we took two months! No wonder I was disappointed at the result."

They had to pick up the pieces quickly—there was a deadline in sight. Motrada was invited to make an official presentation on January 10, 2005. Guillaume knew that this presentation was a once-in-a-lifetime opportunity and he instilled a strong sense of urgency in the team. While he could have lingered on what could go wrong, in Guillaume's mind, there was no other option other than for his idea to succeed. At the end of April 2004, he finally quit Citroen to work on Motrada full time.

Between June and December, the team set up the operational side of the business: company name, registration, and creating an initial marketing concept. The product was launched on October 18, and to Guillaume's delight, he received positive feedback from a man he greatly respected, Wolfgang Sieber, who was an authority on the market. Sieber, the CEO of Denzel Group (the largest car importer in Austria) ordered the product on the spot. He was their first customer and he allowed them to use his company as a reference.

At the international level, Guillaume was still in close contact with people from the used car industry in France, Italy, Spain, and Germany. With those markets in mind, he built the application to be easily translated into different languages. Motrada's short-term goals for market development were

- achieving a market share of 3% of all European B2B sales in 2009,
- finding licensing partners in Spain and Italy by 2007, and in the UK and US by 2008,
- finding a licensing partner for the Asia/Pacific region by 2009, and
- reaching approximately 45% return on sales (ROS) in 2009 (see Table 6).

Motrada went live on February 28, 2005, and the launch was marked by a press conference in one of the trendiest Vienna hotels. Motrada earned good press coverage and started doing business with the Denzel Group. Cooperating with Denzel, Motrada sold four cars in the first week.

To get car dealers to go online and to trade on his platform, Guillaume used direct marketing methods including cold calling and mailings. He also put a publicity banner on another website. After the first quick surge of interest, the press coverage stopped and thorough marketing measures proved excessively expensive.

❖ Table 6 Timing of Market Entrance by Country

	2006	2007		2008		2009	
Country	S2[a]	S1[b]	S2	S1	S2	S1	S2
Austria	X	X	X	X			
Czech Republic/ Slovakia	X	X	X	X			
France	X	X	X	X	X		
Germany		X	X	X	X		
Spain		X	X	X	X		
Italy			X	X	X	X	
Switzerland			X	X	X	X	
Belgium			X	X	X	X	
UK			X	X	X	X	
USA			X	X	X	X	
Asia				X	X	X	X

SOURCE: Motrada Ltd. Business Plan.
[a]S2 = July through December.
[b]S1 = January through June.

There were not enough cars on the platform or enough buyers registered and active. There were many passive registered dealers, but the trust between buyers and sellers had not been established so all sales came gradually to a halt. Before running the whole business into the ground, Guillaume realized that the financial gap was growing too wide. He needed to do two things: modify the concept (it was not attracting enough dealers) and get more financing.

Phase 3: High-Level Professional Support From INiTS

Guillaume knew that adding to the team was essential for Motrada's future success so in December 2005, he sought out the support of a local high-tech business accelerator called INiTS. INiTS Ltd., based in Vienna, is the number one high-tech start-up incubator in Austria. Founded in 2002, INiTS has launched about 60 start-up projects since its founding (www.inits.at).

INiTS start-ups spend about 18 months in the incubator and are subsidized with approximately EUR35,000 to 55,000, depending on the project. About 30% of their start-ups are working in the field of life science/biotechnology, and another 30% in information technology. Through local and European networks, INiTS is able to provide entrepreneurs with access to a broad variety of strategic partners, to fast market entry, and to private equity. The incubator enables start-ups to finalize their business plan, develop a consistent initial product release (IPR) strategy, solve legal and patent issues, and build cross-functional start-up teams. INiTS also helps its start-ups found/incorporate their company, establish a business network, produce prototypes, and so on, and supports pricing decisions and negotiations. When a start-up has been successful in these initial processes, INiTS helps it acquire the financial resources for the next stage of growth, for example, funding from venture capital firms, corporate investors, or public funds.

With intense INiTS support, Guillaume was finally able to complete the business plan he had put off since Motrada's founding. The incubator also enabled him to think about Motrada's strategy, pricing, timing, contracts, quality control, and financial planning. During this time he increased the sources of public financial support for his company.

Guillaume developed the first major stable PAP (private auction platform) while at the incubator. His intentions were to sell the individual platform to the big car-sales and car-leasing companies so that they could use it to monitor their used vehicle resales. Based on customer and user response, the team started implementing countless minor adjustments and changes to the software on a daily basis. Guillaume kept searching and recruiting new team members; despite his budget restrictions, for him, quality was most important. He hired part-time employees from various nationalities to help in their respective countries with the market analysis, initial customer contacts, and implementation of the first negotiations. In addition, he set up co-operation with leading business schools in France and in the United States to get access to fresh management talent.

Guillaume's strategy was to introduce his product to leading customers in all the large European markets. However, after the experiences of his first attempts (prior to working with the incubator), Guillaume knew that he had to decide whether it should grow as a "stand alone" beyond European borders, or if he should sell to a software partner, platform provider, or to user or dealer organizations.

By this time, the programmers were working for very little pay, so Guillaume began offering profit shares to boost team motivation. In October 2005, however, a breakthrough occurred. VolksBank Leasing ordered the first PAP. Despite the uncertainty about when the payment for the PAP would come, Guillaume continued to improve his product. His team finished the Czech, English, French, Spanish, and Italian translations. They focused on turning their European contacts into business opportunities. They developed a partnership system contacting influential players on foreign markets and used them to distribute the platforms in their respective countries.

Once the VolksBank Leasing payments began to come in August 2006, Guillaume was in a position to gain further financing for reinvestment. To gain this financing, Motrada had to prove that it was a useful tool to create a global market for individual sellers. The marketing approach selected was sales through licensing partners. Their target clients were mostly large established companies and to penetrate this market, Motrada needed to build brand recognition. The company achieved brand recognition by distributing Motrada products abroad via licensing partners that were already well known in their respective markets. For Motrada to work with them, a licensing partner had to fulfill three requirements: experience in the industry, successful sales structures, and complete market coverage.

Guillaume was successful at finding good business partners in France and in Germany; in fact, Motrada has already made agreements with these partners. The results achieved by the first user companies have been much better than expected—making 150% more profit as compared to the prices gained through black market methods. Soon sales and technology finally began to run smoothly and normal processes replaced Motrada's earlier chaos. With this new stability, Guillaume had his business plan updated, translated, and handed over to U.S.-based networkers and investors. He also started to sketch out software versions 2.0 and 3.0 to be finished by 2008 and 2009, respectively.

For a product demo of the PAP today, visit http://demo.motrada.com.

Appendix A

Motrada's Competitive Advantage

Motrada has developed a multi-client capable and multi-lingual ASP application. With its application, Motrada can create thousands of adapted platforms, each in only five hours. These platforms offer a secure point of sale where authorized car dealers can buy from known sellers in a trustworthy environment.

Compared to other e-commerce platforms, Motrada is offering significant value added to its product:

1. *Tailor-made platform:* Motrada offers the only easily customized industry solution for the resale of leasing returns, company cars, and dealer cars. Platform customization options allow a customer to convey a professional tool with an individualized appearance. In addition, the customization costs are much lower than if the company were to order a personalized platform.

2. *Improved platform security*: By working only with individually chosen car dealers, the professionalism and confidence in the platform is high.
3. *Larger buyer pool*: The Internet significantly increases the number of potential buyers. With this platform, the selling dealer can use the "buyer group definition" option to enable transactions with other dealers they trust. This raises the probability of finalizing sales contracts and allows sellers to define the size of their buyer group.
4. *More profitable solutions*: Motrada's platform leads to higher profits through modern and efficient sales procedures. Its auction format allows for better prices for sellers and broader options for buyers.
5. *User friendly*: Motrada's platform provides fast and accurate information. Platform users do not need to monitor the system constantly, as they are informed of any new offers or any significant changes automatically.
6. *Less expensive*: The Motrada platform simply charges a monthly fee. This means that users do not have to bear high investment costs and may begin using their professional marketing tool immediately.

Appendix B

Company History

10 Jan 2005	Motrada Handels GmbH founded by Guillaume Hébrard and a financial partner in Vienna, Austria
Jan 2005	First presentation of Motrada at a trade fair (Auto-Zum-Fachmesse) in Salzburg, Austria: More than 120 dealers sign up with www.motrada.com
Feb 2005	Official launch of first platform version
March 2005	First online sale between two registered members
Aug 2005	First release and presentation of the Partner Auction Platform
Dec 2005	Motrada accepted for 18-month incubation program
May 2006	VolksBank Leasing signs client contract for an unlimited period with Motrada (first sales in July 2006)
June 2006	Motrada signs licensee agreement with Le Monde de l'Automobile SA (JTA in France). This important B2B player on the auto market will have exclusive sales rights for Motrada products in France.
July 2006	Client contract signed with PSA Finance Austria AG (first sales in August 2006)
Nov 2006	Client contract signed with PSA Finance Deutschland (first sales in February 2007)
Dec 2006	JTA (in France) sells first PAPs to two car wholesalers (operating on B2B level)

Jan 2007	Additional financing (AWS—ErsteBank) of EUR110,000 and private equity of EUR30,000
Mar 2007	New pilot customers in Spain and Italy

Case Questions

1. Name some crucial aspects of Guillaume's personality that were relevant for the development of his entrepreneurial spirit.
2. Do you think Guillaume represents the "one in a million" entrepreneur? How common is such a person in your own country? How much do you think you have in common with Guillaume in developing Motrada?
3. Is there a market need for Guillaume's idea? Who would be willing to pay for filling this need?
4. Who would be the product's customers and users?
5. Why does the B2B market seem to be more promising than the B2C market?
6. In this situation, what are the crucial criteria for designing the business model and entering the market?
7. Please describe opportunities and risks for this venture based on your knowledge of the market so far.
8. How innovative is this project: a "me too" project, a development and improvement upon existing technology, or a completely new idea?
9. How would you define the sequence of customer importance and of market entry in this scenario?
10. Are there more criteria for further segmenting this market?
11. Do you recognize a systematic structure in the data in Tables 1, 2, 3, and 4?
12. For each of the three phases discussed in the case, please answer the following two questions:
    a. What are the three most important things—good and bad—one can learn from Guillaume's experience?
    b. What would you have done if you were in his position?

Case 8

Parsek LLC

Mateja Drnovšek

"Would you like to have another drink?" a flight attendant asked two partners from the Parsek Group during a flight from Frankfurt, Germany, to San Francisco, California. It was November 2005 when two Parsek Group cofounders, Andrej and Matej, flew to visit their third partner, Aljosa, who recently matriculated in the full-time MBA program at Haas School of Business at the University of California, Berkeley. During the flight, the two cofounders reflected on the past 7 years, which they had spent managing their young company. The company had performed phenomenally during that time: It went from a four-person operation to a multimillion-dollar media giant. With all the divisions operating at different stages, however, the founders faced an interesting challenge. How should they harness their core competencies and strengths and devise a strategy to bring their company to new heights?

Emergence of an Entrepreneurial Team

The story of the Parsek Group illustrates the creation of a technology venture from its early beginnings in a university environment to the company's internationalization to the markets of Southern and Eastern Europe.

The Parsek story began with a group of undergraduate students who worked together on a project called the KOLAP$ journal in a research lab at the Faculty of Economics, University of Ljubljana, Slovenia. The lab was headed at that time by a professor of entrepreneurship who generously supported the entrepreneurial aspirations of students working in his lab. He provided various electronic gadgets and unlimited access to the Internet and computer hardware and software. In addition, the lab cultivated a creative and entrepreneurial spirit with interdisciplinary panel discussions and conferences featuring important speakers from business, the academic world, and politics.

Students working in the lab gained their first business experiences by professionalizing processes for the KOLAP$ journal. However, the first real market opportunity for the team came with the idea of publishing a yearbook for their classmates. This was a novel idea—none of the schools in the University of Ljubljana had their own yearbook.

Source: Used by permission from Mateja Drnovšek.

This was a huge undertaking that involved collecting data and creating profiles of some 8,000 students. Although the team initially did not have any financial resources to implement the idea, they organized a sales force of 20 students who were paid variable commissions for (1) selling advertising space in the yearbook to larger Slovenian companies and banks, and (2) selling the yearbooks in advance at a discount rate. Thus, the needed financing was provided by advertising revenue and advance-copy sales before production ever began. In so doing, the student entrepreneurs managed to start the production and conclude the project with a profit without having to invest any of their own money.

The project led the team to identify a new opportunity by leveraging the automated database-driven application developed for the yearbook. They transformed it into an online version called Studenet, with numerous community portal features students could use. While working on the yearbook project, entrepreneurial roles were assigned to the members of the founding team. As a successful entrepreneurial test, the project and its profits were compelling enough to found a company and face the challenge of commercially harnessing the opportunities identified.

As these enterprising students approached the formal end of their studies, their need for self-realization and autonomy grew stronger. All of them at a certain point agreed they could never work as hired employees. Becoming independent entrepreneurs was their envisioned career choice. That is why they decided to incorporate their activities in 1999 with a minimum start-up capital of EUR9,000. The activities of the start-up firm focused on the three industries the team felt they had some experience in: advertising, publishing, and web development. At that stage, only the three founders were working in the company, with specific roles based on their personal capabilities and competencies. Given the initial success of the yearbook project, they looked for new markets. The yearbook concept was picked up by five other colleges and high schools, but the founders felt the need to consolidate their business and focus on the new opportunities coming with the advent of the Internet.

The available funds they had accumulated were not sufficient to cover the rent for business premises and basic technical equipment. To acquire the resources needed, the founders initiated a partnership with a major Slovenian information technology company. Its CEO was a very charismatic leader and as an entrepreneur, he understood how it felt to see an opportunity, and to have the drive but not the resources to seize it. He wanted to help the young entrepreneurial team, but not for free. He challenged the team with a problem he had in his own company. In order to enter into the new market segment of Internet service provision, he needed a new product to sell bandwidth Internet access to the household market.

Responding to the challenge, the Parsek team developed a packaged software solution that enabled users to set up Internet access autonomously without support from a call center. At that time, such a solution was a clear market innovation. The product solution performed beyond expectations and the founders got their first insights into the real business world. In so doing, they also developed a very broad range of skills and discovered their potential in solving complex problems. During this project, other people joined the start-up company.

The goal the team clearly set for themselves in the very beginning was to secure positive cash flow. To do so, they focused on acquiring projects from only larger, "blue-chip" companies even though the team did not have experience and a track record. Even then, they knew how to use the "foot-in-the-door" strategy of extending a one-time order into a long-term relationship and leverage it to develop new opportunities with clients, which included the largest Slovenian port authority and logistics provider, the Slovenian branch of the carmaker Renault, and several others.

Building the Initial Market

When the start-up entered the market in 1999, the Slovenian information technology (IT) marketplace was growing fast with an increasing number of companies providing Internet solutions. The first wave of firms entered the IT industry at the beginning of the 1990s as resellers of computer hardware. A wide majority of firms then diversified to grow in the local market and only a few went international. After 1995, the IT industry consisted of several niche sub-industries, such as outsourcing, accounting software, system integration, and enterprise resource planning. However, with only 2 million inhabitants, Slovenia's is a small and secluded business community. Being young students directly from university with no prior experience and no social capital seemed to be major obstacles to market entry faced by the entrepreneurial team.

Through the successful implementation of their projects for important Slovenian companies, however, the founding team was confident they were on the right track to fulfill the vision they initially set when starting their company, and that was "world domination." Seeing immense entrepreneurial opportunities in the global market at the time, the team started to question how they could internationalize. Against their most optimistic expectations they were very soon, in early 2000, offered external financing by a UK-based venture fund. Given the start-up's prior revenues of some US$100,000, the expected investment would reasonably amount to some multiple of that figure. Yet, the founders insisted they would not do a deal for less than US$2,000,000. The founders were well aware of the drawbacks of having a strategic investor in the firm—they would lose control over the firm and each founder would remain with a less than 5% stake. The fact that they would now have to work on another person's account was threatening since they understood that with any further capitalization of the firm, they could easily be left without important stakes and control in the company.

On the other hand, they could not deny the direction in which the world Internet industry was headed. The external financing would enable them to develop a concept of an Internet advertising network similar to Google's DoubleClick and 24/7 Real Media to take on a market segment that had recently yielded the highest returns in the global IT industry. In addition, they needed to find a strong international partner to gain a critical push for growth and internationalizing the business. They all agreed that a private placement would enable them to start working on large projects, as they would have enough resources to employ talented designers and engineers. In addition, by leveraging external investors' social networks, they would have easy access to new customers in Slovenia and abroad.

In May 2000, Parsek received US$1.5 million in return for 76% equity stake in the start-up company from a venture capital firm. Besides financial support, the venture capital funds brought a strong impetus to professionalize the organizational structure of the company to correspond to a tighter growth agenda. The business strategy was revised to focus more on the development of Internet technologies in two new divisions: interactive and advertising media. After receiving the financial injection, the company grew at a rate of 35% per annum and expanded business into neighboring Croatia, Bosnia, and Serbia by 2004.

Because of a major restructuring of the venture capital fund that provided the initial financing, the founders were offered the opportunity to buy back their original shares in the company. By the middle of 2005, the founders completed the transaction by executing a management buyout, buying out all other stakeholders, including the venture capital firm.

The Growth Agenda

The company's growth largely depended on trends in the Internet industry in the region and beyond. The initial growth was secured in the local market of Slovenia. The roots of the Internet industry in Slovenia emerged from an intersection of information technologies and advertising industries. The size of the Slovenian IT market in 2006 was estimated at EUR260 million, with about 40% of revenues in software and about 60% in hardware development with average per annum growth of approximately 11%. The major competitors in the industry were system integrators, mostly large companies that sold hardware, provided networking and security, and usually represented a major software vendor (such as IBM, Microsoft, or Oracle) whose technology they implemented in their solutions. Other business opportunities in that segment included support software, video games, Internet banking, and, later, enterprise resource planning software for medium-sized companies. At the same time in 2006, annual advertising expenditures in Slovenia amounted to approximately EUR130 million, with the most important market players being traditionally organized advertising agencies.

Given the industry specifics, human resource–related competencies required to successfully compete in this market segment included web-savvy designers, interactive technologists, and math-minded media planners. Companies that were new entrants to the industry built from agile market approaches, flexibility in customer relations' management, the use of open-source technologies, and maintaining a "perpetual beta mentality," which is related to higher-valued frequency of updates and new features on the costs of application stability. Table 1 summarizes the industry dynamics.

The industry dynamics and new entrepreneurial opportunities that were spotted indeed drove the start-up's strategic decision to organize into four divisions by the year 2004—interactive, professional IT services, SME solutions, and media business—each of which had different growth opportunities in the international arena. Having the four core groups of products organized, Parsek targeted different layers of B2B Internet services–related markets as well as leveraged specific strengths and competencies within the company.

Similarly to many businesses in the Internet industry, the *interactive division* provides interactive communications services and web engineering. Development of corporate websites, portals, intranet, extranets, and online advertising campaigns requires skills in web design, copywriting, service innovation, convergence strategies development, and customer relations' support. The interactive division usually works

❖ Table 1 Industry and Competition in Parsek Divisions, 1999–2005 (in thousands of euros)

Interactive	**Ownership**	**1999**	**2000**	**2001**	**2002**	**2003**	**2004**	**2005**
Top 3 competitors								
Hal	Independent	158	288	446	472	372	440	487
Renderspace	Advertising agency	29	78	373	573	749	1.016	1,206
Innovatif	Advertising agency		42	104	158	151	97	539
Total market size[a]		*662*	*1,102*	*2,246*	*3,210*	*3,981*	*5,535*	*7,032*
Professional IT Services	**Ownership**	**1999**	**2000**	**2001**	**2002**	**2003**	**2004**	**2005**
Top 3 competitors								
BuyITC	Independent			81	157	239	303	326
Trivium	Major agency						17	728
Ice	Independent		280	623	1,301	1,205	1,202	1,819
Total market size[b]		*n.d.*	*n.d.*	*8,170*	*9,988*	*11,290*	*13,331*	*14,704*
SME Solutions	**Ownership**	**1999**	**2000**	**2001**	**2002**	**2003**	**2004**	**2005**
Top 3 competitors								
Celtic	Independent				0	20	44	108
Enki storitve	Independent				99	41	52	98
Digital Team	Independent				54	102	71	63
Total market size[b]		*n.d.*	*n.d.*	*n.d.*	*307*	*331*	*405*	*778*
Media/ Slovenia	**Ownership**	**1999**	**2000**	**2001**	**2002**	**2003**	**2004**	**2005**
Top 3 competitors								
Iprom	Independent			51	83	158	266	347
Najdi Search	Independent				400	500	800	1,255
Other media	Media groups					200	400	600
Total market size[c]				*313*	*767*	*1,198*	*1,937*	*2,952*

SOURCE: Parsek Group.

[a]Combined revenue of 20 largest firms.

[b]Combined revenue of 10 relevant firms.

[c]Estimated.

with marketing departments to accommodate their initiatives. The company's brand in this market segment was positioned as prestigious and above-market. Competitive strengths stemmed from its track record of continuous innovation, professional account and project management, synergies with online advertising handled by the media division, and the highest number of multinational corporate clients in the industry that are present in the local market.

Parsek initiated *professional IT services* in 2004 to serve larger companies. Those typically have larger budgets per project and require comprehensive support of their online businesses embedded in their central information systems. Typical engagements in this segment include e-commerce implementations, enterprise application integration, and custom application development. Implementation of such projects is vital for Parsek's customers because the projects usually involve developing software support and back-office solutions for financial transactions that are embedded within the larger companies' core processes. The most important customers in this sector are IT departments of big corporations and governmental institutions. Budget per project averages in the range of EUR50,000 with an additional fee for maintenance costs. Parsek was able to commoditize some of its originally developed technologies and package them as industry-specific solutions. This contributed to Parsek's more than 80% market share of the online insurance market, which involved four major insurance companies in the country, with the same percentage of all mobile operators using Parsek's e-commerce platform. The division also developed and now operates the leading online payment gateway in the country. Strengths of the professional IT services division spring from a combination of technology and business knowledge, in-company competencies in development of proprietary technologies, and good client management that shows itself in the level of service offered and proactive attitude toward customers.

The third division of the group specialized in the development of *Internet solutions for SMEs*. The leading brand of the division is Easyweb. The Easyweb entails a subscription-based service of bringing a client onto the Internet. A standardized process of customization makes the service cheap and affordable to the customers. Furthermore, by giving up exclusivity of web design the customers get a best practice solution with no upfront fees at low prices. They can pick among different design schemes, service packages, and subscription models. Other services include server hosting, after-sales customer support, and upgrading possibilities that match growth of the client's business. Examples of subscription services include e-presence and e-customer relationship management. Typical customers of the division are SMEs, such as service and manufacturing companies, sole-proprietorships, and craft shops.

Parsek Group entered the online *media business* by launching its subsidiary Httpool in 2000. The market at that time was underdeveloped; there were only a few relevant commercial online media, tiny advertising budgets, and only a 12% user penetration. Httpool implemented world-standard DoubleClick technology, replicated its Internet advertising network model, set standards, and educated marketers and advertising agencies. This was the foundation needed to internationalize company activities. After 5 years of market presence, Httpool became the major online advertising

❖ Figure 1 Synergies among the four divisions of the Parsek Group.

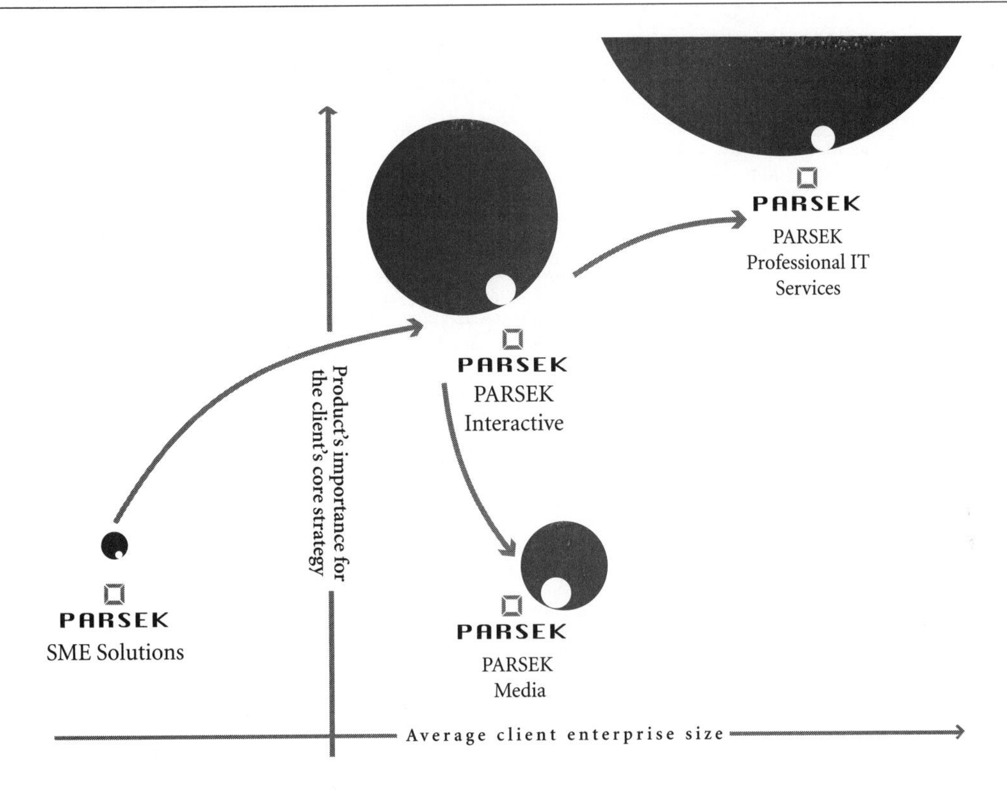

SOURCE: Parsek Group.

provider, representing 50 out of the top 100 online publishers in the world, serving clients with media planning, media buying, ad distribution, optimization, and reporting. The most important customers included advertising agencies and media buyers representing thousands of small and medium-sized firms that had slowly started to switch their budgets from mass media to more targeted forms of advertising.

Figure 1 depicts the business structure of the Parsek Group and Table 2 has an overview of its revenues.

Growth Through Internationalization

Having the company organized into several divisions with varied growth potential driven by industry development, the company was set to embrace international challenges, with each division attacking different international markets and pursuing different growth-related goals.

❖ Table 2 Revenues Per Division in the Parsek Group, 1999–2006 (in thousands of euros)

Parsek Group	Year of Start	1999	2000	2001	2002	2003	2004	2005	2006[a]
Interactive	1999	80	233	313	405	518	589	654	800
Professional IT Services	2004						218	212	320
Media (total)	2001			262	284	518	741	1,251	1,865
Slovenia	2001			262	284	340	472	750	1,013
Croatia	2003					178	269	464	649
Bosnia	2005							30	68
Serbia	2005							3	80
Macedonia	2005							4	55
SME Solutions	2004						28	67	133
Total		**80**	**233**	**837**	**973**	**1,554**	**2,317**	**3,435**	**4,983**

SOURCE: Parsek Group.
[a]2006 projection.

Key elements of their internationalization strategy included

1. Rigorous selection of local partners based on established market position.
2. Building strong client bases, based on leveraging local networks and clients.
3. Purposeful development of capabilities, connections, and credibility to secure a long-term position.

The highest international growth potential that the company had was in the Internet media business market, locally and internationally. The growth of this market was largely dependent on the growth pace of the Slovenian online advertising market, which grew at a 45% average annual rate, reaching EUR2.5 million or 1.5% of total advertising expenditures of Slovenian companies in 2005.

The expected growth in the future for Slovenia was projected at EUR10 million for online advertising or 5% of total advertising by 2010. In the same period, online penetration increased to over 50% of the Slovenian population, due to many new local online media in Slovenia and accessible broadband connections, positioning the Internet as a "must have" in the media mix. The competitive landscape is similar in the former Yugoslavian markets. The major differences are less competition, lower expected user penetration, and less-developed advertising markets, with the exception of the Croatian market, which follows almost the same growth patterns that are identified in the Slovenian market. The perceived prospects of entering this market segment through Httpool activities (based on DoubleClick technology acquired through venture capital financing) were high.

Httpool as an independent business was incubated within the interactive division. This division emerged out of need, because Parsek Group was losing customers in the interactive web-development business, with major customers such as advertising agencies. Parsek realized the need to spin off the interactive business from the core business and provide separate and independent branding. Given that Httpool established its dominant position locally based on first mover advantage, investment in top-notch technology, and know-how, those were competencies that could be easily replicated in new markets, too. Tactically speaking, new international markets were entered by a careful analysis of market conditions and key local players with the goal of finding synergies among markets and the most appropriate partners for establishing joint ventures. Because of the key importance of social capital in those markets, the most viable market entry strategy for a smaller company was organic growth through partnering with local firms. These partnerships provided strong local intertwinement and proven management teams and shared administrative, legal, and other support costs. Moreover, partnering with leading local web developers provided strong mutual synergies, opened access to local clients from the very start, and strengthened both partners' positions in the market.

Parsek expanded first to neighboring Croatia, followed by Httpool Bosnia and Httpool Serbia and Macedonia in 2005 (see Figure 2). All the subsidiaries were successfully locally introduced and gained leadership positions from the start. This was followed by a pan-European marketing initiative through partnerships with leading European Internet advertising networks to participate in promotional activities abroad.

❖ **Figure 2** Expected regional market growth of media industries (in euros).

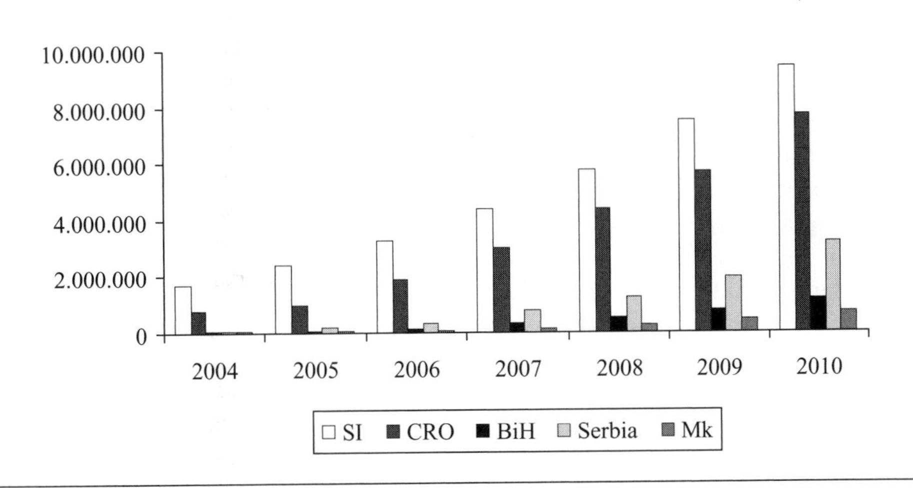

SOURCES: Gospodarska Zbornica Slovenije (n.d.) and primary research.

Other Parsek divisions had less obvious growth potential through internationalization activities and relied more on diversifying in different local markets. By 2006, the interactive division was encountering fierce competition in its market niche. Although the overall revenue in the industry was still increasing, one obvious sign of market maturity was reflected by a strong trend toward industry concentration in 2007. The most recent market trends have opened new opportunities for incumbents as well as newcomers, since the necessary skill set required to compete successfully is now significantly different from the pure advertising business. The largest-budget projects come from regional branches of international corporations and large local corporations.

The professional IT services market was entered because of changing technology. The web industry was being reinvented through the web 2.0 paradigm, which signaled the maturity of the technology as an enterprise application platform. Companies were therefore evaluating hybrid web frameworks, as their new strategic environments required outside professional help to either implement next-generation commercial technologies or build proprietary, open-source-based solutions. Parsek identified opportunities for development of new products in new market segments involving the development of partially customized solutions (i.e., back-office solutions) for corporate customers. The company realized that the approach to the Internet should be built from a company-level perspective. Parsek was able to take on such new opportunities, which offered diversification possibilities, because of a combination of technology and business knowledge, and in-company competencies in the development of proprietary technologies.

Finally, although the product group of *Internet solutions for SMEs* emerged in response to a recognized need for online presence by SMEs, there was also clear international potential for development of a franchisee business in that product group. Similar global online services include, for example, Template Monster. The opportunity to develop Easyweb business came with Parsek's brand recognition in the interactive industry, which was motivated by the demand from small and medium-sized companies. Such an automated approach to web development would also allow Parsek to disrupt the increasingly competitive lower segment of the market and could serve as a foot-in-the-door sales tactic for companies unwilling to pay premium prices. With general growth in the small-firm sector, that market opportunity was growing as well. This market segment also offered a good possibility for expansion to other emerging markets.

In summary, business development within the Parsek Group focused on the market as well as on new product development between 2000 and 2005, local and geographical, which is illustrated in Figure 3. Given that Parsek primarily targeted emerging markets, its growth strategies included substantial investments in building market through their potential customers' awareness that was raised through a personalized, aggressive sales strategy. The costs of new client acquisitions in such markets are initially high and decrease over time. In addition, an overall strategy of acquiring new customers could use the foot-in-the-door strategy to win important business contracts. An important thing to remember when entering the Southern and Eastern European markets is that successful entry depends on breadth and strength of social networks, rather than technological and market sophistication of the product.

❖ Figure 3 Ansoff matrix of business development in the Parsek Group, 2000–2005.

BUSINESS \ MARKET	PRESENT	NEW
PRESENT	Interactive	Httpool SLO
NEW	SMEs solutions Httpool exYu	Professional IT services

SOURCE: Author's interpretation.

Future Challenges

The future development of the company is based on strong product development activities as well as building social networks. In the case of the latter, one of the founders identified networking as so important that he started the Young Executives Society (YES). The organization became a highly prominent club for executives under 40 in building trust and facilitating business connections. Pursuit of an international growth strategy involved development of human resource competencies to provide operational support, which positively affected the bottom line. The majority of new opportunities were incubated within existing operations. For example, professional IT services opportunities emerged within interactive engagements where there were frequent encounters with the client's top management during sales activities. Founders were able to use such opportunities to present IT-related initiatives and were able to win IT contracts from clients directly through top management bypassing the entrenched and conservative IT departments. This was facilitated by a highly capable and motivated core development team. In parallel, the company developed an excellent proprietary software platform. Since there were large commitments to the quality of the projects, clients were usually happy to find that what they received was more than expected at a fixed cost.

❖ **Table 3** Parsek's Value System

People	"The law of crappy people" (the worst employee at any level becomes the de facto standard for that level)
Freedom	"That stimulates creativity and innovation"
Action	"To influence our dreams"
Beauty	"Taste is the enemy of creativeness (Picasso)"
Technology	"New is better"
Fun at work	"Improves the mojo, but not the bottom line"
Hard work	"Mandatory all-nighters"

Given that the markets the Parsek Group is currently serving are heterogeneous and at different life cycle stages, the competitive strengths required are varied and the technology changes are unpredictable. This presents numerous challenges for designing the company's future growth strategy.

What are the strategic alternatives Parsek is confronting? Should the company focus on the strategies of internal growth, such as organic growth in its interactive markets by market penetration through market consolidation and improved long-term agreements with existing and new clients? Should it diversify the interactive business to neighboring regions of the former Yugoslavia, Italy, and Austria? Or rather, why not develop agency businesses by entering into partnership with one of the leading new European search portals? Should Parsek foster its international orientation by opening a spin-off company overseas to capitalize on the technology the company developed and that needs to be marketed? Finally, there is the opportunity to develop traditional advertising agency services. A viable external growth strategy may also result from consolidating its market position in the local market.

As it is with every entrepreneurial venture, the future Parsek story will be greatly influenced by its people. The key human resource in the past was the founding team. There were, however, several other individuals who contributed to the development of the business. The company's value system, represented by people, is composed of freedom and the creative engagement of every individual, along with a passion for technology and beauty (see Table 3).

Case Questions

The following topics could be analyzed in class discussion:

1. *Entrepreneurial event.* What factors contributed to the entrepreneurial event? What was the entrepreneurship opportunity?

2. *Resources needed.* What tangible and intangible assets did the founders invest in Parsek when starting their company? How did they meet their resource needs?

3. *Risks taken.* What were the risks the founders faced in the first year of operation? How did they control and overcome them?

4. *Entrepreneurial growth decision.* Should the founding team have taken the money offered by the private investor? How should the company orient itself for future growth?

5. *Marketing of high-tech products.* What differences exist in the marketing of high-tech products versus the marketing of other goods? Can you identify specific challenges in marketing high-tech products internationally?

6. *International marketing strategies.* Which marketing strategies has Parsek employed so far? Do you believe these strategies will be reasonable in the future, given the industry trends? What international marketing strategies would you suggest Parsek use in the future?

Reference

Gospodarska Zbornica Slovenije. (n.d.). *Catalogue of the Association for Data and Telecommunications.* Retrieved from http://www.gzs.si/katalogi/zacetna_stran_kataloga.asp?kat=037

Case 9

Sedo.com

Christian Koropp and Dietmar Grichnik

When starting a company, it is probably the right thing not to think about an exit at all and instead simply focus on growing the company, but it is at least a valid question to ask yourself once a year.

—Tim Schumacher, CEO of Sedo

Introduction

On a lukewarm spring evening in 2006, Tim Schumacher, Ulrich Priesner, Ulrich Essmann, and Marius Wuerzner, the founders of Sedo GmbH,[1] sat together at a Boston restaurant to discuss the future of their organization. Sedo, a German company with offices in both Germany and the United States, had experienced enormous growth in the 7 years since its inception in 2000 and had become the world's leading online marketplace for domain names. Despite this success, the company's founders were faced with a challenging decision. They had invested all their private wealth in the company, and were now contemplating the benefits of moderating their personal risk by partially divesting from "their" business.

Background

Sedo—an acronym for "search engine for domain offers"—was born from a youthful endeavor of Tim Schumacher, Ulrich Priesner, and Marius Wuerzner. The three knew each other from their school days when they developed a soccer management simulation called Offensiv. They sold this game over the Internet, and bought the domain name offensiv.de to support it.

Authors' Note: This case study was prepared by Christian Koropp under the supervision of Professor Dietmar Grichnik. It is based on publicly available data and on a personal interview with Tim Schumacher, CEO and cofounder of Sedo in May 2007.

Source: Used by permission from Dietmar Grichnik.

After finishing school, the three young men attended university in different parts of Germany. Tim Schumacher studied business administration in Cologne. Ulrich Priesner studied computer engineering in Mannheim. Marius Wuerzner studied history and philosophy in Freiburg. The time commitment needed for their studies ended the Offensiv project. The three friends, however, still owned the domain offensiv.de. It was at this time that they asked themselves: "What can we do with this unused domain name?" The idea to develop a marketplace for used domain names was born and they spent hour after hour outside of their studies to bring their idea to fruition.

In September 1999, the three students created an official partnership to formalize their endeavor and launched their first website to garner feedback from the Internet community. The industry's first offer/counteroffer system enabling domain name buyers and sellers to negotiate directly with each other was now a reality. Despite a lack of marketing, it did not take long for users to begin registering their used domain names.

In early 2000, the young entrepreneurs decided to invest more of their time and money into the business. They booked banner advertisements on websites and cultivated relationships with the press. This occurred at the height of "Internet hype," leading to an overwhelming response from the media and the Internet community. The contacts they gained during this time were invaluable: potential business partners, investors, and future competitors.

One of these competitors was Ulrich Essmann, a medical student working on a project similar to Sedo. He had already acquired the sizable customer base that Sedo lacked. After assessing Sedo's potential, Essmann decided to join the Sedo venture. The Sedo founders, now including Essmann, quickly began negotiations with potential investors.

Negotiations were arduous, as the dot-com crisis was now in full effect. The men persevered, however, and in February 2001 they succeeded in finding a major investor. United Internet, AG[2] (together with their subsidiary 1&1 Internet, AG), at that time Germany's largest registrar for domain names, took a minority stake in the newly founded Sedo GmbH. With a strong and experienced investor backing them, Sedo began offering services in all areas of domain name trading, still not yet foreseeing the tremendous growth ahead.

Sedo's Ownership Structure

Significant changes in Sedo's ownership have occurred in the organization's short history. The first major change was a conversion from the original founded partnership to a limited partnership, SedoGmbH. The second major change occurred when United Internet AG bought 41% of Sedo GmbH for nearly €400,000 while also providing a shareholder's loan. The remaining 59% of shares was still owned by the four founders. This was preserved as a strategic move by both parties.

At the beginning of 2004, United Internet implemented its call option that was agreed upon in the 2001 investment package. As previously arranged, United Internet bought an additional 10% of Sedo's shares for €575,000 (United Internet, 2004). This deal made the company's four founders minority shareholders of their own business. Despite the restructuring, the purchase did not change the everyday functioning of the business. With the new investment, Tim Schumacher, Ulrich Priesner, Ulrich Essmann, and Marius Wuerzner were even more motivated to realize Sedo's global potential.

Only 15 month later, in April 2005, United Internet restructured its own company portfolio. The 51% stake of United Internet and another 1% from one of the founders' holdings were sold to AdLink Internet Media AG, a public, but majority-owned subsidiary of United Internet,[3] for €14.3 million (AdLink Internet Media, 2005). This sale caused some major changes for Sedo's management team. AdLink's company was much smaller than United Internet's, which increased the attention on Sedo and its growth. AdLink provided Sedo with more support but also insisted on greater management intervention. Nevertheless, the entrepreneurial spirit of the founders remained unscathed. Innovations to guarantee Sedo's future success would continue to occur.

The Domain Market

Every company that wants to succeed needs a reasonable and memorable brand name. In the age of e-business and the Internet, companies also need memorable domain names. The market for domain names (domain market) is divided into a primary market and an *aftermarket,* or secondary market.

The primary domain market is the market where new domain names are registered for the first time, using the "first come, first serve" principle. Market partners are the users who want to register a domain name (registrants) and the accredited domain issuers (registrars). The price for a new domain is a standard registration fee, usually only a few dollars.

As most of the promising domain names were already registered, there was a need for a market to buy and sell "used" domain names. This is the domain aftermarket. Transactions in this market are much more complex than primary market transactions. Many changes in the aftermarket regarding transaction procedure, market structure, and market growth have emerged in the last 10 years due to the development of domain name marketplaces like GreatDomains, Afternic, and Sedo. These marketplaces have simplified the domain selling process by reducing relevant transaction costs. For example, search and information costs are reduced by the marketplace's meta-search engine and domain name databases.

Domain aftermarket development has been rapid and unstable. The annual growth rates of the market were tremendous until the beginning of 2000. Then, because of the dot-com crisis, the prices for domain names decreased rapidly along with the total volume on the domain aftermarket. This slump leveled out in 2003, and the domain aftermarket enjoyed a strong rebound—the market volume increased by double-digit rates. By the end of 2006, the total number of aftermarket transactions increased to $96.9 million (www.dnjournal.com).

The structure of the domain aftermarket has changed significantly since Sedo entered the market. In 2000, two companies—Afternic and GreatDomains— dominated the market. The dot-com crisis detrimentally affected these organizations and wiped out the market. Once the crisis ended, the market's growth attracted many smaller competitors leading to today's highly competitive market (see Table 1). Despite this increased competition, Sedo has been the world's leading domain aftermarket since 2004, with a market share of nearly 40%. Predictions of the domain aftermarket's future are highly uncertain and it is likely that today's leaders will not be industry leaders 5 years from now.

Nevertheless, the aftermarket's growth is predicted to be positive. There are greatly underserved markets throughout the world, namely in the emerging countries throughout Asia and Eastern Europe. Millions of people will gain Internet access during the next 10 years. This increase in users will inevitably increase the demand for new and used domain names.

Valuing a Domain Name

The most important issue for domain name vendees and vendors is the determination of the domain name price. As long as a domain name is unregistered, its intrinsic value is equal to the registration fee. But, once that domain name is registered, the resale value is determined by various factors:

- General domain name demand
- Market power distribution
- General economic conditions
- Existence of similar domain names
- Political, regulatory, and sociocultural forces
- Brand name eligibility

❖ Table 1 Market Share for Domain Sales Above $2,000

Marketplace	2004%	2006%
Sedo	41	39.9
Pool	18	1.1
Afternic	10	4.6
GreatDomains	8	–
Moniker DS	8	5.4
Snapnames	7	18.9
Enom's Club Drop	6	0.9
Namewinner	1	–
Moniker TRAFFIC	–	7.9
Pvt Sale	–	14.3
BuyDomains	–	4.1
Forums	–	0.2
Other	1	2.7

SOURCE: www.dnjournal.com.

- Traffic-generating potential[4] (largely dependent on the consumers' ability to remember, recognize the domain name, but also includes the names' descriptive power, length, use of common misspelling or mistyping, and its top-level domain, or TLD[5])
- Pricing mechanism (usually auction system, offer/counteroffer system, or a combination of both)

In 2004, a new method for determining domain value arose in the industry. This method, called "domain parking," connects idle domains with banner advertisements related to the domain's name. Every time a web user accidentally visits the idle domain, the website generates advertisement revenues through pay-per-click fees, generating up to six-figure dollar revenues each month. Aside from the revenue generation potential, this tool establishes a solid track record of revenues and traffic potential for the idle site that simplifies its future appraisal.

Today, domain names are increasingly viewed as assets. Professional domain investors who create domain portfolios own most of the domain names. The prices paid for domain names increased as the aftermarket became more successful. The majority of domain name sales are below $2,000; however, select domain name sales reach seven, or eight figures (see Table 2). Sedo's most profitable deal was the brokerage

❖ Table 2 Top Sales Prices in the Domain Name Aftermarket[6]

Domain Name	Year	Price
sex.com	2005	$ 12,000,000
porn.com	2007	$ 9,500,000
business.com	1999	$ 7,500,000
diamond.com	2006	$ 7,500,000
casino.com	2003	$ 5,500,000
asseenontv.com	n.a.	$ 5,000,000
altavista.com	1997	$ 3,250,000
loans.com	2000	$ 3,000,000
wine.com	2000	$ 3,000,000
vodka.com	2006	$ 3,000,000
creditcheck.com	2007	$ 3,000,000
creditcard.com	2004	$ 2,750,000
tom.com	2000	$ 2,500,000
autos.com	1999	$ 2,200,000
express.com	2000	$ 2,000,000

SOURCE: www.dnjournal.com.

of Vodka.com for $3 million. Sedo brokered the deal between a private U.S. domain holder and the buyer, Russian Standard Vodka Company. Once purchased, Russian Standard used the domain to successfully enter the international vodka market.

Sedo's Business Model

The founders created Sedo to replace the highly fragmented domain name aftermarket. The heart of Sedo's services is a specially developed search engine and database that, by 2007, contained more than 8 million domain names. In addition to its searchable online marketplace, Sedo introduced an escrow service to prevent their clients from fraud within domain name transfers. This was an important service addition as fraud was prevalent in other marketplaces.

To facilitate domain name pricing, Sedo additionally launched a domain name appraisal service based on scientific valuation.[7] Sedo also established a domain brokerage that provided expert negotiation services for domain name buyers or sellers. To generate alternative sources of revenue, the company developed a domain-name parking program, earning revenues from advertisements on idle domains.

Sedo began by operating on the small local domain name aftermarket in Germany, but the four founders had international aspirations. Since its founding, internationalization had been a cornerstone of Sedo's business strategy. The 20 nationalities represented on Sedo's staff displayed the organization's commitment to diversity. The company's network of localized websites included Sedo.com, Sedo.us, Sedo.co.uk, Sedo.de, Sedo.fr, Sedo.dk, Sedo.it, Sedo.nl, Sedo.se, Sedo.at, Sedo.ch, Sedo.jp and Sedo .kr. In addition to the local websites, Sedo offered content in four languages: English, French, Spanish, and German.

In 2004, Sedo opened a second office in Boston, Massachusetts. This was the most significant step toward globalizing the brand and allowed Sedo to grab a firm hold of the U.S. domain market. With an office in Boston, Sedo was able to satisfy U.S. customer demands by facilitating faster bank transfers and more efficient customer service.

Despite its internal innovation efforts (product diversification and internationalization), Sedo also used external strategies such as horizontal integration to foster their first priority: growth. Sedo acquired GreatDomains, a former competitor that specialized in premium domain name auctions. In addition, Sedo built partnerships with major companies along the entire domain name value chain: top registrars in Europe, the United States, and Asia; domain financiers like Domain Capital; and advertising agencies such as Google AdWords.

Sedo's revenue model is based on three major columns:

- *Domain trading:* For every sold domain, Sedo charges 10% of the selling price, at least €50 (for most TLDs); the additional use of the brokerage service runs €69 for the handling fee.
- *Domain parking:* Sedo earns up to 50% of the parked domain name's advertising revenues, depending on the size and negotiating power of the domain name owner.
- *Domain appraisal:* Sedo charges €29 for a standard appraisal and €49 for a premium domain name appraisal. While an important service, its contribution to total revenue is negligible.

The Business Model's Challenges

Despite Sedo's success, there are several challenges that jeopardize the organization's growth. The law rarely protects product and service innovations in the area of Internet applications and this lack of legal protection allows the competition to benefit from Sedo's advancements. A consequence of this void is that most domain name trading marketplaces offer virtually the same services. Furthermore, marketplace designs are often similar. For example, compare the layouts of sedo.com and afternic.com. The opportunities to stay unique and ahead of the market are fast fading, and it is exceedingly difficult for consumers to differentiate between the available marketplaces and their level of quality.

In the last 2 years, competition in the domain name aftermarket has grown rapidly due to the low barriers to entry. Many small companies have taken advantage of the opportunity to enter the market and hope to capitalize on the success of Sedo and its competitors. The existing EBIT (earnings before interest and taxes) margins of the domain name aftermarket are endangered and will presumably decrease in the nearer future.

Sedo's revenue model and the key numbers presented in Table 3 reveal another challenge. Sedo's revenues, and the majority of its profits, are generated by one product: their domain parking service. This single-product dependency is likely to cause challenges for Sedo if competition in this market niche increases and EBIT margins decline.

Sedo's Advantages

Throughout its development, Sedo's greatest advantage was its customer-centric service offerings. In the early 2000s, the uncertainty of the existing auction systems and the prevalence of fraud in the established marketplaces were noticeably dissatisfying domain name customers. These imperfections led Sedo to introduce a pricing system on an offer/counteroffer basis that allowed buyers and sellers to negotiate directly. In addition, they eliminated the danger of fraud by developing a domain escrow service. Even today, Sedo is the only player in the aftermarket to have offices located in both Europe and the United States. This physical presence has proven important for gaining positive press, attracting potential partners, and increasing its customer base. Sedo is the only true multilingual and IDN-ready marketplace.[8] The Sedo team's technical background is another major asset. The technical heart of Sedo's service is the world's largest domain name database, containing 8 million domain names listed for sale, and its meta-search engine. The research and development department is constantly innovating current and future service offerings. Recently, Sedo became the first marketplace to offer financing programs for high-value domains.

November 2006

On that lukewarm spring evening, the four founders sat together late into the night and discussed the prospect of selling a portion of their shares. By the end of the evening, they came to a unanimous decision—they would each sell half of their shares,

❖ Table 3 Key Numbers in Sedo's Success Story

	2000	2001	2002	2003	2004	2005	2006	2007[a]	2008[a]
Revenue	€100,000	€500,000	€635,000	€2,000,000	€7,570,000	€20,780,000	€41,000,000	€62,100,000	€80,400,000
Direct Gross Profit	n.a.	n.a.	n.a.	n.a.	n.a.	€8,000,000	€19,600,000	€27,900,000	€35,800,000
Employees	3	8	15	22	50	80	120	150	180
Transferred Domains	n.a.	n.a.	n.a.	1,927	1,927	10,989	17,850	30,000	50,000
Average Domain Price	n.a.	n.a.	n.a.	€1,416	€1,402	€1,661	€1,720	€1,700	€1,700
Domain Sales Volume	n.a.	n.a.	n.a.	€2,728,632	€7,594,634	€18,252,729	€30,702,000	€51,000,000	€85,000,000
Domains in Database	n.a.	100,000	400,000	800,000	1,600,000	3,000,000	6,000,000	10,000,000	15,000,000
Parked Domains	no service	no service	50,000	400,000	500,000	1,000,000	2,000,000	3,500,000	5,000,000

SOURCE: Tim Schumacher, CEO, Sedo.
[a]Projected.

equaling 24% of all company shares. However, the more difficult decision was deciding to whom they would sell the shares.

AdLink, already a major investor, was an eager prospect. But the founders also considered other investors, particularly private equity companies that were attracted by Sedo's fast growth and future potential. The decision-making process was not as easy as it had been in 2001, when United Internet acquired 41% of Sedo's shares. It took the founders 6 months to reach a decision and, ultimately, it was their intuition and past experiences that allowed them to come to a consensus. Tim Schumacher, Ulrich Priesner, Ulrich Essmann, and Marius Wuerzner decided to sell their shares to their current investor, AdLink, despite higher offers from other bidders.

AdLink increased its stake in Sedo to 76% for nearly 35 million in cash. Today, the four founders still work at Sedo in top management positions. They all hope to remain with the company as it continues to grow and realizes its potential.

Notes

1. "GmbH" is a legal form in Germany comparable to an LLC in the United States.
2. The abbreviation "AG" indicates a corporation.
3. AdLink Internet Media is—like United Internet—publicly noted on the Frankfurt Stock Exchange (Ticker Symbol ISIN DE0005490155), but United Internet owns 82% of the shares, with a small 18% free float remaining.
4. Within this context, traffic means the frequency of visits to a website, measured by the amount of "page impressions" or "unique visitors."
5. Top-level domains are the domain extensions indicating the class of organization behind the website (e.g., .com for commercial organization or .edu for educational organizations) or the country where the website owner is located (e.g., .de for Germany or .cn for China).
6. It should be noted that prices are often not published.
7. The approach was drawn from Tim Schumacher's master's degree thesis, *Price Formation in the Trade of Internet Domain Names.*
8. An internationalized domain name (IDN) is a domain name that can contain non-ASCII characters used in languages such as Arabic or Chinese.

Case Questions

1. How did Sedo's market value develop from 2000 to 2006?
2. To what extent was the 2000 exit strategic for the founders and the investor, AdLink?
3. Was the 2006 exit a bargain, fair valued, or overpriced? Take into account that Sedo's estimated EBIT was 16 million and average EBIT multiples range between 5.5 and 8.1 for companies in the IT industry.
4. How can Sedo's management team sustain the company's current market position in the future?

References

AdLink Internet Media. (2005). *Annual report 2005.* Montabaur: Author.

Schumacher, T. (2002). *Price formation in the trade of Internet domain names.* Unpublished master's thesis, University of Cologne, Germany.

Sedo. (2005). *2004 record year for Internet domain trader* [Electronic press release]. Retrieved from www.sedo.de/presse/presse_190105.php4?tracked=&partnerid=&language=d

Sedo. (2007). *Sedo domain market survey 2006* [Electronic press release]. Retrieved from www.sedo.de/presse/presse_260307.php4?tracked=&partnerid=&language=d

United Internet. (2004). *Annual report 2004.* Montabaur, Germany: Author.

Case 10

Trimo

***Brane Semolic*[1]**

Trimo History

Trimo was founded in 1961 under the name *Kovinsko Podjetje Trebnje* (Trebnje Metal Company). The company was completely restructured and rebranded as Trimo during the national privatization program that occurred in Slovenia during the mid-1990s. Slovenia had been part of the former socialist Yugoslavia until 1990, when the country disintegrated into several independent nations. Slovenia is now a democratic multi-party society. Trimo became a publicly owned company in 1994.

A Summary of Trimo's Product History

In 1974, Trimo began manufacturing thermally insulated plates with polyurethane filling. Thirteen years later, the company turned to manufacturing construction plates filled with mineral wool. And in 1989, it began manufacturing containers. Trimo's first anti-noise fences were manufactured in 1995, while the TPO Dom roof was first presented in 1996. The following year a new technology was developed for the manufacturing of fire-resistant panels. In 2002, the TrimoFORM roof represented an innovative approach to the installation of residential roofing systems because it was marketed to individual customers. In the following year, a new line of TrimoTERM fire-resistant facade panels was launched. As of 2001, a comprehensive approach had been applied to the development of Trimo's new products, technologies, and systems, which led to a range of new products in roofing, facades, prefabricated steel constructions, and decorative elements entering the market (see Figure 1). With the start-up in 2006 of a new development-innovation center, the Trimo Institute, the company entered its next development phase.

Author's Note: Sources for this article included the general manager's response to a company questionnaire, and the Trimo website (http://www.trimo.eu/).
Source: Used by permission from Brane Semolic.

❖ Figure 1 A Trimo installation for the Rossman Company in Germany.

SOURCE: Trimo.

Leadership

One of the most important drivers within the company is Tatjana Fink (see Figure 2). She joined the company immediately after graduating from college in 1980. She began in the controlling department; later she was promoted to director of the finance, sales, design, and commercial divisions. In 1992, she was promoted to general manager of Trimo.

Under her leadership, Trimo flourished and became one of the most successful manufacturing and construction companies in the region. Tatjana Fink has received numerous awards from national and international professional associations. She was named the most powerful and influential female manager in Slovenia in 2006. The next year, she was selected as the most respected manager in Slovenia. Throughout her time as director, Trimo has also received much recognition in its different fields of activities.

Trimo Quality

In 1993, the company acquired the ISO 9001 Quality Certificate, and in 2000, the ISO 14001 Environmental Certificate. The Slovene Committee on Business Excellence granted Trimo its award on behalf of the Republic of Slovenia. This is the highest state

❖ Figure 2 Tatjana Fink, Trimo's award-winning general manager.

SOURCE: Trimo.

honor given to recognize the maintenance of high standards in the quality of products, services, and operations due to the development of knowledge and innovation. Trimo also has placed great importance on the health and safety of its employees. In 2003, the company was awarded the OHSAS 18001 Certificate in recognition of their hard work to ensure safety on the job. In 2004, the European Foundation for Quality Management (EFQM) recognized Trimo for excellence in the industry, and 3 years later Trimo was a finalist for the 2007 EFQM award.

The Trimo Business Network and Its Dynamics

The first foreign subsidiary of Trimo was established in 1990. By the end of 2006, Trimo had 14 subsidiaries, 7 representative offices, and 8 agents in relevant markets. Trimo's story of development, which was primarily Europe oriented, began in 1992 with the motto, "Satisfied customers make the largest profit." Every year, this motto was updated to support and modernize the foundation of Trimo's operations. The 2007 motto, "Innovation for sustainable growth and development," exhibited a new development leap. Trimo is now an international company employing over a thousand people, selling in more than 50 world markets, and manufacturing in Slovenia and abroad.

Comprehensive customer relationship management (CRM) and the establishment of long-term partnerships with all target public groups is a key strategy for Trimo. The company has established strategic partnerships with customers, investors, suppliers, architects, designers, specialists, and others by segmenting its public groups, offering relationships adjusted to their requirements, and organizing work procedures tailored to customer needs. Trimo assesses each of its target groups' satisfaction levels to gain feedback to improve future products, services, and processes.

Trimo's Key Competencies and Strategic Orientations

Trimo strives to ensure complete solutions in the field of prefabricated steel buildings, roofs, facades, steel constructions, and containers. The company's customers are offered efficient and integrated solutions from the very first concept proposal to the final construction, thanks to Trimo's knowledge, research and development, design, advanced technology, and top-quality building materials.

Trimo's main advantages are its clear vision and strategy, capital strength, ambitious and innovative employees, and its extensive marketing and sales network. The company's key competencies are represented by its advanced construction technologies, solutions to complex client problems, quality products and services, and its profound individual and organizational competencies.

At Trimo, special consideration is given to the individual competencies of employees. Employees are encouraged to develop their communication skills, innovation capabilities, teamwork, and self-management. This is how new technical, specific, process, and company knowledge is developed throughout the organization. Throughout the learning process, motivation, creativity, responsibility, and ethics are of utmost importance. Continuous development of competencies by Trimo employees results in added value for all of its customers.

Balanced company growth and development are ensured by the adherence to its development plan, the introduction of new products, and pursuing the company's marketing objectives. These objectives include maintaining the existing and the entering of new strategic markets. For Trimo, an important factor in developing new products is cooperation with independent experts from companies, institutes, and universities, which contributes to its knowledge-creation and innovation abilities as is indicated in the TrimoTERM panel installed in the EUROPARK (see Figure 3).

Construction Industry

Overview

Trimo operates and generates sales from its products and solutions in the construction sector. The construction market is divided into three segments: residential buildings, nonresidential buildings, and infrastructure construction. For Trimo, the most important segment is the development of nonresidential buildings in Europe. In 2005, the size of the European nonresidential building market was estimated at €400 billion. Its largest subsegment was the construction of industrial facilities, followed by commercial and business facilities. Construction of storage facilities is currently on the rise, especially in Eastern Europe and Russia. The nonresidential buildings market in Eastern Europe is increasing by 6% a year, on average, and due to substantial investments in these markets, this growth rate can also be projected into the future.

According to the micro-segmentation of the construction sector, Trimo is a competitor in the global market for insulation sandwich panels. This is part of the

❖ **Figure 3** Trimo product and installation at the Europark shopping mall in Slovenia.

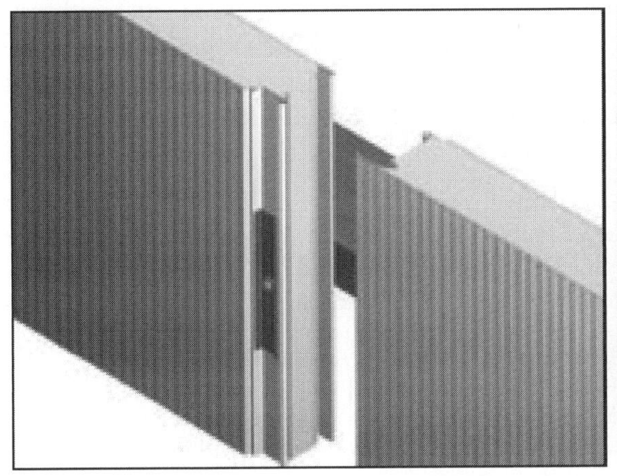

SOURCE: Trimo.

construction mezzo-market of roofs and facades. Insulation sandwich panels are a modern alternative to the classical construction of roofs and facades using concrete, wood, and other materials. Insulation panels differ according to the type of filling. The insulation panels with the largest market share in Europe are filled with polyurethane; however, the use of panels made of mineral wool and extruded polystyrene (EPS) is increasing due to stricter safety legislation.

The entire European panel market is estimated at 140 million square meters, of which 15% to 20% is mineral wool panels. Trimo is the leading European manufacturer of this product. The predominant European manufacturers of PU panels, and Trimo's major competitors, come from Italy, Great Britain, Germany, and France. The strongest markets for insulation panels in Europe are France, Great Britain, Germany, and Spain. Italy is the largest exporter of insulation panels to the European markets.

By providing comprehensive solutions in the field of prefabricated steel buildings, Trimo creates its competitive edge in relation to its competitors. In the European construction market, the top five companies are Vinci, Skanska, Bouygues, Hochtief, and Ferrovial. These major market players are not direct competitors with Trimo because Trimo also serves as their supplier for many projects. With this in mind, Trimo considers the following companies its main competitors: Rukki, Kingspan, Paroc, and Metecno.

Trends in the Construction Industry

Growth in the construction sector is largely dependent on economic trends and investments in the private and public sectors. In the Western European market, the growth of the construction sector is expected to continue at a relatively slow rate. According to projections, this rate will ultimately decrease as interest rates are expected to go up and thus negatively influence credit and loan operations. The interest rate increase will slow consumer spending and lead to less investment in construction projects. In the Western Europe construction market, the fastest growth is expected in the field of building renovation.

Compared to Western Europe, the booming markets of Central and Southeastern Europe represent a great business opportunity. All development prospects and expectations are oriented toward these markets, which are predicted to generate the largest profits in the European construction business through 2010. Market development is focused on the following regions:

1. The markets of new EU member states (i.e., the Czech Republic, Poland, Hungary, and the Baltic states), which together attained a mere 4.5% of the European construction market share in 2004. Growth rates in these markets will be much faster than in Western Europe (5% to 6% a year on average). Growth is expected to level off slowly in this region by 2009.
2. The markets of Southeastern Europe (i.e., Bulgaria, Romania, Croatia, Bosnia-Herzegovina, Serbia, Montenegro, and Macedonia) together constitute just 1.3% of the European construction market. They maintain a fast growth rate that is strongly supported by the programs to move toward EU membership. Growth in their construction market is projected to be in the double digits.
3. The Russian states represent only 3.5% of the European market share in construction. This market, however, is currently in a building boom, thanks to new money coming in from oil and gas reserves. These natural resources have turned Russia into a magnet for foreign investors. The construction growth rate in Russia is expected to exceed 20% a year. Apart from Russia, Belarus and Ukraine are also considered very attractive markets.

Figures 4 and 5 compare the size of the construction sector in 2004 and 2006 in Southeastern Europe and the former Soviet nations. The fastest growth is predicted for the Russian market, followed by Romania, Croatia, Serbia, and Ukraine.

❖ Figure 4 Value of construction output in Southeastern Europe.

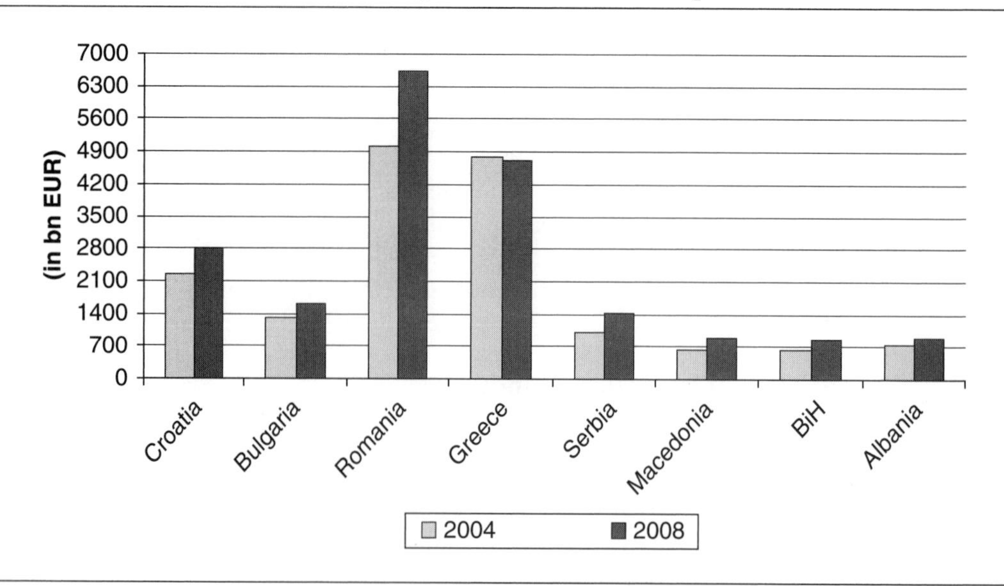

SOURCE: Croatian Government Statistics.

❖ Figure 5 Value of construction output in former Soviet countries.

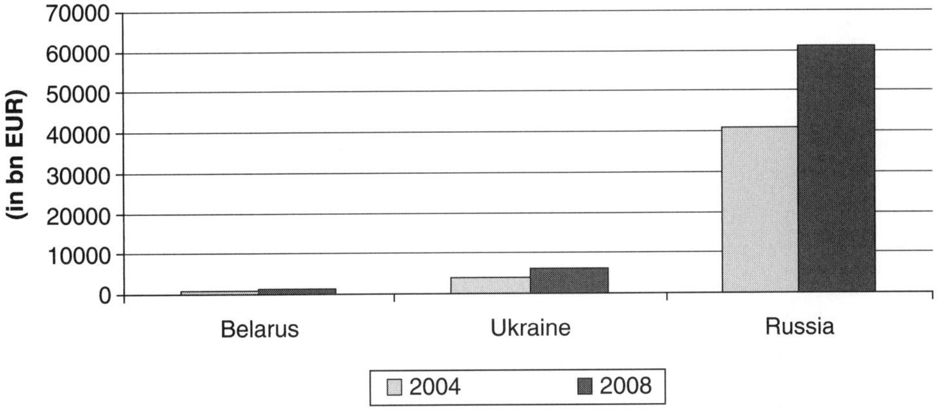

SOURCE: Croatian Government Statistics.

Keys to Success for an Industry Branch

The success of an industry branch strongly depends on the overall economic situation in a particular market. Key factors for the success of an industry branch are the following:

- Fast economic growth
- Substantial foreign direct investment
- Development programs supported by the EU, the European Bank of Reconstruction (EBRD), the European Industrial Bank (EIB), and the World Bank
- Ability to ensure comprehensive solutions in the field of construction
- Strong R&D and technical support
- Launching of new products (new construction materials, new types of construction, speed and ease of assembly, etc.)
- Systematic implementation of customer relations management (CRM) in particular target segments (architects, investors, etc.)

Trimo's Marketing Strategy in Southeastern Europe

Trimo's marketing strategy in Southeastern European is aimed at becoming the leading European company in the provision of comprehensive prefabricated steel building solutions. The company has successfully gained recognition in the Southeastern European market by providing innovative, high-quality, and comprehensive solutions for fireproof roofs, facades, and nonresidential construction. The company focus here is trained on assuring quality solutions, fulfilling the needs of its clients, completing its projects in a timely fashion, and constantly improving its customer support.

Trimo's strategy for entering the Southeastern European markets is divided into three main parts:

1. **Marketing:**

- Approach clients
- Acquire new clients
- Follow strategic clients
- Follow foreign investors
- Set trends in the field of facades
- Expand market network
- Enter new markets
- Increase market share
- Increase regional sales distribution channels

2. **Research & Development**

- Increase innovation
- Joint development with suppliers and clients
- Transfer technology and technological knowledge
- Develop products that are catered to the market/target groups
- Market new products with a higher added value

3. **Production and Purchase**

- Market comprehensive solutions
- Use local sources for purchase of raw materials
- Acquire a less costly work force
- Lower transportation costs
- Find local manufacturers

Trimo's marketing strategy is pursued through the effective use of different tools and steps in market communication. Its strategy is oriented toward producing effective business plans for each region Trimo enters and by raising the company's reputation and recognition within the target markets. The business plans are oriented toward long-term, two-way relationships, strengthening the Trimo brand, supporting sales, and ensuring access for new products and services in new markets. Trimo supports these efforts by giving presentations at specialized trade fairs and for target groups such as architects and investors, advertising in trade magazines, and placing promotional articles and TV advertising.

Because of the size of the Southeastern European market, the expansion and development of the Trimo sales network is carried out by establishing local sales companies and hiring local sales representatives. This ensures that marketing communication is as effective as possible because it is country/region specific.

Trimo and the Croatian Market

Marketing Strategy for the Croatian Market

The Trimo network is based on a unified organizational culture and the high standards it holds for its projects in all markets. The business model for the Croatian market is based on overall corporate strategy, but is targeted specifically to the local market situation, local buyer characteristics, and the development of the local branch.

In 2001, Trimo established Trimo Građenje Ltd. in Croatia (*građenje* is the Croatian word for "construction"). Trimo Građenje's headquarters were located in Croatia's capital, Zagreb, which continues to grow and has more qualified personnel than in the rest of the country. In 2006, the Croatian branch had 14 employees working in sales, project planning, assembly, and imports. Trimo Građenje works closely with the parent company, Trimo.

The Croatian company has successfully established its position in the market. Trimo Građenje organized presentations for architects and investors in Croatia's larger cities (see Figure 6), to continue its networking efforts and increase its brand recognition. The Croatian subsidiary also participated in a construction fair in the town of Split, where it acquired many new and important contacts, extending its network to all regions of Croatia.

Trimo Građenje informs its market about innovations through advertising in specialized magazines. The company also increases its recognition and innovation opportunities through cooperation with local universities and their faculties of civil engineering in Zagreb and Split. For example, the company holds competitions for students in these local universities. Trimo also holds organized visits to its construction sites and the company headquarters in Trebnje, Slovenia, for fourth-year students in civil engineering.

❖ **Figure 6** Trimo Građenje took its marketing efforts to such Croatian cities as Osijek, Rijeka, Zadar, and Zagreb.

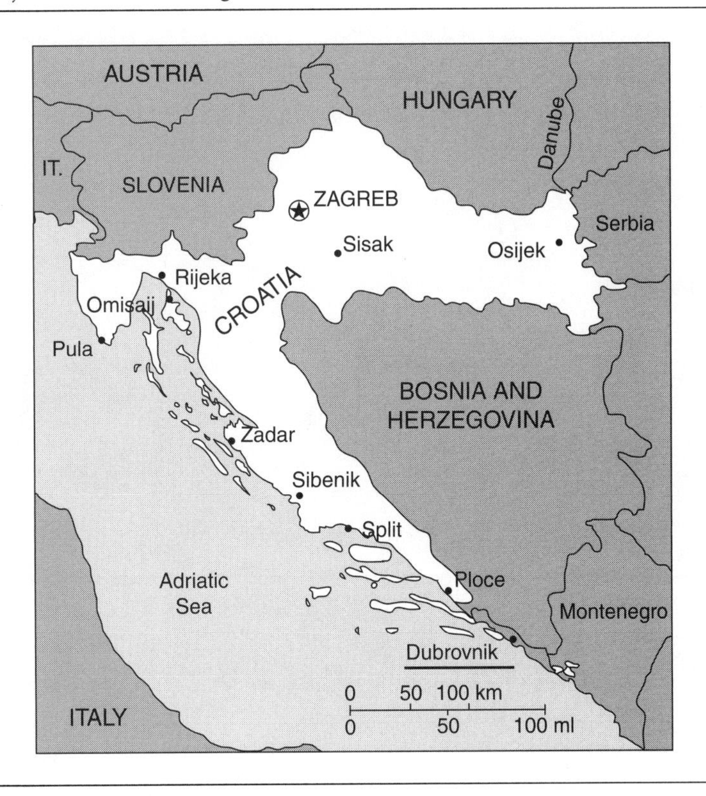

The Marketing Situation, Market Structure, Target Clients, Risks, and Opportunities

Construction is one of the most important industry sectors in Croatia. It alone represents approximately 15% of the Croatian annual gross domestic product (GDP). This fast growth in the construction sector was spurred by the increasing flow of net foreign investments. The growth occurs in the large concentration of construction companies present in the market—the top 10 companies (according to income) account for more than 30% of the entire Croatian construction market. The main foreign companies in the Croatian construction market are Bechtel, Strabag, and Bouygues (through a joint venture with Bina Istra).

Residential construction holds the largest share and represents approximately 40% of all construction activities in the Croatian market. Nonresidential construction and infrastructure construction are gaining value. At first, the growth of nonresidential construction increased due to the restoration of old tourist attractions, but today the number of new buildings in this sector is growing. The construction of shopping centers and logistics centers, and investment in business premises is becoming increasingly essential to the Croatian economy (see Figure 7). Croatia's pending accession into the EU is also providing a significant impetus for the construction and upgrade of nationwide infrastructure.

❖ Figure 7 The GETRO Shopping Mall under construction in Croatia.

SOURCE: Trimo.

Croatia is one of the biggest markets in Southeastern Europe and one of five essential markets for Trimo. As mentioned previously, the road to Trimo's success was paved by strong relationships with clients built upon satisfying clients' needs efficiently and effectively. Trimo Građenje successfully cooperates with existing strategic partners and continues to acquire new clients and potential strategic partners in the Croatian market. The company's target clients and respective partners include investors, architects, project planners, engineering companies, construction companies, assembly companies, licensed partners, tradesmen, and agents.

Trimo Građenje's key advantages in the Croatian market lie in its complete solutions, which are praised by clients, architects, and project planners alike. Trimo's roof assemblies and facades are highly regarded as clients have recognized the quality proven by the many acquired certificates. Trimo Građenje has the additional advantage of being able to offer engineering services, which include project planning, assembly, transport, and construction work. There is strong competition in the Croatian market coming from Italy, Austria, the Czech Republic, and other countries, and the local competition has an increasingly strong position. Nevertheless, Trimo is confident that it will be able to sustain its market share.

The risks for Trimo in the Croatian market are increased local and foreign competition, unsolved economic and political issues, and the unpredictable environment as a whole. There are numerous opportunities in the Croatian market that the company recognizes and builds into its strategic and annual activity plans. It is very clear to Trimo that the need for flexibility and ensuring individual solutions is increasing. Trimo's clients are becoming more demanding, the competition is stronger, and it is vital that the company prepare to react in time to reap the benefits of the changing market conditions. Company results are indicated in Table 1.

❖ Table 1 Key Financial Performance Data for Trimo Građenje, 2003–2006 (in euros)

	2003	2004	2005	2006
Net Sales Revenue	6,272,774	10,466,736	13,171,008	16,729,997
Net Profit	93,172	72,635	217,940	249,335
Assets	2,740,716	4,085,951	5,112,387	9,411,116
Financial Liabilities	0	0	0	0
Average Number of Employees	8	7	11	14

SOURCE: Trimo.

Note

1. Brane Semolic is the director of INOVA Consulting; Professor of Project, Technology Management and Entrepreneurship; Head of Project, Technology Management Institute; Faculty of Logistics, University of Maribor, Slovenia.

Case Questions

1. Describe the nature of the European panel industry in terms of size and characteristics.
2. Explain the trends in the European construction industry.
3. What are the critical factors for success in this industry?
4. Why is a business network so important for the Trimo Company?
5. How does Trimo develop and maintain its competitive advantage?
6. What are the main characteristics of the Trimo marketing strategy in Southeastern Europe?
7. Describe the Trimo marketing strategy for the Croatian market.
8. Why did Trimo establish Trimo Građenje in Croatia?
9. What is the role of Trimo Građenje in the Trimo Company?

Case 11

UniMed and EduMed

Omar M. Zaki

In April 2004, Dr. Michael Zachary and his son, Oscar Zachary, were faced with a critical go or no-go decision. The no-go decision would close an almost 3-year chapter on a vested effort to create a world-class global telemedicine network, which by that point seemed to be unfeasible based on their efforts and capabilities alone. The go decision, however, could potentially create a new business prospect that would help them recapture their investment.

They sat and discussed the new opportunity that was brought to them: teaming up with new business partners who would help facilitate the creation of a new business entity through securing tangible projects in continuous medical education with major multinational pharmaceutical companies.

Dr. Zachary: What do you think Oscar? This is finally an opportunity for us to make our investment into UniMed back and at least break even after all this effort and money spent.

Oscar: But it's a completely different business concept, model, and market strategy than what we've been focused on for the last 3 years. Plus, I'm not sure if I'm comfortable with the idea of partnering with these folks just yet; do you trust them?

Dr. Zachary: Well, I've worked with Ahmed on a separate project before, and the guy is pretty knowledgeable about this market and how to take advantage of its growth opportunities. Plus, he doesn't give me a bad feeling when we discuss ideas, and in fact seems to be a real trustworthy guy. I don't know the other guys very well, but my feeling is they're OK since they came through Ahmed.

Source: Used by permission from Omar Zaki.

Oscar: I don't know, we would be putting all of our relationships and expertise on the line, and who knows what we might lose if something goes sour. I'm almost ready to just say let's pack up for now what we've got, get back to the drawing board, and seek out some stronger financial backing to get the web portal going. That's the real goal here, isn't it? This educational conference stuff just doesn't seem to be what we were trying to do.

Dr. Zachary: I agree with you, but look at it this way: It's a way for us to put to use all the research and relationships we've built thus far and at least see how it works. Although it won't be patient-related services, we will still be providing some benefit to the medical community through these education projects, and we can build some credibility at the same time. Who knows, maybe it's what will lead us to making UniMed a reality instead of a dream down the road.

The Telemedicine Industry

History of Telemedicine

Telemedicine is the practice of rendering medical diagnoses, advice, opinions, education, and even participating in surgery over long distances through current technology and telecommunication applications, without the physical presence of a doctor or patient being required. The idea of performing medical examinations and evaluations through the use of telecommunications is not new. Shortly after the invention of the telephone, attempts were made to transmit heart and lung sounds to a trained expert who could assess the state of the organs; however, poor transmission systems made the attempts a failure. Although it may seem that recent interest in telemedicine can be attributed to advances in the Internet and telecommunications, the truth is that telemedicine has been around since the 1960s, when astronauts first went into space. In fact, NASA built telemedicine technology into early spacecraft and spacesuits to monitor astronauts' physiological parameters. Other milestones mark telemedicine's journey to where it is today.

- 1906: ECG Transmission—Einthoven, the father of electrocardiography, first investigated the use of electrocardiogram transmission over telephone lines.
- 1920s: Help for Ships—Radios were used to link physicians standing watch at shore stations to assist ships at sea that had medical emergencies.
- 1955: Telepsychiatry—The Nebraska Psychiatric Institute was one of the first facilities in the country to have closed-circuit television in 1955. In 1971, the Nebraska Medical Center was linked with the Omaha Veterans Administration (VA) Hospital and VA facilities in two other towns.
- 1967: Massachusetts General Hospital—Telemedicine was established in 1967 to provide occupational health services to airport employees and to deliver emergency care and medical attention to travelers.

Evolution of Telemedicine: A Global Perspective

In the past, access to quality medical care has been restricted both within and between countries by geographic limitations, the inconsistent distribution of physician specialists, and limitations of existing technology. Although telemedicine has been successfully deployed in several countries and in numerous large-scale projects already, recent advances in telecommunications and technology have shown promising opportunities for explosive growth and the ability to provide the highest-quality health care throughout the world.

Limitations to the widespread implementation of telemedicine technologies were imposed by bandwidth, because the transmission of images and interactive video imaging demanded robust communications support. Those barriers have been steadily falling away, however, allowing telemedicine to become a realistic, cost-effective, and timely solution to the problems caused by inconsistent access to health care specialists. Telemedicine has successfully expanded the remote delivery of health care expertise from a broader range of medical specialties and applications, although the various specialty areas are at differing levels of sophistication and acceptance. Examples of those that have been successfully deployed include teleradiology, telecardiology, teledermatology, telepathology, and continuous medical education for health care professionals.

The Benefits of Telemedicine

Telemedicine has allowed for real-time consultations across great distances—whether between physicians, between facilities, or between patients and physicians. High-quality medical care is not delayed by the time required for travel. Not only is the quality of care improved in its timeliness, but the patient is not subjected to the additional stress of long hours of travel and being away from the support of home, family, and friends. With current advances in technology and the growth of telemedicine equipment, software, and service providers, new lines of telemedicine have emerged, such as home care, mobile medical units, and connected rural health centers, which are making medical expertise more readily accessible and simultaneously cutting down on a myriad of health care costs.

Beyond the technology, however, there are many lessons learned from previous telemedicine programs and efforts. Without adequate investment in infrastructure development, quality programs, and careful vendor selection, contracting, and management, the potential benefits to be gained from the use of technology may fall short of expectations. Although physicians have become enamored with the concept of telemedicine, there are different demands in the provision of services to wide geographic areas, and the benefit of an experienced support team becomes critical to the success of a telemedicine project, both in terms of the quality of services offered and maintaining financial viability.

Telemedicine is a reality today and represents the future of how quality health care services can be provided on a global scale. The advantage rests with those countries possessing the adequate communications infrastructure, funding, and innovation. To that degree, therefore, health care access will still be unequally distributed worldwide.

Health Care in the Middle East

History

The Middle East health care market is a very complex one because it is constituted by a number of individual nations each with its own laws, policies, regulative bodies, economies, infrastructure, demographics, and history. Countries such as Egypt, Syria, Jordan, and Saudi Arabia have traditionally been considered major medical markets in the region due to their historical medical academic systems, extensive medical infrastructures, and large market sizes. Thought leaders tend to come out of these markets, making them medical service destinations for many other nations in the region that are close by and have a similar native tongue. Other nations such as Lebanon, Tunisia, Libya, and the Gulf states (Qatar, Bahrain, Kuwait, United Arab Emirates) are still considered either primitive or very young with regard to their capacity for medical services and expertise.

With expanding populations and the emergence of new policies for health care restructuring, nations such as the United Arab Emirates, Qatar, Saudi Arabia, Kuwait, and Bahrain are investing a great deal of money, time, and effort to build and expand their health care infrastructures and capacity to serve their people better, in addition to promoting health care tourism in the region. The reality though is that Western medical care is still far superior in its quality and outcomes, and remains the most trusted destination for those who have the capacity and ability to travel.

The 9/11 Effect

Among the most devastating events to ever occur on U.S. soil were the terrible attacks on New York City, Pennsylvania, and Washington, D.C., that occurred on September 11, 2001. This set of unfortunate events had a definite negative effect on the international patient care market. Before 9/11, many large medical institutions in the United States relied heavily on international patients; for many, 20 to 40% of their profits came directly from international patients. Patients would come to the United States to take advantage of the great medical services available, and get check-ups, diagnoses, and additional treatments or services that they required.

This was a great source of income for U.S. health care and the general economy for two main reasons. First, the sheer volume of patients continually coming to the United States to receive treatment provided a steady base of tourism and spending in the country. Second, the reason international patients are so valuable is that they are generally dollar-for-dollar, cash-basis patients, unlike domestic Medicaid/Medicare patients who pay around $0.40 to the dollar. In other words, institutions receive full payment for services provided to international patients instead of government or insurance-subsidized payments. The events of 9/11 changed everything for these facilities.

After 9/11, the inflow of international visitors decreased dramatically. Visas were harder to come by. Fears led many potential patients to consider other options before coming to the United States to receive medical treatment and diagnosis. Travel declined and was sometimes made too difficult. This opened the floodgates for telemedicine.

Telemedicine: A Natural Fit

Telemedicine solved problems for both the patient who wanted superior medical service and the domestic medical institutions that had lost so much revenue post-9/11. By allowing international patients and medical practitioners to send x-rays, digitized records, and other medical tools across the world in real time, telemedicine instantly connected patients to the great medical institutions in the United States. This process cut costs and time, and it gave both sides the opportunity to overcome problems triggered by 9/11. Through telemedicine, medical institutions would be able to change their business processes slightly and still gain revenue from these international patients who were no longer making the long trip to the United States. Telemedicine had become a natural fit and solution for everyone involved. All that was needed was a company to connect the patients and doctors in the Middle East with the medical prowess of the U.S. medical system. UniMed saw telemedicine's natural fit and sought to capitalize on the opportunity through having a first-mover advantage in the region.

Building a Network

The UniMed Concept

International patients have been coming to the United States and Europe for diagnosis and treatment for many years. In the last decade, increasing numbers of U.S. medical institutions have created programs specifically to serve the needs of international clientele. UniMed's mission was to dramatically improve medical services for patients residing in the Middle East by making Western medicine readily accessible. The concept was spawned through Dr. Zachary's experience managing international patient divisions at leading hospitals in the Washington, D.C., area and the effect he personally witnessed on the international patient business shortly after 9/11.

UniMed's business concept was to combine telemedicine capabilities with a world-class network of medical institutions and physicians to create an efficient, market-leading medical service portal for Middle Eastern patients seeking Western medical services. By providing access to an extensive network of medical institutions through telemedicine technology, UniMed sought to offer second opinions, e-consulting, and patient referral management services for the patients who are able to choose to travel overseas for medical diagnosis and treatment (see Figure 1). Patients' medical files and images would be digitally sent to consulting physicians for review and diagnosis (see Figure 2). Additionally, by having an extensive network of health care constituents, UniMed would be able to offer targeted marketing services for hospitals and physicians who want ready access to these high-margin, high-dollar medical patients.

The Value Proposition

UniMed's first guiding principle was that well-informed patients can and should make their own decisions regarding their health care. UniMed thus took responsibility for helping patients to become informed, get access, and develop reasonable expectations of the process ahead to fully understand the capabilities of participating institutions and physicians, and the associated costs. UniMed's second guiding principle was to ensure a positive experience for the patient. Medical problems are traumatic and the uncertainty of dealing with the unknown makes it more so. The UniMed

❖ **Figure 1** Patient information and service flow.

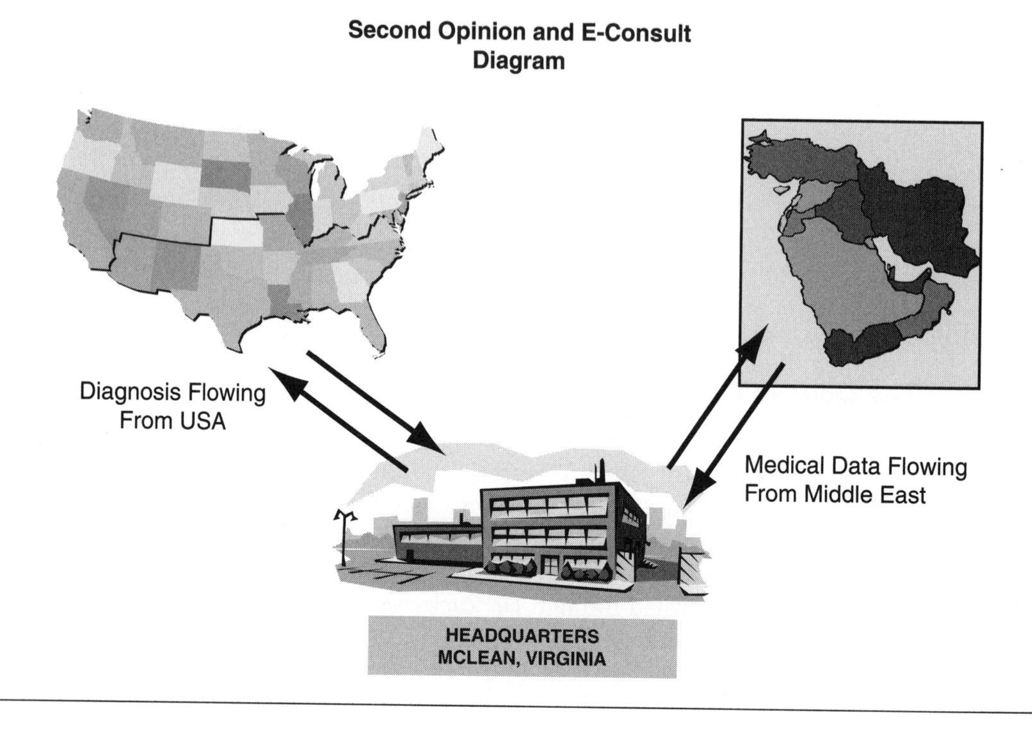

team was committed to working quickly and effectively on the patient's behalf while being a good and empathetic listener. This was considered a global solution-selling concept for the health care industry, because it was a highly customized service for patients and providers alike. UniMed planned to offer the following services: e-consultation, second opinions, and referral management services.

E-Consultations

Patients or their physicians submit questions to Western physicians via e-mail at the satellite UniMed office. The requests are processed, forwarded, and tracked as indicated in Figure 3.

Responses are received, the patient is notified, and the response is then delivered. Assistance is available in understanding and interpreting the response. A fee of US$50 is charged for electronic consultations.

Second Opinions

Patients or their physicians submit medical records for second opinions from Western physicians via the telemedicine workstation at the satellite UniMed office. This typically requires scanning and digitizing the patient's medical records unless the digitized files are brought or e-mailed to the satellite office. Second opinions generate an average of US$400 in fees.

❖ **Figure 2** Transactional flow of patient files.

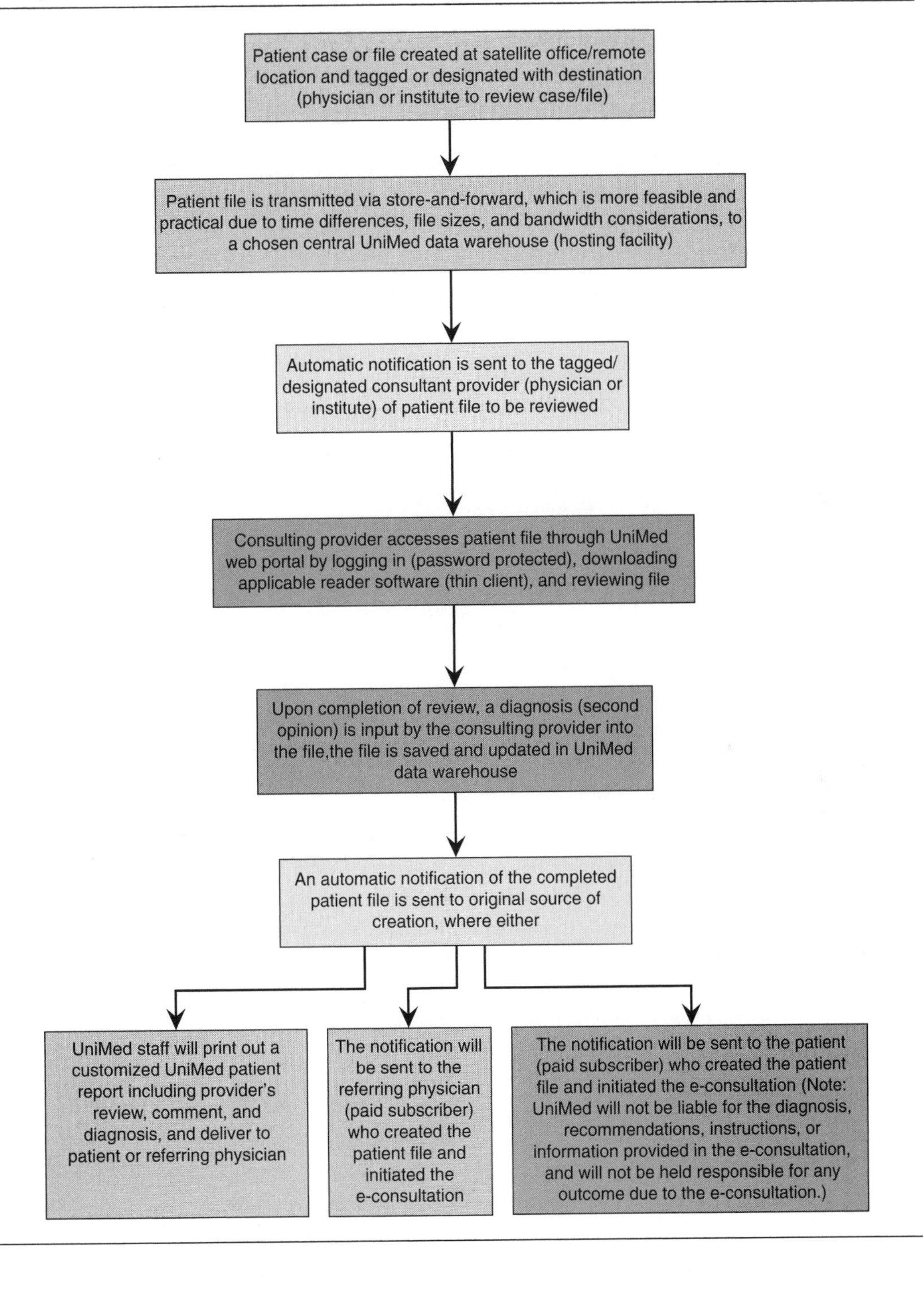

❖ **Figure 3** Sample telemedicine interface used by UniMed personnel.

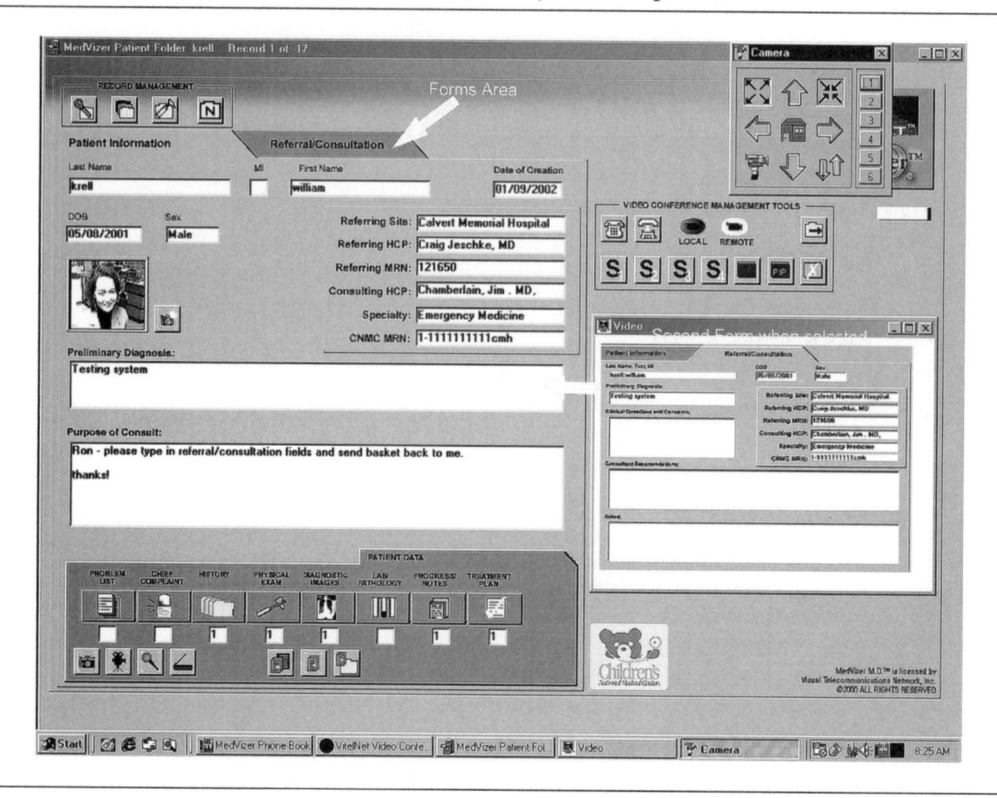

Referral Management Services

Patients who are able to choose to travel outside the Middle East to obtain second opinions or surgery begin their process with an examination of their options at the UniMed office. The staff provides all the options that fall within patients' parameters so that they can make the best decision. Once a patient makes an informed decision, UniMed processes the referral to the participating institution and provides whatever level of support the patient desires on an a la carte basis. Management fees are a flat rate of US$150, in addition to a percentage-based brokerage fee to the institution or physician where the patient is referred.

The benefits of telemedicine as practiced by UniMed include:

- Access to advanced medical resources
- Avoiding the time and expense of travel when telemedicine is an appropriate alternative
- Accelerating the time it takes to connect the patient with a Western physician
- Patients make well-informed decisions based on their own criteria
- Cost-effective services due to UniMed's negotiated arrangements with PPOs, medical institutions, and technology partners

The Early Stages of a Start-Up

UniMed, LLC, was founded by Dr. Zachary and his son Oscar in early 2002, and headquartered in Washington, D.C. The company was based on a functional structure that would maximize the skills and talents of individual consultants and advisers in the early development of the company. The initial strategy was to establish two satellite offices in the Middle East, one in Egypt and one in the United Arab Emirates, as wholly owned subsidiaries owned by the parent UniMed, LLC, and then open additional satellite offices as the company grew. This strategy was based on studies done by both Dr. Zachary and Oscar on establishing a business in those two countries. The offices were to function as patient centers that would process medical documents and records for second opinions and e-consultations. Those two locations were chosen initially as the starting point for UniMed because of their market attractiveness, such as available resources (e.g., staffing, infrastructure); relatively low mobilization costs, especially in Egypt; and market factors, such as demand and growth, and even government tax incentives in Egypt that were available to companies marketing Internet-based services to help promote information and communications technology (ICT) sector growth.

Relationships Are Everything

UniMed was positioning itself as an innovative service that it was hoped would lead to high-margin business. Building relationships was vital to the success of UniMed. Being a start-up company spawned many challenges for UniMed, many of which would prove extremely difficult to overcome. Because UniMed was a new entity in a new industry, the dynamics of building the necessary relationships was different from that of other companies. There were many barriers to entry that UniMed would have to overcome if it was to be successful.

Building the company required intense dedication and a keen feel for the needs and wants of both the customers and the doctors. One of the most difficult obstacles would be raising capital. Without money, the company had no chance of getting off the ground. Gaining access to resources and information were also big barriers to entry for UniMed. There was no existing network set up for this type of service, and there were no tried-and-tested structures to model the company after. The concept was new within a relatively young industry in itself that still had not formalized standards and protocols. The software and equipment providers had not been prepared for this type of service model and much customization and creativity were needed to develop the ideal application service provider (ASP) solution.

The telemedicine industry was not like any other industry. The Internet industry, for example, had an established structure and form, making it possible to follow standards and protocols that had already been set. To gain the necessary support and create a solid network, the founders of UniMed had one choice: to build a network from the ground up bit-by-bit, ensuring each brick in the foundation of the network was sturdy and meshed well with the overall corporate objective. To build a global network of providers and customers, many key relationships and strategic alliances had to be formed; and because the concept was new, the founders of UniMed had to sell the idea.

Much of UniMed's success would come as a direct function of how well it could provide credibility to the service, industry, and business it represented. It had to attract some of the greatest medical institutions and doctors in the world to buy into the idea and therefore help create the credibility it so greatly needed. Names such as Partner's Healthcare, Johns Hopkins, and Cleveland Clinic were industry leaders and sought-after medical destinations for the potential customer base UniMed was targeting. Institutional partners like these would help UniMed get off the ground by leveraging their reputations and experience.

To start the process of building a network, Oscar decided to join the American Telemedicine Association and attended its annual conference in 2002 in Los Angeles. The conference exposed him to the major players in the industry, both companies and individuals, and provided him with tremendous knowledge on the latest developments in the industry. Through the conference, Oscar was able to gain valuable insight and direction from leaders in the telemedicine world and to embark on building the initial relationships that would prove to be vital to UniMed's success.

One such relationship was made with a pioneer in the industry named Dr. Saunders. Dr. Saunders was an accomplished physician and was considered the godfather of telemedicine because of his long-standing involvement, contributions, and impact on the industry. Oscar attended Dr. Saunders' lecture during the conference and was amazed at how he painted such a simple yet compelling picture of the value and benefits of telemedicine. Immediately after Dr. Saunders' presentation, Oscar approached him and discussed with him the idea for UniMed, which Dr. Saunders thought was excellent. They both realized that their offices were very close to each other in Washington, D.C., and scheduled a meeting to discuss the possible business opportunities, paths to follow, and resources required for implementation. Dr. Saunders had extensive relationships and clout in the industry, so without hesitation Oscar retained his services as a chief adviser to UniMed. Immediately, Dr. Saunders began to facilitate introductions that Oscar pursued in an effort to develop needed relationships.

These initial contacts were very good starting points for UniMed. They opened the doors to forming key partnerships with leading medical institutions like Partner's Healthcare and Johns Hopkins, in addition to technology vendors that could help develop web-based solutions for the company. Through these medical institutions, UniMed would be able to cover every major medical specialty and gain the prestige and credibility that would be needed for the start-up of the company.

The Chicken or the Egg?

Client Buy-In or Provider Buy-In?

UniMed's next task was to gain support and buy-in from prospective patients and physicians who would like to use this type of service. Because much of the Middle East used public-sponsored health care services through government and military coverage, the first logical path to pursue was getting the buy-in of the decision makers, and therefore financers, of all the patients traveling abroad for health care services. By the beginning of 2003, UniMed had built several solid industry relationships and had access to many of the resources required to set up a solution. The military in Egypt and the United Arab Emirates were the first two pieces of the puzzle for linking the Middle East with U.S. medical doctors and facilities.

The challenge at this point, however, was that UniMed still did not own its own solution yet. Because it was still only a start-up with limited financial resources, it lacked the significant capital necessary to put the middle part of the solution, the software and hardware, into play. Additionally, it was still only Oscar and Dr. Zachary who were running the show, wearing all hats. Eventually, they would need to build a competent team of managerial, technical, and administrative staff both in the United States and the Middle East for the service model to be operational.

To initiate the process, the plan was to set up a project with the military in either country and have them pay for the consulting and building of the first system. The prospects all thought it was a great, innovative, and desirable solution for the region; but no one wanted to be the first to take a leap of faith with this new idea, and the bureaucracy was astounding. Furthermore, Oscar and Dr. Zachary began to experience the politics and corruption inherent in doing business in the region. For instance, because no legitimate business was yet established with a potential patient base in the region, exclusive contracts still could not be set up between UniMed and the medical institutions in the United States. This then led to some prospective customers in the Middle East wanting to bypass UniMed and go directly to the medical institutions and technology vendors themselves.

Pilot Project

After a little over 2 years of marketing and trying to build a project base that would warrant investing into a system and organizational structure UniMed would require to deliver the service, an opportunity and idea came up to test the concept. The founders obtained the medical records of 20 real patients through Dr. Zachary's extensive relationships with the medical industry in Egypt and sought to use them for a pilot project. They developed a relationship with an independent doctor/computer programmer who claimed to have an open-source electronic patient record (EPR) solution and virtual data center, and had expressed interest in being a part of UniMed's growth. He offered to build a model for the entire company, based on an initial retainer fee to keep the pilot project going, and upon user and provider acceptance, gain equity in the company as it developed its project base.

Oscar and Dr. Zachary wanted to test the concept they had worked so hard on for over 2 years. Piloting the concept by sending real medical records to 5 independent doctors they had strong relationships with was the only way for them to make sure it worked. If they could gain end-user (physicians and patients) acceptance of the system and business model, they would be sure to capture real business and patient transaction flow. The unfortunate outcome, however, was that UniMed was again faced with another example of corruption and deceit with the doctor/computer programmer, who conned the founders by taking his retainer and providing UniMed with a useless, nonfunctioning software solution. UniMed was back to square one again.

End of the Rope

Half a million dollars and 2½ years after the birth of a company and concept, there were still no tangible projects or visible success stories. There were continuous costs to maintain the offices in the United States and Egypt, consultants and advisers, and other expenses, which were becoming too much. Oscar began feeling the frustration of carrying the company's weight all on his shoulders, and started to think he could not continue doing everything on his own anymore. Both he and Dr. Zachary were becoming disheartened with the progress of the company.

After all the trials and troubles, corruption, and deceitfulness UniMed faced, Oscar decided to return to the United States and take a step back from the entire project. With money running out and relationships quickly fading, he felt there was no real way to continue. He started his own job search and agreed with Dr. Zachary to continue attempts to build UniMed on a part-time basis, scaling back all the activities to save on costs. After a couple of months of searching for new work, Oscar was about to accept one of two job offers he had received.

Opportunity Knocks

Just as Oscar was considering new employment, he received an interesting call from his father. Dr. Zachary had just met with a gentleman in Abu Dhabi, named Dr. Ahmed, who had previously worked with him on a medical education project sponsored by a large pharmaceutical entity in collaboration with the hospital Dr. Zachary managed at the time. When Dr. Ahmed heard about what UniMed was attempting to do, he thought it was an amazing concept and had an epiphany. He knew he could use this type of technology in the pharmaceutical industry to train and educate medical doctors in the Middle East, which was a requirement now with recent ethical guidelines in the industry, but was exceedingly difficult to do with quality content after the reality of 9/11. After 9/11, it had become challenging to train and educate doctors because many U.S. and European doctors that had previously come to the Middle East to speak were reluctant to do so now because of fears and anxiety over the geopolitical situation in the region. Additionally, the Middle Eastern physicians who used to travel to the United States for training had more difficulty doing so after 9/11 because of problems with visas and rising travel costs. This ultimately caused major problems for the pharmaceutical industry, making it difficult to maintain the fruitful relationships with health care professionals that allowed the companies to market their products.

Simultaneously, health care in the Middle East was undergoing major restructuring and process and quality improvements, including the implementation of educational requirements for physicians to maintain their licensing in an effort to help raise the standards of care. Pharmaceutical companies were under pressure to keep doctors happy and provide educational opportunities for the doctors through their extensive marketing budgets. Video and web-based communications from the United States, which UniMed specialized in for medical purposes, would help to reunite doctors and the medical sector in the Middle East to those of the Western world for an exchange of best practices and information.

EduMed Is Born

Faced now with a new opportunity to leverage their knowledge and relationships, Dr. Zachary and Oscar considered taking on this new possibility to develop a business slightly different in its objective from UniMed, but nonetheless viable in itself. Dr. Ahmed proposed involving two other associates of his, who he considered influential in the pharmaceutical industry, and proceeded to facilitate a meeting in April 2004, bringing together his associates, Dr. Zachary and Oscar, to discuss the idea and potential for the market. Dr. Zachary, Dr. Ahmed, and his associates discussed starting a new business entity based in Dubai, named EduMed, which would develop, market, and execute continuous medical education (CME) projects (Figure 4) using

❖ **Figure 4** Typical EduMed CME project structure.

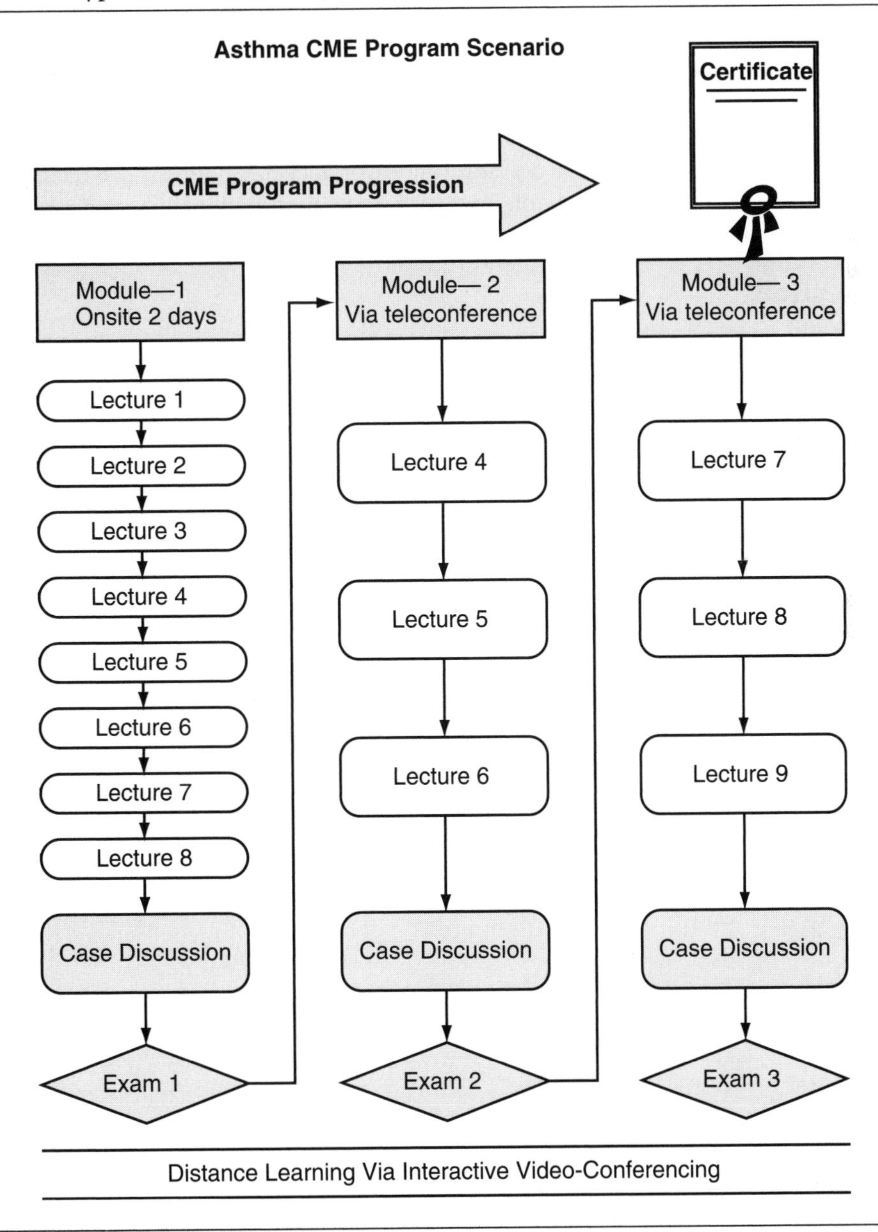

the same technical and academic resources UniMed had developed relationships with. They sought to create a successful profit-generating business by securing tangible projects that could be facilitated through the industry relationships of Dr. Ahmed and his associates. Meanwhile, Oscar sat and observed during the meeting without much involvement, listening to the new potential business partners' suggestions and ideas, with a bit of skepticism based on his previous experiences.

Oscar knew there would be many similar potential pitfalls to what UniMed faced, but the majority of them would be new due to a shift in the market focus and strategy for acquiring the business EduMed would pursue. There was no way to know if EduMed could have a better fate than UniMed, and there was still a sense of attachment and almost parental protection that was felt by both Dr. Zachary and Oscar with regard to letting UniMed's inner core be exposed to these new business partners. The fact remained, however, that UniMed was still not generating any revenue on its own, and for the sake of recapturing the vast investments made into the company, Dr. Zachary and Oscar both realized that EduMed was a necessary endeavor. By 2005, EduMed had secured 12 CME projects throughout the Middle East with many multinational pharmaceutical companies as clients, and the founders had finally recouped their investment in UniMed.

Case Questions

1. What are the key market factors that drove UniMed's business model?
2. What were some of the core elements in creating the UniMed business?
3. What was UniMed's value proposition?
4. What were some of the challenges UniMed faced?
5. What was the dilemma with EduMed?
6. What were the opportunities with EduMed?
7. For EduMed to be a success, what seemed to be required?

Buying Office Supplies—Easy!

Sample Business Plan

Presented by

Joseph Naaman

Submitted in

Glendale, AZ, February 13, 2008

Confidential business plan number: _______

Table of Contents

List of Exhibits

Operations Management Exhibits

Common Exhibits

Executive Summary

The Venture and Its Industry

EGYPT'S PROBLEM

Businesses and consumers alike find purchasing office supplies in Egypt a difficult task. There are no product lists or catalogs to facilitate the process, and there are few choices for office supplies. Traditional local office supply stores are the main medium through which to purchase office goods. Usually, there is no delivery system offered and a minimal variety of products, causing businesses and consumers to spend their time either inefficiently looking for the proper office supply or improvising by making the best of what they have.

OUR SOLUTION

Maktabi provides businesses and consumers with an efficient and inexpensive way to order office supplies from a catalog or online—offering a wide variety of products and diverse styles to choose from at the comfort of one's own desk. The person placing the order can either go online or pick up the phone and dial one of the toll free numbers to order whatever they need. Through operational excellence and efficient distribution systems, the customer will receive the order quickly at a minimal cost.

THE INDUSTRY

Maktabi is in the office supplies industry. Included in this industry are wholesalers, distributors, and retailers. Maktabi fits into each of these categories, making classification difficult but allowing for unique positioning in the minds of businesses and consumers.

The Entrepreneur

Joseph Naaman

Mr. Joseph Naaman started his first business as a sophomore at Boston University, where he earned his degree in finance and marketing. He was a partner in a venture exporting Arizona Iced Tea from the United States to Italy, achieving approximately $2.5 million in sales within the first 2 years. Since then he has joined an established multinational pharmaceutical company, Bristol-Myers Squibb, to gain additional experience in global supply chain and logistics. He continued his professional education globally in business development for a luxury motor yacht company based in Egypt, where he started his second venture exporting organic agricultural products worldwide from Egypt. Along the way Mr. Naaman wrote two award-winning business plans, one for consumer products and one in the services industry. Currently, he is attending the Thunderbird School of Global Management, where he is focusing on entrepreneurship and finance. He has used his time at Thunderbird to refine the skills required to ensure the smooth operation of his new passion—providing office supplies to the Egyptian workplace.

The Board of Advisors

Mahmoud Mohieldin

Dr. Mohieldin has been the Minister of Investment in the Arab Republic of Egypt since 2004. This ministry is responsible for administering investment policy; management of state-owned assets, including privatization and restructuring of public enterprises and joint ventures; and nonbanking financial services, including capital market, insurance, and mortgage finance.

Dr. Mohieldin was born in Egypt in 1965. He received his bachelor of science in economics, with highest honors, first in order of merit, from Cairo University, Egypt. In 1989 he received a diploma in quantitative development economics from University of Warwick, England; in 1990 he received a master of science in economic and social policy analysis from University of York, England; and in 1995 he received his PhD in economics from University of Warwick, England.

Dr. Mohieldin has declared that he will provide his support in this venture by ensuring the efficient flow of orders through the bureaucratic red tape that companies in Egypt sometimes face.

Majid Al-Futtaim

Mr. Majid Al-Futtaim is the founder of several large regional shopping malls and hypermarkets throughout the Middle East. His ventures include such giants as the Mall of the Emirates in Dubai, United Arab Emirates; Ski Dubai in Dubai, United Arab Emirates; and Maadi City Center, Cairo, Egypt. Owning the Carrefour chain of stores in Egypt, Mr. Al-Futtaim hopes to share the expertise of his leadership team in creating a business whose products and service would be used throughout Egypt and the rest of the Middle East. His vision for Maktabi is a Staples for the Middle East.

Tarek Ragheb

Mr. Tarek Ragheb owns several businesses throughout the Middle East, the majority of which are located in Egypt. His contacts and expertise in setting up businesses and seeking funding have made him a crucial member of the Board of Advisors. Additionally, due to his American education, Mr. Ragheb brings a Western ideology of doing business to the Middle East. He is excited about the potential of being part of another winning business opportunity such as Maktabi.

The Management Team

Sherif Naaman

Mr. Sherif Naaman has over 35 years of experience in both the United States and the Middle East, leading projects in the fields of marketing and information technology. Fifteen of his 35 years have been spent as Managing Director in Saudi Arabia for various companies: the Alshaya group, a Kuwaiti holding company; Wardeh Al-Salehiya, a Saudi holding company; and Bristol-Myers Squibb, a U.S. corporation and the fifth largest pharmaceutical company worldwide. With his experience and exposure to the Middle East market, Mr. Naaman is confident that he would efficiently manage the company. He is excited about the opportunity to move back to the Middle East to aid companies in doing business the way they should.

Mahmoud Hindi

Mr. Mahmoud Hindi has over 5 years of experience working for SGS, a global transportation and freight forwarding company whose Egyptian offices were founded by his father. With the exposure that he has received at this high level, Mr. Hindi believes that his experience, contacts, and know-how in distribution and transportation will enable him to manage logistics at Maktabi with excellence.

Nancy Sharkawi

Ms. Nancy Sharkawi has worked for several years in the supply chain and as a sales representative for a large pharmaceutical company in the United States. With this background, Ms. Sharkawi will be able to manage the purchasing department of Maktabi. Naturally a people person, Ms. Sharkawi will foster the relationships required with Eastern and Southeastern Asian countries to ensure the smooth flow of product into Egypt. She is excited to be able to use the skills she has developed in the United States in a global setting.

Christine Chami

Ms. Christine Chami has several years of experience working in the marketing departments of large consumer goods companies. With the beginning of her career based in Canada, she knows how marketing departments are run in the west. She has successfully applied the knowledge she gained from this experience as a high performer at the company she currently works for in Dubai. Living in Dubai has enabled her to learn about doing business in the Middle East.

The Market

A SNAPSHOT

Businesses

- Average combined annual revenues of $1.3 million
- Regular use of office supplies

- Two or more departments in each company that order separately

Consumers

- Average annual household income of $12,000
- Regular use of office supplies
- More than two individuals per household who order office supplies

The Bigger Picture

In interviews conducted with executive assistants and secretaries at small and large corporations, the majority expressed that they would probably or definitely use our service to order office supplies for three reasons:

- It would simplify the processes currently in place in their office.
- There is a trend toward accepting already established ways of doing business in more developed countries.
- Some of the products sold will be considered as trendy or new on the market, making consumers happy to try something different.

Further emphasis will be placed on executive assistants, secretaries, and office buyers because it has been proven that this group is more likely to be into innovations in this type of industry.

Overall, focus has been placed on these users because

- Office supplies are a vital component in the workplace.
- There is no need to double sell consumers on office supplies and the service that we offer.
- These consumers are already familiar with the products and current processes used to order them, and would welcome a service that enhanced the process.
- Our interviews show that these users have a high probability of using our service.

Another market of consumers exists that is not part of a business or an organization, but rather is composed of individuals. These are individuals who have a predisposition for purchasing office supplies because of the nature of their education, hobbies, or interests. Included in this group would be school children and their parents—since it is the parents who would actually purchase the products—artists, hobbyists, and individuals who like to own new and innovative office supplies.

	2008	2009	2010	2011	2012
Total Orders	19,500	202,500	702,500	790,000	917,500
Total Dollars	$215,000	$2,149,000	$7,079,000	$7,951,000	$9,215,500

Figure ES1 5-Year Base Case Sales Projection (US$)

Sales and Profits

In 2008 Maktabi sales will exceed $200,000 by completing over 19,500 different orders. By the 5th year, sales are expected to exceed $9 million (see Figure ES1).

A net loss is expected during the 1st year and the venture will break even by the end of year two. By the 3rd year, the net profit margin is expected to level out at approximately 14%—a net margin that should remain stable throughout the life of the company.

Call for Action

Investors can earn an internal rate of return greater than 32% over the life of the project with an investment of $870,000 that is spread over a 2-year period. The capital investment has an approximate net present value of $1,100,000 with a payback period of less than 2 years. This investment offers you the opportunity to better the Egyptian business environment.

The Maktabi Group has the drive and capabilities to become the leading company in the office supplies industry in Egypt because of its fresh and innovative approach. The detailed business proposal presents our step-by-step process for ensuring the financial success of your investment.

Description of the Business

Description of the Venture

EGYPT'S PROBLEM

Businesses and consumers alike find purchasing office supplies in Egypt a difficult task. There are no product lists or catalogs to facilitate the process and there are few choices for purchasing office supplies. Traditional local office supply stores are the main medium to purchase office goods. Usually, there is no delivery service offered or variety of products, causing businesses and consumers to spend their time either inefficiently looking for the proper office supply or improvising by making the best of what they can find.

OUR SOLUTION

Maktabi provides businesses and consumers with an efficient and inexpensive way to order office supplies from a catalog or online—offering a wide variety of products and diverse styles to choose from at the comfort of one's own desk. The person placing the order can either go online or pick up the phone and dial one of the toll free numbers to order whatever they need. Through operational excellence and efficient distribution systems, the customer will receive the order quickly at a minimal cost.

CRITICAL SUCCESS FACTORS

- Educating businesses and consumers on a new, efficient, and inexpensive way to order office supplies

- Motivating consumers and businesses to change their current ordering practice
- Concentrating on operational excellence as a core competency by maintaining the highest quality standards at the lowest operational costs
- Maintaining constantly updated and original product lines and communicating about them through our catalog and Web site

MISSION STATEMENT

Our mission is to help Egypt fulfill its pursuit of improved and modernized business performance. Our objective is to make Maktabi an integral part of the Egyptian business and home, stressing the importance of an easy and fun office supplies purchasing process. To achieve our mission, we affirm our values of performance, quality, leadership, teamwork, and customers focus.

The Business Model

MARKETING

The target market is split into two distinct groups: businesses and consumers. Our target market is composed of approximately 35,000 businesses and 15 million consumers. The businesses and consumers purchase office supply products on average seven times per year. Special emphasis will be placed on forward-thinking businesses that want to do business like those in more developed countries because they tend to understand the cost-savings of an efficient ordering process. We will reach this primary market by creating a team of salesmen who will aggressively approach these companies to offer our services and free catalog—a salesman "blitz."

Our secondary market will be composed of consumers who purchase office supplies on a regular basis. This group will include school children and their parents, hobbyists, and artists. We will target this group by inciting a feeling of necessity for our products. A more traditional advertising approach will be used to reach them, and an elaborate marketing campaign will be used to introduce the company and the products it offers. Maktabi's products will initially only be found in catalogs and online.

OPERATIONS

Maktabi's products will be organized in essentially two categories: local and outsourced. Through an advanced sourcing model, the buyers at

Maktabi will be faced with a myriad of in-house and outsource decisions, with the majority of our products coming from Southeastern Asia due to its product and export quality, growth, and competitive pricing. The products that Egypt has an advantage in producing will be purchased locally. This careful examination of product sourcing, a state of the art distribution facility located near Cairo, a customer-centric customer service team, coupled with an excellent partnership with a global transportation and distribution third-party logistics provider will enable us to ensure our operational excellence critical success factor (see Figure DB1).

INFORMATION SYSTEMS

There are several information systems that must be in operation in order for Maktabi to run efficiently. These systems include customer order processing, inventory management, warehouse management, accounting and sales representative monitoring, and basic software requirements. All of these systems can be purchased as one package through an enterprise resource planning system.

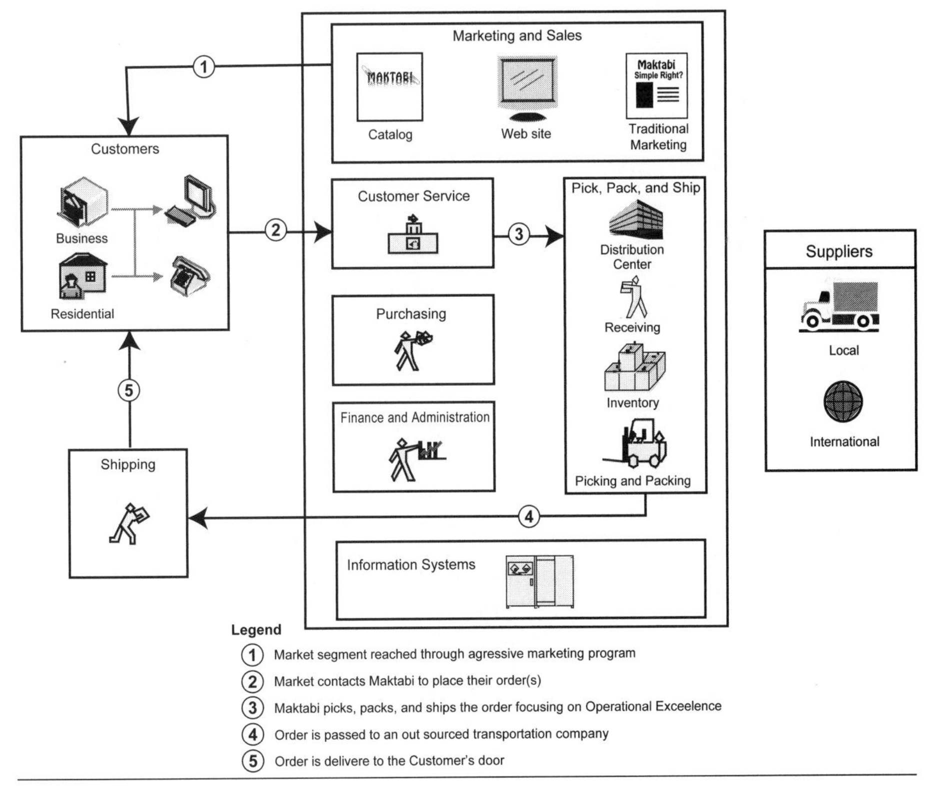

Figure DB1 Maktabi Process Flow Diagram

Competitor, Industry, and Consumer Analysis

Industry Analysis

Maktabi is in the office supplies industry. Included in this industry are wholesalers, distributors, and retailers. Maktabi fits into each of these categories, making classification difficult but allowing for unique positioning in the minds of businesses and consumers.

INDUSTRY AND ENVIRONMENT TRENDS

- Continued economic progress, principally based on Egypt's large, diversified economy, expanding international opportunities, modest external debt levels, fulfillment of debt service requirements, political stability, sustainable GDP growth, and the potential for further economic growth as a result of continued structural reforms.
- A population of over 75 million means a large potential market for investments, particularly in consumer goods and services such as Maktabi's. Demand has kept pace with modernization and is escalating with respect to services and technology.
- Consumer tastes and preferences have evolved with economic liberalization. Egyptian consumers today adapt to change and accept new products far more willingly than was once the case. The younger generations are especially eager to keep up with the latest developments worldwide, and therefore generate a large portion of domestic demand.

- Egyptian middle-income households make up most of Egypt's total household expenditure.
- The middle class is increasingly keen on such equipment as microwaves, stereos, videos, washing machines, and cellular phones, which reflects the change of lifestyle resulting from the recent improvement in the standard of living.
- Egypt offers advantages to multinational companies looking to establish a competitive edge and capitalize on investment decisions. Intermediate goods may be outsourced, and platforms exist for the production and export of goods at different stages of production.

Porter's Five Forces

BARGAINING POWER OF CUSTOMER—MODERATE

- Maktabi's products are sold to businesses large and small as well as consumers. This means that businesses and consumers have some degree of influence on the type of products sold. Though most are standard products, Maktabi will have to follow the patterns of this demand in order to maximize sales.

THREAT OF SUBSTITUTE PRODUCTS—HIGH

- Maktabi's business concept is simple and can easily be copied by any wholesaler, distributor, or retailer already in operation.
- The products that Maktabi sells are standard office supply products that can easily be purchased from local providers or global companies located in regions such as Southeastern Asia.
- The required start-up investment amount is moderate and can be matched by larger competitors who feel their market share is being threatened.

BARGAINING POWER OF SUPPLIERS—VERY LOW

- The products that Maktabi will sell can be purchased from any number of suppliers because the majority are available from other sources and are indistinguishable from one another.

- Global companies, particularly from Asia and Southeastern Asian countries, are hungry for business and will help open barriers to entry.

BARRIERS TO ENTRY—MODERATE TO LOW

- Moderate capital investment paired with a simple business concept allow for development of me-too companies.

CURRENT COMPETITIVE THREAT—MODERATE

- Local office supply stores threaten Maktabi due to their widespread availability throughout Egypt's major areas. The convenience that these stores offer cannot match that of Maktabi because the customer must physically make the purchase and the product variety is limited.

SWOT Analysis

STRENGTHS

- Maktabi is the first company in Egypt to offer office supplies along with their delivery, rendering the process more efficient.
- Beginning a catalog service as well as selling products online will enable Maktabi to sell other products such as furniture and technology related to the office.
- Our core competence is operational excellence. Our sourcing strategy along with our modern distribution facility will enable us to provide products to customers with a minimum error rate in an expected amount of time at little cost.

WEAKNESSES

- No prior experience in the office supplies industry.
- The company's success will depend in large part on an aggressive sales force and a robust marketing and sales promotions plan.
- Ability to find required talent to staff the operation in a forward-thinking, culturally borderless business environment.

OPPORTUNITIES

- Extremely large potential market that is already purchasing the type of product we are offering.
- Introducing a larger variety of products or partnering with companies who would want to use our reputation or our network to sell their own products.
- Expand into other sectors.
- Expand into other countries in the Middle East—borders are less concrete because of the Internet.

THREATS

- Competitors see an opportunity to get into the market using already existing political and economic relations to compete.

Competitive Analysis

Currently, there is one organization and two types of existing business models that directly compete with Maktabi: Speedsend is the former, and traditional office supply stores and hypermarkets are the latter. Consumer perceptions of product attributes are diagramed by Maktabi's positioning matrix in Figure CI1.

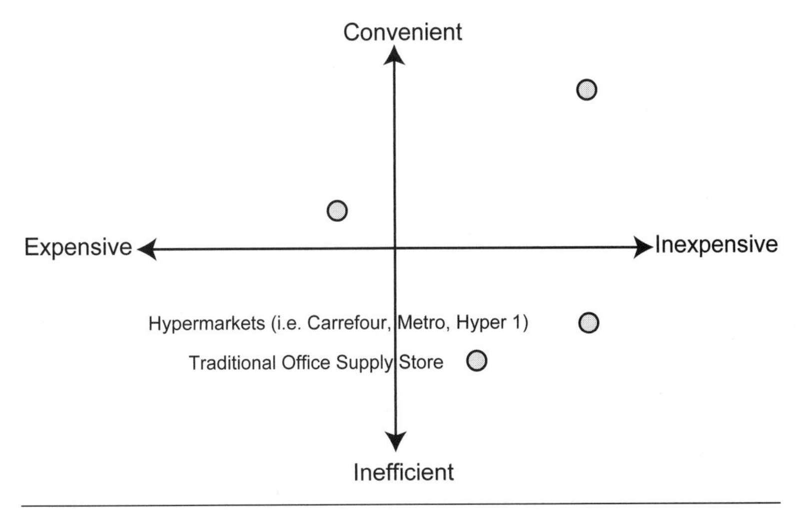

Figure CI1 Maktabi Positioning Matrix

Of the aforementioned competitors, attributes of each are outlined below:

Speedsend (www.speedsend.com)

- In operation since June 2001
- Only offers its services in Cairo
- HP business partner
- Xerox certified corporate reseller
- Make its own brand of paper

Traditional office supply stores (includes high-end stores such as Ali wa Ali and Aswak)

- Located throughout Egypt
- Do deliver locally
- Do not have catalogs
- Do not innovate with the types of product they carry
- Cannot buy in bulk

Hypermarkets

- Increasing in popularity throughout Egypt
- Purchase items in bulk
- Few locations and located primarily outside of the major cities
- Do not innovate with the types of product they carry
- Do not deliver locally
- Do not have catalogs

Target Markets

A SNAPSHOT

Businesses

- Average combined annual revenues of $1.3 million
- Regular use of office supplies
- Two or more departments in each company that order separately

Consumers

- Average annual household income of $12,000
- Regular use of office supplies
- More than two individuals per household who order office supplies

The Bigger Picture

In interviews conducted with executive assistants and secretaries at small and large corporations, the majority expressed that they would probably or definitely use our service to order office supplies for three reasons (see Figure CI2):

- It will simplify the processes currently in place in the office.
- There is a trend toward accepting already established ways of doing business in more developed countries.
- Some of the products sold will be considered as trendy or new on the market, making consumers happy to try something different.

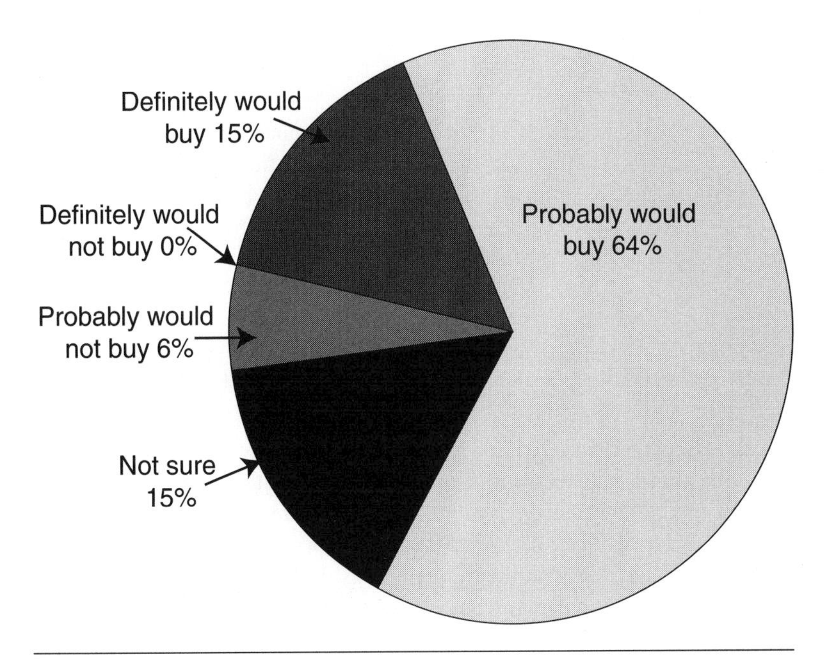

Figure CI2 Usage by Percentage of Population

Further emphasis will be placed on executive assistants, secretaries, and office buyers because it has been proven that this group is more likely to be into innovations in this type of industry.

Overall, focus has been placed on these users because

- Office supplies are a vital component in the workplace.
- There is no need to double sell consumers on office supplies and the service that we offer.
- These consumers are already familiar with the products and current processes used to order them, and would welcome a service that enhanced the process.
- Our interviews show that these users have a high probability of using our service.

Another market of consumers exists that is not part of a business or an organization, but rather is composed of individuals. These are individuals who have a predisposition for purchasing office supplies because of the nature of their education, hobbies, or interests. Included in this group would be school children and their parents—since it is the parents who would actually purchase the products—artists, hobbyists, and individuals who like to own new and innovative office supplies.

Consumer Profiles

Our company is targeting two distinct markets characterized by a combination of psychographics and usage behavior. Particular emphasis will be placed on businesses and we will appeal to women because studies show that they are more likely to use a wide variety of office supplies and are more inclined to make a purchase.

PRIMARY TARGET: TRENDSETTING EXECUTIVE ASSISTANTS, SECRETARIES, AND OFFICE BUYERS

This particular target market is receptive to rationale-based appeals, preferring hard facts over emotional-based motivation. They respond to quick facts that are easily assimilated and applied to their job. This group will be particularly responsive to our sales force strategy and our more traditional advertising strategies, such as billboards, magazines, and advertising. Additional characteristics of these consumers are that they

- are concerned with making their jobs more efficient;
- are aware of the different ways business is being done in more developed countries;
- want to be considered competent and able to make business decisions (no matter the size);
- are influenced by their peers, supervisors, friends, and the media;
- use the Internet often, particularly for work, newsgroups, entertainment, and shopping; and
- value helping the company.

SECONDARY TARGET: OFFICE SUPPLY ENTHUSIASTS

Our secondary target market is less affected by rationale and facts as they are motivated by their hobbies or by their need to own trendy items. This group is not as business-oriented as our primary market, but equally important in our marketing efforts. Catchy advertisements that highlight how trendy our products are and the service that we offer drive them to purchase our product. We assumed less of a consumption rate for this market than the primary target market. Additional characteristics of these consumers are that they

- are excited by new products and new ways of purchasing products;
- are motivated by their hobbies and their emotions;
- are easily influenced by the media, friends, and perceived social leaders; and
- use the Internet for entertainment, online magazines, special interest groups, or gossip columns.

Marketing Strategy

Sales Forecast

In 2008 Maktabi sales will exceed $200,000 by completing over 19,500 different orders (see Figure MK1).

The 5-year sales projection is comprised of several calculations that consider the following (see Exhibits MK1-A, MK1-B, and MK1-C for Base, Best, and Worst Case Sales Projections, page 528–530):

1. Anticipated Demand has been determined by market research through focus groups and surveys (see Exhibits MK2 and MK3). This calculation is contingent upon business and consumer office supply usage (see Figure MK2).
2. Sales Representative Market Penetration determines Maktabi sales with regards to the market awareness created by each of our regional sales representatives (see Figure MK3).
3. Business and Consumer Awareness is a percentage that measures how effective advertising is at making the business user and the consumer aware of the product. Our marketing mix will effectively reach 39% of our target market in year one, with 76% of business

	2008	2009	2010	2011	2012
Total Orders	19,500	202,500	702,500	790,000	917,500
Total Dollars	$215,000	$2,149,000	$7,079,000	$7,951,000	$9,215,500

Figure MK1 5-Year Base Case Sales Projection

users and 2% of consumers becoming fully aware of Maktabi. A lower level of awareness is assigned to the "Office Supply Enthusiasts" group because they do not regularly use office supplies or they are less concerned with office supplies reaching them in an efficient manner; therefore, this group will be less receptive to marketing efforts.

		Purchase Intent	Adjustment	Total Adjusted Trial
Businesses	Definitely Buy	10%	80%	21%
	Probably Buy	62%	20%	
Consumers	Definitely Buy	14%	80%	26%
	Probably Buy	71%	20%	

Figure MK2 Anticipated Demand Calculations

	Year 1	Year 2	Year 3	Year 4	Year 5
Sales Representative 1 (Cairo 1)	2712	2880	2304	2304	2304
Sales Representative 2 (Cairo 2)	2712	2880	2304	2304	2304
Sales Representative 3 (Cairo 3)	2712	2880	2304	2304	2304
Sales Representative 4 (Cairo 4)	2712	2880	2304	2304	2304
Sales Representative 5 (Alexandria and North Coast 1)	2712	2880	2304	2304	2304
Sales Representative 6 (Alexandria and North Coast 2)	2712	2880	2304	2304	2304
Sales Representative 7 (Sinai Peninsula and Red Sea)	2160	2880	2304	2304	2304
Sales Representative 8 (Upper Egypt)	2160	2880	2304	2304	2304
Sales Representative 9 (Upper Egypt)	2160	2880	2304	2304	2304
Total	22,752	25,920	20,736	20,736	20,736
Cumulative	22,752	48,672	69,408	90,144	110,880

Figure MK3 Sales Representative Market Penetration Calculations

Situation Analysis

BEST AND WORST CASE SCENARIOS

Situation analysis considers several internal and external factors that affect sales projection figures. Five-year best case and worst case scenarios have been applied to our sales forecast to anticipate changes in the environment and predict how it could affect the company's performance (see Figure MK4). See Exhibit MK1 for further details.

Factors of Best Case Scenario

- Maktabi earns the support of top companies such as Orascom, ExxonMobil, or EGYPTAIR, increasing business support and awareness by word-of-mouth communication (see Exhibit MK4 for a sample letter of intent to use Maktabi's services, page 538).
- Office supply enthusiasts are more concerned with the efficiency that Maktabi is offering, causing them to be more receptive to the service. This is indicated by 16% of survey respondents that indicated they would definitely buy and 17% that indicated they would probably buy actually purchasing the products, an increase of 6% and 3% respectively from the base case.

Factors of Worst Case Scenario

- Economic downturn equates to less spending by businesses and consumers. This results in a lower adjusted purchase rate with 4% of the consumers who would definitely buy and 11% of the consumers who would probably buy actually purchasing the products.

	Year 1	Year 2	Year 3	Year 4	Year 5
Base	$215,000	$2,149,000	$7,079,000	$7,951,000	$9,215,500
Best	$1,000,000	$5,470,000	$7,990,000	$10,630,000	$10,915,000
Worst	$136,500	$1,875,000	$3,730,000	$2,915,000	$3,000,000

Figure MK4 Anticipated Demand Calculations

- Advertising successfully creates sense of need, but consumers choose to use alternative sources for office supplies. This is represented by lowering awareness.
- After year two's peak of 86% among businesses and year four's peak of 10% among consumers, awareness drops by an average of 18% each year. This decrease in awareness can be attributed to a 13% decrease of consumer reach and 57% lower frequency.

Marketing Strategy

Our promotions and advertising are meant to educate businesses and consumers, which enforces a pull strategy. Heading our marketing efforts, Maktabi's marketing director will focus efforts on informing businesses and consumers about the need to make their work habits more efficient and motivate them to use our services as the solution (see Exhibit MK5 for the curriculum vitae of Maktabi's marketing director candidate, page 539). These marketing strategies support our company's critical success factors. Our marketing efforts must make businesses and consumers aware that they will waste time and money by using traditional office supply ordering habits.

The success of the Maktabi brand is dependent upon how well our marketing efforts align and communicate our companywide strategies and objectives. These objectives manifest themselves as a cohesive theme throughout each level of the marketing and distribution process. Maktabi's marketing strategy can be summarized by a four-stage progression and acronym called REEM:

1. Reason with businesses and consumers about the inefficiencies of current office supply ordering.
2. Educate businesses and consumers about the need to make the office supply ordering process efficient and modern.
3. Empower businesses and consumers to change their office supply ordering habits.
4. Motivate businesses and consumers to use our services.

Market Life Cycle

It will take several years for Maktabi to reach full market saturation. Lack of competitors and high product differentiation indicates that the market is currently in the introduction phase. This will be the longest stage of our market life cycle. This is due to the time and resources it takes to educate businesses and consumers and to motivate them to change their habits, two of our critical success factors. Market growth will occur as our sales increase and businesses and consumers become more aware of the product. We have accounted for this slow growth by taking a more conservative approach in our sales forecasting. We calculated that 80% and 20% of the survey respondents that indicated they will definitely buy and probably buy, respectively, actually purchase the product (see Exhibit MK1-A through MK1-C).

Pricing Strategy

Minimal profit margins will be allocated to each product to undermine the prices set forth by our competitors for similar products. Survey results indicate that the majority of respondents are willing to pay between 5EGP and 9EGP (US$0.87 and US$1.57) for our service (see Exhibit MK2). By providing the business user or the consumer with the choice of several delivery options, the minimum amount will be charged for that service and no gratuity will be required because the delivery will be made by a professional transportation company. Pricing Maktabi's products as competitively or more competitively compared to standard products from other outlets is necessary because consumers consider office supplies low-price commodities. Businesses and consumers will compare the price of our products and service to other alternatives they are familiar with. The more sophisticated consumers will compare Maktabi products to the expensive high-end stores such as Ali wa Ali and Aswak and recognize that we can offer a greater variety of products more efficiently. Similarly, consumers more inclined to make large one-time purchases will compare our products and services to those of the hypermarkets which will have less variety, a less efficient process, and similar or more expensive pricing. We hope that the perception from the beginning will be that Maktabi is the more time- and cost-effective choice.

Product Availability

The large size of our target market requires that our distribution methods ensure that Maktabi's products are available to every potential business and consumer. This is achieved by maintaining accurate forecasts based on historical and analytical data, as well as distributing to all regions of the country. At the beginning of every catalog and on the Web site, a "How to . . ." section will be made available, enabling businesses and consumers to understand how to place orders, how to ask questions, how to complete returns, and more.

Sales Force

During the first 5 years that Maktabi's products and service will be available, the marketing department will employ and train nine sales representatives. All agents will be provided with catalogs, a vehicle, and a laptop computer with access to the Internet from any location for activity tracking and client demonstration purposes. Each representative will earn a base salary of 300EGP (US$52) per month with a 2% increase each year. The nine representatives will earn a 3% commission. The base salary allows the representatives to have a vested interest in the long-term concerns of the company, while the commission motivates them to establish and maintain contacts with businesses. The sales force will be led by a marketing manager who will also be responsible for developing and assessing the marketing mix. For an organizational chart, see Exhibit CM1, page 601.

Advertising Mediums

NEWSPAPER ADVERTISEMENTS

Newspaper advertising will be used as a way to introduce Maktabi to the public. Every newspaper advertisement has a black background and white type that states a bold, high impact, logical statement about better business processes, ending with our recognizable catchphrase "Easy!" These ads act as a stimulant to inform the public about better business practices. This advertising campaign will run for the first 2 years to stir up general awareness about better office supply ordering practices and our products. The advertisement will appear twice a month. Our Web site and our toll free number will be located at the bottom of all newspaper advertisements. Though, based on our analysis, radio, television, and Internet advertising is recognized by businesses and consumers as the medium that will best convey the message about our products and services, we feel newspaper advertising will convey a sense of reliability and urgency to initially create awareness among consumers.

MAGAZINE ADVERTISEMENTS

A continuous magazine advertisement campaign creates awareness among our target consumers. Each magazine selected has been chosen through an extensive cost/reach analysis. Our advertisements will initially be found in *Business Today, Egypt Today, Al-Ahram, Al-Riyadi* and *Kol El-Nas* three times per year per magazine. Our Web site and our toll free number will be located at the bottom of all magazine advertisements.

The advertisements directed at the businesses are meant to create logical relationships to better business practices by using our products and service. These particular advertisements are smart, witty, and filled with images portraying peace and tranquility. The advertisements targeting our consumers are a little less sophisticated in that they demonstrate that every good home must also use our products and services. These advertisements make the consumer feel that they have a problem and that Maktabi is the solution.

RADIO ADVERTISEMENTS

A 30-second radio advertisement will be aired during peak times when our target markets would be tuning in. This will be maintained twice a week after the first 6 months of operation for 6 months to act as a reminder to all businesses and consumers about the company, the free catalogs and where they can be found, as well as the common goal we are both trying to achieve: a more efficient process at no additional cost. After year one, the advertisements will be aired once a week during the programming that best targets our market. The radio advertisement will contain a recognizable tune with lyrics that illustrates, as a message, "This is your office—Easy!"

Other radio advertising will come in the form of free giveaways sponsored by Maktabi during the very same programs that reach our target market.

TELEVISION ADVERTISEMENTS

According to our survey, television advertisement is the number one medium for reaching our potential target market. Television advertisement will come in the form of commercials as well as signage that will be viewable via television (for example on the back of football jerseys of one of Egypt's club teams). The advertisements will include comparisons between Maktabi's process and the traditional office supply ordering process. The commercials will be upbeat and portray a sense of comfort and happiness. The television advertisements will not occur until after year one because it is still necessary for people to know a little about the products that we offer and the service we provide. Coupled with our aggressive sales blitz, the television advertisements will act as support for our marketing strategy. Signage on the football jerseys of one of Egypt's club teams will not occur until after the third year because that is when it will be targeting the business as well as the consumer that already has knowledge about the company.

Promotional Strategy

MAKTABI CLUB CARD AND POINTS

Businesses and consumers will have the ability to sign up for the Maktabi club card (see Exhibit MK6). The idea behind using such a card is to entice businesses and consumers to purchase from Maktabi for two different reasons:

- Special discounts on particular products will be made when the card number is provided.
- The customer will be able to earn points that can be redeemed for any product (predetermined by Maktabi) that the customer needs.

Needless to say, the advantages of providing the club card are numerous:

- Creating repeat customers
- Tracking customer's purchasing trends, and providing them with all the appropriate sales
- Having all customer contact information readily available when an order is placed
- The ability for the card to be used in the future as a credit card on which interest may be charged

GIVEAWAYS AND DISCOUNTS

Maktabi will continually create promotional opportunities by providing free giveaways at contests or when a customer makes a purchase greater than a predetermined amount. Discounts will also be made available during different times of the year to increase sales during slower periods.

Public Relations Efforts

PRESS RELEASES—EDUCATION THROUGH INFORMATION

The following forms of communication are used to create talk within the industries, to sell our products and service to media representatives, and as promotion in the form of word-of-mouth communication and published articles (see Exhibit MK7 for a detailed communication schedule, page 543).

- Press releases to newspapers, magazines, and business journals about Maktabi (see Exhibits MK8-A and MK8-B for sample press releases, pages 547 and 548).
- A sales representative will attend business tradeshows and conferences to solicit endorsements and promote our products and services.

TRADESHOWS AND CONVENTIONS

Tradeshows and conventions are suitable places to promote Maktabi products and services, especially when representatives of businesses in our target market are gathered in one area. Thus, Maktabi participates in the following tradeshows and conventions in Egypt, whether we are exhibiting ourselves or attending to promote the company:

Tradeshows

- Cairo ICT: International telecommunications, information technology, networking, satellite and broadcasting technology trade fair of the Arab World (February)
- APEX: Arab African packaging, paper, and printing exhibition (March)
- Cairo International Fair: General goods and industrials products (March)
- Beem Egypt: Construction and building (June)
- Egypt Invest: International investment and trade forum (November)

Conventions

- International educational conference and exhibition (May)
- Tourism and shopping festival and exhibition (July)
- International exhibition for developing business (November)
- HACE: Hotel supplies and catering equipment (November)
- Office furniture and requirement expo (December)

Catalog Strategy

Though the catalog will be used as a visual aid for customers to see the products that Maktabi is offering, it also serves an important marketing purpose—as a means to communicate with customers to promote new items that have been added to the product line. Market research will determine the products that should be included in the catalog as well as their pricing and the way each item is promoted.

Web Strategy

Maktabi's Web site will be used as an additional outlet for our catalogs as well as an extension of our print media marketing efforts. On the Web site consumers will find all of our available products. They will be able to order them online and find answers to inquiries they may have regarding products, policies, the company, and contacts. Visitors will also be able to give feedback on yet to be released products and advertisements. Banners, links, and online partnerships will be created to ensure maximum exposure to the Web site as well as additional benefits such as support for large customers. Further information about the Maktabi Web site can be found within the Information Systems section of this business plan, page 522.

Company, Product, and Service Presentation

BRAND NAME

After a number of test names, we selected Maktabi as our comany name because it best embodies the qualities of our marketing strategy. Translated into English, the word Maktabi signifies "my office," which carries with it the idea that we are just an extension of the customer's very own office. We want our customers to feel that it is literally that easy to use our service.

POINT OF PURCHASE DISPLAYS

Point-of-purchase (POP) displays are essential, not only to convince business customers to use our service, but also to support our advertising and draw attention to the products in our catalog. Key POP display attributes are

- Displays should be located in businesses where customers who purchase office supplies regularly go, such as shopping malls and grocery stores
- Free catalogs will be made available at the POP displays to encourage consumers to, at a minimum, read about the products and the service that we offer

PACKAGING

The packaging that we will use is an integral element of our marketing mix because it is a visual of our service in action. Just like major brands, such as FedEx or Nike, our brand name and logo must become recognizable upon first glance. Our packaging will come in several different sizes as required by the size of the order (determined by computer systems as discussed in the Organization and Operations Management section).

Our marketing objectives are to educate and motivate consumers, supporting and fulfilling our first two critical success factors. Operations management begins to address our two final critical success factors: operational excellence and original products. Next we review the financial portion of this plan.

Finance

Return on Investment

The project yields a 32% return over a 5-year period.

Investment Requirements and Ownership

The launching of Maktabi requires an initial investment of $690,000 in year one (see Exhibit CM2 for a detailed implementation plan, pages 602–605). Although we break even at the end of year two, an additional investment of $180,000 is needed for the acquisition of capital and expenses in year two (see Exhibits FE1-A through FE1-J for base case

Sources		**Applications**	
Self	$45,000	Vehicles	$74,775
Friends and family	$225,000	Computer system	$643,000
Investor(s)	$600,000	Computers and hardware	$46,130
Bank loan		Furniture and other equipment	—
		Stock/inventory	$84,055
Total	**$870,000**	Working capital	$22,040
		Reserve for contingencies	$45,000
		Other	—
		Total	**$870,000**

Figure FE1 Sources and Uses of Funds

scenario financial statements, pages 549–569). Capital investors will own approximately 70% of all project investments, while the remaining 30% will be owned by management. A breakdown of sources and uses of funds is shown in Figure FE1.

Sensitivity Analysis

A sensitivity analysis was performed to observe the change in IRR when adjusting key variables. In Figure FE2, markup, distribution cost, transportation cost, business orders, and consumer orders were adjusted until the IRR changed to below 20%.

Risk Analysis and Reduction

DECREASE IN MARKUP

Markup can decrease by 5% simultaneously for businesses and consumers before IRR falls below 20%. Key factors that affect markup are supplier relationships and locations.

REDUCING THE RISK

- There is low risk that suppliers will increase their prices due to the abundance of different suppliers.
- To ensure that suppliers do not change their prices, proper, long-lasting relationships with suppliers will be made along with incentives.

Sensitivity Analysis	Percent of Change
Markup	Decrease 5%
Distribution cost	Increase 50%
Transportation cost	Increase 33%
Business orders	Decrease 95%
Consumer orders	Decrease 10%

Figure FE2 Sensitivity Analysis

DISTRIBUTION COST

Distribution cost is based on the quote received from the third-party logistics provider Maktabi will be using. Their costs can increase by 50% before IRR falls below 20%.

REDUCING THE RISK

- A robust contract with the logistics company will provide the fundamental basis for any expected costs related to distribution.
- Providing the sense of partnership between Maktabi and the third-party logistics company will motivate the provider to view Maktabi's success as their own.

TRANSPORTATION COST

Maktabi's orders will be transported to businesses and consumers nationwide; therefore, the variable transportation costs are high and are directly correlated with the fluctuations in fuel prices.

REDUCING THE RISK

- Maktabi's relationship to the transportation company is the same as the one with the distribution company; both services are provided by GSI—Global Structure Industries, precisely to reduce the risk associated with each by managing one company.

BUSINESS AND CONSUMER ORDERS

The sales projections are highly correlated with the accuracy of survey results and the effectiveness of the marketing strategy. Another threat to the company is the introduction of me-too companies.

REDUCING THE RISK

- Each year a portion of the marketing budget is allocated to additional market research. Necessary adjustments on target market, price, and product attributes will be made.
- The marketing director will monitor all elements of the marketing mix and the effect on awareness.

- Strive for continuous improvement. Customer service representatives and the Web site will be ways of communicating with customers to receive feedback.

Situational Analysis

WORST CASE SCENARIO: IRR = 16%
(PROBABILITY OF OCCURRENCE = 10%)

See Exhibits FE2-A through FE2-D for worst case scenario financial statements, pages 570–573. The worst case scenario is based on the worst possible occurrences for the aforementioned risks.

Contingency Plan

- Utilize additional communications vehicles, such as press releases or television. Better identify Maktabi's target market.
- To help prevent me-too companies from stealing the Maktabi concept, Maktabi will establish all necessary documentation to protect its interests with the Egyptian government.

BEST CASE SCENARIO: IRR = 69%
(PROBABILITY OF OCCURRENCE = 5%)

See Exhibits FE3-A through FE3-D for best case scenario financial statements, pages 574–577. The best case scenario is based on the best possible outcomes of the opportunities that Maktabi faces.

Plan of Action

- Increase capacity through appropriate communications with customers, investors, third-party service providers, and management.

Organization

Form of Ownership

Maktabi will incorporate as a limited liability company (LLC) under the Investment Law. Foreign companies prefer to incorporate under the Investment Law to benefit from the privileges that it offers. The Investment Law has one authority that is responsible for investor incentives and guarantees—the General Authority for Investment and Free Zones (GAFI). It also groups over 20 exemptions and incentives under one law, and specifies activities that would automatically accrue benefits to investors. It allows 100% foreign ownership and guarantees the right to remit income earned in Egypt and to repatriate capital.

The LLC itself may be formed with a minimum of 2 shareholders and a maximum of 50 shareholders. The minimum share capital required to form an LLC is 50,000EGP (US$9,078). The capital must be divided into equal shares, either in cash or in kind, and the value of each share must be at least 100EGP (US$18.16). The management of an LLC may be vested in one or more managers. At least one manager must be of Egyptian nationality.

Principals and Management Team

In addition to the Board of Advisors, the principals of Maktabi are key figures on the management team. The Board of Advisors will follow a set of policies that have been predetermined to ensure no conflict of interest. These policies will also ensure that the Board of Advisors, which has a vested interest in the company, makes the right decisions for Maktabi. Both the Chairman and the Chief Executive Officer will participate in board meetings. We feel that with a five-member board, decisions that require a vote will be dealt with efficiently. The credentials of the Board of Advisors are listed here and are followed by the credentials of the principals of the management team. For a breakdown of the organizational structure, refer to Exhibit CM1.

THE BOARD OF ADVISORS

Mahmoud Mohieldin

Dr. Mohieldin has been the Minister of Investment in the Arab Republic of Egypt since 2004. This ministry is responsible for administering investment policy; management of state-owned assets, including privatization and restructuring of public enterprises and joint ventures; and nonbanking financial services, including capital market, insurance, and mortgage finance.

Dr. Mohieldin was born in Egypt in 1965. He received his bachelor of science in economics, with highest honors, first in order of merit, from Cairo University, Egypt. In 1989 he received a diploma in quantitative development economics from University of Warwick, England; in 1990 he received a master of science in economic and social policy analysis from University of York, England; and in 1995 he received his PhD in economics from University of Warwick, England.

Dr. Mohieldin has declared that he will provide his support in this venture by ensuring the efficient flow of orders through the bureaucratic red tape that companies in Egypt sometimes face.

Majid Al-Futtaim

Mr. Majid Al-Futtaim is the founder of several large regional shopping malls and hypermarkets throughout the Middle East. His ventures include such giants as the Mall of the Emirates in Dubai, United Arab Emirates; Ski Dubai in Dubai, United Arab Emirates; and Maadi City Center, Cairo, Egypt. Owning the Carrefour chain of stores in Egypt, Mr. Al-Futtaim hopes to share the expertise of his leadership team in creating a business whose products and service would be used throughout Egypt and the rest of the Middle East. His vision for Maktabi is a Staples for the Middle East.

Tarek Ragheb

Mr. Tarek Ragheb owns several businesses throughout the Middle East, the majority of which are located in Egypt. His contacts and expertise in setting up businesses and seeking funding have made him a crucial member of the Board of Advisors. Additionally, due to his American education, Mr. Ragheb brings a Western ideology of doing business to the Middle East. He is excited about the potential of being part of another winning business opportunity such as Maktabi.

THE MANAGEMENT TEAM

Joseph Naaman—Chairman

Mr. Joseph Naaman started his first business as a sophomore at Boston University, where he earned his degree in finance and marketing. He was a partner in a venture exporting Arizona Iced Tea from the United States to Italy, achieving approximately $2.5 million in sales within the first 2 years. Since then he has joined an established multinational pharmaceutical company, Bristol-Myers Squibb, to gain additional experience in global supply chain and logistics. He continued his professional education globally in business development for a luxury motor yacht company based in Egypt, where he started his second venture exporting organic agricultural products worldwide from Egypt. Along the way Mr. Naaman wrote two award-winning business plans, one for consumer products and one in the services industry. Currently, he is attending the Thunderbird School of Global Management, where he is focusing on entrepreneurship and finance. He has used his time at Thunderbird to refine the skills required to ensure the smooth operation of his new passion—providing office supplies to the Egyptian workplace.

Sherif Naaman—Chief Executive Officer

Mr. Sherif Naaman has over 35 years of experience in both the United States and the Middle East, leading projects in the fields of marketing and information technology. Fifteen of his 35 years have been spent as Managing Director in Saudi Arabia for various companies: the Alshaya group, a Kuwaiti holding company; Wardeh Al-Salehiya, a Saudi holding company; and Bristol-Myers Squibb, a U.S. corporation and the fifth largest pharmaceutical company worldwide. With his experience and exposure to the Middle East market, Mr. Naaman is confident that he would efficiently manage the company. He is excited about the opportunity to move back to the Middle East to aid companies in doing business the way they should.

Mahmoud Hindi—Distribution Director

Mr. Mahmoud Hindi has over 5 years of experience working for SGS, a global transportation and freight forwarding company whose Egyptian offices were founded by his father. With the exposure that he has received at this high level, Mr. Hindi believes that his experience, contacts, and know-how in distribution and transportation will enable him to manage logistics at Maktabi with excellence.

Nancy Sharkawi—Purchasing Director

Ms. Nancy Sharkawi has worked for several years in the supply chain and as a sales representative for a large pharmaceutical company in the United States. With this background, Ms. Sharkawi will be able to manage the purchasing department of Maktabi. Naturally a people person, Ms. Sharkawi will foster the relationships required with Eastern and Southeastern Asian countries to ensure the smooth flow of product into Egypt. She is excited to be able to use the skills she has developed in the United States in a global setting.

Christine Chami—Marketing Director

Ms. Christine Chami has several years of experience working in the marketing departments of large consumer goods companies. With the beginning of her career based in Canada, she knows how marketing departments are run in the west. She has successfully applied the knowledge she gained from this experience as a high performer at the company she currently works for in Dubai. Living in Dubai has enabled her to learn about doing business in the Middle East.

Operations Management

Strategic Value Chain

One of Maktabi's strategic objectives is to focus on operational excellence to provide the customer with the most value at a competitive price while offering a variety of new and original products. To describe the value added at each process, we break down the ordering process into the following areas: purchasing, publications, customer service, distribution and returns,

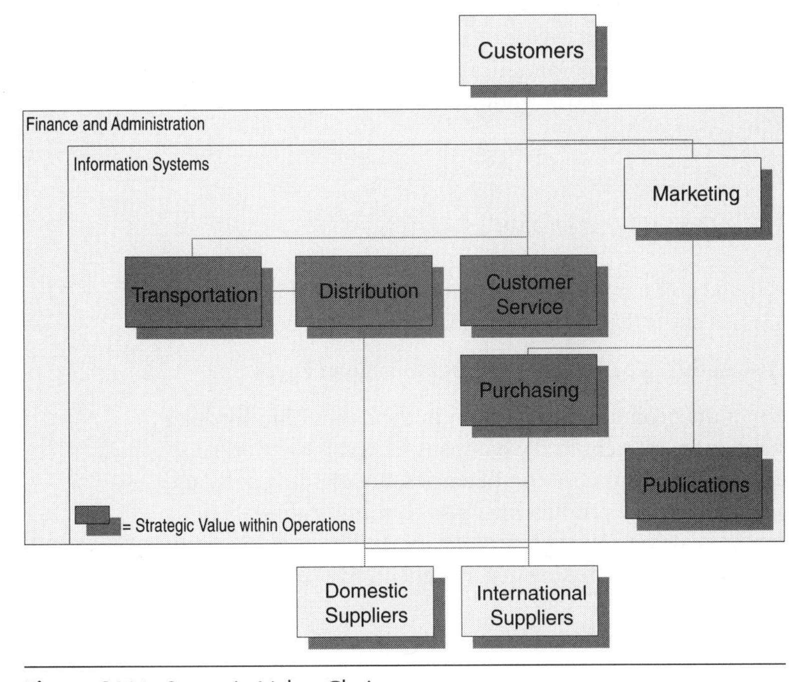

Figure OM1 Strategic Value Chain

transportation and accounts receivables, information systems, and finance and administration. The strategic value chain is depicted in Figure OM1.

The following alternatives have been evaluated using make–buy analysis considering quantitative and qualitative factors to determine the ideal combination of processes that make up the value chain.

Purchasing

Initially, purchasing will consist of a team of two local buyers and two foreign market buyers led by the purchasing manager. The buyers are divided into their area of expertise as determined by the type of products that they purchase (see Exhibit OM1 for a product group listing). The objective of the purchasing department is to supervise the day-to-day purchasing activities of all products that Maktabi purchases domestically and internationally, monitor inventory levels to keep the distribution center stocked at required levels, implement a sourcing strategy to investigate new products in the market, and make recommendations based on assessments to reduce costs and improve the quality of the products that we sell.

FINANCIAL CONSIDERATIONS

The costs of running a purchasing department are minimal because all that is required is employee salaries and benefits, overhead, tools for domestic and international communication, and minor travel expenses for training, tradeshows, and conventions. The total of these costs is broken down in Figure OM2.

STRATEGIC CONSIDERATIONS

- There are no companies in Egypt that offer purchasing as a service, much less at the level that is required.
- Expertise in this department is widely available in Egypt.
- Control of the products must remain in the hands of individuals who have an investment in the company (direct employees) because the last of our core competencies, maintaining constantly updated and original product lines and communicating them through our catalog and Web site, will depend on the skills of the individuals in our purchasing department.

Decision: In-house

	Year 1	Year 2	Year 3	Year 4	Year 5
Number of personnel units	4	4	4	4	4
Wages	$8,846.85	$14,508.11	$15,958.92	$17,554.81	$19,310.29
Bonuses	$0.00	$0.00	$0.00	$0.00	$0.00
Social and other personnel costs	$0.00	$0.00	$0.00	$0.00	$0.00
Office material	$104.50	$172.97	$1,470.27	$1,902.70	$1,902.70
Travel and refreshment	$4,180.18	$6,918.92	$6,918.92	$6,918.92	$6,918.92
Communication	$1,567.57	$2,594.59	$2,594.59	$2,594.59	$2,594.59
Depreciation	$1,028.46	$1,702.27	$1,702.27	$686.26	$20.59
Total Purchasing	$15,727.56	$25,896.87	$28,644.98	$29,657.28	$30,747.10
In % of sales	7%	1%	0%	0%	0%

Figure OM2 Purchasing Financial Consideration

Publications

The publications department will consist of creative associates, catalog editors and their assistants, as well as Web editors and their assistants. The entire department will be overseen by a publications manager. The duties of the two creative associates are to choose the photos to be shown, and determine the content and the layout of both the catalog and the Web site. The catalog and the Web editors' roles are to ensure that the catalog and the Web site are updated regularly to reveal the most recent products available at Maktabi along with their description, prices, and specifications.

FINANCIAL CONSIDERATIONS

Costs for the publications department include employee salaries and benefits, overhead, publishing tools, software, and hardware (see Information Systems section, page 522), as well as printing costs. The total costs for the publications department are estimated in Figure OM3.

	5-year Net Present Value (NPV)
In-house	$760,000
Outsource	$181,000

Figure OM3 Present Value of the Cost of Publications

STRATEGIC CONSIDERATIONS

- Creating, editing, and managing a catalog and a Web site are not considered a core competency.
- The publications department will require a high number of employees to ensure that every detail is addressed.
- A link between purchasing and the publications department needs to be available to manage the information flow of new products that should be placed in either the catalog or on the Web site. The link must be from within the company to maintain efficient communication flows.
- Additional printing machinery needs to be purchased and housed and must be able to print catalogs in thousands of copies.
- Web servers must be managed and housed to ensure smooth Web flow based the capacity for the total number of forecasted users.
- Graphic Art Group based in Alexandria is a company with an excellent reputation, good work ethics, and capacity to handle the required quantities while providing quality results that has already demonstrated their capabilities and has provided us with a competitive offer.

Decision: Outsource to Graphic Art Group with the exception of the publications manager

Customer Service

Customer service is perhaps one of the most valuable areas for the company because it will be the face of Maktabi to the customer, be it by phone or by Web. The customer service department's responsibilities will include, but will not be limited to, answering any inquiries the customer has regarding our products or processes (ordering, returns, payment, etc.), placing the orders, and processing and coordinating any returns. Based on the total orders forecast for the first year, 15 customer service representatives need to be hired. Keeping customer-centric focus (customer relationship management), the customer service representatives will be separated based on the client that they are serving. There will be customer service representatives who will handle businesses and will even be assigned to specific accounts. Other representatives will be assigned to the consumers and another set of representatives will focus on returns only. Representatives who focus on taking orders will also be in charge of reviewing and releasing all orders that come in via the Web. At the head of each customer service area will be a team lead. One analyst will be included in this department to continuously provide reports and analysis on the performance of the customer service representatives, to keep track of customers with issues such as nonpayment, and to offer six-star quality customer service to big customers and their orders. The customer service department will be headed by a manager who will oversee the day-to-day activities and by a director whose responsibility will be to align the department with corporate strategies.

FINANCIAL CONSIDERATIONS

Though a complex area to manage, the customer service department is relatively simple for budgeting; in addition to employee salaries and benefits, training and overhead are included. Technology will play a large role in this department because it will all be automated from the telephone queue, to finding the answers to customer inquiries, to placing orders and processing returns. The information systems portion of the analysis is provided in the Information Systems section, page 522. Figure OM4 is an outline of the costs that will be incurred.

	5-year Net Present Value (NPV)
In-house	$651,000
Outsource	$399,000

Figure OM4 Present Value of the Cost of Customer Service

STRATEGIC CONSIDERATIONS

- Customer service is considered part of operational excellence and needs to be closely monitored.
- Customer service requires a large amount of manpower with skills in servicing, computers, and the Arabic and English languages.
- There are no companies in Egypt that specifically offer this service. If this service is offered, it will be in conjunction with distribution and it is not a core competency of the distribution companies that would be required to gain knowledge of our product and services, even if it is technologically automated.
- Customer service is a delicate issue that must be supported by the dedication of employees who have a direct investment in the company.

Decision: In-house customer service

Distribution and Returns

Maktabi's distribution process is the core of its operational excellence. With the distribution center (DC) located near one of Egypt's largest shipping ports for incoming vessels from Eastern shipping points, Maktabi's 7,000 square meter facility is strategically located for easy access to meet the needs of its customers throughout all of Egypt (see Exhibit OM2, page 596). Included as part of distribution are the processes of customs clearance, inventory stocking, order picking and packing, shipping, quality control, and returns collections.

CUSTOMS CLEARANCE AND TRANSPORTATION TO DISTRIBUTION CENTER

Maktabi expects to receive into the country close to 100–200 shipments per month from many different suppliers mainly located in Southeastern Asian countries (predominantly China, Taiwan, and India). With this many incoming shipments, it is critical that a team with an excellent network within the Egyptian government's Department of Commerce is established. This team would include individuals whose primary role would be to follow up with official processes and ensure that the proper documentation is available for smooth importation. Following the clearance from customs, the shipment must be delivered to the DC.

INVENTORY STOCKING

Once the stock is received, it must be registered with the company's store and placed in an organized manner within the confines of the secured DC. Inventory levels must be closely monitored electronically and low-level notifications sent to the purchasing department. The inventory will also be placed in such a way as to facilitate the next step of the process: picking the order.

ORDER PICKING AND PACKING

The customer service department puts the order through to the DC electronically, at which point a picking document (pick doc) is created. When the pick doc is created, personnel at the DC, using radio frequency technology (RFID), will know where and when to pick each item as stated on the pick doc. The items are placed in a package, which is also electronically determined by the system. Once the order picking and packing process is complete, the order is checked manually by quality control and placed on the appropriate shipping dock according to region, ready for shipment.

QUALITY CONTROL—6 SIGMA

Operational excellence as one of our four core competencies can only be measured through quality control. More specifically, from the time that product is ordered by the purchasing department to the time it reaches the customer, quality will be strictly adhered to. In our case quality is a factor of the variety of products offered, the timing by which they enter the DC (just-in-time), the condition of the products upon acceptance at the DC, efficiency of picking the order, accurate order picking, and accurate and safe delivery. To achieve the superior quality standards required, a total quality management (TQM) approach will be utilized with policies and standard operating procedures (SOPs) completed and signed by management. All workers are to be trained and must sign-off on the training for all applicable policies and SOPs. All policies and procedures will be strictly enforced through disciplinary action.

RETURNS

As a matter of courtesy to all our customers, returns will be accepted as long as firm criteria are followed. There are a limited number of reasons why returns will be accepted, such as damaged product, wrong product (though these will be kept at a minimum due to the quality control in place), and nonpayment. Returns will be properly recorded, closely monitored, and analyzed by the analyst in the customer service department. This point is critical because an investigation and action must take place if any trends are discovered, especially in the case of lost orders.

FINANCIAL CONSIDERATIONS

A summary of all financial considerations are outlined in Figure OM5 (for a more detailed analysis, see Exhibit OM3 on page 597).

STRATEGIC CONSIDERATIONS

- Lease and management of a 4,000 square meter distribution center.
- Fleet of trucks required to transport the shipments from Ain Sukhna port to the distribution center.
- Expertise and network in customs clearance and distribution is required.
- There is a considerable amount of inbound shipments to manage.
- Customs clearance must work closely with the purchasing department to estimate arrival times and have all documentation prepared.
- Flexible shelving must be available according to different seasons when inventory will be higher or lower.
- Large number of unskilled and skilled labor is required for picking and packing, as well as the management of these laborers.
- Time will be required to create the entire set up from scratch.
- Quality control managers must be properly trained and independent of the management of the company in order to remove any conflict of interests. However, senior management must have the flexibility to determine where quality control is required.
- Time and effort will be required to establish all the proper policies and SOPs.

	5-year Net Present Value (NPV)
In-house	$3,250,000
Outsource	$725,000

Figure OM5 Present Value of the Cost of Distribution

- The distribution center must by transparent to the company so as to properly manage and communicate the entire operational process.

Decision: Outsource to GSI—Global Structure Industries with the exception of the quality control director (see Exhibit OM4 for GSIs' letter to provide service, page 598)

Transportation and Accounts Receivables

When a package is ready for shipping, it will be loaded onto a truck along with other packages to be delivered to the same region. Depending on the type of delivery that the customer has requested, the transportation company is contacted by the DC and arrives ready for shipment pickup. A customer service representative then returns a phone call to the customer confirming the shipment and any special delivery notes required. At the destination point, the delivery is considered complete when the driver receives cash or a check for the delivery, unless the cutomer has prepaid by bank card. Those customers who do not pay will not receive the requested shipment and it will be returned to the DC to be restocked into inventory.

FINANCIAL CONSIDERATIONS

Financial considerations for basic transportation include the cost of delivering the shipment with regard to location domestically, the transportation manager's salary and bonus, and overhead (see Figure OM6 for a breakdown of in-house transportation versus outsourcing it).

STRATEGIC CONSIDERATIONS

- Fleet of trucks to be maintained is required.
- Reliable drivers who can pick up payments are required.
- An average of over 8,100 estimated deliveries to be completed per month for year one.

	5-year Net Present Value (NPV)
In-house	$14,580,000
Outsource	$830,000

Figure OM6 Present Value of the Cost of Transportation

- Separate delivery options must be offered, such as next day delivery, 2-day delivery, and regular delivery (with according variation in costs).

Decision: Outsource to GSI—Global Structure Industries with the exception of the transportation director (see Exhibit OM4 for GSIs letter to provide service, page 598).

Information Systems

There are three main information systems that will play a decisive role in the profitability of our company and its continued growth. It is important that the foundations of the system are laid appropriately at the launch of the project to properly support the growth of the company. The Order Processing System (OPS), the Inventory Management System (IMS), and the Warehouse Management System (WMS) will be implemented during the first year. Ensuring that orders placed via customer service or the Web are handled in an efficient and timely manner is vital to sustaining a customer-centric focus and lowering costs. The IMS will enable us to manage our inventory to keep inventory holding costs and purchasing costs low. Finally, the WMS will further develop our core competency of operational excellence by ensuring a smooth flow from order to picking and packing. In addition, important systems that are required are a full accounting system for budgeting, accounts payable and receivable, metrics, and employee payroll. A full marketing system will also be required to ensure that the marketing department has the tools required for market analysis and forecasting. Over and above these systems, the essential Microsoft package will be made available to all employees. With the exception of the Microsoft package, all the other software packages can be summed into one Entity Resource Planning (ERP) system that will allow all the separate systems to operate under one umbrella. This umbrella, as well as the Web site and any internal information technology (IT) issues, will be managed by the IT officer.

FINANCIAL CONSIDERATIONS

Figure OM7 is a summary of the costs between using off-the-shelf software and developing our own software rather than completing a make–buy analysis.

STRATEGIC CONSIDERATIONS

- More than one system will be required if purchased separately. In addition, experts in each software program will be required for training and maintenance purposes.

	5-year Net Present Value (NPV)
In-house	$940,000
Outsource	$195,000

Figure OM7 Present Value of the Cost of Developing a System or Purchasing an Off-the-Shelf System

- The functioning of the company will rely on information systems as its main business tool.
- There needs to be quick turnaround for remedies to any issues that arise with the information systems.
- SAP Corporation has ERP software and expertise in consulting that can handle all systems simultaneously, ensuring proper alignment between all systems as well as addressing any issues that arise.

Decision: Develop system with SAP with the exception of the chief information officer and staff

Finance and Administration

The finance and administration department of Maktabi are referred to as the soul of the company. This department includes the chief executive officer (see Exhibit OM5, page 599), the chief financial officer (heading this department), the accounting manager, two administrative associates, company drivers, and janitors. It is from this department that the company vision stems. The company headquarters will be located near Cairo in approximately 300 square meters of office space. The reason for choosing Cairo as the headquarters is that it is the central commercial hub of Egypt.

FINANCIAL CONSIDERATIONS

The costs of running the finance and administration department are relatively low since all that is required is employee salaries and benefits, overhead, and minor travel expenses for training and networking. The total of these costs is broken down in Figure OM8.

	Year 1	Year 2	Year 3	Year 4	Year 5
Number of personnel units	7	7	7	7	7
Wages	$41,621.62	$78,337.84	$86,335.14	$94,968.65	$104,465.51
Bonuses	$0.00	$0.00	$0.00	$0.00	$0.00
Social and other personnel costs	$0.00	$0.00	$0.00	$0.00	$0.00
Office material	$223.42	$299.10	$302.70	$302.70	$302.70
Travel and refreshment	$1,117.12	$1,495.50	$1,513.51	$1,513.51	$1,513.51
Communication	$3,351.35	$4,486.49	$4,540.54	$4,540.54	$4,540.54
Insurance	$1,074.32	$10,745.50	$35,396.12	$39,755.36	$46,076.75
Prof. services (legal, accounting, etc.)	$121,562.65	$80,727.27	$80,000.00	$80,000.00	$80,000.00
Provisions for unpaid invoices	$0.00	$0.00	$0.00	$0.00	$0.00
Office rent	$17,972.97	$22,702.70	$22,702.70	$22,702.70	$22,702.70
Water, electricity	$513.51	$648.65	$648.65	$648.65	$648.65
Maintenance, repairs	$128.38	$162.16	$162.16	$162.16	$162.16
Depreciation	$2,198.77	$2,943.51	$2,978.98	$841.84	$36.04
Total Finance and administration	$189,764.13	$202,548.72	$234,580.51	$245,436.12	$260,448.57
In % of sales	88%	9%	3%	3%	3%

Figure OM8 Finance and Administration Purchasing Considerations

STRATEGIC CONSIDERATIONS

The roles required to fulfill the finance and administration duties cannot be outsourced to an outside entity.

DECISION: IN-HOUSE

Our efficient means of operation and our required quality standards ensure that our critical success factor of operational excellence will be achieved. Moreover, the introduction of the Enterprise Resource Planning system will help the company offer high-quality service at a lower cost by improving efficiencies and productivity.

Conclusion

The Maktabi Group is presenting a simple, effective solution to the Egyptian public. We are addressing their need to use an efficient and inexpensive way to order office supplies from a catalog or online—offering a large variety of products with a diverse array of styles from the comfort of one's own chair! Current alternatives do not address all requirements for providing this service. Trends in the market indicate that Maktabi's potential market is ripe to be provided with an efficient office supplies ordering process. Our unique positioning and thorough analysis of target consumers gives Maktabi the ability to become a household name.

The Maktabi Group's marketing and operations management unify to meet the company's critical success factors of education, motivation, operational excellence, and innovation. This is achieved through our creative marketing strategy and cost-effective and efficient operating methods.

Maktabi is a low-risk project that offers a 32% return on your investment. This investment offers you the opportunity to better the Egyptian business environment. The Maktabi Group looks forward to the launch of our beneficial service. We hope that through our business plan, you have developed the same enthusiasm and confidence about Maktabi that we have.

Joseph Naaman
Partner

Buying Office Supplies—Easy!

Sample Business Plan Exhibits

Exhibit MK1-A: Base Case Sales Projections

	Year 1—Base*	Year 2—Base	Year 3—Base	Year 4—Base	Year 5—Base
Total Egyptian Consumers	2,501,000	2,568,465	2,637,750	2,708,904	2,781,978
Businesses	31,000	31,775	32,569	33,384	34,218
Households	2,470,000	2,536,690	2,605,181	2,675,521	2,747,760
Businesses	31,000	31,775	32,569	33,384	34,218
Businesses—Definitely Buy	10.34%	10.34%	10.34%	10.34%	10.34%
After 80%	8.28%	8.28%	8.28%	8.28%	8.28%
Businesses—Probably Buy	62.07%	62.07%	62.07%	62.07%	62.07%
After 20%	12.41%	12.41%	12.41%	12.41%	12.41%
Average Order per Year	7	7	7	7	7
Awareness (Sales Reps)	76%	86%	69%	69%	69%
Businesses Purchase	4,864	5,680	4,658	4,774	4,893
Total Orders per Year	6,000	39,760	32,604	33,419	34,254
Households	2,470,000	2,536,690	2,605,181	2,675,521	2,747,760
Households—Definitely Buy	14.29%	14.29%	14.29%	14.29%	14.29%
After 80%	11.43%	11.43%	11.43%	11.43%	11.43%
Households—Probably Buy	71.43%	71.43%	71.43%	71.43%	71.43%
After 20%	14.29%	14.29%	14.29%	14.29%	14.29%
Average Order per Year	5	5	5	5	5
Awareness (Advertisement)	2%	5%	20%	22%	25%
Households Purchase	12,703	32,615	133,981	151,358	176,642
Total Orders per Year	13,500	163,073	669,904	756,790	883,208
Combined Total	19,500	202,833	702,507	790,209	917,462

*First year includes initial set-up period when no orders are placed

Exhibit MK1-B: Best Case Sales Projections

	Year 1—Base*	Year 2—Base	Year 3—Base	Year 4—Base	Year 5—Base
Total Egyptian Consumers	2,501,000	2,568,465	2,637,750	2,708,904	2,781,978
Businesses	31,000	31,775	32,569	33,384	34,218
Households	2,470,000	2,536,690	2,605,181	2,675,521	2,747,760
Businesses	31,000	31,775	32,569	33,384	34,218
Businesses—Definitely Buy	15%	15%	15%	15%	15%
After 80%	12%	12%	12%	12%	12%
Businesses—Probably Buy	75%	75%	75%	75%	75%
After 20%	15%	15%	15%	15%	15%
Average Order per Year	9	9	9	9	9
Awareness (Sales Reps)	76%	86%	86%	86%	86%
Businesses Purchase	6,348	7,412	7,598	7,788	7,982
Total Orders per Year	16,755	66,712	68,380	70,090	71,842
Households	2,470,000	2,536,690	2,605,181	2,675,521	2,747,760
Households—Definitely Buy	25%	25%	25%	25%	25%
After 80%	20%	20%	20%	20%	20%
Households—Probably Buy	90%	90%	90%	90%	90%
After 20%	18%	18%	18%	18%	18%
Average Order per Year	5	5	5	5	5
Awareness (Advertisement)	5%	10%	15%	20%	20%
Households Purchase	46,930	96,394	148,495	203,340	208,830
Total Orders per Year	86,820	481,971	742,476	1,016,698	1,044,149
Combined Total	103,575	548,683	810,857	1,086,787	1,115,990

*First year includes initial set-up period when no orders are placed

Exhibit MK1-C: Worst Case Sales Projections

	Year 1—Base*	Year 2—Base	Year 3—Base	Year 4—Base	Year 5—Base
Total Egyptian Consumers	2,501,000	2,568,465	2,637,750	2,708,904	2,781,978
Businesses	31,000	31,775	32,569	33,384	34,218
Households	2,470,000	2,536,690	2,605,181	2,675,521	2,747,760
Businesses	31,000	31,775	32,569	33,384	34,218
Businesses—Definitely Buy	5%	5%	5%	5%	5%
After 75%	3.75%	3.75%	3.75%	3.75%	3.75%
Businesses—Probably Buy	45%	45%	45%	45%	45%
After 25%	11.25%	11.25%	11.25%	11.25%	11.25%
Average Order per Year	4	4	4	4	4
Awareness (Sales Reps)	76%	86%	69%	59%	49%
Businesses Purchase	3,527	4,118	3,377	2,954	2,515
Total Orders per Year	3,100	20,800	26,600	27,900	29,100
Households	2,470,000	2,536,690	2,605,181	2,675,521	2,747,760
Households—Definitely Buy	14.29%	14.29%	14.29%	14.29%	14.29%
After 75%	5%	5%	5%	5%	5%
Households—Probably Buy	71.43%	71.43%	71.43%	71.43%	71.43%
After 25%	10%	10%	10%	10%	10%
Average Order per Year	3	3	3	3	3
Awareness (Advertisement)	2%	10%	8%	5%	5%
Households Purchase	7,410	38,050	31,262	20,066	20,608
Total Orders per Year	8,700	150,000	320,000	240,000	250,000
Combined Total	11,800	170,800	346,600	267,900	279,100

*First year includes initial set-up period when no orders are placed

Exhibit MK2: Survey Results

Thank you for your participation. This study is being conducted by a team of young entrepreneurs and will be used in the development of a business plan for a new service. This study is being distributed to individuals who we feel may benefit from the service's use. All responses will be kept confidential.

PART I

1. What type of office supplies do you purchase? (check all that apply)

- ☐ Batteries, Surge & UPS **29%**
- ☐ Binders & Accessories **71%**
- ☐ Boards & Easels **17%**
- ☐ Calendars & Planners **46%**
- ☐ Cleaning & Break Room **46%**
- ☐ Desktop Organizers **19%**
- ☐ Envelopes & Forms **35%**
- ☐ Filing Supplies **15%**
- ☐ General Supplies **38%**
- ☐ Luggage & Briefcases **23%**
- ☐ Mail & Ship/Moving **17%**
- ☐ Office Machines & Calculators **38%**
- ☐ Paper & Pads **44%**
- ☐ Self-stick Notes **19%**

2. On average, how many times do you purchase these office supplies in 1 month? (check one)

- ☐ a. 0–1 **37%**
- ☐ b. 2–3 **40%**
- ☐ c. 4–5 **12%**
- ☐ d. 6–7 **4%**
- ☐ e. 8 or more **8%**

3. How much do you typically spend on office supplies at each purchase? (check one)

- ☐ a. 0–49 EGP **52%**
- ☐ b. 50–99 EGP **17%**
- ☐ c. 100–199 EGP **13%**
- ☐ d. 200–499 EGP **12%**
- ☐ e. 500 EGP or more **6%**

4. Where do you primarily purchase your office supply products? (check all that apply)

- ☐ a. Office supply store **75%**
- ☐ b. Large department store **27%**
- ☐ c. Supermarket **15%**
- ☐ d. Internet **10%**
- ☐ e. Catalog **2%**
- ☐ f. Delivery **8%**
- ☐ g. Other ________________ **0%**

5. What is your typical method for purchasing office supply products? (check all that apply)

   ☐ a. Personally purchase the products **77%**

   ☐ b. Someone else purchases the products **21%**

   ☐ c. Products delivered **10%**

6. What is your primary reason for using office supplies? (check all that apply)

   ☐ a. Personal use **67%** ☐ b. Business use **56%**

7. Please rate how important the following qualities are in relation to purchasing office supplies:

	Not at all Important		**Somewhat Important**		**Very Important**
Convenience	☐ a. 1 **4%**	☐ b. 2 **6%**	☐ c. 3 **44%**	☐ d. 4 **10%**	☐ e. 5 **37%**
Variety of Products	☐ a. 1 **8%**	☐ b. 2 **4%**	☐ c. 3 **44%**	☐ d. 4 **17%**	☐ e. 5 **27%**
New Products	☐ a. 1 **6%**	☐ b. 2 **10%**	☐ c. 3 **44%**	☐ d. 4 **15%**	☐ e. 5 **25%**
Time	☐ a. 1 **12%**	☐ b. 2 **2%**	☐ c. 3 **42%**	☐ d. 4 **12%**	☐ e. 5 **33%**
Price	☐ a. 1 **2%**	☐ b. 2 **4%**	☐ c. 3 **58%**	☐ d. 4 **10%**	☐ e. 5 **27%**
Usefulness	☐ a. 1 **6%**	☐ b. 2 **6%**	☐ c. 3 **19%**	☐ d. 4 **21%**	☐ e. 5 **48%**
Quality	☐ a. 1 **6%**	☐ b. 2 **2%**	☐ c. 3 **21%**	☐ d. 4 **12%**	☐ e. 5 **60%**

PART II

A new service will be offered in the market. It is a new method for viewing, ordering, and receiving office supply products. This business will offer office supplies (from pens to paper clips and everything in between), office furniture, and technology products via catalog and an online Web site. Using these catalogs and the Web site, customers can view products they can order via phone or Web site and expect possible next-day delivery. This new process will save time and be more financially efficient.

8. On a 1 to 5 scale, where 1 is strongly disagree and 5 is strongly agree, please rate the business concept on the following characteristics:

	Strongly Disagree		Somewhat Agree		Strongly Agree
Convenient	☐ a. 1 **4%**	☐ b. 2 **2%**	☐ c. 3 **48%**	☐ d. 4 **10%**	☐ e. 5 **37%**
Expensive	☐ a. 1 **12%**	☐ b. 2 **13%**	☐ c. 3 **54%**	☐ d. 4 **8%**	☐ e. 5 **13%**
Easy to Use	☐ a. 1 **0%**	☐ b. 2 **8%**	☐ c. 3 **44%**	☐ d. 4 **6%**	☐ e. 5 **42%**
Efficient	☐ a. 1 **2%**	☐ b. 2 **4%**	☐ c. 3 **42%**	☐ d. 4 **15%**	☐ e. 5 **37%**
Useful	☐ a. 1 **2%**	☐ b. 2 **4%**	☐ c. 3 **38%**	☐ d. 4 **13%**	☐ e. 5 **42%**
Trendy	☐ a. 1 **17%**	☐ b. 2 **15%**	☐ c. 3 **46%**	☐ d. 4 **4%**	☐ e. 5 **17%**
Modern	☐ a. 1 **0%**	☐ b. 2 **6%**	☐ c. 3 **44%**	☐ d. 4 **12%**	☐ e. 5 **38%**

9. Where would you be most likely to hear about this service? (check all that apply)

☐ a. Office supply store **46%**
☐ b. Television ad **48%**
☐ c. Newspaper ad **44%**
☐ d. Newspaper article **8%**
☐ e. Business magazine ad **15%**
☐ f. Business magazine article **4%**
☐ g. People magazine ad **15%**
☐ h. People magazine article **6%**
☐ i. Radio **17%**
☐ j. Internet **58%**
☐ k. Other ____________________ **0%**

10. Which name do you think best fits this service?

☐ a. Maktabi **54%**
☐ b. Dabbasa **12%**
☐ c. Maktaba Depot **19%**
☐ d. Other __________ **0%**

11. What is the maximum price you expect to pay, in addition to the office supplies, for this service? **85 EGP**

12. What price, in addition to the office supplies, would you expect to pay for this service?

☐ a. 0–4 EGP **21%**
☐ b. 5–9 EGP **31%**
☐ c. 10–14 EGP **21%**
☐ d. 15–19 EGP **10%**
☐ e. 20 EGP or more **17%**

13. Given your above chosen price, how likely would you be to use our service?

    ☐ a. Definitely buy **15%** ☐ b. Probably buy **63%** ☐ c. Don't know **15%**
    ☐ d. Probably not buy **6%** ☐ e. Definitely not buy **0%**

14. Given your answer to the above question, how many times per year would you use our service to purchase office supplies?

    ☐ a. 0–3 **23%** ☐ b. 4–6 **33%** ☐ c. 7–9 **15%**
    ☐ d. 10–12 **23%** ☐ e. 13 or more **6%**

PART III

15. What is your gender?

☐ a. Female **42%** ☐ b. Male **58%**

16. What is your age?

☐ a. 18 and under **4%** ☐ b. 19–24 **46%** ☐ c. 25–34 **10%**

☐ d. 35–44 **6%** ☐ e. 45–54 **2%** ☐ f. 55 and above **0%**

17. How many employees are there in your company?

☐ a. 10 and under **27%** ☐ b. 11–19 **13%** ☐ c. 20–49 **7%**

☐ d. 50–99 **20%** ☐ e. 100–499 **13%** ☐ f. 500 and above **20%**

18. What is the approximate annual revenue of your company?

☐ a. 0–49,999 EGP **17%** ☐ b. 50,000–99,999 EGP **0%**

☐ c. 100,000–499,999 EGP **13%** ☐ d. 500,000–999,999 EGP **17%**

☐ e. 1,000,000–9,999,999 EGP **4%** ☐ f. 10,000,000 EGP or more **50%**

19. What is the name of your company? ______________________

SIDPEC
TRANSMISR
HAKETEGP
CHILDCARE ACADEMY
STIA
EXXONMOMBIL
ORASCOM
SAUDI ARABIAN AIRLINES
ABB
BMW
SHAVING SYSTEMS
GT EGYPT
ALMUTAHIDA GROUP
DEBIRS YACHTS

20. What is a telephone number we may be able to reach you at in order to verify any information? __________

21. Your opinion is extremely valuable to us. Please express any additional comments about the service or the survey in the space provided.

____

____

____

____

Thank you for your time and participation.

Exhibit MK3: Focus Group Results

Moderator: Mahmoud Hindi
Location: Beano's
Heliopolis, Cairo, Egypt

Observer: Joseph Naaman
Date: June 5, 2007
Time: 21:00 – 22:00

Participants	Age
Mohamad Humeyda	23
Mohamad Medhat	25
Ayman El-Bedihwi	26
Sherif Ezzat	23
Mai El-Ashry	22
Hoda El-Mankabadi	23

Focus Group Description
Office supply enthusiasts

How do you feel about the current office supplies industry in Egypt? Are there any trends that are occurring? Or, do you think they have been pretty similar over the last few years/decades?

Trends recognized: Office supplies in Egypt does not constitute a hot industry mainly because of the lack of variety of products available in the market. Not only is there no variety of products, but part of the reason is the lack of a modern store that offers the latest office supplies. Participants acknowledge that it is a little easier in Cairo, however, it is not enough. They noticed that trends in the office supply industry have been stagnant and there have been no major changes to the industry over the last few decades. Also, most of the time when searching for something specific for a hobby or an interest, they rarely find the products they are looking for. The general feeling is that there is nothing to get excited about when it comes to the office supply industry in Egypt.

The Maktabi concept was then introduced.

What do you think of this new way to purchase office supplies? Do you think it will be useful? More convenient?

Feelings and thoughts: All participants reacted with great enthusiasm about the concept and maintained their enthusiasm throughout the focus group. Once the background of the idea was explained, all participants related the same experiences and said they always wished for something that would enhance the process. They also became very excited by the idea that the variety of products available in different sizes and colors would be greater than what they were actually accustomed to. They thought the process itself would be convenient and simple.

What do you think about the catalog? The Internet? What type of products would you expect to see in the catalog or on the Internet? Talk about variety.

Thoughts: Being that it is a free catalog, the participants loved the idea because they now don't have to waste their time searching for the product they are looking for. They also liked the idea that the products would be delivered to their residence or work as soon as the next day, if that was required. They were interested in the idea of being able to place orders on the Internet because this is now the next logical step for Egypt's Internet industry. They felt it is starting to head in that direction, but needs more support from companies like Maktabi. They did however feel that people need to start trusting the Internet before using it and this might take a few more years.

What is the best way to reach people to advertise this idea? What type of advertisement do you feel would most appropriately target this segment of the market?

How to advertise and promote: All participants felt that the best way to reach the target market would be via television advertising as well as radio, magazine, and Internet promotions. They felt like the advertising would be rather simple because it is only logical that this new concept offers products and service that are better than what most people are used to. They also said that the novelty of the idea would encourage the use of the service.

How much do you expect to pay for Maktabi's products and services compared to other office supplies companies? Would you use this service? At what price?

Pricing: All participants expected to pay a premium for this service, but most did not want to. When they were told that the only increase in price would be the delivery and that this would be kept at a minimum because it can sometimes, depending on location, be equivalent to paying a tip, or "bakshish," they were very excited.

Exhibit MK4: Sample Letter of Intent

26/07/08

From: xyZyx
Ibn Jubier Street
Attarine Alexandria
ARE
Tel: 203.999.4901
Fax: 203.990.4901
E-mail: xyZyx_egypt@xyZyx.com

To: Maktabi Group

Re: Letter of intent to purchase office materials.

Dear Maktabi Group:

It is our pleasure to inform you of our intent to make Maktabi Group our main supplier of office materials. We believe that the concept the Maktabi Group has presented to xyZyx will offer our company greater efficiency and value.

We hope that the concept presented will be embraced throughout Egypt and the Middle East.

Sincerely,

Sabah Tawil
Vice President of Technical Affairs

Exhibit MK5: Sample Marketing Director Resume

(For more information on this candidate, please contact the Maktabi Group directly.)

Candidate: Louise Cham

Date of birth: October 6, 1978

Citizenship: Canadian and Egyptian

Profile

- Excellent organization and communication skills, strong presentation and negotiating aptitudes, diverse background resulting in the ability to be adaptable and to work well both independently and within a team environment, proven to be resourceful in a variety of fast-paced business environments.

Education

Bachelor of Commerce (International Business), 2002
John Molson School of Business
Concordia University, Montreal, Canada
Semester abroad : "École Superieure de Commerce à Montpellier," France, Fall 2001

Diplôme d'Études Collégiales (DEC) in Social Sciences and Mathematics, 1998
Collège Jean-de-Brébeuf, Montreal, Canada

Professional Experience

ExTech, Pune, India, 2006–Present

Marketing Executive

- Conduct detailed market and trend analysis, identify threats and opportunities, and develop targeted marketing strategies.
- Lead the proposal process for specific clients including pricing development, proposal writing, and contract negotiations.
- Create marketing and financial business plans for the launch of new products.
- Construct innovative promotional programs to ensure market growth.
- Write, edit, and revise content of marketing materials, such as the company Web site, catalogs, and brochures.

Accomplishments:

- Coordinated the launch of a new product line for the company.
- Created a company newsletter informing current and potential customers of the company's business activities and latest industry news.

Barens, Dubai, United Arab Emirates, 2005–2006

Marketing Coordinator

- Developed, designed, and produced marketing collaterals.
- Performed cost and benefit analysis on current market conditions and prepared reports as well as forecasts.
- Organized and attended seminars, board meetings, and conferences.

Accomplishments:

- Created two new databases for the marketing and sales departments.

TRC (Food Supply Specialist), Montreal, Canada, 2003–2005

Buyer/Market Researcher

- Identified and analyzed markets to be developed resulting in new private brand and product labels for goods sold in North America, Europe, and the Caribbean.
- Negotiated prices with multinational suppliers. Negotiated rate quotes with shippers, brokers, and freight forwarders.
- Monitored customers' inventory. Coordinated the logistics and documentation process for local and international transactions.
- Prepared tenders and managed the financials relevant to all new offers.

Accomplishments:

- Earned the position of new business coordinator for the region.

Sports Plus Inc. (Health Centre), Laval, Canada, 2001–2002

Customer Service/Receptionist (part-time)

- Advised clients about various membership plans while managing reception in a fast-paced environment.
- Resolved complaints and solidified continuous customer satisfaction.

Accomplishments:

- Consulted in the development of new internal software.

Life Carrier, Montreal, Canada, Summer 2000

Disability Support Associate—Group Life and Health

- Coordinated medical appointments and carried out follow-ups with the insured after their return to work.

Life Carrier, Montreal, Canada, Summer 1999

Administrative Support Associate—Group Life and Health

- Managed data conversion from in-house software to a new software.
- Provided administrative support to disability analysts.

Davis Promotions, Inc., Montreal, Canada, Summers 1997 and 1998

Administrative Assistant

- Organized U.S. and Canadian promotions.
- Ordered office supplies and insured on-time delivery.
- Prepared and validated accounts payables and receivables.

Linguistic Skills

- French and English: perfectly bilingual; Arabic: fluently spoken; Spanish: basic understanding

Computer Skills

- Microsoft Office: Word, Excel, Access, PowerPoint, Project, Outlook; Paint, Photoshop, Maximizer, SAP, Planosoft
- Expert in navigating and researching the World Wide Web

Other Activities and Interests

Member of Sakaar, April–December 2005, Pune, India

- Social committee bringing aid to the underprivileged in the local community.
- Coordinated events such as the sponsorship of a child's education and tree plantations.

Executive Vice President, 2001–2002, CASA Cares (Commerce & Administration Student Association), Concordia University—mandate of raising funds for different charities

- Organized and planned various social events.
- Raised almost $10,000 for UNICEF, Centraide, and the Cure Foundation.
- Managed task delegation.

Other Activities

- Scuba diving, tennis (participated in multiple amateur tournaments), snowboarding, and physical fitness.
- Travel throughout Europe, North Africa, India, and the United States.

Exhibit MK6: Maktabi Club Card

Buying Office Supplies – Easy!

4290 6239 7922 4350

BMW Egypt

Exp: 01/2009

Front

Authorized Signature:

Save 10% every time you use your Maktabi Club Card!

Back

Exhibit MK7: Detailed Communication Schedule

Year 1	**Jan**	**Feb**	**Mar**	**Apr**	**May**	**Jun**	**Jul**	**Aug**	**Sep**	**Oct**	**Nov**	**Dec**
Newspaper Advertisements												
Al-Ahram (2x/mos)								X			X	
Akhbar El-Yom (2x/mos)										X		
El-Misri El-Yom (2x/mos)									X			X
Magazine Advertisements												
Business Today									X			
Egypt Today										X		
Al-Ahram Al-Riyadi											X	
Kol El-Nas								X				X
Radio Advertisements								X	X	X	X	X
Television Advertisements												
Tradeshows												
Cairo ICT												
APEX												
Cairo International Fair												
Beem Egypt												
Egypt Invest											X	
Conventions												
International educational conference and exhibition												
Tourism and shopping festival and exhibition												
International exhibition for developing business											X	
HACE—Hotel supplies and catering equipment											X	
Office furniture and requirement expo												X
Sales Rep Visits								X	X	X	X	X
Year 2	**Jan**	**Feb**	**Mar**	**Apr**	**May**	**Jun**	**Jul**	**Aug**	**Sep**	**Oct**	**Nov**	**Dec**
Newspaper Advertisements												
Al-Ahram (2x/mos)		X			X			X			X	
Akhbar El-Yom (2x/mos)	X			X			X			X		
El-Misri El-Yom (2x/mos)			X			X			X			X
Magazine Advertisements												
Business Today	X				X				X			
Egypt Today		X				X				X		
Al-Ahram Al-Riyadi			X				X				X	
Kol El-Nas				X				X				X
Radio Advertisements	X	X	X	X	X	X	X	X	X	X	X	X
Television Advertisements	X	X						X	X			X

(Continued)

Exhibit MK7 (Continued)

Year 2	**Jan**	**Feb**	**Mar**	**Apr**	**May**	**Jun**	**Jul**	**Aug**	**Sep**	**Oct**	**Nov**	**Dec**
Tradeshows												
Cairo ICT		X										
APEX			X									
Cairo International Fair			X									
Beem Egypt						X						
Egypt Invest											X	
Conventions												
International educational conference and exhibition					X							
Tourism and shopping festival and exhibition							X					
International exhibition for developing business											X	
HACE—Hotel supplies and catering equipment											X	
Office furniture and requirement expo												X
Sales Rep Visits	X	X	X	X	X	X	X	X	X	X	X	X
Year 3	**Jan**	**Feb**	**Mar**	**Apr**	**May**	**Jun**	**Jul**	**Aug**	**Sep**	**Oct**	**Nov**	**Dec**
Newspaper Advertisements												
Al-Ahram (2x/mos)		X			X			X			X	
Akhbar El-Yom (2x/mos)	X			X			X			X		
El-Misri El-Yom (2x/mos)			X			X			X			X
Magazine Advertisements												
Business Today	X				X				X			
Egypt Today		X				X				X		
Al-Ahram Al-Riyadi			X				X				X	
Kol El-Nas				X				X				X
Radio Advertisements	X		X		X		X		X		X	
Television Advertisements	X	X						X	X			X
Tradeshows												
Cairo ICT		X										
APEX			X									
Cairo International Fair			X									
Beem Egypt						X						
Egypt Invest											X	
Conventions												
International educational conference and exhibition				X								
Tourism and shopping festival and exhibition							X					
International exhibition for developing business											X	
HACE—Hotel supplies and catering equipment											X	
Office furniture and requirement expo												X
Sales Rep Visits	X	X	X	X	X	X	X	X	X	X	X	X

Year 4	**Jan**	**Feb**	**Mar**	**Apr**	**May**	**Jun**	**Jul**	**Aug**	**Sep**	**Oct**	**Nov**	**Dec**
Newspaper Advertisements												
Al-Ahram (2x/mos)		X			X			X			X	
Akhbar El-Yom (2x/mos)	X			X			X			X		
El-Misri El-Yom (2x/mos)			X			X			X			X
Magazine Advertisements												
Business Today	X				X				X			
Egypt Today		X				X				X		
Al-Ahram Al-Riyadi			X				X				X	
Kol El-Nas				X				X				X
Radio Advertisements	X		X		X		X		X		X	
Television Advertisements	X	X						X	X			X
Tradeshows												
Cairo ICT		X										
APEX			X									
Cairo International Fair			X									
Beem Egypt						X						
Egypt Invest											X	
Conventions												
International educational conference and exhibition					X							
Tourism and shopping festival and exhibition							X					
International exhibition for developing business											X	
HACE—Hotel supplies and catering equipment											X	
Office furniture and requirement expo												X
Sales Rep Visits	X	X	X	X	X	X	X	X	X	X	X	X
Year 5	**Jan**	**Feb**	**Mar**	**Apr**	**May**	**Jun**	**Jul**	**Aug**	**Sep**	**Oct**	**Nov**	**Dec**
Newspaper Advertisements												
Advertise in the two most effective newspapers from the past two years		X		X		X		X		X		X
	X		X		X		X		X		X	
Magazine Advertisements												
Advertise in the two most effective magazines from the past two years	X		X		X		X		X		X	
		X		X		X		X		X		X
Radio Advertisements	X		X		X		X		X		X	
Television Advertisements	X	X						X	X			X
Tradeshows												
Cairo ICT		X										
APEX			X									
Cairo International Fair			X									
Beem Egypt						X						
Egypt Invest											X	

(Continued)

Exhibit MK7 (Continued)

Year 5	Jan	Feb	Mar	Apr	May	Jun	Jul	Aug	Sep	Oct	Nov	Dec
Conventions												
International educational conference and exhibition					X							
Tourism and shopping festival and exhibition							X					
International exhibition for developing business											X	
HACE—Hotel supplies and catering equipment											X	
Office furniture and requirement expo												X
Sales Rep Visits	X	X	X	X	X	X	X	X	X	X	X	X

Exhibit MK8-A: Sample Press Release 1

Buying Office Supplies—Easy!

National Launch of Maktabi

On January 1, 2007, HINA Business & Investment Group will launch MAKTABI, a company that offers a new solution to the traditional way of ordering office supplies.

Maktabi provides businesses and consumers with an effective and inexpensive way to order office supplies from a catalog or online—offering a large variety of products with a diverse array of styles from the comfort of one's own chair! The person placing the order can either order online or pick up the phone and dial one of the toll free numbers to order whatever they require. Through operational excellence and efficient distribution systems, the order will be received quickly at a minimal cost.

The Maktabi Web site is being developed to accommodate all the necessary information for customers to view product information and place orders online.

Exhibit MK8-B: Sample Press Release 2

Helping Egyptian Businesses

December 21, 2007

CAIRO—What do Yasser Refaat, Essam Ali, and Abir Mansour have in common? Their smarts—they have all decided to use Maktabi as the sole source for all their office supply needs.

Yasser Refaat is the General Manager for Guest Relations at the Conrad Hotel located in Mohandiseen, Cairo. He has a staff of over 25 employees who are in constant commotion to ensure that every request a guest has is granted. This seems easier said than done.

Refaat says that he has developed a way of staying organized by creating a color-coded filing system using colored paper and pens. During an interview, he remarked, "It is difficult (work), but, when the shift is over, each employee feels that they have done their utmost to make the guests' experience an unforgettable one." He further comments: "If it were not for the office supplies we purchase from Maktabi, we would be 40%–50% less efficient. Maktabi is so simple to use, I don't know if I would be where I am today without it."

Ali is a Sales Manager for ABX Logistics, whose Egyptian headquarters are in Nasr City, Cairo. He lived in the United States for several years and confesses: "When I first returned to Egypt, I almost got depressed at the process that was in place for ordering office supplies. I often found myself pen-less or paper-less in front of customers—something that never happened to me in the United States!" He then says: "Maktabi is a small piece of the West that has turned business into art. The best part is they are Egyptian!"

Our third interview was with the Executive Assistant for ExxonMobil whose offices are located in Alexandria. Everyday at least 20 (of the 50 or so) employees come to her to ask for specific office supplies. "All I do is have them (the employees) pick what they want from the catalog, mark it down, call Maktabi's call center, place the order, and swish! It's here within 48 hours or less," she exclaims. She says that she orders items about 15 times a month with an average of 100EGP per order.

Although Maktabi sells office supplies, its mission statement is grand and humanitarian to a certain extent: to make business processes in Egypt efficient. More than 30,000 orders have been placed since they first opened their doors in July 2007.

Egypt thanks Maktabi.

Exhibit FE1-A: Base Case—Assumptions

Maktabi

Assumptions for the Financial Plan (Summary)

All figures shown in Egyptian Pounds

SALES

- The first sales will take place in 10/08
- Average order price structure:
  Business orders 14
  Consumer orders 10

COSTS OF SERVICES PROVIDED

- Average material costs per order:
  Business orders 8
  Consumer orders 6

OPERATING COSTS

- Monthly wages reflect current market rates
- Social costs as percentage of wage costs 0.00%
- Annual rise in wages 10.00%
- The model for the number of employees is given in the financial plan
- Import customs and transportation to distribution center 216 / inbound shipment
- Picking and packing 0 / order
- Shipping 1 / order
- Catalog design will be paid at market rates
- Catalog photos 0 / photo
- Catalog printing 2 / catalog
- Information systems will be paid at market rates
- Sales representative commission on sales 3.00%
- Commissions on sales 0.00%
- Advertising media as a percentage of sales 0.25%
- Promotions as a percentage of sales 0.75%
- Public relations as a percentage of sales 0.25%
- Other marketing expenses as a percentage of sales 0.25%
- Consultants for special projects and auditors will be paid at market rates
- Additional costs per person calculated as follows:

Cost per Person/Month	Training	Office Material	Travel	Communication
Customer service	5	7	4	54
Purchasing	0	4	144	54
Distribution	0	4	11	18
Transportation and AR	0	4	4	18
Publications	0	4	4	18
Information Technologies	0	4	4	18
Marketing and Sales*	4	4	4	18
Finance and Administration	0	4	18	54

*Marketing and Sales training for sales representatives only

- Rent per square metre per month 35.00%
- Provisions for unpaid invoices in percentage of sales 0.00%
- Interest income on liquid assets 0.00%
- Returns as a percentage of sales 0.50%
- Income tax 20.00%

BALANCE SHEET

- Debitors are settled within 30 days, creditors within 30 days
- Goods are purchased on average 30 days before the sale of the product/service
- Fixed assets include computers, software, office equipment, and property
- Individual depreciation periods per asset and cost center
- Provisions for wages represent half a monthly salary
- Taxes are paid at the end of the tax period

Exhibit FE1-B: Base Case—Profit and Loss Statement (US$)

Maktabi

Profit and Loss Statement

Sales	2008	2009	2010	2011	2012
Business orders	81,081	533,784	440,541	451,351	462,838
Consumer orders	133,784	1,615,315	6,638,684	7,499,721	8,752,512
Total sales	214,865	2,149,099	7,079,225	7,951,072	9,215,350
Cost of services provided	129,993	1,300,205	4,282,931	4,810,399	5,575,286
Gross margin	84,872	848,894	2,796,294	3,140,673	3,640,063
In % of sales	40%	40%	40%	40%	40%
Operating costs					
Customer Service	18,631	52,157	137,705	179,163	186,520
In % of sales	9%	2%	2%	2%	2%
Purchasing	15,728	25,897	28,645	29,657	30,747
In % of sales	7%	1%	0%	0%	0%
Distribution	33,355	118,051	320,718	363,790	410,644
In % of sales	16%	5%	5%	5%	4%
Transportation and Accounts Receivables	17,397	120,430	391,653	439,572	509,201
In % of sales	8%	6%	6%	6%	6%
Publications	22,875	63,947	52,937	53,099	53,555
In % of sales	11%	3%	1%	1%	1%
Information Technologies	27,661	53,633	60,107	60,531	61,274
In % of sales	13%	2%	1%	1%	1%
Marketing and Sales	41,949	149,718	373,491	417,236	479,376
In % of sales	20%	7%	5%	5%	5%
Finance and Administration	189,764	202,549	234,581	245,436	260,449
In % of sales	88%	9%	3%	3%	3%
Total operating costs	367,359	786,381	1,599,835	1,788,486	1,991,766
In % of sales	171%	37%	23%	22%	22%
Operating profit	-282,488	62,513	1,196,458	1,352,188	1,648,297
In % of sales	-131%	3%	17%	17%	18%
Financing expenditure	0	0	0	0	0
Financing income	0	0	0	0	0
Profit before tax	-282,488	62,513	1,196,458	1,352,188	1,648,297
Income tax	0	0	195,297	270,438	329,659
Net profit	-282,488	62,513	1,001,162	1,081,750	1,318,637
In % of sales	-131%	3%	14%	14%	14%

Exhibit FE1-C: Base Case—Profit and Loss Statement (US$) Details Year 1

Maktabi

Profit and Loss Statement

	Month 1 Jan 08	Month 2 Feb 08	Month 3 Mar 08	Month 4 Apr 08	Month 5 May 08	Month 6 Jun 08	Month 7 Jul 08	Month 8 Aug 08	Month 9 Sep 08	Month 10 Oct 08	Month 11 Nov 08	Month 12 Dec 08	Total 2008
Sales													
Business orders	0	0	0	0	0	0	0	0	6,757	20,270	27,027	27,027	81,081
Consumer orders	0	0	0	0	0	0	0	0	14,865	29,730	39,640	49,550	133,784
Total sales	0	0	0	0	0	0	0	0	21,622	50,000	66,667	76,577	214,865
Expenditure													
Costs of performance													
Material costs	0	0	0	0	0	0	0	0	12,973	30,000	40,000	45,946	128,919
Returns	0	0	0	0	0	0	0	0	108	250	333	383	1,074
Total costs of performance	0	0	0	0	0	0	0	0	13,081	30,250	40,333	46,329	129,993
Gross profit	0	0	0	0	0	0	0	0	8,541	19,750	26,333	30,248	84,872
In % of sales	0%	0%	0%	0%	0%	0%	0%	0%	40%	40%	40%	40%	40%
Operating costs													
Customer Service													
Wages	0	0	0	450	450	901	1,351	1,351	1,351	1,351	1,802	1,802	10,811
Bonuses	0	0	0	0	0	0	0	0	0	0	0	0	0
Social and other personnel costs	0	0	0	0	0	0	0	0	0	0	0	0	0
Training	0	0	0	5	5	9	14	50	50	50	86	86	351
Office material	0	0	0	7	7	14	22	79	79	79	137	137	562
Travel and refreshment	0	0	0	4	4	7	11	40	40	40	68	68	281
Communication	0	0	0	54	54	108	162	595	595	595	1,027	1,027	4,216
Depreciation	0	0	0	31	31	62	93	340	340	340	587	587	2,409

(*Continued*)

Exhibit FE1-C (Continued)

	Month 1 Jan 08	Month 2 Feb 08	Month 3 Mar 08	Month 4 Apr 08	Month 5 May 08	Month 6 Jun 08	Month 7 Jul 08	Month 8 Aug 08	Month 9 Sep 08	Month 10 Oct 08	Month 11 Nov 08	Month 12 Dec 08	Total 2008
Purchasing													
Wages	0	450	450	667	667	667	667	883	1,099	1,099	1,099	1,099	8,847
Bonuses	0	0	0	0	0	0	0	0	0	0	0	0	0
Social and other personnel costs	0	0	0	0	0	0	0	0	0	0	0	0	0
Office material	0	4	4	7	7	7	7	11	14	14	14	14	105
Travel and refreshment	0	144	144	288	288	288	288	432	577	577	577	577	4,180
Communication	0	54	54	108	108	108	108	162	216	216	216	216	1,568
Depreciation	0	35	35	71	71	71	71	106	142	142	142	142	1,028
Distribution													
Wages	0	0	0	818	818	818	818	818	818	818	818	818	7,364
Bonuses	0	0	0	0	0	0	0	0	0	0	0	0	0
Social and other personnel costs	0	0	0	0	0	0	0	0	0	0	0	0	0
Import customs and transportation to distribution center	0	0	0	0	0	9,730	865	1,081	1,081	1,081	1,946	2,162	17,946
Picking and packing	0	0	0	0	0	0	0	0	721	1,622	2,162	2,523	7,027
Office material	0	0	0	4	4	4	7	7	7	7	7	7	54
Travel and refreshment	0	0	0	11	11	11	22	22	22	22	22	22	162
Communication	0	0	0	18	18	18	36	36	36	36	36	36	270
Depreciation	0	0	0	35	35	35	71	71	71	71	71	71	532
Transportation and Accounts Receivables													
Wages	0	0	0	541	541	541	721	721	721	721	721	721	5,946
Bonuses	0	0	0	0	0	0	0	0	0	0	0	0	0
Social and other personnel costs	0	0	0	0	0	0	0	0	0	0	0	0	0

	Month 1 Jan 08	Month 2 Feb 08	Month 3 Mar 08	Month 4 Apr 08	Month 5 May 08	Month 6 Jun 08	Month 7 Jul 08	Month 8 Aug 08	Month 9 Sep 08	Month 10 Oct 08	Month 11 Nov 08	Month 12 Dec 08	Total 2008
Shipping	0	0	0	0	0	0	0	0	1,081	2,432	3,243	3,784	10,541
Office material	0	0	0	4	4	4	7	7	7	7	7	7	54
Travel and refreshment	0	0	0	4	4	4	7	7	7	7	7	7	54
Communication	0	0	0	18	18	18	36	36	36	36	36	36	270
Depreciation	0	0	0	35	35	35	71	71	71	71	71	71	532
Publications													
Wages	0	0	0	360	360	360	360	360	360	360	360	360	3,243
Bonuses	0	0	0	0	0	0	0	0	0	0	0	0	0
Social and other personnel costs	0	0	0	0	0	0	0	0	0	0	0	0	0
Catalog design	0	0	0	0	1,818	0	0	0	0	0	0	0	1,818
Catalog photos	0	0	0	0	721	0	0	0	0	0	0	0	721
Number of catalogs	0	0	0	0	0	0	0	720	1,152	1,440	2,160	2,160	7,632
Catalog printing	0	0	0	0	0	0	0	1,557	2,491	3,114	4,670	4,670	16,502
Office material	0	0	0	4	4	4	4	4	4	4	4	4	32
Travel and refreshment	0	0	0	4	4	4	4	4	4	4	4	4	32
Communication	0	0	0	18	18	18	18	18	18	18	18	18	162
Depreciation	0	0	0	40	40	40	40	40	40	40	40	40	364
Information Technologies													
Wages	0	0	0	270	270	270	270	541	541	541	541	541	3,784
Bonuses	0	0	0	0	0	0	0	0	0	0	0	0	0
Social and other personnel costs	0	0	0	0	0	0	0	0	0	0	0	0	0
Service and maintenance	0	0	0	0	0	0	1,725	1,725	1,725	1,725	1,725	1,725	10,349
Office material	0	0	0	4	4	4	4	4	4	4	4	4	32
Travel and refreshment	0	0	0	4	4	4	4	4	4	4	4	4	32
Communication	0	0	0	18	18	18	18	18	18	18	18	18	162
Depreciation	0	0	0	472	903	1,334	1,765	1,765	1,765	1,765	1,765	1,765	13,301

(*Continued*)

Exhibit FE1-C (Continued)

	Month 1 Jan 08	Month 2 Feb 08	Month 3 Mar 08	Month 4 Apr 08	Month 5 May 08	Month 6 Jun 08	Month 7 Jul 08	Month 8 Aug 08	Month 9 Sep 08	Month 10 Oct 08	Month 11 Nov 08	Month 12 Dec 08	Total 2008
Marketing and Sales													
Management													
Management wages	0	0	0	2,587	2,858	2,858	2,858	2,858	3,128	3,128	3,128	3,128	26,530
Management bonuses	0	0	0	0	0	0	0	0	0	0	0	0	0
Management social and other personnel costs	0	0	0	0	0	0	0	0	0	0	0	0	0
Office material	0	0	0	4	7	7	7	7	11	11	11	11	76
Travel and refreshment	0	0	0	4	7	7	7	7	11	11	11	11	76
Communication	0	0	0	18	36	36	36	36	54	54	54	54	378
Sales Representatives													
Sales representatives wages	0	0	0	0	0	324	324	324	486	486	486	486	2,919
Sales representatives commissions, bonuses	0	0	0	0	0	0	0	0	649	1,500	2,000	2,297	6,446
Sales representatives social and other personnel costs	0	0	0	0	0	0	0	0	0	0	0	0	0
Training	0	0	0	0	0	22	22	22	32	32	32	32	194
Office material	0	0	0	0	0	22	22	22	32	32	32	32	195
Travel and refreshment	0	0	0	0	0	22	22	22	32	32	32	32	195
Communication	0	0	0	0	0	108	108	108	162	162	162	162	973
Advertising media	0	0	0	0	0	0	0	0	54	125	167	191	537
Promotions	0	0	0	0	0	0	0	0	162	375	500	574	1,611
Public relations	0	0	0	0	0	0	0	0	54	125	167	191	537
Other	0	0	0	0	0	0	0	0	54	125	167	191	537
Consultancy	0	0	0	0	0	0	0	0	0	0	0	0	0
Depreciation	0	0	0	35	71	71	71	71	106	106	106	106	745

	Month 1 Jan 08	Month 2 Feb 08	Month 3 Mar 08	Month 4 Apr 08	Month 5 May 08	Month 6 Jun 08	Month 7 Jul 08	Month 8 Aug 08	Month 9 Sep 08	Month 10 Oct 08	Month 11 Nov 08	Month 12 Dec 08	Total 2008
Finance and Administration													
Wages	0	0	1,171	1,171	1,802	1,802	5,946	5,946	5,946	5,946	5,946	5,946	41,622
Bonuses	0	0	0	0	0	0	0	0	0	0	0	0	0
Social and other personnel costs	0	0	0	0	0	0	0	0	0	0	0	0	0
Office material	0	0	14	14	22	22	25	25	25	25	25	25	223
Travel and refreshment	0	0	72	72	108	108	126	126	126	126	126	126	1,117
Communication	0	0	216	216	324	324	378	378	378	378	378	378	3,351
Insurance	0	0	0	0	0	0	0	0	108	250	333	383	1,074
Professional services (legal, accounting, etc.)	10,811	10,811	10,811	10,811	10,811	10,811	10,811	10,811	10,811	10,811	6,727	6,727	121,563
Provisions for unpaid invoices	0	0	0	0	0	0	0	0	0	0	0	0	0
Office rent	315	315	315	1,892	1,892	1,892	1,892	1,892	1,892	1,892	1,892	1,892	17,973
Water, electricity	9	9	9	54	54	54	54	54	54	54	54	54	514
Maintenance, repairs	2	2	2	14	14	14	14	14	14	14	14	14	128
Depreciation	0	0	142	142	213	213	248	248	248	248	248	248	2,199
Total Finance and Administration	11,137	11,137	12,753	14,386	15,239	15,239	19,494	19,494	19,602	19,744	15,744	15,794	189,764
In % of sales	0%	0%	0%	0%	0%	0%	0%	0%	91%	39%	24%	21%	88%
Total operating costs	11,137	11,825	13,441	21,407	25,561	34,231	32,637	35,935	40,785	45,079	46,855	48,467	367,359
In % of sales	0%	0%	0%	0%	0%	0%	0%	0%	189%	90%	70%	63%	171%
Operating profit (EBIT)	(11,137)	(11,825)	(13,441)	(21,407)	(25,561)	(34,231)	(32,637)	(35,935)	(32,245)	(25,329)	(20,521)	(18,219)	(282,488)
In % of sales	0%	0%	0%	0%	0%	0%	0%	0%	-149%	-51%	-31%	-24%	-131%
Financing expenditure	0	0	0	0	0	0	0	0	0	0	0	0	0
Financing income	0	0	0	0	0	0	0	0	0	0	0	0	0
Profit before tax	(11,137)	(11,825)	(13,441)	(21,407)	(25,561)	(34,231)	(32,637)	(35,935)	(32,245)	(25,329)	(20,521)	(18,219)	(282,488)
Income tax	0	0	0	0	0	0	0	0	0	0	0	0	0
Net profit	(11,137)	(11,825)	(13,441)	(21,407)	(25,561)	(34,231)	(32,637)	(35,935)	(32,245)	(25,329)	(20,521)	(18,219)	(282,488)
In % of sales	0%	0%	0%	0%	0%	0%	0%	0%	-149%	-51%	-31%	-24%	-131%

Exhibit FE1-D: Base Case—Profit and Loss Statement (US$) Details Years 2 and 3

Maktabi

Profit and Loss Statement

	Qtr 1 2009	Qtr 2 2009	Qtr 3 2009	Qtr 4 2009	Total	Qtr 1 2010	Qtr 2 2010	Qtr 3 2010	Qtr 4 2010	Total
Sales										
Business orders	128,378	81,081	175,676	148,649	**533,784**	110,135	81,081	175,676	148,649	**440,541**
Consumer orders	267,568	406,306	475,676	465,766	**1,615,315**	1,659,671	406,306	475,676	465,766	**6,638,684**
Total sales	395,946	487,387	651,351	614,414	**2,149,099**	1,769,806	487,387	651,351	614,414	**7,079,225**
Expenditure										
Costs of performance										
Material costs	237,568	292,432	390,811	368,649	**1,289,459**	1,061,884	292,432	390,811	368,649	**4,247,535**
Returns	1,980	2,437	3,257	3,072	**10,745**	8,849	2,437	3,257	3,072	**35,396**
Total costs of performance	239,547	294,869	394,068	371,721	**1,300,205**	1,070,733	294,869	394,068	371,721	**4,282,931**
Gross profit	156,399	192,518	257,284	242,694	**848,894**	699,073	192,518	257,284	242,694	**2,796,294**
In % of sales	40%	40%	40%	40%	**40%**	40%	40%	40%	40%	**40%**
Operating costs										
Customer Service										
Wages	5,946	5,946	5,946	5,946	**23,784**	24,200	5,946	5,946	5,946	**96,800**
Bonuses	0	0	0	0	**0**	0	0	0	0	**0**
Social and other personnel costs	0	0	0	0	**0**	0	0	0	0	**0**
Training	302	324	324	324	**1,275**	459	324	324	324	**1,838**
Office material	483	519	519	519	**2,040**	735	519	519	519	**2,941**
Travel and refreshment	241	259	259	259	**1,020**	368	259	259	259	**1,470**
Communication	3,622	3,892	3,892	3,892	**15,297**	5,514	3,892	3,892	3,892	**22,054**
Depreciation	2,069	2,224	2,224	2,224	**8,741**	3,151	2,224	2,224	2,224	**12,602**

	Qtr 1 2009	Qtr 2 2009	Qtr 3 2009	Qtr 4 2009	Total	Qtr 1 2010	Qtr 2 2010	Qtr 3 2010	Qtr 4 2010	Total
Purchasing										
Wages	3,627	3,627	3,627	3,627	**14,508**	3,990	3,627	3,627	3,627	**15,959**
Bonuses	0	0	0	0	**0**	0	0	0	0	**0**
Social and other personnel costs	0	0	0	0	**0**	0	0	0	0	**0**
Office material	43	43	43	43	**173**	368	43	43	43	**1,470**
Travel and refreshment	1,730	1,730	1,730	1,730	**6,919**	1,730	1,730	1,730	1,730	**6,919**
Communication	649	649	649	649	**2,595**	649	649	649	649	**2,595**
Depreciation	426	426	426	426	**1,702**	426	426	426	426	**1,702**
Distribution										
Wages	2,700	2,700	2,700	2,700	**10,800**	2,970	2,700	2,700	2,700	**11,880**
Bonuses	0	0	0	0	**0**	0	0	0	0	**0**
Social and other personnel costs	0	0	0	0	**0**	0	0	0	0	**0**
Import customs and transportation to distribution center	6,486	3,892	10,811	11,459	**32,649**	13,514	3,892	10,811	11,459	**54,054**
Picking and packing	13,153	16,937	21,982	20,901	**72,973**	63,289	16,937	21,982	20,901	**253,154**
Office material	22	22	22	22	**86**	22	22	22	22	**86**
Travel and refreshment	65	65	65	65	**259**	65	65	65	65	**259**
Communication	108	108	108	108	**432**	108	108	108	108	**432**
Depreciation	213	213	213	213	**851**	213	213	213	213	**851**
Transportation and Accounts Receivables										
Wages	2,378	2,378	2,378	2,378	**9,514**	2,616	2,378	2,378	2,378	**10,465**
Bonuses	0	0	0	0	**0**	0	0	0	0	**0**
Social and other personnel costs	0	0	0	0	**0**	0	0	0	0	**0**
Shipping	19,730	25,405	32,973	31,351	**109,459**	94,933	25,405	32,973	31,351	**379,732**
Office material	22	22	22	22	**86**	22	22	22	22	**86**
Travel and refreshment	22	22	22	22	**86**	22	22	22	22	**86**
Communication	108	108	108	108	**432**	108	108	108	108	**432**
Depreciation	213	213	213	213	**851**	213	213	213	213	**851**

(Continued)

Exhibit FE1-D (Continued)

	Qtr 1 2009	Qtr 2 2009	Qtr 3 2009	Qtr 4 2009	Total	Qtr 1 2010	Qtr 2 2010	Qtr 3 2010	Qtr 4 2010	Total
Publications										
Wages	1,189	1,189	1,189	1,189	**4,757**	1,308	1,189	1,189	1,189	**5,232**
Bonuses	0	0	0	0	**0**	0	0	0	0	**0**
Social and other personnel costs	0	0	0	0	**0**	0	0	0	0	**0**
Catalog design	1,818	0	0	0	**1,818**	455	0	0	0	**1,818**
Catalog photos	541	0	0	0	**541**	135	0	0	0	**541**
Number of catalogs	6,480	6,480	6,480	6,480	**25,920**	5,184	6,480	6,480	6,480	**20,736**
Catalog printing	14,011	14,011	14,011	14,011	**56,043**	11,209	14,011	14,011	14,011	**44,835**
Office material	11	11	11	11	**43**	1	11	11	11	**4**
Travel and refreshment	11	11	11	11	**43**	1	11	11	11	**4**
Communication	54	54	54	54	**216**	5	54	54	54	**18**
Depreciation	121	121	121	121	**486**	121	121	121	121	**486**
Information Technologies										
Wages	1,784	1,784	1,784	1,784	**7,135**	1,962	1,784	1,784	1,784	**7,849**
Bonuses	0	0	0	0	**0**	0	0	0	0	**0**
Social and other personnel costs	0	0	0	0	**0**	0	0	0	0	**0**
Service and maintenance	5,175	5,175	5,175	5,175	**20,698**	5,175	5,175	5,175	5,175	**20,698**
Office material	11	11	11	11	**43**	1	11	11	11	**4**
Travel and refreshment	11	11	11	11	**43**	1	11	11	11	**4**
Communication	54	54	54	54	**216**	5	54	54	54	**18**
Depreciation	5,296	5,296	7,021	7,884	**25,497**	7,884	5,296	7,021	7,884	**31,534**
Marketing and Sales										
Management										
Management wages	10,322	10,322	10,322	10,322	**41,289**	11,354	10,322	10,322	10,322	**45,418**
Management bonuses	0	0	0	0	**0**	0	0	0	0	**0**
Management social and other personnel costs	0	0	0	0	**0**	0	0	0	0	**0**

	Qtr 1 2009	Qtr 2 2009	Qtr 3 2009	Qtr 4 2009	Total	Qtr 1 2010	Qtr 2 2010	Qtr 3 2010	Qtr 4 2010	Total
Office material	32	32	32	32	**130**	32	32	32	32	**130**
Travel and refreshment	32	32	32	32	**130**	32	32	32	32	**130**
Communication	162	162	162	162	**649**	162	162	162	162	**649**
Sales Representatives										
Sales representatives wages	1,605	1,605	1,605	1,605	**6,422**	1,766	1,605	1,605	1,605	**7,064**
Sales representatives commissions, bonuses	11,878	14,622	19,541	18,432	**64,473**	53,094	14,622	19,541	18,432	**212,377**
Sales representatives social and other personnel costs	0	0	0	0	**0**	0	0	0	0	**0**
Training	97	97	97	97	**389**	8	97	97	97	**32**
Office material	97	97	97	97	**389**	8	97	97	97	**32**
Travel and refreshment	97	97	97	97	**389**	8	97	97	97	**32**
Communication	486	486	486	486	**1,946**	41	486	486	486	**162**
Advertising media	990	1,218	1,628	1,536	**5,373**	4,425	1,218	1,628	1,536	**17,698**
Promotions	2,970	3,655	4,885	4,608	**16,118**	13,274	3,655	4,885	4,608	**53,094**
Public relations	990	1,218	1,628	1,536	**5,373**	4,425	1,218	1,628	1,536	**17,698**
Other	990	1,218	1,628	1,536	**5,373**	4,425	1,218	1,628	1,536	**17,698**
Consultancy	0	0	0	0	**0**	0	0	0	0	**0**
Depreciation	319	319	319	319	**1,277**	319	319	319	319	**1,277**
Finance and Administration										
Wages	19,622	19,473	19,622	19,622	**78,338**	21,584	19,473	19,622	19,622	**86,335**
Bonuses	0	0	0	0	**0**	0	0	0	0	**0**
Social and other personnel costs	0	0	0	0	**0**	0	0	0	0	**0**
Office material	76	72	76	76	**299**	76	72	76	76	**303**
Travel and refreshment	378	360	378	378	**1,495**	378	360	378	378	**1,514**
Communication	1,135	1,081	1,135	1,135	**4,486**	1,135	1,081	1,135	1,135	**4,541**
Insurance	1,980	2,437	3,257	3,072	**10,745**	8,849	2,437	3,257	3,072	**35,396**
Profesional services (legal, accounting, etc.)	20,182	20,182	20,182	20,182	**80,727**	20,000	20,182	20,182	20,182	**80,000**
Provisions for unpaid invoices	0	0	0	0	**0**	0	0	0	0	**0**

(Continued)

Exhibit FE1-D (Continued)

	Qtr 1 2009	Qtr 2 2009	Qtr 3 2009	Qtr 4 2009	Total	Qtr 1 2010	Qtr 2 2010	Qtr 3 2010	Qtr 4 2010	Total
Office rent	5,676	5,676	5,676	5,676	**22,703**	5,676	5,676	5,676	5,676	**22,703**
Water, electricity	162	162	162	162	**649**	162	162	162	162	**649**
Maintenance, repairs	41	41	41	41	**162**	41	41	41	41	**162**
Depreciation	745	709	745	745	**2,944**	745	709	745	745	**2,979**
Total Finance and Administration	49,995	50,193	51,273	51,088	**202,549**	58,645	50,193	51,273	51,088	**234,581**
In % of sales	13%	10%	8%	8%	**9%**	13%	10%	8%	8%	**3%**
Total operating costs	175,508	184,828	214,542	211,504	**786,381**	399,959	184,828	214,542	211,504	**1,599,835**
In % of sales	44%	38%	33%	34%	**37%**	44%	38%	33%	34%	**23%**
Operating profit (EBIT)	(19,109)	7,690	42,742	31,190	**62,513**	299,115	7,690	42,742	31,190	**1,196,458**
In % of sales	-5%	1%	6%	5%	**3%**	-5%	1%	6%	5%	**17%**
Financing expenditure	0	0	0	0	**0**	0	0	0	0	**0**
Financing income	0	0	0	0	**0**	0	0	0	0	**0**
Profit before tax	(19,109)	7,690	42,742	31,190	**62,513**	299,115	7,690	42,742	31,190	**1,196,458**
Income tax	0	0	0	0	**0**	0	0	0	0	**195,297**
Net profit	(19,109)	7,690	42,742	31,190	**62,513**	250,290	7,690	42,742	31,190	**1,001,162**
In % of sales	-5%	1%	6%	5%	**3%**	-5%	1%	6%	5%	**14%**

Exhibit FE1-E: Base Case—Balance Sheet (US$)

Maktabi

Balance sheet at end of accounting year

	2008	2009	2010	2011	2012
Assets					
Liquid assets					
Cash	55,478	124,026	829,547	1,880,907	2,764,140
Net receivables from customers	76,577	199,099	589,935	662,589	767,946
Stock/inventory (30, 60, or 90 days)	84,054	353,961	397,554	460,767	0
Total liquid assets	216,108	677,086	1,817,036	3,004,264	3,532,086
Gross fixed assets	329,982	439,243	450,775	462,306	462,306
Minus cumulated depreciation	21,111	63,459	115,742	157,039	189,300
Net fixed assets	308,871	375,784	335,033	305,267	273,007
Total assets	**524,980**	**1,052,870**	**2,152,070**	**3,309,531**	**3,805,093**
Liabilities					
Debt					
Short-term debt					
Open third-party invoices (creditors)	110,017	394,649	440,100	494,631	525,315
Provisions for wages	7,451	8,196	11,958	14,353	15,789
Provisions for taxes	0	0	48,824	67,609	82,415
Total short-term debt	117,468	402,845	500,883	576,594	623,519
Long-term debt					
Loans and mortgages	0	0	0	0	0
Total long-term debt	0	0	0	0	0
Total debt	**117,468**	**402,845**	**500,883**	**576,594**	**623,519**
Equity					
Share capital	690,000	870,000	870,000	870,000	0
Reserves	0	0	0	0	0
Profit/loss carried forward	-282,488	-219,975	781,187	1,862,937	3,181,574
Total equity	407,512	650,025	1,651,187	2,732,937	3,181,574
Total liabilities	**524,980**	**1,052,870**	**2,152,070**	**3,309,531**	**3,805,093**

Exhibit FE1-F: Base Case—Balance Sheet (US$) Details Year 1

Maktabi

Balance Sheet

	Month 1 Jan 08	Month 2 Feb 08	Month 3 Mar 08	Month 4 Apr 08	Month 5 May 08	Month 6 Jun 08	Month 7 Jul 08	Month 8 Aug 08	Month 9 Sep 08	Month 10 Oct 08	Month 11 Nov 08	Month 12 Dec 08	Total 2008
ASSETS													
Liquid assets													
Cash	54,820	47,160	54,686	56,179	49,544	52,095	50,547	49,575	49,596	51,973	49,310	55,478	55,478
Gross receivables from customers (30, 60, or 90 days)	0	0	0	0	0	0	0	0	21,622	50,000	66,667	76,577	76,577
Provisions for bad debts	0	0	0	0	0	0	0	0	0	0	0	0	0
Net receivables from customers	0	0	0	0	0	0	0	0	21,622	50,000	66,667	76,577	76,577
Stock/inventory (30, 60, or 90 days)	0	0	0	0	0	0	0	12,973	30,000	40,000	45,946	84,054	84,054
Total liquid assets	**54,820**	**47,160**	**54,686**	**56,179**	**49,544**	**52,095**	**50,547**	**62,548**	**101,217**	**141,973**	**161,923**	**216,108**	**216,108**
Fixed assets													
Vehicle	64,865	64,865	74,775	74,775	74,775	74,775	74,775	74,775	74,775	74,775	74,775	74,775	74,775
Computer system	0	0	0	51,748	103,495	155,243	206,991	206,991	206,991	206,991	206,991	206,991	206,991
Computer hardware and software	0	1,261	6,306	15,315	19,099	20,180	25,045	34,955	37,477	37,477	46,126	46,126	46,126
Furniture and other equipment	0	36	180	468	577	649	829	1,441	1,514	1,514	2,090	2,090	2,090

	Month 1 Jan 08	Month 2 Feb 08	Month 3 Mar 08	Month 4 Apr 08	Month 5 May 08	Month 6 Jun 08	Month 7 Jul 08	Month 8 Aug 08	Month 9 Sep 08	Month 10 Oct 08	Month 11 Nov 08	Month 12 Dec 08	Total 2008
Property, buildings, and plant	0	0	0	0	0	0	0	0	0	0	0	0	0
Total fixed assets	64,865	66,162	81,261	142,306	197,946	250,847	307,640	318,162	320,757	320,757	329,982	329,982	329,982
Cumulated depreciation													
Vehicle	360	721	1,136	1,552	1,967	2,382	2,798	3,213	3,629	4,044	4,459	4,875	4,875
Computer system	0	0	0	431	1,294	2,587	4,312	6,037	7,762	9,487	11,212	12,937	12,937
Computer hardware and software	0	35	210	636	1,166	1,727	2,422	3,393	4,434	5,475	6,757	8,038	8,038
Furniture and other equipment	0	0	3	8	15	23	33	50	68	86	111	136	136
Property, buildings, and plant	0	0	0	0	0	0	0	0	0	0	0	0	0
Total cumulated depreciation	0	35	213	1,075	2,475	4,337	6,767	9,480	12,264	15,048	18,079	21,111	21,111
Net fixed assets	**64,865**	**66,127**	**81,048**	**141,231**	**195,471**	**246,510**	**300,872**	**308,682**	**308,492**	**305,708**	**311,903**	**308,871**	**308,871**
Total assets	119,685	113,287	135,734	197,410	245,015	298,605	351,419	371,229	409,710	447,681	473,825	524,980	524,980
Liabilities													
Debt													
Short-term debt													
Open third-party invoices (creditors)	10,822	11,024	11,327	11,787	14,503	21,936	14,999	30,501	50,902	64,203	70,643	110,017	110,017
Provisions for wages	0	225	811	3,433	3,883	4,270	6,658	6,901	7,225	7,225	7,451	7,451	7,451
Provisions for taxes	0	0	0	0	0	0	0	0	0	0	0	0	0
Total short-term debt	10,822	11,249	12,137	15,220	18,386	26,206	21,656	37,402	58,127	71,428	78,094	117,468	117,468

(Continued)

Exhibit FE1-F (Continued)

	Month 1 Jan 08	Month 2 Feb 08	Month 3 Mar 08	Month 4 Apr 08	Month 5 May 08	Month 6 Jun 08	Month 7 Jul 08	Month 8 Aug 08	Month 9 Sep 08	Month 10 Oct 08	Month 11 Nov 08	Month 12 Dec 08	Total 2008
Long-term debt													
Loans and mortgages	0	0	0	0	0	0	0	0	0	0	0	0	0
Total long-term debt	0	0	0	0	0	0	0	0	0	0	0	0	0
Total debt	10,822	11,249	12,137	15,220	18,386	26,206	21,656	37,402	58,127	71,428	78,094	117,468	117,468
Equity													
Share capital	120,000	125,000	160,000	240,000	310,000	390,000	480,000	520,000	570,000	620,000	660,000	690,000	690,000
Reserves	0	0	0	0	0	0	0	0	0	0	0	0	0
Profit/loss carried forward	(11,137)	(22,962)	(36,403)	(57,810)	(83,370)	(117,601)	(150,238)	(186,173)	(218,418)	(243,747)	(264,268)	(282,488)	(282,488)
Total equity	108,863	102,038	123,597	182,190	226,630	272,399	329,762	333,827	351,582	376,253	395,732	407,512	407,512
Total liabilities	119,685	113,287	135,734	197,410	245,015	298,605	351,419	371,229	409,710	447,681	473,825	524,980	524,980

Exhibit FE1-G: Base Case—Balance Sheet (US$) Details Years 2 and 3

Maktabi

Balance Sheet

	Qtr 1 2009	Qtr 2 2009	Qtr 3 2009	Qtr 4 2009	Total	Qtr 1 2010	Qtr 2 2010	Qtr 3 2010	Qtr 4 2010	Total
Assets										
Liquid assets										
Cash	142,290	148,342	144,998	316,328	**124,026**	207,387	207,387	207,387	207,387	**829,547**
Gross receivables from customers (30, 60, or 90 days)	395,946	487,387	651,351	614,414	**199,099**	147,484	147,484	147,484	147,484	**589,935**
Provisions for bad debts	0	0	0	0	**0**	0	0	0	0	**0**
Net receivables from customers	395,946	487,387	651,351	614,414	**199,099**	147,484	147,484	147,484	147,484	**589,935**
Stock/inventory (30, 60, or 90 days)	241,081	318,378	404,865	595,042	**353,961**	99,388	99,388	99,388	99,388	**397,554**
Total liquid assets	779,317	954,108	1,201,214	1,525,785	**677,086**	454,259	454,259	454,259	454,259	**1,817,036**
Fixed assets										
Vehicle	224,324	224,324	224,324	224,324	**74,775**	18,694	18,694	18,694	18,694	**74,775**
Computer system	620,973	620,973	827,964	931,460	**310,487**	77,622	77,622	77,622	77,622	**310,487**
Computer hardware and software	149,189	153,333	154,595	154,595	**51,532**	15,586	15,586	15,586	15,586	**62,342**
Furniture and other equipment	6,991	7,315	7,351	7,351	**2,450**	793	793	793	793	**3,171**
Property, buildings, and plant	0	0	0	0	**0**	0	0	0	0	**0**
Total fixed assets	1,001,477	1,005,946	1,214,235	1,317,730	**439,243**	112,694	112,694	112,694	112,694	**450,775**
Cumulated depreciation										
Vehicle	17,117	20,856	24,595	28,333	**9,860**	3,711	3,711	3,711	3,711	**14,845**
Computer system	49,160	64,685	83,084	106,083	**37,948**	17,249	17,249	17,249	17,249	**68,997**
Computer hardware and software	32,252	45,065	57,913	70,796	**25,030**	11,453	11,453	11,453	11,453	**45,811**
Furniture and other equipment	569	831	1,093	1,355	**481**	233	233	233	233	**934**
Property, buildings, and plant	0	0	0	0	**0**	0	0	0	0	**0**

(Continued)

Exhibit FE1-G (Continued)

	Qtr 1 2009	Qtr 2 2009	Qtr 3 2009	Qtr 4 2009	Total	Qtr 1 2010	Qtr 2 2010	Qtr 3 2010	Qtr 4 2010	Total
Total cumulated depreciation	81,981	110,580	142,089	178,234	**63,459**	28,935	28,935	28,935	28,935	**115,742**
Net fixed assets	919,496	895,366	1,072,145	1,139,496	**375,784**	83,758	83,758	83,758	83,758	**335,033**
Total assets	1,698,813	1,849,474	2,273,359	2,665,282	**1,052,870**	538,017	538,017	538,017	538,017	**2,152,070**
Liabilities										
Debt										
Short-term debt										
Open third-party invoices (creditors)	338,480	421,926	530,479	718,048	**394,649**	110,025	110,025	110,025	110,025	**440,100**
Provisions for wages	24,587	24,512	24,587	24,587	**8,196**	2,990	2,990	2,990	2,990	**11,958**
Provisions for taxes	0	0	0	0	**0**	12,206	12,206	12,206	12,206	**48,824**
Total short-term debt	363,066	446,438	555,066	742,635	**402,845**	125,221	125,221	125,221	125,221	**500,883**
Long-term debt										
Loans and mortgages	0	0	0	0	**0**	0	0	0	0	**0**
Total long-term debt	0	0	0	0	0	0	0	0	0	0
Total debt					**402,845**	125,221	125,221	125,221	125,221	**500,883**
Equity										
Share capital	2,220,000	2,300,000	2,525,000	2,610,000	**870,000**	217,500	217,500	217,500	217,500	**870,000**
Reserves	0	0	0	0	**0**	0	0	0	0	**0**
Profit/loss carried forward	(884,253)	(896,964)	(806,707)	(687,353)	**(219,975)**	195,297	195,297	195,297	195,297	**781,187**
Total equity	1,335,747	1,403,036	1,718,293	1,922,647	**650,025**	412,797	412,797	412,797	412,797	**1,651,187**
Total liabilities	1,698,813	1,849,474	2,273,359	2,665,282	**1,052,870**	538,017	538,017	538,017	538,017	**2,152,070**

Exhibit FE1-H: Base Case—Cash Flows (US$)

Maktabi

Cash Flow Calculation

	2008	2009	2010	2011	2012
Cash at beginning of year	**0**	**55,478**	**124,026**	**829,547**	**1,880,907**
Cash inflow					
Net profit	-282,488	62,513	1,001,162	1,081,750	1,318,637
Plus depreciation/amortization	21,111	42,349	52,282	41,297	32,261
Plus changes in:					
Liabilities from performance	110,017	284,632	45,451	54,531	30,684
Wage provisions	7,451	745	3,763	2,395	1,435
Tax provisions	0	0	48,824	18,785	14,805
Long-term debt/loans	0	0	0	0	0
Total cash inflow	-143,910	390,239	1,151,482	1,198,759	1,397,822
Cash outflow					
Minus changes in:					
Net receivables from performance	76,577	122,523	390,836	72,654	105,356
Stock	84,054	269,907	43,592	63,214	-460,767
Gross fixed assets	329,982	109,261	11,532	11,532	0
Total cash outflow	490,613	501,691	445,960	147,399	-355,411
Cash increase/decrease	-634,522	-111,452	705,522	1,051,360	1,753,233
Financing (increase in equity)	690,000	180,000	0	0	-870,000
Cash at end of year	**55,478**	**124,026**	**829,547**	**1,880,907**	**2,764,140**

Exhibit FE1-I: Base Case—Cash Flows (US$) Details Year 1

Maktabi

Cash Flow Calculation (Indirect Calculation)

	Month 1 Jan 08	Month 2 Feb 08	Month 3 Mar-08	Month 4 Apr 08	Month 5 May 08	Month 6 Jun 08	Month 7 Jul 08	Month 8 Aug 08	Month 9 Sep 08	Month 10 Oct 08	Month 11 Nov 08	Month 12 Dec 08	Total 2008
Cash at start of month/year	0	54,820	47,160	54,686	56,179	49,544	52,095	50,547	49,575	49,596	51,973	49,310	0
Cash inflow													
Net profit	(11,137)	(11,825)	(13,441)	(21,407)	(25,561)	(34,231)	(32,637)	(35,935)	(32,245)	(25,329)	(20,521)	(18,219)	(282,488)
Plus depreciation/amortization	0	35	177	862	1,400	1,862	2,430	2,713	2,784	2,784	3,031	3,031	21,111
Plus changes in:													
Liabilities from performance	10,822	202	303	461	2,715	7,433	(6,937)	15,503	20,401	13,301	6,440	39,374	110,017
Wage provisions	0	225	586	2,622	450	387	2,387	243	324	0	225	0	7,451
Tax provisions	0	0	0	0	0	0	0	0	0	0	0	0	0
Long-term debt/loans	0	0	0	0	0	0	0	0	0	0	0	0	0
Total cash inflow	(315)	(11,363)	(12,375)	(17,462)	(20,995)	(24,548)	(34,756)	(17,476)	(8,736)	(9,245)	(10,825)	24,186	(143,910)
Cash deployed													
Minus changes in:													
Net receivables from performance	0	0	0	0	0	0	0	0	21,622	28,378	16,667	9,910	76,577
Stock	0	0	0	0	0	0	0	12,973	17,027	10,000	5,946	38,108	84,054
Gross fixed assets	64,865	1,297	15,099	61,045	55,640	52,901	56,793	10,523	2,595	0	9,225	0	329,982
Total cash deployed	64,865	1,297	15,099	61,045	55,640	52,901	56,793	23,495	41,243	38,378	31,838	48,018	490,613
Increase/decrease in cash	(65,180)	(12,660)	(27,474)	(78,507)	(76,634)	(77,449)	(91,549)	(40,972)	(49,979)	(47,623)	(42,662)	(23,832)	(634,522)
Financing (increase in equity)	120,000	5,000	35,000	80,000	70,000	80,000	90,000	40,000	50,000	50,000	40,000	30,000	690,000
Cash at end of month/year	54,820	47,160	54,686	56,179	49,544	52,095	50,547	49,575	49,596	51,973	49,310	55,478	55,478

Exhibit FE1-J: Base Case—Cash Flows (US$) Details Years 2 and 3

Maktabi

Cash Flow Calculation (Indirect Calculation)

	Qtr 1 2009	Qtr 2 2009	Qtr 3 2009	Qtr 4 2009	Total	Qtr 1 2010	Qtr 2 2010	Qtr 3 2010	Qtr 4 2010	Total
Cash at start of month/year	13,870	13,870	13,870	13,870	**55,478**	31,007	31,007	31,007	31,007	**124,026**
Cash inflow										
Net profit	15,628	15,628	15,628	15,628	**62,513**	250,291	250,291	250,291	250,291	**1,001,162**
Plus depreciation/amortization	10,587	10,587	10,587	10,587	**42,349**	13,071	13,071	13,071	13,071	**52,282**
Plus changes in:										
Liabilities from performance	71,158	71,158	71,158	71,158	**284,632**	11,363	11,363	11,363	11,363	**45,451**
Wage provisions	186	186	186	186	**745**	941	941	941	941	**3,763**
Tax provisions	0	0	0	0	**0**	12,206	12,206	12,206	12,206	**48,824**
Long-term debt/loans	0	0	0	0	**0**	0	0	0	0	**0**
Total cash inflow	97,560	97,560	97,560	97,560	**390,239**	287,871	287,871	287,871	287,871	**1,151,482**
Cash deployed										
Minus changes in:										
Net receivables from performance	19,144	19,144	19,144	19,144	**76,577**	97,709	97,709	97,709	97,709	**390,836**
Stock	21,014	21,014	21,014	21,014	**84,054**	10,898	10,898	10,898	10,898	**43,592**
Gross fixed assets	82,496	82,496	82,496	82,496	**329,982**	2,883	2,883	2,883	2,883	**11,532**
Total cash deployed	122,653	122,653	122,653	122,653	**490,613**	111,490	111,490	111,490	111,490	**445,960**
Increase/decrease in cash	-27,863	-27,863	-27,863	-27,863	**-111,452**	176,381	176,381	176,381	176,381	**705,522**
Financing (increase in equity)	45,000	45,000	45,000	45,000	**180,000**	0	0	0	0	**0**
Cash at end of month/year	31,007	31,007	31,007	31,007	**124,026**	207,387	207,387	207,387	207,387	**829,547**

Exhibit FE2-A: Worst Case—Assumptions

Maktabi

Assumptions for the Financial Plan (Summary)

All figures shown in Egyptian Pounds

SALES

- The first sales will take place in 11/06
- Average order price structure:
  Business orders 15
  Consumer orders 10

COSTS OF SERVICES PROVIDED

- Average material costs per order:
  Business orders 9
  Consumer orders 7

OPERATING COSTS

- Monthly wages reflect current market rates
- Social costs as percentage of wage costs 0.00%
- Annual rise in wages 10.00%
- The model for the number of employees is given in the financial plan
- Import customs and transportation to distribution center 243 / inbound shipment
- Picking and packing 0 / order
- Shipping 1 / order
- Catalog design will be paid at market rates
- Catalog photos 0 / photo
- Catalog printing 2 / catalog
- Information systems will be paid at market rates
- Sales representative commission on sales 2.00%
- Commissions on sales 0.00%
- Advertising media as a percentage of sales 0.25%
- Promotions as a percentage of sales 0.75%
- Public relations as a percentage of sales 0.25%
- Other marketing expenses as a percentage of sales 0.25%
- Consultants for special projects and auditors will be paid at market rates
- Additional costs per person calculated as follows:

Cost per Person/Month	Training	Office Material	Travel	Communication
Customer service	4	7	3	52
Purchasing	0	3	139	52
Distribution	0	3	10	17
Transportation and AR	0	3	3	17
Publications	0	3	3	17
Information Technologies	0	3	3	17
Marketing and Sales*	3	3	3	17
Finance and Administration	0	3	17	52

* Marketing and Sales training for sales representatives only

- Rent per square metre per month 35.00%
- Provisions for unpaid invoices in percentage of sales 0.00%
- Interest income on liquid assets 0.00%
- Returns as a percent of sales 0.50%
- Income tax 20.00%

BALANCE SHEET

- Debitors are settled within 30 days, creditors within 30 days
- Goods are purchased on average 30 days before the sale of the product/service
- Fixed assets include computers, software, office equipment, and property
- Individual depreciation periods per asset and cost center
- Provisions for wages represent half a monthly salary
- Taxes are paid at the end of the tax period

Exhibit FE2-B: Worst Case—Profit and Loss Statement (US$)

Maktabi

Profit and Loss Statement

Sales	**2007**	**2008**	**2009**	**2010**	**2011**
Business orders	45,826	307,478	393,217	412,435	430,174
Consumer orders	90,783	1,565,217	3,339,130	2,504,348	2,608,696
Total sales	136,609	1,872,696	3,732,348	2,916,783	3,038,870
Cost of services provided	86,747	1,189,162	2,370,041	1,852,157	1,929,682
Gross margin	49,862	683,534	1,362,307	1,064,626	1,109,187
In % of sales	37%	37%	37%	37%	37%
Operating costs					
Customer Service	12,084	28,695	83,488	104,443	108,942
In % of sales	9%	2%	2%	4%	4%
Purchasing	12,344	17,827	19,596	20,153	21,015
In % of sales	9%	1%	1%	1%	1%
Distribution	32,041	120,977	222,365	200,821	206,458
In % of sales	23%	6%	6%	7%	7%
Transportation and Accounts Receivables	11,579	110,349	217,932	170,398	177,823
In % of sales	8%	6%	6%	6%	6%
Publications	21,629	61,075	50,390	50,528	50,912
In % of sales	16%	3%	1%	2%	2%
Information Technologies	37,563	51,001	56,706	59,959	63,771
In % of sales	27%	3%	2%	2%	2%
Marketing and Sales	31,676	110,526	175,336	150,422	158,923
In % of sales	23%	6%	5%	5%	5%
Finance and Administration	78,101	104,222	118,183	117,369	122,830
In % of sales	57%	6%	3%	4%	4%
Total operating costs	237,017	604,673	943,997	874,094	910,675
In % of sales	174%	32%	25%	30%	30%
Operating profit	-187,155	78,861	418,310	190,532	198,512
In % of sales	-137%	4%	11%	7%	7%
Financing expenditure	0	0	0	0	0
Financing income	0	0	0	0	0
Profit before tax	-187,155	78,861	418,310	190,532	198,512
Income tax	0	0	62,003	38,106	39,702
Net profit	-187,155	78,861	356,307	152,425	158,810
In % of sales	-137%	4%	10%	5%	5%

Exhibit FE2-C: Worst Case—Balance Sheet (US$)

Maktabi

Balance Sheet at End of Accounting Year

	2007	2008	2009	2010	2011
Assets					
Liquid assets					
Cash	169,597	310,272	638,212	817,830	1,136,001
Net receivables from customers	43,826	189,130	311,029	243,065	253,239
Stock/inventory (30, 60, or 90 days)	45,853	195,948	153,131	159,541	0
Total liquid assets	259,276	695,351	1,102,372	1,220,436	1,389,241
Gross fixed assets	180,522	230,296	234,991	239,687	239,687
Minus cumulated depreciation	12,006	34,808	61,951	81,991	96,829
Net fixed assets	168,515	195,488	173,040	157,696	142,858
Total assets	**427,792**	**890,839**	**1,275,412**	**1,378,133**	**1,532,099**
Liabilities					
Debt					
Short-term debt					
Open third-party invoices (creditors)	62,184	231,008	241,135	195,924	189,631
Provisions for wages	5,806	6,386	9,024	10,505	11,555
Provisions for taxes	0	0	15,501	9,527	9,926
Total short-term debt	67,990	237,394	265,660	215,955	211,112
Long-term debt					
Loans and mortgages	0	0	0	0	0
Total long-term debt	0	0	0	0	0
Total debt	**67,990**	**237,394**	**265,660**	**215,955**	**211,112**
Equity					
Share capital	546,957	761,739	761,739	761,739	761,739
Reserves	0	0	0	0	0
Profit/loss carried forward	-187,155	-108,294	248,013	400,438	559,248
Total equity	359,802	653,445	1,009,752	1,162,177	1,320,987
Total liabilities	**427,792**	**890,839**	**1,275,412**	**1,378,133**	**1,532,099**

Exhibit FE2-D: Worst Case—Cash Flows (US$)

Maktabi

Cash Flow Calculation

	2007	2008	2009	2010	2011
Cash at beginning of year	**0**	**169,597**	**310,272**	**638,212**	**817,830**
Cash inflow					
Net profit	-187,155	78,861	356,307	152,425	158,810
Plus depreciation/amortization	12,006	22,801	27,144	20,039	14,838
Plus changes in:					
Liabilities from performance	62,184	168,823	10,127	-45,211	-6,293
Wage provisions	5,806	581	2,638	1,481	1,050
Tax provisions	0	0	15,501	-5,974	399
Long-term debt/loans	0	0	0	0	0
Total cash inflow	-107,158	271,066	411,716	122,760	168,804
Cash outflow					
Minus changes in:					
Net receivables from performance	43,826	145,304	121,899	-67,964	10,174
Stock	45,853	150,095	-42,817	6,410	-159,541
Gross fixed assets	180,522	49,774	4,696	4,696	0
Total cash outflow	270,201	345,173	83,777	-56,859	-149,367
Cash increase/decrease	-377,359	-74,108	327,939	179,619	318,171
Financing (increase in equity)	546,957	214,783	0	0	0
Cash at end of year	**169,597**	**310,272**	**638,212**	**817,830**	**1,136,001**

Exhibit FE3-A: Best Case—Assumptions

Maktabi

Assumptions for the Financial Plan (Summary)

All figures shown in Egyptian Pounds

SALES

- The first sales will take place in 11/06
- Average order price structure:
  Business orders 13
  Consumer orders 10

COSTS OF SERVICES PROVIDED

- Average material costs per order:
  Business orders 8
  Consumer orders 6

OPERATING COSTS

- Monthly wages reflect current market rates
- Social costs as percentage of wage costs 0.00%
- Annual rise in wages 10.00%
- The model for the number of employees is given in the financial plan
- Import customs and transportation to distribution center 174 / inbound shipment
- Picking and packing 0.35 / order
- Shipping 0.35 / order
- Catalog design will be paid at market rates
- Catalog photos 0.09 / photo
- Catalog printing 2 / catalog
- Information systems will be paid at market rates
- Sales representative commission on sales 3.00%
- Commissions on sales 0.00%
- Advertising media as a percentage of sales 0.25%
- Promotions as a percentage of sales 0.75%
- Public relations as a percentage of sales 0.25%
- Other marketing expenses as a percentage of sales 0.25%
- Consultants for special projects and auditors will be paid at market rates
- Additional costs per person calculated as follows:

Cost per Person/Month	Training	Office Material	Travel	Communication
Customer service	4	7	3	52
Purchasing	0	3	139	52
Distribution	0	3	10	17
Transportation and AR	0	3	3	17
Publications	0	3	3	17
Information Technologies	0	3	3	17
Marketing and Sales*	3	3	3	17
Finance and Administration	0	3	17	52

* Marketing and Sales training for sales representatives only

- Rent per square metre per month 35.00%
- Provisions for unpaid invoices in percentage of sales 0.00%
- Interest income on liquid assets 0.00%
- Returns as a percent of sales 0.50%
- Income tax 20.00%

BALANCE SHEET

- Debitors are settled within 30 days, creditors within 30 days
- Goods are purchased on average 30 days before the sale of the product/service
- Fixed assets include computers, software, office equipment, and property
- Individual depreciation periods per asset and cost center
- Provisions for wages represent half a monthly salary
- Taxes are paid at the end of the tax period

Exhibit FE3-B: Best Case—Profit and Loss Statement (US$)

Maktabi

Profit and Loss Statement

Sales	2007	2008	2009	2010	2011
Business orders	218,543	863,674	891,913	914,217	936,522
Consumer orders	830,451	4,610,157	7,101,949	9,724,935	9,987,509
Total sales	1,048,994	5,473,831	7,993,862	10,639,153	10,924,030
Cost of services provided	634,641	3,311,668	4,836,286	6,436,687	6,609,038
Gross margin	414,353	2,162,163	3,157,575	4,202,465	4,314,992
In % of sales	40%	40%	40%	40%	40%
Operating costs					
Customer Service	17,451	50,342	132,915	172,506	179,350
In % of sales	2%	1%	2%	2%	2%
Purchasing	15,181	24,996	27,649	28,626	29,678
In % of sales	1%	0%	0%	0%	0%
Distribution	58,487	228,838	338,452	443,752	454,841
In % of sales	6%	4%	4%	4%	4%
Transportation and Accounts Receivables	42,644	201,262	293,544	390,023	400,972
In % of sales	4%	4%	4%	4%	4%
Publications	18,018	51,430	42,606	42,763	43,203
In % of sales	2%	1%	1%	0%	0%
Information Technologies	87,419	117,699	130,540	138,202	146,897
In % of sales	8%	2%	2%	1%	1%
Marketing and Sales	79,113	298,990	412,864	536,258	554,142
In % of sales	8%	5%	5%	5%	5%
Finance and Administration	135,233	183,191	204,931	225,804	237,274
In % of sales	13%	3%	3%	2%	2%
Total operating costs	453,545	1,156,748	1,583,500	1,977,935	2,046,358
In % of sales	43%	21%	20%	19%	19%
Operating profit	-39,193	1,005,415	1,574,075	2,224,531	2,268,634
In % of sales	-4%	18%	20%	21%	21%
Financing expenditure	0	0	0	0	0
Financing income	0	0	0	0	0
Profit before tax	-39,193	1,005,415	1,574,075	2,224,531	2,268,634
Income tax	0	193,244	314,815	444,906	453,727
Net profit	-39,193	812,171	1,259,260	1,779,625	1,814,907
In % of sales	-4%	15%	16%	17%	17%

Exhibit FE3-C: Best Case—Balance Sheet (US$)

Maktabi

Balance Sheet at End of Accounting Year

	2007	2008	2009	2010	2011
Assets					
Liquid assets					
Cash	31,310	784,897	1,849,392	3,600,926	5,942,327
Net receivables from customers	220,387	518,139	666,155	886,596	910,336
Stock/inventory (30, 60, or 90 days)	194,807	399,693	531,958	546,202	0
Total liquid assets	446,504	1,702,729	3,047,505	5,033,724	6,852,663
Gross fixed assets	318,504	423,965	435,096	446,226	446,226
Minus cumulated depreciation	20,415	61,291	111,755	151,122	181,579
Net fixed assets	298,089	362,675	323,341	295,104	264,647
Total assets	**744,594**	**2,065,404**	**3,370,846**	**5,328,828**	**7,117,311**
Liabilities					
Debt					
Short-term debt					
Open third-party invoices (creditors)	226,647	458,955	483,003	626,164	595,751
Provisions for wages	10,183	11,201	15,162	17,835	19,619
Provisions for taxes	0	60,531	78,704	111,227	113,432
Total short-term debt	236,830	530,687	576,869	755,226	728,801
Long-term debt					
Loans and mortgages	0	0	0	0	0
Total long-term debt	0	0	0	0	0
Total debt	**236,830**	**530,687**	**576,869**	**755,226**	**728,801**
Equity					
Share capital	546,957	761,739	761,739	761,739	761,739
Reserves	0	0	0	0	0
Profit/loss carried forward	-39,193	772,978	2,032,238	3,811,863	5,626,770
Total equity	507,764	1,534,717	2,793,977	4,573,602	6,388,509
Total liabilities	**744,594**	**2,065,404**	**3,370,846**	**5,328,828**	**7,117,311**

Exhibit FE3-D: Best Case—Cash Flows (US$)

Maktabi

Cash Flow Calculation

	2007	2008	2009	2010	2011
Cash at beginning of year	**0**	**31,310**	**784,897**	**1,849,392**	**3,600,926**
Cash inflow					
Net profit	-39,193	812,171	1,259,260	1,779,625	1,814,907
Plus depreciation/amortization	20,415	40,876	50,464	39,368	30,456
Plus changes in:					
Liabilities from performance	226,647	232,308	24,048	143,161	-30,413
Wage provisions	10,183	1,018	3,961	2,674	1,784
Tax provisions	0	60,531	18,173	32,523	2,205
Long-term debt/loans	0	0	0	0	0
Total cash inflow	218,052	1,146,904	1,355,906	1,997,350	1,818,939
Cash outflow					
Minus changes in:					
Net receivables from performance	220,387	297,752	148,016	220,441	23,740
Stock	194,807	204,886	132,265	14,244	-546,202
Gross fixed assets	318,504	105,461	11,130	11,130	0
Total cash outflow	733,699	608,099	291,411	245,815	-522,462
Cash increase/decrease	-515,647	538,805	1,064,495	1,751,535	2,341,401
Financing (increase in equity)	546,957	214,783	0	0	0
Cash at end of year	**31,310**	**784,897**	**1,849,392**	**3,600,926**	**5,942,327**

Exhibit OM1: Product Group Listing, Phase I

Phase I Beginning at Year 0

Phase I			
Product Group	**Product Category**	**Product Type**	**Product Item**
Office Supplies	Binders and Accessories	Presentation Binders	0.5" Presentation Binders
Office Supplies	Binders and Accessories	Presentation Binders	1.0" Presentation Binders
Office Supplies	Binders and Accessories	Presentation Binders	1.5" Presentation Binders
Office Supplies	Binders and Accessories	Presentation Binders	2.0" Presentation Binders
Office Supplies	Binders and Accessories	Presentation Binders	Easel Binders
Office Supplies	Binders and Accessories	Reference Binders	0.5" Reference Binders
Office Supplies	Binders and Accessories	Reference Binders	1.0" Reference Binders
Office Supplies	Binders and Accessories	Reference Binders	1.5" Reference Binders
Office Supplies	Binders and Accessories	Reference Binders	2.0" Reference Binders
Office Supplies	Binders and Accessories	Reference Binders	3.0" Reference Binders
Office Supplies	Binders and Accessories	Storage Binders	4.0" Storage Binders
Office Supplies	Binders and Accessories	Storage Binders	5.0" Storage Binders
Office Supplies	Binders and Accessories	Storage Binders	Archival and Heavy Duty Storage Binders
Office Supplies	Binders and Accessories	Binder Accessories	Multiple
Office Supplies	Binders and Accessories	Index Dividers	Customizable Tabs
Office Supplies	Binders and Accessories	Index Dividers	Preprinted Tabs
Office Supplies	Binders and Accessories	Index Dividers	Insertable and Write-On Tabs
Office Supplies	Binders and Accessories	Index Dividers	Untabbed Dividers
Office Supplies	Binders and Accessories	Index Dividers	Adhesive Tabs
Office Supplies	Binders and Accessories	Report Covers	Clear Front Report Covers
Office Supplies	Binders and Accessories	Report Covers	Fastener Folders With Pockets
Office Supplies	Binders and Accessories	Report Covers	Fastener Folders Without Pockets
Office Supplies	Binders and Accessories	Report Covers	Presentation Folders
Office Supplies	Binders and Accessories	Sheet Protectors	Presentation Sheet Protectors
Office Supplies	Binders and Accessories	Sheet Protectors	Specialty Sheet Protectors
Office Supplies	Binders and Accessories	Specialty Binders	Data, Post, and Hanging Binders
Office Supplies	Binders and Accessories	Specialty Binders	Specialty-Sized Binders
Office Supplies	Binders and Accessories	Two-Pocket Portfolios	Presentation Folders
Office Supplies	Binders and Accessories	Two-Pocket Portfolios	Two-Pocket Portfolios
Office Supplies	Boards and Easels	Dry-Erase Boards	Dry-Erase Premium Magnetic
Office Supplies	Boards and Easels	Dry-Erase Boards	Dry-Erase Premium Non-Magnetic
Office Supplies	Boards and Easels	Dry-Erase Boards	Dry-Erase Commercial
Office Supplies	Boards and Easels	Dry-Erase Boards	Dry-Erase Economy
Office Supplies	Boards and Easels	Dry-Erase Boards	Electronic Whiteboards
Office Supplies	Boards and Easels	Dry-Erase Boards	1.5 × 2 Boards
Office Supplies	Boards and Easels	Dry-Erase Boards	2 × 3 Boards
Office Supplies	Boards and Easels	Dry-Erase Boards	3 × 4 Boards
Office Supplies	Boards and Easels	Dry-Erase Boards	3 × 5 Boards

Phase I			
Product Group	**Product Category**	**Product Type**	**Product Item**
Office Supplies	Boards and Easels	Dry-Erase Boards	4 × 6 Boards
Office Supplies	Boards and Easels	Dry-Erase Boards	4 × 8 Boards
Office Supplies	Boards and Easels	Bulletin Boards	Bulletin Boards—Premium
Office Supplies	Boards and Easels	Bulletin Boards	Bulletin Boards—Commercial
Office Supplies	Boards and Easels	Bulletin Boards	Bulletin Boards—Economy
Office Supplies	Boards and Easels	Bulletin Boards	1.5 × 2 Boards
Office Supplies	Boards and Easels	Bulletin Boards	2 × 3 Boards
Office Supplies	Boards and Easels	Bulletin Boards	3 × 4 Boards
Office Supplies	Boards and Easels	Bulletin Boards	3 × 5 Boards
Office Supplies	Boards and Easels	Bulletin Boards	4 × 6 Boards
Office Supplies	Boards and Easels	Bulletin Boards	4 × 8 Boards
Office Supplies	Boards and Easels	Bulletin Boards	Bulletin Boards—Stylish
Office Supplies	Boards and Easels	Easels and Easel Pads	Pads Easels
Office Supplies	Boards and Easels	Cubicle and Personal-Size Boards	Cubicle and Personal-Size Bulletin Boards
Office Supplies	Boards and Easels	Cubicle and Personal-Size Boards	Cubicle and Personal-Size Dry-Erase Boards
Office Supplies	Boards and Easels	Chalkboards and Accessories	Chalkboards and Accessories
Office Supplies	Boards and Easels	Letter/Message Boards and Accessories	Letter/Message Boards and Accessories
Office Supplies	Boards and Easels	Cubicle Management Systems	Cubicle Management Systems
Office Supplies	Boards and Easels	Conference Cabinets	Conference Cabinets
Office Supplies	Boards and Easels	Dry-Erase Markers and Accessories	Dry-Erase Accessories
Office Supplies	Boards and Easels	Dry-Erase Markers and Accessories	Dry-Erase Marker Kits
Office Supplies	Boards and Easels	Dry-Erase Markers and Accessories	Dry-Erase Markers
Office Supplies	Boards and Easels	Dry-Erase Magnetic Accessories	Dry-Erase Magnetic Accessories
Office Supplies	Boards and Easels	Presentation Boards	Presentation Boards
Office Supplies	Boards and Easels	Dry-Erase and Bulletin Board Systems	Dry-Erase and Bulletin Board
Office Supplies	Calendars and Planners	Calendars and Planners	2006 Calendars and Planners
Office Supplies	Calendars and Planners	Calendars and Planners	Academic (Aug-Jul)
Office Supplies	Calendars and Planners	Calendars and Planners	Calendars and Planners
Office Supplies	Calendars and Planners	Calendars and Planners	Personal Organizers
Office Supplies	Calendars and Planners	Calendars and Planners	Undated Organizers and Calendars
Office Supplies	Cleaning and Breakroom	Paper Products	Paper Towels
Office Supplies	Cleaning and Breakroom	Paper Products	Facial Tissue
Office Supplies	Cleaning and Breakroom	Paper Products	Bathroom Tissue
Office Supplies	Cleaning and Breakroom	Cleaning Supplies	All-Purpose Cleaners
Office Supplies	Cleaning and Breakroom	Cleaning Supplies	Pre-Moistened Wiped

(*Continued*)

Exhibit OM1 (Continued)

Phase I			
Product Group	**Product Category**	**Product Type**	**Product Item**
Office Supplies	Cleaning and Breakroom	Cleaning Supplies	Hand Soaps, Sanitizers, and Lotions
Office Supplies	Cleaning and Breakroom	Breakroom Supplies	Cups and Lids
Office Supplies	Cleaning and Breakroom	Breakroom Supplies	Cutlery
Office Supplies	Cleaning and Breakroom	Breakroom Supplies	Plates and Bowls
Office Supplies	Cleaning and Breakroom	Trash Bags and Cans	Trashbags
Office Supplies	Cleaning and Breakroom	Trash Bags and Cans	Plastic Wastebaskets
Office Supplies	Cleaning and Breakroom	Trash Bags and Cans	Fire Safe and Metal
Office Supplies	Cleaning and Breakroom	Trash Bags and Cans	Wastebackets
Office Supplies	Cleaning and Breakroom	Lightbulbs and Extension Cords	Extension Cords
Office Supplies	Cleaning and Breakroom	Lightbulbs and Extension Cords	Light Bulbs
Office Supplies	Cleaning and Breakroom	Equipment, Storage	Padlocks
Office Supplies	Cleaning and Breakroom	Equipment, Storage	Step Stools and Ladders
Office Supplies	Cleaning and Breakroom	Equipment, Storage	Flashlights
Office Supplies	Desktop Organizers	Desktop Organizers, Holders, and Accessories	Business Card Holders
Office Supplies	Desktop Organizers	Desktop Organizers, Holders, and Accessories	Desk Pads
Office Supplies	Desktop Organizers	Desktop Organizers, Holders, and Accessories	Desktop File Sorters
Office Supplies	Desktop Organizers	Desk Sets/Organizers	Desk Organizer Collections—Plastic
Office Supplies	Desktop Organizers	Desk Sets/Organizers	Desk Organizer Collections—Wire Mesh and Metal
Office Supplies	Desktop Organizers	Desk Sets/Organizers	Desk Organizer Collections—Wood and Faux Leather
Office Supplies	Desktop Organizers	Drawer Organizers	Drawer Organizers
Office Supplies	Desktop Organizers	Wall Art	Wall Art
Office Supplies	Desktop Organizers	Wall Organizers and Pockets	Wall File Organizer Systems
Office Supplies	Desktop Organizers	Wall Organizers and Pockets	Wall Files
Office Supplies	Desktop Organizers	Rolodex Card Organizers	Business Card Books
Office Supplies	Desktop Organizers	Rolodex Card Organizers	Card Files and Accessories
Office Supplies	Desktop Organizers	Cubicle and Partition Organizers and Accessories	Cubicle and Partition
Office Supplies	Desktop Organizers	Cubicle and Partition Organizers and Accessories	Organizers and Accessories
Office Supplies	Desktop Organizers	Index Cards, Guides, and Files	Index Card Files
Office Supplies	Desktop Organizers	Index Cards, Guides, and Files	Index Cards Guides

Phase I			
Product Group	**Product Category**	**Product Type**	**Product Item**
Office Supplies	Desktop Organizers	Index Cards, Guides, and Files	Index Cards
Office Supplies	Desktop Organizers	Desktop Computer Accessories	Desktop Copyholders
Office Supplies	Desktop Organizers	Desktop Computer Accessories	Desktop Drawers
Office Supplies	Desktop Organizers	Desktop Computer Accessories	Keyboard Wrist Rests
Office Supplies	Desktop Organizers	Bookends, Book Shelves, and Magazine Files	Bookends and Book Shelves
Office Supplies	Desktop Organizers	Bookends, Book Shelves, and Magazine Files	Magazine Files
Office Supplies	Desktop Organizers	Decorative Accessories	Clocks
Office Supplies	Desktop Organizers	Decorative Accessories	Frames
Office Supplies	Desktop Organizers	Decorative Accessories	Maps, Magnifiers, and Flags
Office Supplies	Desktop Organizers	Supply Closet Organizers	Supply Closet Organizers
Office Supplies	Envelopes and Forms	Business Envelopes	Gummed Closure
Office Supplies	Envelopes and Forms	Business Envelopes	Pull and Seal/Self-Sealing
Office Supplies	Envelopes and Forms	Business Envelopes	Security
Office Supplies	Envelopes and Forms	Mailers and Tubes	Bubble Mailers
Office Supplies	Envelopes and Forms	Mailers and Tubes	Corrugated Mailers
Office Supplies	Envelopes and Forms	Mailers and Tubes	Flat/Media Mailers
Office Supplies	Envelopes and Forms	Large Format/ Catalog Envelopes	Clasp
Office Supplies	Envelopes and Forms	Large Format/ Catalog Envelopes	Gummed Closure
Office Supplies	Envelopes and Forms	Large Format/ Catalog Envelopes	Padded
Office Supplies	Envelopes and Forms	Specialty Envelopes	Coin and Media
Office Supplies	Envelopes and Forms	Specialty Envelopes	Colored and Invitation
Office Supplies	Envelopes and Forms	Specialty Envelopes	Document and Booklet
Office Supplies	Envelopes and Forms	Forms	Pads—Message/Memo
Office Supplies	Envelopes and Forms	Forms	Automotive
Office Supplies	Envelopes and Forms	Forms	Clipboards
Office Supplies	Envelopes and Forms	Columnar Pads, Journal, and Record Keeping	Columnar Pads
Office Supplies	Envelopes and Forms	Columnar Pads, Journal, and Record Keeping	Journals and Record Keeping
Office Supplies	Envelopes and Forms	Tax Forms	Tax Forms
Office Supplies	Filing Supplies	Filing Supplies	File Folders
Office Supplies	Filing Supplies	Filing Supplies	Hanging File Folders
Office Supplies	Filing Supplies	Filing Supplies	File Jackets and Sorters
Office Supplies	Filing Supplies	Filing Supplies	Filing Accessories
Office Supplies	Filing Supplies	Filing Supplies	End Tab Filing
Office Supplies	Filing Supplies	Filing Supplies	Expandable Files
Office Supplies	Filing Supplies	Filing Supplies	Medical Filing
Office Supplies	Filing Supplies	Filing Supplies	100% Recycled Filing

(*Continued*)

Exhibit OM1 (Continued)

Phase I			
Product Group	**Product Category**	**Product Type**	**Product Item**
Office Supplies	General Supplies	Tape, Glue, and Adhesives	Invisible Tape
Office Supplies	General Supplies	Tape, Glue, and Adhesives	Tape Dispensers
Office Supplies	General Supplies	Tape, Glue, and Adhesives	Mounting and Specialty Tapes
Office Supplies	General Supplies	Tape, Glue, and Adhesives	VELCRO Brand Fasteners
Office Supplies	General Supplies	Tape, Glue, and Adhesives	Glue and Adhesive Products
Office Supplies	General Supplies	Tape, Glue, and Adhesives	Vinyl Numbers and Letters
Office Supplies	General Supplies	Clips, Tacks, and Rubber Bands	Binder Clips
Office Supplies	General Supplies	Clips, Tacks, and Rubber Bands	Paper Clip Holders
Office Supplies	General Supplies	Clips, Tacks, and Rubber Bands	Paper Clips
Office Supplies	General Supplies	Clips, Tacks, and Rubber Bands	Pins and Tacks
Office Supplies	General Supplies	Clips, Tacks, and Rubber Bands	Rubber Bands
Office Supplies	General Supplies	Clips, Tacks, and Rubber Bands	Specialty Clips and Fasteners
Office Supplies	General Supplies	Scissors, Rulers, and Paper Trimmers	Scissors
Office Supplies	General Supplies	Scissors, Rulers, and Paper Trimmers	Scissors for Kids
Office Supplies	General Supplies	Scissors, Rulers, and Paper Trimmers	Paper Trimmers
Office Supplies	General Supplies	Scissors, Rulers, and Paper Trimmers	Paper Trimmer Accessories
Office Supplies	General Supplies	Scissors, Rulers, and Paper Trimmers	Rulers
Office Supplies	General Supplies	Scissors, Rulers, and Paper Trimmers	Letter Openers
Office Supplies	General Supplies	Scissors, Rulers, and Paper Trimmers	X-Acto and Utility Knives
Office Supplies	General Supplies	Scissors, Rulers, and Paper Trimmers	Drafting Supplies
Office Supplies	General Supplies	Scissors, Rulers, and Paper Trimmers	Clipboards
Office Supplies	General Supplies	Staplers and Staples	Desktop Staples
Office Supplies	General Supplies	Staplers and Staples	Electic Staplers
Office Supplies	General Supplies	Staplers and Staples	Heavy-Duty Staplers
Office Supplies	General Supplies	Staplers and Staples	Stapel Removers
Office Supplies	General Supplies	Staplers and Staples	Staples
Office Supplies	General Supplies	Paper Punches	Desktop Paper Punches
Office Supplies	General Supplies	Paper Punches	Heavy-Duty Paper Punches
Office Supplies	General Supplies	Paper Punches	Electric Paper Punches
Office Supplies	General Supplies	Paper Punches	1-Hole Paper Punch
Office Supplies	General Supplies	Paper Punches	2-Hole Paper Punch

Phase I			
Product Group	**Product Category**	**Product Type**	**Product Item**
Office Supplies	General Supplies	Paper Punches	Paper Punch Accessories
Office Supplies	General Supplies	Batteries	Alkaline/Lithium Batteries
Office Supplies	General Supplies	Batteries	AA/AAA/9V Rechargeale
Office Supplies	General Supplies	Batteries	AA/AAA/C/D/9V Chargers
Office Supplies	General Supplies	Batteries	Digital Camera Batteries
Office Supplies	General Supplies	Batteries	Camcorder Batteries
Office Supplies	General Supplies	Batteries	Camcorder/Digital Camera Chargers
Office Supplies	General Supplies	Batteries	Camcorder/Digital Camera Power Supplies
Office Supplies	General Supplies	Batteries	Notebook Batteries
Office Supplies	General Supplies	Batteries	PDA Batteries
Office Supplies	General Supplies	Batteries	MP3 Batteries
Office Supplies	General Supplies	Batteries	Portable DVD Player Batteries
Office Supplies	General Supplies	Batteries	Cordless Phone Batteries
Office Supplies	General Supplies	Batteries	Cell Phone Batteries
Office Supplies	Luggage and Briefcases	Luggage and Briefcases	Briefcases
Office Supplies	Luggage and Briefcases	Luggage and Briefcases	Catalog Cases
Office Supplies	Luggage and Briefcases	Luggage and Briefcases	Computer Backpacks
Office Supplies	Luggage and Briefcases	Luggage and Briefcases	Computer Bags and Accessories
Office Supplies	Luggage and Briefcases	Luggage and Briefcases	Gift Gallery
Office Supplies	Luggage and Briefcases	Luggage and Briefcases	Luggage
Office Supplies	Luggage and Briefcases	Luggage and Briefcases	Messenger Bags
Office Supplies	Luggage and Briefcases	Luggage and Briefcases	Padfolios
Office Supplies	Luggage and Briefcases	Luggage and Briefcases	Presentation Portfolios
Office Supplies	Luggage and Briefcases	Luggage and Briefcases	Travel Accessories
Office Supplies	Luggage and Briefcases	Luggage and Briefcases	Women's Totes
Office Supplies	Mail and Ship/Moving	Mailers and Tubes	Bubble Mailers
Office Supplies	Mail and Ship/Moving	Mailers and Tubes	Corrugated Mailers
Office Supplies	Mail and Ship/Moving	Mailers and Tubes	Flat/Media Mailers
Office Supplies	Mail and Ship/Moving	Shipping and Moving Boxes	Shipping Boxes—Fixed Depth
Office Supplies	Mail and Ship/Moving	Shipping and Moving Boxes	Shipping Boxes—Multi Depth
Office Supplies	Mail and Ship/Moving	Shipping and Moving Boxes	Moving Boxes and Kits
Office Supplies	Mail and Ship/Moving	Bubble Wrap and Packing Material	Bubble Wrap—Adhesive
Office Supplies	Mail and Ship/Moving	Bubble Wrap and Packing Material	Bubble Wrap—Standard
Office Supplies	Mail and Ship/Moving	Bubble Wrap and Packing Material	Foam Rolls
Office Supplies	Mail and Ship/Moving	Packaging Tape and Dispensers	Masking and Duct Tape
Office Supplies	Mail and Ship/Moving	Packaging Tape and Dispensers	Packaging Tape
Office Supplies	Mail and Ship/Moving	Packaging Tape and Dispensers	Packaging Tape Dispensers

(*Continued*)

Exhibit OM1 (Continued)

Phase I			
Product Group	**Product Category**	**Product Type**	**Product Item**
Office Supplies	Mail and Ship/Moving	Mailroom Equipment and Supplies	Handtrucks and Dollies
Office Supplies	Mail and Ship/Moving	Mailroom Equipment and Supplies	Letter Folders
Office Supplies	Mail and Ship/Moving	Mailroom Equipment and Supplies	Literature Holders—Wall Style
Office Supplies	Mail and Ship/Moving	Poly Bags	Flat Poly Bags
Office Supplies	Mail and Ship/Moving	Poly Bags	Reclosable Poly Bags
Office Supplies	Mail and Ship/Moving	Poly Bags	Reclosable Poly Bags with White Block
Office Supplies	Mail and Ship/Moving	Recycled Mailing Supplies	Recycled Mailers
Office Supplies	Mail and Ship/Moving	Recycled Mailing Supplies	Recycled Mailing Tubes
Office Supplies	Mail and Ship/Moving	Recycled Mailing Supplies	Shipping Boxes—Fixed Depth
Office Supplies	Mail and Ship/Moving	Postal Scales and Meters	Postage Meters
Office Supplies	Mail and Ship/Moving	Postal Scales and Meters	Shipping and Postal Scales
Office Supplies	Mail and Ship/Moving	Shipping and Mailing Labels	Inkjet Address Labels
Office Supplies	Mail and Ship/Moving	Shipping and Mailing Labels	Label Printers
Office Supplies	Mail and Ship/Moving	Shipping and Mailing Labels	Laser Address Labels
Office Supplies	Mail and Ship/Moving	Stretch Wrap and Dispensers	Clear Stretch Wrap
Office Supplies	Mail and Ship/Moving	Stretch Wrap and Dispensers	Goodwrappers Stretch Wrap
Office Supplies	Mail and Ship/Moving	Stretch Wrap and Dispensers	Strapping Kits
Office Supplies	Mail and Ship/Moving	Stamps and Pads	Electronic Stamps
Office Supplies	Mail and Ship/Moving	Stamps and Pads	Pre-Inked Stamps
Office Supplies	Mail and Ship/Moving	Stamps and Pads	Self-Inking Stamps
Office Supplies	Paper and Pads	Paper and Pads	Cards and Badges
Office Supplies	Paper and Pads	Paper and Pads	Brochure and Specialty
Office Supplies	Paper and Pads	Paper and Pads	Colored Paper
Office Supplies	Paper and Pads	Paper and Pads	Computer Paper
Office Supplies	Paper and Pads	Paper and Pads	Cover and Card Stock
Office Supplies	Paper and Pads	Paper and Pads	Fax Paper
Office Supplies	Paper and Pads	Paper and Pads	Inkjet Paper
Office Supplies	Paper and Pads	Paper and Pads	Laser Paper
Office Supplies	Paper and Pads	Paper and Pads	Multiuse and Copy Paper
Office Supplies	Paper and Pads	Paper and Pads	Notebooks, Pads, and Filler Paper
Office Supplies	Paper and Pads	Paper and Pads	Photo Paper
Office Supplies	Paper and Pads	Paper and Pads	Printing Paper
Office Supplies	Paper and Pads	Paper and Pads	Recycled Paper

Phase I			
Product Group	**Product Category**	**Product Type**	**Product Item**
Office Supplies	Paper and Pads	Paper and Pads	Register and Calculator Rolls
Office Supplies	Paper and Pads	Paper and Pads	Stationary
Office Supplies	Paper and Pads	Paper and Pads	Wide Format Paper
Office Supplies	Self-Stick Notes	Super Sticky Notes	Super Sticky Notes
Office Supplies	Self-Stick Notes	Staples Sticky Notes	Flat Notes
Office Supplies	Self-Stick Notes	Staples Sticky Notes	Memo Cubes
Office Supplies	Self-Stick Notes	Staples Sticky Notes	Pop-Up Notes
Office Supplies	Self-Stick Notes	Self-Stick Notes	Flat Notes
Office Supplies	Self-Stick Notes	Self-Stick Notes	Memo Cubes
Office Supplies	Self-Stick Notes	Self-Stick Notes	Pop-Up Notes
Office Supplies	Self-Stick Notes	Recycled Self-Stick Notes	Recycled Flat Notes
Office Supplies	Self-Stick Notes	Recycled Self-Stick Notes	Recycled Pop-Up Notes
Office Supplies	Self-Stick Notes	Self-Stick Note Dispensers	Bonus Packs
Office Supplies	Self-Stick Notes	Self-Stick Note Dispensers	Flat Note Dispensers
Office Supplies	Self-Stick Notes	Self-Stick Note Dispensers	Pop-Up Note Dispensers
Office Supplies	Self-Stick Notes	Self-Stick Flags and Index Tabs	Flags
Office Supplies	Self-Stick Notes	Self-Stick Flags and Index Tabs	Flag Dispensers
Office Supplies	Self-Stick Notes	Self-Stick Flags and Index Tabs	Page Markers and Tabs
Office Supplies	Self-Stick Notes	Index Cards, Guides, and Files	Index Card Files
Office Supplies	Self-Stick Notes	Index Cards, Guides, and Files	Index Card Guides
Office Supplies	Self-Stick Notes	Index Cards, Guides, and Files	Index Cards
Office Supplies	Self-Stick Notes	Message Pads and Memo Slips	Pads—Message/Memo
Office Supplies	Self-Stick Notes	Self-Stick Easel Pads and Self-Stick Boards	Self-Stick Easel Pads
Office Supplies	Self-Stick Notes	Self-Stick Easel Pads and Self-Stick Boards	Self-Stick Accessories
Technology	Batteries, Surge, and UPS	Batteries, Surge, and UPS	Batteries
Technology	Batteries, Surge, and UPS	Batteries, Surge, and UPS	Battery Backups/UPS
Technology	Batteries, Surge, and UPS	Batteries, Surge, and UPS	Surge Protectors
Technology	Office Machines and Calculators	Office Machines and Calculators	Calculators

Exhibit OM1: Product Group Listing, Phase II

Phase II Beginning at Year 2

Phase II			
Product Group	**Product Category**	**Product Type**	**Product Item**
Office Supplies	Cleaning and Breakroom	Food and Beverage	Beverages
Office Supplies	Cleaning and Breakroom	Food and Beverage	Snack
Office Supplies	Cleaning and Breakroom	Food and Beverage	Coffee
Office Supplies	Cleaning and Breakroom	Appliances	Refrigerators
Office Supplies	Cleaning and Breakroom	Appliances	Water Dispensors and Filtration
Office Supplies	Cleaning and Breakroom	Appliances	Heaters
Office Supplies	Cleaning and Breakroom	First Aid and Safety	Aspirin and Pain Relievers
Office Supplies	Cleaning and Breakroom	First Aid and Safety	Band-Aids and Bandages
Office Supplies	Cleaning and Breakroom	First Aid and Safety	First Aid Kits
Office Supplies	Cleaning and Breakroom	Healthcare Products	Bandages, Wraps, and Masks
Office Supplies	Cleaning and Breakroom	Healthcare Products	Cleaners and Sanitizers
Office Supplies	Cleaning and Breakroom	Healthcare Products	Diagnostic Equipment
Technology	Computer Accessories	Notebook Accessories	Adapters, Cords, and Power
Technology	Computer Accessories	Notebook Accessories	Computer Cases—Nonrolling
Technology	Computer Accessories	Notebook Accessories	Keypads and Headphones
Technology	Computer Accessories	Mouse Pads and Wrist Pads	Keyboard Wrist Rests
Technology	Computer Accessories	Mouse Pads and Wrist Pads	Mouse Pads
Technology	Computer Accessories	Mouse Pads and Wrist Pads	Mouse Pads With Wrist Rests
Technology	Computer Accessories	Monitor and Machine Stands	CPU Stands
Technology	Computer Accessories	Monitor and Machine Stands	LCD Monitor/Plasma Mounts
Technology	Computer Accessories	Monitor and Machine Stands	Monitor Arms
Technology	Computer Accessories	Screen Filters/Protectors	CRT 13"–15" Filters
Technology	Computer Accessories	Screen Filters/Protectors	LCD 13"–15" Filters
Technology	Computer Accessories	Screen Filters/Protectors	Notebook Filters
Technology	Computer Accessories	Keyboard Drawers	Articulating Drawers
Technology	Computer Accessories	Keyboard Drawers	Desktop Drawers
Technology	Computer Accessories	Keyboard Drawers	Underdesk Drawers
Technology	Computer Accessories	Copyholders	Desktop Copyholders
Technology	Computer Accessories	Copyholders	Monitor Mount Copyholders
Technology	Computer Accessories	Media Storage	Case Storage
Technology	Computer Accessories	Media Storage	Desktop Storage
Technology	Computer Accessories	Media Storage	Filing/Binder Storage
Technology	Computer Accessories	Cleaning and Maintenance	Air Dusters
Technology	Computer Accessories	Cleaning and Maintenance	CD/DVD Maintenance
Technology	Computer Accessories	Cleaning and Maintenance	Cloths and Wipes
Technology	Computer Accessories	Back and Foot Rests	Back/Seat Rests
Technology	Computer Accessories	Back and Foot Rests	Foot Rests
Technology	Computer Accessories	Keyboards	Corded Keyboard

Phase II			
Product Group	**Product Category**	**Product Type**	**Product Item**
Technology	Computer Accessories	Keyboards	Cordless Keyboard
Technology	Computer Accessories	Keyboards	Keypads and Headphones
Technology	Computer Accessories	Mice	Corded Mice
Technology	Computer Accessories	Mice	Cordless Mice
Technology	Computer Accessories	Mice	Mice and Keyboard Bundles
Technology	Computer Accessories	Speakers and Headsets	Headsets
Technology	Computer Accessories	Speakers and Headsets	Speakers
Technology	Computers and PDAs	Build Your Own Pc	Build Your Own Desktop
Technology	Computers and PDAs	Build Your Own Pc	Build Your Own Notebook
Technology	Computers and PDAs	Pre-Configured PCs	Desktops
Technology	Computers and PDAs	Pre-Configured PCs	Notebooks
Technology	Computers and PDAs	PDAs and Handheld PCs	Palm Powered
Technology	Computers and PDAs	PDAs and Handheld PCs	Pocket PC Based
Technology	Computers and PDAs	Electronic Organizers	Electronic Organizers
Technology	Computers and PDAs	Electronic Organizers	Electronic Reference
Technology	Computers and PDAs	Notebook Accessories	Adapters, Cords, and Power
Technology	Computers and PDAs	Notebook Accessories	Computer Cases—Nonrolling
Technology	Computers and PDAs	Notebook Accessories	Internal Notebok Hard Drives
Technology	Computers and PDAs	Notebook Accessories	Keypads and Headphones
Technology	Computers and PDAs	Notebook Accessories	Locks, Lights, and Fans
Technology	Computers and PDAs	Notebook Accessories	Notebook Batteries
Technology	Computers and PDAs	Notebook Accessories	Notebook Memory
Technology	Computers and PDAs	Notebook Accessories	Notebook Stands and Pads
Technology	Computers and PDAs	Notebook Accessories	Travel Mice
Technology	Computers and PDAs	PDA Accessories	PDA Adapters and Cables
Technology	Computers and PDAs	PDA Accessories	PDA Anti-Virus Software
Technology	Computers and PDAs	PDA Accessories	PDA Cases and Protectors
Technology	Computers and PDAs	PDA Accessories	PDA Cradles and Chargers
Technology	Computers and PDAs	PDA Accessories	PDA Expansion
Technology	Computers and PDAs	PDA Accessories	Cards/Modems
Technology	Computers and PDAs	PDA Accessories	PDA Financial Software
Technology	Computers and PDAs	PDA Accessories	PDA Input Devices
Technology	Computers and PDAs	PDA Accessories	PDA Productivity Software
Technology	Computers and PDAs	PDA Accessories	PDA Reference Software
Technology	Copiers and Fax	Copiers and Fax	All-in-One Machines
Technology	Copiers and Fax	Copiers and Fax	Copiers
Technology	Copiers and Fax	Copiers and Fax	Fax Machines
Technology	Digital Scanners and Scanners	Digital Scanners and Scanners	Digital Cameras
Technology	Digital Scanners and Scanners	Digital Scanners and Scanners	Digital Camera Accessories
Technology	Digital Scanners and Scanners	Digital Scanners and Scanners	Digital Camcorders
Technology	Digital Scanners and Scanners	Digital Scanners and Scanners	PC and Web Cameras

(*Continued*)

Exhibit OM1 (Continued)

Phase II			
Product Group	**Product Category**	**Product Type**	**Product Item**
Technology	Digital Scanners and Scanners	Digital Scanners and Scanners	Scanners
Technology	Digital Scanners and Scanners	Digital Scanners and Scanners	Flash Memory
Technology	Digital Scanners and Scanners	Digital Scanners and Scanners	Photo Paper
Technology	Digital Scanners and Scanners	Digital Scanners and Scanners	Photo Printers
Technology	Digital Scanners and Scanners	Digital Scanners and Scanners	Security Cameras
Technology	Digital Scanners and Scanners	Digital Scanners and Scanners	Photo Center
Technology	Digital Scanners and Scanners	Digital Scanners and Scanners	Instant Cameras and Film
Technology	Drives and Media	Drives and Media	CD Drives
Technology	Drives and Media	Drives and Media	CD Media
Technology	Drives and Media	Drives and Media	Floppy Drives
Technology	Drives and Media	Drives and Media	Media Labels
Technology	Drives and Media	Drives and Media	Floppy Diskettes
Technology	Drives and Media	Drives and Media	Hard Drives
Technology	Drives and Media	Drives and Media	Media Storage
Technology	Drives and Media	Drives and Media	Tape Backup and Data Cartridges
Technology	Drives and Media	Drives and Media	USB Flash Drives
Technology	Drives and Media	Drives and Media	Zip Drives
Technology	Drives and Media	Drives and Media	Zip Media
Technology	Drives and Media	Drives and Media	REV Media
Technology	GPS and Satellite Radio	GPS and Satellite Radio	Portable Automotive GPS
Technology	GPS and Satellite Radio	GPS and Satellite Radio	PDA and Notebook GPS
Technology	GPS and Satellite Radio	GPS and Satellite Radio	Handheld GPS
Technology	GPS and Satellite Radio	GPS and Satellite Radio	Marine GPS
Technology	GPS and Satellite Radio	GPS and Satellite Radio	GPS Accessories
Technology	GPS and Satellite Radio	GPS and Satellite Radio	XM Satellite Radio
Technology	Ink and Toner Finder	Ink and Toner Finder	All Brands
Technology	MP3 and Media Players	MP3 and Media Players	MP3/Digital Audio Players
Technology	MP3 and Media Players	MP3 and Media Players	MP3 Accessories
Technology	MP3 and Media Players	MP3 and Media Players	Media Players
Technology	Monitors and Digital Projectors	Monitors and Digital Projectors	CRT Monitors
Technology	Monitors and Digital Projectors	Monitors and Digital Projectors	LCD (Flat Panel) Monitors
Technology	Monitors and Digital Projectors	Monitors and Digital Projectors	Plasma and LCD Televisions
Technology	Monitors and Digital Projectors	Monitors and Digital Projectors	Monitor Accessories

Phase II			
Product Group	**Product Category**	**Product Type**	**Product Item**
Technology	Monitors and Digital Projectors	Monitors and Digital Projectors	DVD Players and Televisions
Technology	Monitors and Digital Projectors	Monitors and Digital Projectors	Digital Projectors
Technology	Networking and Cables	Networking and Cables	Wireless-G with MIMO
Technology	Networking and Cables	Networking and Cables	Wireless-G Enhanced
Technology	Networking and Cables	Networking and Cables	Wirless-G
Technology	Networking and Cables	Networking and Cables	Wireless-A/G
Technology	Networking and Cables	Networking and Cables	Accessories
Technology	Networking and Cables	Networking and Cables	Wires (Ethernet)
Technology	Networking and Cables	Networking and Cables	Internet Phone (VoIP)
Technology	Networking and Cables	Networking and Cables	Cables, Hubs, Connectors, and Switches
Technology	Networking and Cables	Networking and Cables	Modems
Technology	Office Machines and Calculators	Office Machines and Calculators	Binding Machines and Supplies
Technology	Office Machines and Calculators	Office Machines and Calculators	Cash Registers and Credit Card Terminals
Technology	Office Machines and Calculators	Office Machines and Calculators	Copiers
Technology	Office Machines and Calculators	Office Machines and Calculators	DVD Players and Televisions
Technology	Office Machines and Calculators	Office Machines and Calculators	Digital Projectors
Technology	Office Machines and Calculators	Office Machines and Calculators	Fax Machines
Technology	Office Machines and Calculators	Office Machines and Calculators	Label Markers and Printers
Technology	Office Machines and Calculators	Office Machines and Calculators	Laminators and Supplies
Technology	Office Machines and Calculators	Office Machines and Calculators	Office Machines Supplies
Technology	Office Machines and Calculators	Office Machines and Calculators	Overhead Projectors and A/V Equipment
Technology	Office Machines and Calculators	Office Machines and Calculators	Paper Folders
Technology	Office Machines and Calculators	Office Machines and Calculators	Printers and All-in-One Machines
Technology	Office Machines and Calculators	Office Machines and Calculators	Recorders and Transcribers
Technology	Office Machines and Calculators	Office Machines and Calculators	Shredders
Technology	Office Machines and Calculators	Office Machines and Calculators	Time Clock and Cards
Technology	Office Machines and Calculators	Office Machines and Calculators	Typewriters
Technology	Peripherals and Memory	Peripherals and Memory	CD Drives
Technology	Peripherals and Memory	Peripherals and Memory	DVD Drives

(*Continued*)

Exhibit OM1 (Continued)

Phase II			
Product Group	**Product Category**	**Product Type**	**Product Item**
Technology	Peripherals and Memory	Peripherals and Memory	Floppy Drives
Technology	Peripherals and Memory	Peripherals and Memory	PC and Web Cameras
Technology	Peripherals and Memory	Peripherals and Memory	Hard Drives
Technology	Peripherals and Memory	Peripherals and Memory	USB Flash Drives
Technology	Peripherals and Memory	Peripherals and Memory	Zip Drives
Technology	Peripherals and Memory	Peripherals and Memory	Components and Upgrade Equipment
Technology	Peripherals and Memory	Peripherals and Memory	Flash MEmory
Technology	Peripherals and Memory	Peripherals and Memory	Gaming
Technology	Peripherals and Memory	Peripherals and Memory	Keyboards
Technology	Peripherals and Memory	Peripherals and Memory	Mice
Technology	Peripherals and Memory	Peripherals and Memory	Modems
Technology	Peripherals and Memory	Peripherals and Memory	PC Memory
Technology	Peripherals and Memory	Peripherals and Memory	Sound, Video, and Upgrade Cards
Technology	Peripherals and Memory	Peripherals and Memory	Speakers and Headets
Technology	Peripherals and Memory	Peripherals and Memory	Touchpads and Pens
Technology	Printers and All-in-Ones	Printers and All-in-Ones	All-in-One Machines
Technology	Printers and All-in-Ones	Printers and All-in-Ones	Dot Matrix Printers
Technology	Printers and All-in-Ones	Printers and All-in-Ones	Inkjet Printers
Technology	Printers and All-in-Ones	Printers and All-in-Ones	Label Printers
Technology	Printers and All-in-Ones	Printers and All-in-Ones	Laser Printers
Technology	Printers and All-in-Ones	Printers and All-in-Ones	Photo Printers
Technology	Printers and All-in-Ones	Printers and All-in-Ones	Portable Printers
Technology	Printers and All-in-Ones	Printers and All-in-Ones	Printer Accessories Finder
Technology	Printers and All-in-Ones	Printers and All-in-Ones	Wide Format Printers and Plotters
Technology	Shredders	Cross-Cut Shredders	Light/Med Duty Cross-Cut
Technology	Shredders	Cross-Cut Shredders	Heavy-Duty Cross-Cut
Technology	Shredders	Cross-Cut Shredders	Commercial Cross-Cut
Technology	Shredders	Strip-Cut Shredders	Light/Med Duty Strip-Cut
Technology	Shredders	Strip-Cut Shredders	Heavy-Duty Strip-Cut
Technology	Shredders	Strip-Cut Shredders	Commercial Strip-Cut
Technology	Shredders	Micro-Cut Shredders	Micro-Cut Shredders
Technology	Shredders	Media Destroyers	Media Destroyers
Technology	Shredders	All Shredders	All Shredders
Technology	Shredders	Shredder Oil and Bags	Shredder Oil
Technology	Shredders	Shredder Oil and Bags	Shredder Bags
Technology	Software	Software	Accounting and Finance
Technology	Software	Software	Anti-Virus and Internet Security
Technology	Software	Software	Business Productivity
Technology	Software	Software	Communications

Phase II			
Product Group	**Product Category**	**Product Type**	**Product Item**
Technology	Software	Software	Digital Media
Technology	Software	Software	Graphics and Design
Technology	Software	Software	Learning and Reference
Technology	Software	Software	Macintosh
Technology	Software	Software	Microsoft
Technology	Software	Software	Operating Systems
Technology	Software	Software	System Utilities
Technology	Software	Software	Tax Software
Technology	Telephone and Communications	Corded Phones	Multi-Line Phones—Corded
Technology	Telephone and Communications	Corded Phones	Single-Line Phones—Corded
Technology	Telephone and Communications	Cordless Phones	Single-Line Phones—Cordless
Technology	Telephone and Communications	Cordless Phones	Multi-Line Phones—Cordless
Technology	Telephone and Communications	Cordless Phones	Expandable Phone Systems—Cordless
Technology	Telephone and Communications	Headset Telephone Systems	Headset Telephone Systems
Technology	Telephone and Communications	Mobile Headsets	Mobile Headsets
Technology	Telephone and Communications	Office Headsets	Office Headsets
Technology	Telephone and Communications	Answering Machines and Caller ID Devices	Answering Machines
Technology	Telephone and Communications	Answering Machines and Caller ID Devices	Caller ID Devices
Technology	Telephone and Communications	Telephone Accessories	Cordless Phone Batteries
Technology	Telephone and Communications	Telephone Accessories	Cords, Couplers, Amplifiers, and Adapters
Technology	Telephone and Communications	Telephone Accessories	Stands, Shoulder Rests
Technology	Telephone and Communications	Wireless Accessories	All Brands
Technology	Telephone and Communications	Two-Way Radios	Two-Way Radios
Technology	Telephone and Communications	Two-Way Radios	Accessories Two-Way Radios Accessories
Technology	Telephone and Communications	Internet Phone (VoIP)	Internet Phone (VoIP)
Technology	Telephone and Communications	Broadband and Internet Services	Broadband Services
Technology	Telephone and Communications	Broadband and Internet Services	Dial-Up Services
Technology	Telephone and Communications	Weather/Alert Radios	Weather/Alert Radios

(Continued)

Exhibit OM1 (Continued)

Phase II			
Product Group	**Product Category**	**Product Type**	**Product Item**
Technology	Telephone and Communications	Wireless and Cellular	Wireless and Cellular
Furniture	Armoires	Armoires	Armoires
Furniture	Bookcases	Bookcases	Commercial Wooden Bookcases and Systems
Furniture	Bookcases	Bookcases	Small Office/Home Wooden Bookcases
Furniture	Bookcases	Bookcases	Commercial Metal Bookcases
Furniture	Bookcases	Bookcases	Small Office/Home MetalBookcases
Furniture	Bookcases	Bookcases	Furniture Collection Bookcases
Furniture	Bookcases	Bookcases	Literature Holders
Furniture	Carts and Stands	Carts and Stands	Audio/Visual Carts
Furniture	Carts and Stands	Carts and Stands	Computer Carts
Furniture	Carts and Stands	Carts and Stands	Craft Stands
Furniture	Carts and Stands	Carts and Stands	Lecterns
Furniture	Carts and Stands	Carts and Stands	Mail Carts
Furniture	Carts and Stands	Carts and Stands	Mobile Workstations
Furniture	Carts and Stands	Carts and Stands	Printer/Machine Carts
Furniture	Carts and Stands	Carts and Stands	Utility Carts
Furniture	Chairmats and Floormats	Chairmats and Floormats	Chairmats—Anti-Static
Furniture	Chairmats and Floormats	Chairmats and Floormats	Chairmats—Carpet
Furniture	Chairmats and Floormats	Chairmats and Floormats	Chairmats—Hard Floor
Furniture	Chairmats and Floormats	Chairmats and Floormats	Floormats—Anti-Fatigue
Furniture	Chairmats and Floormats	Chairmats and Floormats	Floormats—Carpeted
Furniture	Chairmats and Floormats	Chairmats and Floormats	Floormats—Industrial
Furniture	Chairmats and Floormats	Chairmats and Floormats	Floormats—Outdoor
Furniture	Chairs	Executive Chairs	Fabric Executive
Furniture	Chairs	Executive Chairs	Leather and Chrome
Furniture	Chairs	Executive Chairs	Leather and Wood
Furniture	Chairs	Executive Chairs	Leather Executive
Furniture	Chairs	Executive Chairs	Mesh Fabric
Furniture	Chairs	Management Chairs	Big and Tall
Furniture	Chairs	Management Chairs	Ergonomic
Furniture	Chairs	Management Chairs	Fabric Executive
Furniture	Chairs	Management Chairs	Leather
Furniture	Chairs	Management Chairs	Mesh Fabric
Furniture	Chairs	Commercial Chairs	Commercial
Furniture	Chairs	Task and Drafting Chairs/Stools	Fabric Task
Furniture	Chairs	Task and Drafting Chairs/Stools	Leather Task
Furniture	Chairs	Task and Drafting Chairs/Stools	Drafting Supplies

Phase II			
Product Group	**Product Category**	**Product Type**	**Product Item**
Furniture	Chairs	Task and Drafting Chairs/Stools	Stools
Furniture	Chairs	Reception and Guest Chairs	Fabric
Furniture	Chairs	Reception and Guest Chairs	Rception
Furniture	Chairs	Reception and Guest Chairs	Guest
Furniture	Chairs	Reception and Guest Chairs	Futons
Furniture	Chairs	Wood Chairs	Bankers
Furniture	Chairs	Wood Chairs	Side
Furniture	Chairs	Stacking and Folding Chairs	Stacking
Furniture	Chairs	Stacking and Folding Chairs	Folding
Furniture	Chairs	Educational Furniture	Chairs and Desks
Furniture	Chairs	Accessories	Casters
Furniture	Chairs	Accessories	Chair Arms
Furniture	Chairs	Accessories	Chair Carts
Furniture	Chairs	Accessories	Ottomans
Furniture	Desks	Desks	Compact and Student Desks
Furniture	Desks	Desks	Computer Desks
Furniture	Desks	Desks	Corner Desks
Furniture	Desks	Desks	Writing Desks
Furniture	Desks	Desks	"L" Shaped Desks
Furniture	Desks	Desks	Mobile Workstations
Furniture	File Cabinets	File Cabinets—Vertical	All Vertical File Cabinets
Furniture	File Cabinets	File Cabinets—Vertical	Commercial Metal
Furniture	File Cabinets	File Cabinets—Vertical	Small Office/Home Metal
Furniture	File Cabinets	File Cabinets—Vertical	Wood Vertical File Cabinets
Furniture	File Cabinets	File Cabinets—Lateral	All Lateral File Cabinets
Furniture	File Cabinets	File Cabinets—Lateral	Commercial Metal
Furniture	File Cabinets	File Cabinets—Lateral	Small Office/Home Metal
Furniture	File Cabinets	File Cabinets—Lateral	Wood Lateral File Cabinets
Furniture	File Cabinets	File Cabinets—Lateral	Open File Shelves
Furniture	File Cabinets	File Cabinets— Wood Lateral	Wood File Cabinets
Furniture	File Cabinets	File Cabinets— Wood Vertical	Wood File Cabinets
Furniture	File Cabinets	Fire Resistant	Fire Proof
Furniture	File Cabinets	Flat and Roll Files	Drafting and Printout File Systems
Furniture	File Cabinets	Flat and Roll Files	Flat File Systems
Furniture	File Cabinets	Storage Cabinets	Metal Storage Cabinets
Furniture	File Cabinets	Storage Cabinets	Lockers
Furniture	File Cabinets	Storage Cabinets	Storage Cubes
Furniture	File Cabinets	Mobile File Cabinets and Carts	Mobile File Cabinets
Furniture	File Cabinets	Mobile File Cabinets and Carts	Mobile File Carts
Furniture	File Cabinets	Locks and Accessories	Locks and Accessories

(Continued)

Exhibit OM1 (Continued)

Phase II			
Product Group	**Product Category**	**Product Type**	**Product Item**
Furniture	File Cabinets	Safes Sentry	Fire-Safe Chests
Furniture	File Cabinets	Safes Sentry	Fire-Safe Files
Furniture	File Cabinets	Safes Sentry	Fire-Safe Safes
Furniture	File Cabinets	Safes Sentry	Security Safes
Furniture	File Cabinets	Safes Sentry	Waterproof Fire-Safe Safes
Furniture	Furniture Accessories	Furniture Accessories	Chairmats and Floormats
Furniture	Furniture Accessories	Furniture Accessories	Ottomans
Furniture	Furniture Accessories	Furniture Accessories	Clocks
Furniture	Furniture Accessories	Furniture Accessories	Desk Sets/Organizers
Furniture	Furniture Accessories	Furniture Accessories	Pads and Protectors
Furniture	Furniture Accessories	Furniture Accessories	Coat Hangers
Furniture	Furniture Accessories	Furniture Accessories	Coat Racks and Hooks
Furniture	Furniture Accessories	Furniture Accessories	Costumers/Garnment Racks
Furniture	Furniture Accessories	Furniture Accessories	Chair Arms
Furniture	Furniture Accessories	Furniture Accessories	Frames
Furniture	Furniture Accessories	Furniture Accessories	Maps, Magnifiers, and Flags
Furniture	Furniture Accessories	Furniture Accessories	Door Stops
Furniture	Furniture Accessories	Furniture Accessories	Casters
Furniture	Furniture Collections	Furniture Collections	Commercial Grade Collections
Furniture	Furniture Collections	Furniture Collections	Small Office/Home Office Collections
Furniture	Home and Office Furnishings	Home and Office Furnishings	Accent Furniture
Furniture	Home and Office Furnishings	Home and Office Furnishings	Area Rugs
Furniture	Home and Office Furnishings	Home and Office Furnishings	Audio Towers
Furniture	Home and Office Furnishings	Home and Office Furnishings	Breakroom and Kitchen
Furniture	Home and Office Furnishings	Home and Office Furnishings	Contemporary Seating
Furniture	Home and Office Furnishings	Home and Office Furnishings	Entertainment Centers
Furniture	Home and Office Furnishings	Home and Office Furnishings	Entertainment Furniture
Furniture	Home and Office Furnishings	Home and Office Furnishings	Entertainment Stands
Furniture	Home and Office Furnishings	Home and Office Furnishings	Folding Screens
Furniture	Home and Office Furnishings	Home and Office Furnishings	Futons
Furniture	Home and Office Furnishings	Home and Office Furnishings	Media Storage
Furniture	Lamps and Lighting	Desk Lamps	Contemporary—Desk Lamps

Phase II			
Product Group	**Product Category**	**Product Type**	**Product Item**
Furniture	Lamps and Lighting	Desk Lamps	Functional—Desk Lamps
Furniture	Lamps and Lighting	Desk Lamps	Traditional—Desk Lamps
Furniture	Lamps and Lighting	Floor Lamps	Contemporary—Floor Lamps
Furniture	Lamps and Lighting	Floor Lamps	Tasks—Floor Lamps
Furniture	Lamps and Lighting	Table Lamps	Contemporary—Table Lamps
Furniture	Lamps and Lighting	Table Lamps	Traditional—Table Lamps
Furniture	Lamps and Lighting	Magnifying Lamps	Magnifying Lamps
Furniture	Lamps and Lighting	Under-Cabinet and Panel Lamps	Under-Cabinet and Panel Lamps
Furniture	Lamps and Lighting	Light Bulbs	Light Bulbs
Furniture	Office Décor and Plants	Office Décor and Plants	Desk Sets/Organizers
Furniture	Office Décor and Plants	Office Décor and Plants	Wall Art
Furniture	Office Décor and Plants	Office Décor and Plants	Accent/Coffee Tables
Furniture	Office Décor and Plants	Office Décor and Plants	Decorative Chalkboards
Furniture	Office Décor and Plants	Office Décor and Plants	Decorative Corkboards
Furniture	Office Décor and Plants	Office Décor and Plants	Mirrors
Furniture	Office Décor and Plants	Office Décor and Plants	Plants
Furniture	Office Décor and Plants	Office Décor and Plants	Privacy Screens
Furniture	Office Décor and Plants	Office Décor and Plants	Rugs
Furniture	Office Décor and Plants	Office Décor and Plants	Umbrella Stands/Coat Racks
Furniture	Panel Systems/ Accessories	Panel Systems/Accessories	Panel Systems
Furniture	Panel Systems/ Accessories	Panel Systems/Accessories	Panel Systems Hardware
Furniture	Panel Systems/ Accessories	Panel Systems/Accessories	Cubicle and Parition Organizers/Accessories
Furniture	Panel Systems/ Accessories	Panel Systems/Accessories	Panel Accessories
Furniture	Panel Systems/ Accessories	Panel Systems/Accessories	Under-Cabinet and Panel Lamps
Furniture	Shelving	Shelving	Literature Holders
Furniture	Shelving	Shelving	Metal Shelving
Furniture	Shelving	Shelving	Plastic Shelving
Furniture	Storage Cabinets	Storage Cabinets	Lockers
Furniture	Storage Cabinets	Storage Cabinets	Media Storage Cabinets
Furniture	Storage Cabinets	Storage Cabinets	Metal Storage Cabinets
Furniture	Storage Cabinets	Storage Cabinets	Storage Cubes
Furniture	Storage Cabinets	Storage Cabinets	Wood, Resin, and Laminate
Furniture	Storage Cabinets	Storage Cabinets	Storage Cabinets
Furniture	Tables	Tables	Folding and Banquet Tables
Furniture	Tables	Tables	Utility and Special Tables
Furniture	Tables	Tables	Meeting/Conference Room Tables
Furniture	Tables	Tables	Drafting Tables
Furniture	Tables	Tables	Training Room Tables
Furniture	Tables	Tables	Reception Area Tables

Exhibit OM2: Location in Egypt

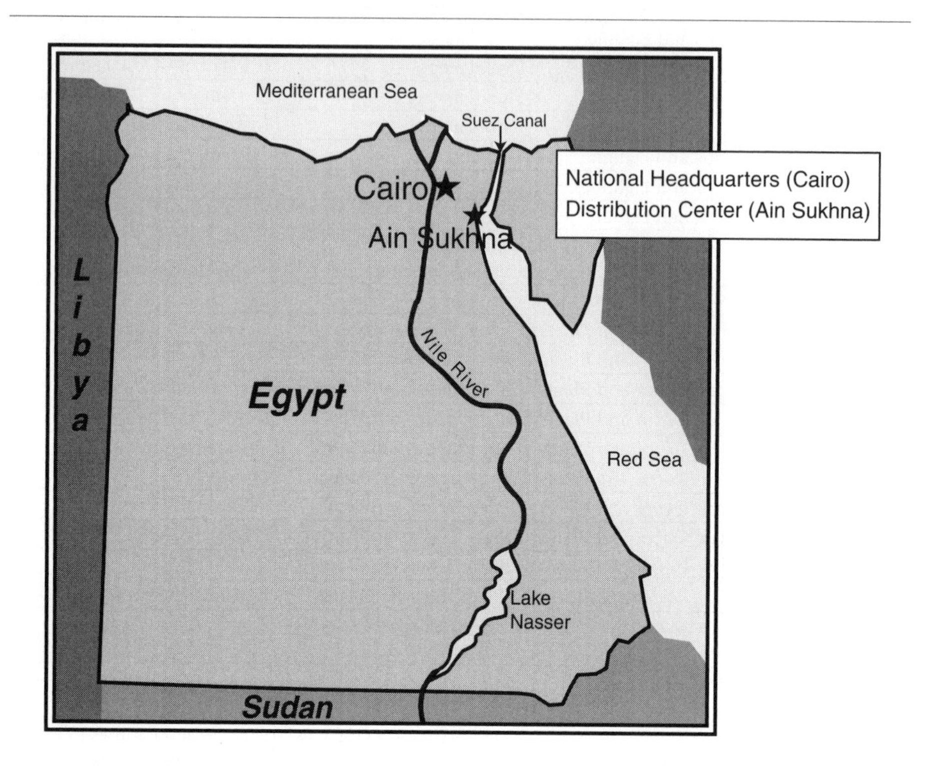

Egyptian Transportation

Railways: total: 5,063 km standard gauge: 5,063 km 1.435-m gauge (62 km electrified) (2004)

Highways: total: 64,000 km paved: 49,984 km unpaved: 14,016 km (1999 est.)

Waterways: 3,500 km note: includes Nile River, Lake Nasser, Alexandria-Cairo Waterway, and numerous smaller canals in delta; Suez Canal (193.5 km including approaches) navigable by oceangoing vessels drawing up to 17.68 m (2004)

Pipelines: condensate 289 km; condensate/gas 94 km; gas 6,115 km; liquid petroleum gas 852 km; oil 5,032 km; oil/gas/water 36 km; refined products 246 km (2004)

Ports and harbors: Alexandria, Damietta, El Dekheila, Port Said, Suez, Sukhna, Zeit

Merchant marine: total: 77 ships (1,000 GRT or over) 1,194,696 GRT/1,754,815 DWT by type: bulk carrier 14, cargo 34, container 2, passenger/cargo 5, petroleum tanker 14, roll on/roll off 8 foreign-owned: 10 (Denmark 1, Greece 6, Lebanon 2, Turkey 1) registered in other countries: 34 (2005)

Airports: 87 (2004 est.)

Heliports: 2 (2004 est.)

Exhibit OM3: Detailed Analysis of Distribution Costs (US$)

	Year 1	Year 2	Year 3	Year 4	Year 5
Number of personnel units	2	2	2	2	2
Wages	$7,363.64	$10,800.00	$11,880.00	$13,068.00	$14,374.80
Bonuses	$0.00	$0.00	$0.00	$0.00	$0.00
Social and other personnel costs	$0.00	$0.00	$0.00	$0.00	$0.00
Number of inbound shipments	$83.00	$151.00	$250.00	$300.00	$300.00
Import customs and transportation to distribution center	$17,945.95	$32,648.65	$54,054.05	$64,864.86	$64,864.86
Number of orders	$19,500.00	$202,500.00	$702,503.59	$790,190.00	$917,458.00
Picking and packing	$7,027.03	$72,972.97	$253,154.45	$284,753.15	$330,615.50
Office material	$54.05	$86.49	$86.49	$86.49	$86.49
Travel and refreshment	$162.16	$259.46	$259.46	$259.46	$259.46
Communication	$270.27	$432.43	$432.43	$432.43	$432.43
Depreciation	$531.96	$851.14	$851.14	$325.61	$10.30
Total distribution	**$33,355.06**	**$118,051.14**	**$320,718.02**	**$363,790.01**	**$410,643.83**
In % of sales	16%	5%	5%	5%	4%

Exhibit OM4: GSI—Global Structure Industries Letter to Provide Services

GSI—Global Structure Industries
221 Hafaz Badwy
Nasar City
Seventh District
Cairo, Egypt
Telephone: +2 0105853129
Fax: +2 0105853137

August 19, 2008

To: Mr. Stephan Shar
Vice President, Maktabi

Re: Service Agreement

Dear Mr. Shar,

I am pleased to confirm GSI's agreement with Maktabi to provide third-party services to your company. These services are to include, but are not limited to:

- Freight forwarding and customs clearance
- Renting or construction of a distribution center near Cairo
- Transportation to distribution center
- Management of distribution center
- Picking and packing
- Order fulfillment
- Customer tracking

The details of services to be rendered will be discussed at the meeting scheduled during the second week of October and the final contract will drawn up for approval and signature in December.

We are looking forward to developing a close relationship with you and the Maktabi Group.

Sincerely,

A.M. Mahmood

A. M. Mahmood
Sales Manager
GSI

Exhibit OM5: Sample Chief Executive Officer (CEO) Resume

(For more information on this candidate, please contact the Maktabi Group directly.)

Objective

To obtain a challenging position that utilizes my diverse experience in the U.S. and international market including, but not limited to, sales, technical operations, supply chain, and financial analysis.

Experience

June, 2004–Present, InterMed

Pharmaceutical Sales Representative and Associate Territory Business Manager

Pharmaceutical Sales Representative for assigned medicines in a territory that includes greater New York. Sales goals have been exceeded every quarter, with an annual sales volume of over $10 million.

- Overall sales portfolio and goal attainment is above 110%, exceeding sales quota and achieving top ten ranking nationwide.
- Currently ranked in the top 2% of sales in the neuroscience group.
- Ranked top sales representative for numerous contests.
- Converted targeted physicians to 100% market share expansion.

September, 2002–June, 2004, InterMed

Senior Analyst, U.S. Market Planning

Responsibilities included the detailed analysis and the production of reports concerning product demand, management of the Materials Planning System, organiztion of logistical fulfillment, and coordinaton of production efforts with third-party manufacturers.

- Coordinated with marketing, finance, and sales departments, production operations, customer service, and the regulatory group to develop overall marketing strategies.
- Evaluated market trends to ensure inventory and manufacturing goals were on target.
- Responsible for the rollout of the company's new central planning system, which will be used for the global coordination and execution of materials replenishment and logistical delivery.
- Managed a global inventory that supported over $10 billion in sales revenue.
- Provided direction to site production planners to ensure adequate production to meet market demand.

August, 2000–September, 2002, Baya Cosmetics

Supply Chain Analyst

Responsible for ensuring the integrity of the global supply chain.

- Resolved capacity issues and ensured the balance of supply across regions and manufacturing plants.
- Achieved a significant reduction in backorders within 6 months.
- Improved Customer Service fill rates from 65% in 2000 to 96% in 2002.

February, 1995–May, 2000, Best Cleaners (Family Business)

Manager

- Hired, trained, and managed a staff of five.
- Initiated a new automation process by computerizing the establishment and training the staff in the new mode of operation, resulting in increased productivity.
- Performed all financial aspects including payroll, income tax, billing, and charge accounts.

Education

Rutgers University, New Brunswick, New Jersey

Bachelor of Arts in Political Science with Economics Minor, May 2000

- Graduated with Departmental Honors—GPA in Major 3.60/4.00
- Dean's list from 1997 to 2000
- Volunteer/Teaching Assistant, Paul Robinson Community School of the Arts: taught grammar, reading, and math to over 20 students with learning disabilities for academic year 1999/2000.

Skills

Advanced skills in SAP, MRP I/II, Business Warehouse, Dendrite, and Microsoft Office

Other

- Languages: Arabic and basic understanding of Spanish
- Member, Toastmasters International; received many speech awards
- Completed the Dale Carnegie Seminar
- Occupational Safety & Health Association (OSHA) Certified for Hazardous Materials Emergency Response
- Member of Minority Pharmaceutical Sales Representative Organization

Exhibit CM1: Organizational Chart

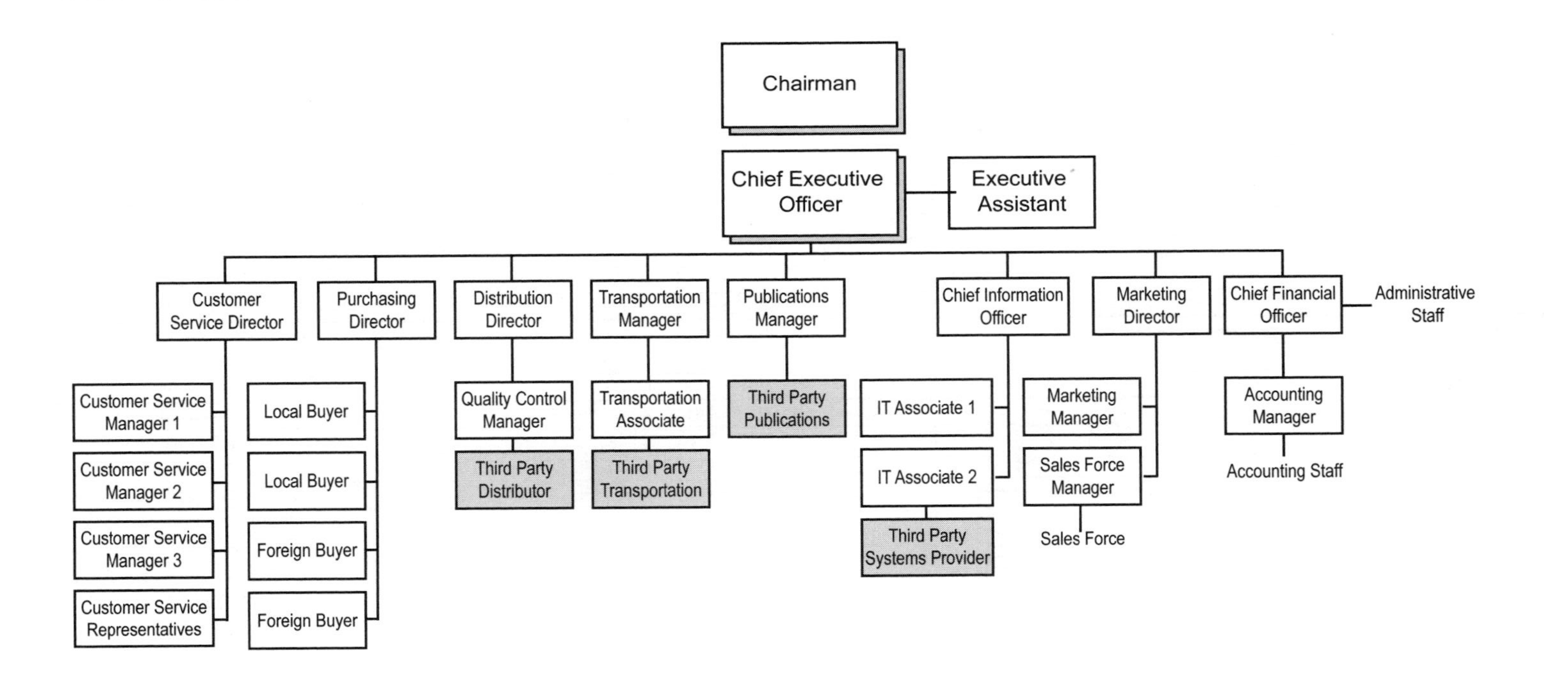

Exhibit CM2: Implementation Plan

ID	Task Name	Duration	Start	Finish	Predecessors	1st Half: Jan Feb Mar Apr May Jun / 2nd Half: Jul Aug Sep Oct Nov Dec
1	Maktabi Implementation	183 days	Sun 2/3/08	Tue 8/5/08		
2	**Phase I: Business setup and sourcing**	**40 days**	**Sun 2/3/08**	**Thu 3/27/08**		
3	**Initial setup**	**10 days**	**Sun 2/3/08**	**Thu 2/14/08**		
4	Office space search and move-in	1 week	Sun 2/3/08	Thu 2/7/08		CEO, CIO
5	Computer hardware and software purchase	1 week	Sun 2/3/08	Thu 2/7/08		CIO
6	Furniture and other equipment purchase	1 week	Sun 2/10/08	Thu 2/14/08	4	CEO, CIO
7	Office material purchase	2 days	Sun 2/10/08	Mon 2/11/08	4	CEO, CIO
8	Telephone and mobile line purchase	1 day	Sun 2/10/08	Sun 2/10/08	4	CIO
9	**Legal and financial business setup**	**40 days**	**Sun 2/3/08**	**Thu 3/27/08**		
10	Required legal formalities setup	2 months	Sun 2/3/08	Thu 3/27/08		CEO, CIO
11	Open small business bank account	1 week	Sun 2/3/08	Thu 2/7/08		CEO, CIO
12	**Phase II: Pre-sales setup**	**159 days**	**Thu 2/7/08**	**Tue 9/16/08**		
13	**Administration setup**	**71 days**	**Thu 2/28/08**	**Thu 6/5/08**		
14	Directive, policy and procedure creation	3 months	Thu 2/28/08	Wed 5/21/08	31	CEO
15	CFO search and hire	3 weeks	Sun 5/4/08	Thu 5/22/08	4FS + 60 days	CEO, CIO
16	Insurance purchase	2 weeks	Sun 5/25/08	Thu 6/5/08	15	CFO
17	Executive assistant search and hire	2 weeks	Sun 5/25/08	Thu 6/5/08	15	CEO
18	**Customer service setup**	**90 days**	**Sun 5/4/08**	**Tue 9/1608**		
19	Customer service director search and hire	3 weeks	Sun 5/4/08	Thu 5/22/08	4FS+ 60 days	CEO, CIO, CFO
20	Customer service setup plan creation	1 month	Sun 5/25/08	Thu 6/19/08	19	Customer service director
21	Customer service setup plan approval	0 days	Thu 6/19/08	Thu 6/19/08	20	6/19
22	Customer service manager search and hire	3 weeks	Thu 6/12/08	Thu 7/2/08	19FS + 14 days	Customer service director
23	Computer hardware and software purchase	1 week	Wed 9/10/08	Tue 9/16/08	95FF	CIO
24	Furniture and other equipment purchase	1 week	Wed 9/10/08	Tue 9/16/08	95FF	CFO
25	Office material purchase	2 days	Mon 9/15/08	Tue 9/16/08	95FF	CFO
26	Telephone and mobile line purchase	1 day	Tue 9/16/08	Tue 9/16/08	95FF	CFO

ID	Task Name	Duration	Start	Finish	Predecessors	1st Half / 2nd Half (Jan–Dec)
27	**Purchasing setup**	**90 days**	**Thu 2/7/08**	**Wed 6/11/08**		
28	**Sourcing initiation**	**55 days**	**Thu 2/7/08**	**Wed 4/23/08**		
29	Purchasing director search and hire	3 weeks	Sun 2/10/08	Thu 2/28/08	4	CEO, CIO
30	Final product selection	3 weeks	Thu 2/7/08	Wed 2/27/08	29SF+ 14 days	CEO, CIO, Purchasing director
31	Final product selection approval	0 days	Wed 2/27/08	Wed 2/27/08	30	2/27
32	Local supplier search	1 month	Thu 2/28/08	Wed 3/26/08	31	CEO, CIO, Purchasing director
33	Foreign market supplier search	2 months	Thu 2/28/08	Wed 4/23/08	31	CEO, CIO, Purchasing director
34	Purchasing department setup	35 days	Thu 4/24/08	Wed 6/11/08		
35	Purchasing manager search and hire	3 weeks	Thu 4/24/08	Wed 5/14/08	33	Purchasing director
36	Product order and purchase plan	1 month	Thu 5/15/08	Wed 6/11/08	35	Purchasing director, purchasing manager
37	Product order and purchase plan approval	0 days	Wed 6/11/08	Wed 6/11/08	36	9/11
38	Computer hardware and software purchase	1 week	Thu 5/8/08	Wed 5/14/08	35FF	CIO
39	Furniture and other equipment purchase	1 week	Thu 5/8/08	Wed 5/14/08	35FF	CFO
40	Office material purchase	2 days	Tue 5/13/08	Wed 5/14/08	35FF	CFO
41	Telephone and mobile line purchase	1 day	Wed 5/14/08	Wed 5/14/08	35FF	CFO
42	**Distribution setup**	**57 days**	**Sun 5/4/08**	**Mon 7/21/08**		
43	Distribution director search and hire	3 weeks	Sun 5/4/08	Thu 5/22/08	4FS+ 60 days	CEO, CIO
44	Contract with distribution provider	3 weeks	Thu 6/12/08	Wed 7/2/08	43FS+ 14 days	Distribution director
45	Quality control manager search and hire	3 weeks	Tue 6/3/08	Mon 6/23/08	43FS+ 7 days	Distribution director
46	Quality control policy creation	1 month	Tue 6/24/08	Mon 7/23/08	45	Quality control manager
47	Quality control plan approval	0 days	Mon 7/21/08	Mon 7/21/08	46	7/21
48	Computer hardware and software purchase	1 week	Sun 5/18/08	Thu 5/22/08	43FF	CIO
49	Furniture and other equipment purchase	1 week	Sun 5/18/08	Thu 5/22/08	43FF	CFO
50	Office material purchase	2 days	Wed 5/21/08	Thu 5/22/08	43FF	CFO
51	Telephone and mobile line purchase	1 day	Thu 5/22/08	Thu 5/22/08	43FF	CFO

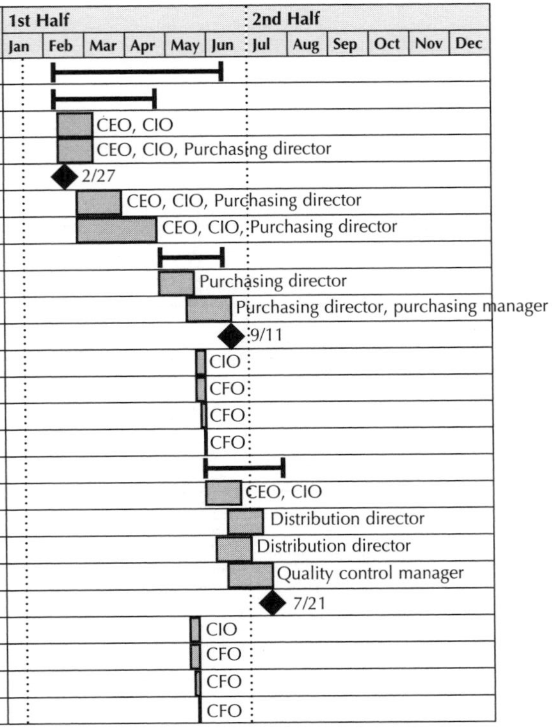

(*Continued*)

Task ▭ Milestone ◆

Split .... Summary ├──┤

Exhibit CM2 (Continued)

ID	Task Name	Duration	Start	Finish	Predecessors	1st Half / 2nd Half: Jan Feb Mar Apr May Jun Jul Aug Sep Oct Nov Dec
52	**Transportation setup**	**57 days**	**Sun 5/4/08**	**Mon 7/21/08**		
53	Transportation director search and hire	3 weeks	Sun 5/4/08	Thu 5/22/08	4FS+ 60 days	CEO, CIO
54	Contract with transportation provider	3 weeks	Thu 6/12/08	Wed 7/2/08	53FS+ 14 days	Distribution director
55	Transportation associate search and hire	3 weeks	Tue 6/3/08	Mon 6/23/08	53FS+ 7 days	Distribution director
56	Transportation plan policy creation	1 month	Tue 6/24/08	Mon 7/21/08	55	Quality control manager
57	Transportation plan approval	0 days	Mon 7/21/08	Mon 7/21/08	56	7/21
58	Computer hardware and software purchase	1 week	Sun 5/18/08	Thu 5/22/08	53FF	CIO
59	Furniture and other equipment purchase	1 week	Sun 5/18/08	Thu 5/22/08	53FF	CFO
60	Office material purchase	2 days	Wed 5/21/08	Thu 5/22/08	53FF	CFO
61	Telephone and mobile line purchase	1 day	Thu 5/22/08	Thu 5/22/08	53FF	CFO
62	**Publications setup**	**37 days**	**Sun 5/4/08**	**Mon 6/23/08**		
63	Publications manager search and hire	3 weeks	Sun 5/4/08	Thu 5/22/08	4FS+ 60 days	CEO, CIO
64	Contract with publisher	3 weeks	Tue 6/3/08	Mon 6/23/08	63FS+ 7 days	Publications director
65	Computer hardware and software purchase	1 week	Tue 5/13/08	Mon 5/19/08	63FS+ 7 days	CIO
66	Furniture and other equipment purchase	1 week	Tue 5/13/08	Mon 5/19/08	63FS+ 7 days	CFO
67	Office material purchase	2 days	Tue 5/13/08	Wed 5/14/08	63FS+ 7 days	CFO
68	Telephone and mobile line purchase	1 day	Tue 5/13/08	Tue 5/13/08	63FS+ 7 days	CFO
69	**Information technologies setup**	**57 days**	**Sun 5/4/08**	**Mon 7/21/08**		
70	IT associate search and hire	3 weeks	Sun 5/4/08	Thu 5/22/08	4FS+ 60 days	CIO
71	IT requirements draft	1 month	Tue 6/3/08	Mon 6/30/08	70FS+ 7 days	IT associates
72	IT requirements approval	6 days	Mon 6/30/08	Mon 6/30/08	71	6/30
73	Contract with IT service provider	3 weeks	Tue 7/1/08	Mon 7/21/08	72	CIO
74	Computer hardware and software purchase	1 week	Sun 5/18/08	Thu 5/22/08	70FF	CIO
75	Furniture and other equipment purchase	1 week	Sun 5/18/08	Thu 5/22/08	70FF	CFO
76	Office material purchase	2 days	Wed 5/21/08	Thu 5/22/08	70FF	CFO
77	Telephone and mobile line purchase	1 day	Thu 5/22/08	Thu 5/22/08	70FF	

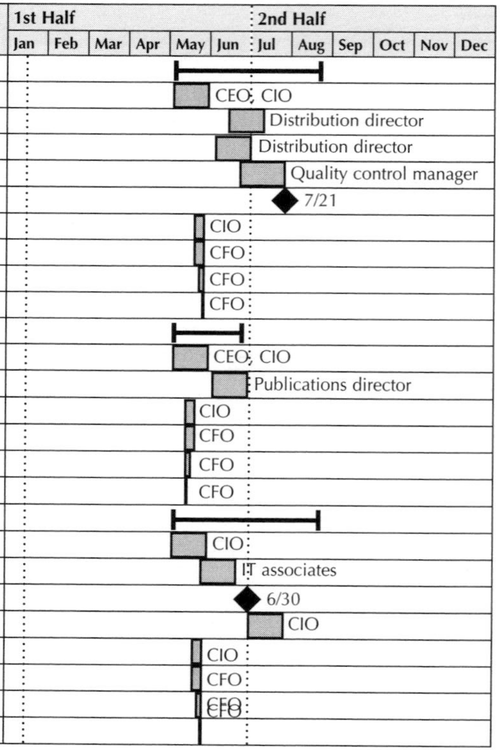

ID	Task Name	Duration	Start	Finish	Predecessors	1st Half / 2nd Half
78	**Marketing and sales setup**	**49 days**	**Sun 5/4/08**	**Wed 7/9/08**		
79	Marketing director search and hire	3 weeks	Sun 5/4/08	Thu 5/22/08	4FS+ 60 days	CEO, CIO
80	Marketing promotions and advertising sales creation	1 month	Thu 6/12/08	Wed 7/9/08	79FS+ 14 days	Marketing director
81	Marketing promotions and advertising sales approval	0 days	Wed 7/9/08	Wed 7/9/08	80	7/9
82	Marketing manager search and hire	3 weeks	Tue 6/3/08	Mon 6/23/08	79FS+ 7 days	Marketing director
83	Computer hardware and software purchase	1 week	Sun 5/18/08	Thu 5/22/08	79FF	CIO
84	Furniture and other equipment purchase	1 week	Sun 5/18/08	Thu 5/22/08	79FF	CFO
85	Office material purchase	2 days	Wed 521/08	Thu 5/22/08	79FF	CFO
86	Telephone and mobile line purchase	1 day	Thu 5/22/08	Thu 5/22/08	79FF	CFO
87	**Phase III: Pre-sales operations**	**164 days**	**Thu 2/28/08**	**Mon 8/11/08**		
88	**Administration operation**	**15 days**	**Sun 5/4/08**	**Thu 5/22/08**		
89	New office search and move in	3 weeks	Sun 5/4/08	Thu 5/22/08	4FS+ 60 days	CFO
90	New office approval	0 days	Thu 5/22/08	Thu 5/22/08	89	5/22
91	Accounting manager search and hire	3 weeks	Sun 5/4/08	Thu 5/22/08	4FS+ 60 days	CFO
92	Personnel (drivers, janitors, etc.) search and hire	3 weeks	Sun 5/4/08	Thu 5/22/08	89FF	CFO, Executive assitant
93	**Customer service operation**	**60 days**	**Wed 7/23/08**	**Mon 9/22/08**		
94	Customer service training preparation	1 month	Wed 7/23/08	Tue 8/19/08	22FS+ 14 days	Customer service manager (CSM)
95	Customer service representatives search and hire	1 month	Wed 8/20/08	Tue 9/16/08	94	CSM
96	Customer service representatives training	1 month	Wed 9/17/08	Tue 10/14/08	95	CSM
97	**Purchasing operation**	**185 days**	**Thu 2/28/08**	**Wed 8/6/08**		
98	**Sourcing operation**	**117 days**	**Thu 2/28/08**	**Tue 6/10/08**		
99	Local supplier visits	1 month	Mon 3/10/08	Sun 4/6/08	32SS+ 7 days	CEO, CIO, Purchasing director
100	Foreign supplier market visits	2 months	Wed 3/19/08	Tue 5/11/08	33SS+ 14 days	CEO, CIO, Purchasing director
101	Temporary warehouse space search and rent	1 week	Thu 2/28/08	Wen 3/5/08	31	Purchasing director
102	Purchase/receipt of local supply samples	1 month	Mon 3/10/08	Sun 4/6/08	32SS+ 7 days	CEO, CIO, Purchasing director
103	Purchase/receipt of foreign supply samples	3 months	Wed 3/19/08	Tue 6/10/08	33SS+ 14 days	CEO, CIO, Purchasing director

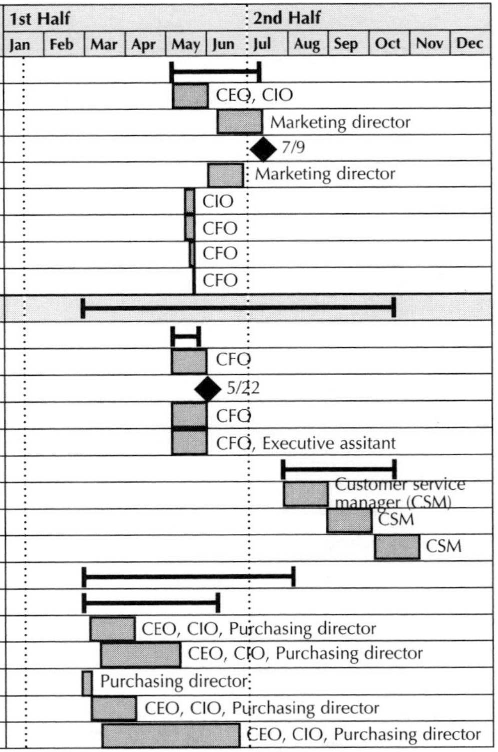

(Continued)

Task ▭ Milestone ◆
Split .... Summary ├──┤

Exhibit CM2 (Continued)

ID	Task Name	Duration	Start	Finish	Predecessors	1st Half / 2nd Half (Jan–Dec)
104	**Purchasing department operation**	**40 days**	**Thu 6/12/08**	**Wed 8/6/08**		
105	Pre-sales product orders and purchase plan execution	2 months	Thu 6/12/08	Wed 8/6/08	37	Purchasing director, Purchasing manager
106	**Distribution operation**	**60 days**	**Thu 7/3/08**	**Wed 9/24/08**		
107	Operations setup with distribution provider	3 months	Thu 7/3/08	Wed 9/24/08	94	Distribution director
108	**Transportation operation**	**60 days**	**Thu 7/3/08**	**Wed 9/24/08**		
109	Operations setup with transportation provider	3 months	Thu 7/3/08	Wed 9/24/08	54	Transportation provider
110	**Publications operation**	**40 days**	**Tue 6/24/08**	**Mon 8/18/08**		
111	Initial catalog design	1 month	Tue 6/24/08	Mon 7/21/08	64	Publications director (PD), Publications manager (PM)
112	Photos of sample products	3 weeks	Tue 7/22/08	Mon 8/11/08	113SS	PD, PM
113	Initial catalog design	1 month	Tue 7/22/08	Mon 8/18/08	111	PD, PM
114	Final catalog approval	0 days	Mon 8/18/08	Mon 8/18/08	113	8/18
115	**Information technologies operation**	**60 days**	**Tue 7/22/08**	**Sun 9/21/08**		
116	Operations setup with IT service provider	3 months	Tue 7/22/08	Mon 10/13/08	73	CIO, IT service provider
117	**Marketing and sales operation**	**60 days**	**Thu 7/10/08**	**Wed 10/1/08**		
118	Pre-sales marketing promotions and advertising plan execution	3 months	Thu 7/10/08	Wed 10/1/08	81	Marketing director
119	Sales representative training preparation	1 month	Mon 7/14/08	Sun 8/10/08	82FS+ 14 days	Marketing manager
120	Sales representative search and hire	1 month	Mon 8/11/08	Sun 9/7/08	119	Marketing manager
121	Sales representative training	3 weeks	Mon 9/8/08	Sun 9/28/08	120	Marketing manager
122	Sales representative visits execution	0 days	Sun 9/28/08	Sun 9/28/08	121	9/28
123	**Phase IV: Operations kickoff**	**0 days**	**Wed 10/1/08**	**Wed 10/1/08**		10/1

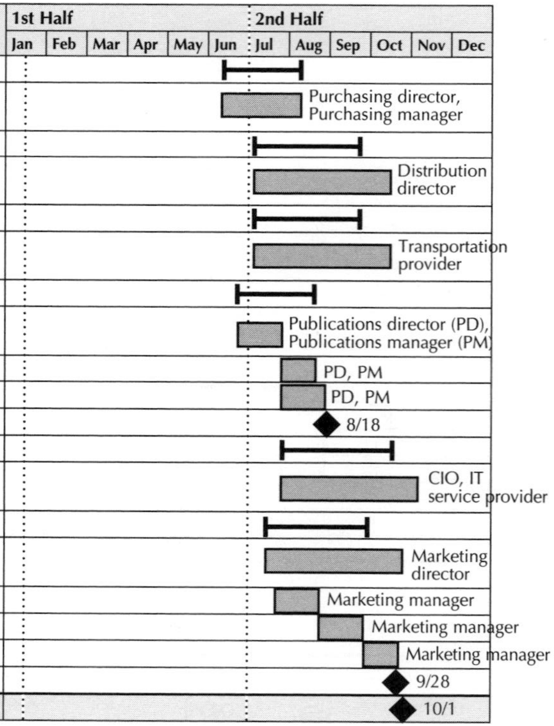

Task — Milestone — Split — Summary

Index

About the Author

Robert D. Hisrich is the Garvin Professor of Global Entrepreneurship and Director of the Walker Center for Global Entrepreneurship at Thunderbird School of Global Management. He holds an MBA and a doctorate from the University of Cincinnati. Professor Hisrich's research pursuits are focused on entrepreneurship and venture creation: entrepreneurial ethics, intrapreneurship, women and minority entrepreneurs, venture financing, and global venture creation. He teaches courses and seminars in these areas, as well as in marketing management and product planning and development. His interest in global management and entrepreneurship resulted in two Fulbright Fellowships in Budapest, Hungary; honorary degrees from universities in Russia and Hungary; and visiting faculty positions in universities in Austria, Australia, Ireland, and Slovenia. Professor Hisrich serves on the editorial boards of several prominent journals in entrepreneurial scholarship, is on several boards of directors, and is author or coauthor of over 300 research articles appearing in such journals as *Journal of Marketing, Journal of Marketing Research, Journal of Business Venturing, Journal of Small Business Finance, Small Business Economics, Journal of Developmental Entrepreneurship, and Entrepreneurship Theory and Practice.* Professor Hisrich has authored or coauthored 25 books, including *Entrepreneurship: Starting, Developing, and Managing a New Enterprise* (translated into nine languages), *The 13 Biggest Mistakes that Derail Small Businesses and How to Avoid Them, and Marketing: A Practical Management Approach.*